BRITAIN'S ENTRY INTO THE EUROPEAN COMMUNITY

FOREIGN AND COMMONWEALTH OFFICE (FCO) PUBLICATIONS

Series Editors: Gill Bennett and Keith Hamilton

ISSN: 1471-2083

FCO historians are responsible for editing *Documents on British Policy Overseas (DBPO)* and for overseeing the publication of FCO Internal Histories.

DBPO comprises three series of diplomatic documents, focusing on major themes in foreign policy since 1945, and drawn principally from the records of the Foreign and Commonwealth Office. The latest volumes, published in Series III, are composed almost wholly of documents from within the thirty-year 'closed period', which would otherwise be unavailable to the public.

Since the early 1960s several Internal Histories have been prepared by former or serving officers, the majority of which concentrated upon international developments and negotiations in which the UK has been directly involved. These were initially intended for use within the FCO, but some of the more substantial among them, studies that offer fresh insights into British diplomacy, are now being declassified for publication.

Forthcoming FCO publications:

Détente in Europe, 1972–1976
Documents on British Policy Overseas, Series III, Volume III
Gill Bennett and Keith Hamilton (eds)

The Southern Flank in Crisis, 1973–77
Documents on British Policy Overseas, Series III, Volume IV
Gill Bennett and Keith Hamilton (eds)

BRITAIN'S ENTRY INTO THE EUROPEAN COMMUNITY

Report by Sir Con O'Neill on the Negotiations of 1970–1972

Edited and with a Foreword by

Sir David Hannay, GCMG

WHITEHALL HISTORY PUBLISHING
in association with
FRANK CASS
LONDON • PORTLAND, OR

First published in 2000 in Great Britain by
FRANK CASS PUBLISHERS
Newbury House, 900 Eastern Avenue
London IG2 7HH

and in the United States of America by
FRANK CASS PUBLISHERS
c/o ISBS, 5804 N.E. Hassalo Street
Portland, Oregon, 97213-3644

Website: www.frankcass.com

British Library Cataloguing in Publication Data

O'Neill, Sir Con, 1912–1988
Britain joins the European Community: report by Sir Con O'Neill on the negotiations of 1970–1972. – (Foreign and Commonwealth office publications)
1. European Union 2. Great Britain – Foreign relations – European Union countries 3. European Union countries – Foreign relations – Great Britain
I. Title II. Hannay, David
327.4'1'04

ISBN 0-7146-5117-6 (cloth)
ISSN 1471-2083

Library of Congress Cataloging-in-Publication-Data

O'Neill, Con, Sir, 1912–1988.
Britain joins the European Community: report by Sir Con O'Neill on the negotiations of 1970–1972 / Sir Con O'Neill; edited with a foreword by Sir David Hannay.
p. cm.
Includes index.
ISBN 0-7146-5117-6 (cloth)
1. European Union–Great Britain–History–Sources. 2. International and municipal law–Great Britain–History–Sources. I. Hannay, David, Sir. II. Title.
KD4015.O545 2000
341.242'2'0941–dc21

00-043124

Typeset by Vitaset, Paddock Wood, Kent
Printed in Great Britain by
MPG Books Ltd, Bodmin, Cornwall

Contents

* Not printed

Editor's Foreword

When I first read this report, shortly after it was written in 1972, I can recall feeling regret that, for some thirty years or so, it was fated to be read by relatively few people and that, as Sir Con O'Neill himself observed, 'the only people able to read it will lack the time to do so'. The reasons for confidentiality were understandable. The subject matter was controversial in domestic political terms, some of the judgements were more so; and the comments on and assessments of the governments of our European Community partners were sufficiently perceptive and acerbic to risk complaint. My other immediate reaction, as one who had been directly involved throughout the negotiations in a junior capacity, was sheer admiration at the way in which the trees were marshalled into recognisable and well-explained woods; and at the broad sweep of the analysis of negotiations whose course and outcome at the time, only a few months before the report was written, had been far from clear even to those who were closely involved. This might not, properly speaking, be history, as its author modestly asserts, but it was evidently a remarkably valuable source for the subsequent writing of history.

It is usually unwise to claim that something is unique, but it is safe to assert that this report is highly unusual. Firstly it is, with a few minor exceptions, entirely written by one person, whereas the frequent but not invariable practice with such internal records, as was indeed the case with the report that was written on the earlier, unsuccessful negotiations for accession to the Community in 1961–63, is to follow a more collective pattern. In addition, this report is one man's personal work, the assessments and judgements contained in it having been submitted to no screening process. Moreover the author reporting directly to Ministers and having advised them throughout the negotiations, was well placed to comment on the main policy issues as well as to be abreast of the technicalities and the detailed ins and outs of the actual negotiating process. The fact that the report was written for a small audience (it was in fact considered sufficiently sensitive to be sent only to named and numbered recipients) and was clearly destined to remain confidential for a substantial period of time, freed it of the need for excessive discretion and also of the almost obligatory Panglossian spin which is so often given to immediate reporting on a ministerial visit or negotiation destined to be circulated more widely. And being written so soon after the events that it described, the author has avoided even the slightest temptation to benefit from hindsight or to adjust the judgements to fit the development that followed the negotiations.

The report provides the anatomy of a negotiation, at times going into almost excruciating detail, at others standing back and giving a broad-brush overview of what was at stake. The view is, of course, a very British view, illuminated with much information and speculation about the positions and motivations of the other governments principally involved, but with such information derived almost exclusively from British sources or from those who knew that what they said would end up being analysed by their British negotiating partners. Within these limitations, the anatomy is defined with great clarity. The negotiating machinery is explained; the dealings with the Community, with the governments of the original Six member states, with the other applicants and with the EFTA non-candidate countries, with the Commonwealth countries most affected and with the Press are all fully spelled out. The process by which the British government itself defined its negotiating position, then deployed that position, and the results that were achieved, is there in detail. The insight thus given into how a negotiation such as this actually works, indeed in some cases what it feels like to be involved in it, goes far beyond that usually available.

This was not, however, a negotiation just like any other. It was a new species with a new style, which had emerged in the period after the Second World War, as part of the rapid expansion of multilateral diplomacy; and within that new species it was one of the earliest in a sub-species relating to negotiating with, or about the development of, the European Community. The reader will only have gone a few pages before realising that this is not a negotiation which bears the slightest resemblance to the Congress of Vienna, to the Paris Conference of 1919 or even to the conclaves which followed the Second World War and gave birth to the Cold War. Not only had all the graces and glitter of those earlier negotiations disappeared, shrunk to a series of working dinners at which discussion was more likely to focus on the minutiae of agricultural or trade policy than on grand strategy, and to a single glass of Luxembourg sparkling wine masquerading as champagne drunk at 5 a.m. when the back of the negotiations had been broken; but the subject matter had entirely changed too. Many of the issues involved were not those formerly considered as a suitable subject of international negotiation at all. And while the international implications of many aspects of the negotiation were clearly visible and far-reaching in their consequences, they derived from decisions and compromises, which were based on considerations of domestic policy. Seldom had technical issues assumed such an importance at a multilateral level.

Moreover the multilateral nature of the negotiation, involving not only the formal negotiating sessions in Brussels or Luxembourg but also a multiplicity of diplomatic contacts in individual capitals developed into a kind of three-dimensional game of chess of a complexity which was new to at least some of the participants, particularly to those who had not been party to the negotiations setting up the Community in the first place. The idea that the conduct of technically complex negotiations in Brussels somehow marginalised or put out of business the embassies in national capitals does not survive a study of this report and the evidence of how much of the real negotiation actually took place away from Brussels, in this case as often as not in Paris. Another novel feature of this new sub-specie of negotiation was the extent to which substance was determined or at least foreshadowed by procedure. The technique, described in detail in the report, by which the British sought to ensure that discussion of individual issues remained locked up within the Six until an outcome was discernible that could be accepted by the United Kingdom is one example of this. The question of whether or not to hold a summit of the Six (the original member states), the Seven (the Six plus the United Kingdom) or the Ten (all members and all candidates) or, as in the end happened, just of two (Britain and France), is another.

While the report is written very much from the position of a senior official and not that of a politician, the author does not mince his words when analysing Britain's fundamental vulnerability as the negotiations unfolded. The lost opportunities of the 1950s are always present in his thinking. 'What mattered was to get into the Community and thereby restore our position at the centre of European affairs which, since 1958, we had lost. The negotiations were concerned only with the means of achieving this objective at an acceptable price' was how he put it, foreshadowing later Prime Ministerial references to being 'at the heart of Europe'. That same analysis led him to the conclusion that the Community's prescription for handling decisions which had been taken before Britain joined—'Swallow the lot, and swallow it now', unpalatable though it was, could not be avoided. And, although the natural tendency of any negotiator is to overestimate the significance of the negotiating process and the triumphs achieved at the negotiating table, Sir Con O'Neill delivered a crushing rebuke to any such illusions when he described the negotiations as 'in a certain sense ... peripheral, accidental and secondary', a conclusion he reached on the basis both of Britain's fundamental interest in accession and of the evidence that President Pompidou had in fact decided as early as the Hague Summit in December 1969, long before the negotiations began, that Britain's accession could no longer be resisted by France and could perhaps be welcome.

Perhaps the most interesting aspects of the report are those where the author analyses the outcome and subjects this to a rigorous consideration of whether it was as good as it might have been or whether a better deal could have been obtained. Mistakes are admitted; a reasonable degree of success is claimed. Broadly these judgements have stood the test of time over the succeeding twenty-seven years. In only one case, that of fisheries, does it seem reasonable to question the balance struck between success and shortcomings.

The author identified four key issues on which the success of the negotiations turned—Commonwealth sugar, New Zealand butter, Community finance and fisheries. None of the many dozens of other matters resolved in the negotiations has emerged subsequently to challenge the validity of that short-list. Commonwealth sugar, the first to be settled, was also the one where the deal struck was most questioned at the time. It did indeed require a considerable act of confidence to accept that a few words committing an enlarged Community to have as its firm purpose the safeguarding of the interests of the developing Commonwealth sugar producers was likely to prove a more valuable assurance than even the least ungenerous quantitative commitment that looked obtainable if Britain had pursued the matter further down the latter path. And yet it turned out to be so. When the Sugar Protocol of the Lomé Convention came into force in 1975 it gave guaranteed access for 1.2m tons of Commonwealth sugar at a price close to the Community price and well above the world price. This compares with the figure guaranteed under the pre-existing Commonwealth Sugar Agreement of 1.373m tons and figures such as 500,000 which were being mentioned in Brussels before the negotiations turned towards a general rather than a specific commitment. Moreover the commitment has been sustained through subsequent re-negotiations of the Lomé Convention, albeit with some erosion of the quantities guaranteed. When one adds to that the monies made available by the Community under its scheme for stabilising the export receipts of the Lomé associates from primary commodities and also the successive increases in the development aid packages at each Lomé re-negotiation, it is hard to avoid the conclusion that those developing Commonwealth countries which were enabled to become associates of the Community benefited more than they would have done if Britain had remained outside the Community, the sole support for their sugar industries and their principal source of overseas development aid.

The deal that was struck for New Zealand dairy products was in marked contrast to that for Commonwealth sugar. In place of the latter's vague and general assurances, was precision as to the quantities of imports in each year, as to the method of determining prices and as to the institutional arrangements for taking decisions on such imports beyond the five-year transitional period. This high degree of specificity reflected a political reality. The New Zealand government would not have been satisfied with anything less; and without the acquiescence of the New Zealand government it was rather doubtful whether the terms of Britain's accession would have been approved by the House of Commons. The author of the report considers that the deal struck, precisely because of these political considerations, was unduly generous; his complaint is not that New Zealand deserved less but that Britain had to pay more than it would otherwise have had to in the transitional arrangements for Community finance. This judgement is difficult to contest, given the very clear linkage established in the final stage of the negotiations by the French between the terms to be negotiated on New Zealand and those on Community finance. Nevertheless it does assume that the French could have been beaten down to lower figures on finance, which cannot be asserted with any certainty. It is also the case that the figures on finance finally accepted were within the bracket of acceptability established in advance by the British Cabinet. And when the time came to negotiate further arrangements for New Zealand butter imports post-1977, the higher figures established in the accession negotiations could be read across and a higher base existed to which to apply the degressivity on which the Community was always going to insist.

No-one aware of the battles which raged subsequently between 1979 and 1984 over Britain's net budget contribution can fail to regard the negotiations over Community finance as the heart of the matter. One thing is clear. The British negotiators cannot be accused of having failed to identify the scale of the problem that would arise once all transitional constraints on the British contribution were removed. The calculations put forward from the British side, although not borne out in every respect by subsequent developments, were a great deal closer to the truth than the less closely reasoned figures put forward from the Community side. The latter in particular reflected a hopelessly optimistic view of the Community's ability to restrain the rise in spending on the Common Agricultural Policy. And both sets of calculations underestimated the way in which the Community's budget would expand overall, thus making even heavier the burden on a member state of below average prosperity. The real question that arises is whether the British government was right to assume, as it did, that any fundamental change in the Community's financial arrangements would be unnegotiable. At first sight this seems surprising, given that the Community did, when taking its decisions on finance in 1969/70, at least appear to leave the door open to some change. But all the evidence available to the British government at the time was that any attempt to change the basic decisions, taken so recently and with such difficulty by the Community, would put the success of the accession negotiations at risk. Not only would any change be bitterly resisted by the French but it would, by definition, mean a higher contribution for all the existing member states. The experience of the negotiations of 1979–84, when it took five years of tough negotiation to move from short-term palliatives to the lasting solution of the abatement in the Fontainebleau agreement does not encourage confidence that a fundamental change could have been negotiated in 1970–71. When the matter was re-opened in the renegotiations undertaken by the Wilson government in 1974–75, the corrective mechanism then negotiated failed completely to produce any effective remedy against the day when the transitional constraints on Britain's contribution ran out. So when it came to that point Britain's case for re-opening the arrangements on Community finance had to rest on the 'unacceptable situations' statement made by the Community in the accession negotiations. In the event there never was any serious effort made to contest that the situation that had by then developed was other than unacceptable, nor that the absence of any legal obligation was an obstacle to addressing it. The problem lay in finding an appropriate degree of remedy; and that surely could not have been achieved in the accession negotiations.

The fourth of the main pillars of the negotiations, fisheries, was different in every way from the other three. In place of the careful manoeuvring across well-reconnoitred ground, resembling in some ways the set-piece campaigns of eighteenth-century European warfare, the negotiating armies lurched into confrontation, collided almost haphazardly and seemed for much of the time bemused as to what they were actually trying to achieve. On the British side the contrast was particularly sharp with the other sectors. Preparation for the negotiations was inadequate; the Community's adoption of a Common Fisheries Policy on the same day that the negotiations opened came like a bolt from the blue to a government which prided itself on being exceptionally well informed about internal Community developments and pretty expert by then at influencing them; and thereafter the formulation of policy was subjected to a tug of war between the interests of the deep sea fishing fleet and the inshore fishermen, a struggle which the final compromise resolved in favour of the latter but not before normally amicable Anglo-Norwegian relations were put to severe strain in an unavailing attempt to claw back lost access to Norwegian waters. The Community's performance was even more open to criticism. The original decision to press ahead with adoption of a fisheries policy without taking any account of the interests of four candidate countries whose fish catch more than doubled that of the six original member states was irresponsible in the extreme. One unintended consequence (if one sets aside the conspiracy theories which held that France always wanted Norway to be excluded to avoid the Community's centre of gravity becoming too northerly) was that the Norwegian referendum on the terms of accession failed and to this day Norway, despite a second attempt to join, remains outside a grouping, of which, in most other respects, it is a natural member. Moreover the Community found itself saddled with basic provisions on access to fisheries (the provisions on market management and structural policy have never been controversial to the same degree) which were exceptionally difficult to reconcile with the pressures arising from a whole series of developments; the extension of fishing zones to 200 miles; the loss of access to distant waters by Community fishing fleets; the accession of two new members, Spain and Portugal, with large fishing capacity and relatively few fish; and the urgent need to conserve over-fished stocks from increasingly effective fishing techniques. Not all this could easily be foreseen in 1970 but some of these developments were not far over the horizon when the Community sets its course so irrevocably.

The question naturally arises whether all this could have been avoided. It is unwise to be categorical in such judgements since a negative cannot easily be proved. But it is hard to believe that, if the British government had joined the Norwegians and pulled out all the stops in a campaign to slow the progress towards the Community's decisions on a fisheries policy, it would not have had some degree of success. Once the basic decisions had been delayed beyond the opening of the accession negotiations, it should have proved progressively easier to argue that any policy in a sector where the candidates played such a predominant economic role would better be devised by an enlarged community—as was in fact tacitly recognised in the case of the sheepmeat regulation. The author of the report partly recognises the validity of the criticism that the British government did not pull its weight on this occasion and excuses this on the ground that a general election campaign was under way at the time matters came to a head. Given the damaging consequences that flowed from the fisheries policy over the years to come that reads more like an explanation than a justification.

Napoleon used to require that his marshals be lucky. The same gift is desirable in diplomacy, and the author was surely right to underline how extraordinarily lucky the British government was during the period of the accession negotiations. He contrasted it with all the misfortunes of the 1961–63 negotiations. But the contrast can now be taken wider than that. This was one of the few, if not the only, occasions during the chequered history of Britain's membership of the Community when the cards really fell the right way. The inflationary upheavals of the mid and late 1970s deprived Britain of that close association between Community membership and economic prosperity which, throughout the 1960s, so cemented the loyalty to it of the population of the original six member states. This, and the collapse in 1992 of Britain's membership of the Exchange Rate Mechanism following the strains set up by German reunification, are only two among many examples of bad luck, laced with some bad judgement, which dogged the subsequent history of Britain in Europe.

DAVID HANNAY

The back of Britain's accession negotiations is broken at 4.30 a.m., 23 June 1971. The British delegation files into the Council chamber in Luxembourg for the final session of the Eighth Ministerial Meeting of the Conference.
(Photograph from *Paris Match* of 3 July 1971, courtesy of Scoop.)

Sir Con O'Neill

Note on the Author

When Con O'Neill sat down in January 1972, the week after the signature of Britain's Treaty of Accession to the European Community, to write his report on the negotiations for entry, he was close to the end of a long, but distinctly unusual, career in the Diplomatic Service. Not only was there the interruption suffered by most members of his generation, arising from military service in the Second World War, but in addition he resigned three times from the Service and was three times re-employed. Not that these interruptions prevented his rising rapidly to a number of senior and influential posts, the last of which involved heading at the official level the inter-departmental negotiating team charged with Britain's second, and this time successful, accession negotiations.

O'Neill was born in 1912, the second son of Hugh O'Neill, later Lord Rathcavan, an Ulster politician who was a member of Parliament for Antrim North from 1915 to 1952 and first Speaker of the Northern Ireland Parliament. He was educated at Eton, where he won a history scholarship to Balliol College, Oxford. He took a first class honours degree in English in 1934 and the year after was elected a fellow of All Souls College. In 1936 he was called to the Bar and shortly afterwards joined the Diplomatic Service. During his time at Oxford he began an association with Germany which was to be something of a *leitmotif* of his subsequent career, becoming friendly with a number of Germans who were at the university at the time, including Adam von Trott and Helmut von Moltke, both of whom became active in the 1944 conspiracy to overthrow Hitler.

His first posting abroad, early in 1938, was to the British Embassy in Berlin. As a junior member of the staff of Sir Nevile Henderson he had a ringside seat for the policy of appeasement which culminated in the Munich agreements in September of that year. Like many he was deeply marked and shocked by the experience but, alone among his colleagues in the Diplomatic Service, he resigned in disgust. In 1939 he worked for the embryo Ministry of Information and served as a private secretary to the Parliamentary Secretary; but when the Foreign Office sought to re-employ him this was frustrated by the veto of Sir Horace Wilson, by then Head of the Civil Service, who had been Prime Minister Chamberlain's chief adviser at the time of Munich and who had neither forgotten nor forgiven O'Neill's action in resigning in protest.

In 1940 he joined the armed forces in which he served until 1943 in a number of capacities, all related to psychological warfare, intelligence and propaganda. He was No. 2 in the German section of the Political Warfare Executive where he worked with Richard Crossman, later to be a leading figure in the Labour governments of Harold Wilson. He was sent to interrogate Rudolf Hess, Hitler's Deputy, who had flown to Scotland in circumstances which have never been clearly explained; O'Neill's recollection was that Hess held deranged views of Britain, of politics and of the possible. He worked at Woburn with German refugees on the preparation of material for broadcasting to Germany. In the autumn of 1941 he went as intelligence officer to the Guards Armoured Division at Wincanton; and in late 1942 he was sent to the headquarters of the Allied First Army in Tunisia where he organised the bombardment of German and Italian positions with leaflets designed to undermine the morale of the defenders. In 1943 he rejoined the Foreign Office on a temporary basis and worked there until 1946, when he resigned for the second time, thereafter taking up a full-time job as leader writer for *The Times*.

In 1947 O'Neill returned to the Foreign Office and began a rapid rise through its ranks. He was posted in 1948 to the Allied Control Commission in Germany and served in Frankfurt as British representative in the U.S. Sector, later moving on to Bonn where he was one of the closest advisers to the British High Commissioner, Sir Ivone Kirkpatrick. Then, after returning to London, he did a spell at the Imperial Defence College and was, in 1954, appointed head of the Foreign Office News Department, always an exceptionally demanding job involving the handling of contacts with the Press. Between 1955 and 1957 he served as Chargé d'Affaires in Peking, effectively the British representative to China since relations were only raised to ambassadorial level some time after his period there. After a spell as Assistant Under-Secretary of State in the Foreign Office, dealing with disarmament, he was sent as ambassador to Finland and spent the period 1961–63 in Helsinki. From there he was chosen by Edward Heath, immediately after the collapse of Britain's first attempt to join the European Communities, to go as ambassador and head of the small observer mission to the European Community in Brussels. His two years there laid the foundations for the detailed knowledge of the daily working of the Community as well as enabling him to acquire a grasp of its wider political significance and aims which were to be essential when he headed the negotiating team at the end of that decade.

On his return from Brussels in 1965 he was appointed Deputy Under-Secretary of State in charge of economic affairs and as such became closely involved in the shift of policy which led the Wilson government in 1967 to re-submit Britain's application for membership to the Community. He was in charge of the mass of detailed work which was done at the time to prepare for the resumption of negotiations and which culminated in Foreign Secretary George Brown's opening statement of the British position on 4 July 1967. In the event the opening of negotiations was frustrated by General de Gaulle's second veto; but the basic positions from which Britain began negotiating in 1970 were those defined in the earlier period of preparation. It was at the time not obvious that an opportunity to open negotiations would re-emerge so quickly and, deeply frustrated by George Brown's decision not to send him as ambassador to Bonn when that post fell vacant, O'Neill resigned for a third time in early 1968. In the event, a little over one year later General de Gaulle had himself resigned and it became clear that there was a real possibility of negotiating Britain's accession. O'Neill was recalled and again put in charge of preparations for negotiation, which gradually gathered pace through the latter part of 1969 and the first half of 1970.

The Con O'Neill who led the British delegation into the successive meetings of the Conference of Deputies and who sat at the side of Geoffrey Rippon, UK head of delegation for the ministerial meetings, was an imposing and, to some at least, a quite austere figure. A high, domed forehead, a prominent nose and a remarkably sepulchral voice combined to give an impression that was perhaps more episcopal than diplomatic. The British position was set out at slow dictation speed in language which, for all the technicalities of the subject matter, brooked of no misunderstanding or confusion. But closer contact revealed a sharp, if acerbic, sense of humour and great integrity, that essential attribute for any successful negotiator. In the internal British delegation meetings he rode his team of prima donnas from the different Whitehall departments on a loose rein, chain-smoking, intervening seldom but always pertinently and to good effect, and ensuring that fascination with matters of detail, always a feature of any Community negotiation, was not allowed to cut across or undermine achievement of the strategic objective.

His views were never those of an uncritical advocate of Britain's membership, as he showed in an article written for *European Review* in the summer of 1969:

> Some people argue that it is wise to proclaim maximum objectives because thereby we can convince the Europeans of our sincerity and give a good European impression. Those already in the Community can allow themselves all sorts of dangerous thoughts without losing their European status; they are Europeans by election. We, who want to get in, are expected to become Europeans by continual and uninterrupted grace. This does not worry me much. Those who wish to cast doubt on our vocation will always find plenty of ammunition to hand. Others are already convinced. The European game has become professional. Its adepts are not impressed by players who keep their head in the air instead of their eyes on the ball.[1]

He was always determined to avoid straying off what he later described in the report as the strait and narrow path leading to membership. Nor was he ever guilty of implying in his public utterances, as some were, that Britain's

[1] Sir Con O'Neill, 'Reality and Illusion', *European Review*, Vol. XIX, No. 3 (1969), 4–5.

accession was simply an economic calculation, with no wider political implications. In the Stamp Memorial Lecture, which he delivered in 1972, just after the negotiations, he pointed out:

> The true purpose of the Community is security as well as prosperity, and gradually, by the consent of its members, to extend the advantages of working together into new spheres. Its objectives, whatever the forms through which they first expressed and still express themselves, are not usually economic.

And his judgement on Britain's own predicament in the post-war world and its failure to come to terms with it was both scathing and regretful:

> Britain's experience had been different, or had seemed different; and for a long time we misinterpreted it. The world still seemed our oyster, though in fact we lacked the power to open it. We had escaped defeat and occupation; we had been spared the collapse of our society and institutions. But we had not escaped exhaustion and diminution, the common lot of our European neighbours.

After he left the Diplomatic Service for the last time in 1972, O'Neill held a number of business positions and was Chairman of the Intervention Board for Agricultural Produce. He played an active role in the 1975 referendum campaign on Britain's membership of the Community. He died on 11 January 1988.

Technical Note

The general approach which has been followed in the editing for publication of Sir Con O'Neill's Report on the Negotiations for Entry into the European Community is to leave the report substantially as it was originally written in the spring and summer of 1972. Everything written by Sir Con O'Neill himself and all the documents that he identified and annexed to this report, both the classified and unclassified ones, are now being published in this volume. It has, however, been decided not to publish the texts of Annex I of the report dealing with Secondary Legislation and Authentic English Texts. These chapters were not written by Sir Con O'Neill himself and are extremely technical and difficult to follow without access to additional material; but the main reason for not publishing them is to avoid making an already lengthy text even longer. The text of this annex, like the original text of the report itself, will be available in the Public Record Office under the normal procedures applied after the expiry of thirty years.

It was also decided to publish two texts, which were not included with Sir Con O'Neill's report. The first of these is the full text of Mr. Soames' despatch from Paris reporting and analysing the Heath–Pompidou meeting of 20–21 May 1971. The document annexed to the report by Sir Con O'Neill contained only paragraphs 2–6 of that despatch. Since the report in any case does not go into much detail on that meeting, publication of the full text of the despatch should add to the understanding of its scope and significance. The second text is the statement made by Mr. Rippon on sterling at the meeting of the Negotiating Conference on 7 June 1971, which was subsequently annexed to the Act of Accession. The addition of this text too should add to the general understanding of the report itself.

One further set of additions has been made. Where the report speculates about the likely follow-up to the accession negotiations or about the implementation of agreements reached during these negotiations footnotes are provided setting out the facts as the situation developed in the years following the United Kingdom's accession. These footnotes reflect the views of the editor alone. While there is some risk of seeming to make an excessive use of hindsight, the value of demonstrating where Sir Con O'Neill's judgements about future developments were validated, and where they were not, would seem to outweigh this.

Technical Note

Glossary

Achèvement (completion)	One of a triptych of policies (the other two being élargissement (enlargement) and approfondissement (deepening)) endorsed by the European Community Hague Summit meeting of December 1969. Completion was sometimes given a wide interpretation, including, for example, adoption of a Common Fisheries Policy. But more often, as The Hague Summit communiqué did, it was limited to the adoption of definitive financial arrangements for the common agricultural policy. These arrangements were contained in the Budget Treaty of April 1970.
Act concerning the Conditions for Accession	The title given to the document annexed to the much shorter Treaty of Accession; the Act contained the vast majority of the transitional and other arrangements for the new member states.
Agence Europe	The name of an Italian-owned news agency, first set up in Luxembourg after the establishment there of the European Coal and Steel Community's High Authority and subsequently, when the Commissions of the European Economic Community and of Euratom were established in Brussels, moved to the latter city. It published a daily news sheet which was remarkably well informed about all European Community developments and documents and which therefore became required reading for diplomats and Commission officials.
The Anglo-Irish Free Trade Area (AIFTA)	A free trade area agreement between the United Kingdom and the Republic of Ireland. It was separate from EFTA, of which the Republic of Ireland was not a member, and had some

	different provisions. It lapsed when the United Kingdom and the Republic of Ireland entered the European Community.
American Selling Price	A system applied in the United States to imported chemical products under which they were assessed for the purpose of tariff treatment not at their cost of production or market price but at the price based on the cost of similar US products. Its removal became a major bone of contention in the Kennedy Round of trade negotiations.
Article 220 Conventions	Inter-governmental conventions referred to in Article 220 of the EEC Treaty on such matters as double taxation, the mutual recognition of companies, enforcement of judgements on bankruptcy, etc. These were not treated as part of the *acquis communautaire* which had to be accepted before accession.
British Wine	Not to be confused with wine grown in Britain (of which, at the time of accession, there was very little). A product made from imported grape under conditions which were not consistent with EC wine regulations and therefore gave rise to problems in the negotiations.
British Honduras	Known after its independence as Belize.
BIS	Bank for International Settlements.
Budget Treaty	The European Community treaty negotiated in April 1970 and ratified later that year which provided the European Community with its own revenue resources derived from customs duties, levies on agricultural imports and up to 1% of a VAT assessed on a Community-wide basis.
Capital Movements	The European Community legislation adopted to achieve the EEC Treaty objective of freedom of movement of capital.
Commission	A term used both for the members of the executive set up under the treaties and also their (much more numerous) officials.
Commission 'opinion'	A formal document which, under the provisions of the Treaties, the Commission had to produce before the Member States could take a decision to admit a new member. But, unlike Commission 'proposals', which subsequently constrained the way in which the Council could take decisions, there was no need for the Member States to

	accept any recommendations or proposals made in the 'opinion'.
Common Agricultural Policy (CAP)	The corpus of treaty provisions and European Community legislation which regulated the markets in agricultural products and trade in them and provided for structural reforms and expenditure.
Common Commercial Policy	The corpus of treaty provisions and European Community legislation which regulated the Community's external trade policy. It thus covered tariffs and quota arrangements towards third countries but also such matters as anti-dumping, rules of origin and arrangements for inward processing.
Common External Tariff	The tariff rates charged on imports into the European Community from third countries once the member states had completed the transition from their own national external tariff rates to the common rates negotiated when the European Community was established. This transitional process had been completed by the time the United Kingdom joined; so the progressive dismantling of tariffs by the European Community on UK exports and the adjustments to the UK's tariffs on its imports from third countries were calculated on the basis of the rates in the Common External Tariff.
Common Fisheries Policy (CFP)	The corpus of treaty provisions and European Community legislation which regulated access to fisheries, market arrangements for fish and the structural reform of the fishing industry.
Commonwealth Sugar Agreement	An agreement between the United Kingdom and Commonwealth sugar exporting countries under which the former guaranteed to import specified quantities of sugar at prices well above the world market rate.
Community Preference	The mechanisms by which European Community agricultural producers were given a market advantage and a degree of protection against agricultural imports from outside the European Community, sometimes by means of a levy calculated on the basis of the European Community's own guaranteed prices, sometimes by a tariff and sometimes by a combination of the two.

Conference	The abbreviated term for 'The Conference between Member States of the European Communities and other States which have applied for membership of the Communities'. The conference met at either ministerial or deputy or expert level.
Coreper	The French acronym for the Committee of Permanent Representatives, which met on a weekly basis to prepare European Community business for decisions by Ministers.
Conference Secretariat	The small joint secretariat which was set up between officials of the European Community's Council secretariat and officials from the candidate countries to service the meetings of the Conference.
Derogations	A term of art used to describe provisions negotiated during the accession negotiations which went beyond simple transitional arrangements or temporal adaptations and which amounted in effect to changes in or exceptions from European Community legislation, such as, for example, the provisions for New Zealand butter, for fisheries or Norwegian agriculture.
European Atomic Energy Community (Euratom)	Established at the same time as the European Economic Community in 1957.
European Court of Justice (ECJ)	The court established under the European Community treaties to judge cases involving disputes over the application of Community law or breaches of that law.
European Coal and Steel Community (ECSC)	Established at the same time as the European Economic Community. The founder members were Belgium, France, Germany, Italy, Luxembourg and the Netherlands.
European Free Trade Association (EFTA)	Established in 1959. Its members consisted of Austria, Finland (associate member), Iceland, Norway, Portugal, Sweden, Switzerland and the United Kingdom.
EFTA Non-Candidate Countries	Austria, Finland, Iceland, Portugal, Sweden and Switzerland.
European Investment Bank (EIB)	Institution established at the same time as the EEC, but separate from it, to encourage investment in major infrastructure and other projects.

Economic and Monetary Union (EMU)	An objective defined in the communiqué of the Hague Summit in 1969 but on which no progress had been made at the time of the accession negotiations.
Fusion Treaty	A treaty signed in 1957 which fused the executives of the three European Communities (the ECSC High Authority and the EEC and Euratom Commissions). But the treaty did not fuse the three communities nor the three treaties on which they were based. The single Commission therefore exercised different powers under different procedures depending on which of the three treaties the subject matter fell under.
The Five	(Sometimes known as the Friendly Five). Belgium, Germany, Italy, Luxembourg and the Netherlands.
Generalised Scheme of Preferences (GSP)	A scheme launched by the Organisation for Economic Co-operation and Development in 1970 under which the developed countries would apply nil or reduced tariff rates to imports from developing countries.
Groupe Atomique	The working group of expert representatives from the member states of Euratom which prepared decisions to be taken by Ministers under the Euratom Treaty.
Groupe CECA	The working group of expert representatives from the member states of the European Coal and Steel Community which prepared decisions to be taken by Ministers under the ECSC Treaty.
Interim Period	The period between the cut-off date for secondary legislation (10 November 1971) and the entry into force of the Treaty of Accession (1 January 1973) during which any decisions taken by the European Community would first be the object of consultation with the candidate countries.
International Sugar Agreement	An international commodity agreement, with its headquarters in London, but containing no provisions on guaranteed quantities or prices.
Kennedy Round	A world trade negotiation carried out under the auspices of the General Agreement on Tariffs and Trade. Agreement was reached in 1967, resulting in substantial mutual reductions in tariffs affecting, among others, the European

Community's Common External Tariff and the United Kingdom's tariff.

Multilateral Group on Tariff Quotas — A working group composed of the members of the European Community, the Commission and the candidate countries which was set up by the Conference to deal with the UK's requests for tariff quotas.

Multilateral Treaty Drafting Group — A working group composed of the members of the European Community, the Commission and the candidate countries which was set up by the Conference to draft the Treaty of Accession and all the associated documents.

New Hebrides — Known after its independence as Vanuatu.

Negotiating Team — The United Kingdom's negotiating team, headed by Mr. Rippon and, at official level, by Sir Con O'Neill. It was mainly London-based but a number of its members were based in Brussels.

Secretariat of the Council of Ministers — An organisation completely separate from the Commission, which serviced all the meetings of the European Community member states at expert, official, ambassadorial and ministerial level.

The Six — The founding members of the European Community: Belgium, France, Germany, Italy, Luxembourg and the Netherlands.

Southern Rhodesia — Known after its independence as Zimbabwe.

Summit meeting (The Hague) — The summit meeting in The Hague in 1969 was the first meeting of the Heads of State and Government of the European Community for operational rather than largely ceremonial purposes. There was no regular pattern for such meetings for some years thereafter and none was in fact held between the 1969 meeting in The Hague and the end of the accession negotiations.

Tariff Quotas — (Not to be confused with quantitative restrictions or quotas.) A device for importing a stated quantity of a product or commodity at less than the full tariff rate (or even at a nil tariff rate). Once the stated quantity is filled, imports can still continue, but only at the full tariff rate.

Vue d'Ensemble — The title the Commission gave to the paper, which they circulated to the member states in November 1970. It had no formal status under the treaty, i.e. it was not an 'opinion' in terms of Article 237 of

	the EEC Treaty, but was simply an overall view of the issues that had so far arisen in the accession negotiations. It was never transmitted to the candidate countries.
Value-added Tax (VAT)	Value-added taxes replaced the pre-existing turnover taxes, which considerably distorted intra-Community trade in the founding member states and became a requirement for membership.
Western European Union (WEU)	Sometimes known as the Seven: Belgium, France, Germany, Italy, Luxembourg, the Netherlands and the United Kingdom. A security organisation set up in 1954 after the collapse of the proposed European Defence Community. Because its membership brought together the UK and the founding members of the European Community its meetings were used as a forum for discussion of the relationship between the UK and the European Community during the years after the first French veto.
Yaoundé	The agreement which associated the European Community with their newly independent ex-colonies. Replaced in 1974 by the Lomé Convention, which brought in the newly independent ex-colonies of the United Kingdom in the African, Caribbean and Pacific regions.

REPORT ON THE NEGOTIATIONS FOR UK ENTRY INTO THE EUROPEAN COMMUNITY

June 1970–January 1972

by

SIR CON O'NEILL

Foreign and Commonwealth Office,
London, S.W. 1
27 July, 1972.

The Right Honourable
Sir Alec Douglas-Home, KT, MP
etc.

Sir,

On 24th January this year the News Department of the Foreign Office announced that I would be giving up my departmental duties at the end of that month; and added: 'The Secretary of State for Foreign and Commonwealth Affairs has, however, asked Sir Con to conclude his assignment by writing a personal account of the negotiations for official purposes.' I now have the honour to forward to you, with this despatch, a Report on the Negotiations for Entry into the European Community, from June 1970 to January 1972.

2. I have called it a Report, not a History, for two reasons. First of all, it is too soon, too close to the events I describe, to write their history. Second, my Report is too narrowly based on my experience and my own view of the course of events to deserve the name of a history.

3. I have stuck closely to the actual negotiations. There are therefore many things which this Report omits. It makes no attempt to cover the long background of events which eventually led us to our successful negotiations for membership. One could start the story in 1945, or 1950, or 1959. I have started in 1967, the year of our second application for membership; and I have covered events from 1967–1970 only in a single short introductory chapter. Nor in my Report do I attempt to deal at all with political and Parliamentary developments in the United Kingdom, or with those of public opinion, which accompanied our negotiations. Nor do I deal with the question sometimes called 'European Political Unification', which has quite a long history, which came to life again with The Hague Summit Meeting of December 1969, and has involved much work since then, especially in the last six months preceding the start of our negotiations, and in the last six months since they ended.

4. Nor have I dealt at all fully with what was certainly the most important event of the negotiations—the meeting in May 1971 between Mr. Heath and President Pompidou. I think a full description of this meeting is best left for a later date. I have however referred, in numerous chapters of my Report, to its impact on various sectors of the negotiations; and I have included a chapter describing how the meeting came about.

5. My main problem in preparing this Report was, within the time I had for the task, its scale and length. I thought at first I could write a much shorter Report than it has turned out to be. Equally of course, given time, I could have written a much longer one; for the negotiations were long and complicated and embraced a wide field. They did not, to be sure, quite descend to the kitchen sink; but they approached it. Much time and many telegrams were spent, for

example, on gas meters. As it turned out, the amount of what seemed to me necessary detail and explanation dictated the length of the Report, which with its Annexes and Appendices amounts to well over 200,000 words. I fear it has become too long for its purpose, and that the only people able to read it will lack the time to do so.[1]

6. I have seen it as my task not only to describe the actual course of the negotiations but also, in many cases, to explain the background to particular problems in enough detail to make them more easily comprehensible. And in addition to describing and explaining I have also commented, partly as I went along but also more generally in Part IV of the Report.

7. I have avoided a chronological treatment of the negotiations, though I have included a couple of chapters—Chapters 8 and 9—to summarise the actual sequence of events over the nearly 19 months of negotiations. In the main, however, I have separated out the principal topics of the negotiations and dealt with them one by one in different chapters or groups of chapters. This gives of course a totally misleading impression of tidiness, control and order. I hope readers of the Report will correct this impression by bearing in mind that in fact, and on the whole, almost everything was going on almost everywhere at all times and at once.

8. I was invited to write a personal history, and this is indeed a personal Report in two different ways. First, and inevitably, the selection of topics and the importance I attach to them reflects a personal view, and records the way things struck me. Second, my Report is indeed a personal one in that, apart from a few sections, I have produced it entirely by myself. All the research has been my own, as well as the composition. The former took much more time than the latter; I needed, for instance, well over a week merely to read the files on fisheries. The files accumulated by the Foreign Office alone on the negotiations in 1970 and 1971 would cover, I suppose, about 150 feet of shelf space; so I have achieved a certain compression. I have not read all the files; but I have read a good proportion of them, including all the most important ones. As a result, I feel I can truly claim to have a far fuller and more accurate comprehension of the negotiations than I have ever had while they were proceeding.

9. If my Report is a personal one, it is also inevitably a rather Foreign Office-centred one. I have read only the Foreign Office files; but of course a high proportion of them consists of papers and correspondence originating in other Departments. Nevertheless, I feel I owe some apology to my colleagues from other Departments on the Negotiating Delegation. Inevitably the perspective from which I write cannot be exactly the same as theirs; and the balance of my

[1] The Report was given a very restricted distribution, reflecting the sensitivity, at the time at least, of some of the judgements contained in it and also of the comments made about the performance and motives of a number of foreign governments. Copies were numbered and limited to those who had some responsibility for European affairs. The report therefore escaped the fate of some less weighty official contributions to the debate on Britain's entry into the European Community and did not quickly end up in the public domain.

Report may do less than justice to what were their principal concerns. In particular I am very conscious that, mainly through lack of knowledge, I have dealt too briefly and superficially with many matters deriving from the complexities of the Community's Common Commercial Policy.

10. I have included two appendices each of a dozen or fifteen documents, one of published documents, one of confidential ones. I was in a difficulty here. A reasonably full documentary history of the negotiations could easily fill a score of large volumes. My selection of confidential documents is particularly arbitrary; I could have chosen several other dozens of equal importance, but these happened best to illustrate the narrative as I wrote it. I might have reproduced no documents at all, but I decided to include this very limited number for two reasons. First, including them enabled me in many cases to shorten my narrative. Second, they give a valuable taste of the immediacy, actuality and suspense of events which my Report, written with knowledge of the outcome, could not convey.

11. I must add one point on nomenclature. There are three European Communities, though by now they have a single common set of institutions. There is the European Coal and Steel Community, the European Economic Community and the European Atomic Energy Community. We had applied to join each of the three separately. Should one therefore write about 'the Community' or 'the Communities'? The latter is usually correct. But it is also, it seems to me, usually pedantic. I have therefore used the singular, and written of 'the Community' except where a quotation, or the sense, dictated otherwise.

12. I am very proud to have been the leader of the Official Negotiating Team; and I believe we did on the whole a good job. Leading it was not always easy. It comprised some very senior officials from other Departments, with wide and direct responsibilities to their Permanent Secretaries and Ministers. Sometimes there were differences of approach. But before too long we had shaken down fairly well together as a team, and long before the end we were operating, I think, with real efficiency and harmony.

13. I wish to record my gratitude, not only to all the members of the Negotiating Team including its successive Ministerial leaders, Mr. Thomson, Mr. Barber and especially Mr. Rippon, but also and particularly to those who have helped me by writing sections of this Report: Mr. Christofas, Mr. Marshall, Mr. Coates and Mr. Elkin for Annex I;* Mr. Sinclair for Annex II; and Mr. Shovelton for Chapter 21 on the Coal and Steel Community and Euratom. I could have delved in the files and produced a chapter of a kind on these two Communities, but without the real comprehension and familiarity which 18 months of negotiations about them had given Mr. Shovelton.

14. Two further debts of gratitude I wish to acknowledge. The first is to Miss Sheila Butler, my Personal Assistant, who has now worked with me for almost three years, in London, Brussels and Luxembourg, to which she came with me

* Not printed

to every single meeting of the Ministers or their Deputies. But I most wish to thank her for her help with this Report, drafts of which I have dictated to her chapter by chapter, and for which she compiled the Chronology in Appendix III.

15. The second debt is the greatest of all—to Mr. John Robinson. During the negotiations he was known, rather quaintly, as my 'Special Assistant'; but he was far more than that. For some 15 years he has worked, in Paris, Brussels and London, uninterruptedly on Community affairs, and has become an unrivalled authority upon them. For nearly seven of these years he and I worked together, first in Brussels and then in London. I have sought his advice many hundreds of times, and can scarcely remember an occasion when I failed to follow it. In the negotiations he knew everyone, understood everything, foresaw everything, did everything. His strategic and tactical appreciation throughout the negotiations was much more valuable even than his detailed knowledge. Yet his most important service, I think, came in the years between the first and the last negotiations. To get into the Community—and of course we are not quite there yet—this country had to follow an extremely strait and narrow path, maintaining the true objective, overcoming disappointments, above all resisting the temptations of plausible but inadequate alternatives. The man who did most for many years, by rigorous argument and strong determination, to hold us to this strait and narrow path is Mr. John Robinson.

16. I have dated this despatch 27 July, 1972, the day on which I despatched the last sections of my Report to the printer. I have thus completed my task in just under six months. And in ending my Report I end (I imagine) the last task I shall undertake for the Foreign Office, which I shall leave in a few days' time. I first came to work in this building in October 1936; since then I have had seven separate spells of work in it, amounting in all to over 15 years. I shall be sad to leave it.

I have, etc.,

CON O'NEILL

PART I
PRELIMINARIES, PROCEDURES, ORGANISATION, OBJECTIVES AND TACTICS

I

From May 1967 to June 1970

The British application for membership of the European Community which was made on 11 May, 1967 (it is reproduced in Appendix II) led over three years later to the negotiations which began in June 1970 and ended in January 1972. There was no discontinuity between this application and its success, or between the policy of the successive British administrations which made it, and which converted it through negotiations into the Accession Treaty signed in Brussels on 22 January, 1972.

2. The application of 11 May, 1967, was preceded by the then Prime Minister's statement in the House of Commons of 2 May (published as Cmnd. 3269), which declared the Government's decision to apply for membership of the Community; and by the vote of the House of Commons of 10 May, 1967, at the end of a three-day debate. The Motion ('That this House approves the statement contained in the Command Paper, Membership of the European Communities (Command Paper No. 3269)') was adopted by 488 votes to 62. The Prime Minister's statement, and the vote on it, had been preceded by the tour of the Six Community capitals which Mr. Wilson and Mr. Brown made between 16 January and 8 March, 1967. The Irish Republic and Denmark applied for membership of the Community immediately after we did, Norway some two months later.

3. These developments in British policy and the British application to join the Community were received in Europe with varying degrees of enthusiasm or scepticism. They were welcomed warmly by the Five, and received coolly by the French. The first reaction from General de Gaulle himself could hardly have been worse. In his Press Conference of 16 May, he rehearsed all the problems our entry raised for the Community, as he saw them. He spoke of three alternatives, none of them consisting of straightforward British entry, and one consisting of the 'association' he had offered us after his veto of January 1963. As to that, he declared that 'for our part there could not be, and moreover has never been, any question of a veto'. He also said 'Naturally I do not prejudge what the negotiations could be should there be negotiations. I say again should there be negotiations.' At the Summit meeting of the Six in Rome at the end of May, held to celebrate the Tenth Anniversary of the Signature of the Treaty

of Rome in March 1957, General de Gaulle took the line that the terms of the relevant Treaties should be strictly applied in dealing with the British and other applications for membership; the Council of Ministers should examine them, and the Commission's opinion should be sought. The other Five agreed.

4. On 7 June a formal acknowledgment of the British application was addressed by the President of the Council of Ministers to the Prime Minister. The Prime Minister visited Paris between 18 and 20 June for conversations with General de Gaulle, at which the latter was guarded and noncommittal. He did not exclude our membership or forecast the rejection of our application; but he stressed his doubts of Britain's European vocation. He did not refer to alternatives to membership. He stressed the need for our application to be considered by the Community in the utmost detail, which would naturally take some time.

5. Meanwhile work was proceeding on a statement of the British position for the negotiations. A problem existed as to how, when and where to make it. It was evident that no formal meeting between ourselves and the Six could take place until a formal and favourable reaction to our application had been received; and it was far from certain that such a reaction would be forthcoming. It was decided that the Foreign Secretary, Mr. George Brown, should take advantage of a meeting of the Ministerial Council of Western European Union in The Hague on 4 July to make our statement. The statement was approved by the Cabinet and duly—though somewhat in defiance of the agenda and procedure of the meeting—delivered on 4 July. It was published on the same day as Cmnd. 3345. (Had it not proved possible to make the statement on 4 July, the British Government would have communicated it in writing to all concerned.)

6. This statement was, and remained, of the first importance. Although the negotiations to which it looked forward did not open until almost exactly three years later, after a change of administration in the United Kingdom, the statement remained the basis on which the new Conservative administration opened its negotiations on 30 June, 1970.*

7. The White Paper 'The United Kingdom and the European Communities' published on 7 July, 1971, recorded that: 'When the present Government took office, they confirmed their predecessor's decision to open negotiations at a first Ministerial meeting on 30 June. They picked up the hand which their predecessors had prepared for the negotiating table.' This hand was, in all essentials, the statement by Mr. George Brown of 4 July, 1967, and its subsequent elaboration in numerous detailed briefs.

8. But three years earlier, in 1967, things did not run smoothly. On 10 July the Council of Ministers, in accordance with the relevant article of the three Community Treaties, asked the Commission to prepare its 'Opinion' on the British application for membership; and this Opinion was forwarded to

* See Appendix II

the Council of Ministers on 29 September, 1967. After a full and on the whole fair examination of the problems involved, the Commission concluded 'that, in order to dispel the uncertainty which still attaches to certain fundamental points, negotiations should be opened in the most appropriate forms with the States which have applied for membership, in order to examine in more detail, as is indeed necessary, the problems brought out in this document and to see whether arrangements can be made under which the indispensable cohesion and dynamism will be maintained in an enlarged Community.' The publication of the Opinion coincided with the 1967 Annual Conference of the Labour Party, at which the Government's decision to apply for membership was endorsed. But October and November passed with few if any signs of progress from across the Channel.

9. On 18 November sterling was devalued. This event, and the British economic weakness which it acknowledged, much strengthened the hand of the French Government in their resistance to the opening of negotiations. At a Press Conference on 27 November General de Gaulle spoke in terms of quite exceptional bitterness, hostility and scorn about the British application, and concluded: 'What France cannot do is to enter at present into a negotiation with the British and their associates which would lead to the destruction of the European structure of which she is a part.' The Governments of all the member states of the Community except the French continued to express (with varying degrees of resolve) their welcome for our application and their hope that negotiations could begin; but at a meeting of the Council of Ministers of the Community on 18 and 19 December the French Delegation refused to agree to the opening of negotiations. The President of the Council of Ministers of the Community (Professor Schiller) sent a letter to the Prime Minister, dated 19 December, recording the deadlock reached in the Council, but adding that the British application would remain on its agenda (*see* Appendix II). On 20 December, in a statement in the House of Commons, Mr. George Brown said 'The Communiqué which was issued after yesterday's meeting of the Community Council of Ministers made clear that our application, as well as those of the other countries, remain on the agenda of the Council of Ministers. We, in turn, confirm that our application stands. We do not intend to withdraw it.'

10. Thus the application of May 1967 was rebuffed seven months later; and the door the British Government had attempted once again to open remained closed.

11. There followed a period of 16 months in which no serious progress was made. It was by no means a period of inactivity. Throughout it the British Government, holding to Mr. Wilson's declaration that it would 'not take no for an answer', maintained its determination to join the Community and declined to endorse any objective falling short of that. Early in 1968 there were various initiatives from Member States of the Community, some of which the British Government supported and some of which it opposed. It supported, by and large, proposals made in January and February 1968 by the Benelux

Governments, and somewhat separately by the Italian Government, which sought to make progress in British relations with the Community in areas which would not compromise the aim of membership; that is to say, in the main, in areas falling outside the Treaty of Rome. It opposed the German plan for a 'commercial arrangement' because this would have compromised the aim of membership; but it expressed its readiness to consider any proposals provided they came from the whole Community and were firmly linked to British membership as their culmination. Nevertheless, these German ideas were developed, taken up by the French and indeed in April 1968 received considerable endorsement in another 'Opinion' from the Commission. Throughout this period the main formal British contact on Community affairs with the Member Governments of the Community continued to take place, as indeed it had ever since October 1963, on the 'economic day' of the quarterly meetings of the Council of Ministers of Western European Union.

12. In May 1968 the European atmosphere, and even British prospects, were changed, though not yet decisively, by 'les événements' in France. In June elections for the French Assembly confirmed the Gaullists in absolute control. M. Pompidou soon after left the scene; M. Couve de Murville became Prime Minister and M. Debré Foreign Minister. This was a constellation which seemed to make our prospects of membership of the Community more remote than ever.

13. In the new circumstances, the Community's desultory consideration of the problem proceeded. The British Government's application continued to 'remain on the table'. The Germans continued to develop their unsatisfactory ideas for a 'commercial arrangement' and the French continued to make these ideas even more unsatisfactory from our point of view. Pursuing the alternative line based on the Benelux and Italian proposals of January and February 1968, the British Government sought, with the help at this stage in particular of the Belgian and Italian Governments, to advance its cause by broadening co-operation in Western European Union; but at a meeting of its Ministerial Council in Rome in November 1968 Belgian attempts to enlarge the tasks of the organisation met with a sharp rebuff from the French. In February 1969, at another Western European Union Council meeting in Luxembourg, British pressure brought matters to a head, and led, soon after, to French withdrawal from work in Western European Union. They did not return to the organisation until June 1970, shortly before our negotiations with the Community eventually opened.

14. On the very day when the Foreign Ministers of the Seven were assembling, on 4 February, 1969, in Luxembourg for the Western European Union meeting, a new and major event occurred which, in its sequence, embittered our relations with the French much more. This was the 'Soames Affair'. On that day, General de Gaulle received Mr. Soames and made proposals to him which there is no need to recapitulate here. A week later, at a meeting with Dr. Kiesinger in Bonn, Mr. Wilson informed him of the proposals the General had

made; and 10 days after that the substance of his proposals became public. French resentment at what they chose to regard as British perfidy was intense; and if there had ever been any hope—in my judgment there never had been—for British entry into the Community while General de Gaulle remained President of France, there could now be none.

15. For my part, while as I have said this is not the place to describe or analyse the 'Soames Affair', I feel no doubt whatever that what General de Gaulle said to Mr. Soames was not intended to be, and could not possibly have developed into, a move which could bring us nearer to membership of the European Community. Nevertheless, it led to a somewhat strange, and from our point of view a definitely helpful, development in the later attitude of some of de Gaulle's most loyal supporters, both Ministerial and official. A year or two later, after the General had gone, the legend grew up, and was in some such quarters eagerly believed, that the General's intention in speaking to Mr. Soames as he did had in fact been to begin the process of admitting us to membership of the Communities. By believing this many Frenchmen in important positions in the administration were able to justify to themselves, in 1970 and 1971, our admission to the Communities as being a process which, early in 1969, the General himself, still in the plenitude of his authority, had decided to initiate.[1]

16. But in the immediate aftermath of the 'Soames Affair' no such vision beckoned. The freeze in Anglo-French relations was total, and French obstruction of our objective seemed bound to become more ruthless even than before. Yet this period proved short. Little more than two months after the 'Soames Affair' had broken upon the public, General de Gaulle lost his referendum and immediately resigned.

17. The door was now open. The transformation of our prospects, by this single event, was complete. Everywhere, except at first in France, this was assumed to be the case. In France, M. Pompidou was elected President on 15 June. M. Couve de Murville, after the General perhaps our most bitter opponent for a decade, disappeared from the scene. M. Debré became Minister of Defence and M. Maurice Schumann became Foreign Minister. His appointment, in the light of his earlier European enthusiasms, was regarded as signalising the return of France to more European paths.

18. While biding its time as things developed in France, the Labour

[1] The ideas floated by General de Gaulle at his lunch with Mr. Soames related more to the field of co-operation on foreign and security policy, at this stage quite outside the Community's sphere of activity, than to the question of British membership of the Community as such, about which he was entirely unclear as to whether his objections, which had led to his two vetoes, had been overcome. He foresaw co-operation on foreign and security policy between the main European powers (France, Britain, Germany and Italy) in what came to be called a directoire. Whether these ideas were actual proposals, intended to be followed up in a systematic manner, was also not clear. The subsequent diplomatic row over the disclosure of the lunchtime discussion meant that it never was possible to establish what precisely General de Gaulle had in mind nor whether this was intended to be a genuine opening or a diversionary tactic fraught with risk to Britain's chances of entering the Community.

Government immediately recognised that our prospects for membership of the Community had changed from nil to good. (My own experience confirms this: less than four weeks after the General's departure I was approached and invited to return to the Foreign Office to take charge of the departments concerned with European integration and to be the official leader of the negotiations now foreseen. I did so on 1 September, 1969.) Before the summer holidays, one very significant event occurred: on 22 July, 1969, the Council of Ministers of the Community requested the Commission to prepare an up-to-date version of its 1967 'Opinion' on the British application for membership. This revised Opinion was completed on 1 October; and as the 1967 Opinion had done it recommended the opening of negotiations, but this time 'as soon as possible'. On 5 October Mr. George Thomson was appointed Chancellor of the Duchy of Lancaster, with a seat in the Cabinet, to work in the Foreign Office on European affairs and to be the Ministerial leader of negotiations with the Community.

19. Things were now moving forward. The elections in Germany on 28 September led to Herr Brandt becoming Federal Chancellor on 21 October. The floating of the Deutsche Mark on 29 September, and its revaluation in October, led to difficulties between France and Germany in the Community over agricultural prices and procedures. The Summit meeting of the Six, proposed by the French Government in July and agreed to by its partners in September, took place on 1 and 2 December at The Hague. The Communiqué issued after this meeting became, on the side of the Community, the charter for the opening of negotiations. Its contents are dealt with in another chapter; the text of the Communiqué is reproduced in Appendix II.[2]

20. The great feature of The Hague decision from our point of view was that, even though it provided for other developments less congenial to us, in particular the completion of the Common Agricultural Policy through a definitive agreement on its financing, it marked the formal consent of the French Government at the highest level to the proposition that, on certain firm and rather exacting conditions, the United Kingdom and the other applicants should be admitted to membership of the Community. Almost 18 months later, when the negotiations had been in progress for nearly a year, we were still in doubt as to whether they would succeed. These doubts, as later chapters will show, were not without justification. But looking back, with the benefit of wisdom after the event, my own conclusion is that M. Pompidou and the French Government did in fact effectively take at this Summit meeting the decision which admitted us to the Community. The rest, agonising though it often was, was no more than the process of negotiation. Accidents could have happened.

[2] The Summit meeting at The Hague in 1969, while not the first occasion on which the Heads of State and Government of the Member States had met, was the first meeting which had an operational rather than largely ceremonial significance. Summit meetings were not yet a regular feature of the life of the European Community as they were to become from the late 1970s onwards. The next summit meeting did not take place until the autumn of 1972 after the accession negotiations were over and was attended by the candidate countries as well as the Member States.

The French Government could have reversed its decision. We could have refused some of the stiff tests to which we were subjected. But barring these possibilities, it was in fact The Hague Summit meeting which opened the way to success.

21. The story unfolded rather slowly. Before the end of 1969 the Council of Ministers of the Community reached agreement in principle on definitive arrangements for agricultural finance-arrangements which could scarcely have been less welcome from our point of view, and which were correspondingly welcome to some unreconstructed French Gaullists as likely to make our membership impossible. It was not until April 1970 that these arrangements were finally worked out in detail, and a Treaty incorporating them was signed. Its ratification by the Six Member States took most of the rest of the year, and until the last of them had ratified it the French remained determined not to commit themselves far in the negotiations with us.

22. The Hague Communiqué provided for the opening of negotiations (on certain conditions) with the candidate countries and decided that 'the preparatory work essential to the establishment of a common negotiating position' should be put in hand at once. The Community took six months to complete this work. Meanwhile, in parallel with it, the preparation of the British negotiating position was intensified in London. Mr. Thomson, in January, March and April, visited the Six Community capitals. In January M. Schumann, and in March Herr Brandt, visited London. In February the British Government published its White Paper 'Britain and the European Communities: An Economic Assessment'. In April the composition of the official British Delegation for the negotiations was announced (see Appendix II); it remained unchanged under the Conservative administration.

23. The British Government pressed for the earliest possible date for the opening of negotiations; and in the course of Mr. Thomson's various visits it emerged that a meeting at the very end of June would prove acceptable. This was to be a formal meeting of the Foreign Ministers of the Six Member States with Ministers of the four candidate states. A meeting before the end of June happened to be especially welcome to some of the parties concerned. It would take place before the end of M. Harmel's Chairmanship of the Council of Ministers. It would have, under standing Community arrangements, to be held in Luxembourg. And it would enable the outgoing Commission to be present on the eve of the expiry of their term of office. The date of 30 June was fixed, and a first bilateral Ministerial meeting with the United Kingdom was fixed for 21 July in Brussels.

24. Meanwhile, in London, Parliament was dissolved on 29 May and a General Election took place on 18 June. The Conservatives won and formed a new administration. On 20 June Mr. Anthony Barber was appointed Chancellor of the Duchy of Lancaster, to work as a Cabinet Minister in the Foreign Office and to lead the negotiating team. The election campaign had necessarily led to some interruption of preparations for the opening of negotiations. When the President of the Council of Ministers, in a formal letter dated 9 June replying

for the first time to the United Kingdom's application of 11 May, 1967, invited the United Kingdom to begin negotiations on 30 June, it was impossible, pending the outcome of the election, to give a formal reply; but, as the Government's White Paper of July 1971 recorded (paragraph 21): 'the Head of the United Kingdom Delegation to the European Communities was able to say, when the formal invitation to open negotiations on 30 June, 1970, was conveyed to him on 11 June, that he was confident that the date proposed would be acceptable to Her Majesty's Government'. M. Harmel's letter of 9 June, 1970, is reproduced in Appendix II.

25. Not surprisingly, the new Conservative administration, unfamiliar with all the preparations which had been made and the policies which had been adopted by their predecessors, hesitated a little before accepting the dates proposed. They rapidly agreed to attend the formal opening meeting in Luxembourg on 30 June, and the Council of Ministers was so informed on 22 June. The Belgian Ambassador in London, on behalf of M. Harmel as President of the Council of Ministers, suggested next day that it would be well understood by the Community if the new British Government preferred to delay the first bilateral Ministerial meeting fixed for 21 July. After some doubts, this temptation was rejected and the date of 21 July confirmed. This was a valuable decision. A couple of months delay in the start of the negotiations could have led to a corresponding delay in their conclusion.

26. At Luxembourg on 30 June negotiations opened, at a formal session attended by the Community and the four candidate states. The Foreign Secretary attended the meeting; Mr. Barber made the British Government's opening statement. M. Harmel, on his last day in office as President of the Council of Ministers, made the formal statement which embodied the conclusions of the Community reached over the last six months as to their own negotiating position. This statement is reproduced in Appendix II. It was a statement of the greatest importance for the conduct, course and character of the negotiations. It is discussed in the next chapter.

2

The Basis of the Negotiations

The basis on which the negotiations took place can be defined by reference to a very small number of texts. The first is of course Article 237 of the Treaty of Rome (and the corresponding articles of the two Treaties establishing the Coal and Steel Community and the Atomic Energy Community). Article 237 reads as follows:

> 'Any European State may apply to become a member of the Community. It shall address its application to the Council whose decision, after the opinion of the Commission has been obtained, shall be unanimous thereon.
>
> The conditions of admission and the adjustments to this Treaty necessitated thereby shall be the subject of an agreement between the Member States and the applicant State. That agreement shall be submitted for ratification by all the contracting States in accordance with their respective constitutional rules.'

2. The other relevant texts, in the chronological order of their coming into existence, are:

(A) Mr. George Brown's statement of 4 July, 1967, to the Ministerial Council of Western European Union;
(B) the Final Communiqué of the Conference of the Heads of State and Government of the Member States of the Communities held at The Hague on 1 and 2 December, 1969;
(C) the Opening Statement made on behalf of the Community at Luxembourg on 30 June, 1970, by M. Harmel. as President of the Council of Ministers; and
(D) the Opening Statement made immediately thereafter on behalf of the United Kingdom by Mr. Barber.

These four documents are reproduced in Appendix II.

3. Anyone reading these four texts might well wonder why the negotiations were so elaborate and took so long. The concordance of objectives stated, and of conditions stated and accepted, as between these various texts is close. But

it had to be, if the negotiations were to succeed; and it is no accident that it was. Had the negotiating margin been larger, we should no doubt have stated our own objectives in more optimistic and far-reaching terms. But over the years we had had to make a judgment of what was possible and what was not; and we had had to accept that the Community would inevitably set the limits of negotiation with any aspirant for membership at a rather narrow span. The way that span had narrowed since 1961 is interestingly demonstrated by a comparison between Mr. Heath's Opening Statement of 10 October, 1961 (Cmnd. 1565 of November 1961) and Mr. Brown's statement of 4 July, 1967. By 1967 we were still asking for as much as we believed there was any hope of achieving; but it had become much less than six years earlier.

4. The relevant passage (paragraph 13) of The Hague Communiqué of 2 December, 1969 reads as follows:

> 'They reaffirmed their agreement on the principle of the enlargement of the Community, as provided by Article 237 of the Treaty of Rome.
>
> *In so far as the applicant states accept the treaties and their political finality, the decisions taken since the entry into force of the treaties and the options made in the sphere of development the heads of state or government have indicated their agreement to the opening of negotiations* between the Community on the one hand and the applicant state on the other.
>
> They agreed that the essential preparatory work could be undertaken as soon as practically and conveniently possible. By common consent, the preparations would take place in a most positive spirit.'

The critical element in this paragraph is the statement, in the passage italicised, of the conditions the candidate States were required to accept.

5. Another passage from this Communiqué which seemed relevant to our negotiations, but in the end did not prove so, was paragraph 7, which came at the end of the passage devoted to the Community's decisions on a definitive agreement on agricultural finance and reads as follows:

> 'The acceptance of a financial arrangement for the final stage does not exclude its adaptation by unanimous vote, in particular in the light of an enlarged Community and on condition that the principles of this arrangement are not infringed.'

6. I shall not in this chapter enter into the reasons for which the Community adopted this stern and conditional line about the basis on which it was prepared to negotiate with the candidates for membership; nor shall I discuss the reasons for its re-affirmation and elaboration in M. Harmel's statement of 30 June, 1970. There will be some discussion of this in a later chapter.

7. Mr. Brown's statement of 4 July, 1967, which remained throughout the negotiations the principal definition of the British negotiating position and objectives, was a clear and relatively simple one. 'We seek to reduce the area of negotiations to the minimum' (paragraph 16). 'We want to keep the negotiations

as short as possible' (paragraph 17). 'We accept all three Treaties, subject only to the adjustments which are required to provide for the accession of a new member ... Her Majesty's Government accept without reserve all the aims and objectives of the three Treaties and will implement them' (paragraph 19). 'The questions to be settled before our entry are few' (paragraph 21). 'All of us, you no less than we, will need a transitional period or periods to permit mutual adaptation to the circumstances of an enlarged Community. I would like to propose, following your example at the outset of the Community's life, that the first year of the transitional period should be a standstill period' (paragraph 22). 'In the case of Euratom we seek nothing more than this 12 month initial period. In the case of the European Coal and Steel Community we seek only a limited period of transition. Thereafter we are prepared fully to implement these two Treaties and all the arrangements made under them' (paragraph 24). 'Many of the necessary adaptations could be made immediately following on a twelve months standstill. In other cases, we shall be able to adapt our arrangements with very little delay; but some of the changes which we shall be called on to make, particularly in the field of agriculture, will be very considerable and an adequate period of adaptation will be needed' (paragraph 25).

8. Mr. Brown then proceeded to deal with certain special cases—the Annual Agricultural Review; milk, pigmeat and eggs. He referred to the financing of the Common Agricultural Policy, outlining our special difficulties and expressing the hope that we could take part as a full member of the Community in the negotiation of the agricultural finance arrangements for the period after the end of 1969: this was the hope the French at that time were especially determined to frustrate. In the same paragraph (paragraph 31) Mr. Brown referred to the problem of hill farmers. He went on to deal with the special cases of sugar and New Zealand. On sugar, he declared that we must fulfil our commitment under the Commonwealth Sugar Agreement until the end of 1974 but would wish to discuss with the Community how the interests of Commonwealth sugar producers in the developing countries and territories (thus Australia was already excluded) could be safeguarded in the longer term. On New Zealand, while observing that New Zealand's economy largely depends on her trade in butter, cheese and lamb, Mr. Brown asked nothing for lamb. It had already been decided that we should not seek a change in the Common External Tariff of 20 per cent on lamb, which we believed would not interfere with New Zealand exports to our market, given other circumstances which would operate when we were a member; and the possible contingency of a Community sheepmeat regulation being adopted was catered for by the fact that the whole of Mr. Brown's statement was made 'subject to developments in the Community in the meantime'. For butter, he said that more precise provision would have to be made but 'in the case of cheese it may be found that in practice there will be little or no problem. But we could turn out to be wrong about this.'

9. He went on to deal with the arrangements we should require for Commonwealth dependent territories, for the independent Commonwealth countries in

Africa and the Caribbean and for developing independent Commonwealth countries for whom association was not thought appropriate; in these cases he referred to what had already been provisionally agreed in the negotiations from 1961–63. He said we would accept the obligations of membership in respect of capital movements subject only to a transitional period; and that we should be prepared to accept the Common External Tariff subject to discussing 'how our tariff structure will be adjusted to that of the Community within the period of adjustment to which I have referred earlier'.

10. He then remarked 'there will be a limited number of other points which will need to be considered', instancing our accession to the agreements associating Greece and Turkey with the Community and certain matters affecting the harmonisation of laws in the agricultural and food field. He added 'we think that most of these could be settled after we join the Community' (paragraph 43). He then stated: 'In all other fields we accept, as I have already made clear, the obligations of the Treaty establishing the European Economic Community and the regulations, directives and other decisions taken under it, subject only to a transitional period and, of course, to developments in the Community in the meantime' (paragraph 44). He added that Member States of the Community might wish to propose other questions for consideration and we should be perfectly ready to discuss them. He concluded that our own list was not a formidable one.

11. This statement by Mr. Brown remained the basis on which we conducted the negotiations from 1970 to 1972; and it was certainly also one of the bases on which the Community prepared their own negotiating position in the first six months of 1970. The basis of the Community's negotiating position was set forth in M. Harmel's statement of 30 June, 1970 at Luxembourg, which summed up and declared the position established by the Community as a result of numerous meetings held in the first six months of 1970. He declared that 'the context of the negotiations is that of a three-fold movement, decided upon at the Summit meeting at The Hague: the transition to the final period of the Common Market, the internal development of the Communities and their enlargement'. This was the famous triptych of The Hague Communiqué: 'achèvement, approfondissement, élargissement'. M. Harmel added (though it was hardly true of achèvement): 'These three themes are not linked in such a way that one is a pre-condition for the others'. He went on to deal with achèvement in the context mainly of the definitive financial regulation and remarked that it had been adopted 'without excluding the possibility of adapting it unanimously, to meet the demands of an enlarged Community, but on condition that the principles of the regulation shall not be changed'. He then turned to the internal development of the Community (approfondissement) and referred in particular to economic and monetary union, technological development, the Euratom research programme and the reform of the social fund. Work on these various subjects, as on others, was being actively continued within the Community. 'I refer to this work', said M. Harmel, 'because it is the Community's

intention that, as the examination of these problems leads within the Community either to guidelines or to resolutions for action, these will be put to the applicant States in the negotiations as Community positions. As for the decisions in question, the applicant States will be asked to accept them on the same basis as the other decisions which have been taken since the Treaties came into force.' Thus the 'acquis communautaire' which the candidates were required to accept became extended not merely to all that the Community had done up to 30 June, 1970, but to all that it might do between then and the entry into force of the Treaty of Accession.

12. After this general introduction, M. Harmel went on to describe 'the positions ... which the Community has decided upon for the purpose of the negotiations'. This was the kernel of his statement. He declared the Community's assumption that the applicant States accepted 'the Treaties and their political objectives, all the decisions of every type which had been taken since the Treaties came into force, and the choices made in the field of development.' These decisions, he added, included the agreements concluded by the Community with third countries. Accordingly, 'the Community wishes, at the opening of the negotiations, to state a certain number of principles which it intends to apply'.

13. The first of these principles was: 'The rule which must necessarily govern the negotiations is that the solution of any problems of adjustment which may arise must be sought in the establishment of transitional measures and not in changes in the existing rules.' The duration of transitional measures must be restricted to that required to allow for necessary adjustments: 'They must incorporate detailed timetables and must commence with an initial mutual significant tariff reduction on the entry into force of the Accession Treaties.' The next principle M. Harmel enunciated was the outcome of much difficult discussion within the Community and was accordingly characterised by some rather ambiguous phrasing: 'The transitional measures must be conceived in such a way as to ensure an overall balance of reciprocal advantages. With this in mind, it will be necessary to ensure an adequate synchronisation (parallélisme) of the progress of freedom of movement of industrial goods with the achievement of the agricultural Common Market. This consideration must be taken into account in respect of the duration of the transitional measures in the industrial and agricultural sectors.' The next principle offered a little more latitude: 'In the other fields in which transitional measures prove to be necessary, the duration of such measures could, if possible and desirable, be varied according to their subject matters and the applicants involved.' M. Harmel added two further principles—that in the field of trade the duration of the transitional period should be the same for all the applicants, and that the various Accession Treaties should come into force on the same date.

14. M. Harmel went on to refer to the new responsibilities which the enlarged Community would have towards developing countries. The enlarged Community, he said, 'must be ready to continue its policy of association, both as

regards the existing associated African and Malagasy states and for the benefit of the independent African countries of comparable structure and level of development which request association'; but the possible extension of the policy of association 'should not lead to a weakening of relations with the present associated states'. He added that 'the terms and conditions of association with all these African countries' could be defined during negotiations to replace the present Yaoundé Convention, which were to begin in August 1973. It should be noted that the above related to African countries only. Caribbean and other independent Commonwealth developing countries were not referred to, unless in the following sentence: 'When, during the course of the negotiations, we reach the most important problems concerning the relations with the Commonwealth, we will suggest guidelines as regards Commonwealth countries other than the African countries which I have mentioned.' This vagueness reflected the fact that the Community had so far reached no conclusions on the possible association of developing Commonwealth countries other than those in Africa; and presumably this sentence must be taken as having referred also to the questions of sugar and New Zealand, and indeed to many other Commonwealth questions not mentioned explicitly in M. Harmel's statement.

15. M. Harmel added that his statement was not exhaustive and did not therefore touch on all the problems which would arise during the negotiations. He instanced questions concerning Euratom and the European Coal and Steel Community, and also 'the discussions which we shall be having with the United Kingdom on certain special questions relating to the economic, monetary and financial problems connected with accession'. M. Harmel's statement also described the Community's position on the procedure for the negotiations; this will be dealt with in the next chapter.

16. Mr. Barber's statement of 30 July, 1970, made almost immediately after M. Harmel's statement and drafted in ignorance of the precise terms of that statement, did not in fact add much to the definition of the basis on which the negotiations were opening. The key passage in this statement was the following:

> 'Both Mr. Heath, in a speech last month, and the previous British Government have made it clear that we accept the Treaties establishing the three European Communities and the decisions which have flowed from them. I confirm that this is the position of Her Majesty's Government, subject to the points to which I now turn.
>
> The list of questions which we wish to see covered in negotiations remains the same as those put forward by the previous British Government in July 1967. For Euratom and the European Coal and Steel Community we seek only a very short transitional period. Adaptation to the obligations of the European Economic Community will clearly require more time than that. And it would be unrealistic not to face up to the fact, at the outset, that there are some very difficult problems to be solved. Our main problems, as you know, concern matters of agricultural policy; our contribution to Community

budgetary expenditure; Commonwealth sugar exports; New Zealand's special problems; and certain other Commonwealth questions.

The position which the previous British Government took in July 1967 was, of course, subject to developments in the Community in the meantime. Fisheries policy may prove to be one such development.'

Mr. Barber went on to add a strong statement about the special difficulties in the field of Community finance. He spoke of sharing the Community's determination to go on from what had been already achieved into new spheres of co-operation beginning with economic and monetary matters; but he naturally stopped short of any formal acceptance of what the Community might choose to do in these spheres, though he referred to the recent statement by Mr. Heath to the effect that in all these problems 'we should seek to achieve solutions which are Community solutions'. He added: 'We hope the negotiations can be kept short and confined to essentials.'

17. Thus—apart from crucial matters such as the length and terms of the transitional period or periods, and the details of the settlements in respect of New Zealand and of the problems of the developing Commonwealth, especially sugar, of the other matters described in Mr. Brown's statement of three years before and now possibly of fisheries (for the Community was about to adopt a Common Fisheries Policy that very afternoon)—the positions set out by the two sides seemed to have much in common. The Community insisted that the candidates must accept everything they had done; we for our part, subject to our list of special problems and 'subject to developments in the meanwhile', declared our agreement to do so. The Community asserted (subject to leaving open one chink in respect of a possible unanimous adaptation of the finance regulation) that transitional measures and transitional measures alone must provide 'the solution of any problems of adjustment'. We for our part had gone far to accept that transitional measures and periods would be the main mechanism for adaptation, but had never formally accepted that they could be the only possible solution; though in fact, in the main and subject perhaps to some measure of definition, they proved to be so. Otherwise, the only clear discrepancies between the opening positions of the two sides were to be found in what may have seemed two relatively minor points. We asked for a period of 12 months 'initiation' in which Community obligations should not take effect, while making it clear that this period would be a part of the general transitional period. And we adhered to the view that a number of minor questions could be left to be settled after we had joined the Community.

18. There was nothing in the statement of the Community position which indicated any readiness to accept either of these proposals; and neither was accepted. In the event, we agreed as early as October 1970 to 'set aside' these two proposals; and we never reverted to them. As for the 'period of initiation' we got in the end, through a combination of agreed transitional measures and agreed delays for the entry into force of particular regulations or directives,

enough of the substance of what we had been seeking by our proposal for the period of initiation; but at the cost, of course, of infinitely more complex and detailed negotiations on a vast range of matters than would have been required had our proposal been accepted. As for our suggestion that minor matters could be left to be settled until after we had joined the Community, we met throughout the negotiations a steady and consistent refusal on the part of the Community to agree to anything of the kind. The reasons for this are discussed in Chapter 4. There are it is true (quite apart from those cases where the main issues of the negotiations—for instance sugar, New Zealand and fisheries—will require further discussion at a later stage in the enlarged Community) a number of relatively small matters relating to the details of transitional arrangements which could not by their nature be settled during our negotiations and remain for settlement either in the interim period between signature of the Treaty of Accession and its entry into force or even in the early stages of our membership. But in the main the Community insisted that every conceivable question must be settled, or the conditions of its later settlement precisely provided for, in the negotiations themselves. This we had to accept; and in doing so we accepted also a prolongation and complication of the negotiations to no small extent.

19. One other apparent discrepancy between the Community's conception and our own might be found in the insistence, both in Mr. Brown's statement and in Mr. Barber's, on our hope that 'the negotiations can be kept short'. This contrasts with M. Harmel's remark that 'the task which awaits our negotiators is vast; the problems which they will have to solve are numerous and complex'. But in fact we had no doubt that M. Harmel's formula was likely to prove the more accurate. If we urged speed and simplicity it was mainly a reflection of the tactical requirement for meeting a necessary timetable which dominated our conduct of the negotiations. We knew and accepted from the outset that we should probably need 18 months to conclude them. (Luckily enough, this estimate of the time which would be needed coincided exactly with that most generally accepted within the Community.) M. Harmel's statement, on the other hand, reflected the Community's view that speed was less important than thorough deliberation; and the fact that the Community was not prepared to cut any corners or run any risks for the sake of a group of *demandeurs*.[1]

[1] The Harmel statement has in fact become the paradigm for the opening of all subsequent accession negotiations. The European Community statements made at the opening of negotiations with Greece, with Spain and Portugal, with Austria, Sweden, Finland, and Norway and, more recently, with the Central and East European applicants and Cyprus have all been cast in the same classical mould. While there have been minor differences, the broad principles, the need for the applicants to accept the entire Acquis Communautaire, the broad limitation of flexibility to transitional measures, the insistence that all details be worked out in advance of accession, have been common to all of them.

3

Procedure in the Negotiations

There were important differences between the procedure adopted in the negotiations from 1961 to 1963 and that adopted in the negotiations from 1970 to 1972. This is clearly reflected in the difference between the titles of the two Conferences in which the negotiations were conducted. The first negotiations took place in a 'Conference between Member States of the European Communities and other States which have applied for membership of the Communities'. The title of the Conference which began on 30 June, 1970, declared by M. Harmel in the statement he made that day, was 'Conference between the Communities and the States which have applied for membership of the Communities'. Thus the first Conference was a Conference between States—the Member States on the one hand and the applicant States on the other. The second Conference was a Conference between the Community and the applicant States. The difference was extremely significant.

2. There was a great deal of discussion and uncertainty over the eight or nine months before negotiations began in 1970 as to what their character and their procedure should be. The controversy was begun by the Commission, which stated its views on the point at length in paragraph 59 of its up-dated Opinion of 1 October, 1969. The Commission argued strongly that it should itself, in the main, be entrusted with the conduct of the negotiations. It made no claim for exclusive responsibility; and of course it accepted that it could in any case only negotiate on the basis of a mandate given to it by the Council of Ministers. But it did suggest that the Commission should take the lead in negotiations on 'the problems posed by common policies already in operation or in course of elaboration (Common External Tariff, Common Agricultural Policy and so on) for which Community-type negotiations seem particularly appropriate'. Problems of this kind, of course, were certain to constitute at least nine-tenths of the total negotiation. The Commission went on to propose that in a second phase of negotiation, conducted by the Member States meeting within the Council, the Community would 'decide on the acceptability of the results achieved during the first phase', and the Member States would then, in negotiation with the candidate States, devote themselves 'first and foremost to the more peculiarly political issues, such as the general political problems

resulting from the enlargement of the Community, institutional problems, and the adjustments to be made to the texts of the Treaties'.

3. For the next six months, this problem was discussed in a fairly desultory way within the Community, and the positions of a number of Member States began to crystallise. There was evident reluctance on the part of the Member States openly to controvert the Commission's thesis, which of course seemed to have a highly respectable Community character. As time passed, the Belgians in particular came out in support of the thesis advanced by the Commission. This attitude seems to have been related largely to their hope that it would help M. Rey to remain the President of the new Commission which was to take office at the beginning of July 1970. At first the French also seemed to support the idea that the Commission should be the principal negotiator. When M. Schumann visited London in January 1970 he spoke, though rather noncommittally, in this general sense. The Germans, Italians and especially the Dutch were however in different degrees opposed to allowing the Commission to play so prominent and exclusive a role in the negotiations.

4. We for our part were strongly opposed to the idea put forward by the Commission. But we felt inhibited from openly declaring our position for two reasons. First of all, it was clearly a matter for the Community, not for us, to decide the basis on which they, on their side, wished to negotiate. Secondly, Mr. George Brown, in his statement of 4 July, 1967, had said: 'I will not make any suggestions at this stage about the procedures we might adopt for the conduct of these negotiations. I am sure that we shall be able to fall in with whatever is proposed.' Our primary reason for objecting to the Commission's proposal lay in the fact that it was the governments of the six Member States of the Community, and not its institutions, who would in reality have to take the final decision as to whether the results of the negotiations were acceptable or not. Moreover, it was evident that these governments would not in fact leave any real margin of discretion to the Commission as a negotiator. Negotiations with the Commission would therefore clearly entail a continual process of reference back by the Commission to the Council of Ministers for revision of their mandate; or alternatively might proceed for long periods without any certainty that the solutions they developed would prove acceptable to the member governments. In negotiating with the Commission we should have been negotiating at one remove from the real source of authority and decision in the Community. Moreover, and this was perhaps the most decisive consideration of all, we felt it was essential that the member governments of the Community, and above all their Ministers, should become actively engaged in the negotiations and committed to their success; and our own Minister leading our negotiating team must have the opportunity of really getting to grips with Ministers of the member governments. While, as stated above, we felt unable to make clear our views publicly or represent them formally to the member governments, it was made unmistakably clear at least to the German, Italian and Dutch Governments that we did not like the Commission's proposals;

and there is no doubt that the French Government were also aware of our view.

5. Fortunately for us the Commission's ideas tended to grow more unpopular in the Community as time passed. Even the French grew more doubtful of the wisdom of the Commission's proposal, to which they had never become strongly attached. By April it had become clear that the Permanent Representatives of the Member States in Brussels were themselves anxious to play an active part in the negotiations; and although no formal decision was taken that month the Foreign Ministers of the Member States in fact virtually decided at a meeting in Luxembourg on 20 April against the Commission's proposal. This did not however mean that they favoured the same procedure as had been adopted in 1961 to 1963. There was a clear consensus of view among the member governments that this time the Community must negotiate as such, and not as a collection of Member States. This thesis was particularly strongly insisted on by the French; but it found no opposition from the other members. In 1961 to 1963 the Community had indeed, and necessarily, spent a great deal of time in arriving at common views to present and defend in the negotiations with us. But they did not then, because of the character of the Conference, confine themselves when they met us to negotiating through a single spokesman operating on behalf of the Community as a whole. On the contrary, at meetings of the Conference representatives of each Member State were free to express their views as debate developed, and did so. This certainly made the negotiations in 1961 to 1963 very much more interesting and lively than they were in 1970 to 1972. But it led to a strong feeling on the part of some of the Member States of the Community, and not only the French, that an undesirable consequence of this state of affairs had been that we were given opportunities of 'dividing the Six'. The French were determined, and on the whole the others tended to agree with them, that we should not be given such opportunities again.

6. It was probably in our own interest that we should not be put in a position where we might appear, even if unjustly, to be aiming at such a division. In any event, the essential feature of the Community's final decisions on procedure was that the negotiations should be conducted at all levels by a single spokesman—the Chairman for the time being—on behalf of the Community as a whole; and this concept underlay the title of the Conference proposed by M. Harmel. The Community also proposed that the Conference should take place at Ministerial, at senior official and at Working Group level; and that the senior officials on their side should be their Permanent Representatives in Brussels. These proposals were decided on at a meeting of the Council of Ministers in Brussels on 8 June; and after this meeting the Council published a communiqué declaring the procedure they intended to adopt. This communiqué is reproduced in Appendix II. At the meeting on 30 June M. Harmel, in his statement, declared that the Community would employ a uniform negotiating procedure at all levels and for all questions. There can be no doubt whatever that we were fortunate to avoid the dangerous consequences—in terms of delay, uncertainty

and remoteness from the real centres of decision—which would have flowed from a decision that the Commission should be the principal negotiator for the Community. After the negotiations were over, M. Wellenstein, leader of the Commission's negotiating 'task force', told me that we had been quite right to oppose the proposals advanced by the Commission in its Opinion of October 1969.

7. It was not clear, and for a long time remained uncertain, whether the negotiations would, after the formal opening meeting on 30 June at which all four candidates were present, be of a mainly or indeed exclusively bilateral character (that is to say, separately between the Community and each of the four applicant countries) or whether they would acquire to some extent a multilateral character. M. Harmel referred to this point too. He remarked that the Community were aware that the applications for membership raised both problems peculiar to each of the applicant States and problems which would have to be examined jointly. The organisation of the negotiations, he added, must therefore take this situation into account 'it being understood that, during the first stage in any case, most of the work will have to be done on a bilateral basis'. In fact, as things turned out, the bilateral basis was preserved throughout the negotiations, at all events at the level of the Ministers and of the Deputies.

8. That this would be so remained for a long time uncertain; for instance, we ourselves proposed at the Ministerial meeting in July 1971 that the next Ministerial meeting should be a multilateral one, devoted to fisheries, at which Ministers of all candidate States should negotiate together with the Community. It was perhaps rather fortunate for us that this proposal proved unacceptable to the other candidate States. But some of the tasks of the Conference were performed, and had to be performed, on a multilateral basis. Thus the prolonged and intensive work of the group on Secondary Legislation was carried out simultaneously between all four candidate countries and the Commission. Solutions to the problems of tariff quotas were worked out in a multilateral group between representatives of the six Member States and the four candidate States. The drafting of the Treaty was performed by a multilateral group on which all four candidate States, all six Member States, the Commission and the Secretariat of the Council of Ministers were all represented. But, though right to the end of the negotiations the possibility was felt to exist that a multilateral meeting at Deputy or Ministerial level might yet prove necessary, it did not do so. This gave rise to the technical problem which became known as 'multilateralisation', because it was necessary, given the decision that there should be a single multilateral Treaty of Accession, that each of the candidate States should accept all the solutions reached bilaterally with each of the other candidate States. This process, as it turned out, gave rise to few difficulties.

9. After the formal proposals made by the Community on the procedure and character of the Conference, which we were glad to accept, it was necessary to take a decision on the rhythm and periodicity of meetings. At our first bilateral Ministerial meeting on 21 July the Community proposed that in principle there

should be two Ministerial meetings with us each quarter and that the Deputies should meet for two days every fortnight. They also proposed that this pattern could be changed and accelerated if the need for such action became clear. We had been inclined to feel that rather more frequent meetings at both levels might be desirable; but given the possibility of having more frequent meetings if the need for them could be demonstrated—as later on it was—we accepted these proposals. Mr. Rippon in particular, who soon after this meeting succeeded Mr. Barber as Chancellor of the Duchy of Lancaster and Minister in charge of the negotiations, took the view that frequent Ministerial meetings would be undesirable, and that they should only take place when there was real and useful work for them to do. The schedule thus agreed was on the whole adhered to. In the 19 months of negotiation, we had 13 meetings of Ministers and 38 of Deputies. Apart from summer holiday and Christmas interruptions, Deputies' meetings were in fact held as a rule every other week. Occasionally, and particularly in the last two months of the negotiations, they were rather more frequent. Ministerial meetings sometimes took place only at intervals of about two months; but in two periods, May to July 1971 and November to December 1971, four and three Ministerial meetings were held respectively in periods of nine weeks and five weeks. The remaining six Ministerial meetings were thus spread over a period of about 60 weeks. Compared with the negotiations from 1961 to 1963, Ministerial meetings were somewhat less numerous and lasted rather less long.

10. How did these arrangements work? I shall write more on this in the next chapter on the character of the negotiations. Here it suffices to say that the arrangements made worked out all right in the end, while producing negotiations which were, on the surface at least, of a rather strange and stilted character. It is also true that the procedures agreed on had the result of relieving us from the accusation directed against us to some extent during the earlier negotiations and still more in retrospect after them—that we had spoiled our chances and deserved our failure by 'seeking to divide the Six'.

11. All was of course not quite so formal and stilted as the impression given by the surface appearance of Ministerial and Deputies' meetings. Contacts outside the formal meetings of the Conference became increasingly frequent and increasingly important as the negotiations moved forward. At first, as recorded elsewhere in this Report, it was not easy to arrange useful contacts with the Commission; but as initial suspicions on the part of some of the member Governments thawed—and at the outset they were remarkably lively—our contacts with the Commission (at all levels below that of members of the Commission) grew increasingly frequent, informal and fruitful. Senior members of the visiting Delegation and many members of the resident Delegation took part frequently in such contacts. In the process of informalising and accelerating the negotiations contacts with the Presidency also came to play an increasingly useful role. Throughout the negotiations, and especially after he became acting head of the Permanent Delegation in Brussels on Sir J. Marjoribanks'

retirement in March 1971, Mr. Christofas maintained close touch with the Presidency between formal meetings of the Conference. Before every meeting of the Deputies I had a bilateral private meeting with their Chairman, partly to discuss and agree on the agenda of the meeting about to take place, partly to provide an opportunity for the raising, by either side, of other questions on an informal basis. Before every Ministerial meeting Mr. Rippon spent a short time with the Chairman of the Council of Ministers for a similar purpose.

12. My own regular contacts with the Chairman of the Deputies before formal meetings grew increasingly useful as the end of the negotiations approached, and were more and more used for exchanging views about the position of the two sides on matters which, usually in order to protect them from premature publicity, it was agreed not to ventilate in the formal Conference. After such meetings, the Six Permanent Representatives frequently held a short meeting among themselves, at which their Chairman would communicate what I had told him; and he would then, still outside the formal meeting, communicate to me the Community's reaction. In this way, supplemented of course as a rule by further expert contacts with the Commission, a number of sensitive questions were advanced towards solution but withheld from discussion in formal Conference until agreement, or virtual agreement, had been reached and the risks of premature publicity had passed.

13. Some examples of matters so handled are given in paragraph 17 of Chapter 6. Another was the desire of certain elements in the Community, towards the close of the negotiations, to oblige us to acknowledge in a formal agreement the supremacy of Community law over our own municipal law. This was an attempt to dictate the character of our implementing legislation; it was quite superfluous, and had it happened would have been widely regarded as unwarranted interference and would have drawn public attention in an unwelcome manner to a delicate issue. Fortunately, in this case, the French were on our side. The matter was discussed with the Presidency on several occasions; it never leaked; and in the end the Community dropped the point.

14. The procedures of the formal Conference were slow, and in the early stages we did not seek to short-circuit them. Often there was so little ripe for discussion at any particular meeting that we and the Community preferred to keep what little we had to say for the meeting, rather than invent devices for the advance exchange of papers or statements. But we did, especially in the early stages of exposition and exploration, table longer and more important papers in the intervals between meetings, in order to give the Community time to consider them before a meeting took place. Usually only a few days passed before the substance of these papers, if of sufficient interest, leaked and was published by the Agence Europe. In the last stages of the negotiations, when time pressed, more rapid procedures were devised and both sides frequently exchanged written papers or statements in the intervals between meetings or during adjournments of them. Another device regularly adopted throughout

the proceedings was the communication, after any statement of more than routine significance had been made, of its text by each side to the other.

15. The Conference Secretariat played a useful role. To it we contributed two officials who helped to ensure that the records of the Conference adequately reflected our own point of view. These formal records of Deputies and Ministerial meetings were kept on what proved a sensible basis: extremely brief and summary reference to views exchanged, but full and careful records, often in long Annexes to the Minutes, of agreements reached. Even so, there were a number of cases where—through no fault of the Secretariat—agreements recorded proved ambiguous or incomplete, and led to later difficulties in the Treaty Drafting Group. The Secretariat played little part in the policy developments of the Conference, though occasionally, in the latter stages, they contributed to the task of bridging gaps. The Head of the Conference Secretariat was M. de Schacht, the Belgian Deputy Secretary-General of the Council of Ministers. At the outset he seemed somewhat reserved and suspicious in his attitude towards us; but by the end of the Conference he had become much more forthcoming and helpful, and was clearly committed to a successful outcome. The Secretary-General of the Council of Ministers, M. Calmes, appeared only at Ministerial meetings; as indeed did M. Deniau and other Members of the Commission.

16. Another procedural point deserves to be mentioned, for anyone who examines the records of the Conference might find it a little surprising. Such examination would show that in virtually every case, from whatever side a problem had been raised (and of course most of them had to be raised by us), eventual formal agreement was reached on the basis of a proposal put forward by the Community. This was no more than a little habit of vanity on the Community's part: they liked having the last word. It by no means implies that the elements of agreement had been contributed by the Community rather than by us; but we saw no reason to object if they preferred to do the final 'summing up'. It may indeed be partly because the Community could never utter the first word that they were so keen to have the last one. Examination of the records will reveal another fact: the Community never once took the initiative on a major issue with a concrete proposal. They were able to propose principles and procedures; but in no single major case—such as Community finance, New Zealand butter, tariff or agricultural price movements or fisheries—could they overcome their internal differences and deal in hard practical terms of figures or periods till we had broken the ice by doing so ourselves.

17. To conclude this chapter, something should be recorded about the procedures adopted by the United Kingdom Delegation. The crucial decision about the composition and work of the United Kingdom Delegation was that whereby I and its other senior members retained our position in the Whitehall Departments to which we belonged, and only visited Brussels when we were required to do so for formal sessions of the Conference, or occasionally for other purposes. I myself was lucky enough to attend every Ministerial and Deputies

meeting; and thus, with one or two other expeditions thrown in, I made during the course of the negotiations well over 50 return journeys from London to Brussels or Luxembourg.

18. The author of the commentary on the Narrative Report on the Brussels Negotiations from 1961 to 1963 described the similar practice which was followed during those negotiations and added:

'This form of organisation had several advantages. Most important, it enabled Departments in Whitehall to be kept fully and constantly informed of developments in Brussels. There were, however, disadvantages as well. The fact that the travelling members of the Delegation were not only concerned with the conduct of the negotiations, but also with the preparation of their own instructions in London, led to some blurring of responsibility. It was difficult for the Delegation to form, and to express to London, a corporate view based purely on the needs of the negotiations. Such a view might often have been helpful in the formulation of policy. After meetings with the Six, the travelling members usually had to leave at once. Consequently it was seldom possible for the Delegation to make a considered assessment of the current position and decide what fresh instructions were needed before we saw the Six again and what should be done and said in the meanwhile. We consider that the disadvantages of the system clearly outweighed the advantages. Should there ever be another negotiation of comparable character, we think it would be more effective if it were conducted from the British side by a Delegation anchored more firmly on the spot. The Delegation should concentrate entirely on the negotiations themselves.'

19. I feel it is fortunate that, in spite of this recommendation, we adhered to the practice of our predecessors. We did not, in my judgment, suffer from the disadvantages described above. This may perhaps have been due to the fact that meetings in Brussels requiring the attendance of the senior officials of the Delegation were rather less frequent and less prolonged than they had been nine years before. Had we frequently had meetings with the Six at intervals of no more than four or five days, similar difficulties might have arisen; but as a rule we had 12 days in London between meetings to sort things out. As it turned out, during our own negotiations the senior members of the Delegation spent considerably less than one-quarter of their time in Brussels, and the rest in London. And their presence for most of their time in London was indispensable. In each Department it was the senior members of the Delegation who bore the main daily responsibility, subject of course to the views of their Permanent Secretaries and Ministers, for the formulation of policy on the issues which were being negotiated in Brussels. Most of them regularly attended, as the senior representatives of their Departments, the meetings of the Cabinet Office official committees which determined policy on secondary issues, and formulated it for decision by Ministers on major ones. We were thus able to avoid any serious conflicts of appreciation, interest or attitude between Whitehall and Brussels;

and largely as a result of this interlinking there were virtually no cases in which the Delegation received instructions which it felt it had no chance of carrying out successfully. The only such case I recall occurred in the very last stage, while the whole Delegation was away in Brussels for over a week.

20. The Delegation's corporate existence in London naturally and properly became merged in the general Whitehall machinery for determining negotiating policy, though occasionally meetings of the Delegation as such were held in London. In Brussels, however, the Delegation preserved its corporate identity and common approach by holding a Delegation meeting before every Deputies meeting and almost every Ministerial meeting. The Delegation meetings in Brussels were often long and sometimes arduous, especially when, as was generally the case before Deputies meetings, they took place from 10 p.m. to midnight, shortly after arrival from London. At these meetings tactics were settled, the texts of statements to be made were finally agreed and any Press aspects of an impending meeting discussed. These meetings also served the useful purpose of strengthening the links between the visiting members of the Delegation from London and the Permanent Delegation in Brussels; and an essential feature of them was, naturally, that the latter were able to convey the very latest news and information on events in Brussels to the former.

4

The Character of the Negotiations

The character of the negotiations was the resultant of their basis and their procedure, described in the two previous chapters. Their basis determined their content; their procedure determined their style. In this chapter I shall describe the style and content of the negotiations, beginning with the former.

2. It is perhaps worth sketching briefly the scene presented by a formal meeting of the Conference. In a large room, equipped with simultaneous interpretation, the British Delegation sat at one end of a long hollow rectangle of tables. Opposite them sat the President and the Secretariat. The two longer sides of the rectangle were occupied by the Delegations of the six Member States and of the Commission. There was no lack of people present. In a Ministerial meeting, those present in the room often amounted to one hundred or more; attendance at Deputies meetings fluctuated around seventy or eighty. There was room for about fifty at the table; the rest sat behind. These large groups of people assembled to listen to a stilted dialogue, or rather a series of short and stilted dialogues, between the President of the Community Delegation and the British Delegation. In the meetings of Deputies we at least contributed a little variety in that, while I made the more general statements and conducted the proceedings from our side, our statements on monetary affairs (capital movements, the European Investment Bank, tax harmonisation) were made by Mr. Bell of the Treasury; our statements on agricultural matters were made by Mr. Kearns of the Ministry of Agriculture, Fisheries and Food; those on industrial trade and tariffs and the Common Commercial Policy were made by Mr. Denman of the Department of Trade and Industry; and those on the European Coal and Steel Community and Euratom by Mr. Shovelton of the same Department.

3. But on the Community side only the President spoke. At the first Deputies meeting the Dutch Permanent Representative, deliberately experimenting, ventured a few words though not in the Chair. After the meeting he was jumped on by his French colleague and the rule was never broken again. Once at a Ministerial meeting Dr. Luns ventured to suggest that a matter of procedure—the date of future meetings—might be discussed by all concerned in the presence of the British Delegation; Signor Moro supported him. But M.

Schumann, in the Chair, soon put a stop to that. Not even the Commission had—as it did in the earlier negotiations—the right to speak. The representatives of the Commission did occasionally make some remarks, but only on the invitation of the President, and probably not more than half a dozen times in the course of all our formal meetings. He was only called upon for occasional factual contributions, or when the President was stumped on a matter of procedure or the interpretation of Community texts. Naturally, however, the Commission played a full and prominent part in the internal deliberations of the Six. It was made very clear throughout by the Six that the Commission must be regarded, and must regard itself, as the servant of the Six, rather than of the Conference as a whole.

4. The fact that the Community could only speak with one voice meant that they could only speak after they had decided among themselves what that voice was to say. This made an extended dialogue impossible; the Community could not react to any proposal we might advance until they had had the opportunity to consider it among themselves; and such consideration, though occasionally it took only hours, frequently took months. It thus became one of our objectives in the negotiations to offer the Community every possible chance to get together for discussion among themselves, since things could not move forward until such discussions had taken place. Adjournments of a meeting, while we cooled our heels and the Six carried on their argument, though superficially frustrating to us, were in fact a fruitful device and one which we promoted as much as we could. At the first Ministerial meeting on 21 July the pattern was inaugurated when a five-and-a-half-hour adjournment took place to enable the Community to deliberate on some proposals Mr. Barber had just made. The result (though accompanied by a semi-successful effort by the French to stiffen up the basis of the negotiations against us) was a large measure of agreement with us, which could not have been reached in any other way. It was a characteristic of the negotiations that much more and much longer negotiation took place within the Community than between them and us. Deliberations on the negotiations between the Permanent Representatives or their Deputies and in the Council of Ministers probably took up twenty or thirty times as much time, during the 19 months of the negotiations, as did their formal meetings with us.

5. The formal meetings with us, whether at Ministerial or Deputies level, were indeed brief. On occasions they were embarrassingly so. There were times, during the six most barren months of the negotiations, from November 1970 to April 1971, when we were at our wits end to scrape together enough topics for discussion to give a meeting a duration of minimum respectability. We had piled in a series of proposals already; but the Community was not able to react to them. Although in principle two days had been allotted to each Deputies meeting with us, we very seldom, except in the last two months, used more than one. We tried, in January 1971, to make use of both days, in the hope that the interval between them would enable the Community to respond on the second day; but the device proved barren. It was hard enough at this stage to make

good use of one day, let alone two. We used to time the duration of Deputies meetings, and I think the record for brevity was held by one which took place in November 1970; it lasted 23 minutes. But this characteristic, though embarrassing at this stage, was to some extent common to all the formal negotiations from the beginning to the end. Even the all-night sessions, of which our Conference produced perhaps six or seven apiece at Ministerial and Deputy level, were by no means what they may have seemed to those who read about them in the Press. Perhaps the general image was conveyed of the British Delegation locked for 15 or 20 hours at a stretch in debate with the Community Delegation, as statement or proposal, reply, rebuttal or rejoinder, compromise or counter-compromise were volleyed across the table. This was not the case.

6. What happened was very different. I do not think there was a single continuous session between Ministers of the Community and Mr. Rippon which lasted as much as an hour; and only on a few occasions, as the agenda became more charged and detailed towards the end, did single sessions of the Deputies last for much more than an hour. Instead, where a meeting was prolonged at all, it consisted of an alternation of relatively brief sessions with us and much longer sessions between the Six, in which they deliberated after we had withdrawn. The most successful of all the Ministerial meetings, that from 21 to 23 June, 1971, at Luxembourg, though it had two all-night sessions each of which lasted until about 5 in the morning, probably did not entail, in its 30 hours of meetings spread over two days and two nights, more than a couple of hours if that during which the British Delegation was formally seated in the Conference chamber with the Six. For the rest of the time (apart from interventions for meals, which were on this as often on other occasions highly constructive interludes from the point of view of the negotiations) the Community was deliberating by itself. And for much of the time, as things advanced towards solutions, the Community itself was doing no more than sitting twiddling its thumbs while various emissaries, mainly from the Commission, armed with the Community's latest position, were sent forth to contact us, to bargain with us and to return again to the Six—while we wrestled and bargained with Mr. Marshall on New Zealand butter and cheese.

7. It is thus true to say that there was in fact no real negotiation at the formal sessions of the Conference. There could not be. We, having no partners to consult, had more liberty than the Community. We were therefore in general a little better than they at keeping the discussion going, even in a formal session. Except on procedural matters, their President could barely reopen his mouth once he had discharged a statement of their position. Thus in general the formal sessions of the Conference, at either level, had two purposes only: to make statements or proposals and develop the arguments in support of them; and to record formal agreements once these had been reached through the elaborate variety of methods pursued outside the formal Conference. During, as opposed to at, Ministerial meetings negotiation in the most genuine sense did of course take place. Political pressure was applied and yielded the most important results of

the Conference, as over sugar, New Zealand butter or fisheries. The same process, for less momentous results, even took place during the Deputies meetings of the last six weeks of the Conference. But in general the Conference at Deputy level was no more than a steering committee for the Conference as a whole. As such it was indispensable; but it could seldom be, and scarcely ever was, a genuine negotiating forum. To some extent, especially in the early stages of the Conference, the Deputies deliberately minimised and sought to conceal their achievements. This was because an important part of our tactics was to ensure if we could that at least each Ministerial meeting had some solid, even if not always very significant, agreement and achievement to record. Thus there were many occasions when agreement was carefully prepared and indeed completed in the Deputies, but the degree of agreement attained was somewhat minimised with the Press in order to hold the achievement back for the next Ministerial meeting.

8. So much for the character of the negotiations in so far as it was expressed through their style; I now turn to the way in which their character was dictated by their content, which in turn was dictated by the basis of the negotiations agreed between the two sides before, at or soon after their opening. I say 'soon after' because we continued, at the first Ministerial meeting in July 1970 and for some time thereafter, to reserve formally both the possibility of changing some of the Community's policies and rules and the possibility of leaving matters over for settlement after we had entered the Community. By October 1970 we had shelved these possibilities as formal objectives; although of course to some extent each of them was met by some of the solutions eventually achieved in one or other field of the negotiations.

9. The only participant in the negotiations who was able, so far as I am aware, to publish, even before the Treaty was finally drafted or signed, a history of them was Dr. Nass, a member of the Commission's staff (Englands Aufbruch nach Europa, Europäische Schriften, Europa Union Verlag GmbH). His small book was a little premature (he records that he completed his manuscript in October 1971), and it is perhaps not so much a history of the negotiations as a commentary on them. What Dr. Nass wrote was somewhat schematic and extremely juridical; was written almost exclusively from the standpoint of the Commission; and seems to me rather to overestimate the degree to which the candidates, including ourselves, were obliged to accept in full all the doctrines and positions of the Community. This error may have been a bit more excusable in October 1971, before some of the later decisions of the Conference, for example those on fisheries, the Channel Islands and animal health, had undermined Community positions rather more than was common in the earlier stages. Nevertheless Dr. Nass, whose part in the negotiations was concerned principally with secondary legislation, does give an interesting analysis of the proceedings and does make some penetrating remarks. Thus he writes: 'All those who took part both in the first and in the second negotiations with the United Kingdom agreed that the second negotiations were much more boring.' Though I myself

found the negotiations entirely absorbing throughout, I agree that in a sense this is true. It was a consequence of the character imposed upon them by their basis and their procedure. But even if they were more boring, the limits imposed on them enabled them to be more practical and more businesslike; and they produced a happier result.

10. Dr. Nass remarks that the 'great issues' of European integration were never discussed in the negotiations, by which he means questions such as the future policies of an enlarged Community, its relations with the rest of the world, what its institutions should become and how they should work. This again is true; and it is fortunate. The negotiations only took place because all Governments had become convinced that, on matters such as this, there was a sufficient congruence of view between all concerned to make a success of the enlarged Community. But matters such as these were for discussion between Mr. Heath and M. Pompidou, or in a future Summit Conference, not in the negotiations for entry.

11. What made the negotiations tedious, and forced them to deal at such length with so many subjects of a highly technical character and only secondary significance, were two principles, one of which we accepted in advance and one of which we had to accept as we went along. These two principles (they are in fact two facets of a single principle) entailed, first, that (in Mr. George Brown's words), 'We accept ... the obligations of the Treaty establishing the European Economic Community and the regulations, directives and other decisions taken under it'; and, second, that nothing would be left over for settlement after we had entered the Community. The principle of accepting all the decisions of the Community had far-reaching consequences. Dr. Nass sets them out in a long passage which is reproduced in Appendix II. I will quote here, because they well illustrate a major difference between our negotiations and those which had taken place nine years earlier, the first four sentences of this passage: 'In the negotiations in the years 1961–63 the Treaties represented not indeed the only, but certainly the decisive, sector of European law which Great Britain had to accept. It was in consequence of this that these negotiations were concerned above all with these Treaties. By 1970, the situation was fundamentally altered. An almost inconceivable flood of European law had since then been enacted and had to be accepted by the candidates.'

12. What Dr. Nass describes in the long passage which these sentences introduce is the 'Acquis Communautaire', a concept which haunted us throughout the negotiations, which proved almost indefinable (I know no better definition than that given by Dr. Nass) and which seemed at times to be capable of almost indefinite extension. It was sometimes also referred to as the 'patrimoine' of the Community. Everything, beginning with the Treaties themselves, on which any of the three Communities, through any of their institutions, had ever reached agreement in any form, even if it had never been published, was, provided it had not clearly lapsed or been rescinded, a part of it. And we were asked to endorse, accept and be bound by it all. The generality of our acceptance

is expressed (sometimes rather obscurely) in Articles 2 to 9 of the 'Act Concerning the Conditions of Accession'. And one can say not unfairly that the whole of the remaining 300 or so pages of the Treaty of Accession, including in particular all its Protocols and Annexes and its Final Act, record no more than the instances in which and the degree to which, largely but by no means exclusively through transitional periods and mechanisms, the Community agreed that the acceptance by each of the Candidate States of the Acquis Communautaire should be qualified, modified and eased.

13. The second facet of the Community's principle of 'swallow the lot' was involved in our contention that certain relatively minor matters should be left over to be settled after we had joined the Community. We had advanced this proposition for years, and had frequently made clear our acceptance that they should be so settled 'in accordance with Community principles and procedures'. Over the years, representatives of certain Member States, and even at times of the Commission itself, had assented to this proposition. Thus in its updated opinion of 3 October, 1969, the Commission wrote: 'It would be well to concentrate on essentials during the negotiations, leaving to the institutions of the enlarged Community the task of settling less important problems not resolved during the negotiations.' But when the negotiations opened we rapidly found (as so many in their dealings with the Community have found) that this assent from individual Community quarters was based on weak foundations, in some cases perhaps on little more than politeness and a desire to please. The Community as a whole would have none of it. The French at least had not misled us. Speaking to Sir J. Marjoribanks on 3 March, 1970, M. Boegner, the French Permanent Representative, observed that 'there was one attitude ascribed to us on which he felt obliged to utter a word of warning. This was the thesis that only major problems should be tackled in the negotiations and the more detailed questions could be settled after entry—the wrong approach so far as he was concerned. We must not be too concerned if by going into the details as well the negotiations were to last three or four months longer.'

14. Here again Dr. Nass explains the juridical reasons for the Community's attitude clearly enough: 'Negotiations between the enlarged Community and one of its new members would have given the newcomer, compared with the founder members, a privileged status: accordingly they had to be excluded.' He adds that to seek solutions within an enlarged Community by means of its appropriate organs and procedures need not have been excluded; but postponing problems in this way would have necessitated a provision in the Accession Treaty to establish what the position would be in the enlarged Community between accession and the solution of the problem so postponed. (This device was in fact adopted in a few cases.) But Dr. Nass goes on: 'In this connection the attitude of the Community was clear: failing agreement to the contrary in the accession negotiations, the existing Community rules apply without restriction.' This doctrine had to be accepted; and it had the effect of throwing upon us the onus of raising every case in which we sought an adaptation

of existing rules, or transitional measures or a period of delay in their application.

15. In this crucial question it is of course necessary to probe deeper than merely into juridical considerations and arguments. It is legitimate to ask why six friendly European Governments were so determined to make things so difficult for others who wished to join them. None of them would have denied that the rules of the Community were based on the interests of the Six, and had been framed without taking any account of the interests of the four candidates, which were necessarily different. None would have denied that enlarging the Community was an enterprise of supreme political as well as economic significance. Here, one might have thought, some compromises, some fresh starts, some changes of existing rules and policies, would be a natural and reasonable accompaniment of the process of enlargement. Why therefore did the Six—in principle at least—so resolutely reject any accommodation of this kind?

16. In the first place, the Community is an organisation within which, in its dealings with the world outside, the hardest of the positions adopted by any of the Member States is the one which tends to prevail. We would of course have had a much easier passage but for the French. Yet, as so often, it was not only the French, and there were acceptable arguments they could use to make their own principles palatable to their partners. Chief among these was the proposition that the negotiation was one to admit new members to the existing Community, not one for joining with them to found a new Community. The applicants had applied to join the Community; they had declared their acceptance of its rules (for their application to be acceptable, they had had to); and they must be taken at their word. Behind this argument lay two others, which remained unspoken. First, almost every conceivable Community policy or rule or enactment is the resultant of a conflict of interests between the members, and has embedded in it features representing a compromise between these interests. Open it up at any point, and the whole laborious basis of the compromise will fall apart. Each member of the Community could see how undesirable that would be. Second, as in all negotiations, exceptions are dangerous, for they create precedents. Admit a change in this or that case, just because British arguments are strong and the matter is of no great importance, and you will find it hard to resist change in other cases where the matter is vital. So the two facets of the Community's principle became embodied in one precept: 'Swallow the lot, and swallow it now.'

17. This, by and large, we had to do. We achieved many mitigations, many adaptations of secondary importance, many important modifications through exceptional measures expressed in the main as holding good for transitional periods only, though in a number of cases open to possible prolongation or further modification by agreement at various specified dates after our entry. But in the main the doctrine of accepting everything, unless a good case for some mitigation could be shown, had to be adopted. This, deriving as it did from the

basis on which the negotiations had opened, was what more than anything else gave them their prolonged, complicated, technical and perhaps tedious character.

18. Nor was it only the secondary issues in the negotiations to which this doctrine applied. All the most important issues too—Community Finance, New Zealand butter, Commonwealth sugar, fisheries—all had to be raised and fought for because otherwise existing and unacceptable Community policies and enactments would have applied without modification or transitional arrangements. Occasionally, as in the case of association with the Community for our dependent territories, or the offer of the three options to certain independent developing Commonwealth countries, the existing policies of the Community suited us and we were able to take advantage of them, though not without a certain struggle. But in the main we had to fight all the way against existing Community policies and rules. The corollary was that we did not need, even where we felt certain apprehensions, to negotiate about areas where the Community had no policies or rules. Thus we did not need, in spite of New Zealand concern, to negotiate about access for New Zealand lamb to our market; the Community had no sheep-meat regulation; and we were prepared to accept the 20 per cent tariff on lamb. We were never, in the negotiations, concerned with the formulation or enactment of new policies or rules: that had to await our membership. We were however obliged by the same Community doctrine to concern ourselves in the negotiations in exactly the same way with new policies or rules which the Community adopted or enacted after the negotiations began, just as we are obliged now, under the agreed procedures for the interim period, to defend our interests in respect of any new policies or rules adopted or enacted between 10 November, 1971 and the entry into force of the Treaty of Accession. In a sense, the process of negotiation will move on without interruption into the process of membership.

5

Organisation

A.—ORGANISATION IN THE FOREIGN OFFICE

I am not competent to describe the organisation adopted by the other Government Departments principally concerned to cope with the Brussels negotiations, but I shall describe briefly the organisation adopted for this purpose in the Foreign Office. It was a fairly simple and economical organisation. Until October 1971, a single Department dealt with all aspects of our relations with the Community including the negotiations—the European Integration Department. It was responsible for questions concerning political integration in the Community as well as those concerning economic integration, and thus handled in addition to the negotiations the work deriving from paragraph 15 of The Hague Communiqué. This work was fairly considerable in volume during the six months before the negotiations began, and again of course after they had ended. But during the negotiations themselves it did not involve a great deal of effort.

2. Mr. John Robinson was Head of this Department from 1968 until shortly before the negotiations began. He was then released from departmental responsibilities to become my Special Assistant, as he had been in 1967 when I had been nominated as official leader for the negotiations which did not take place. As such, from the start of the negotiations, Mr. Robinson was one of the senior members of the Delegation who, while remaining based in London, attended all formal meetings of the Conference. In London he shared a general responsibility with his successor as Head of European Integration Department for work on the negotiations, and in particular played much the largest part in representing the Foreign Office in the official Cabinet Office Committees concerned with the co-ordination of policy for the negotiations. His successor in May 1970 as Head of European Integration Department was Mr. Norman Statham, who returned from South America for a second stint in the Department he had headed from 1965 to 1968.

3. There was also established early in 1970 a special 'European Communities Information Unit' with responsibility for all information (as opposed to Press) work concerning the Foreign Office arising from the negotiations. Its first Head

was Miss Caroline Petrie; she was succeeded in March 1971 by Mr. James Adams, until then an Assistant in European Integration Department. In April 1970 Mr. John Ford returned to the Foreign Office to work as the Assistant Under-Secretary supervising European Integration Department and the European Communities Information Unit. It was his responsibility to take charge of European Community affairs during my own frequent absences in Brussels, and in addition he specialised on work in the monetary and information fields. He left the Foreign Office again in July 1971. Mr. Ian Sinclair was Legal Adviser to the Delegation throughout the negotiations, and as such travelled regularly from London to Brussels for all formal meetings of the Conference until September 1971, when he took up residence in Brussels and concentrated in the last four months of the negotiations on the work of drafting the Treaty.

4. As the end of the negotiations approached, increasing strain fell on the European Integration Department. A much greater variety of issues were under active negotiation, and the work they demanded grew more complex, technical and detailed. Moreover, Mr. Statham was posted abroad in October 1971. It was decided at that point to establish a second European Integration Department, of which Mr. Adams became Head. Many of the more detailed tasks of the first European Integration Department were transferred to it. It became responsible for all the work on secondary legislation and authentic texts; for the work arising from the drafting of the Treaty; and for Foreign Office aspects of the work of preparing the European Communities Bill. It also incorporated the European Communities Information Unit. Mr. Robinson, who had been promoted to be an Assistant Under-Secretary in July 1971, took over superintendence of these two departments early in October, when Mr. Statham left and was succeeded as Head of the first European Integration Department by Mr. John Mason.

5. There was one further and rather unusual unit working in the Foreign Office during the negotiations which should be mentioned; this was the group of translators who were responsible for all the work leading up to the preparation of authentic English texts. They worked under Mr. Elkin, Special Adviser in the Foreign Office on Community Law. As this work grew more intense throughout 1971 the total number of translators and revisers employed on it in the Foreign Office rose to 25 or 30, with a correspondingly large complement of typing staff.

6. The organisation described above worked, first through Mr. Ford and later through Mr. Robinson, to myself; and I worked direct to Mr. Rippon, as I had to Mr. Barber and Mr. Thomson before him. In September 1971 Mr. Rippon transferred his office as Chancellor of the Duchy of Lancaster from the Foreign Office to the Cabinet Office, since it was felt that he should now concentrate more on the impending tasks of legislation. But he continued as leader of the Negotiating Delegation until the Treaty was signed, and the relationship with him of the Delegation as a whole, and of the Foreign Office organisation described above in particular, was not affected by his move from the Foreign Office.

B.—ORGANISATION OF THE DELEGATION

7. The official members of the negotiating team were designated, and their appointment announced, on 10 April, 1970. The announcement is reproduced in Appendix II. Under myself as Leader at the official level the senior members of the Delegation were Mr. G.R. Bell, a Third Secretary in the Treasury; Mr. G.R. Denman, a Deputy Secretary in the Board of Trade; Mr. F.M. Kearns, a Deputy Secretary in the Ministry of Agriculture, Fisheries and Food; and Mr. W.P. Shovelton, an Under-Secretary in the Ministry of Technology. When the Board of Trade and the Ministry of Technology were later amalgamated to form the Department of Trade and Industry, Mr. Denman and Mr. Shovelton continued their respective functions in the Delegation. The structure of the Delegation—as also the co-ordination of policy in Whitehall described in the next section of this chapter—was considerably simplified, as compared with the 1961–63 situation, by the fact that in the meanwhile the Colonial Office and the Commonwealth Relations Office had ceased to exist as independent Departments, and their functions had been transferred, in the main, to the Foreign Office.

8. The Delegation as announced in April 1970 remained unchanged throughout the negotiations, except for the withdrawal of Sir J. Marjoribanks when he reached retiring age in March 1971 and left Brussels. He was succeeded by Mr. Palliser in October 1971. Sir J. Marjoribanks, the Head of the Permanent Delegation in Brussels, and his Deputy Mr. Christofas, had been nominated as members of the Negotiating Delegation. This was to provide a link between two organisations which had in theory, and to some extent in practice, a separate existence. There were of course tasks which the Permanent Delegation had to continue to discharge which were quite separate from the negotiations. The distinction was carried further, in that some more junior officials were appointed to the Negotiating Delegation but resided permanently in Brussels. They included a Principal from the Ministry of Agriculture, Fisheries and Food, and two First Secretaries from the Foreign Service, among the latter being Mr. Hannay, who had already spent nearly five years on the Permanent Delegation in Brussels. This had given him an exceptionally thorough knowledge of the Community which was very valuable to the Negotiating Delegation. Mr. Mellon, Head of Chancery in the Permanent Delegation before negotiations began, thereafter fulfilled this function for the two Delegations together. In this capacity he played a very useful co-ordinating role, and provided a necessary hinge for the smooth turnover of the work of the combined Delegations, including the work of organisation and administration. A valuable asset to the Negotiating Delegation was the fact that three of its senior London-based members—Mr. Bell, Mr. Robinson and Mr. Sinclair—were veterans of the 1961–63 negotiations.

9. There were of course a number of officials other than those named in the formal announcement of the Delegation who came out from London to

help from time to time with the work of the formal sessions of the Conference. Since the heaviest burdens fell on the Ministry of Agriculture and on the Department of Trade and Industry, additional officials from these Departments were frequently in Brussels, including most regularly Mr. Franklin and Mr. Preston, Under-Secretaries in these two Departments respectively. The prolonged and intensive work on secondary legislation, which began in July 1970 and lasted until the end of the Conference, also involved visits to Brussels by a very large number of officials from many different Whitehall Departments. Mr. Christofas took charge of this work from the outset, as well as performing numerous other tasks in the negotiations. From March till October 1971 he was Acting Head of the Permanent Delegation. He too had acquired outstandingly detailed and thorough knowledge of the Community, its personalities, its ways and its laws, which was of the greatest value to the Delegation's work.

10. At the Ministerial level Mr. Rippon, after he had succeeded Mr. Barber at the end of July 1970, was our only representative throughout virtually the whole of the negotiations. As such he made a statement in the House of Commons after each Ministerial meeting. For the last four or five Ministerial meetings, when fisheries was the main outstanding issue, Mr. Rippon was accompanied at Ministerial meetings by Mr. Buchanan-Smith, Parliamentary Under-Secretary in the Scottish Office; and at the last two Ministerial meetings, at which the question of fisheries was respectively deadlocked and solved, Mr. Rippon was also accompanied by Mr. Prior, Minister of Agriculture, Fisheries and Food.

C.—ORGANISATION IN WHITEHALL FOR THE CO-ORDINATION OF POLICY FOR THE NEGOTIATIONS

11. In this section I shall summarise very briefly a subject which, if thoroughly treated, would require a report and indeed documentation which taken together might substantially exceed in length the whole of this Report on the negotiations. I cannot possibly treat this subject with the thoroughness it deserves, and therefore will cover it in outline only. Nor shall I deal at all (partly because in the main they were no concern of the Foreign Office) with the contacts between Government Departments and non-Governmental economic organisations in the United Kingdom—especially, but by no means exclusively, the Confederation of British Industry and the National Farmers' Union—which over a wide area played an important part in preparing British policy and ensuring that it remained broadly acceptable to those who would be so much affected by it.

12. A very great deal of work was of course done throughout most of 1967 on the preparation of detailed briefs covering the main issues foreseen in the negotiations for which we then hoped but which never took place. The Official Committee in which most of this work was co-ordinated was presided over by Sir William Nield of the Cabinet Office. The work was not wasted. When in

1969 the prospect of joining the Community reopened, a great deal of the necessary material for future negotiations was available. In October 1969, after the demise of the Department of Economic Affairs of which he was the last Permanent Secretary, Sir William Nield returned to the Cabinet Office to take charge of economic affairs in general and in particular of the preparations for negotiations with the Communities. Much detailed work on the preparation of briefs ensued in the next eight months. In addition to the EURO Committee over which Sir William Nield presided, an informal Working Group on Europe was established under the Chairmanship of Mr. Thornton, a Deputy Secretary in the Cabinet Office, which did most of the preparatory work. Ministerial consideration of the results of this work had not been completed by the time of the General Election in June 1970. Nevertheless, the incoming Conservative Administration found no lack of briefs ready for their consideration. A paper prepared in the latter part of June 1970 summarised in 17 pages the general conclusions of the more important briefs which had been prepared.

13. The Ministerial and official committee structure was somewhat, though not fundamentally, reorganised by the new administration. A 'Ministerial Committee on the Approach to Europe' was established on 26 June, 1970. It was to be presided over by the Foreign Secretary; its other members were the Chancellor of the Exchequer, the Lord President of the Council, the Chancellor of the Duchy of Lancaster, the Minister of Technology, the Secretary of State for Scotland, the Lord Privy Seal, the Minister of Agriculture, Fisheries and Food and the President of the Board of Trade. Its terms of reference were: 'To supervise the negotiations in connexion with our applications for membership of the European Communities; and to report as necessary to the Cabinet.' On 3 July, 1970, an 'Official Committee on the Approach to Europe' was established, under the Chairmanship of Sir William Nield. Its terms of reference were: 'To co-ordinate preparations for, and to advise on, the negotiations in connexion with our application for membership of the European Communities; and to report to the Ministerial Committee on the Approach to Europe.' Apart from the Cabinet Office, it was to include representatives of the Treasury, the Foreign Office, the Ministry of Technology, the Ministry of Agriculture, Fisheries and Food, the Board of Trade and the Bank of England.

14. Intensive work on the final elaboration and approval of briefs continued in July, August and September 1970; meanwhile the first meetings of the negotiations took place. The Ministerial Committee held 8 meetings in 1970 (4 of them in July) and 12 in 1971. The Official Committee met much less frequently, partly because Sir William Nield was detached from time to time from European work for other tasks, and partly because a habit grew up which led to the bulk of the work of co-ordinating Departmental positions being carried out in the Working Group on Europe, from which Group papers usually went direct to the Ministerial Committee. It was in the Working Group that the steady flow of policy papers and briefs, which the negotiations continued to engender right up to their conclusion, was processed. The Group met some 35 times in 1970

and 25 times in 1971. Mr. Robinson was the Foreign Office representative on the Group; and Mr. Thornton was its Chairman from start to finish. He also acted as the Secretary of the Ministerial Committee, and because of his central position in the work of policy co-ordination he attended most of the Ministerial meetings held in Brussels or Luxembourg in 1971 as a member of the Delegation.

15. Though there were few formal meetings of the AEO Committee, Sir William Nield held fairly frequent informal meetings of its principal members (who included all the senior members of the negotiating team) to review the state of the negotiations, to take decisions on further work required, and to set in hand other general tasks, such as the preparation of briefs for the meeting between Mr. Heath and M. Pompidou, the briefing for major Parliamentary debates or the drafting of the White Paper of July 1971, which was inaugurated at such a meeting held on 4 June, 1971.

16. The Official Committee on the Approach to Europe did however establish certain sub-committees for specialised tasks. These included a Sub-Committee on European Information Policy, under Mr. Maitland, which in fact seldom met. Information policy and activity was intensively studied and pursued throughout the negotiations, but on a more *ad hoc* and informal basis. In this work Mr. Royle, Parliamentary Under-Secretary in the Foreign Office, came to take the lead. Another Sub-Committee on Financial and Monetary aspects of the negotiations was established, under the Official Committee, on 6 July, 1970; its Chairman was Sir Frank Figgures. Its sphere of action included economic and monetary union, sterling and capital movements; and it also dealt with the Questionnaire on sterling and the British economy received from the Community in December 1970. to which we replied in February 1971. This Sub-Committee held two meetings in 1970 and four in 1971. A third Sub-Committee was that on legislation, under Sir Charles Sopwith; its task was to consider the scope of legislation to provide for our entry into the Communities and to comply with the obligations we should assume under the Treaty of Accession. The first report of this Sub-Committee was circulated on 1 January, 1971, and its second report on 7 June, 1971.

17. In the autumn of 1971, as the end of the negotiations approached, new official and Ministerial machinery was established to cope with the rather different tasks of the future. A 'European Interdepartmental Unit' was established under Sir William Nield's Chairmanship on 14 October, 1971. It had virtually the same membership as the Official Committee on the Approach to Europe, and its terms of reference were: 'To compare experience and to co-ordinate thinking and action by Departments in the preparations for accession to the European Communities.' The Unit in fact held only two meetings before the negotiations ended; but it established an important subordinate body, in the shape of the Working Group on Legislation under the Chairmanship of Mr. Cubbon of the Cabinet Office, which was responsible for carrying forward the work inaugurated by the Sopwith Committee and preparing a draft of the European Communities Bill.

18. Similarly, a new 'Ministerial Committee on Europe' was set up on 18 November, 1971. It did not supersede the Ministerial Committee on the Approach to Europe, as it was given rather different tasks less directly concerned with the negotiations. Its terms of reference were: 'To co-ordinate inter-Departmental action in relation to the preparation and passage of the legislation required to give effect to British accession to the EEC; and to supervise, in consultation with other inter-Departmental Committees as appropriate, Departmental preparations for accession, particularly in the field of economic, scientific and technological policies.' Mr. Rippon was Chairman of this Committee. It included some of the Ministers who were members of the Ministerial Committee on the Approach to Europe; but also a number of others, such as the Secretaries of State for Employment, for the Environment, and for Wales, and the Solicitor General. It held only one meeting before the negotiations ended. Its principal task, apart from future legislation, was to consider a number of papers on future British policy in the enlarged Community which had been prepared in the summer and autumn of 1971 by the Working Group on Europe.[1]

[1] This structure for handling issues related to the United Kingdom's membership of the European Communities, with a rather more elaborate and policy-orientated function for the Cabinet Office (through what came to be known as the European Secretariat) than was usual in other policy areas, has, with a number of changes in title and precise mandate but few of substance, survived to the present day.

6

Information

A.—INFORMATION ON COMMUNITY DEVELOPMENTS

Paragraph 22 of the Introductory Commentary on the 'Narrative Report on the Brussels Negotiations' prepared by the United Kingdom Delegation after the negotiations which ended in January 1963 reads as follows:

> 'Whereas, during the period between our application and the beginning of the negotiations there was intense consultation and discussion with Commonwealth countries, our contacts with the Member Governments of the Community, with whom we were about to negotiate, were confined to questions of procedure; we were not in touch at all with the Commission except in the normal way through our then very small permanent Mission in Brussels. At the time there was little knowledge in London of the manner in which the Member Governments, and the Institutions of the Community, were interpreting the provisions of the Treaty of Rome. It is at least possible that, if we had initiated during this period preliminary consultations on matters of substance with the Member Governments, and still more with the Commission, we might have acquired information on which we should have been able to base a more informed judgment.'

2. Lack of information about the activities, procedures and views of the Community was not, fortunately, a handicap from which we suffered in the negotiations of 1970–72. To this extent, the intervening years had been put to good use. It is true that the Permanent United Kingdom Delegation to the Communities, up to 1963, was extremely small; and until a fairly short time before our negotiations began in 1961 its attention had been directed even more to the European Coal and Steel Community than to the European Economic Community. But after the first negotiations ended in 1963 a decision was taken by the British Government, at the time when I was appointed in the spring of 1963 to be Head of the Delegation in Brussels, that that Delegation should be considerably strengthened; and this was done. Over the intervening years until 1970 our Delegation in Brussels acquired a very thorough knowledge of the

procedures, personalities and development of the three Communities; and reported very fully to London on all their multifarious activities.

3. Thus by 1970 we had the advantage, which apparently our Delegation in the earlier negotiations felt they did not have, of pretty widespread and accurate knowledge spread throughout Whitehall of what the Community was and how it worked; and accordingly of what could reasonably be hoped for, or could not be achieved, in negotiations with them. Apart from the Foreign Office, the Whitehall Departments principally concerned—the Treasury, the Board of Trade, the Ministry of Agriculture, Fisheries and Food and the Ministry of Technology—had acquired a high degree of familiarity with the operations of the Community in their respective spheres. In building up this corpus of information a special debt was incurred to a few members of the Delegation in Brussels who, through exceptionally long service there, acquired especially good knowledge of the way the Community worked. It was this background of information and appreciation, increasingly available throughout Whitehall from 1963 onwards, which enabled our judgment of negotiating possibilities to be, as the outcome proved, reasonably realistic.

4. Apart from this indispensable corpus of background information, the Negotiating Delegation were admirably served throughout the negotiations by an uninterrupted flow of rapid and accurate information about developments and attitudes within the Community and on the part of the individual member governments. Such information, at least in general outline, is not difficult to acquire in Brussels. One merit of the Community—at least for those outside it—is that they find it almost impossible to maintain any security for their transactions. But the information available to us went infinitely further and deeper than that available, for example, to a competent journalist in Brussels. Friendly Delegations among the Six kept us closely and continuously informed of what was going on; and our Embassies in the capitals of the Six filled in the background with constant reports.

5. From these and other sources we had a picture not merely of general dispositions and attitudes on the other side of the hill, but of individual positions and nuances, which was virtually complete. And we had it in good time. It was thus very rare for any proposal to be made to us in the negotiations of the substance of which we were not aware in advance; and in very many cases we had seen the text of Community statements before they were made to us. We tended during the negotiations to take this for granted, so familiar had such detailed information been to us so long. Nevertheless, to enjoy information so good, so full and so prompt was, throughout the negotiations, of inestimable advantage.

6. In later chapters of this Report, especially in those dealing with the various issues covered in the negotiations, there will be continual reference to what happened in various meetings of the Six, and to the attitudes adopted and statements made by individual representatives among them. These are all based on reports received, mostly by telegram, from our permanent Delegation in

Brussels; and they in turn were based on a rapid collation of information received—and often volunteered—from a large variety of friendly sources who knew exactly what had transpired. I sometimes feel that the information we received about the doings of the Six may in many cases have been virtually as complete and as accurate as that received by the Governments of the Six; and frequently more rapid—for we needed it more rapidly.

7. Another routine activity which had grown up since 1963, through co-operation between our Delegation in Brussels and Departments in London, also proved of the greatest practical utility during the negotiations. This was the steady and regular process of translating into English the innumerable regulations and directives of the Community as they had been enacted over the years. The availability of these translations, even though in some respects they proved inadequate and had to be improved, was an indispensable basis for the gigantic task of preparing authentic texts in English of all the Community's legislation.

B.—INFORMATION FOR INTERESTED GOVERNMENTS

8. A necessary accompaniment to the negotiations was a procedure for keeping interested third governments, especially those of the Commonwealth, of EFTA and of the other candidate countries, informed of their progress. These governments were closely concerned, though in somewhat different degrees, by the way our negotiations went; and it was important to ensure that they should not feel that matters affecting them were proceeding without their being given an opportunity to make their views known. This they could only do if they were promptly and fully informed.

9. On 7 May, 1970, the then Prime Minister sent a message to Commonwealth Prime Ministers making proposals for regular machinery of information and consultation in the course of the negotiations. At the same time proposals were put to our EFTA partners, and agreed with them at a meeting of the EFTA Ministerial Council in Geneva on 14 and 15 May. As a result of these preparations a procedure was inaugurated when the negotiations began and adhered to throughout them.

10. After each of our formal meetings in the negotiations, both at Deputy and at Ministerial level, information about what had transpired was given to Commonwealth and EFTA representatives. In the case of Deputies meetings, this was done in Brussels only; in the case of Ministerial meetings, information was given in Brussels for EFTA representatives and both in Brussels and in London for Commonwealth representatives. The meeting in London was made necessary by the fact that not all Commonwealth countries were represented in Brussels, though those mainly concerned were. By the end of the negotiations between 15 and 20 Commonwealth countries were represented in Brussels. The procedure was as follows. After each Deputies meeting, separate meetings were held in Brussels for EFTA Ambassadors to the Community or their

representatives, and for corresponding Commonwealth representatives. Depending on the amount of ground to be covered, each meeting lasted between forty minutes and an hour. Almost without exception, I chaired these meetings and described what had transpired. After Ministerial meetings, Mr. Rippon held similar successive meetings with the same people in Brussels; and in addition, on returning to London, he held a meeting for all Commonwealth High Commissioners, which was attended by a representative of the Commonwealth Secretariat. Similarly, after each meeting of the Deputies or Ministers, I or Mr. Rippon met with the Irish Ambassador in Brussels to give him an account of what had occurred. Representatives of the other candidate countries, Denmark and Norway, were of course informed at the meetings with EFTA representatives. A representative of the EFTA Secretariat attended all EFTA briefing meetings, and prepared a report which, after clearance with our Delegation in Brussels, was sent to the EFTA Council in Geneva and distributed to Delegations there.

11. At all these meetings extremely full information was given and questions were answered. The procedure was laborious and time-consuming. But it was necessary, and in my judgment it worked successfully. The objective was to ensure that all concerned felt that they were receiving the information they needed. Proof that they were satisfied is provided by the fact that there were no complaints and hence presumably the minimum of suspicions. The procedure also served to reduce bilateral enquiries in London. Naturally, those EFTA and Commonwealth governments most affected continued to keep closely in touch with the Foreign Office in London; but by and large the procedures adopted appear to have satisfied them.

12. Similar procedures applied in reverse. Thus Norwegian and Danish negotiators in Brussels regularly briefed their EFTA partners there, including us, on the progress of their own negotiations; and the Irish negotiators in Brussels regularly briefed us in bilateral meetings. Informally, and at a lower level, we also kept United States representatives in Brussels regularly informed after each meeting in the negotiations of its outcome.

C.—PRESS AND PUBLICITY

13. Given the open character of the Community, and the fact that virtually all its developments and disputes become public knowledge with the minimum of delay, it was clear that our own negotiations with the Community would have the same character. Anything we might wish to conceal would be hard to conceal, at all events as soon as it was discussed at a formal meeting of the Conference. These considerations dictated our action on publicity and relations with the Press.

14. We took the view, since everything that transpired at Ministerial meetings, and scarcely less at Deputies meetings, would inevitably become public knowledge, that it would be better tactics for us to assist this process and ensure

thereby at least that our version of events, rather than a version slanted in a different direction or simply garbled, should become available. Accordingly, the resident Press Officer of the Delegation (Mr. Richards) regularly briefed the Press after (and sometimes even during) every Deputies meeting, and with a few exceptions conveyed to them as full an account as they wished to have of what had transpired. These briefings were open to all correspondents who wished to attend them, not only to British correspondents. After Ministerial meetings, a procedure developed (it began rather accidentally at the first of them) in accordance with which, as soon as the meeting concluded, a joint Press briefing was held by the Foreign Minister of the Six who was in the Chair and Mr. Rippon. Mr. Rippon also arranged, after most though not all Ministerial meetings, a separate meeting with the Press at the British Delegation offices. These were attended mainly but not exclusively by British correspondents. Mr. Rippon's personal Press Officer, Mr. Beetham, accompanied him to all Ministerial meetings (and on most of his many other journeys abroad) and in between worked in the Foreign Office News Department as a specialist on Community affairs.

15. On the whole, these arrangements worked satisfactorily. The seven or eight British correspondents resident in Brussels and specialising in Community affairs became fairly expert in the course of the Conference; other British correspondents who regularly came out from London for the Ministerial meetings also contributed their share. With few exceptions, the British daily Press supported the Government's efforts to enter the Community; and on the whole we had the advantage throughout the negotiations of full, fair and sympathetic coverage of events in Brussels in the British press, and on television and radio.[1]

16. But of course the fact that the Conference was so open necessarily operated as an inhibiting factor on our conduct of the negotiations. This inhibition operated from other quarters besides the Press, especially from Parliament. Since everything we attempted was bound to become public, it became a maxim of negotiating tactics that we must not attempt too much, and be seen to fail. This inevitably imposed a restraint—perhaps a healthy one on the way in which we approached individual questions. Another continual restraint imposed upon us by the openness of the proceedings was the need to ensure that certain secondary issues, of whose eventual outcome we could be fairly confident but which were capable of raising much public anxiety, were dealt with, before the prospect of a satisfactory outcome was clear, in as private a way as possible.

17. There were a number of such issues, especially towards the end of the Conference. These we handled where we could by taking advantage of the fact

[1] This account of the methods used for briefing the Press rather understates the degree and complexity of the Press briefing which actually went on. Several of the senior, London-based members of the Negotiating Delegation were extremely assiduous in briefing the Press, both British and others, on a background basis, thus ensuring that even the most technical areas of the negotiations, particularly those dealing with agriculture and commercial policy, were fully covered.

that, whereas everything raised in a formal session of the Conference inevitably became public, it still remained possible to handle matters outside the Conference, with the Presidency or the Commission, in a way which protected them from leakage. There were a number of matters of this character (nationality, units of measurement, certain aspects of agreement on the ECSC and the detailed arrangements for the 'status quo' in Commonwealth trade are examples) on which we succeeded in developing successful solutions through contacts and discussions outside the formal Conference. Thus the Press, unaware of what was afoot and of the various stages in the discussion, had no opportunity to speculate on the consequences of failure. By the time formal agreement was recorded in the Conference and became known, it was often scarcely worth reporting. In this we were helped by the fact that, towards the end of the negotiations, journalists in Brussels had become thoroughly bored with the multiplicity of highly technical subjects still under discussion and were ready to be content with fairly superficial information.

7

United Kingdom Objectives and Tactics

Before moving on to Part II of this Report, which will deal with the way in which individual problems in the negotiations, major and minor, were settled, it will I think be useful, in this final chapter of the introductory Part of the Report, to describe United Kingdom objectives and tactics in the negotiations. This Part of the Report is concerned with a number of general matters relevant to the negotiations as a whole. The generality of United Kingdom objectives and tactics can thus best be considered here. Any negotiation, of course, involves continual concentration on negotiating tactics as it proceeds; and their details change significantly from time to time. I shall not be concerned in this chapter with lesser and individual tactical issues; some of them will emerge in the next Part of the Report where the individual issues of the negotiations are dealt with. This chapter will therefore concentrate on our major objectives—that is to say our strategy and those major tactical considerations which influenced us especially strongly at the start of the negotiations and in the main throughout their course.[1]

2. Our overriding strategic objective was to sign a satisfactory Treaty of Accession. But scarcely less important as a strategic objective was to ensure that we signed it at the right time. A major objective of our strategy in the negotiations, and hence of our tactics, was to ensure that the negotiations should not drag on indefinitely but should be concluded in time to permit us to enter the Community on 1 January, 1973. Had an earlier date seemed feasible, we would have preferred it; but it did not. We did not believe the negotiations could be completed in less than 18 months. The date of 1 January, 1973, for entry suited us, moreover, in terms of the Government's general objectives. By this date the new Conservative administration would have run almost exactly half its maximum course; and it naturally hoped that there would be time before the next General Election for the United Kingdom to have settled down as a member of the Community and for some, but not all, of the consequences of

[1] This chapter also brings out very clearly the fact that the distinction between strategy and tactics in a European Community negotiation is rather unreal and that many of the most far-reaching decisions taken in such negotiations are foreshadowed by the procedural handling of them.

our entry to be operating. This date moreover was one which had come, during the first half of 1970, to be fairly generally accepted within the Community, and by the Commission, as a reasonable target date for the enlargement of the Community. 1 January, 1973, became accordingly a fixed pole in our planning; and it was by working back from this date that earlier target dates in the process of entry were established.

3. It was accepted that roughly a year would be required, after the signature of a Treaty of Accession, for the process of its ratification, by the old and new Member States alike, to be completed. We for our part reckoned that we might need the best part of a year to pass through Parliament the legislation which would be necessary to provide for our accession and to comply with the obligations we should undertake in the Treaty. This legislation, it was hoped, might pass through both Houses of Parliament before they rose for the Summer Recess of 1972. But this could not be certainly assumed; and a prolongation of the session of more than customary length into the autumn might prove necessary. In any case the legislation must be completed in the 1971–72 session of Parliament. This in turn meant that ideally the Treaty of Accession must be signed not later than the end of 1971; though it was accepted from the start that a very short spill-over into January 1972 might be acceptable. The objective was that the necessary legislation should be introduced in the House of Commons at the latest by early February 1972. (In fact, though the Treaty was not signed until 22 January, 1972, the European Communities Bill was introduced and had its first reading in the House of Commons as early as 25 January.)

4. Thus, with the opening date of negotiations set for 30 June, 1970, we reckoned that we had 18 months, or if necessary a week or two longer, for the process of negotiation. This, as indicated above, corresponded pretty well with what seemed to have become a generally, though not a universally, accepted view within the Community by the time negotiations opened. It became necessary therefore to consider how best from our point of view, within this span of time, the negotiations should be handled and should develop. It was clear that, as in every major negotiation, there would have to be a climax and a crunch. When, ideally, should this take place? There were various factors to consider. First of all, it was evident that even after the crunch on the main issues there would remain a great deal of detailed negotiation to do and the laborious task of drafting the Treaty of Accession. Second, there were important political as well as psychological reasons for seeking to ensure that the crunch came before the summer holidays of 1971. The political reasons were mainly the expectation that Parliament and the political parties would wish to know, before they dispersed for the summer break of 1971, and before the Annual Party Conferences in the early autumn, whether the negotiations were going to succeed or not and, in the favourable case, that they were over the hump. Psychological considerations of a more general character pointed the same way. We feared—and in this we were influenced to a considerable extent by the experience of the negotiations in 1962—that if the Conference dispersed in

July 1971 for the summer holidays without the negotiating climax having been reached and successfully passed, and therefore in a mood still of doubt and uncertainty about eventual success, it might prove difficult if not impossible to revive enthusiasm and the conviction that success remained possible when the Conference resumed its work in September 1971.

5. For all these reasons it had become, even by the time negotiations opened, a generally accepted assumption in Whitehall that we should have to work to bring them to a successful climax before the summer holidays of 1971; and it was also widely accepted that this objective might not be capable of being reached without the holding of a Summit Conference of Heads of Government in one form or another. As evidence of the early date at which the general views described above had been formed, a paper, and a timetable, prepared by Mr. Robinson for Mr. Barber, and submitted on 17 July, 1970, is reproduced in Appendix I.

6. It is worth analysing this document in a little detail to see where, in July 1971, [*sic*: 1970] we were already more or less right in our forecasts and where we were to some extent mistaken. The timetable proved pretty well exactly right; except that it (and the paper) assumed more of a gap between the 'conclusion of negotiations on major questions of substance' and the signature of the Treaty of Accession than in fact occurred. As things turned out, the gap was very small indeed; the last major question—fisheries—was concluded by us on 12 December, 1971 (though not by the Norwegians until January 1972); and detailed negotiations on many issues by the Deputies continued to within four days of the signing of the Treaty. The paper was a bit too pessimistic about the Italian Chairmanship, which in fact proved effective and highly co-operative in the last half of 1971. But it already contained the arguments which led us to welcome rather than to fear the fact that the French would hold the Chairmanship for the first half of 1971. The paper tended perhaps to regard the question of Community finance as likely to prove rather more exclusively central to the negotiations than in fact turned out to be the case, even though, from our own national point of view, it certainly remained by far the most important issue the negotiations had to deal with. The paper already foresaw that the Eastern policy of the new German Government would play a large part in affecting the general background of the negotiations. Above all, it foresaw that a summit meeting of some kind would prove necessary, though it suggested that this meeting might have to concentrate more exclusively on Community finance than proved to be the case, and it contemplated a summit meeting of the Seven rather than the bilateral Anglo-French summit meeting which in fact took place. It argued that such a summit meeting should be held between March and July of 1971 and tended to favour the earlier date.

7. Thus even though there were some points on which this forecast of events proved slightly wrong, it demonstrates nevertheless that the scenario we had in mind for the negotiations at the time when they began was not very far removed from the manner in which and the pace at which they in fact developed.

8. Given the general objectives so described, it became a very important matter of tactics to work for decisions on the major issues in the early summer of 1971 and to communicate to the Community the conviction that this was the right course to adopt. Mr. Rippon's phrase about 'breaking the back of the negotiations in the summer of 1971' became one of our main themes at a fairly early date. Mr. Rippon told M. Deniau at a meeting in Brussels on 14 October, 1970, that 'he hoped that the back of the negotiations would have been broken by July 1971'. He developed the same theme forcefully to Dutch Ministers in The Hague two days later. And he formally repeated it in the Conference at the Ministerial meeting on 27 October, 1971. By dint of constant repetition from our side this objective came gradually to be accepted by the Community as a reasonable and desirable one; and indeed we necessarily came, right from the start of negotiations, to press continually for rapid progress.

9. This had its dangers; we were aware of them, but we accepted that they were unavoidable. The Federal German Minister, Herr Ehmke, said to Sir Alec Douglas-Home on 15 March, 1971: 'He thought the French were currently guided by an understandable intention to squeeze every advantage out of the British desire for early progress. They no doubt calculated that by going slow at this stage they could induce the impatient British to make concessions.' There was a danger also that insistence on breaking the back of the negotiations before the summer holidays might rebound upon us with dangerous effects if we failed to achieve the objective; and for this reason we were careful to formulate it as something highly desirable, while always falling short of describing it as something absolutely essential. At one stage, indeed, Mr. Rippon, quite deliberately, turned the screw even tighter. At the Ministerial meeting on 16 March, 1971—a meeting peculiarly barren in practical results—he said that it seemed to him 'entirely reasonable and possible that we should reach agreement on all the main issues at or shortly after our next meeting on 11 May'. We decided not long after that this bid to 'break the back in May' was asking too much and should be dropped; but it may have helped to persuade the Community that they should join us in doing the job in June.

10. Another general tactical requirement of much importance which influenced us throughout the negotiations was the need to ensure that our proposals, when we came formally to put them forward, were not pitched too high. It was obviously equally undesirable that they should be pitched too low; and it was not always easy to strike the right balance. But the dangers of asking for much too much, in a Conference every move in which became public as soon as it had been made, always seemed to us the greater. Nothing could have created a more damaging impression, in the Press and in Parliament, than for us to have demanded a particular solution, and then to be seen to be beaten back by the pressure of circumstances and the Community into having to accept something much more modest.

11. In some cases, it is true—and indeed in the most important cases—we did put forward maximum demands. But there were special reasons for doing

so. In the case of sugar and New Zealand dairy products our first proposals were for the maintenance of existing supplies to our market subject to review after the transitional period. We knew perfectly well that this was more than we could get. But we felt it tactically wise to open with a bid which would satisfy the sugar producers and the New Zealanders, and which would therefore not have to be preceded by painful negotiations with them. It seemed better to allow the Community reactions we foresaw to play upon them, rather than merely our own arguments. And in both cases we made it clear to our friends that, although we were asking for the maximum on their behalf, we did not expect to get it. On the issue of Community finance we also, in our first and only proposals tabled on 16 December, put forward a somewhat extreme demand. We did so deliberately by way of reaction to the extreme proposals in the other direction contained in the Commission's so-called 'Vue d'Ensemble' which they circulated in November 1970. This was perhaps a tactically dangerous move, since we knew well that we should have to pay more than the 3 per cent to 15 per cent scale we proposed. But in this case, oddly enough, our intransigence did not rebound upon us too dangerously when, in the event, we had to agree to pay more. This was because in spite of our efforts and largely because of the Community's indignant reactions, and even though we maintained our proposal without modification for six months (though we began to hint at modification a good deal earlier)—the British Press on the whole, and even Parliament, always regarded our opening bid as purely tactical and as bound to suffer increase, and were thus not unduly critical when an increase had to be accepted. But in spite of the fact that in these three major fields our opening bid was a high one, we did take care in almost every other field, for the reasons given above, not to make proposals which went too far beyond what we anticipated might be the eventual outcome. The corollary of this was that, when we had made a proposal, we stuck to it as long as we could (usually until the final solution was in sight) and refused to become engaged in a descending process of compromise.

12. In the early days of the negotiations we had three other main tactical principles. First, we sought to start the negotiations on a fairly broad front by deliberately opening up a considerable number of questions. Thus in a paper dated 10 July, 1970, which he circulated to the AE Committee, Mr. Barber, putting forward his proposals for the start of work at the first Ministerial Committee on 21 July, wrote that we should perhaps work on several subjects in parallel. We should not concentrate either on the easier subjects or on the more difficult ones, but take some of each. In particular, we should not limit our proposals only to the problem of our contribution to the Community's budget, since this would both give the impression that we were only interested in the cost of joining and risk the Community seeking to turn the solution of this issue into a precondition for considering other issues. Furthermore, we must avoid giving the impression that we were concentrating solely on domestic problems and open up from the start some of the principal problems of the Commonwealth. This line was endorsed; and in the next five or six months we

followed it up by steadily putting forward our proposals on virtually every aspect of the negotiations, undiscouraged by the Community's inability to react, until early in 1971 almost every topic then foreseen (except a few which we wished to leave till later) had at least been broached.

13. The second of these main tactical principles was to try as hard as we could to get the member governments of the Community, and in particular their Ministers most concerned with the negotiations, to give them what we regarded as the necessary priority. This was not easy. At first, Community Governments and Ministers were as much preoccupied with the general current work of the Community (and with their multifarious other duties) as they were with our negotiations. It was hard to get them to agree on dates for Ministerial meetings. Only four such meetings took place in the almost ten-month period between the first Ministerial meeting on 21 July, 1970, and the first 'breakthrough' Ministerial meeting on 11 and 12 May, 1971. By then, helped by the prospect of the Heath–Pompidou meeting announced on 8 May, 1971, the necessary momentum and interest had indeed been engendered; and it was maintained until the end of the negotiations.

14. The third of these main tactical principles was to go as far as we could in representing ourselves as seeking, not so much our own protection and advantage, as Community solutions to Community problems. This theme was one employed by Mr. Rippon in most of his formal statements, and still more in his bilateral conversations, throughout the negotiations. As he put it in the House of Commons on 20 January, 1971, 'the negotiations are a collective endeavour, not a game of poker or beggar-my-neighbour'. This line probably helped to make our general approach, and even our requirements, somewhat more acceptable; and it helped also to relieve us of the old accusations that we 'lacked Community spirit' or were 'seeking to divide the Six'. The record of a conversation held in Paris on 9 November, 1970, between Mr. Rippon and M. Schumann is reproduced in Appendix I, simply as an illustration of Mr. Rippon's negotiating style. Almost any one of many scores of similar records of bilateral talks between Mr. Rippon and Community Ministers, EFTA Ministers or Commonwealth Ministers would illustrate it equally well.

15. Another tactical principle we followed throughout was that of negotiating only where we had to. We avoided expanding the scope of the negotiations beyond what was necessarily involved in our acceptance of or adaptation to existing Community policies—including, regrettably but necessarily, all the new rules or policies adopted by the Community during the negotiations. We eschewed in the negotiations the raising either of delicate issues (such as New Zealand lamb) where, though we feared they might, the Community had not yet created obstacles; or of general issues of policy which were better left to be pursued when we had become a member. This principle also implied something else, equally important. We naturally considered whether there were any issues extraneous to the negotiations of which we might take advantage in order to 'do a deal', above all of course with the French. In a minute dated 27 July, 1970

to the Permanent Under-Secretary I wrote: 'I think we must make an effort to convince all concerned that, if there is a summit meeting, its purpose will be to seek decisions enabling the negotiations to proceed to success within their own terms and scope, and not to introduce extraneous issues to clinch the deal.' It became clear as time passed that the French felt the same way; and this line was in fact adhered to.

16. A further important tactical principle had special relevance in the period from January to May 1971 when the Six were endeavouring, with great difficulty and with major divergence between some of their individual positions, to achieve a common policy among themselves with which to confront us on some of the essential issues, such as sugar, New Zealand and Community finance. Our objective in this situation was to ensure if we could, through frequent appropriate suggestions to the Five, that they should not, simply for the sake of apparent progress and helping the Community to make some proposal however bad, move towards the more extreme positions being adopted by the French. In this connexion a minute from Mr. Rippon to the Prime Minister of 17 March, 1971, reproduced in Appendix I, well describes our concern. In this minute Mr. Rippon, describing what we had learnt of the discussion in the Council of Ministers on 15 March (the day before a Ministerial meeting with us) wrote that: 'In each case the French took an extreme position, and although there are differences of detail in the views of the Five and the Commission, the French were on this occasion isolated, and seen to be isolated, on all the three main issues remaining to be settled in our negotiations.' Similarly, in a paper written on 24 April, 1971, in contemplation of our next Ministerial meeting with the Community in May, Mr. Robinson wrote of 'the all-important point that, if the Community cannot make joint proposals to us which lie within the range of what we would regard as reasonably negotiable, we want the Community to fail to agree on joint proposals to us. We want the crisis on each subject to be within the Six rather than between the Six and ourselves if we cannot have reasonable proposals.'

17. A further aspect of our tactics in the early stages was our view that it would be advantageous to leave certain issues to be raised only at a late stage in the negotiations. Thus we were concerned from the start, partly in order to allow the new Government's general economic policies time to develop, and partly because of considerations affecting the timing of the opening of negotiations to renew the sterling area agreements and the Basle Facility, that the discussions we knew we should have to have with the Community on sterling and the state of our economy should be postponed at least until 1971. In the event, this did not prove difficult; the Community's action in beginning the process with a written Questionnaire in December 1970 enabled us to put off our written reply until February 1971; and not until March did this topic come to the boil, though still outside the formal Conference.

18. In the same way, we decided at the start that it would be wiser to leave the questions of fisheries and of the Channel Islands and the Isle of Man to the final stages of the negotiations, after the summer break of 1971. We felt that

the major difficulties of principle involved in both these questions could best be tackled at a time when the negotiations were regarded as having succeeded, and nothing but a clearing up process remained. At that stage, we reckoned, there would be less dogmatism on the Community side, and a better chance of practical solutions. Our plan worked in the case of the Channel Islands and the Isle of Man, even though it was at times difficult to persuade the Islanders that they were not being unwarrantably neglected. We made our first proposal on the subject in June 1971, and left negotiation thereon till the last three months of the year. In the case of fisheries however, growing public and Parliamentary pressure forced Ministers to decide late in May 1971 that an attempt must be made to solve the problem of fisheries, together with the other major questions of the negotiations, at the anticipated 'back-breaking' meeting in June. This decision may have been politically inevitable, but it is questionable whether from the point of view of the negotiations it was a wise one. We failed to reach agreement on fisheries in June; and the proposals we then made probably made it harder rather than easier to reach, eventually, a satisfactory solution.

19. One or two other tactical needs of the negotiations, though less lasting, deserve to be recorded. After the meeting between Mr. Heath and M. Pompidou, we ran into an unusual and potentially awkward situation. The meeting had clearly been a great success. But just what its results had been, and in particular how far, if at all, it had led to detailed agreement on the main issues, was not made known. The Five tended for a time to assume that virtually everything had been settled at the meeting and that accordingly they could relax and wait for the Anglo-French rabbits to be produced from the hat. In particular our friends among them saw no reason to exert themselves by working for solutions which might even go beyond what, they felt, we might have accepted; they did not want, they said, to be more royalist than the King. This feeling became clear very soon after the summit meeting was over, and we had to devote much effort to disabusing the Five of their unfounded impressions. When in fact at the Ministerial meeting on 7 June a totally unexpected settlement on sterling was reached, evidently as a result of a previous understanding between ourselves and the French which could only have been arrived at or initiated at the meeting between Mr. Heath and M. Pompidou, these feelings revived with redoubled strength, and once again we had to take steps to counteract them. The instructions we telegraphed on 11 June to our Ambassadors in the Five posts are reproduced in Appendix I.

20. Occasional minor tactical requirements were imposed on us by developments outside the Conference. As an instance of these, I recall the concern with which, in the two or three weeks preceding the crucial Parliamentary debate and the final vote of principle of 28 October, 1971, I besought the Italian Chairman of the Deputies to avoid raising at any Deputies meeting controversial matters which might lead to embarrassing reactions from the Press, even though at all other times we were urging the Community to get on with everything as fast as possible. I met with the fullest understanding and co-operation.

PART II
THE PROBLEMS OF THE NEGOTIATIONS AND HOW THEY WERE SOLVED

8

Summary and Sequence: From the Start to the Breakthrough: 30 June, 1970, to 23 June, 1971

Chapters 10 to 27 of this Part of the Report describe in some detail the course of events concerning the major and minor topics dealt with in the negotiations. This and the following chapter consist of a relatively brief summary of the course of the negotiations as a whole.

2. They have a two-fold purpose. First, to provide an outline and chronology of developments which may perhaps prove useful for reference, and for any reader who may not wish to dig more deeply into the course of events. Second, to show, in a general and summary way and without entering into the substance of individual sectors, how the negotiations as a whole developed and how individual topics within them moved in parallel: to show, in short, their build-up, pace and rhythm. Though in the main no more than a summary, these two chapters do however deal with a number of matters not referred to elsewhere in this Report.

3. The negotiations fell into three main phases, characterised, somewhat accidentally, by the successive Chairmanships of the different member countries of the Community. The opening meeting on 30 June, 1970, took place on the last day of the Belgian Chairmanship. For the next six months the Germans were in the Chair; during this phase there were three Ministerial meetings and nine meetings of Deputies. It was in the main a phase of exploration, exposition and manoeuvre, in which few decisions were reached. Things moved slowly in this phase; but though we had expected them to do so, the Community's inability in the last two months of 1970 to react to our various proposals proved frustrating.

4. In the following six months of French Chairmanship there were five Ministerial meetings and 13 meetings of Deputies. This phase of the negotiations proved—once again, as we had expected and planned—the decisive one. Late in June we 'broke the back of the negotiations'. But the break was long in coming. Although progress was made during them on some issues, in the main the first four months of 1971 were months of stagnation, exasperation, virtual deadlock and increasing apprehension about the outcome. Then things began to move. The 43 days from 11 May to 23 June were the golden period of the negotiations—three successful Ministerial meetings, with the Heath–Pompidou meeting between the first and second of them.

5. During the Italian Chairmanship in the second half of 1971 there were five Ministerial meetings and 13 meetings of Deputies. This was a phase of clearing up, consolidation and conclusion. Four times as many decisions were taken in this phase as in the whole of the first year of the Conference. Only one issue of first-class political difficulty—fisheries—had to be settled in this phase, but a dozen or more other issues of considerable significance were also disposed of. The pace of work increased sharply. Much work of a highly complex and detailed character was completed, and most of the Accession Treaty was drafted. In the first three weeks of 1972, which, though the Luxembourgers were in the Chair, can be regarded as falling within the same phase as that of the Italian Chairmanship, there were three Deputies meetings of a considerably more prolonged and intense character than most earlier meetings in the series. At the last of them, at about 3 a.m. in the morning of 18 January, 1972, the final outstanding issues were settled.

6. After the opening meeting on 30 June, 1970, which was confined to programmatic statements by the Community and the four candidates and at which no business was transacted, the first working meeting was our bilateral Ministerial meeting of 21 July. It was agreed that there should be two Ministerial meetings with the United Kingdom every quarter, and a two-day meeting at Deputy level every fortnight; if necessary, meetings could be held more frequently, by mutual agreement. Important agreements were reached on procedure and working methods, and, on the basis of proposals put forward by Mr. Barber, areas of work on which to start were agreed and the 'fact finding period' was inaugurated. The Community Delegation 'invited the Commission' to undertake a number of studies of data to be supplied by the United Kingdom; but the Community made it very clear that the Commission must operate as the servant of the Six, not of the Conference as a whole. Its reports were to be addressed to the Council of Ministers. Work put in hand included the European Coal and Steel Community but not EURATOM; for a long period the Community were reluctant to take up the latter, because of problems related to the Non-Proliferation Treaty.[1] A decision at this meeting inaugurated the work on technical adaptations to Community legislation and on English texts, which was to last throughout the Conference. At this meeting also Mr. Barber, in his opening statement, repeated in categorical language our readiness to accept the Common Agricultural Policy of the Community. This was implicit in what we had already said; but the Community—or some of its members—were showing some signs of doubting it, or of being reluctant to proceed to

[1] These problems related to the difference in status vis-à-vis the Non-Proliferation Treaty of both the existing and the candidate Member States and the implications for the interface between EURATOM and the International Atomic Energy Agency. Of the original Member States, five (Belgium, Germany, Italy, Luxembourg and Netherlands) were signatories of the Non-Proliferation Treaty and one (France) was not. All four of the candidate States (Denmark, Ireland, Norway and the United Kingdom) were signatories, but one (the United Kingdom) was categorised as a Nuclear Weapons State which had implications for its status.

genuine negotiations until it had been made clear beyond a peradventure. Immediately after this meeting the United Kingdom Delegation tabled papers on the Commonwealth Sugar Agreement, on the Common External Tariff and tariff quotas, on English texts of Community instruments and (most important of all) on the financial arrangements in an enlarged Community.

7. At the five Deputies meetings which took place in July, September and October before the next Ministerial meeting on 27 October, only modest progress was made. Working arrangements were agreed to start examining some technical aspects of our adoption of the Common External Tariff; the problems of liquid milk, pigmeat and eggs, and the annual agricultural review, were examined. Further British papers of a factual kind were tabled in September and October (on dairy products in relation to New Zealand, on the consequences for sugar of the enlargement of the Community, on the Common Fisheries Policy, on British Dependent Territories, and on Hong Kong). At the second meeting of Deputies on 16 September we put forward our proposal for a transitional period of three years for eliminating internal industrial tariffs and adopting the Common External Tariff. At the third Deputies meeting on 1 October, the United Kingdom Delegation proposed, and it was agreed, that its suggestions (to which the Community clearly felt strong objection) about the 'period of initiation' and about leaving certain matters for settlement after entry should be 'set aside' for the time being. They were never reverted to. At the fourth Deputies meeting on 14 October the Community declared themselves 'prepared in principle to consider association of Commonwealth dependent territories', reserving their position on Hong Kong and Gibraltar. Also at this meeting we put forward our proposal for a six-year agricultural transitional period. There were discussions on the Common Commercial Policy, and the United Kingdom Delegation urged, not for the first time and still in vain, that work should begin on the question of tariff quotas, on which it had made proposals in July.

8. At the second Ministerial meeting, on 27 October in Luxembourg, the somewhat modest fruit of this early period was gathered in and decisions were recorded on liquid milk, pigmeat and eggs; on the annual agricultural review; on the association of dependent territories; and on some aspects of the Common Commercial Policy. Mr. Rippon made a statement, very welcome to the Community, about the introduction in the United Kingdom of levies on certain food imports.[2] The Community, which at French insistence had declared at the first Ministerial meeting on 21 July that all problems must be solved by transitional measures only, now went one step further, again at French insistence, and declared that all questions should be settled on the basis of a single identical transitional period. In their statement putting forward this proposition the

[2] The statement was welcome because it was seen as a clear step away from the United Kingdom's traditional policy of protecting agricultural incomes by means of deficiency payments to farmers and towards the European Community policy whereby import levies linked to an internal price level above that of world commodity prices provided the protection.

Community referred to 'questions lying at the very heart of the negotiations', and included among them 'economic, financial and monetary problems connected with accession which must be examined under appropriate conditions'. It was also agreed at this Ministerial meeting—somewhat prematurely—that the 'period of fact-finding' was now over. And this meeting was the first occasion on which Mr. Rippon made plain to the Community as a whole our determination that the 'back of the negotiations must be broken' before the summer holidays next year.

9. There then ensued a period, which was to last well into 1971, in which the British Delegation continued the process begun in September and October of steadily building up a large structure of proposals in various fields to which, with few exceptions, the Community found itself unable to react.

10. In October, the Commission at length completed its unilateral study of the material we had supplied on sugar and dairy products; and its papers on these two subjects were transmitted by the Community to the Conference shortly after the sixth Deputies meeting on 4 November. These were somewhat non-committal papers, which eschewed proposals. A more important paper by the Commission on financial arrangements in an enlarged Community was also transmitted to the Conference in early November. It was at the sixth meeting of Deputies on 4 November that the Community, in promising to transmit this paper to us, expressed its agreement with the general lines of the paper's conclusions and a particular endorsement of those expressed in paragraph 20, which contained the important sentence 'should unacceptable situations arise within the present Community or an enlarged Community the very survival of the Community would demand that the institutions find equitable solutions.' This sentence was later quoted in paragraph 96 of the British White Paper of July 1971.[3]

11. We for our part made proposals at this meeting on 4 November on transitional measures in the agricultural sector. We tabled on 6 November proposals for New Zealand dairy products and for Commonwealth sugar, both of which requested the maintenance of existing supplies to the British market subject to review at the end of the transitional period. In this period also the United Kingdom Delegation continued, at meetings of Deputies, to unfold in successive statements its ideas on agricultural transition. At the seventh meeting of Deputies on 17 November the United Kingdom Delegation broached the question of the European Investment Bank; and at the same meeting the Community at length gave a partial reaction to our request for tariff quotas, and a procedure was agreed for carrying this matter forward. At this meeting also the United Kingdom Delegation raised the question of transitional periods for capital movements and for fiscal harmonisation.

[3] When, in 1979, following the end of the transitional arrangements for Community finance, the British Government insisted that its burden was inequitable and must be alleviated, this statement by the founder members served as the political basis for that demand. It continued to be so used until the decision on a rebate mechanism was taken at the Fontainebleau European Council in 1984.

12. On 17 November, 1970, the Commission completed its paper giving a 'Vue d'ensemble' of the principal elements of the negotiations. This paper (which was never formally circulated to the Conference, though we had copies of it by 19 November) was notable especially for its extremely unhelpful proposals on Community Finance. On 26 November we circulated a proposal on independent Commonwealth Developing countries in Africa, the Caribbean, the Indian Ocean and the Pacific.

13. At the eighth meeting of Deputies on 1 December more progress was made, and some of the Community's reactions proved relatively swift. They accepted that the Declaration of Intent of 1963 with its alternative options including association should apply to Commonwealth developing territories in Africa (subject to a reserve in respect of Lesotho, Botswana and Swaziland because of their Customs Union with South Africa), but reserved their position on the other Commonwealth territories in the Caribbean, the Pacific and the Indian Ocean. Progress was also made at this meeting on the European Investment Bank and Gibraltar.

14. The third Ministerial meeting took place on 8 December. Little by way of formal agreement was achieved, but it was notable for Mr. Rippon's proposal to combine our previous separate proposals for transitional periods (three years in the industrial sector and six years for agriculture) and to adopt a period of five years for both. This received at first a somewhat grudging welcome from the Community, to which Mr. Rippon reacted strongly; but eventually the Community 'noted with satisfaction' our proposals and it was from this date that it came to be accepted that the general transitional period should in fact be five years. Some earlier partial agreements (on independent developing Commonwealth countries, Gibraltar and the European Investment Bank) were endorsed; and Mr. Rippon stated that the United Kingdom Delegation would make detailed proposals on Community Finance before the next meeting of the Deputies. This was done in a paper circulated on 16 December; and on the same day Mr. Rippon described our proposals in a statement to the House of Commons.

15. Little more progress was made before the end of 1970, though at the ninth Deputies meeting on 18 December the Community accepted in principle our proposal—revived from the earlier negotiations of 1961–63 and put forward in a paper circulated shortly before the meeting—that trade agreements should be offered to the Asian Commonwealth countries ineligible for association. At this meeting also the United Kingdom Delegation put forward more precise proposals for transition for agricultural and industrial trade; and made further statements on capital movements and fiscal harmonisation. The Community expressed their readiness to start work on EURATOM early in 1971.

16. The way in which, in this period, the Conference marked time can be illustrated by the following extract from a statement which I made at the 10th meeting of Deputies (the first meeting under French Chairmanship) on 12 January, 1971:

'As we resume our work in 1971 I must say that we do feel some concern at the pace at which the Conference is proceeding. We have made proposals in a number of fields on which we are now awaiting the Community's views. The major proposals concern Community finance and *ressources propres*, New Zealand and the interest of the developing Commonwealth sugar producers. Other problems are independent Commonwealth countries in the Caribbean, Indian Ocean and the Pacific; Botswana, Lesotho and Swaziland; the possibility of further questions from the Community side regarding our dependent territories in respect of which the Community have asked for material which they are now examining; Hong Kong (on which we hope to have a statement from the Community during the meeting); transitional arrangements in industrial and in agricultural trade; tariff quotas on which we await the Community's views on the remaining five items which we have raised; fiscal harmonisation; capital movements; the Community's agreements with third countries; the ECSC and EURATOM.

On all this large range of questions we are awaiting replies from the Community. We recognise that on some of them you still require some time to reach a view. Most of them have been before us for a number of weeks and, looking forward to the next Ministerial meeting on 2 February, I have the impression that, unless special efforts are made, the Conference may be able on that occasion to reach agreement only on a small number of questions, such as the Asian Commonwealth countries and, we hope, perhaps the withdrawal of your reserve relating to dependent territories. If that were all it would be a modest achievement for the two months period between Ministerial meetings.'

17. At this meeting on 12 January, however, one significant agreement was reached in principle: namely, that the Community would include Hong Kong in its generalised preference scheme. The United Kingdom Delegation made proposals for transitional periods in some further sectors, including that of transport; and made a statement on its proposals on Community Finance. And at this meeting the Community announced a significant new procedural decision; they established a Committee of the Six 'Deputies of Deputies', to prepare their positions for the Conference. This Committee remained in being for the remaining year of the negotiations, and proved invaluable in intensifying work on the Community side.[4] The 11th Deputies meeting on 26 January produced some further inconclusive discussion on tax harmonisation and definite progress on EURATOM. Otherwise it was confined mainly to further refinement of the agreements to be recorded at the next Ministerial meeting.

18. At the fourth Ministerial meeting on 2 February, 1971, agreement was

[4] The members of this Committee were normally the Political Counsellors of the Permanent Representatives. By establishing this piece of machinery the Permanent Representatives not only took some of the burden off themselves but ensured that their meetings and those of the Ministers were properly prepared and the groundwork laid for taking the necessary decisions.

confirmed on the Asian Commonwealth countries, on Botswana, Lesotho and Swaziland, on Hong Kong and on association for the New Hebrides. Mr. Rippon raised the special case of Papua and New Guinea. Agreement was virtually reached (it was confirmed on 10 February) on the precise timetable for tariff movements in the industrial field, both in respect of the dismantling of internal tariffs and of the movement by the candidate countries to the Common External Tariff. This meeting was also the occasion of a strong statement by Mr. Rippon on Community finance. In the preceding seven weeks since we had tabled our proposals on this subject deadlock had prevailed, with the Community indicating from time to time that they could not proceed further with the matter unless we tabled fresh proposals. At this meeting, however, after Mr. Rippon's statement, the Community at length declared their intention to make in due course certain procedural proposals to facilitate a solution. But over three months were to pass before they did so, in May.

19. At the 12th Deputies meeting on 10 February the Community lifted its reserve on the agreement previously reached on dependent territories; and there were further exchanges on Community Finance. At the 13th meeting of Deputies on 23 February some further progress was made on tariff quotas. Capital movements and the European Investment Bank were further discussed; and a procedure was agreed for work on the United Kingdom's adaptation to the Community's Generalised Preference Scheme. At the following meeting on 9 March the Community made a first important statement on agricultural transition, which it completed at the 16th Deputies meeting on 6 April. Further significant progress was made on tariff quotas. The European Investment Bank was further discussed, and the United Kingdom Delegation made a statement on New Zealand. In reply, the Community Delegation 'recalled its favourable reply on the principle of derogations for New Zealand dairy products'. This was in fact the first completely clear statement by the Community of this important principle.[5]

20. As a general comment on the progress of negotiations so far, it should be recorded that the Community Delegation had shown itself, at the outset, extremely jealous and suspicious about contacts between the United Kingdom and the Commission. It endeavoured to ensure that these should take place only on the basis of principles it had previously approved, and to maintain the position that the Commission was exclusively the servant of the Six, with no authority to take negotiating initiatives of any kind. Gradually this suspicion abated. In the early months of 1971 it became much easier for us to secure approval by the Conference that we should consult the Commission on various issues, though always on the basis that we should be seeking information only.

[5] In European Community parlance the term 'derogation' implies a change going beyond a simple transitional arrangement. The clear implication of this statement was therefore that, so far as arrangements for New Zealand dairy products were concerned, the European Community was moving away from its earlier insistence that all problems should be dealt with by transitional arrangements.

Finally, at the Deputies meeting on 9 March, 1971, 'the Community Delegation took this opportunity to state that, generally speaking, the Commission was prepared to supply the United Kingdom Delegation with all the technical clarification it might wish to have'. Thereafter our contacts with the Commission became more regular and fruitful, and frequently went far beyond 'technical clarification' into the substance of possible solutions.

21. The fifth Ministerial meeting took place on 16 March, 1971. It was particularly barren of results, though we earned some useful credit with the Community by the uncomplaining fortitude with which Mr. Rippon, in dealing with the Press after the meeting, was able to refrain from expressing disappointment and continued to express his confidence for the future. In the meeting itself he exerted strong pressure on the Community in successive statements on sugar and New Zealand; and by pressing hard for real progress in May he succeeded in getting the Community to allot more time to the May Ministerial meeting and to contemplate the possibility of an additional Ministerial meeting not long thereafter. This eventually led to the additional meeting on 7 June.

22. Meanwhile, in the background, intense consideration was already being given to the desirability of a meeting between President Pompidou and Mr. Heath; and it was becoming clear that the following Ministerial meeting of the Conference, due on 11 and 12 May, would be a critical one at which progress must be made. Also in the background, and outside the Conference, the question of sterling and the British economy began to emerge as a major factor. On this we had received a written questionnaire from the Commission in December and had replied to it in February. On 18 March the French Permanent Representative made a strong statement on these subjects at a meeting of the Six, which immediately leaked and created a considerable sensation. The British reaction to it, however, was studiously moderate and calm—a line which paid off later.

23. By now a little more progress was perceptible in the routine dealings of the Conference. Work on tariff quotas moved forward; on 22 March the United Kingdom Delegation circulated a paper with detailed proposals for consideration by the Multilateral Group which had been set up after the 13th meeting of Deputies to deal with this question. At the 15th Deputies meeting on 24 March progress was made on the European Investment Bank, Capital Movements, Third Country Agreements, secondary legislation and Article 220 Conventions. At the next meeting on 6 April, in consequence of the Budget statement, the United Kingdom Delegation was able to withdraw its request for a five-year transitional period for fiscal harmonisation (Value Added Tax).[6] It made further proposals for the transport sector. The Community Delegation made its further promised statement on agricultural transitional measures, and a statement on EURATOM.

[6] The announcement in the Budget that the United Kingdom had decided to introduce a Value Added Tax before the probable date for the United Kingdom's accession to the European Community removed the need for any transitional period.

24. On 21 April, at the 17th Deputies meeting, the United Kingdom Delegation made a carefully considered reply to the proposals the Community had put forward on agricultural transition. It was already clear—indeed it had been since January—that in this sector our attitude to the Community's proposals on Community Preference was crucial. The 18th meeting of Deputies on 28 April made notable progress on transitional measures in the sector of industrial trade (safeguard clauses, anti-dumping measures, State monopolies, taxes having an equivalent effect to duties); and there was an advance towards settling the issue of third-country agreements. Meanwhile the work of the multilateral group on tariff quotas went forward well. The Deputies meeting on 4 and 5 May noted that the group had settled nine of the 13 products under discussion, and settled three of the remaining four. Only alumina remained. At the same meeting outstanding problems on the European Coal and Steel Community and EURATOM moved forward, and we raised for the first time a further awkward question, animal health.

25. On 8 May the impending meeting between Mr. Heath and President Pompidou was announced. On the previous day we were able to act on a decision which, in retrospect, can be seen to have unlocked the door and opened up the prospect of success in the negotiations: we instructed our posts in the Community capitals, and the Delegation in Brussels, to communicate the draft of a statement Mr. Rippon intended, if he could be assured in advance that it would be acceptable, to make at the Ministerial meeting on 11 May on agricultural transition. This statement made a number of proposals about the mechanisms of agricultural transition, and it accepted the Community's insistence that Community Preference must apply in full from the start. This was well received; and the Ministerial meeting on 11 to 13 May in effect began the decisive move of the Conference towards success.

26. This meeting, after fairly severe difficulties met with on the first day and night (mainly on sugar) began to be resolved, acquired a character and atmosphere completely different from that of its predecessors. Genuine negotiations took place outside the formal Conference sessions; and during the long meeting that lasted most of the second night matters were resolved in hours which, on previous form, could have occupied months. At this meeting agreement was reached (albeit somewhat untidily, which led to difficulties later, and subject to much further detailed definition which in various forms occupied the Conference till the very end of the negotiations) on agricultural transition, including the question of horticulture. Agreement was also reached on sugar, thanks in part to the Community's extension to independent Commonwealth territories in the Caribbean, the Indian Ocean and the Pacific of its offer of the three options, including association. (This agreement was necessarily subject to its proving satisfactory to the Commonwealth sugar producers.) Final agreement was confirmed on 12 of the 13 commodities in respect of which we had asked for tariff quotas. It was agreed that matters concerning EURATOM need no longer trouble the Conference at Ministerial level. Progress was made

on Community finance, in so far as the Community side put forward a conceptual framework on the basis of which agreement was reached six weeks later. Mr. Rippon 'placed on record' a number of statements by British Ministers about sterling which helped towards later agreement; and it was also agreed that an additional Ministerial meeting should be held on 7 June. At six in the morning of 13 May, not long after the meeting had ended, I met with EFTA representatives in Brussels to brief them on its results. They were anxious to get reports to their Ministers in Reykjavik before Mr. Rippon arrived there, later that morning, for a meeting of the EFTA Ministerial Council.

27. At the 20th meeting of Deputies on 18 May agreement was recorded on tariffs in the EURATOM sector. Some loose ends left over from the Ministerial meeting were taken up, especially on sugar. This meeting was also notable for the second transmission by the Community to the Conference of a report deriving from the work of the group on Secondary Legislation—the first such report had been transmitted on 4 May. Similar reports (on nearly all of which we had to make detailed comments) followed with increasing frequency throughout the remainder of the negotiations, till almost their last day. They will not be further noticed in this summary. At the 21st Deputies meeting on 1 June, the United Kingdom Delegation made a proposal on fisheries requesting six-mile limits. Among other matters raised was the free movement of labour in Northern Ireland, and animal health was again taken up by us, though without progress. At the seventh Ministerial meeting, on 7 June in Luxembourg, the last of the tariff quota items (alumina) was settled; so was, thanks to the meeting between Mr. Heath and President Pompidou, the question of sterling. Mr. Rippon also raised the fisheries question and, for the first time, the problems of the interim period between signature of the Treaty and its entry into force. He also informed the Conference of the outcome of the meeting with the Commonwealth sugar producers held in London on 2 and 3 June. At the 22nd Deputies meeting on 16 June we proposed for the first time a solution for the problems of the Channel Islands and the Isle of Man. The British contribution to the European Coal and Steel Community funds was settled; and the Community Delegation made proposals on certain institutional changes made necessary by enlargement. Numerous other proposals in this area were made as the Conference proceeded, and in the main they proved entirely uncontroversial.

28. There followed on 21 to 23 June at Luxembourg the most crucial Ministerial meeting of all. Agreement was reached on New Zealand dairy products and Community finance. Agreement was also reached on hill farming and, subject to further definition and refinement, on the interim period. A first agreement on institutional changes consequent upon the enlargement of the Community was recorded; and it was agreed that sufficient progress had been made on questions concerning the European Coal and Steel Community for it to be unnecessary for the matter to arise again at Ministerial level. The agreement reached included the important understanding that the Community had no intention of calling in question the size and legal position of the British

Steel Corporation or the National Coal Board. An attempt by the United Kingdom Delegation to settle the question of fisheries did not get very far, though the Community accepted that their regulations would require revision. We also proposed that at the next Ministerial meeting, on 12 July, the question of fisheries should be discussed multilaterally between the Community and the four applicants together. This proposal did not prove acceptable to the Norwegians, nor therefore to the Community.

29. Thus 'the back of the negotiations was broken'. When, after two all-night sessions, the meeting ended a little before 5 a.m. on 23 June, all were convinced that the negotiations would succeed.

9

Summary and Sequence: From the Breakthrough to the End: 29 June, 1971, to 22 January, 1972

The 23rd Deputies meeting on 29 June produced good progress on capital movements and some advance in the transport sector. With the Italian Chairmanship which began on 1 July, the final phase of the Conference started. A few major questions remained, especially fisheries, and in terms of detailed work on an immense variety of topics it proved—and it was no surprise—that much more remained to be concluded than had been concluded in the first year of the negotiations.

2. The further Ministerial meeting on 12 July produced no major advances, but some useful progress. It was agreed that the question of capital movements had in the main been settled, though some further work remained for the Deputies. It was agreed also that most matters concerning the Common Commercial Policy were now settled, though here too much in fact remained to be done. Mr. Rippon made a further statement on fisheries, making it clearer than it had been before that our proposal for 6-mile limits could only be maintained if it proved acceptable to all concerned including the other candidates; and he put forward as an alternative solution the maintenance of the status quo in respect of fishery limits for all concerned, subject to later decisions by the enlarged Community. At this meeting also we raised for the first time the question of work on drafting the Treaty, and urged that it should begin immediately after the summer holidays. A further Ministerial meeting arranged for 27 July was cancelled.

3. At the 24th Deputies meeting on 20 July it was agreed that the Northern Ireland Maintenance of Employment Act might remain in force for a transitional period of five years. At the 25th meeting on 28 July the Community made a statement on the structure of the Accession Treaty and agreement was reached that the drafting of the Treaty should start in September. The Community put forward a precise proposal for the interim period. There were further exchanges on the Channel Islands and the Isle of Man.

4. The summer holidays then intervened, and the 26th meeting of Deputies did not take place until 14 September. At this meeting the principal matter outstanding in relation to the European Investment Bank—our contribution to its reserves—was settled. Agreement was reached on the interim period, subject to

confirmation by the next Ministerial meeting. Less progress than we had hoped had been made over the holidays on initiating Treaty drafting, but it was agreed that the first meeting of the Multilateral Drafting Group should take place on 20 September. The 10th Ministerial meeting took place a week later, on 21 September. This was a short meeting at which little progress was made; and the main outstanding issue of the negotiations, fisheries, was not even raised. But agreement was confirmed on procedure for the interim period. Mr. Rippon expressed some concern at the pace of work on secondary legislation and the preparation of authentic English texts, and began to apply pressure, which was to be maintained till early December, for signature of the Treaty before the end of 1971.

5. The next four meetings of Deputies, between 28 September and 3 November, made fairly steady but unspectacular progress on a large variety of subjects. Many highly significant matters relating to conditions of trade—tariff structure and nomenclature, drawback, export credits and other matters—were agreed or advanced towards agreement. The question of export restitutions on grain-based spirits was first raised in the Conference on 12 October—it had been the subject of much discussion over earlier months in the course of the work on secondary legislation.[1] Fruit and vegetable grading was discussed. Agreement was reached that the Commission of the enlarged Community should be an entirely new one, with all present members retiring at the end of 1972; and other institutional questions, including those related to the European Court of Justice, were settled. On 3 November the complicated question of additives and colorants in food and animal feeding stuffs, which we had raised earlier in the year, was broadly settled, though much remained over for later detailed discussion. The outline of a settlement on fiscal duties, including in particular the difficult problem of tobacco, was agreed; so was the 'exchange of knowledge' in the field of EURATOM. The conditions for the status quo till 31 January, 1975, for trade between the United Kingdom and dependent and independent Commonwealth territories qualifying for association was agreed, after prolonged negotiations conducted outside the Conference. The cut-off date of 10 November for secondary legislation was agreed; and the Community offered a three-year transitional period for drivers' hours as a compromise between the two years it had offered earlier and the four years for which we had then asked. The work of the Treaty Drafting Group went forward at steadily increasing pressure, though there were still delays in tackling some areas, especially agriculture.

[1] The problem over grain-based spirits (mainly whisky and gin) was that their cost base was being sharply raised by the need for the United Kingdom to accept European Community prices and levies on the raw material, but without compensating export restitution. Under existing European Community legislation, European spirits were for the most part based on wine—for which there were no similar price and levy provisions, and therefore no disadvantage with their competitors on third country markets. By contrast, a high proportion of the United Kingdom's production of whisky and gin was exported to third countries, so the problem was a substantial one.

6. Already in October we had been forced to the conclusion that the aim of signing the Treaty by the end of the year would almost certainly prove unattainable, so many and complex were the matters still remaining to be agreed. We continued, however, from time to time (and indeed up until December) to press strongly for signature in 1971. Our main objective in doing so was to maintain the spur of shortage of time in order to move things forward; but a useful by-product of its maintenance was the agreement (on 3 November) on the cut-off date of 10 November for the consideration by the Conference of secondary legislation and for the initiation of the interim period procedure. If by the time this agreement was reached the objective of signing in 1971 had been abandoned, the cut-off might have been a month later.

7. At the 11th Ministerial meeting on 9 November, Signor Moro, in response to pressure from Mr. Rippon, confirmed the objective of signature before Christmas. Agreement was reached on the Channel Islands and the Isle of Man, subject to later confirmation that it was acceptable to the Island authorities. An agreement previously reached in Deputies on an important point relating to export credits was confirmed. We raised again the question of Papua and New Guinea. Arrangements were confirmed for consultation with the candidates on the mandate for the Commission for negotiation with the EFTA non-candidates. There was much rather unfruitful discussion on fisheries, which led at least to the giving of a mandate to the Commission to consult the candidates. An additional Ministerial meeting on 29 November, to deal with fisheries, was agreed. The other three applicants were also to have Ministerial meetings on the same day.

8. On 16 November a multilateral meeting of the Community and the four candidates was held for consultation on the draft mandate to the Commission prepared by the Community for negotiations with the EFTA non-candidate States. While the candidates expressed some criticisms of the draft mandate, it was agreed by all that the negotiations should be opened as soon as possible.

9. The 31st Deputies meeting on 24 November covered much ground. By now the agenda of each Deputies meeting tended to be two or three times as long as it had been during the first year of the negotiations. On this occasion the first United Kingdom statements relating to disputed points in the Treaty drafting exercise were made; a procedure for the multilateralisation of agreements reached by the Community with the various candidates separately was agreed. (Already, throughout the year, the other candidates had frequently been invited to accept agreements reached with us, and had done so; though so far the reverse procedure had not been applied.) The question of travellers' franchise within the enlarged Community was settled; so were details concerning the adoption by the candidates on 1 January, 1974, of the Community's generalised preference scheme, and the question of Papua and New Guinea. Agreement was also reached, after much delicate discussion outside the Conference, on the last outstanding matters concerning the European Coal and Steel Community. But deadlock persisted on the question of animal health. Here it had proved

impossible, over months, to get the Community's agreement to the establishment of a multilateral working party; but on this occasion, at least, the Community formally authorised the Commission to 'continue', with us, the examination of the problems involved. Deadlock also persisted on the question of restitution on grain-based spirits.

10. At the 12th Ministerial meeting on 29 and 30 November, Mr. Rippon reported the consent in principle of the Channel Islands and the Isle of Man, secured in the course of visits he had made to them, to the arrangements negotiated for them; though it was still necessary for these arrangements to be endorsed by their legislatures, as they were by mid-December. He maintained our objective of signing before Christmas, though by now the Community were much more reluctant to commit themselves. He made to the Conference the statement on United Kingdom nationality required in the context of the free movement of labour. But on the main topic for which this meeting had been arranged—fisheries—complete deadlock persisted, in spite of an all-night session held in a somewhat tense and frustrated atmosphere. No better progress was made in the brief separate meetings between the Community and the other candidates. It was agreed to meet again to discuss fisheries on 11 and 12 December; and on that occasion also parallel meetings were to be held between the Community and the other three candidates on the same subject.

11. The 32nd meeting of Deputies intervened on 7 December, at which a number of points were settled, including the problems of British wine and drivers' hours, and United Kingdom adhesion to the Community's non-preferential agreements with third countries. It was becoming clear by now that the final task of the Conference would be to settle the couple of dozen points, some of them of major significance, on which it was proving impossible to reach agreement in the Treaty Drafting Group. By now also certain accelerated procedures were being adopted by the Deputies, which proved useful in the new year. Thus new proposals by either side, or reactions to or acceptance of earlier proposals, were frequently circulated in writing between meetings, or during adjournments of meetings.

12. The 13th Ministerial meeting on 11 and 12 December succeeded in settling the problem of fisheries, subject to further work required on the marketing regulation. Denmark and the Irish Republic accepted the fisheries settlement; Norway did not. Animal health was also at length settled, subject again to some minor points and to the fact that the Irish were holding out for more; this suited us, since we also had to obtain more for Northern Ireland, as Mr. Rippon made clear. It was agreed that the Treaty would be signed towards mid-January and that unless something unforeseen were to occur no further Ministerial meeting between the United Kingdom and the Community would be required. But Norway and the Irish Republic secured dates for Ministerial meetings early in the new year.

13. There remained a large number of points to be settled in the Deputies, and six further meetings, spread over 10 days between 15 December and 18

January, 1972, were required to complete the task. On 15 December some of the outstanding Treaty drafting points were inconclusively raised; animal health was tidied up; fruit and vegetable grading was settled; a transitional period for liquid milk was agreed, as also for pharmaceutical products. So was our participation in the EURATOM five-year research programme. On 17 December various institutional questions were agreed, including those concerning the European Investment Bank. So were delays in the implementation of non-agricultural directives and a transitional period for flax and ramie yarn. A few (but still not the last) outstanding points on the Channel Islands were cleared up and the date of 22 January, 1972, was agreed for signature of the Treaty. On 22 December most outstanding questions on the fish marketing regulation were settled. The question of units of measurement, which had been for long a delicate problem discussed mainly outside the Conference, was more or less concluded, though it was yet to give trouble. The delays required for the implementation of agricultural directives were agreed; some outstanding points on EURATOM third country agreements and the Common Commercial Policy were settled. Matters discussed but not settled included hops and grain-based spirits.

14. A good deal remained for 1972, and for the Luxembourg chairmanship. The 36th meeting of Deputies was held on 6 and 7 January. Fish marketing was finally concluded. Questions arising from the hops regulation were at last settled. So was the problem of grain-based spirits, and an awkward last-minute problem about the date at which the Community would take further decisions on regional policy was settled to our satisfaction. Maritime freights for coal and steel, the further problems of EURATOM third country agreements, the composition of numerous Community Committees and the question of sugar stocks were settled. It was agreed that the Community's agricultural regulations would operate in all candidate countries from 1 February, 1973, subject to a solution being found for the outstanding problem of apples and pears. Progress was made with the classification of pig carcasses, though not on regulations concerning beef and veal. The exchanges on Treaty drafting points continued, and statements by the Community reduced the number of points outstanding.

15. The 37th meeting of Deputies was spread over three days, 12, 13 and 14 January. At this and the next meeting, work continued till the early hours of the morning, and frequent and often prolonged adjournments gave the opportunity for detailed drafting and informal consultation to promote agreements. In this the Presidency and the Commission played, as usual, the leading part on the Community side; in fact, only at this late stage did it prove possible to apply in the Deputies meetings the techniques which had been successfully employed in several of the Ministerial meetings since May 1971.

16. At this 37th meeting, a point concerning the future of the Guidance Section of the Agricultural Guidance and Guarantee Fund was settled. Animal health was finally concluded (the Irish having meanwhile got certain further concessions at their Ministerial meeting). Beef and veal was settled, largely by

leaving matters over for final consideration during the interim period. A difficult problem concerning the marketing of seeds was finally solved. The Community accepted that (with some exceptions) the United Kingdom need not apply the nomenclature of the Common External Tariff till 1 January, 1974—a conclusion they had been resisting for some weeks. The question of the definition of United Kingdom nationals for the purpose of the Community's rules on free movement of labour was finally cleared up. The Dutch in particular (but not only they) had developed some anxieties which proved hard to allay, and some rather delicate contacts outside the Conference had proved necessary over recent weeks to secure agreement. In the same agreement a national of Gibraltar was defined; and a separate agreement finally spelt out a number of matters concerning Gibraltar which had been insufficiently clarified in the agreements of principle reached in the autumn of 1970, and had caused some difficulties since then. The last remaining points concerning the Channel Islands and the Isle of Man were cleared up. Units of measurement were finally settled. A number of the less difficult points outstanding from the work of the Treaty Drafting Group were settled; and the Community Delegation at length produced a text for the 'entry into force' article of the Treaty, which was close enough to a text we had informally circulated some months earlier to prove acceptable. A problem which characterised this meeting of Deputies, and the next and last one, was that of 'multilateralisation'—in several cases it had to be agreed that solutions would only prove acceptable if they were accepted by all other candidates. This arose especially, but not exclusively, in the spheres of fisheries and animal health.

17. The 38th and last meeting of Deputies began on 17 January, and ended with final agreement at about 3 a.m. on 18 January. Before this meeting started the Norwegians had finally reached agreement with the Community on fisheries. The Deputies meeting had two tasks: to settle a few outstanding issues of substance and to reach agreement on the disputed provisions of the draft Treaty. The latter was the more difficult and the more important. The issues of substance—including sugar import arrangements to conclude the obligations of the Commonwealth Sugar Agreement, compensatory amounts for apples and pears, an outstanding point on liquid milk and dairy products, Protocol XVII of List G on 'Flying Machines', a point on iron and steel scrap, some points relating to the Anglo-Irish Free Trade Area Agreement, some problems concerning pigmeat were settled without too much difficulty. The United Kingdom Delegation accepted the fisheries agreement reached with Norway, placing on record a brief statement of its views and insisting that the other candidates should not go further than it did in any unilateral statements they might make, nor reopen in any other way the balance of the settlement now reached.

18. There remained the disputed Treaty points. Considerable further progress in settling them was made on 17 January, and by the evening only some seven or eight of the most difficult points remained outstanding. They included

deficiency payments, corrective action in the event of difficulties arising in the Community in the application of agricultural transitional provisions, safeguards for third-country agricultural trade, the question whether or not the agreement reached in June 1971 about unanimity in decisions on New Zealand trade after 1977 should be explicitly recorded in the New Zealand Protocol, and a group of articles (to which it was clear the Community attached paramount importance) relating to the financing of the Common Agricultural Policy. It was evident that only a package deal could bring agreement; and during an adjournment late on 17 January the United Kingdom Delegation proposed a package through the Presidency. It became evident that the Community had contemplated a rather different package, and at first difficulties arose. Some rather intense negotiations ensued outside the Conference with the Presidency and the Commission; and eventually our package was broadly accepted. The Conference resumed for its formal endorsement, and at about 3 a.m. final agreement in the negotiations was recorded.

19. All was not quite over. The process of 'multilateralisation' was successfully concluded by the Community during 18 January with the Danes, Norwegians and Irish, not without much concern on our part over fisheries. Late on 18 January we learnt that the French Delegation were seeking their partners' assent to requesting a further agreement from us on general safeguard provisions in the Treaty, but after a little time—helped perhaps by an indignant reaction from us—this project failed to get off the ground. On 21 January a final formal meeting of the Conference was held to approve the records of the last three or four meetings (the Secretariat had not been able to keep pace) of the Conference at Deputy level with each of the candidates. The Multilateral Drafting Group worked at high pressure till 20 January to embody the final decisions of the Conference in the draft of the Treaty of Accession. The Multilateral Group of Jurists-Linguists meanwhile put the final touches to each of the eight language versions of the Treaty of Accession. On 22 January the Treaty of Accession was signed.

10

Transitional Measures and Periods

With the exception of one dismal period in the autumn of 1967, it had always been accepted by all concerned that a principal, if not the principal, feature of any agreement on the admission of new States to the European Community would be the negotiation with them of transitional measures and periods to ease their adjustment to membership of the Community. In the autumn of 1967, when the French were casting around for ways to thwart our attempt to open negotiations, they developed a new doctrine, based largely on the opportunity given them by manifest British economic weakness around the time of the devaluation of sterling at the beginning of November 1967. According to this new French doctrine, applicant States must qualify for membership by reaching certain standards of economic health, and by themselves adapting their practices to those of the Community. Only when their practices had been so adapted, according to this doctrine, could negotiations for membership begin; and then of course they could be extremely short, for neither derogations nor transitional periods would be needed. In other words, the whole process of adaptation and transition must precede negotiations, not begin from entry as a member. When M. Schumann was in London on 23 January, 1970, some words he had used in a public speech the previous evening were interpreted by some of the British Press as an echo of this doctrine; but he hastened to assure both the Foreign Secretary (Mr. Stewart) and the Prime Minister (Mr. Wilson) at separate meetings that he had been misunderstood, and that he fully accepted that in the negotiations due to begin later that year transitional periods must be provided for the applicant States.

2. The positions adopted in advance of the negotiations of 1970 to 1972, both by ourselves and the Community, have been described in some detail in Chapter 2. It is worth repeating the main features of them here, in so far as they dealt with transitional measures and periods. Our own position had been briefly stated by Mr. Brown in July 1967: 'All of us, you no less than we, will need a transitional period or periods to permit mutual adaptation to the circumstances of an enlarged Community.' M. Harmel was rather more categoric. There must indeed be transitional measures; but there must be nothing else. 'The rule which must necessarily govern the negotiations is that the solution of

any problems of adjustment which may arise must be sought in the establishment of transitional measures and not in changes in the existing rules.' He went on to say: 'The transitional measures must be conceived in such a way as to ensure an overall balance of reciprocal advantages. With this in mind, it will be necessary to ensure an adequate synchronisation (parallélisme) of the progress of freedom of movement of industrial goods, with the achievement of the agricultural Common Market.' 'Adequate parallelism' became a very significant feature of the negotiations. M. Harmel went on to say: 'In the other fields in which transitional measures prove to be necessary, the duration of such measures could, if possible and desirable, be varied according to their subject matters and the applicants involved.'

3. On the whole, the Community got their way. The negotiation proved to be a negotiation about transitional measures and periods, and about relatively little else. This is reflected in the structure of the Treaty of Accession. Part IV of the 'Act Concerning the Conditions of Accession and the Adjustments to the Treaties' is entitled 'Transitional Measures' and contains no less than 108 of the 161 Articles of the Act. And most of the remaining Articles are concerned either with adjustments to the texts of the Treaties which followed more or less automatically from enlargement, or with formal provisions such as those in Part V. Most, but by no means all, of the 30 Protocols attached to the Act are also concerned with transitional provisions. So are Annexes V, VII, X and XI. But Annexes I and II (which, together with the four Annexes just mentioned, comprise the enormous output of the work on Secondary Legislation) are not transitional. They record permanent adaptations to the laws of the Community, some of them of much significance.

4. The transitional periods provided for in the Act are anything but uniform. Paragraph 2 of Article 9 of the Act reads: 'Subject to the dates, time limits and special provisions provided for in this Act, the application of the transitional measures shall terminate at the end of 1977.' It is thus formally laid down that in principle the transitional period is five years. But in fact, and indeed the last quotation above from M. Harmel's statement foresaw it, many different periods are laid down in a great variety of cases.

5. Moreover, the Act provided for very different types of transitional measures. The normal concept of transition is a gradual process by which a new situation is reached in successive steps and stages. This concept applies in a number of cases provided for in the Act; but in the great majority of cases (though not the most important) transition is provided simply through the establishment of a period in which nothing is to occur and no steps are to be taken, but at the end of which an obligation is assumed in full. Such a form of transition, in the work on Secondary Legislation, came to be termed a 'temporal adaptation', to distinguish it from an adaptation of substance. The term could well be applied in many other cases. It is necessary, in analysing the Act, to distinguish between these two types of transition: temporal adaptation and transition by stages. One might even establish a third type, a mixture of the other two. For instance, are

the arrangements made for capital movements to be regarded as of the first type or of the second? Admittedly, they provide for adoption by the United Kingdom of the Community rules on capital movements by successive stages, after two years, after 30 months and after five years. But in each case a particular part of these rules is to be adopted in full after the agreed period, and not necessarily approached step by step. Though the great majority of cases in which transition of some kind is provided fall into the category of 'temporal adaptation', yet in the most important cases of all the genuine system of transition by successive steps to the complete adoption of Community rules was the one adopted. It was adopted, for instance, in the cases of Community finance and of New Zealand butter and cheese; and also for tariff changes and for the move to new agricultural prices.

6. In most of the cases where genuine transition of this sort, on the step-by-step basis, was adopted, it was agreed that at the end of the period laid down Community rules should prevail. The cases in which the possibility was agreed of further exceptional measures being applied after the expiry of the period established are relatively few. They are in fact confined to New Zealand butter (not cheese), fisheries, animal health, units of measurement, and additives to foodstuffs and animal feeding stuffs. Only in one case, that of New Zealand butter, do the terms of the agreement reached make it absolutely clear that there must be further special measures after the first transitional period concludes. Thus, paragraph 2 of Article 5 of Protocol No. 18 on New Zealand butter and cheese lays down that 'appropriate measures to ensure the maintenance, after 31 December, 1977, of exceptional arrangements in respect of imports of butter from New Zealand ... shall be determined by the Council.' In the case of fisheries, animal health, units of measurement and additives to food and to animal feed there is the possibility of further special measures after the expiry of the period laid down, but no obligation that there shall be such further special measures. Only in one case, in the whole Treaty complex, was the rule that nothing more than transitional measures could be admitted explicitly breached. This was in Protocol No. 20 on Norwegian Agriculture, in which the parties to the Treaty 'recognise in principle that the transitional period could not solve these problems and that it is therefore necessary to envisage specific arrangements—which should not be regarded as constituting a precedent'.[1]

7. The periods agreed for transitional measures, whether in the classic step-by-step form or as a 'temporal adaptation', varied very widely. The longest period of all was granted in Protocol No. 7 to the Irish for the maintenance of

[1] There was however one important exception, Commonwealth sugar. Although specific provisions were not agreed in the accession negotiations, it was clear that something more than transitional arrangements was envisaged. And so it turned out. The commitment by the European Community to buy specific quantities of sugar at a guaranteed price related to the European Community and not to the world price, continues to the present day as an integral part of successive Lomé Conventions (the successors, from 1975 onwards to the Yaoundé Convention).

their system of motor vehicle assembly: it was 12 years. Next came fisheries, with 10 years. The transitional period for Community finance was seven years. For units of measurement it was also seven years, though here as in the case of fisheries there is the possibility of prolongation.[2] At the other end of the scale, periods of delay before the application of certain regulations or directives vary, in several hundreds of different cases, from one month up to five years. The one-month delay after entry into force of the Treaties applied only in the case of the application of the agricultural marketing regulations on 1 February, 1973, by all the candidates. The other periods of delay in the application of particular regulations or directives by various candidate countries are set out sometimes in the body of the Act (examples are Articles 68, 69, 76, 84, 89, 151 and 154); in a few cases in Annex I; but for the most part in Annexes V, VII, X and XI. In some of these cases an agreed period of delay can by further agreement be prolonged (though not beyond the end of 1977); in a few cases such a period can, by agreement, be shortened.

8. Yet the period of five years laid down in paragraph 2 of Article 9 of the Act as the standard period of transition is by no means without meaning. Above all, it governs the transitional period in respect of agricultural prices. For tariff movements, we succeeded in getting a somewhat shorter period, namely four and a half years; the final abolition of internal tariffs and the final moves to the Common External Tariff are to be completed by 1 July, 1977, six months before the last move to agricultural prices. It was of course as between these two processes that the main tussle over 'adequate parallelism' took place. The four and a half year period for tariffs was provisionally settled first; and there is no doubt that the French had hoped that we should be obliged to accept an identical period for agricultural price movements, completing our transition in the course of 1977 as the various crop years began. Indeed, when we at length succeeded, at the Ministerial meeting on 11 and 12 May, 1971, in getting it accepted that, for agricultural prices, we should be allowed to make six movements over five full years, the French made an attempt to reopen the provisionally agreed period for tariff changes and move it up likewise to the full five years. Fortunately, in the co-operative atmosphere which had at that meeting suddenly and for the first time developed, the attempt failed. The minutes of the meeting record Mr. Rippon as observing that 'the Community had generously decided not to request' the modification of the provisional agreement on tariffs, 'and he welcomed this as another expression of goodwill'.

9. Although transitional measures and 'temporal adaptations' were agreed in so many fields, there was one field of the greatest importance in which the Community refused to grant us any transition at all (except the one month's grace till 1 February, 1973). This is the field of Community Preference in agriculture, which turned out to be one of the key areas of the whole negotiation.

[2] In many cases this was subsequently further prolonged; and in some (for example pints, miles) a derogation in perpetuity was subsequently agreed.

A case could be made for the view that this constitutes an unwarranted exception to the general pattern of the negotiations. In this field we made clear from the start our acceptance of the proposition that Community Preference was an essential feature of the Common Agricultural Policy and that we were prepared to introduce it; but we argued for months that it should be introduced by stages over the transitional period. There was some dispute as to whether this was technically possible; but the Commission at least accepted that it was, and indeed there can be no real doubt on the matter. Some of the Member States of the Community accepted it too. Thus a telegram from Brussels of 29 January, 1971, which summed up a discussion on transitional measures held by the Six Permanent Representatives the previous day, concluded as follows: 'The major point to be resolved is Community Preference. The French, Belgians, Luxembourgers and Dutch are for the immediate and full introduction of Community Preference. The German and Italian Delegations question this proposal: to introduce Community Preference immediately would be against the principles of transition as such.' Against this proposition it can be argued, and this of course was the French view, that the full operation of Community Preference was no more than one aspect of the mechanisms of the agricultural Common Market which we had agreed to install from the outset. Be that as it may, it is difficult to accept that the arrangement on Community Preference which we were obliged to adopt was not an exception to the general principle that there should be transitional measures or periods to help the new Member States in adapting to Community rules.

10. Before leaving transition as a general theme, certain further peculiarities of its use in the Treaty should be noted. First, there were a couple of cases in which the Treaty did not record completed agreements, but laid down that agreements should be completed. The first case is paragraph 2 of Article 3 of the Act, in which the new Member States undertake (without time limit) to accede to the Conventions provided for in Article 220 of the Treaty of Rome, and to enter into negotiations with the original Member States in order to make the necessary adjustments thereto. (These Conventions cover matters such as the reciprocal enforcement of judgments, and the present Member States themselves have so far made relatively little progress in completing them or bringing them into force.) Second, Article 108 provides that the new Member States shall apply the provisions of certain agreements concluded by the Community with third countries from the date of accession; and that this application shall be the subject of Protocols (to be negotiated, it follows, before accession) which may themselves include transitional measures.

11. Perhaps the most peculiar transitional arrangements of all were those concluded in the case of fisheries, in so far as, in this case alone, a part at least of the transitional arrangements agreed was made available not only to the applicant States but to the original, Member States. Thus the first major part of the exceptions agreed—for fisheries—the general limit of 6 nautical miles—was set out as something which 'the Member States of the Community'

as a whole were authorised to adopt. And in the second general exception—12-mile limits—one Member State, France, joined as well as all the candidate States. This is proof that the Community's Fisheries Regulation suffered greater damage and distortion in the negotiations than any of its other rules. Its provisions on access must be admitted, unfortunately, to have survived in spite of Articles 100 to 103 of the Act; but only in a somewhat spectral form.

12. Finally, this general consideration of transition provides a convenient opportunity to mention a very important topic which, fortunately for us, never arose in the negotiations. This is the question, much canvassed over many years, whether the fact that the new Member States would not from the outset be assuming in full all the obligations of membership, but would have this assumption slowed and mitigated by transitional measures and periods, should or should not have the consequence that their participation in the institutions of the Community and in the rights of membership should be in any way limited. The question was raised in the first Opinion of 29 September, 1967, by the Commission on our application for membership. Paragraph 26 of this Opinion read: 'Since the establishment of a transitional period creates a time-lag in application of the Community regulations to new members, it must be asked whether or not these new members should nevertheless be fully entitled to participate in the adoption of decisions which would not be immediately applicable to them because of the transitional arrangements from which they benefit. This is a particularly difficult problem for which there is no point in seeking a solution until we know how long the transitional period will be and what the obligations of new members will be during that period.' The Commission's updated Opinion of 3 October, 1969, contained no reference to the point. We had of course always maintained most strongly that there could be no question of our entering the Communities with anything less than the full rights of a Member State, including in particular its full voting rights. The Community were well aware that this was our view, and must have appreciated that it would be dangerous to challenge it.

13. In the event, they did not. The possibility that we might have to accept less than full voting rights if we accepted less than full obligations from the start was occasionally brandished in the background. During the first six months of 1970, when the Community were preparing their negotiating position, the point arose from time to time; but they decided not to seek to limit our rights. The Commission's 'Vue d'ensemble' of November 1970 discussed the question, and concluded: 'In the opinion of the Commission, a transitional period of the nature described in this document justifies, from the start, full participation of the new Member States in the institutional life of the enlarged Community.' This did not mean that the danger had passed. From time to time, even in the first six months of the negotiations, there were reports that the French might bring the argument back into play. Nor was it only the French. Thus in November 1970 Mr. Lardinois, Dutch Minister of Agriculture, told reporters on returning to Holland from conversations in England with Mr. Prior that he

had impressed on the latter that we must switch over rapidly to the EEC agricultural system 'if Britain wanted from the very beginning to obtain a say and voting rights as a full member of the Common Market'. In the same month Dr. Mansholt told Mr. Marshall (who passed it on to Mr. Rippon on 24 November) that once the applicants had joined, they could vote; but the price of the vote was Community Preference. Other problems besides agriculture could, in this period, have triggered off a Community reaction. Had we not, in October 1969, agreed to 'set aside' our original request (which we had always regarded as a potential discard) for a one-year period of initiation, the Community might well have countered by threatening that if we were to enjoy such a year we should have to accept an abatement of our rights during it.

14. But it was at the end of 1970 and in the first few months of 1971 that this danger arose in its sharpest form, as a prelude and a reaction to the proposals on Community finance which we tabled on 16 December, 1971. On 1 December in Brussels M. Deniau of the Commission told me emphatically that if we sought escape from the appropriate financial burden we should put at risk our participation as a full member from entry. After our paper was tabled, rumblings about voting rights from Paris increased. German officials raised the issue in conversation with our Embassy in Bonn. One of them, on 3 February, remarked that settling our contribution to Community finance 'was rather like buying a share in a going concern: one had to pay the market price. The market price included an element for voting rights.' We grew seriously concerned at the risk involved; and our concern and the arguments we used are clearly shown in Foreign Office telegram No. 51 of 22 January, 1971, to Bonn and other posts, reproduced in Appendix I. We even judged it necessary to make the point firmly in the Conference; and in his statement on Community finance at the Ministerial meeting of 2 February, 1971, Mr. Rippon included the following passage:

> 'Some people even suggest that, because under our proposals our initial payment would be small in the first year compared to what it would be in later years, we should not from the outset enjoy our full status as a member of the Community. This argument about status and voting rights is another whose logic I do not perceive. And of course my colleagues will recognise that Britain's position in the institutions of the Community raises a very clear and simple political question; either Britain enjoys a full voice from the start in the institutions of the Community, or we do not join.'

15. Whether or not in consequence of this firm warning, less was heard thereafter about an abatement of our voting rights. The question was never formally raised; and the proposition that new members of the Community would enjoy from their entry the full rights of membership was never challenged, though in one respect, reasonable enough, the Treaty of Accession does provide that new members shall not, for a certain period, vote on certain Community

decisions. This exception is expressed in Article 114 of the Act, which provides that (until, by virtue of Article 115, 31 January, 1975) only the votes of the original Member States shall be counted when the Council of Ministers decides on matters relating to the existing Yaoundé and Arusha Conventions, by which new Member States will not be bound.

11

Transitional Measures for Tariffs and Agricultural Prices

After the analysis in the last chapter of transitional measures and periods as they emerged in the Treaty as a whole, it is time to turn to the details of the way in which transitional measures and periods were negotiated in certain fields. I will deal in later chapters with those adopted in the cases of Community finance, New Zealand dairy products, fisheries and a number of less important matters. This chapter will give an account of the way in which agreement was reached on transitional measures and periods in the two fields of tariffs and agricultural prices.

2. We had been extremely careful throughout our preparations for the negotiations not to commit ourselves in public to any definite period of transition as a target. On their side, the Community had done the same. Perhaps there was already a general impression in the air that something like five years might prove to be the outcome; but if so, it rested on no concrete base of suggestion from either side. For our part, we were anxious that transition should be more rapid in the field of tariff movement—both the dismantling of internal tariffs within the enlarged Community and the move by the candidates to the Common External Tariff—than in the field of agriculture. We considered, and so did the Confederation of British Industry, that it would be to our advantage to move rapidly rather than slowly to full free trade in the industrial field. But we knew that a longer period would be necessary for agricultural transition, because of the major adjustments it would involve, both for producers in this country and above all for consumers in the moves they would have to make towards higher food prices. We knew too that the Community would insist strongly on at least 'adequate parallelism' in these two fields. We had decided—and the Confederation of British Industry agreed—that if we could not get our objective of two completely different transitional periods (and we hardly expected to) then agricultural considerations should take priority, and we should accept if we had to a longer period of tariff movements in order to get a longer period for agricultural transition.

3. This was an area where we made an early start. At the first Deputies meeting after the summer break of 1970 we proposed, on 16 September, that there should be a transitional period of three years for eliminating internal

industrial tariffs and adopting the Common External Tariff, while making it clear that a longer transitional period would be needed for agriculture. We proposed a first tariff movement of 40 per cent on 1 January, 1974; and two subsequent movements of 30 per cent each on 1 January, 1975, and 1 January, 1976. This was reasonably well received by the Community; but they immediately made it clear that there would have to be 'adequate parallelism'. 'The industrial sector', said Herr Sachs, the Chairman of the meeting, 'cannot be isolated. It is connected with agriculture and it is therefore necessary to preserve a certain balance.' A month later, at the fourth Deputies meeting on 14 October, we proposed a six-year transitional period for agriculture. This caused some uproar; the French in particular expressed (outside the Conference) a good deal of indignation that we should contemplate transitional periods in the two fields of which one was twice as long as the other. Already in fact we were reckoning that we might end up with a compromise of five years for both.

4. The French counter-attacked. At the Ministerial meeting on 21 July they had succeeded in somewhat hardening against us the opening position of the Community by getting the Community to agree, and state to us, that all problems in the negotiations must be solved by transitional measures and nothing else. This went beyond M. Harmel's statement of 30 June by excluding the highly qualified possibility of adapting the definitive financial regulation (see paragraphs 11 and 13 of Chapter 2). At the Ministerial meeting on 27 October they went further, and got the Community to agree to a statement made to us which clearly implied that there could be one period of transition only for all problems, including not only industrial tariffs and agriculture, but New Zealand, sugar and Community finance. This was a distinct change from the position previously adopted by the Community and expressed in M. Harmel's opening statement. That had referred to 'adequate parallelism' in movement to industrial free trade and to the Common Agricultural Market, which itself implied the possibility of some distinction; but it had declared also that in fields other than that of trade the duration of transitional measures could be varied according to their subject matter and the applicants involved.

5. This Community statement did not however prove the obstacle that we feared. In the next month in Brussels we continued in Deputies meetings to explain our ideas on the mechanisms of agricultural transition; and at the Ministerial meeting on 8 December Mr. Rippon put forward a new proposal. Ministers had agreed that we could abate our agricultural proposal by one year; and accordingly on 8 December in Brussels Mr. Rippon proposed that there should be a single transitional period of five years for tariffs and for agricultural prices.

6. This proposal, which we regarded as a major concession and move forward, was by no means there and then agreed, indeed it received at first a rather grudging welcome from the Community, though they did, after a three-hour adjournment, 'note it with satisfaction'. The Community's hesitations may have been due in part to the fact that the speech in which Mr. Rippon made

his proposal concluded with a long passage on Community Finance which was bound to be less popular. Be that as it may, it came to be generally accepted, after the making of this proposal, that something like a general five-year transitional period would be the outcome. This indeed corresponded to the Commission's own proposal, put forward in their 'Vue d'ensemble' of 17 November: 'The Commission is of the opinion that a five-year transitional period ... would constitute an appropriate framework'. At the next Ministerial meeting on 2 February, 1971, agreement was recorded on a timetable for industrial tariff moves. The Community, to be sure, made clear that it could be no more than a provisional agreement, and that it depended on satisfactory measures and periods being agreed for agriculture. Nevertheless, the eventual programme of tariff movements was now established. So far as internal tariff dismantlement was concerned, there were to be five successive moves of 20 per cent each, on 1 April, 1973, 1 January, 1974, 1975 and 1976 and 1 July, 1977. For the adoption by the candidates of the Common External Tariff there would be a first move of 40 per cent on 1 January, 1974; and subsequent moves of 20 per cent on 1 January, 1975 and 1976, and on 1 July, 1977. We thus achieved to a considerable extent our objectives in the field of tariff movements. To be sure, we had to agree to a period of more than three years. Nevertheless, under this arrangement, 80 per cent of tariffs would be removed at the end of three years; and the whole process would be completed in four and a half years rather than five.

7. The agreement on agricultural transition was much more complicated and took much more time. It became apparent at an early stage that the acceptance in full by the candidates of Community Preference at the start was something on which the French were totally insistent. Thus already on 27 January, 1971, our Embassy in Bonn reported that State Secretary von Braun, in giving an account of the talks between Herr Brandt and M. Pompidou in Paris on 25 and 26 January, said that M. Pompidou had mentioned the importance of our giving full Community Preference from the very beginning in the agricultural field. In the internal discussions of the Community resistance by some Member States to this French position continued; but at a meeting of the Council of Ministers on 1 and 2 March, 1971, the French secured agreement to their requirement. They had however to concede, in the course of doing so, that something should be done to meet the main problem we foresaw should we have to accept Community Preference in full from the start—namely the disruption which might be caused to traditional supplies from third countries, such as Australia. To meet this point the Council for the first time adopted something like the formula which eventually, almost a year later and after much modification, led to paragraph 5 of Protocol No. 16 of the Treaty, and to its rather peculiar footnote.[1] At the same meeting of the Council the Germans

[1] This was one of those problems which loomed a great deal larger in the negotiations than in the period after accession. Although patterns of trade between the United Kingdom and its main developed Commonwealth suppliers underwent considerable change, no claims of

and Italians finally abandoned the support they had given to our insistence that our moves towards Community agricultural prices must take place in six movements over five full years. The Council decided that there should be five movements only, the last step being completed by July 1977. This would have meant in fact that we should have had only a four-year period for agricultural transition, since of course the first price moves would only take effect at the beginning of the various crop years in 1973; but it would have provided for total parallelism with the movements provisionally agreed on in the tariff field. In a public speech in Brussels on 2 March M. Schumann declared: 'On 1 March the Six agreed on Community Preference, which is the foundation of its other rules. Great Britain will certainly accept this principle.'

8. Against the background of this decision by the Council, negotiation on agricultural transition continued actively in Brussels. The French Chairman of the Deputies made two long and detailed statements of the Community's position at meetings with us on 9 March and 6 April. At the Ministerial meeting on 16 March Mr. Rippon continued to urge that it was essential for us to spread the process of adjusting to the Community's agricultural prices by being able to make six movements over five full years. Frequent meetings took place in Brussels between Mr. Kearns and his assistants and groups of experts from the Commission, usually led by M. Rabot, Director-General of Agriculture. The outlines of practicable solutions began to emerge, but they were always predicated, from the Community side, on our acceptance of Community Preference in full from the start. On 21 April, 1971, Mr. Kearns, at the 17th meeting of Deputies, made a further long statement of our position in this field, in reply to the two Community statements of 9 March and 6 April. In this statement he insisted on the need for five full years of transition and six agricultural price movements. He argued that it was both possible and desirable to introduce Community Preference gradually throughout the transitional period; but, in his comments on the ideas the Community had put forward for resolving the problems of disruption of third country trade which immediate full Community Preference would involve, he probably succeeded in indicating to them that our position on Community Preference was no longer absolute. He did however maintain that certain quota provisions regulating our imports, including those for apples and pears, should be phased out gradually. He indicated also that we might be able to accept something like the Community's timetable for tariff cuts on agricultural trade (this of course was most important in the field of horticulture) provided that the first cut was made, not as they had suggested in 1973, but at the beginning of 1974. He welcomed ideas that had begun to emerge from the Community side about a possible small margin of flexibility, both in the annual price movements and in the annual tariff movements, especially for horticultural products. He concluded: 'It would therefore be easier for us to

disruption were made in the terms of this protocol or at least none requiring action by the European Community. This was certainly in part due to the high level of world agricultural prices in the period immediately following accession.

consider your approach to agricultural transition, including your proposals on Community Preference, as a basis for agreement, if it were clear to us that a limited number of practical problems could be solved.'

9. The first Community reaction to this statement was somewhat critical. The criticism extended even to M. Pompidou, who grumbled a few days later that we were now even making trouble about apples and pears. But when, after considerable procedural difficulties instigated by the French, we succeeded in overcoming their reluctance to allow us to engage in further discussions with the Commission to clarify the position reached, it began to be recognised, on both sides, that the outlines of an agreement were becoming perceptible. The Ministerial meeting arranged for 11 and 12 May was rapidly approaching. The meeting between Mr. Heath and M. Pompidou had already been in principle agreed; its date was settled at the beginning of May and announced on 8 May. We felt it was of the greatest importance that, as a prelude to that meeting, the Ministerial meeting in Brussels of 11 and 12 May should make major progress. Accordingly, the whole problem of agricultural transition and Community Preference was reconsidered by Ministers in London; and in the light of their decisions we were able to take action on 7 May which, in my judgment, led to the turning point in the Brussels negotiations. On that day, two telegrams of instructions were despatched to our posts in the Community which set out the statement Mr. Rippon was prepared to make in the Conference on 11 May 'provided it was clear in advance that an approach on these lines would be acceptable to the member countries and the Commission, and could lead to an agreement'. These two telegrams are reproduced at Appendix I.

10. The reaction to these proposals was on the whole welcoming and good; the Commission in particular promised its best efforts in helping things forward. When the Ministerial meeting began on 11 May Mr. Rippon judged that the prospect of agreement was clear enough to enable him to circulate his statement. There was no lack of confusion during the following 36 hours before the end of the meeting, and I will not attempt to unravel it in detail. The Community insisted on modifying our proposals by various insertions designed to tie them more closely to existing provisions of the Common Agricultural Policy. There were prolonged and useful expert sessions with the Commission during adjournments of the Conference. M. Deniau was able for the first time, once this work with the Commission experts had yielded results, to play an active and useful part in mediating, outside the Conference, between the British and the Community Delegations. A determined effort by Dr. Luns to insist that we must start dismantling horticultural tariffs in 1973 received no support whatever from the French, and accordingly failed. By the early morning of 13 May agreement had been reached more or less on the basis of our proposals. We would accept Community Preference in full from the start. In return, there would be provision in the Treaty for dealing with disruption caused to third country trade. There would be provision for dealing with problems arising within the Community (this meant essentially in our own market) should things go wrong in the course

of transition. We should be granted five full years with six movements to adapt to Community agricultural prices, though the last of these movements must take place not at the beginning of crop years through 1978 but at the very beginning of 1978. Agricultural tariffs would be dismantled in five equal steps of 20 per cent beginning only on 1 January, 1974. And there would be a permissible 10 per cent margin of flexibility in both price and tariff moves, confined in the latter case to horticultural tariffs only.

11. This was a satisfactory agreement to us, provided in particular that the measures to deal with disruption proved workable. There was a good deal of blurring of the edges of the agreement reached, which gave trouble later in formulating Treaty texts. There was a considerable number of significant agricultural transitional problems not covered by the agreement at all—just as the agreement at the Ministerial meeting of 2 February on industrial tariff moves had left many detailed problems of the Common Commercial Policy to be sorted out. A great deal of the remaining work of the Conference had to be devoted to these two tasks, and aspects of them occupied it until the very end of its work. Nevertheless, this agreement of 13 May, 1971, on the mechanisms and the period of agricultural transition, together with the agreements on sugar and association for the developing sugar-producing countries of the Commonwealth which were reached at the same meeting, marked the first real breakthrough in the Conference. That in turn provided the prelude which was needed to increase the chances of success of the meeting which took place just over a week later between Mr. Heath and M. Pompidou.

12. This chapter has concentrated heavily on Community Preference in agriculture. What is it? The Conference never found it easy to define. But I think it worth giving here a couple of definitions which the Community side gave in the course of the negotiations in the hope of clarifying a little what all the argument was about. First, a definition given in the course of our informal contacts with the Commission by Herr von Verschuer, a very able official in the Commission's Agricultural Directorate-General. I extract the following from a telegram from Brussels of 24 February, 1971:

> 'Asked to give a general definition of the concept of Community Preference von Verschuer said it was that (a) producers in an enlarged Community should receive prices above the world prices and (b) Community producers should when necessary have a degree of priority over third country suppliers in selling in the Community market. The degree of this preference would be greatest when market prices were at or near the intervention price and would fall to zero when they rose above the threshold price. Thus it would vary from time to time and from product to product: indeed for some commodities, e.g. rice and maize in some parts of the present Community, there was an effective preference in favour of third country imports over supplies from the southern parts of the Six.
>
> Von Verschuer in explaining the application of their proposals to cereals

said the point of departure would be the Community threshold price at the end of the transitional period. From this the intervention price at United Kingdom ports could be derived either taking the level as being 7 per cent below the threshold price (this representing the standard differential at Community ports) or by adding transport and handling charges to intervention prices obtaining in nearby exporting areas in the Six. In practice he expected that the minimum price at which grain from the Six could be sold in the United Kingdom market would be somewhat above the United Kingdom intervention prices: in other words the cost of transport across the Channel would give an effective measure of protection to the United Kingdom market against imports from the Six hence reducing the degree of preference against third country exports.

Asked what the concept of Community preference meant in sectors where protection against imports was not, or not primarily, afforded by a levy related to a threshold price, von Verschuer said that, on products such as ornamental plants for which the Community had a simple tariff, there was no preference except in the sense that Community producers could enjoy better returns than third country suppliers because of the imposition of duty. On processed products there was a two-part levy on imports, with one element related to the levy on the basic product (cereals, sugar, etc.) and another element providing protection for the processing industries. Community preference was represented by the latter element, which had more or less the same effect as a tariff and would be treated as such. Finally on some products such as beef there was a tariff as well as a levy: on beef, where the levy only came into force periodically, the tariff was the most significant element. The Commission had not been able to decide how the application of full Community preference in this sector would be worked out.'

13. As an alternative, the following is a second definition of Community preference taken from the statement made on behalf of the Community on 9 March, 1971, by M. Boegner, the French Permanent Representative, at that time Chairman of the Conference at Deputy level:

'This concept refers to the special situation, resulting from a combination of measures and conditions varying from one product to another, which arises from the common organisation of the market. The main characteristic of this organisation of the market is that it enables intra-Community trade to develop in conditions comparable with those existing in an internal market. The actual size of the preference depends, on the one hand, on the interplay of the various elements of the market organisation and, on the other hand, on the developments of the market situation and a number of other factors. These factors may vary from one marketing year to the next and even during a given marketing year. It is therefore impossible to know the extent of the preference in advance. It is thus not practicable to obtain gradual introduction of this preference by isolating a single factor among all the conditions which determine it (the compensatory amount, for example) and attaching a pre-determined scale of variations to this factor.'

14. It will be seen from the above definitions that it is not easy to forecast how important our acceptance of Community Preference in full from the start will prove in practice to be. Its effects will depend on a number of detailed arrangements yet to be established, and on the state of markets and supply. The main risk involved in the immediate application of full Community Preference in our market is, of course, that to its traditional suppliers. Arrangements were agreed to mitigate this risk which could prove effective. Our ability to resist pressure for full Community Preference from the start—led as it was by the French and the Dutch as agricultural exporters—was somewhat weakened by the fact that two of our fellow-candidates, the Danes and the Irish, were themselves, as agricultural exporters, strongly in favour of the Community's requirement.

12

Sugar, and Association for Developing Commonwealth Territories: The Background

In the eventual settlement of the problem of sugar in our negotiations with the Community, two decisions taken in 1967 and in 1968 played a crucial part. They related to the Commonwealth Sugar Agreement, which dated from 1951. It was then concluded for a duration of eight years, and year by year thereafter its duration was 'rolled forward' for a single year to maintain the eight-year limit. But in 1967, since we had in that year applied for membership of the Communities, we declined to roll the date forward for a further year. Thus the terminal date for the agreement remained 1974, as established in the previous year. When the time came in 1968 to reconsider the duration of the agreement, our application for membership had been rebuffed almost 12 months earlier and nothing seemed less likely than that we could soon successfully revive it. All the sugar producing members of the Commonwealth Sugar Agreement were therefore determined that the lost year should be made good and that it should be decided to 'roll forward' the agreement, in 1968, for two years. This we resisted, for a variety of reasons, included among which was our hope of being able once again to renew our efforts to join the Community. After a good deal of consideration by Ministers, we made proposals which in December 1968 the sugar producers accepted. Under these proposals the agreement became 'of indefinite duration', by virtue of Article 6.1 of Chapter III of its amended text. But Article 6.3 (*b*) of Chapter III read as follows:

> '(*b*) The provisions of this Article are subject to the understanding that the United Kingdom Government, if it successfully completes negotiations for the accession of the United Kingdom to the European Economic Community,
>
> (i) cannot be committed to continuing contractual obligations under the Agreement after 31 December, 1974;
>
> (ii) shall, in the event that it does not accept such contractual obligations after 31 December, 1974, consult with the other Parties to the Agreement with a view to seeking means of fulfilling the objectives which those obligations would otherwise fulfil.'

Thus we had the opportunity, should we successfully complete negotiations for accession to the Community, of terminating our obligations under the Agreement at the end of 1974.

2. It so happened that this was a date which coincided fairly closely with some other important dates fixed for future stages of development within the Community. First of all the current sugar regulation of the Common Agricultural Policy, which had been introduced in 1968, was due to expire at the end of June 1975. It seemed possible that on renewal important alterations might be made in it, possibly modifying the whole system of national quotas on which it is based; and of course it would be necessary for the revised regulation to be discussed and agreed well before June 1975, probably in the course of 1974. Another closely parallel, and closely relevant, date was that established, on its renewal in 1969, for the expiry of the renewed Yaoundé Convention. This was to take place on 31 January, 1975. Another date which had a good deal of relevance, though not quite so direct, was that for the expiry of the International Sugar Agreement (to which we were a party but the Community was not) at the end of 1973.

3. In the light of these dates, the possibility of terminating our obligations under the Commonwealth Sugar Agreement at the end of 1974, should we join the Community, was extremely significant. Had we 'rolled forward' the agreement in 1967 to 1975; or had we (even with the Community escape clause) 'rolled it forward' in 1968 to 1976, then the agreement we eventually reached with the Community in 1971 might not have been available to us. The Community gave us an exemption of two years after accession until the end of 1974 to fulfil our obligations under the agreement because it coincided so neatly in time with the requirement to renegotiate their own sugar régime. Would they have given us three years until the end of 1975, or four years until the end of 1976? Probably not; at the best, we should have had to enter into the Community negotiation of 1974 to settle its new sugar régime with an obligation to the Commonwealth producers extending beyond the date from which that régime was to operate; and this would have caused immense difficulties. As it was, the general coincidence of dates was a major advantage. Nor did this advantage relate only to sugar, or to sugar-producing territories. It was the target-date of 1 February, 1975, for the entry into force of the association agreement to replace the renewed Yaoundé agreement which made possible Community assent to the whole 'status quo' arrangement, up to date, for our trading relations with all Commonwealth developing territories which became eligible for association, including our dependent territories.

4. The question of sugar in our negotiations meant primarily, but by no means exclusively, the problem of continuing to provide a market after our entry into the Community for the quantities of sugar which we were obliged to buy at negotiated prices (which had regularly been far above the world price) from the producing members of the Commonwealth Sugar Agreement. It turned out to be both technically and politically one of the most complex, if not the most complex, of all the problems of the whole negotiation. There was

a great variety of parties involved, whose interests were often diametrically opposed.

5. First among them were of course the developing territories whose sugar industries were party to the Commonwealth Sugar Agreement. It is necessary here to give some figures. The quantities we were obliged under the agreement to buy each year at a negotiated price were as follows:

Developing countries	*Thousand metric tons raw value*
West Indies and Guyana	769
Mauritius	403
Fiji	148
Swaziland	90
India	27
British Honduras	22
East Africa	7
	1,466
Developed country	
Australia	355
	1,821

In addition, Southern Rhodesia had a quota of 27,000 tons which was in suspense.[1] Among the developing countries involved, the degree of dependence on sugar exports varied greatly. Mauritius, Fiji, Barbados, St. Kitts, and British Honduras all depended so heavily on sugar exports (which represented from 50 per cent to over 90 per cent of their total exports) that the question could fairly be described as a matter of life and death for them. Next most heavily dependent were Guyana, Jamaica and Swaziland. Apart moreover from their direct dependence on exports, each of these territories was heavily dependent on sugar production as a source of employment and, therefore, of social stability. Thus although Trinidad, for example, depended on sugar for only 5 per cent of its total exports, nevertheless sugar production accounted for 12 per cent of its total employment. This meant that the prospect of exporting lower quantities to the enlarged Community, even at higher prices for the same total money return, was very unpopular with the producers.

6. Among the developing sugar-producing territories, those with dependent status had a different position which might have complicated matters further. In this context, this meant the West Indian Associated States (among whom only St. Kitts was highly dependent on sugar exports) and British Honduras. We secured the offer of Part IV Association for our dependent territories—including these—very early in the negotiations. Not till many months later was

[1] This quota had been suspended following Southern Rhodesia's Unilateral Declaration of Independence.

a comparable offer of association made to the independent sugar-producing territories in the Caribbean, the Indian Ocean and the Pacific.

7. Australia was a separate problem. It was the only country benefiting from the Commonwealth Sugar Agreement which was not a developing country. And although its sales to us under the agreement were large, they represented a relatively small proportion of Australian sugar production and exports as a whole. In any case, it should have been perfectly clear to the Australians from Mr. Brown's statement on 4 July, 1967, that we did not regard ourselves as obliged to fight for Australian sugar in the same way as we were obliged to fight for that from the other Commonwealth producers. Nevertheless, the Australians were reluctant to accept and acknowledge this, even though Mr. Rippon made it clear enough to them when he visited Australia in September 1970. As late as 11 November, 1970, shortly after we had made our formal proposal on sugar to the Communities, the Australians presented us with an *aide-mémoire* complaining of our disregard for their interests; and there was to be more trouble later. The Queensland Sugar Producers' Association were also active lobbyists of Ministers and Members of Parliament.

8. Then there was the staff of the International Sugar Organisation and its members. Throughout the negotiations they (with Australia again to the fore) were seriously concerned at the effect on the Organisation which certain possible solutions in our negotiations might have. At a meeting of the Council of the International Sugar Organisation on 26 March, 1971, the Cuban delegate urged an approach to the countries involved in our negotiations, and was supported by the delegates of Mexico, Brazil, Australia, South Africa and the Soviet Union. On 18 May, 1971, a delegation from the ISO visited Dr. Mansholt in Brussels to express their concern; but our agreement on sugar with the Community had been reached six days before. A similar Delegation called on Mr. Rippon on 28 May.

9. The existing associates of the Community also had anxieties. Only two of them (Madagascar and Congo Brazzaville) were sugar exporters, and not in a very big way. But they had lost their market in the Community and hoped to cash in if other developing sugar producers should succeed in maintaining one. Moreover, and quite apart from sugar, the Community, led by the French, insisted strongly that if new territories were to benefit from association with the Community this must in no way dilute the advantages already enjoyed by existing associates. This concept had to be enshrined in the Treaty of Accession; and the French gave more than adequate notice in the course of the negotiations that, if sugar receives specially favourable consideration in future arrangements for association, they for their part may fight for similar arrangements for other products such as groundnuts.

10. There were also strongly conflicting interests in the United Kingdom. The industry refining cane sugar in particular were deeply concerned and disturbed at the prospect of any reduction in raw cane sugar imports into the United Kingdom, on which they were almost completely dependent. Tate and

Lyle and Co., Ltd. were particularly active. Mr. F.H. Tate and Mr. John Lyle presented their apprehensions to the Foreign Secretary in detail on 16 February, 1971, and they lobbied other Ministers from time to time. The company also conducted something of a Press campaign by advertisements in support of their interests. In this they were matched, on the other side of the Channel, by the French Confédération Générale des Planteurs de Betteraves, who took a full page of *Le Monde* on 4 May, 1971, to proclaim their case. They maintained (in close concert with what had been French policy till shortly before) that access for Commonwealth Sugar Producers to the Community should be limited to 500,000 tons, with compensation through higher prices. This rather aggressive advertisement spoke of the 'sugar war', and reminded readers, fairly enough, that sugar beet had only come into existence as an industrial crop because of the British Continental Blockade of Napoleon.

11. On the opposite side to the cane refiners in the United Kingdom, British farmers had a strong interest in being allowed to grow more beet sugar, and to escape from the rigid acreage restrictions long imposed on them to ensure a place in our market for Commonwealth sugar. (Roughly one-third of sugar consumed in the United Kingdom is derived from sugar beet grown here, and two-thirds from raw cane sugar imported under the Commonwealth Sugar Agreement.) The Ministry of Agriculture favoured an expansion of home sugar beet production, partly because, with our cereals output expanding in the Community, sugar beet would provide an exceptionally useful break crop. But they favoured it much more, and so did the Treasury, because of the exceptionally large savings to the balance of payments which would be yielded by any additional sugar beet production in this country. As our main brief on sugar in the negotiations stated: 'It is estimated that each additional ton of United Kingdom beet sugar production that saved importing a ton of sugar from the rest of the Community would represent a saving to the balance of payments, taking account of resource considerations, of about £55. Each ton of Commonwealth sugar that saved importing sugar from the rest of the Community would save us about £17 to £19.'

12. Apart from the material interests involved, there were strong political feelings and pressures and correspondingly strong lobbies. There was a widespread feeling, fully represented in Parliament as elsewhere, that it was essential to protect, in our negotiations with the Communities, the interests of the developing sugar producers. No aspect of the negotiations (except possibly fisheries) produced a larger number of letters to the Foreign Office from members of the public than sugar. And Foreign Office Ministers received a flood of letters from MPs of all parties reflecting their constituents' concern. The Overseas Development Administration took a special interest in the sugar producing territories, which led it on some occasions to argue for policies which other Departments were unable to accept.

13. Continual pressure was also exercised, naturally and fairly enough, by the overseas interests involved. Ministers and representatives of growing and

trading associations from the Commonwealth sugar producers descended on London in droves from June 1970 till June 1971. They came mainly from the West Indies, but Mauritius, Fiji and Swaziland were not far behind. More than any other sector of the negotiations, sugar obliged Mr. Rippon to devote a high proportion of his time and powers of persuasion to the interests involved. This he did with great success. The confidence he built up in the West Indies during his visit in February 1971 stood him in good stead at the critical Lancaster House Meeting on 2 and 3 June. Finally, the British end of the Commonwealth sugar lobby played its part sturdily, led by Lord Campbell as Chairman of the Commonwealth Sugar Exporters. In the end, at Lancaster House, he did us proud; but he gave us plenty of qualms on the way.

14. On the other side of the Channel, the Community had no less strong an interest in this question. They wished in the main for two things: not to have to reduce—indeed if possible to increase—their own sugar beet production, and to be able to export significant quantities of their sugar surplus to the British market at the high Community price. Within the Community the French had by a wide margin the largest production of sugar. They also had the highest yields, and were probably the most efficient producers. They could most easily provide a major expansion of output; and the influential organisations of French growers and processors were most anxious to be able to do so. Here again it is necessary to quote some figures to show the real dilemma which was involved:

PRODUCTION/CONSUMPTION POSITION IN THE TEN IN 1969–70
(thousand tons)

	Consumption	*Production*	*Balance*
United Kingdom	2,820	940	−1,880
Norway	190	—	−190
Ireland	190	150	−40
Denmark	250	300	+50
	3,450	1,390	−2,060
Six	6,600	8,100	+1,500
	10,050	9,490	−560

Thus in 1969–70 the Six had an estimated current annual surplus of about 1.5 million tons of sugar, while the Four had a net import requirement of over 2 million tons, leaving a current net import requirement for the Ten of about half a million tons. As against this, we had ideally to preserve access to our market for between 1¼ and 1½ million tons of sugar from the developing producers of the Commonwealth Sugar Agreement. Obviously, the sum would not work out; and this was the dilemma.

15. There were only two hopeful factors. First, sugar consumption in Europe is rising fairly rapidly. It was estimated that sugar consumption in the Ten might be about 1 million tons higher in 1978 than it was in 1970. But there was reason

to fear that, without some further restraint, beet sugar production in the Six might easily rise over this period to produce the whole of the extra million tons. Second, the Community, and not least the French, wished to avoid appearing ungenerous in their dealings with developing countries.

16. With all these conflicting interests and considerations, and with the technical and political difficulties they involved, it is no wonder that the problem of sugar was hard to solve. Nor did we solve it. We postponed it. Probably, as things went, this was the best possible outcome, not only in terms of concluding the negotiations but even in terms of a good chance to reach a much more satisfactory settlement at a later date than we could ever have reached in 1971. But it necessarily involved taking a good deal on trust, and persuading Commonwealth sugar producers, and their many supporters in this country, to do likewise. This was certainly the most difficult part of the exercise; and in retrospect it seems to me rather remarkable that we succeeded with it as well as we did.

13

Sugar, and Association for Developing Commonwealth Territories: The Outcome

The basis for our position on sugar, as on so much else, was as usual to be found in Mr. Brown's statement of 4 July, 1967. Paragraph 33 of that statement read as follows:

> 'For sugar, as you know, we have an agreement with Commonwealth sugar producers which runs until the end of 1974. Your own transitional arrangements are due to expire six months later. The commitment we have under the Commonwealth Sugar Agreement is a contract which we must fulfil. We believe that the sugar exported to Britain under the Commonwealth Sugar Agreement can be accommodated within a reasonable production quota under existing Community arrangements, and without departure from the precedents which you have set for yourselves. We have also to look to the longer-term interests of the developing countries and territories many of whose economies are overwhelmingly dependent on their exports of sugar and we believe that it is in the Community's longer-term interest that we should do so. In due course, we shall wish to discuss with you how these interests can be safeguarded in the longer term.'

2. Our policy was developed, when things got going again in 1969, in a long and detailed brief which was taking shape in the spring of 1970. A final version was completed and circulated on 30 June, and provisionally approved by Ministers in the AE Committee on 8 July. The brief observed that negotiations would be primarily concerned with the arrangements for the period after 1974, when our commitments under the Commonwealth Sugar Agreement would have ended. It went on—interestingly in the light of the eventual outcome—as follows: 'The first question, however, is whether we need seek specific provision for the post-1974 period at all. It might be argued that we could leave this to be settled after entry, or that we should simply seek a general assurance from the Six about the future treatment of the Commonwealth. Neither course would however effectively safeguard Commonwealth interests. We could not count on being able, as one voice among Ten, to secure reasonable or lasting provision for them. A general assurance would not be appropriate for a period as imminent as 1975.' Instead, the brief recommended that we must negotiate specific

provision for Commonwealth sugar in the post-1974 period, while recognising that this would lead the Six to insist in the course of the negotiations on setting a production quota for British home-grown sugar for the period after 1974. Our aim would be to secure as large a United Kingdom production quota as possible. For the developing Commonwealth countries, our aim should be to maintain their export earnings from sales of sugar in our market.

3. The brief recognised that any reduction for the Commonwealth sugar producers in quantitative access to our market would be most unwelcome to them, because of its effect on employment and hence social stability. 'The extreme position in response to this attitude', it went on, 'would be to continue to import the same quantity as now from them at the same price ... The extreme low position consistent with the maintenance of their export earnings from our market would be the purchase of 1.04 million tons at prices reflecting full EEC price levels.' Thus we were at this stage prepared to contemplate, at the limit, a reduction of sugar imports from the developing Commonwealth countries of 426,000 tons, or around 30 per cent. 'At this stage we need not decide precisely what figure to aim at for the Commonwealth quota. It seems clear, however, that if we are to secure our central aim of keeping the balance of payments cost to a minimum by negotiating as large as possible a United Kingdom production quota we shall almost certainly have to accept a substantial reduction in the quantity we now take from Commonwealth developing countries. If it proved necessary we should be prepared to accept the minimum quantity which could maintain their present earnings, i.e. 1.04 million tons on a levy free basis.' The brief also recommended that the United Kingdom should seek a production quota which would permit sugar beet production some 50 per cent greater than now. As it happened, we never had to put forward in the negotiations the policy which this brief recommended, or to reveal to our Commonwealth clients that we had contemplated accepting reduced quantities of sugar from them, albeit at higher prices. Things developed differently.

4. Only four papers on this subject were circulated to the Conference before the sugar problem was settled in May 1971, three by us and one by the Commission, and none of them proved of much significance in the end. On 23 July, 1970, we circulated a descriptive paper about the Commonwealth Sugar Agreement. On 14 September, 1970, we circulated a further paper analysing the consequences for sugar of the enlargement of the Community. In October the Commission produced an entirely non-committal study of these two papers, which reached us at once and which was circulated to the Conference on 12 November. But already, on 6 November, we had circulated our formal proposal for a solution of the sugar problem, making (as in some other cases) a proposal which we did not expect to be accepted. We asked that after 1 January, 1975, there 'should be specific provision to permit the import into the Community from the developing countries and territories whose industries are parties to the Commonwealth Sugar Agreement of the quantities of sugar which the United Kingdom at present purchases from them at a negotiated price'. These

quantities, we added, are equivalent to approximately 1,373,000 metric tons of refined sugar. There should be a special rate of levy to ensure a remunerative price to the exporter and to enable the sugar to be sold within the Community. There should be suitable provision for periodic review of these arrangements.

5. The producing countries were informed on the previous day what our proposal was to be; naturally it was acceptable to the developing territories, so there was no need for advance consultation. The Australian Government was informed that our proposal provided for maintenance of the existing situation up to the end of 1974 but 'thereafter what is suggested for Australia is suitable arrangements for phasing-out, within the transitional period to be agreed for agriculture'.

6. Meanwhile, through this period of the opening papers, we were subject to the opening pressures. Already in July and August many representations, and many visits, were received from the sugar-producing countries, including Fiji, Mauritius, Swaziland and India, and pressure built up for an early meeting between Commonwealth sugar producers and Her Majesty's Government. This we resisted, arguing that there was no point in such a meeting until a much later stage. But at a meeting which took place on 3 September between Mr. Rippon and Mr. Lightbourne (Minister for Trade and Industry of Jamaica) and other Ministers from the West Indies, Mr. Rippon accepted in principle a suggestion from Mr. Lightbourne that there should be a meeting with Commonwealth Sugar Agreement producers as a whole at an appropriate time. This led to further pressures and suggestions from time to time over the next eight months that such a meeting should be held. We knew that at some stage it would have to be held. The anxiety of the West Indian producers to have such a meeting was materially reduced by Mr. Rippon's tour of the Caribbean in February 1971; and in the end we were able to defer agreeing to a general meeting with the Commonwealth Sugar producers until after the Ministerial meeting in Brussels of 11–13 May, 1971, when a provisional settlement of the question of sugar was reached with the Community. Thereupon we at once suggested such a meeting, which eventually took place at Lancaster House on 2 and 3 June, 1971.

7. In the early stages of the Conference, the Community's consistent reaction to our proposals for the association with the Community of independent developing sugar-producing Commonwealth territories was invariably that the question of association could not be settled until the question of sugar had been settled. This they continued to maintain until early May 1971. Then, paradoxically, the opposite occurred. At a meeting of the Council of Ministers on 10 May the French circulated a paper which, almost completely unexpectedly, proposed offering the options of the 1963 declaration not merely to African Commonwealth territories (this had been agreed five months earlier) but to comparable territories in the Caribbean, the Indian Ocean and the Pacific. This the Five at once accepted; and it was on the basis of agreement on the possibility of association that agreement was reached on sugar.

8. At this point I must deal rather summarily with the question of association for independent developing Commonwealth territories. It deserves fuller treatment than I can give it; but I think it is convenient to describe it in the general context of sugar, although of course sugar was relevant to less than half the total number of territories concerned. This was an area where precedents from the negotiations of 1961–63, and their aftermath, proved of advantage to us. In the earlier negotiations it had been generally accepted that opportunities must be given to Commonwealth developing territories to associate with the Community. Later in 1963, when the Community's first Association Convention was signed in Yaoundé, the representatives of the Community States meeting in the Council declared their readiness to negotiate in a sympathetic spirit agreements with any non-member countries who so requested and whose economic structure and production were comparable to those of the associated States. Such agreements could take the following forms:

(a) Accession to the Yaoundé Convention according to the procedure laid down in Article 58 thereof, or
(b) Association agreements with mutual rights and obligations, particularly in matters of trade, or
(c) Commercial agreements to facilitate and expand trade between the Community and these countries.

9. But a number of years had elapsed since 1963 and when negotiations opened in 1970 it was by no means certain that the Community were prepared to regard this offer as still holding good. The question of association for dependent Commonwealth territories, under Part IV of the Treaty of Rome, was easier; and accordingly we tested this question first by proposing in September 1970 that our dependent territories should be so associated. On 14 October, 1970, the Community told us it was prepared in principle to consider such association; and in fact from that point the matter was agreed in principle, with the exception of course of Gibraltar and Hong Kong which were special cases. On 26 November, 1970, we proposed that independent developing Commonwealth territories, of which we circulated a list which now figures as Annex 6 to the Treaty of Accession, should be offered the options described in the 1963 Declaration quoted above. The Community, for once, accepted part of this proposition rapidly. On 1 December, 1970, they agreed (subject to a special problem relating to Botswana, Lesotho and Swaziland) that the independent developing Commonwealth countries of Africa should be offered these options. But they declared, as described above, that they could give no answer in respect of Commonwealth developing territories in the Caribbean, the Indian Ocean and the Pacific (which included almost all the sugar-producing territories) until the question of sugar had been solved.

10. Five months then elapsed without any real progress either on sugar or on the question of the association of these territories. And as time passed the prospect of the Community ever agreeing to offer the 1963 options to these

territories seemed to grow more dim. There were various reasons for this. First of all—and M. Deniau made clear that this consideration weighed particularly strongly with him—the Community had become sensitive to the charge that its association and other preferential arrangements were turning into a serious obstacle to the free development of world trade. They were in any case exposing the Community to strong criticism, particularly from the United States and Latin America. To those who felt this way it seemed dangerous that the enlargement of the Community should be the occasion of more than doubling the number of territories enjoying preferential agreements with it, and vastly extending the geographical area covered by such agreements. The Community felt able to defend its preferential agreements in Africa and the Mediterranean area as a consequence of the history of its present members; but was reluctant to take a leap across the Atlantic on to the very doorstep of the United States in the Caribbean, or another leap into the remote Pacific. Apprehension about the attitude of the United States to a new extension of preferential agreements by the enlarged Community proved well founded. In this respect United States policy (which will be dealt with in a later chapter) was ambivalent. It wanted the enlargement of the Community; it wanted to stop the spread of Community preferential trading arrangements. Somewhat half-heartedly, the latter consideration for a time prevailed; and at the turn of the year the United States Government made formal representations to us and to the Governments of the Community.

11. On 30 December, 1970, a fairly junior official in the United States Embassy spoke on instructions to the Foreign Office. He said that the United States Administration had strong objections to the offer of associated status to the Commonwealth countries in Africa and the Caribbean on the grounds that association would enlarge an already discriminatory trade bloc and would be a backward step in liberalisation of world trade. The Americans would regard any such arrangement as contrary to Articles I and XXIV of GATT. The Americans were not prepared to extend the benefit of generalised preferences to developing countries who refused to eliminate the preferences which they accorded to developed countries. This would apply to any African or Caribbean country accepting association with the EEC as a result of arrangements which we succeeded in negotiating in Brussels. The Americans were making this clear to the Governments concerned as well as to the European Commission and the Six. The American official said that his instructions were 'to put American views on record'.[1]

[1] The most deep-rooted US objections were to what was described as 'reverse preferences' i.e. to the preferences which the European Community insisted its developing associates should grant to its exporters in their markets, thus putting US exporters at a disadvantage to European Community ones. These 'reverse preferences' existed under the Yaoundé Convention; but its successor, the Lomé Conventions, which came into effect in 1975 and which for the first time also included countries in the Caribbean and the Pacific, placed no such requirement on the developing country associates.

12. We reacted strongly to this; nevertheless we had to accept that United States action had reduced the likelihood of association becoming available to our Caribbean, Indian Ocean and Pacific territories. By the time Mr. Rippon left on his tour of the Caribbean, early in February 1971, the prospects of these territories being offered the 1963 options did not seem good. On 9 March Mr. Wellenstein of the Commission told me without qualification that the Community would not agree to association for independent Commonwealth Caribbean countries; though he said that such association would probably be available for the Indian Ocean and Pacific territories. (On 4 May, however, he told me that opinion was swinging towards the idea that reviving the 1963 options for the Caribbean countries would not be too difficult.) On 26 March an official in Bonn told us that the Germans were basically opposed to association for the Caribbean territories. But only four days later, on 30 March, we received (and at that stage paid little attention to it) the first indication that the French in fact thought differently On that date Sir Laurence Lindo, High Commissioner for Jamaica in London, who had also been accredited to the Community, was formally received, in the process of such accreditation, by M. Schumann as President of the Council of Ministers of the Six. Sir Laurence Lindo told us that on this occasion M. Schumann had told him that 'an offer of association would be made to us when sugar had been disposed of'. This solitary indication of a new French line (it was not really a change: they at least had never said they would refuse association for the Caribbean territories) was almost all we had until unexpectedly, at the Council of Ministers on 10 May, a French paper was circulated which proposed an offer of association to the territories in question, a proposal which the rest of the Community at once accepted.

13. Why did the French so decisively lead their partners away from the consensus that had been developing among them against offering the options of 1963 to the Caribbean territories? One is tempted to believe that they may have done so partly by way of reaction against the United States representations. Yet this is to impute to French policy in 1971 its attitudes of some years earlier; in fact, by 1971 the French Government seemed to be seeking accommodation and relaxation over wide areas of its relations with the United States, rather than the reverse. I do not find the question easy to answer. But the answer may well lie in the fact that, over the spring of 1971, the French, in their discussions with their Five partners in Brussels, had frequently suggested that sugar from Commonwealth developing territories ought not to be the only new commodity to benefit from the enlargement of the Community. They had repeatedly referred to groundnuts from their African associates, and to one or two other commodities as well, which ought to receive preferential treatment if sugar did. Yet it would be difficult to ensure such preferential treatment for groundnuts—I hope it will be difficult enough in any case for other good reasons—except on the basis of an extension of the existing association arrangements with African territories. Thus, the French may have argued, since sugar is likely to receive a degree of preferential treatment in the enlarged Community in any case, let us

ensure that it does so within a framework which increases the opportunity of extending preference to other commodities of particular interest to our own existing associates, especially groundnuts.[2] Whatever the reason, as from 10 May, 1971, the offer to all our independent developing Commonwealth territories concerned of the 1963 options was assured.

14. However convenient this link between association and sugar proved, it is worth pointing out nevertheless that it was not essential. By this I do not mean merely that we could have secured some—if almost certainly not a satisfactory quantitative offer for the post—1974 period. I mean that there were methods other than association theoretically available for solving the sugar problem not during the negotiations but after enlargement. It could have been deferred and solved (as indeed the Commission suggested) in the context of settling the Community's sugar regulation for the period after 30 June, 1975. It could even (provided the Community had become a member of the International Sugar Organisation, and this was perhaps in the timescale not likely) have been settled in the context of the renegotiation of the International Sugar Agreement in 1972. It is all the same perhaps fortunate that neither of these two possibilities was pursued, and that it was the offer of the option of association which, in the end, did the trick. For association offered even more obvious advantages for certain other commodities than for sugar.

15. I must now go back to sugar and to November 1970. As recorded above, the early exchanges of formal papers on sugar, culminating with our proposals of 6 November, 1970, had not advanced matters much. But later in November a paper was produced which did. This was the Commission's 'vue d'ensemble', completed on 17 November. It has already been referred to in this report, together with the fact that it was never formally communicated to us although we were well aware of its text. The proposals in this paper on sugar proved in the end to be as positive and constructive as its proposals on Community finance were, to us, unwelcome and negative. We summarised them as follows, in a telegram of 27 November, 1970, to Kingston and other posts:

> 'The United Kingdom should be permitted to fulfil its obligations under the Commonwealth Sugar Agreement until the end of 1974 on condition that it limited its own domestic production for that period to the present level. The institutions of the enlarged Community should be left to determine the definitive sugar régime in 1975, and this would include the régime to be applied to developing sugar producers and members of the Commonwealth Sugar Agreement. The Community and the candidates should give assurances

[2] This explanation is clearly the correct one. The Lomé Convention, which succeeded the Yaoundé Convention in 1975, contained provisions for stabilising the export receipts of the developing associates for a whole range of primary products, including groundnuts (the scheme known as STABEX). Subsequently a similar scheme was put in place to cover mineral exports (SYSMIN). But these schemes, beneficial as they were in particular to former French overseas territories, were not, like the Sugar Protocols to successive Lomé Conventions, a guarantee to purchase specified quantities at prices linked to the European price.

to the developing sugar producers that their interests would be taken into account when the definitive régime was drawn up, preferably in the context of a new international sugar agreement. The sugar-producing interests of certain of the Yaoundé associates and of the overseas territories should also be taken into consideration. If all the developing members of the Commonwealth Sugar Agreement become associates of the Community (on which the Council had reserved its position) a special regime for sugar could be included in the framework of the associations. If, as the United Kingdom appeared to wish, the régime for sugar imports from developing sugar producers after 1975 was to be settled now, then the Community's definitive sugar régime would also have to be settled: but the Commission would regard this as inopportune.'

16. This proposal by the Commission proved in fact the turning point in the negotiations on sugar; though it was not clear for a very long time that it would do so. It was based on the idea, which as described above we had considered and rejected in our own main brief on sugar, of leaving the crunch on sugar until later, for settlement within an enlarged Community, and being content in the negotiations themselves with a declaration defining the intentions of the enlarged Community. We had realised the advantages of this course well enough; but had doubted our ability to secure the assent to it of the Commonwealth sugar producers and the many organisations and individuals who had their interests at heart. But in the light of the negative reactions of the Community, as they developed over the next few months, to our own proposals we came increasingly—and indeed pretty rapidly—to the conclusion that this was the best option available to us. We were persuaded to this conclusion particularly strongly by the factor referred to in the last sentence of the summary of the Commission's proposals given above: namely that, if a specific quantitative degree of access after 1974 to the Community market for Commonwealth sugar was to be settled in our negotiations, then inevitably it would be necessary to settle also in the course of our negotiations the Community's definitive sugar régime for the period from 1975—including of course our own definitive domestic production quota. But this was virtually impossible; and indeed it would have been absurd, so numerous and significant were the unforeseeable factors involved, to settle in 1971 a régime which touched so many important Community interests so sensitively and acutely, but was to be inaugurated only four years later.

17. It became moreover increasingly clear, as the spring of 1971 advanced, that while we probably could, if we continued to press for them, secure specific guaranteed quantitative outlets for Commonwealth sugar after 1974, the quantities would be disappointingly low, and likely to prove degressive. To secure a 1975 guarantee for as much as 1 million tons might prove impossible. And to reconcile Commonwealth producers to such an outcome might prove as hard as, or harder than, reconciling them to accepting instead a general assurance for the future. It became a choice between figures or words.

18. Long before Mr. Rippon set off, early in February 1971, on his tour of the Caribbean, we had concluded that the Commission's ideas formed the best foundation for progress, if only we could persuade the sugar producers that this was the case. As early as 25 November, 1970, I had a conversation with Sir Laurence Lindo, and asked him about his reaction to the Commission's paper, of which he already knew as well as I did. He said that it had not been encouraging. In reply I 'pointed out that it could have been more discouraging. In effect the Commission agreed to the continuance of the Commonwealth Sugar Agreement until 1975 and proposed a review of the situation after that date. One point stood out from this: such a review would be made by the enlarged Community, including the United Kingdom. It could be argued that a better deal might emerge as a result of our efforts within the enlarged Community than through our efforts from outside.' This is the first instance I can trace of what became prolonged efforts to 'soften-up' the sugar producers and persuade them that postponement until after enlargement, with appropriate assurances, was a better bet than efforts to establish post-1974 quantitative guarantees in the current negotiations.

19. The proposition was thoroughly considered by Departments in Whitehall, and a further paper was prepared for Ministers. Its consideration became linked to the preparation of briefs for Mr. Rippon's Caribbean tour. At a meeting of the AE Committee on 26 January, 1971, Ministers concluded 'that this was a highly sensitive issue which required very careful handling'. During his forthcoming visit to the Caribbean, Mr. Rippon would need to make it clear that we intended to do our utmost to get quantitative post-1974 guarantees, and were not contemplating the possibility of abandoning the proposals we had made in November. Mr. Rippon would, however, be able to refer to the proposals for sugar which the Commission had made and 'could then lead on to a purely exploratory discussion of the various alternative forms of assurance which the Six might be prepared to offer'. We were thus already more or less committed to the Commission's line, provided only we could reconcile the sugar producers to it.

20. From 7 to 19 February, 1971, Mr. Rippon toured the Caribbean. He took with him a massive brief, with 12 annexes and 15 appendices. Apart from sugar, the annexes covered in detail such matters as bananas, citrus, coffee, cocoa and spices, cigars and rum, all of which were matters of serious concern to one or other of the West Indian territories. I shall not attempt to describe the long and intricate consideration to which these various commodities had from the start given rise, and will only say that satisfactory solutions for every one of them seemed reasonably probable in the event of the territories concerned being offered and opting for association with the Community, and much more difficult to secure in other circumstances. Moreover, if association were offered and accepted, then, like sugar, the details of the treatment of these commodities could be worked out after enlargement during the negotiations on the content of new association agreements instead of having to be worked out during the negotiations for entry.

21. I will not refer further to Mr. Rippon's Caribbean discussions; records of them are available in a printed volume of 75 pages. But they went well; and though nothing the Caribbean Governments said committed them to the new concept of decisions after instead of before enlargement—on the contrary, they made plain their dislike of the idea—they were by now considering it as a possibility. On his return from the Caribbean, Mr. Rippon despatched a special message to the Six Community Foreign Ministers describing his impressions and underlining the importance of the issues involved.

22. Meanwhile, the Community continued to discuss sugar among themselves at frequent intervals and at great length. In meetings with us, no more than routine and programmatic statements were occasionally exchanged. At the Ministerial meeting on 16 March, which was so singularly unproductive, Mr. Rippon made a strong statement in support of the proposals we had tabled in November. On the Community side, there was for a long time no disposition to take up the line recommended by the Commission, and argument continued to centre on the level of access which should be offered to the Commonwealth producers after 1974. Here the Dutch in particular were stout in their defence of the interests of the sugar producers, and continued for months to urge that they should be entitled after 1974 to export to the Community the whole of the present negotiated price quantities. The French were at the other end of the scale, and they for their part insisted that access for Commonwealth sugar should be reduced to 500,000 tons, or about 35 per cent of existing quantities. At one point, in March, M. Schumann conceded that the amount should be 'not less than' 500,000 tons. Throughout this long discussion the French suggested from time to time that, if specific quantities were to be guaranteed to the Commonwealth sugar producers after 1974, then it would be necessary for the Community's post-1975 sugar arrangements to be settled at the same time in the course of our negotiations. A variety of formulae were discussed by the Six—*avantages comparables, une place comparable, une place raisonnable*—each of which was capable of being converted into higher or lower quantities. The Six were far from agreement; and, as in other contexts, we urged our friends that we much preferred no agreement by the Six to agreement by them on something unacceptable to us.

23. In London, the process of 'softening-up' the sugar producers towards acceptance of a solution based on the Commission's ideas developed. On 4 February, 1971, Mr. Rippon said to Lord Campbell that we were really faced with a choice, and explained it. What did Lord Campbell think was best? He replied, somewhat enigmatically, that he thought the best solution would be to obtain a general assurance from the Community, plus a clause providing access for not less than the existing quantities. Still earlier, and before he went to the Caribbean, Mr. Rippon had written a letter on 11 January, 1971, to Mr. Lightbourne in reply to a letter from him of 29 December, 1970. In this letter Mr. Rippon wrote:

'You say in your letter that you regard the proposals in the Commission's *vue d'ensemble* as 'totally unsatisfactory' because they provide no undertaking with regard to volume or price of imports of CSA sugar into an enlarged Community. As I have said, none of the Commission's suggestions in the *vue d'ensemble* has so far been approved by the Community, and in these circumstances it would obviously be unwise for us to make any official reaction. It is certainly true that the Commission's suggestions do not go as far as we should all like. At the same time I think it is clear that there are some undeniably positive elements in the Commission's approach to the problem; and I think it would be wrong to overlook these. The first of these positive elements is that the Commission specifically recognises that this problem constitutes a 'special case', a solution to which must be sought outside the framework of the transitional period for agriculture. Second, the Commission accepts our obligations deriving from the CSA, and suggests that the provisions of that Agreement should be maintained—in derogation from the Common Agricultural Policy—until their expiry at the end of 1974. Third, the Commission recognises that the Community's sugar policy after 1975 must be such as to leave reasonable room for imports from developing CSA countries and from other countries in association with an enlarged Community. In short, therefore, while the Commission's suggestions do not tally with what we have proposed, they do at least constitute an explicit recognition that an enlarged Community will be under an obligation to ensure reasonable opportunities for the continuation of exports by developing CSA countries. This is, in my view, a significant step forward at the present stage. We must now await the Community's reaction to our own proposals.'

24. This provides a good summary of the themes and arguments which, from the beginning of 1971, we began informally and tentatively suggesting to the sugar producers. They for their part countered with the theme—invented by Mr. Lightbourne—of 'bankable assurances'. When Mr. Rippon and Mr. Lightbourne met in London on 27 January, 1971, 10 days before Mr. Rippon began his trip to the Caribbean, Mr. Lightbourne said that the prospect that there would be a cut-off date for the obligations of the Commonwealth Sugar Agreement at the end of 1974 'had already caused bank managers and others to become very chary about granting the necessary credits to sugar producers'. Nor, he argued, could they be persuaded to do so without quantitative commitments for the period after 1974. 'Specific assurances were urgently necessary.' What, Mr. Rippon asked, would the Caribbean countries think if we could get a general assurance? Mr. Lightbourne said that the Caribbean countries needed an assurance about the future quantities of sugar they could hope to export.

25. So it went on through February, March and April. The Six were still arguing about the level of the quantitative assurance that should be offered. We, while never withdrawing or moving away from our own proposals of November 1970, continued to insinuate to the sugar producers that a general assurance for the period after 1974 might suffice. But by now the Five were

beginning to come round to the Commission view. A report we had of the discussion at the meeting of the Council of Ministers on 15 March, at which no agreement was reached, recorded that the French still insisted that the Community should not guarantee more than half a million tons of sugar to Commonwealth producers after 1974. These producers would get adequate compensation for loss of volume in increased prices; and the French referred once again to the *vocation sucrière évidente* of France, which M. Brunet had proclaimed to the Council of Ministers on 1 March. But 'the other Member States argued that the questions of precise quantities and prices should be left over until after enlargement'. M. Schumann said this would be doing the British no service. Mr. Rippon had made it clear that what he wanted was a guarantee on prices and quantities. On 26 March, at a meeting of the Permanent Representatives, the French urged that since the existing Yaoundé associates would derive very little benefit from the proposed arrangements on sugar, the balance should be redressed by giving them a similar guarantee for groundnuts. For good measure, they threw in bananas and palm kernels as well.

26. By now not only we but the Commission as well, in their direct contacts with representatives of the Commonwealth sugar producers, were recommending their own ideas and strongly pointing out the virtual impossibility of getting a quantitative guarantee in the course of the negotiations which would be adequate for the period after 1974. At the end of April the High Commissioners of the four independent Caribbean countries in London made a journey to Brussels, together with Mr. Demas, Secretary-General of CARIFTA. They visited me on 26 April before they left for Brussels. I said that as far as sugar was concerned, the Delegation might encounter in Brussels reticence and differing attitudes on the part of national Delegations. 'But the Commission, which was inclined towards a more generous line, was very conscious of a dilemma. This was the choice between an agreement on fixed quantities or a more general agreement.' On 30 April, after visiting Brussels, the same Delegation called on me again. They had met in Brussels with each of the Six Permanent Representatives, with Signor Malfatti, M. Deniau, Herr Dahrendorf and M. Wellenstein. M. Deniau had left them rather unhappy. 'He had said there might be difficulties about the 1963 Declaration, but what he had said about sugar worried them still more.' He had said there were only two possible solutions, the first involving guarantees of quantities—and here he had mentioned 500,000 tons—and the second being a 'political solution containing a general declaration without figures'. M. Deniau had made it clear that he thought the second was the better solution. While the High Commissioners remained troubled, Mr. Demas remarked on 30 April 'that if the political solution for sugar included a very precisely worded guarantee this would be satisfactory'.

27. The crunch came very suddenly. We had indeed, since our abortive Ministerial meeting with the Community on 16 March, hoped that sugar might be one of the issues we could settle at the next Ministerial meeting on 11 and

12 May. But no progress seemed to have been made towards solving the difficulties within the Community as these dates approached. However, very significant progress had been made elsewhere. A meeting between Mr. Heath and M. Pompidou had been arranged for 20 and 21 May, and it was announced on 8 May. It was accepted between us and the French that the Ministerial meeting on 11 and 12 May should if possible make significant progress. It was—of this I feel, in retrospect, there can be no doubt—as a contribution to such progress that the French advanced their new proposals at the meeting of the Council of Ministers on 10 May. If proof were needed, it can in my judgment be found in a conversation which took place on the afternoon of 12 May in Paris, that is to say in the middle of the Ministerial meeting in Brussels, between Mr. Soames and M. Jobert, and at a moment when, as the result of the way things had gone in Brussels late on 11 November [*sic*: May], the outlook seemed stormy. M. Jobert said he was very concerned at the tone of the remarks attributed to Mr. Rippon in that day's Press, which had given the impression in Paris that Mr. Rippon thought the French proposals on sugar were designed to complicate rather than facilitate the negotiations. 'He wanted to give me his word of honour that this was the reverse of the truth. M. Pompidou had instructed M. Schumann, as we had requested, that the meeting between M. Pompidou and the Prime Minister should not be used as an excuse not to make progress in the Brussels meeting'; and the French proposals on sugar were designed as a positive contribution to this end.

28. These proposals, as already described above, had been tabled by the French in the Council of Ministers on 10 May. They contained the offer of the 1963 options to the sugar-producing countries, and also provided for a status quo in British trade relations with these countries until the date set (1 February, 1975) for the entry into force of a renewed Yaoundé Convention. But they said very little indeed on sugar. The Five, in the Council of Ministers on 10 May, had urged the need for more specific reference to sugar; the French had explained that their formula could even mean an increase in the sugar exports of the developing Commonwealth countries and was therefore preferable to anything more precise. Finally, after further pressure from the Five, the French had agreed to add the following sentence on sugar to their paper. 'It is within this framework and bearing in mind, with regard to exports of sugar, the importance of this product for the economies of several developing countries, in the Commonwealth in particular, that the case of this product will be settled.' M. Schumann had said that if one read between the lines of this formula it clearly meant that every effort would be made to maintain the present outlets, but he was not prepared to say this explicitly, because he did not want to have to give guarantees to the French African associates. With this addition, the Five had accepted the French paper, and it was put to us early in the Ministerial meeting which began on the following day.

29. Mr. Rippon warmly welcomed the offer of the 1963 options, of the acceptance of our Commonwealth sugar obligations until the end of 1974 and

of the status quo in our trade relations until the end of January 1975. But, he said, something more was needed on sugar. There then took place (in the intervals of progress on the equally important matter of agricultural transition, also settled at this meeting) various adjournments. But late on the evening of 11 May the Community had still made no improvement on their proposal on sugar. Before that day's session concluded, a little before midnight, Mr. Rippon urged the Six in strong language to do better. What he said reached the Press, and it accounts for M. Jobert's concern recorded above.

30. Meanwhile, in informal discussions between ourselves and the Commission, ideas for an improvement in the Community's paper in respect of sugar had been developed. On the afternoon of 12 May M. Schumann returned to Paris for the regular weekly meeting of the French Cabinet. When he returned to Brussels that evening, he was able to accept an addition to the Community's paper. This consisted simply of the following phrase, which was to become familiar during the next few weeks: 'In this connexion, the enlarged Community will have as its firm purpose (*aura à coeur*) the safeguarding of the interests of all the countries mentioned above, whose economies depend to a considerable extent on the exports of primary products and in particular of sugar.' The translation of '*aura à coeur*' by 'will have as its firm purpose' was suggested by us to the Community's translators late on the evening of 12 May; and it became accepted as the official Community translation into English of the phrase.[3]

31. Mr. Rippon, in the early hours of 13 May, when the Community formally proposed this addition to their paper, 'warmly welcomed this declaration and said that I was confident that we had found the way forward'. M. Schumann pressed him to conclude the matter then and there by a final acceptance on behalf of Her Majesty's Government, and thus 'close the sugar dossier'. But Mr. Rippon said he could not do so until he had consulted the countries concerned. 'I nevertheless said that I believed that these countries would acknowledge, as I did, the sincerity with which the Community had approached and understood their problems, and that I would certainly emphasise to them my conviction that the Community had come forward with a solemn declaration indicating their determination to safeguard their interests'. Mr. Rippon promised to let the Community know the results of his consultations as soon as possible and in any case by the next Ministerial meeting on 7 June. Later that day (13 May) instructions were sent to our posts in Commonwealth sugar-producing countries explaining the solution reached and proposing that consultations should take place with the developing members of the Commonwealth Sugar Agreement in Kingston or in another Caribbean country on 1 and 2 June. Later that day also (while Mr. Rippon was arriving in Reykjavik for the EFTA

[3] The translation of 'aura à coeur' as 'will have as its firm purpose' gave the professional translators a good deal of pain but the United Kingdom Delegation had made it clear in the Conference at the time agreement was reached that this was dependent on that particular wording being used in the English version. And so it was throughout the treaty drafting process until it emerged in Protocol 22 of the Act concerning the Conditions of Accession.

Ministerial meeting) the Cabinet recorded its conclusion that the settlement reached on sugar in Brussels 'probably represented the best outcome which we could expect'.

32. The Community's proposals did not cover the small Indian sugar quota, for India was not offered the option of association. Mr. Rippon at once raised the point. The Community made no difficulty; and at the next Ministerial meeting on 7 June a satisfactory formula was agreed to cover the Indian case.

33. This settlement on sugar produced at first, it must be admitted, a good deal of confusion and some disappointment. Already in a letter to *The Times* published on 12 May, when the general nature of the Community's proposals but not their final addition to them had become known, Lord Campbell expressed his indignation and disappointment. 'The French offer as reported makes no concession whatever to the British proposals and solves none of the problems.' After 13 May, the first reactions from the Governments and producers of the Commonwealth countries concerned were not good. The Minister of External Affairs of Trinidad was quoted in the local Press on 14 May as saying that he was very worried about the Community's proposals. The first reaction reported from Jamaica was one of concern and doubt, with the impression that the assurances given by the Community were inadequate and unacceptable. On 14 May Mr. Lightbourne issued a relatively restrained and moderate statement which nevertheless said: 'I would be bound to summarise the proposal of the Six on sugar as being a political guarantee which, however sincerely meant, would nevertheless be inadequate in bankable terms to safeguard the Commonwealth Caribbeans' sugar industry.' The Mauritian Chamber of Agriculture said that the news from Brussels had been received with great consternation, for the formula adopted was no more than an expression of good intentions and contained none of the guarantees and precise assurances which the Commonwealth demanded. Similar criticism was reported from Fiji and St. Kitts.

34. Meanwhile Mr. Heath and M. Pompidou met in Paris. The communiqué issued after their meeting 'expressed their joint desire to resolve the problems which will arise from the renewal of the Yaoundé Convention in a positive spirit and having regard to existing rights. It will equally be necessary to take account of the need to safeguard the countries who are, or will have the opportunity to become, signatories of that Convention and who are largely dependent upon the markets of the enlarged Community for their exports of sugar or other primary products.'

35. It rapidly appeared that most of the Governments of the Commonwealth sugar-producing countries, while eager for the meeting we had proposed, were not happy that it should be held in the Caribbean. A strong consensus emerged in favour of holding it in London. Mr. Lightbourne himself had at first liked the idea of a meeting in Kingston but our High Commissioner there reported on 18 May that 'he finally admitted when I put it to him squarely that sugar interests in Britain had been bringing pressure on Caribbean Governments to

meet in London where presumably they might hope to exert maximum leverage on all Governments concerned including Britain'. We bowed to the consensus and on 25 May sent a message to all concerned that we agreed to the meeting taking place in London on 2 June.

36. It duly took place in Lancaster House on that and the following day. (Mr. Lightbourne and Mr. Rippon met for a talk on 1st June.) A large number of representatives from all the countries concerned attended. A full account of the proceedings has been printed so I will deal with them extremely briefly here. Mr. Rippon presided and Mr. Prior was also present. Mr. Rippon made a long opening speech arguing the advantages of the solution reached with the Community. Mr. Lightbourne replied with an opening speech for the sugar producers from which the following are extracts. 'You see before you a group of bewildered people—people filled with deep concern about the future of our oldest and most sensitive industry—sugar. Bewildered because but a short time ago, we felt that you were in full accord with us—in accord as to the need for bankable assurances—in accord that to be bankable such assurances had to be specific in terms of volume, price and continuity ... Then all of a sudden out of a clear blue sky, without any warning, we heard that the United Kingdom, in lieu of the specific assurances she had previously been seeking on our behalf, had instead endorsed as adequate to our needs acceptance of a statement which, with great respect, we would normally regard merely as an expression of goodwill ... To say we were amazed would be an understatement. For if we take what has happened at face value then we have witnessed a complete turnabout by the United Kingdom ... By no stretch of the imagination, with the information we currently have to hand, can we regard the proposed formula as containing any specific commitment.' There was a good deal more in this strain. But Mr. Lightbourne courageously concluded his speech by saying: 'If a political solution is the only one that is now available—if indeed abandonment of seeking precise commitments from the EEC is inevitable—if figures are politically unacceptable to the EEC but the intention to accommodate our sugar production on the terms we need is nevertheless genuine, then let us put those assumptions to the test. Let us get together and seek a formula with which we can all live one which is truly bankable.'

37. The general discussion which followed was full of criticism and complaint. Many delegates urged that the Community must be asked for something better. Some were somewhat comforted when Mr. Rippon told the meeting that Tate and Lyle, with whom he had discussed the Community's assurance, had been able to tell him that they were confident enough to be able to go ahead, as sugar producers in the Caribbean and as refiners in Britain, to plan for the import into Britain of approximately the present tonnages of raw cane sugar. Mr. Demas, Secretary-General of CARIFTA, said the best course would be for Her Majesty's Government to return to Brussels and negotiate a new formula. At the end of the day a drafting group was set up in order, in Mr. Rippon's words, 'to produce a statement which would set out what the developing

countries would like the Brussels formula to mean'. If such a statement could be agreed, 'he would be willing to take this statement back to Brussels and inform the Six that this was the interpretation which we believed should be placed on the formula'.

38. I missed this meeting. I only got back from a Deputies meeting in Brussels late on the afternoon of 2 June. I therefore cannot describe at first hand how what seems to me almost a miracle took place. For before the end of the morning of 3 June agreement had been reached on a communiqué, the text of which is reproduced at Appendix II. No doubt it was the product of much hard and ingenious work behind the scenes. Almost more remarkable, when the communiqué had been agreed and representatives of the sugar-producing industries were invited to join the meeting, Lord Campbell observed: 'I can only say that I personally would have wholly accepted this settlement as satisfactory and constructive for the developing countries.'

39. Thus the Lancaster House Conference ended successfully. But there was one further task to be performed. Mr. Rippon had undertaken, as the communiqué recorded, to inform the Council of Ministers of the European Community of the outcome of the meeting and to communicate to them the text of the agreed statement embodied in the communiqué. This was done on 7 June at a Ministerial meeting in Luxembourg. Mr. Rippon made a brief statement and simultaneously copies of the agreed statement were circulated. We had undertaken no obligation to the Commonwealth Governments to ask the Community to agree to this statement or to seek their reaction to it. We had indeed strongly resisted pressures to this end. It was perfectly clear that the Community would not agree to the interpretation which we and the Commonwealth Governments had put on the settlement reached; it was highly undesirable that they should make any comment on it at all. We therefore waited, with somewhat bated breath, for the Community's reaction.

40. It came in a muted and casual form; but it came. M. Schumann paused for a moment, and remarked in a low voice: 'Of course this statement can only engage the United Kingdom.' He then passed on to other business. But M. Schumann played fair. When at the end of the meeting he and Mr. Rippon held their usual joint Press conference, M. Schumann was asked whether the Community agreed with the interpretation given in London by the British and Commonwealth countries to the agreed declaration. He replied that the Community had given no interpretation. The United Kingdom Government had given the text to the Community Delegation for information and the Community had taken note of it on this basis. However, M. Schumann's brief statement at the meeting that the statement communicated by Mr. Rippon to the Community 'can only engage the United Kingdom' was duly recorded in the minutes of the meeting and remains on the record. Fortunately, it did not attract very much attention. Like everything else it leaked; but rather late and without emphasis. It was however duly noted in *Le Monde* of 9 June and attributed to a spokesman of the Council of Ministers.

41. M. Schumann, in treating this matter as he did, cannot have been unaware that the outcome of the Lancaster House Conference had caused concern in Paris. Mr. Soames and M. Jobert had met again in Paris on 4 June (their meeting was mainly concerned with sterling, and is referred to elsewhere in this Report). M. Jobert said that President Pompidou was deeply concerned at the wording of the communiqué issued after Mr. Rippon's meeting with representatives of the sugar-producing countries. This seemed to him to be an attempt to reopen the agreement so painfully achieved in Brussels, which he had believed the Prime Minister and himself were agreed in regarding as satisfactory. If this were the case, the whole atmosphere of the Luxembourg negotiations could be soured. Mr. Soames assured M. Jobert that this was not in the least our intention. The Lancaster House communiqué was simply intended as a unilateral statement. Our plan was to read it into the record at Luxembourg but not to invite any comments on it from the Six. M. Jobert noted this, but without much satisfaction. We seemed, he said, to be 'paving the way for a battle royal in 1974'.[4]

[4] This prediction turned out to be a bit over-pessimistic. The negotiations which took place in 1974–75 over what came to be called the Sugar Protocol of the Lomé Convention and those for the Community's internal sugar régime were certainly hard-fought and arduous but they gave rise to no major political crisis nor to any questioning of the commitment to the developing Commonwealth sugar producers which had been established in Protocol 22 of Britain's Treaty of Accession. In the event the Sugar Protocol guaranteed access to the Community of 1.2 million tons per year mainly (there were moderate quantities allocated to the francophone Sugar producers) from the Commonwealth associates at prices in the range of the Community's own. This figure needs to be compared with the 500,000 tons which was the most the French ever said they were prepared to contemplate during the accession negotiations and the British opening bid of 1.373 million tons.

14

Sterling

No subject which entered into the negotiations was more elusive and mysterious, both in the way in which it developed and in the way in which it was solved, than the problem of sterling. In no case was it harder to grasp clearly and firmly what were the issues at stake and what we would be asked by the Community to do. I felt this throughout the course of the negotiations, and I feel it even more strongly as I study the way things went. Nobody on the Community side, least of all the French who were virtually alone in wishing to raise the subject at all, seemed to know clearly what they wanted or to maintain a consistent attitude about it as the months passed. We at least knew fairly well, and stuck fairly closely to, the limits of what we could do.

2. Throughout the preparation by the Community of their negotiating position a very important distinction was observed between questions relating to sterling and the state of the British economy, and all other questions. The former, unlike the latter, were for discussion only, not for negotiation. Accordingly in December 1969 the Community decided not to include problems of sterling and the British economy among those on which they required to prepare common negotiating positions; and in fact they made no attempt to do so, until after the French suddenly brought the question to the forefront in March 1971. But even in the preparatory stage, before negotiations began, the Six had agreed on a rough definition of what it was they wanted to discuss with us. At that stage it was the evolution and perspective of the British balance of payments, including the repayment of debts and the problem of growth rates; and the international status of sterling including its reserve role and the rights and obligations which Britain had in relation to sterling area countries. When on 30 June, 1970, M. Harmel made the Community's opening statement he did refer to these problems, but his reference was carefully severed from the passage in his speech dealing with the issues for negotiation and thrown in almost as an afterthought. He said that what he had just stated on the Community's position was not exhaustive. He was thinking, among other things, 'of the discussions we shall be having with the United Kingdom on certain special questions relating to the economic, monetary and financial problems connected with accession'. This concept of discussion, as opposed to negotiation, was extremely

welcome to us, and we sought to maintain the distinction as things developed.

3. The background to the problem which the Six perceived is too vast for any attempt to sketch it here. It included the whole history of international monetary development in recent years, and in particular the record of our own disappointing economic performance in the 'sixties, the balance of payments problems we had had and the international indebtedness we had incurred. It included also, as a concomitant to the negotiations, the Community's ambition and efforts to establish an economic and monetary union. Perhaps fortunately for us, these efforts were put into cold storage after the exchange crisis of early May, 1971, and did not revive till after our negotiations ended.

4. When the French succeeded in frustrating our application for membership in 1967, they were immensely helped by our economic weakness, and above all by the devaluation of sterling which occurred at the crucial period in November of that year. This they well remembered. Nevertheless, throughout 1970 and part of 1971, their position always struck us as confused. In the first place, it was never quite clear whether the reserve role of sterling was more objectionable to the French as something which gave us an unusual privilege and advantage, or as something which would represent an unacceptable liability and risk to the Community should we enter it. Different aspects were stressed by different people in the French administration at different times; and to some extent they seemed themselves aware of this confusion. Reporting on a discussion with an official of the French Ministry of Finance early in May, 1971, a member of the staff of our Embassy in Paris wrote that while it threw some light on the intentions of this particular sector of the French machine, it tended as always to leave more in the dark than it illuminated. Some Frenchmen outside the official machine found its concern as obscure as we did. In a conversation with Mr. Rippon of 12 December, 1970, M. Marjolin said he had been enquiring in Brussels about the proposed discussions on sterling. But he did not see their point. They could produce no information which was not known already. Those who thought that sterling's reserve role or the particular problems of the British balance of payments should rule out British membership of the Community were the same people who had been negotiating with Britain since June. If they thought there was no solution to the problem, they should never have agreed to start the negotiations.

5. It was clear that this was an issue on which M. Pompidou felt very strongly. On 20 November, 1970, he told Mr. Soames that what he did not like was the reserve role of sterling. The reality of things today was that there could be only one reserve currency and that was the dollar. The last thing he wanted to have was a monetary war with the United States. He saw no role for another reserve currency based either on sterling or on a European currency. It would be wrong to seek to create a European reserve currency. M. Pompidou went on to say, in reply to a question from the Ambassador, that he did not think of the reserve role of sterling as giving an undue competitive advantage to Britain; indeed, he saw it much more as a disadvantage. When M. Pompidou was touring Africa

early in 1971, he was asked a question about the sterling area at a Press conference in Yaoundé on 11 February. His reply stressed once again the major problems he foresaw in this context if Britain should enter the Community, especially the problems of the sterling balances and British debts. These were difficulties which it would be utterly foolish to ignore.

6. And yet the French Finance Minister, M. Giscard d'Estaing, seemed for a long time to take a much more relaxed view. When he was in London on 24 November, 1970, he told the Chancellor of the Exchequer that, so far as sterling was concerned, he wished to make it clear that the French Government would not bring this question into the negotiations for entry, though the matter would certainly need to be discussed at some stage. On the same day he told Mr. Rippon that the Six would not raise British balance of payments problems during the negotiations nor the question of British monetary organisation. He said the French had had these problems themselves, and they had not admitted that they were a matter for negotiation. When would we want to discuss these problems, as opposed to negotiating about them? Yet six months later, at a meeting of the Council of Ministers of the Six in Brussels, it was M. Giscard who, with the help of a dictionary, tried to demonstrate to his colleagues that there was no difference between discussion and negotiation.

7. Why, in spite of the way they tended to blow hot and cold, did the French raise these issues so strongly in the spring of 1971? Partly perhaps it was a hangover from 1967. French files and briefs at that time must have been bulging with unanswerable objections based on our economic weakness; and it cannot have been easy to forget them even in 1971. Partly it was their desire not to discard a valuable argument to justify their action were they to decide after all, in the last resort, that they did not want us in. Partly it was the application of the 'Community preference' argument which weighed so strongly with the French in other fields; this aspect governed in particular the line they took on the United Kingdom's exports of capital to the sterling area, a matter they pressed extremely hard in April and May 1971 and then suddenly and completely dropped. Partly, at least in so far as the argument of British economic weakness was concerned rather than merely that of the reserve role of sterling, it was that up until quite a late stage the French seem to have suffered from an ambiguity, and been aware of a dilemma, in their policy towards us. On the one hand they were determined to make us pay as high a price for entry as they could. On the other hand they doubted if we could afford it. Thus we had a report in December, 1970, which we regarded as completely reliable, that at a restricted session of the Permanent Representatives at the beginning of that month M. Boegner had declared that France sincerely wanted Britain to become a member of the Community; but that France did not believe that Britain could afford membership. The length of the transitional period scarcely mattered; for it would emerge that the British economy could not sustain membership. Partly again it may be that among the reasons the French had for raising the matter so abruptly as they did in March, 1971, was a decision by M. Pompidou

that, in the light of the now clearly discernible prospect of a meeting between himself and Mr. Heath, it was good tactics to raise the stakes and the temperature, and sharpen up the issues for the crunch.

8. If these, or something like them, were the reasons why the French kept the sterling issue simmering so long, and brought it so sharply to the boil in the spring of 1971, then it is easy (at least in retrospect) to see why, in the end, they dropped it so suddenly, and were content with assurances which we found it so painless to give. Once the decision had been finally confirmed that our entry was acceptable, this became the easiest of all the issues to drop, because it was the most artificial. Unlike so many other cases, there was here no solid and substantial French national interest to defend.

9. We for our part had a fairly clear and sustained line as to what we could and could not do, whatever we might in the end be asked to do. First of all, we were perfectly prepared, as a number of statements by Ministers had made clear so—indeed had some statements by Ministers in the last Administration—to contemplate changes in the reserve role of sterling so long as these were brought about in a way which did no serious damage to international liquidity, imposed no unacceptable extra burdens on our balance of payments and took account of the interests of holders of sterling. We had begun indeed to make it clear that we would see positive advantage in a gradual and orderly liquidation of the reserve role of sterling. But it was perfectly evident to us that this was a process which would not only involve more Governments than merely those of the Community but would above all take much more time than was available for our negotiations. The negotiations had to be concluded in something like 18 months; arrangements for dealing with the reserve role of sterling might well take the whole of the decade. It was thus of vital importance to preserve the distinction between discussion and negotiation, and the principle that our negotiations with the Community were not the right forum for even attempting to seek a definitive settlement of the major issues involved in sterling's reserve role. Correspondingly, we feared throughout that, if the French tried to insist that these issues must be settled in the negotiations, it would be clear evidence that they did not want them to succeed, for they must have known as well as we did that the time-scale simply would not fit.

10. Against this background of confusion and uncertainty, greater and more shifting than was the case in other area of the negotiations, things moved, as might have been expected, on a rather fluctuating course. For a long time we hoped the discussions which we knew we would have to have would give rise to no major problems. Nothing happened till the Ministerial meeting of 27 October, 1970, when at French insistence the Community declared to us that sterling was among the matters 'which lay at the very heart of the negotiations'. Thereafter, matters developed in a fairly leisurely way, with our exchange of written questions and answers with the Commission, until mid-March of 1971. Suddenly the French, on 18 March, hotted things up. The temperature rose all through April and the first half of May, and when Mr. Heath met M. Pompidou

we feared this might prove almost the most difficult problem. It was fully discussed, and in the end it appeared to have been simply and satisfactorily settled. A few days later, in Brussels, it seemed to have arisen again as sharply as before. Suddenly, in bilateral contacts with the French, we found this was all a mistake. It had been settled after all. At the Ministerial meeting in Luxembourg on 7 June the rather peculiar settlement achieved was duly recorded; and the great issue of sterling ended not with an ugly bang but with what was, from our point of view, a very small and satisfactory whimper.

11. Although I wrote in paragraph 3 above that the background to this problem was too vast for any attempt to sketch it here, nevertheless I must at this point refer to one element in the background which was moving decisively in our favour throughout the period of the negotiations—and indeed over the previous year. This was the progress, to use the current Treasury jargon, of 'reserve/debt improvement'; and indeed nothing played a more effective part in drawing the poison out of the sterling issue (and out of much else besides) than the steady increase in our reserves and the steady reduction of our international indebtedness. At the end of 1968 our medium and short-term international indebtedness had reached a peak of $8,071 million. At that time our published reserves amounted to $2,636 million—thus they were in fact in a high degree negative reserves. At the end of June 1970—the moment when the negotiations opened—our corresponding international indebtedness had fallen to $3,506 million. By the end of March 1971 the figure was $1,640 million—a reduction of $6,431 million from the peak at the end of 1968. At the end of 1970 our reserves amounted to $2,827 million; at the end of 1971, as the negotiations were concluding, they had reached $6,582 million, a figure several times greater than that to which by then our remaining medium and short-term international debt had sunk.

12. To complete the picture, it should be stated, because it became highly relevant to the discussions on sterling, that throughout this period the official sterling area balances were rising. In September 1968, at the time of the Basle Arrangement, they had reached their low point of £1,506 million. By the end of 1970 they stood at £2,244 million. Some elements in the Commission claimed to see in this rise of the official sterling area balances a kind of counterpart of the reduction in our medium and short-term international debts; but this was special pleading, and in any case the orders of magnitude were strikingly different. Nevertheless, much was made by the Community of the risks of the rise in the official sterling area balances; and in the end we gave, with very little reluctance, an undertaking that we would be 'prepared to envisage an orderly and gradual rundown of official sterling balances after our accession'.

13. I shall not attempt to describe in any detail the actual course of discussions about sterling and its related issues during the negotiations. More than with almost any other problem—though with a number of other problems something similar happened—events in the early stages proved to have led in irrelevant directions, and completely new paths were suddenly found to the solution. Our

main concern, in the early months of the negotiations, was not to get involved in discussions on sterling too soon. We wanted to postpone them at least until the beginning of 1971. A telegram to Paris of 23 October, 1970, summarised 'our main reasons for preferring to hold these discussions some time next year'. There were three of them. First, until some significant progress had been made in the negotiations proper, it would be premature to discuss the effects of accession on our economy and sterling. Second, since the new Government had not yet had time to develop and explain its general economic policies, it would be better to postpone discussions about our economic prospects until these policies had been presented and the course of the economy charted over the months and years ahead. Third, we wanted to make some progress towards the renewal of the sterling area agreements (which had to be completed by September 1971) before embarking on substantive discussions on the status of sterling in Brussels.

14. There was a good deal of desultory discussion in the autumn of 1970 with various representatives of Community Governments as to how, when they took place, the discussions should be held. Here our main concern was that they should be held in as discreet and expert a forum as possible. We felt that to discuss these matters in the leaky sieve of the Brussels Conference itself could have damaging consequences, even for confidence and exchange rates. But as time passed it became clear that the French, and M. Boegner in particular, strongly preferred that the discussions should not be altogether divorced from the normal negotiating forum and that, at least on the Community side, the Permanent Representatives should play their customary part.

15. The Commission was also anxious to play its part. That is to say M. Barre, the French Vice-President responsible for economic and monetary affairs in the Commission, was anxious to do so. This prospect gave us little pleasure. We knew that of all the members of the Commission M. Barre was the most hostile to our membership of the Community. There is little doubt that he saw the sterling issue as one barrel of a gun to shoot us down with, the other being our contribution to the Community Budget. He succeeded in playing a major part in the discussion of sterling within the Community. In November 1970 he explained to the six Permanent Representatives all the difficulties he foresaw; and in January 1971 he was preaching the doctrine that the Basle Facility should not be renewed without some modifications to ensure that the growth of the sterling balances should be reduced. Later he took the lead in developing within the Commission a critical and rather hostile analysis of our replies to the Commission's questionnaire. M. Barre was however discomfited in the end, as we shall see later.

16. As already described in Chapter 8, the Community made a statement to us at the Ministerial meeting in Luxembourg on 27 October, 1970, in which they described the sterling issue as one of the matters which 'lay at the very heart of the negotiations', and which must be opened up before the end of the year. It was this commitment to get started in 1970 which led to the

communication to us of a series of written questions about sterling and our economy, which M. Deniau sent to Mr. Rippon on 21 December, 1970. We were asked to reply in writing, and it was intimated that the Community hoped we should reply before the end of January. We set about preparing written replies of considerable length and complexity, and but for a few rather unexpected delays we might have delivered our replies about the end of January; as it turned out, and it did not matter, we did not deliver them until 17 February, 1971.

17. Meanwhile it had become clear that one of the elements on which the French at least were likely to concentrate was the 'Community preference' aspect of our exports of capital to the developed Commonwealth. These were of course severely restricted by the 'voluntary programme' of restraint on investment from the United Kingdom in Australia, New Zealand, South Africa and the Irish Republic. Nevertheless, it was clear that the French felt that our capital outflows in recent years had been a luxury which a country with our balance of payments record should never have allowed itself; and were anxious to ensure that, right from the start of our membership, we should not discriminate in any degree against the Community in our rules governing capital movements. Yet the Community had already accepted in principle that we should have a transitional period for compliance with their existing directives on capital movements within the Community, so that it would be some years before we approached even the relative freedom of capital movements existing within the Community. The French doctrine of total non-discrimination against the Community from the start would have been both awkward for us and inconsistent with, for example, the transitional arrangements which were already shaping up in the field of industrial tariffs. The Chancellor of the Exchequer wished, in the 1971 Budget, to abolish the voluntary programme, which would of course have made discrimination against the Community in capital movements more evident. But he accepted arguments put forward by the Foreign Secretary and Mr. Rippon to the effect that this would seriously embarrass us in our negotiations with the Community, by raising the issue of non-discrimination in a starker and less defensible form; and the abolition of the voluntary programme was deferred until 1972.

18. Meanwhile also, and before any discussions with the Community had begun, we were able to make a start on the process of renewing the sterling area agreements—which were due to lapse in September 1971 but were renewable for two years—and the associated Basle Facility. An approach to the sterling area countries concerned was made on 4 March, 1971; and a day or two later the Governor of the Bank of England, at one of the regular meetings of the Bank for International Settlements in Basle on 7 and 8 March, raised the question of the renewal of the Basle Facility. He did so with unexpectedly rapid success. It was agreed on by the Central Banks concerned there and then, though the French, as before, stood aside. Some trouble was caused later by French suggestions that they had been inadequately consulted or excluded from consideration; but the record is clear that the Governor of the Bank of France

was informed in advance of our intentions, and himself elected to take no part in the decisions of his colleagues. The process of renewing the sterling area agreements ran smoothly and later in the year, after the sterling issue had been disposed of in our negotiations with the Community, they were duly renewed for two years until 1973.

19. In spite of the most elaborate precautions on the part of the Commission, their December questionnaire to us leaked fairly rapidly; and our replies to it began being published in Brussels as early as 3 March. But in fact the whole exercise of question and answer proved irrelevant as time passed. The Commission and the Community were still considering our replies when the French made an unexpected move. Though we did not learn it until a little later, this move was in fact decided on at a special meeting held in Paris on 17 March between M. Pompidou, M. Chaban-Delmas, M. Schumann and M. Giscard d'Estaing. They decided—the background to and the reasons for their decision are suggested in paragraph 7 above—that the question of sterling should be raised at once with their colleagues in the Community, and instructions were immediately despatched to M. Boegner in Brussels. He carried them out by making a statement in the Committee of Permanent Representatives the following day.

20. The statement was fairly short and fairly sharp. France wished that the Council of Ministers, at its meeting on 30 March, should succeed in elaborating a common position to be rapidly transmitted to the British with a view to the discussions on economic, financial and monetary problems which had been foreseen. M. Boegner went on to describe the French position. France considered that there would be a contradiction between membership of the Community, moving as it was to an economic and monetary union, and responsibility by a member for maintaining an international reserve currency; since this would make such a member the centre of a non-European monetary zone and subject it to factors external to the Community. Such a situation could gravely disturb the proper functioning of the Community. This did not imply that the Community must insist that Great Britain should terminate the reserve role of sterling at the moment of accession, but at least it was necessary that during the period of transition Britain should ensure that the volume of the sterling balances should progressively diminish. France also considered that the provisions of Articles 108 and 109 of the Treaty of Rome could not operate in favour of a member country unless the difficulties it was experiencing derived from problems of its own economy and not from external influences. Furthermore, the entry of Britain into the Community should be accompanied by the immediate suppression of discrimination in respect of capital movements which at present operated in favour of the white Commonwealth (essentially Australia and New Zealand) in comparison with Community members. Moreover, such capital exports had the effect of increasing the volume of the sterling balances and the external monetary vulnerability of Britain. It was in an essentially Community spirit, concluded M. Boegner, that he raised these problems in order

that the Council of Ministers should adopt as rapidly as possible a common attitude on which discussions with Great Britain could be based.

21. M. Boegner's statement leaked immediately. This was much to our advantage. The immediate reactions of the other five members to it were without exception critical and indignant; and this fact leaked too. The general reaction of the Press was to assume that a new and major obstacle to the success of the negotiations had been raised in a notably sharp and hostile form. The French were most indignant at the leakage, and genuinely embarrassed at the interpretation put upon their action. We began almost immediately to hear that M. Boegner had carried out his instructions in too sharp a manner and thus distorted their constructive and moderate intentions. While in no way displeased by the sharp reactions of the Five, we at once decided that for our part we should take this new development calmly and coolly. That we did so was undoubtedly deeply appreciated by the French, and it contributed not a little to restoring a more friendly atmosphere and helping things forward, not only in this field.

22. Nor did we by any means take this line only as a prudent tactical move. We genuinely felt little concern at the substance of M. Boegner's statement, and were rather surprised—useful though it was to us—at the strength of the reaction from the Five. In particular, we welcomed the fact that the French statement in no way raised the question of the general state of the British economy or its rate of growth; and only touched indirectly on our balance of payments and our indebtedness. The day after M. Boegner's statement, on 19 March, we sent guidance to our posts abroad making it clear that we had always anticipated that we should have to discuss with the Community certain special questions relating to the economic, monetary and financial problems connected with accession; and that we saw nothing new or surprising in the request by a Member State that the Council of Ministers should take this matter up. Five days later, in a minute to the Prime Minister, the Chancellor of the Exchequer wrote that the questions raised by M. Boegner were ones which we had known throughout we should have to answer; and the Treasury did not find it really surprising that the French should have brought them forward at this point. Mr. Barber did not feel that the tone of the French statement was either unreasonable or hostile. He added that these moves did not of themselves provide any evidence that the French had introduced these questions at this point in order to disrupt or delay the negotiations. He concluded: 'To my mind the French attitude remains as enigmatic as ever, and the recent developments afford no firm evidence one way or the other.'

23. The Council of Ministers met on 30 March. They took procedural decisions only. The Permanent Representatives and the Commission were charged to work out a Community position, with the assistance of an *ad hoc* group of senior civil servants of the member countries and the Commission; the *ad hoc* group was at liberty to meet with British representatives. But M. Giscard d'Estaing, who attended the meeting, took a line no less hard—in fact a little harder—than M. Boegner had taken 12 days before. He elaborated all

the respects in which, as France saw it, the reserve role of sterling remained incompatible with British membership of the Community; and made much in particular of the problem of British capital exports and their potentially discriminatory character. He concluded by saying that the Community should ask that the sterling balances should be progressively reduced. When Dr. Luns insisted that, in accordance with the Community's earlier decisions, all these were matters for discussion with the British, not for negotiation, M. Giscard said it was hard to see any difference. He quoted from Larousse to demonstrate that discussion and negotiation were much the same, and he said he preferred negotiation, which was merely an attempt to reach agreed conclusions. Dr. Luns maintained there was no need to solve these problems in the negotiations; they could be postponed and dealt with later.

24. Soon after Mr. Barber produced the 1971 Budget. Its measures, including the decision to move next year towards a Value-added Tax, were extremely well received within the Community. There can be no doubt that the impression of Community commitment conveyed by the Budget, and the impression (not altogether borne out by the events of the next nine months) that the United Kingdom economy was well on the way to recovery, helped to make French insistence on subjecting us to so many severe economic tests and questions seem even less relevant and important to the Five. Coupled above all with the favourable progress of our balance of payments, our reserves and our debts (see paragraph 11 above) the general climate was moving in our favour. The sterling area agreements were known to be on the way to renewal; the renewal of the Basle Facility was assured. We had made it perfectly clear that we were prepared, given time, for major changes in the reserve role of sterling. What, the Five felt more and more, were the French worrying about?

25. The *ad hoc* group set up by the Council of Ministers on 30 March to study these questions held its first meeting on 16 April and, as authorised by the Council of Ministers, invited British representatives to join it at its next meeting in Brussels on 21 April. We accepted this invitation, and were represented at this meeting by Mr. Bell of the Treasury and Mr. Morse of the Bank of England. A relatively calm and friendly discussion took place. A few days later, on 26 and 27 April, the Finance Ministers of the Six met in Hamburg. Their meeting was somewhat more stormy, but not because of sterling which as it happened they never discussed at all. They regarded their meeting as a specially confidential one; but as usual much of what had transpired leaked almost at once, including the story that M. Giscard d'Estaing had pressed for an increase in the price of gold. For some reason, apparently only because the leaks were first reported by Reuters, we were in various quarters held responsible for them, even though we had not been present at the meeting. But what was most significant of all was that the Six Finance Ministers, at the time of this meeting, were beginning to feel serious disquiet at the pressures on the exchanges caused by the weakness of the dollar. This was also one of the occasions on which French irritation with and dislike of Professor Schiller came most strongly and visibly to the surface.

These feelings, compounded of reactions to what the French regarded as the intellectual pretensions, academic arrogance and ruthless tactics of the Professor, helped on a number of occasions to make us seem a preferable partner.

26. The *ad hoc* group resumed its meeting, this time without us, on 28 and 29 April, to draft its report for the Permanent Representatives. The French continued to take a hard line. On 6 May the Permanent Representatives met to consider a report (far from unanimous) by the *ad hoc* group, which was to be presented to the Council of Ministers on 10 May, the day before our next Ministerial meeting with the Community. But already on 5 May the dollar crisis had become acute, and in Germany the foreign exchange market was closed. The Community convened a special meeting of its Monetary Committee for 6 May. The French, deeply concerned at the effect on the Common Agricultural Policy of any change in the parities of Community currencies, were by now strongly and bitterly critical of German policy. Suddenly, the bogy of sterling was replaced by the reality of the dollar and the Deutschemark, which on 8 May was set free to float.

27. 8 May was also the day on which the impending meeting between Mr. Heath and M. Pompidou was announced. The stage was set for a confrontation at the highest level on the problem of sterling; but meanwhile the scenery had been very significantly shifted. In the somewhat chaotic circumstances of the European exchange markets and of intra-Community agricultural trade, the Council of Ministers when it met on 10 May took no decisions on a common position for discussions with us on sterling. M. Giscard continued to take a hard line, and to concentrate in particular on the problem of capital movements to the developed sterling area. (He also displayed extreme bitterness over the German action in floating the Deutschemark.) But the Finance Ministers of the Five, who were all present, unanimously declined to follow the French line. The Italians, the Germans and the Belgians all suggested that discussion should be held with the United Kingdom on these questions *en marge* of the negotiations with a view to working towards a unilateral declaration by the British Government.

28. We ourselves had long had the idea that the way out of these difficulties might be the making by us of a unilateral statement of some kind and its acceptance by the Community. When the Ministerial meeting with us took place from 11 to 13 May—a meeting at which for the first time so much real progress was made in other fields—the Community had nothing to say to us on sterling. But Mr. Rippon, in the early hours of 13 May, took the opportunity, in line with our ideas about an eventual unilateral declaration, to place on record in the Conference 'a number of public statements by Her Majesty's Government on the particular question of the future of the role of sterling'. He quoted from a statement he had himself made in the House of Commons a few months before on 21 January: 'Sterling's international role has been declining significantly over the past decade or more. ... It is clear to most observers that the reserve role of sterling is no longer an advantage to Britain. Indeed, the reverse is more easily

argued, and these trends in the trading and reserve uses of sterling will probably continue. In the long term the Government do not propose to stand in the way of these developments.' He also, quoted from a more recent statement in the House of Commons by the Chancellor of the Exchequer, who on 27 April had said: 'Early changes in the reserve role of sterling are not practicable. At an appropriate time the Government will be willing to explore possibilities for change with all those concerned, including the official holders of sterling. ... The Government would be ready to consider such a move provided that means could be found which avoided an unacceptable burden on the United Kingdom, promoted the healthy development of the international monetary system, and protected the interests of the sterling holders.' M. Schumann, in the chair, thanked Mr. Rippon for making this statement to which, he said, he had listened with lively interest.

29. A week later Mr. Heath and M. Pompidou met in Paris. The problem of sterling was very thoroughly discussed; and the upshot was agreement that the problem was nothing like so difficult as it had been made to appear. In particular M. Pompidou did not raise at all the special problem of discrimination in capital movements to the advantage of the developed sterling area, on which M. Boegner and M. Giscard d'Estaing had concentrated so much, and which from our point of view could have been perhaps the most awkward problem to overcome. Nor did the question of the availability to us of the provisions of Articles 108 and 109 of the Treaty of Rome—a question which had engendered much interest and discussion in 1967—prove at all insurmountable. Everything seemed to have been satisfactorily settled; although of course it was left to the Negotiating Conference to put the final touches to the agreement reached.

30. This was immensely satisfactory. But we were not to emerge from all these troubles without some further alarms. The Five of course had only the minimum of information about what had passed between Mr. Heath and M. Pompidou in Paris. So did the French Administration. The Permanent Representatives were due to resume on 27 May their discussions on the *ad hoc* committee's report. The Dutch asked us what advice we had to give them on tactics in the light of the meeting between Mr. Heath and M. Pompidou. We replied on 26 May instructing our Embassy in The Hague to tell the Dutch that it was our expectation that in the light of the Prime Minister's talks with President Pompidou the French Government would not wish to press for further discussion on sterling questions before the negotiations were concluded. But a telegram from Brussels on the morning of 27 May reported that, when the Permanent Representatives had met earlier that day, 'the French had just tabled a paper which appeared to be a mere restatement of the line which Giscard had taken in the Council of Ministers on 10 May'. The Five were said to be solidly against the proposals in the paper, subject to a slight wavering on the part of Belgium. No conclusions were reached.

31. This puzzled us. And indeed it alarmed us not a little. Mr. Armstrong, the Prime Minister's Private Secretary, had written on 25 May to Mr. Soames

in Paris asking him to take up with M. Jobert, the Secretary-General of the Elysée, the question how, in the light of the recent meeting between Mr. Heath and M. Pompidou, the question of sterling should be disposed of in Brussels. Mr. Soames was to say that we presumed that, following the talks between the President and the Prime Minister, this matter would now be put aside, at least to the extent that any further questions on sterling would be dealt with after the conclusion of an accession agreement in the context of progress towards European economic and monetary union. But before Mr. Soames had had time to act reports reached us of the developments in the Committee of Permanent Representatives on 27 May. A telegram from Mr. Armstrong, despatched that evening, asked Mr. Soames to add, in carrying out his earlier instructions, that we had now heard of the new paper the French Delegation had tabled in Brussels. 'We find this surprising in the light of the recent Paris meeting. Can M. Jobert give you any explanation?'

32. Mr. Soames saw M. Jobert early on 28 May. As soon as he mentioned sterling, M. Jobert interrupted him to say that he doubtless knew that the French had put a paper to the Five in Brussels on sterling the previous day. It was not very different from the theme they had been pursuing before the Heath–Pompidou meeting. The reason for this was that, had they not acted in this way, they would have been faced with all sorts of questions from the Five which they would have found it impossible to answer. 'Their action was therefore a smoke-screen.' M. Jobert wanted to know from us how we would like them to play the hand on sterling from now on. When the Prime Minister had left Paris the President had understood that he wanted him to say nothing to anyone. And indeed he had not. Giscard had been knocking on his door, but he had refused so far to see him. How did we wish the President to play his hand from now on?

33. This complex situation led to fairly complex exchanges, which lasted for a few days, during which the Five, not unnaturally, remained in a state of considerable confusion. The idea was worked out between Mr. Soames and M. Jobert that at the next Ministerial meeting in Luxembourg on 7 June the Community should ask us to make a statement about the place of sterling in the enlarged Community, and that we should then make one. The outline of such a statement was put by Mr. Soames to M. Jobert. Numerous exchanges on the details of the text followed on 3 and 4 June between London and Paris, and Mr. Soames and M. Jobert had successive encounters and conversations. Finally, late on the evening of 4 June, all was agreed by M. Pompidou, and M. Jobert told Mr. Soames that 'Giscard would act accordingly both within the Six in their deliberations, and at the negotiating meeting with us, in response to Mr. Rippon's proposed statement.' He added that it would no doubt be for us to do what we could to ensure that the Five responded satisfactorily.

34. Meanwhile, the Six continued their by now somewhat embarrassing labours in Brussels. The French paper of 27 May did not disappear from the table; worse still, some of the Five began to move in some respects towards it;

and others toyed with the idea of proposing alternative texts. On 3 June the Permanent Representatives finally approved a paper to be submitted to the Council of Ministers on 7 June; it was of course a disagreed paper, recording different points of view, but in some respects some of the Five were moving closer to the French. Some of the Five also, in particular the Italians, expressed to us a certain hesitation about continuing to oppose the French, since they feared that what the French in Brussels were proposing might represent what Mr. Heath in Paris had agreed to.

35. On Saturday, 5 June (the Council of Ministers was to meet in Luxembourg on Monday morning, and thereafter to have a Ministerial meeting with us), we sent instructions to our posts in the Community capitals and our Delegation in Brussels. They were to inform representatives of the Five (including their Permanent Representatives in Brussels) that we had been discussing with the French how we might handle the questions of sterling and associated matters in the context of the negotiations: as a result we now saw our way to making a statement on this subject at the meeting on 7 June which the French would accept as satisfactorily disposing of it. We gave no instructions, which in retrospect appears a little unkind, for any communication to the Commission. Reactions to communications made on the basis of these instructions reached us on Saturday evening and on Sunday, 6 June; they showed general satisfaction.

36. When the Council of Ministers met on 7 June, M. Barre of the Commission 'circulated a detailed paper in an attempt to reach a compromise between what Barre still thought were French views and those which had been expressed by the other member States'. But the Council decided to await the meeting with us. At this meeting, Mr. Rippon duly made his statement. M. Schumann proposed an adjournment to allow the Council to consider it before making a reply to us later in the evening. After the adjournment had concluded, M. Schumann made a brief reply to Mr. Rippon's statement. The Community had taken note of his declaration with satisfaction. They agreed to it. They proposed that this agreement should be recorded in an exchange of letters to be annexed to the Treaty of Accession. Mr. Rippon thanked M. Schumann, and said that the matter was thus satisfactorily disposed of. It appears that during the adjournment, when the Council considered Mr. Rippon's statement, M. Giscard said at once that he could accept it. 'This was greeted with some laughter from other Delegations, and some indignation from the Commission.' Later, M. Barre is said to have remarked that what Mr. Rippon had said 'amounted to zero plus zero plus zero' and he could not understand why Giscard had agreed to it. He also made a statement, quoted in the Press, to the effect that 'it was regrettable that the agreement contained none of the necessary guarantees, given the importance of the matter'.

37. This immensely satisfactory outcome—I will not describe Mr. Rippon's statement as it is annexed to the Act of Accession*—led to some confusion, as

* See Document N in Appendix II.

well as surprise. Among the Five it created a strong disposition, against which we subsequently had to take what action we could (see Chapter 7 above), to suspect that other outstanding matters in the negotiations had likewise been settled bilaterally between Mr. Heath and M. Pompidou, and a corresponding reluctance to commit themselves to further action on our behalf. In the United Kingdom too there was some incredulity, and a disposition to suppose that we must have made to the French some more substantial concessions than were apparent from the terms of Mr. Rippon's statement. Mr. Rippon's report to the House of Commons on 9 June did not succeed in allaying this concern. The Prime Minister found it necessary to make a statement in the House of Commons on 10 June. He pointed out that it was an advantage to us, not a weakness, that these problems were left for discussion after our accession. We had not been asked for and had not entered into any specific undertakings or commitments on methods or timetables. We were committed only, as Mr. Rippon's statement had recorded, to envisage an orderly and gradual rundown of official sterling balances after our accession. No undertaking had been given about the method to be used or the time-phasing on which this should be done, and therefore the rate at which it should be done, for the reason that it must not be done in a way which would at any time be a burden on the balance of payments.

15

New Zealand: The Background

The following table gives the shortest and clearest answer to the question why New Zealand was a major problem in the negotiations, and Australia and Canada (unlike the position nine years earlier) were not.

EXPORTS TO THE UNITED KINGDOM AS PERCENTAGE OF TOTAL EXPORTS

Year	*Canada*	*Australia* [1]	*New Zealand* [2]
1938	38.2	54.2	83.8
1950	15.1	32.7	66.2
1959	15.6	26.4	56.4
1969	7.5	11.8	35.9
1970	8.9	11.1	34.4
1971	7.7	N.A.	N.A.

[1] Years beginning June.
[2] Years beginning June for 1969 and 1970.
N.A. = Not yet available.

Yet while this table shows the New Zealand problem, it suggests also that, steadily over the years, it was becoming less grave. New Zealand's dependence on the British market was still great; but it was not, as it had been not so long ago, almost total. There was moreover reason to believe that the decline in the importance of the British market to New Zealand would continue steadily and fairly rapidly. This was not because New Zealand was likely to export, other things being equal, less to Britain in the future. It was because she was increasingly likely to export more to other markets. Her exports of meat (which as it turned out were not likely even in the case of lamb to be reduced in our market because of our entry to the Community) were growing much more rapidly than her exports of dairy products, and were being directed with increasing success to new markets such as the United States (for beef) and Japan (for mutton). Her exports of forestry products and manufactured goods were at last beginning to become really significant, and were likely to increase fast. In another five years it might have been by no means so easy to argue that our entry into the

Community without special safeguards for New Zealand would be a disaster to her.

2. In some ways, the problem of New Zealand in the negotiations was one of the most simple. Not that it did not create an infinity of work and paper almost more than any other subject. But it was clear and straightforward. Solving it was just a matter of securing its recognition and maintaining pressure. The number of parties concerned was limited—far more so than in the case, for example, of sugar. Ourselves, the Community, New Zealand—that was all. Our other important butter and cheese suppliers outside the enlarged Community, such as Australia, Poland and Finland, could only hold their breath and fear the worst. There was no fundamental switch of emphasis or definition during the negotiations such as took place with the problems of sugar or sterling. The potentially grave problem of lamb was successfully kept out of the negotiations from start to finish. Only one unexpected development occurred, and it was helpful to the outcome. This was the sudden transformation, beginning late in 1970, hardly realised till the spring of 1971 and culminating not long after the question was solved, in the supply situation of butter, where a world shortage emerged. The nature and effects of this development are discussed later. Here I will only record my view that, quite apart from its effects on New Zealand, this was one of the most fortunate developments which took place during the negotiations. For it demonstrated to the British public that they had, even outside the Community, no natural and eternal right to buy their butter (apart from New Zealand butter) at or below half its cost price.

3. The Government of New Zealand played a much larger part in the negotiations than any other third Government. Their concern was intense. The prospect of our entering the Community had been their major problem for the last 10 years, and they had brought to bear on it all their resources of study, skill and tactics. These were considerable, and they played their hand well. They were competent and sophisticated in their approach, not only to us. They were well represented in London, in the capitals of the Community and in Brussels. Mr. Marshall, Deputy Prime Minister and Minister for Overseas Trade, had been living with the problem since 1961. He knew it inside out. He was experienced, lucid, cool and determined; and his quiet and modest approach, in contrast to that of some other Commonwealth statesmen, was much appreciated in the Community. The New Zealand Government was moreover well supported by non-governmental pressure groups who had excellent means for making themselves felt in London. Sir John Ormond, President of the New Zealand Meat Board; Mr. Onion, President of the Dairy Board; Mr. Begg, President of the Federated Farmers of New Zealand—they all visited London during the negotiations and kept up their pressures at home. The New Zealand Government were even able to exploit the weakness of their political position—they had a tiny majority in Parliament and seemed scarcely likely to survive the next election—and the hostility of their Labour Opposition. Mr. Kirk, its Leader, visited London as the guest of Mr. Harold Wilson in April 1971. He did

what he could to appeal to British public opinion on New Zealand's behalf, and criticised the New Zealand Government for not doing more.

4. The New Zealand Government skilfully supported their case by inviting visitors to New Zealand to study it on the spot. Apart from Mr. Rippon, who went there in September 1970, they gave the full on-the-spot treatment to Ministers from Belgium and Holland (M. Fayat and Mr. de Koster) in 1970, and from France (M. de Lipkowski) in 1971; and to senior officials from Italy and Germany. They also invited journalists from Community countries. Just at the right moment, on 5 June, 1970 they published a long and persuasive study of their problem by the New Zealand Monetary and Economic Council which, while ostensibly an entirely independent body, not surprisingly produced a report skilfully presenting the Government's case and even preserving its negotiating nuances. The report was translated into French and German and widely circulated within the Community. Finally, the New Zealand Government had fixed the Australians in advance. The Australians sent some 65,000 tons of butter to our market each year, over a third of New Zealand's supply. But Mr. Marshall quietly pointed out from time to time that the Australian Government had agreed to do nothing to thwart New Zealand's more critical case.

5. New Zealand, as Mr. Marshall explained to Mr. Barber in July 1970, is a country with rather less than three million people, rather more than three million dairy cattle and 60 million sheep plus, in the period from July to December, 40 million lambs. In spite of the figures, it was the dairy cows. rather than the sheep, which gave rise to the problem. This problem was, in essence, the same as with sugar. The Community had a milk surplus, which had shown itself mainly in the creation of the 'mountain' of surplus butter, still at its peak when the negotiations began. Two of the other three candidates, Denmark and Ireland, also had large milk surpluses and exported major quantities of dairy products mainly, like New Zealand, to the British market. Britain for its part had of course a major milk deficit. The Community countries with the main milk surpluses (France and the Netherlands) wanted, as in the case of sugar, to be able to export these surpluses in the form of butter and cheese to the British market, displacing non-Community suppliers. (The Dutch are especially provoking in that, while producing vast quantities of butter, they consume next to none of it themselves, and live thriftily on margarine.) But in the British market there would not be room for everyone. Once again, as with sugar, the problem was how to get both a Community pint and a Commonwealth pint into a single pint pot. (It is worth pointing out that two of our fellow-applicants, Denmark and the Irish Republic, had a strong interest, as major exporters of butter and cheese, in maintaining maximum access to our market. It is to their credit that they did not try, so far as we ever discovered, to put a spoke in our New Zealand wheel.)

6. It is necessary to realise the unique position of the British market as a destination for overseas butter and cheese. Our average butter imports in recent years had been 440,000 tons, of which New Zealand had supplied on average

about 175,000 tons, or 40 per cent. The total butter trade in the whole of the rest of the world, excluding intra-EEC trade, had amounted on average in the five years to 1968 to some 224,000 tons, or half British imports. The United Kingdom was also the world's largest importer of cheese, though it took only one-third of world exports of cheese, as opposed to two-thirds in the case of butter. We had operated a quota system for butter imports since 1962 (in order to protect New Zealand and other traditional suppliers from dumping rivals) and 'voluntary restraint' arrangements for cheddar cheese imports since 1969. In 1970–71 New Zealand was expected to provide 56 per cent of our cheddar cheese imports. Furthermore, it was clear that our entry into the Community would have two significant consequences for butter. Our own domestic butter (and cheese) production was certain to rise and our consumption of butter, with rising prices, was certain to shrink. Thus the prize for which all contended—the British butter deficit—was going in any case to be a smaller one.

7. We set out the problem in statistical form in a table, reproduced at the end of this chapter, showing the butter, cheese and milk balance for the EEC and the applicant countries in 1969. This was 1 of 10 tables annexed to a paper on the consequences for dairy products of the enlargement of the Community, which we circulated, after consultation with New Zealand on its contents, to the Conference in September 1970. It showed that on the 1969 basis there would be, in the enlarged Community, a modest deficit for milk and milk products as a whole—but a deficit not nearly big enough to leave room for New Zealand exports to the British market. Furthermore, our paper argued, the situation in the enlarged Community was bound to deteriorate from that of 1969. The milk surplus of the Six existing Member States of the Community would not, we estimated, be greatly different from the present level. But milk output would rise a little in Denmark and a lot in the Irish Republic. There might in the United Kingdom be a small rise in milk output, but there would be a marked decline as prices rose in the consumption of dairy products, leading to reduced import requirements. We concluded: 'It seems probable, therefore, that the net effect of the application of the Common Agricultural Policy in the United Kingdom and the other applicant countries would be that the present deficit for the 10 countries taken together of about 1.75 million metric tons of milk (equivalent to an import requirement of 75,000 metric tons of butter) would become a surplus of milk in the enlarged Community.' Accordingly, a still worse prospect for New Zealand.

8. Thus the New Zealand problem was a serious one and something had to be done about it. It had been made worse in recent years by the dumping of Community surplus butter at give-away prices in many of the remaining small markets for butter which New Zealand had striven to develop. But was their problem quite so serious as the New Zealanders always claimed? Among British officials there was, right from the start of the negotiations and all through them, a certain scepticism. This was shared by our High Commissioner and his

staff in New Zealand. Sir Arthur Galsworthy (whose continual, thorough and illuminating reports and analyses from Wellington made him, after Mr. Soames in Paris, the British representative abroad who contributed most to the negotiations) never understated the New Zealand case; but he never overstated it either. He was well aware of its weaknesses and exaggerations; and always prepared to urge the New Zealanders in the direction of moderation. At the end of March 1971 he advised us that they would be prepared to accept less than they claimed was essential, and considerably less than in the end we achieved for them.

9. Even the report of the New Zealand Monetary and Economic Council revealed, on a close reading, some weaknesses in their case. While not failing to give all the relevant statistics, it did convey the impression that New Zealand stood or fell with exports of butter and cheese to Britain. It stressed also the critical value of lamb exports to our market, but rather underplayed the much greater value (about three times as great) of wool and meat (including beef) exports to other markets. At one point it compared the effects on New Zealand of having no more than transitional arrangements giving them time to adjust to our adoption of the Common Agricultural Policy with the effects on New Zealand of the decline in wool prices in 1967, and suggested that they would be rather graver. That had been no doubt a grave crisis for New Zealand, but hardly a total disaster. It calculated too that the value of exports New Zealand stood to lose permanently if she failed to maintain her outlets in Britain for butter and cheese and lamb (which in 1969 almost equalled in value the other two put together) would (after costly re-structuring of the economy) be 85 million New Zealand dollars, or some £40 million; that is to say less than 8 per cent of total New Zealand exports in 1969. Mr. Marshall met the challenge of this figure fairly enough. At his meeting with Mr. Barber on 7 July, 1970, he said that the report of the New Zealand Monetary and Economic Council 'had concluded that, on the most favourable estimate, if the dairy and lamb industries had to be converted into beef and forestry industries, the permanent loss of export earnings would amount to 85 million dollars per annum. This was equivalent to a loss of £600 million for Britain or 8,000 million dollars for an enlarged Community.' The point was legitimate (though he could have halved his figures had he admitted that lamb was not at risk); and the threat to New Zealand was certainly grave, though perhaps not disastrous.

10. Whether Mr. Marshall's repeated public assertions that New Zealand faced either sudden death (if her dairy exports were cut off at once) or slow strangulation (if she received only a transitional period leading eventually to third country treatment) were entirely justified is perhaps another matter. It is necessary, to justify the scepticism of British officials to which I have referred, to give some more figures. The following table, constructed from figures of overseas exchange transactions published by the New Zealand Government on 30 October, 1970, illustrate the argument:

NEW ZEALAND EXPORTS (IN YEAR ENDED SEPTEMBER)
(NZ$ million)

Exports	*Butter, Cheese Other Dairy Products*	*Meat, Wool Other Animal Products*	*Forest Products, Other Primary Products Manufactured Exports and Miscellaneous*	*Total*
1967	229.4	431.5	80.3	741.2
1968	210.4	539.7	137.3	887.5
1969	218.8	671.6	171.1	1061.5
1970	245.2	727.1	196.7	1169.0

Thus exports of dairy products, which amounted in 1967 to just under 31 per cent of total exports, had fallen by 1970 to just under 21 per cent. Exports of butter and cheese to Britain, which constituted the problem, were just under 150 million New Zealand dollars in 1969, or about 14 per cent of total New Zealand exports. Meat exports to the United States in 1970 were nearly 25 per cent greater in value than butter exports to Britain. Cheese exports to Britain in 1970 were worth less than exports to Australia of manufactured goods.

11. In a letter of 28 May, 1970, Sir Arthur Galsworthy wrote: 'Ever since 1967—indeed especially since 1967—the New Zealanders have achieved remarkable results in diversifying their pattern of exports generally, even though the results of their undoubted efforts to diversify the markets for their dairy products have been exceedingly disappointing. Thus they have doubled the value of their exports of meat, and achieved notable success with other lines, particularly forest products, and manufactures; and there has been steady growth in their tourist trade. With every year that has passed the significance of the New Zealand dairying industry in relation to other segments of their economy has diminished in terms of export earnings.' But he added, and it is fair to add it here: 'The real problem for New Zealand lies in the fact that any substantial scaling down of their dairying industry necessitated by our entry into the EEC, unless it can be accomplished over a lengthy transitional period, will give rise to very serious political, sociological and administrative problems for any New Zealand Government.'

12. A certain scepticism of the validity of the extreme New Zealand case in no way diminished the efforts which all concerned on the British side, officials included, made to get the best possible settlement for New Zealand. Our scepticism, throughout the negotiations and right up to the moment of the final solution, should be seen not so much against the background of an expectation that we would get a settlement—as we did—which would in our view more than meet all New Zealand's requirements, but rather against the background of an expectation that we might fail to do so. Then, we anticipated, we would have to exert ourselves to demonstrate to New Zealand, and to British public

and Parliamentary opinion, that even a settlement less good than they had hoped for was in fact a fair and satisfactory settlement and offered New Zealand all the protection she really needed. As it was, things ended much better for New Zealand than we had dared to hope. The settlement we got for them seemed to me at the time, and seems in retrospect, almost extravagantly favourable. In some respects, as some New Zealanders have admitted, it may have been too favourable even for New Zealand, and may operate to retard the diversification of products and markets which is in any case necessary.

13. We also believed New Zealand would in fact have been content to settle for a good deal less than they eventually got. On 9 March the New Zealand Ambassador in Brussels told me (somewhat incautiously) that he for his part would be very pleased if the opening bid by the Community was no worse than the proposal at that time being put forward by the Commission. This would have given New Zealand 45 per cent of the milk equivalent of their present butter and cheese supplies to our market in 1977, as opposed to the 71 per cent they eventually got. In a telegram from Wellington dated 30 March, 1971, Sir Arthur Galsworthy wrote: 'Our feeling here is that it should in due course be possible to sell the Dutch formula, equivalent to 62 per cent of current exports of butter and cheese, to the New Zealanders.' He added: 'I rather doubt whether anything below the figure of 60 per cent milk equivalent (in 1977) would be thought a tolerable outcome in New Zealand, politically or economically: 60 per cent looks to us at present to be about the breaking point.' They got 71 per cent, decorated with all kinds of delightful last-minute additional garnishings, such as a specially slow run-down for cheese in 1973 and 1974, an unexpectedly firm formula on continuity for butter after 1977, an undertaking by the Community to promote the conclusion of an international agreement on milk products, and another undertaking that the Community would strive not to frustrate New Zealand's efforts towards diversification of its economy and exports.

14. Nor is it enough, to rebut the thesis I am putting forward, simply to say: 'But even as it was the New Zealanders only accepted the outcome rather grudgingly.' This is true, but it was inevitable. In a minute of 26 March, 1971, to Mr. Rippon I wrote of the risk that we were giving New Zealand a veto over our entry into the Community and added: 'It is too much to expect that any agreement we are likely to reach with the Community on New Zealand dairy products will be in the slightest degree popular in New Zealand, or will be easy for the New Zealand Government—especially so weak a one as the present one—to acquiesce in, let alone support. Reluctant and indignant acquiescence in the best of a bad job is perhaps the most we can hope for.' We got a better reaction than that; but then we got much more out of the Community than I was expecting. Even so, the first official New Zealand reactions to the settlement, including especially Mr. Marshall's, were a bit grudging. This should be no surprise. They virtually had to be; and I expect Mr. Marshall had long before decided that, however good the outcome, they would be. All the same, there

seemed before long, in less official reactions from New Zealand, to be a note of positive glee.

15. We were in a dilemma. The New Zealanders had us over a political barrel. They did indeed, to some extent, hold a veto over our entry into the Community. If we accepted a settlement and they rejected it, the chances of Parliamentary approval would be very much diminished. Moreover in the circumstances prevailing we could not possibly, either in our public presentation of the issue here or in our dealings with the Community, cast any scintilla of doubt on the merits of the New Zealand case. We did, towards the end, carefully prepare arguments and statistics to justify a less good outcome—which we expected—than we got. We made a little discreet use of these arguments with the Press in May and June 1971; but in the end we did not need to fall back on them. New Zealand undoubtedly enjoyed extremely strong and widespread political support in this country; and she knew it. Right at the start, in a despatch from Wellington dated 1 July, 1970, Sir Arthur Galsworthy wrote: 'The situation is further complicated by the fact that the present New Zealand Government (whose term of office lasts until October 1972 unless it should be upset as a result of by-elections) is very far from being a strong or effective Administration, and is unlikely to be willing or able to take vigorous steps to persuade public opinion here to accept any solution which falls appreciably short of their present expectations. Rather, I would expect them in such circumstances to devote their energies to mounting a publicity campaign in Britain directed to trying to persuade British opinion to reject entry on such terms.' This was a risk we always had in mind; and from time to time, as the negotiations progressed, we fancied we detected signs of New Zealand preparations to do precisely this.

16. There is little doubt that New Zealand's political support in this country was more widespread and more fundamental, and would have been more effective, than even the support enjoyed by the developing sugar producers. To a certain extent, support for the sugar producers came from the Left and for New Zealand from the Right. But this is an oversimplification. Because New Zealand was small, because she was far away, because of her support in war—for these and many other reasons the way the Community would treat her had become a touchstone, for millions of ordinary people, of their attitude towards our entry. Support for New Zealand ran right across the political spectrum. Mr. Thorpe, the leader of the Liberal Party, suggested to the Prime Minister on 24 May, 1971, that the main difficulty in securing Parliamentary assent to proposals for entry into the Common Market could be over New Zealand. He suggested it might help if Britain were able to offer assistance—say £200 million spread over five years or more—for industrial development in New Zealand. Mr. Duncan Sandys told the French Prime Minister in May 1971 that, though he believed passionately in European unity, he would find it impossible to support an agreement which betrayed New Zealand's trust in Britain. 'Without a generous arrangement for New Zealand ... no settlement, however satisfactory on other points, would stand a chance of being approved by Parliament.' Mr.

Sandys sent copies of his record of this conversation to the Prime Minister, the Foreign Secretary and Mr. Rippon. Mr. Wilson made the alleged inadequacy of our settlement for New Zealand, in terms of its failure to last for a generation, one of his points of strongest attack on the Government.[1]

17. The New Zealanders were confident of the strength of this political support. Mr. Marshall visited M. Schumann in Paris early in June 1971. A few days later, on 15 June, M. Cuvillier, M. Schumann's Chef de Cabinet, remarked to Mr. John Galsworthy of our Embassy that 'Mr. Marshall had left M. Schumann in no doubt whatever of his ability to sway votes at Westminster'. Mr. Marshall was usually too tactful, and too careful, to make this point to us; but not always. At the beginning of the crucial meeting in Luxembourg on 21 June I went to the airport to meet Mr. Marshall on his arrival from Brussels. Driving back with him I told him of the information we had received two days before that the French were prepared to make a major move forward (to a point in terms of milk equivalent even higher than the Dutch had been defending) and asked him, on Mr. Rippon's behalf, if he could accept the new French position. Mr. Marshall, 'while welcoming the news that the French were prepared to move so far, said he would not be prepared to accept their figures. He did not think the House of Commons in London would accept them either.'

18. Mr. Marshall was probably not far out in his appreciation of what the House of Commons would or would not accept. Ministers in London broadly shared his estimate. The New Zealand case was regarded as politically crucial. The Foreign Secretary, when he read the account the New Zealand Prime Minister sent Mr. Rippon of his conversation with M. Pompidou on 26 April, 1971, minuted: 'This is going to be very difficult. I have always felt in my bones that Parliament might reject the whole on the New Zealand question and the French know it.' Earlier that month, Mr. Rippon had prepared a paper on the 'Shape of the Final Package in the EEC Negotiations'. In it he wrote that 'New Zealand could probably be brought to accept diminishing quantities to 60 per cent of the present total in the fifth year but she would expect her income to be maintained and there to be provision for a review or some continuing arrangements after the first five years'. Mr. Rippon went on to suggest that the likely outcome could take two forms, neither providing for even as much as 60 per cent in the fifth year. Commenting on this, the Foreign Secretary wrote: 'I do not think that either of the proposals at present put forward is politically saleable. I do not feel that in the fifth year we could ask New Zealand to go below 70 per cent of current levels in terms of milk equivalent.' This requirement was met; and in the end the milk equivalent in the fifth year was jacked up to about 71 per cent.

[1] This dissatisfaction led to an attempt being made by the Wilson government after it came to power in 1974 to re-open the arrangements in the accession treaty. While no change was made to the quantities established for the transitional period (1973–77), quantitites were established for a further period beyond that (1978–80) i.e. the provisions of paragraph 2 of Article 5 of Protocol 18 were applied by anticipation.

19. Probably we were helped, though it is hard to estimate how much, in achieving this result by the sudden change in the butter supply position. During 1970 and the spring of 1971 the Community's 'butter mountain' suddenly melted away. It dropped from 302,000 tons at the beginning of 1970 to 131,000 tons at the end, and by April 1971 was probably below the Community's 'ideal' stock figure of 100,000 tons. The main reason for the world-wide change was a decline in milk production in the Community itself and in a number of important butter producing countries including Denmark, Australia and New Zealand. Already in November 1970 British supplies of butter were growing short and we had to authorise 5,000 tons of additional imports. What happened can best be demonstrated by the movement of New Zealand butter and cheese prices on the British market. In 1969 the United Kingdom first-hand price for New Zealand bulk butter was £300 per ton. By the end of 1970 it stood at £330 per ton. In 1971 it was increased by successive steps in March, April, May, June, August, October and November to £530 per ton. On 10 January, 1972, it rose to £550 per ton. In the same way New Zealand cheddar cheese, standing at £241 per ton in 1969, rose steadily from May 1970 to £481 per ton (almost exactly double) on 24 January, 1972. In parallel with this process, the Community on 27 March, 1971, abolished its export restitution on bulk butter (which stood at £407 per ton on 1 January, 1971) for all destinations except the United Kingdom; and on 29 April, 1971, it abolished it for exports to the United Kingdom too. If the butter and cheese position should remain indefinitely what it was in June 1971, the month in which we reached our agreement with the Community, then there would have been no need for any special arrangements for New Zealand at all.

20. These developments, while they may have made it easier for the Community to give us the settlement we got for New Zealand, came too late for the United Kingdom to profit by them. In retrospect, one might think the Community should have been able (though of course the whole development in butter supply may prove temporary, and less than a year after our New Zealand settlement was already switching back again in the other direction) to be generous to New Zealand without exacting too high a price for their generosity. But they made us pay for what we got.

21. This is the reason why I have concentrated so much in this chapter on the flaws in the New Zealand case. Why, it may be asked, should we worry? If the New Zealanders in the end got more than they expected, and more than we really believed they deserved, is not this a matter only for satisfaction? It would be but for one factor. We had to pay a high price for it, as a result of the link established by the Community, which we had foreseen and feared for many months, between a settlement on New Zealand and a settlement on Community finance. I will not write more on this subject here; it is referred to in the next chapter, in the chapters on Community Finance and in Chapter 35.

22. Nevertheless, though we may have mixed feelings, the New Zealanders deserve nothing but admiration for the way they manoeuvred towards their

success. By their skill and persistence they deserved it. Their first great problem was to maintain the recognition which, with our help, they established in 1962 that New Zealand was a special case and must receive special treatment. With our help again, they did so throughout the negotiations of 1970 and 1971, and this recognition was not diminished by the changes in New Zealand's economic prospects which had taken place meanwhile. Mr. Marshall played his hand, both economic and political, with coolness, resolution and a certain ruthlessness. His officials sometimes seemed to waver a bit, but Mr. Marshall never. When, from March 1971 onwards, we were urging the New Zealand Government that they must consider what their fall-back position would be, we found a good deal of readiness among New Zealand officials to prepare to do so, though they insisted the process must be left to Mr. Marshall. Even Sir Keith Holyoake, in a conversation with the Foreign Secretary in London on 14 April, himself volunteered that New Zealand would indeed have to consider a fall-back position. But Mr. Marshall resolutely refused to be pinned down. He evaded any discussion of the subject with us—to which we tried, from the beginning of May 1971, to compel him—until almost the very end, and only began to speak tentatively of possible alternatives to New Zealand's full demands in a conversation with Mr. Rippon in London on 14 June. In the two critical days and nights of the Ministerial meeting in Luxembourg from 21 to 23 June, he stood firm and went on asking for more until, in almost every respect, he got it. In my judgment, Mr. Marshall was more successful in the negotiations than anybody else.

BUTTER, CHEESE AND MILK BALANCE FOR EEC AND APPLICANT COUNTRIES, 1969
'000 metric tons
(see paragraph 7 of this chapter)

	Butter			*Cheese*			*Total Milk*		
	Production	*Consumption*	*Surplus/ Deficit*	*Production*	*Consumption*	*Surplus/ Deficit*	*Production*	*Consumption*[1]	*Surplus/ Deficit*
The Six	1,325	1,100[2]	+215	1,575[2]	1,525[5]	+50[5]	73,308	66,941[2]	+6,366
Denmark	147	46	+101	109	46	+63	4,868	2,107	+2,761
Norway	19	19	Nil	46	28	+18	1,755	1,592	+164
Irish Republic	74	30	+44	112	27	+85	3,745	2,434	+1,311
The Three	240	95	+145	267	101	+166	10,369	6,133	+4,236
United Kingdom[4]	60	466	−406	123	284	−161	12,826	25,185	−12,359[6]
The Ten	1,625	1,671	−46	1,965	1,910	+55	96,503	98,259	−1,756

1 Includes milk fed to stock except in United Kingdom.
2 Excludes about 90,000 tons of butter sold withaid of subsidy.
3 Estimate based upon 1968 date.
4 Year ending March 1970.
5 Excludes curd. 6 Of which New Zealand supplied 46 per cent.

16

New Zealand: Negotiations and Outcome

Having dealt at some length in the previous chapter with the background, it may not be necessary in this chapter, long though it is bound to be, to deal in too much detail with the negotiations. Some interesting twists and turns in our negotiations with New Zealand will accordingly have to be omitted. I say with New Zealand, because in fact we negotiated far more with New Zealand than with the Community. Our continual contacts with New Zealand Ministers and officials were described as consultations, or keeping closely in touch; but they were in fact, at least in the first and in the final stages, negotiations in the fullest sense. With the Community the usual pattern prevailed: a preliminary factual paper by us and formal comments thereon by the Commission; a formal proposal by us on 6 November, 1971; a proposal by the Commission in their 'Vue d'ensemble' of 17 November, 1970; and then a long gap till eventually and suddenly a solution was reached in June 1971. This gap was filled, as usual, by occasional formal statements from our side in the Conference in support of our proposals; by continual informal conversations and consultations in capitals and corridors; by continual negotiation, mostly by the Permanent Representatives, among the Six themselves; and by steady pressure on us from New Zealand.

2. As usual again, the story begins with Mr. Brown's statement of 4 July, 1967. What he said on New Zealand was as follows:

> 'Turning to New Zealand: in 1962, and again when the Prime Minister and I visited the capitals of the Community countries in the first months of this year, we found general recognition that her case was of an altogether special kind, and should be treated by the Community as such. I do not believe that this should present the Community with problems which we cannot resolve together. New Zealand's economy largely depends on her trade in butter, cheese and lamb. Because of the size of the British market for dairy produce, we believe that provisions for exports of butter and cheese from New Zealand would in no way be inconsistent with substantial benefits accruing to other members of a wider Community; and we shall need to discuss such provisions with you. In the case of cheese it may be found that in practice there will be little or no problem. But we could turn out to be wrong about this. So we

shall ask you to agree to a review procedure to enable action to be taken if it is necessary. For butter, more precise provision will have to be made. I am confident that in discussion together we can find a constructive and realistic solution. Community farmers have a strong interest with New Zealand in wishing to see the level of butter consumption maintained in Europe.'

3. This formulation, by 1970 at least, had become very unpopular with the New Zealand Government. They thought it deficient on lamb; and they did not like the passage on cheese. They maintained that cheese must be treated in the same way as butter. On the whole they were right, because, as Mr. Brown had foreseen, the situation had changed. Production of cheddar in Community countries for our market, negligible in 1967, had increased considerably in the Netherlands and in France. Although the quantities they sent us in 1968 and early 1969 were still small compared with those coming from our traditional suppliers, they were enough to contribute to a disruption of the market, and had caused us to introduce, in 1969, the 'voluntary restraint arrangements' for cheddar cheese which established fixed shares of our market for its various suppliers.

4. As soon as the possibility of successful negotiations emerged in 1969, the New Zealanders were afoot. In October 1969 Mr. Marshall visited London. It was to be the first of four visits he made to Europe before the negotiations ended. He was here again in July 1970; in October and November 1970; and in May and June 1971. On most of these occasions he visited Brussels and various capitals of the Community and the other applicant countries as well as London. And he was in at the death at Luxembourg at the final meeting on 21–23 June, 1971.

5. Early in 1970, along with all the other briefs, we began refurbishing the brief on New Zealand. It was eventually circulated on 29 June to the AE Committee. After describing the problem, the brief went on: 'The essential need is to provide New Zealand with a breathing space long enough for her to have a reasonable chance to make the necessary painful adjustments to her economy and in the meantime to have reasonable outlets for her existing dairy industry.' The conclusion of the brief was very like the conclusion of the sugar brief:

'Our negotiating objective should therefore be to maintain New Zealand earnings from butter and cheese at their present level for a period lasting for some years beyond the end of the agricultural transitional period, with provision for review of subsequent arrangements.'

Once again, we contemplated a reduction in outlets in our market coupled with an increase in price to maintain total earnings. This would, we knew—and so it proved—be extremely unpopular with New Zealand, because maintained earnings would be no real compensation for the elimination of a large proportion of the dairy industry. But once again, as in the case of sugar, our opening bid was different; and we were never obliged formally to avow this purpose either to the New Zealanders or to the Community. In the end, rather accidentally, this was much what was achieved; but the increase in the price for New Zealand was the consequence less of negotiation than of the natural movement of the market price for butter and cheese throughout 1971.

6. In April 1970 Mr. Marshall asked to visit the United Kingdom again and it was arranged he should come to London early in June. But then came the dissolution of Parliament and the election campaign, and his visit was postponed. Nevertheless it was agreed to hold discussions with New Zealand officials in London pending Mr. Marshall's later arrival, and these discussions took place on four or five separate occasions between 9 and 17 June. They were rather formal and extremely detailed. Mr. Moriarty, Secretary of the New Zealand Department of Industries and Commerce, led the New Zealand Delegation; and I led the group of British officials. The objective of the New Zealand officials was to force our hand and commit us to various far-reaching negotiating objectives. They were particularly concerned about the way in which we should deal with New Zealand in our opening statement on 30 June; they wanted to promote cheese from the position Mr. Brown had left it in three years earlier; they tried promoting lamb into a matter for the negotiations, and to commit us to securing a reduction of the 20 per cent common external tariff on lamb. They wanted us to accept the objective of trying to change the nature of the Common Agricultural Policy in respect of dairy products during our negotiations; and they made clear their repugnance at any deal which should involve a reduced volume of exports of butter and cheese compensated by a higher price. They tried also to secure our agreement that New Zealand should take part in our negotiations with the Community on her problems.

7. We resisted most of these objectives; and at the end of the meetings the New Zealanders expressed their disappointment with them, which Sir Keith Holyoake repeated in a message to Mr. Heath. Our official discussions clarified one other issue. It was theoretically possible that New Zealand's problem could be settled by a form of preferential association with the Community, or indeed by a trade agreement. These possibilities were known as 'the institutional approach'. We asked the New Zealanders if they were interested in these ideas, hoping, as we did, to receive a negative reply. However satisfactory preferential arrangements of this kind might have been to New Zealand (if they were obtainable which was hardly likely), the New Zealanders could not afford to ask for them because of their important trading relations with other countries, and in particular because of their free trade agreement with Australia.

8. Mr. Marshall arrived in London on 6 July. Mr. Barber's opening statement of 30 June had meanwhile been made. He had referred briefly to 'New Zealand's special problems', and the New Zealanders accepted that this was 'satisfactory at this stage'. Mr. Marshall had two long meetings with Mr. Barber on 7 and 9 July, in which he rehearsed the New Zealand problem at great length. He urged us to make a full 'statement of claim' on behalf of New Zealand at the first

bilateral Ministerial meeting due to take place on 21 July. He pressed particularly hard on lamb. We continued to maintain, while recognising the vital importance of lamb exports for New Zealand—they were about as important as butter and cheese exports put together—that it would be extremely unwise to raise lamb in the negotiations. We maintained that, because of the prospective rise in meat prices in our market after entry, New Zealand's trade in lamb would continue equally profitably over the 20 per cent tariff which in any case, we explained, was necessary for our own lamb producers, who would be losing much of the protection they now enjoyed in the form of deficiency payments on lamb and a guaranteed price for wool. We agreed, however, as we had already told New Zealand officials, that if the Community were to produce a sheepmeat regulation during our negotiations (as they were obliged by the Common Agricultural Policy to do at some stage) this would produce a new situation which we should have to discuss with New Zealand. To meet New Zealand's concern on lamb, Mr. Marshall and Mr. Barber agreed on a joint statement, issued to the Press, which included the following sentence: 'The special position of New Zealand rests on its extreme dependence on the British market for its exports of butter, cheese and lamb and the vital role which these products play in preserving the economic and social well-being of New Zealand.' A passage in these terms was included by Mr. Barber in the statement he made at the Ministerial meeting on 21 July.

9. At this point, to avoid too much later reference to it, I should explain that the question of lamb, though we deliberately never raised it formally with the Community, haunted our negotiations with them about New Zealand from beginning to end. The Community were indeed, and had for some time been, considering the introduction of a sheepmeat regulation, as a result of pressure from France. While an appropriate sheepmeat regulation could have been of much advantage to New Zealand, we and they feared that, if it were introduced in a form best suited to French interests, its pricing arrangements might be such as to do immense damage to New Zealand trade. Throughout the negotiations, from time to time, the introduction of a sheepmeat regulation appeared imminent. We steadily refused to raise the matter formally in the Conference, insisting to the New Zealanders that we could not breach our principle of not negotiating about 'spectres'—the Community's hypothetical future arrangements. But from November 1970 onwards we continually let the Community and all its member Governments know informally how dangerous it might be for them to proceed with a sheepmeat regulation. This was made clear especially to the Commission: on separate occasions Mr. Rippon put the point extremely forcibly to Signor Malfatti and Dr. Mansholt. The Commission took the point, and did their best to stall. But French pressure continued from time to time, and New Zealand anxieties rose and fell with it They were not allayed until in June 1971 M. Schumann himself told Mr. Marshall that the French would not seek a sheepmeat regulation during our negotiations; whereupon New Zealand fears were transferred from the period of the negotiations to the interim period

between signature of the Treaty and our accession. This, we assured the New Zealanders, would be looked after by our agreed arrangements for the interim period. But they insisted nevertheless on some statement to this effect to which they could refer; and it was finally provided in paragraph 76 of the White Paper we published in July 1971. As for the 20 per cent common external tariff on lamb, the New Zealanders continued for long to grumble about the damage it would do them; and not till the late spring of 1971 did they finally accept that it was reasonable that we should not challenge it.[1]

10. Late in July Mr. Rippon succeeded Mr. Barber, and all the hard work Mr. Marshall had put in on the latter was lost. In September Mr. Rippon took up the invitation Mr. Marshall had given to Mr. Barber, and visited New Zealand. On the same journey he spent a few days in Hong Kong and in Australia. Mr. Marshall had also invited me to New Zealand; and I spent six days there with Mr. Rippon, between two meetings of the Deputies in Brussels. We received in New Zealand the same thorough indoctrination from Ministers and officials that Mr. Barber had had in London in July; and we also saw innumerable cows and sheep.

11. In September we circulated to the Conference in Brussels a detailed paper, with a long statistical appendix, on the consequences of the enlargement of the Community for dairy products—that is to say on the problem of New Zealand. This paper is described in paragraph 7 of the previous chapter. In its later comments on our paper the Commission made no attempt to challenge its figures or arguments. One incidental objective of our paper was to refute an argument the French used from time to time, and which we had heard from M. Schumann in August. He had said the New Zealand problem was perfectly simple: all they had to do was to export their butter and cheese to Japan instead of to the United Kingdom. Our paper therefore said: 'For example, in the new development plan promulgated by the Japanese planning agency in 1969 it was envisaged that the four or five-fold rise in demand for beef, milk and dairy products expected between 1965 and 1985 would be met largely, if not entirely, by increased livestock numbers in Japan itself.' In fact, the small outlets for dairy products in Japan, which the New Zealanders had worked hard to secure, had been steadily dwindling in recent years. Nevertheless, the notion that Japan was the answer to New Zealand's dairy products problem was not extinguished, and continued to crop up from time to time.

12. Mr. Marshall was back again in Europe late in October and in November. After a visit to London (he had a long conversation with Mr. Rippon on 30 October) he was to tour the Community. This fact had some influence on the timing of the proposal we had decided to put forward to the Conference. We had concluded that we must begin by asking for the maintenance of existing

[1] The decision not to raise the question of sheepmeat in the accession negotiations was fully justified by the subsequent course of events. Not only was no European Community sheepmeat regulation adopted either during the accession negotiations or during the interim period, but a market regulation for sheepmeat was not finally adopted until 1982.

levels of access to our market for New Zealand butter and cheese. We had no illusion that we could secure these; but to ask for less would have involved immense difficulties with New Zealand. We felt it would be as well that our proposal should be on the table in the Conference before Mr. Marshall toured Europe, so that he could find out for himself how small was the chance of it being accepted. Mr. Marshall was informed in advance of our proposal, and of course he found it entirely satisfactory. It was also made perfectly clear to him from the start that we did not believe we could possibly get the Community to concede so much.

13. Our proposal was tabled in Brussels on 6 November. It explained that New Zealand's basic entitlement for butter imports into the United Kingdom was 172,720 metric tons, and under the voluntary restraint arrangement she was currently sending 76,200 metric tons of cheddar cheese. These figures represented the equivalent of just over 4,945,000 metric tons of milk. We proposed that, for the duration of the agreed transitional period for the adaptation by the United Kingdom to the Common Agricultural Policy of the Community, New Zealand should have the opportunity to sell annually to the enlarged Community these quantities of butter and cheese. A review should be held 12 months before the end of the agricultural transitional period in order to ensure the continuance of arrangements to meet New Zealand's interest in the exports of butter and cheese to the enlarged Community.

14. This proposal did not forestall by more than a week or two the Commission's 'Vue d'ensemble' paper of 17 November on the main problems of the negotiations. This paper has already been referred to, and will be again. From our point of view, it was good in one part only—namely sugar, as described in Chapters 12 and 13 above. It was extremely bad on Community finance. It was bad on New Zealand too. The Commission proposed degressive access for New Zealand butter to our market over a five-year transitional period so that, by the end of the period, it 'will not have decreased by more than 50 per cent'. For cheddar, there should be total abolition of quantitative guarantees at the end of the five years. New Zealand should receive compensation through gradually higher prices over the five years. The Community should try to promote, immediately on enlargement, an international agreement on dairy products in order to improve for New Zealand the conditions ruling on the world market. If no such agreement could be reached, the institutions of the enlarged Community should examine and decide on measures to be taken at the end of the five years.

15. The scene was now set for the ensuing struggle. The New Zealanders, of course, found the Commission's proposals deeply distasteful. When Mr. Marshall returned to London after his European tour—he admitted that none of the Governments concerned had, in conversations with him, said they would accept our proposal, but insisted that equally none of them had said that they rejected it—his main objective, in conversations with Mr. Rippon and the Prime Minister, was to elicit an undertaking from us that we would stick rigorously to

our own proposal. He was by now, in the light of developments in the butter supply position, beginning to press the argument that Community milk production would continue over the years to decline, and that in eight or ten years' time the Community would need New Zealand production. Why therefore cripple it in the interval? But on 24 November Mr. Rippon told Mr. Marshall that, though we had put in the highest possible bid for New Zealand, 'at some stage one must face up to reality'.

16. On the following day discussion of the problem began among the Permanent Representatives in Brussels, and it continued inconclusively for the next six months. The different members of the Community adopted different positions. From the start, the Dutch were much the most generous, and the French the least. As these were the two countries which had the greatest interest, among Community members, in exporting dairy products to our market, the Dutch deserve great credit for their attitude. The visit of Mr. de Koster, the Minister of State in the Dutch Foreign Office, to New Zealand in August and September 1970 had perhaps helped to turn him into the staunch champion of the New Zealand case which he became; and in this context the fact that a considerable number of Dutchmen had emigrated to New Zealand since the war, and in many cases established themselves in dairy farming there, may have helped. Mr. de Koster and Mr. Marshall remained in close touch throughout the negotiations. There was a somewhat strange episode in April 1971 when Mr. de Koster assured Mr. Rippon, in The Hague, that the proposals the Dutch were then supporting in Brussels (which would have provided for the export of about 62 per cent of New Zealand butter and cheese in terms of milk equivalent in 1977) had been accepted by Mr. Marshall as adequate to meet New Zealand requirements. When later Mr. Rippon taxed Mr. Marshall with this, he denied it; and he wrote to Mr. de Koster to repeat his denial. Mr. de Koster still seemed to believe that he had in fact had Mr. Marshall's agreement; but he was not discouraged and continued to fight loyally for New Zealand, though he told Sir Edward Tomkins on 18 June that it would be embarrassing for the Dutch Government to have to support in public even higher New Zealand claims, 'their interest in the British market being greater than that of any other member of the Community'.

17. But Mr. de Koster soldiered loyally on. It cannot have been easy for him. He had told me six months earlier, on 8 December, 1970, that the opening Dutch position—70 per cent of existing quantities of butter only for New Zealand after five years—had only been established in the Netherlands Cabinet 'after a great fight in which he and Lardinois had opposed each other'. Mr. Lardinois was the Dutch Minister of Agriculture. After the formation of a new Netherlands Government at the end of June 1971, Dr. Luns disappeared and Mr. de Koster became Minister of Defence. But Mr. Lardinois remained Minister of Agriculture. From that time on the Dutch line in the whole negotiations was very different; but the question of New Zealand had already been solved.

18. In the meeting of the Permanent Representatives on 25 November no

Delegation tabled formal proposals in respect of New Zealand, but the negative French attitude was made extremely clear. Over the next two months, the national attitudes of the Six developed. By 26 February, 1971, a consensus had been reached that there should be a derogation in favour of New Zealand, that it should last for the five years transitional period and that the quantities of New Zealand dairy products covered by the derogation should be degressive over this period. The Commission, Belgium, Luxembourg and Germany wanted the derogation to cover cheese as well as butter. The Dutch (by now joined by the Italians) wanted it to cover the milk equivalent of New Zealand's current butter exports to the United Kingdom, leaving it to New Zealand whether they should use some of this guaranteed access for cheese. The French wanted the derogation to relate only to butter. As for the degree of degressivity in the transitional period, the Commission were still maintaining that butter should be reduced by 1977 to 50 per cent of present exports to the United Kingdom and cheese to nil. The Dutch and the Italians supported a reduction to the milk equivalent of 70 per cent of present New Zealand butter exports. The Germans, Belgians and Luxembourgers were in general supporting the Commission. The French wanted butter reduced to zero at the end of the transitional period, and no derogation of any sort on cheese.

19. A fortnight later, on 12 March, positions had not much altered. The Commission had not moved; their proposal would have given New Zealand in 1977 a guarantee of 44 per cent of current exports in terms of milk equivalent. The Dutch and Italians, arguing for 70 per cent of the milk equivalent of New Zealand exports of butter, were offering 56 per cent of milk equivalent in 1977. The French position was still no guarantee at all for cheese and butter to reach zero in 1978; this represented a guarantee of 17 per cent of milk equivalent in 1977. The Germans, Belgians and Luxembourgers were still, with minor variations, supporting the Commission. The New Zealanders were of course as well aware of these developments as we. They were alarmed by them. On 17 February, 1971, Mr. Marshall wrote to Mr. Rippon urging that we should make a strong statement at a Deputies meeting. Mr. Rippon replied on 5 March agreeing that this would be done, and that he would also make a statement at the next Ministerial meeting. Accordingly, statements in strong terms urging the merits of our own proposal were made by me at a Deputies meeting on 9 March and by Mr. Rippon at the Ministerial meeting a week later. This gratified the New Zealanders considerably; but probably played little part, beyond what general pressure was in any case contributing, in changing positions within the Community.

20. However, they did change. Meetings of the Permanent Representatives on 25 and 26 March saw significant movement. On 25 March the Dutch accepted the view of their partners that the guarantee should be expressed in specific quantities of both butter and cheese, and proposed 70 per cent of New Zealand's current butter exports to the United Kingdom and 20 per cent of New Zealand's current cheese exports for 1977. The Italians immediately

supported this new Dutch proposal; the Luxembourgers and Germans showed readiness to move up from their previous position. Only the Belgians stuck with the Commission. The French too made no move. Before very long, the example of the Dutch and Italians had drawn the Germans and Luxembourgers upwards, and by early May all but the Belgians and French were supporting the Dutch proposal. We exercised various forms of pressure on the Belgians, and at last they too moved up to join the Dutch, leaving the Commission and the French in their original positions. As in the case of the Dutch, the Belgian position was the result of an inter-Ministerial struggle, which in the six months till May was won by the Belgian Minister of Agriculture, M. Héger. (After holding this post interruptedly since 1960 M. Héger finally left the Belgian Government the day before we signed our Treaty of Accession in January 1972; things might have been marginally easier for us, and not only in respect of New Zealand, if he had left a year earlier.) In May also a new gambit—long anticipated—appeared from Paris. The French floated the idea that instead of a five-year transitional period, with zero in year six, there should be a transitional period of eight or nine years before access for New Zealand butter was cut off.

21. By now we hoped it had been borne in on the New Zealand Government that there was no possibility of agreement to our formal proposal. On 18 March Sir Arthur Galsworthy asked Mr. Lloyd White (the Deputy Secretary in the New Zealand Foreign Ministry who, with Mr. Moriarty, was Mr. Marshall's principal adviser on these issues and who also accompanied him on all his trips to Europe) whether any thought was being given in Wellington to the kind of compromise solution that would not be too painful or unbearable for New Zealand. Mr. Lloyd White replied that officials in the Ministry of Foreign Affairs were beginning to feel that the time had come when they should start thinking seriously about this, although he thought New Zealand Ministers might not yet be ready to face up to the problem. We encouraged Sir Arthur Galsworthy to pursue these probings. On 30 March, as recorded in the preceding chapter, he expressed the view that it should in due course be possible to sell the Dutch formula (62 per cent of current exports of butter and cheese in 1977) to the New Zealanders, adding that '60 per cent looks to us at present to be about the breaking point'. I have already described in the previous chapter how Ministers in London came to feel, as a result of increasing political and Parliamentary pressures, that 62 per cent would not suffice. And indeed, as time passed, Sir Arthur Galsworthy too was forced to change his view. He had stuck to it and repeated it as late as 10 June, 1971; but on 21 June, within a few hours of the opening of the crucial meeting in Luxembourg, he had to report that New Zealand opinion had hardened, and a good deal of it was 'now probably fairly confident of a settlement based on anyhow 75 per cent of present dairy trade with provision for review'.

22. I have no doubt that Sir Arthur Galsworthy was right and that New Zealand expectations had grown in the previous couple of months, as their political leaders and their Press had hardened their views and hopes. A lesson

seems to emerge from our experience with the politically critical topics of our negotiations—fisheries and finance as well as New Zealand. It is that—as in the more bitter of industrial disputes—the passage of time means that more not less has to be paid for a settlement. In the end, both for New Zealand and fisheries, we made the Community pay more; but in the case of New Zealand we had also to pay more ourselves.

23. By April, we felt, the New Zealanders were consciously stepping up their pressure on British public opinion as well as on the British Government; though in a formal respect they never overstepped the bounds of decorum. Sir Keith Holyoake arrived in London on 12 April. He had interviews with the Prime Minister and Mr. Rippon; and he saw M. Pompidou in Paris on 26 April. M. Pompidou took a hard line on New Zealand, but he said something which looked more significant in the light of the later meeting between Mr. Heath and M. Pompidou than it did at the time. M. Pompidou told Sir Keith that: 'If he were to look at French farming in the long term, he might be tempted to talk about cheese more than butter'.

24. On 30 April Mr. Marshall told Sir Arthur Galsworthy that the Dutch proposal would be 'acceptable as a start'. By this he meant it would be a tolerable opening bid by the Community; but he went on to say that New Zealand was not prepared to accept less than present quantities. Sir Arthur Galsworthy told him that sooner or later New Zealand would have to start thinking in terms of a realistic compromise. It would be better to face and examine this problem now, rather than leave it to a last-minute scramble. Mr. Marshall finally said that he recognised this problem would have to be faced, and that he would be ready to discuss it with Mr. Rippon when next he went to London—though he added that this should not be until the Six had given a formal response to our proposals. From this point on Mr. Marshall became increasingly reluctant to be pinned down to a discussion of fall-back positions, and he continued with much success to evade our efforts to force him to face the issue.

25. By now the meeting between Mr. Heath and M. Pompidou was imminent, though of course the New Zealanders did not know it. We decided it would be important to press Mr. Marshall further before the Ministerial meeting in Brussels on 11 and 12 May. Accordingly, on 3 May, Sir Arthur Galsworthy was instructed—since Sir Keith Holyoake had said that Mr. Marshall was ready to pack his bags and come to London at any time—to invite Mr. Marshall to come to London at once for talks with Mr. Rippon on 7 and 8 May. Mr. Marshall resolutely declined. He did not understand the hurry. He could not in any case get away. He did not expect any developments at next week's Ministerial meeting which would make it necessary for New Zealand to be rushed into a decision. It would be time enough for him to come to London when the Six had reacted to the British proposals. On 8 May the meeting between Mr. Heath and M. Pompidou fixed for 20 and 21 May was announced; and probably Mr. Marshall understood why we had pressed him to come so quickly. In any case, when Mr. Rippon offered to see him in London on 18 May,

Mr. Marshall accepted. He left New Zealand on 14 May, and did not return until 29 June, after the negotiations on New Zealand had been concluded in Luxembourg.

26. Early in May Ministers in London had reviewed the position. They were by now extremely conscious of the pressures that had developed in public and Parliamentary opinion in support of New Zealand. They decided only that before we indicated to the Six our readiness to move to a compromise solution, it would be necessary to have further discussions with Mr. Marshall in London. These discussions did not as it turned out change things much. Mr. Marshall renewed his pressure on lamb; he needed some assurance in the negotiations that New Zealand's trade in lamb would continue. He continued to evade any commitment on a fall-back position for butter and cheese, but he told the Prime Minister on 17 May that New Zealand would not regard it as an unreasonable opening if the Six were to agree on the Dutch position. They would then hope we could get the Community to move higher, and it would be very difficult for New Zealand if the Community refused to do so. By now Mr. Marshall and New Zealand officials had at least come to acknowledge the inevitability of some compromise on quantities. But by now too Mr. Marshall—having for so long rejected the idea that higher prices should compensate for lower quantities—was stressing strongly how essential it was that, if quantities went down at all, New Zealand should receive higher prices. He was also engaged with our help in a campaign directed towards the Six to prove that New Zealand was no longer, as the Six were still inclined to believe, one of the richest countries in the world in terms of income per head. It had been 12 years earlier (fifth in the world league, when we were seventh). But by now it had dropped to fifteenth place, even faster than our own decline to thirteenth. This was mainly, but perhaps not entirely, due to the way the terms of trade had moved against agricultural producers.

27. Two days after he saw the Prime Minister, Mr. Marshall saw Mr. Rippon and his tune had changed a little. 'He hoped the Community would not put forward the Dutch proposal. If this happened he would have to say it was unacceptable.' He pressed hard for higher prices; and he changed his insistence on some assurance about lamb in the negotiations to a readiness to accept a unilateral assurance from us. This led, after complicated negotiations with New Zealand officials in London, to paragraphs 109 and 110 of our White Paper of July 1971.

28. When Mr. Heath and M. Pompidou met in Paris on 20 and 21 May, they discussed New Zealand thoroughly. An understanding emerged that M. Pompidou would be prepared to offer New Zealand more generous treatment; but it was clear that this was linked in M. Pompidou's mind to the outcome of discussions on Community finance. M. Pompidou made it clear to Mr. Heath that, as between butter and cheese, the French were more concerned about the latter. On 24 May Mr. Marshall saw the Prime Minister again, with Mr. Rippon; and that afternoon he saw the Foreign Secretary. Sir Alec Douglas-Home told

him it would be impossible to get any but a fair deal for New Zealand through the House of Commons.

29. Four weeks remained before the crucial Ministerial meeting in Luxembourg. During them, with two exceptions, relatively little significant movement on the New Zealand problem took place. We had complicated and repeated discussions with New Zealand officials in London. Mr. Marshall went to The Hague and saw Mr. de Koster on 17 June. He had further discussions with Mr. Rippon in London on 3, 14 and 18 June, in the course of which he made it absolutely clear that a longer transitional period for New Zealand, with degression at the end of it to zero, was quite unacceptable. In Brussels, things hung fire; it was clear that the French—who, apart from floating the idea of a longer transitional period degressive to zero, never formally moved from their earlier position until the Luxembourg meeting—were determined not to show their hand until the crunch came. The Commission, embarrassed at finding themselves in a less generous position towards New Zealand than that adopted by Five out of the Six Member countries, concentrated, with encouragement from us, on some of the peripheral but immensely significant elements of a New Zealand deal other than quantities. These were—and simultaneously the New Zealanders were pressing these points with us in London—the nature and conditions of a review clause, the question of an international agreement on dairy products and the possibility of some undertaking that the Community would not thwart market diversification by New Zealand through subsidised dairy products exports. In New Zealand itself, as Sir Arthur Galsworthy reported, there were stirrings of criticism of the Government's line. Some distinguished private New Zealanders (beginning with Sir Edmund Hillary) and a few New Zealand journalists expressed their repugnance at their Government's passive and lachrymose attitude, and their confidence that New Zealand could deal with its economic problems whatever the outcome of the negotiations in Brussels. The New Zealand Government, compelled by the even stronger line adopted by the official Opposition, rebuked these stirrings and, though we carefully noted them against the worst case, they had no influence on the outcome.

30. The two exceptions referred to above were the following. First of all, the AE Committee met again on 3 June to consider a further paper on New Zealand. This paper stated: 'The New Zealand Government would probably be well content, as far as their economic interests are concerned, with a figure between 60 per cent and 70 per cent. But they will not be prepared to say publicly that a figure of this order is acceptable.' Yet that was by now the requirement: not merely to get a satisfactory settlement but to get a settlement which the New Zealand Government would publicly endorse. The paper accordingly recommended that we must seek a solution which would give New Zealand not less than 70 per cent in terms of milk equivalent in 1977. In a brief for Mr. Rippon on this paper the dilemma was summed up as follows: 'The New Zealand Government's weak position, the increasingly critical attitude of the Opposition

in Wellington, and the position which the New Zealanders believe they enjoy in Parliament here, mean that they are most unlikely to say publicly that they find acceptable any offer which the Community are likely to make to us. They could hardly reject an offer of 90 per cent; but we shall not get 90 per cent. A lower figure would be likely to be criticised, whether it was 60 per cent or 70 per cent.' Ministers approved the proposals in the paper on 3 June; and Mr. Rippon was saddled with what seemed an almost impossible task. The second exception came just a week later, and made Mr. Rippon's task look not quite so insuperable. On 10 June M. Schumann at last began talking turkey to Mr. Soames. He moved up to 50 per cent in 1977, adding that if the Community were to have to agree to this the French could not come down below 9 per cent as the figure for our financial contribution in 1973: it was thus that he saw a package deal being struck

31. Mr. Soames argued vigorously against both these proposals; and by 18 June M. Schumann had moved much further. He told Mr. Soames that he had been working on a new proposal on which he intended to seek M. Pompidou's approval. The proposal was that cheese (which up to now the French had excluded altogether) should be reduced by 20 per cent per annum, thus reaching zero in 1977; butter would be reduced by five per cent per annum down to 75 per cent in 1977. (This was better even than the current Dutch proposal; it amounted to almost 63 per cent in terms of milk equivalent in 1977, as opposed to almost 62 per cent.) There would also be review provisions. Having gone as far as this on New Zealand, he would have to ask us to agree to a first year's contribution to the budget of 9 per cent. Could Mr. Soames reach agreement with him before Monday 21 June on a package deal along these lines? Mr. Soames said he was afraid it would not be possible. We needed more on New Zealand and less on the budget. M. Schumann later telephoned him to say that M. Pompidou had agreed to his New Zealand formula provided we would accept an initial contribution of 9 per cent.

32. When Mr. Marshall saw Mr. Rippon alone in London on 14 June, he at last unveiled a little of his thinking on a fall-back position. At this time, not yet knowing that the French were prepared to move on cheese, we were pressing the New Zealanders to consider dropping quantitative guarantees for cheese altogether in exchange for a higher figure for butter. Mr. Marshall was prepared to consider this on a variety of conditions. As for butter, Mr. Marshall said that his Cabinet would probably agree to degressivity down to 85 per cent of present quantities at the end of a five-year transitional period. Mr. Marshall and Mr. Rippon agreed that Mr. Marshall should be present in Luxembourg during the Ministerial meeting.

33. This meeting—the most critical, and in the end the most successful, of the whole negotiation—began late on 21 June. Mr. Marshall arrived earlier that day from Brussels; I have already recorded in the previous chapter his immediate rejection of the latest French proposals as we knew them. This hardly surprised us. In the early hours of the following morning the Community put forward its

first proposal on New Zealand. This already constituted an advance beyond even the latest French proposal. It proposed 75 per cent for butter and 20 per cent (instead of zero) for cheese in 1977, that is to say some 66 per cent in terms of milk equivalent. There was to be a review in 1976 and a unanimous decision of the Council would be needed to maintain quantitative guarantees for butter beyond 1977. There would be no such guarantees for cheese. Quantities of butter and cheese could be varied provided the total milk equivalent was preserved. The whole proposal was made subject to a satisfactory agreement on the British contribution to the Community budget.

34. Mr. Marshall and his advisers had been flitting in and out of the Conference building by a back door to consult with the British Delegation. As soon as we told him of the Community's proposal he categorically rejected it. Mr. Rippon accordingly, about 4 a.m. on 22 June, told the Conference that he welcomed their movement towards our position but that their figures and their statement generally were unsatisfactory; we would revert to the matter later in the day. Meanwhile knowledge of the 66 per cent proposal had reached New Zealand, and provoked a strongly hostile reaction. '66 per cent is just too hard a blow', said a speaker on New Zealand Radio. And Sir Keith Holyoake, in a long television interview, said: 'I want to make this point, that immediately Mr. Marshall made the comment that this is unacceptable to New Zealand, I and the whole of the Cabinet and Dairy Board too have strongly confirmed this. This is the opening position of the Six countries of the Common Market and we argue from there.'

35. Later in the morning of 22 June Mr. Marshall and Mr. Rippon had a further long interview. Mr. Rippon agreed to table a new proposal in the Conference that day which would aim at getting 71 per cent milk equivalent in 1977. He told Mr. Marshall that our chances of getting this were not good. (The previous night's experience justified this pessimism. M. Schumann, Chairman of the Conference, had been behaving in a strangely hysterical fashion, with dire threats of disaster and breakdown directed to the Five and leaked to the Press.) He agreed with Mr. Marshall that we should aim at 80 per cent for butter and 20 per cent for cheese in the fifth year, since Mr. Marshall preferred this; but Mr. Marshall said he might be prepared to accept 85 per cent for butter and zero for cheese in 1977 as an alternative. Mr. Marshall agreed to put to his Government that if we got a 71 per cent milk equivalent result they should accept and welcome it. He told Mr. Rippon his previous instructions only allowed him to accept 75 per cent milk equivalent. In our new paper to the Conference, we omitted any reference to a unanimous decision for continuation after 1977; and we made it clear that this would be hard to accept.

36. By now the luck was running New Zealand's way. The Commission, perhaps unaware how far the French Government and the other Governments would be prepared to go on quantities, had been concentrating on the surrounding arrangements, in respect of which the Community's first proposal had been notably barren. In frequent contacts with all concerned in the corridors we

encouraged this process. Meanwhile the Governments were moving too. Late at night on 22 June, they completed and passed to us their new proposals. With Mr. Marshall's agreement (save on the question of price: see below) we accepted them. They were subject of course, as before, to 'satisfactory agreement being reached on the amount of the United Kingdom contribution to Community financing'. This final proposal from the Community accepted Mr. Rippon's proposal of 80 per cent for butter and 20 per cent for cheese, making 71 per cent milk equivalent, in 1977. It also contained all the other agreeable provisions relating to the timing and conditions for a review; to the virtual guarantee of continuity for butter after 1977; to efforts by the Community to achieve a world agreement on milk products and not to frustrate New Zealand's progress towards diversification of its economy and markets—all of which now feature in Protocol No. 18 to the Act of Accession. The Community's proposal said nothing about unanimity being required for a decision on continuity after 1977; but they asked us to accept in return for its elimination, and we did so, that the minutes of the Conference should record agreement that this decision should in fact be taken unanimously. This caused trouble with New Zealand later.

37. The formula the Community proposed on price was (as Protocol No. 18 records) that it should be such as to 'enable New Zealand to realise a price representing the average price (for butter and cheese) obtained by that country on the United Kingdom market during 1969, 1970, 1971 and 1972'. We had already, in contacts in the corridors, got the Community to drop the year 1968 from this catalogue. But the four years left in still included two (1969 and 1970) of low prices. Mr. Marshall begged Mr. Rippon to get 1969 struck out, and he agreed to try. To my surprise—for by now the Community were in a thoroughly giving mood—they refused. Had Mr. Rippon made this request in person to the Conference I think he would have got his way. But at this stage our various assents and dissents and the Community's reactions thereto were being ferried to and fro between our Delegation office and the Six by M. Deniau. We heard later that he represented our request as only halfhearted, which was not the case. But in retrospect I find it hard to regret this failure. Success would have meant still more for us to pay.

38. One critical element, perhaps the most critical of all, remained: the New Zealand reaction. Mr. Marshall had gone to bed. Clearly he could make no public comment till the related matter of Community finance had also been settled, which needed two or three more hours. But he had left a statement with a spokesman; and this first reaction, uttered to the Press soon after 5 a.m. on 23 June, was somewhat grudging. The package agreed, he said, represented on the whole a substantial acknowledgment of the New Zealand. case. But the quantities of butter and cheese New Zealand would still be able to export to Britain were not as great as they had asked for and hoped to get. He was however satisfied that the result was the best which the British could in the circumstances obtain for New Zealand; though he regretted very much that he could not endorse it in respect of the price formula.

39. The Prime Minister had sent an urgent telegram in the early hours of 23 June from London to Sir Keith Holyoake in New Zealand in which he said that looked at as a whole the agreement was remarkably satisfactory—indeed well beyond what seemed likely or possible earlier that week. He realised the prices agreed were not ideal; but they guaranteed New Zealand a price around £400 a ton for her butter compared with £311 which they were getting only two years before. He appealed to Sir Keith Holyoake to make his public comments as positive and welcoming as he could.

40. This message arrived in time for Sir Arthur Galsworthy to deliver it to Sir Keith Holyoake an hour or two before he made a statement in the New Zealand House of Assembly on the evening (still the European morning) of 23 June; and there is no doubt that it helped to make his statement rather more positive. Sir Arthur Galsworthy reported that Sir Keith Holyoake 'obviously regretted Marshall's generally lukewarm tone'. He said Mr. Marshall should clearly have made no comment until he had seen the final draft of the statement to be made in Wellington. He had been going, said Sir Keith, to make a positive and forthcoming statement. and 'now this has damn well happened'. Nevertheless, Sir Keith Holyoake's statement was a positive one. Mr. Marshall in Luxembourg met the Press and made a second statement on 23 June, warmer than his first one. Over the next week or 10 days New Zealand reactions, official and still more unofficial, grew still more positive as time passed. It was left to Mr. Tallboys (who has now succeeded Mr. Marshall as Minister for Overseas Trade in Mr. Marshall's own Administration) to make, on 16 September, 1971, an interesting comment on the agreement, when he pointed out that: 'In fact, our shipments of butter to the United Kingdom this year will be little higher than the tonnage we shall be entitled to ship in 1977': This was because in 1971 New Zealand did not have enough butter to meet its quota on the British market. That year they sent us 145,000 tons. In 1977, under the agreement, they will be able to send us 138,000 tons.

41. Our troubles with New Zealand were not quite over. Six months later. during the drafting of the New Zealand Protocol to the Treaty of Accession, a problem arose. As recorded in paragraph 37 above, the Community had agreed to omit from the text of our agreement on New Zealand of 23 June any reference to unanimity being required when the Council should take its decision on 'appropriate measures to ensure the maintenance, after 31 December, 1977, of exceptional arrangements in respect of imports of butter from New Zealand'. But in return we had agreed to record in the minutes that in fact unanimity would be required. As soon as the New Zealand Protocol began taking shape towards the end of the year the French made it clear that they wanted the requirement of unanimity explicitly stated. We replied that we fully accepted that we were and would remain bound by the agreed minute; but the presentational advantage of not spelling out the need for unanimity was just as great as it had been in June. None of the other Five had strong feelings; so before the end of December we had taken the matter up bilaterally with the French.

42. Various possibilities were canvassed. We could have written a confidential letter placing on record our acknowledgment of the permanent and binding character of the minute; but we were reluctant to have any unpublished exchanges accompanying the signature of the Treaty. At one stage we said we would agree to the recording of a formal minute in the proceedings of the final Conference to be held on the occasion of signature which would restate the contents of the minute of June 1971. But the French lawyers still felt there was a risk that a published agreement not referring to unanimity could be held to override a mere minute of the Conference. In the end, on 17 January, the French agreed to drop their request for including unanimity in the Protocol; but asked instead for a letter from the British Delegation setting out the position. This, for the reason given above, we were reluctant to agree to.

43. The New Zealand Protocol was by no means the only point in dispute on the drafting of the Treaty in these very last stages of the Conference. There were seven or eight others, several of them of much greater importance to us, in particular the provisions dealings with the steps to be taken in the event of abrupt disruption of the trade of traditional suppliers of our market, and provisions to express the Community's readiness to deal effectively with disturbances which might take place during the operation of our own transitional arrangements for agriculture. We decided we had done enough for New Zealand; and towards midnight on 17 January, during the last Deputies' meeting, I was glad to receive instructions from London authorising me to accept the mention of unanimity in the New Zealand Protocol 'on the understanding that you will use this to seek to obtain a satisfactory outcome on intra-Community agricultural trade'.

44. This we did. The New Zealanders suspected that we had done so, but we have never avowed it. The Community had expected us to pocket a concession on New Zealand, escaping from a public reference to unanimity, and to give ground elsewhere. So at first there was some confusion. But in the end we got what we wanted on the points of major concern to us and we agreed to including the word 'unanimity' in paragraph 2 of Article 5 of the New Zealand Protocol. We explained this to the New Zealanders as best we could, and much telephoning between Brussels, London and Wellington took place on each side of midnight 17–18 January. Rather surprisingly, it suddenly transpired that the New Zealanders might never have been aware of the agreement we had reached with the Community on 23 June, 1971, about the entry in the minutes of the Conference. I still have my doubts on this; though I have since been assured by a New Zealander who ought to know that they were in fact ignorant of this agreement. The action we took led to some trouble in Wellington. There was a good deal of criticism in the Press and Mr. Marshall (who during the night of 17–18 January had sent a message to Mr. Rippon saying that New Zealand expected the original agreement at Luxembourg to be honoured, and would take the strongest exception to any departure from it) made some rather disobliging comments in a radio interview. But in fact the

point was of little substance; and the New Zealanders soon realised it. Their criticism was echoed by some of the Government's critics in London; but in the end it removed only a very little of the gilt from New Zealand's ample gingerbread.[2]

[2] The argument over whether or not to mention in the Protocol the requirement for unanimity in deciding any prolongation of New Zealand's derogation was more a legal one than anything else. The strict legal interpretation is that where a precise decision-making procedure is not specified then the decision should be taken by a simple majority. Since the European Community's dairy products regulation was, like all other agricultural market regulations, based on Article 43 of the EEC Treaty which provides for qualified majority voting, the presumption against unanimity in the case of no explicit mention of unanimity was strengthened. So the agreement to mention unanimity avoided a distinctly ambiguous situation developing.

17

Community Finance: The Background

Settling our contribution to the Community's budget was the most important issue for us in the whole negotiation. As things turned out, it was rivalled—some might say surpassed—in strictly political importance by the three questions of New Zealand dairy products, Commonwealth sugar and fisheries. But in terms of its economic importance to ourselves it completely transcended any of these. It was also by far the most important issue in the negotiations for the French, in their case both in economic and in political terms. It is worth, for so important an issue, describing the background in some detail, before proceeding to describe how the problem developed and was settled.

2. To set out very briefly what was at stake, I will give a few figures. Assuming (as did the White Paper of July 1971) a total Community budget of £1,400 million in 1973, the first year of our membership, and of £1,600 million in 1977, 1 per cent of the budget would equal £14 million in 1973 and £16 million in 1977. Thus arguments over percentage points of our annual contribution to the budget were anything but trivial. Each 0.1 per cent of the 1973 budget meant £1,400,000. These were sums worth arguing about.

3. We had seen this problem coming from the earliest days of our attempts to enter the Community; though of course in 1962 total Community expenditure was extremely small (the Common Agricultural Policy having been barely inaugurated) and the problem was correspondingly less significant. Year by year thereafter it grew. The Community were obliged to settle, before the end of their original transitional period of 31 December, 1969, the definitive method for financing their expenditure, and to move over to the system of '*ressources propres*' by which certain national revenues—customs duties and levies on agricultural imports had always been foreseen as the principal source—would accrue as of right not to the national State in which the revenue was collected but to the Community. This was a target on which the French had long had their eyes fixed, and a consummation they were determined to force.

4. When in 1967 we made our application for membership, we were already well aware that this was the major problem. We hoped that, if we could get negotiations started soon and complete them in time, we should already be a member of the Community by the time it came to take these crucial decisions.

Thus in his statement of 4 July, 1967, Mr. Brown said: 'We shall look forward to taking part as a full member of the Community in the negotiation of the agricultural finance arrangements for the period after the end of 1969.' Whatever other reasons the French Government had in 1967 for frustrating our application—and no doubt they had quite a few—the importance of frustrating the hope that we should be able to take part from within the Community in determining these crucial financial arrangements, and thereby bend them to our own advantage, must have weighed with them very heavily.

5. When, after de Gaulle's resignation in April 1969, things changed, these crucial negotiations in the Community had not yet seriously begun. But the French continued to attach the highest importance to them, and to getting them concluded and ratified by all the existing Member States before we could appear on the scene. It was thus a critical point of the policy with which President Pompidou went to The Hague Summit meeting in December 1969 that, if he had to accept the opening of negotiations on our application, he must ensure that these negotiations did not begin until the Six had completed their agricultural finance regulation, and did not conclude until they had all ratified the resulting Treaty. This was the factor which produced the link, in The Hague Communiqué, between 'the completion of the Community' (*achèvement*) and its enlargement. The third wing of the triptych, reinforcement or *approfondissement*, was less important. It related to ensuring continual progress by the Community in a variety of other fields, without allowing negotiations for enlargement to inhibit progress. But *élargissement* was made clearly conditional on *achèvement*.

6. The Summit Conference did not complete the job of working out the definitive finance regulation but it took the essential decision of principle. The Communiqué recorded that the Heads of State or Government reaffirmed their will 'to lay down a definitive financial arrangement for the Common Agricultural Policy by the end of 1969. They agreed progressively to replace, within the framework of this financial arrangement, the contributions of member countries by their own resources ... with the object of achieving in due course the integral financing of the Communities' budgets in accordance with the procedure provided for in Article 201 of the Treaty establishing the European Economic Community.'

7. It was already December; and though much progress was made the job could not be completed by the end of 1969. But it was completed soon after. By February 1970 virtually final agreement had been reached; in April it was embodied in a Treaty which, in accordance with Article 201, had to be adopted by the Member States in accordance with their respective constitutional rules, that is to say formally ratified. Parallel with this process, in the first four months of 1970, the Community was already working out the lines of its position for negotiations with us. We made clear to the Member States, as their work on the financial regulation proceeded, how crucial a matter it was from the point of view of our interests and of our future negotiations; but our representations availed little against French determination. The financial arrangements

eventually adopted proved to be, as we had always foreseen they were likely to be, extremely disadvantageous from our point of view. One chink of hope had been left open, as the result of the efforts of our friends, in The Hague Communiqué, paragraph 7 of which read: 'The acceptance of a financial arrangement for the final stage does not exclude its adaptation by unanimous vote, in particular in the light of an enlarged Community and on condition that the principles of this arrangement are not infringed.' This chink was narrow and bristled with conditions; and as things turned out we were not able to take advantage of it.

8. The problem of Community finance dominated our preparations for the negotiations. It dominated in particular the White Paper 'Britain and the European Communities: An Economic Assessment' which the Labour Government published in February 1970. By May of that year the brief for Ministers on Community Finance, distilled from much more copious studies, had become a document of 60 pages. I will set out briefly the problems we foresaw and the reasons for them.

9. Well over 90 per cent of Community expenditure is absorbed by the Common Agricultural Policy. This policy was of course tailored to the advantage of agricultural exporters in the Community (the French and the Dutch in particular). But we were bound to remain a large agricultural importer. We should have (quite apart from the budget) to pay higher prices for our food imports, whether from the Community or elsewhere. If from the Community, we should simply pay a higher price; if from elsewhere, we should not only pay the higher price but be obliged to surrender a large proportion of it (represented by the levy) to the Community budget. Under the finance regulation we should have to pay 90 per cent of all our import levies on foodstuffs and animal feed, and 90 per cent of all our customs duties, to the Community budget. As a large food importer, geared in particular to imports from outside the Community, the levies we should pay on agricultural imports would be far higher than those paid by any other member. And because our general imports of articles other than food were drawn, and would for a long time be bound to continue to be drawn, much more from outside the Community than was by 1971 the case in any of the existing Member States, we should also have to make disproportionately high payments derived from customs duties.

10. The additional element required to top up the Community budget, if income received from levies and duties was inadequate to meet expenditure, was to be an amount equal to the yield of up to 1 per cent of a Value Added Tax, or an equivalent sum calculated on the basis of Gross National Product. This we did not mind. Being based on GNP, it contained an element of equity which in our case the levies and the duties would in no way reflect. But so large would our levy and duty contributions be that it was anticipated that only a very small additional sum, if anything, from the third source of income would be required to balance the enlarged Community's budget; thus the only inadequate element of equity was liable to be ousted. On top of this profound bias against us on the revenue side, there was bound to be an equally profound

bias against us on the expenditure side. The sum of money we could hope to recover from the Community budget in respect of agriculture was certain to be small, mainly because, since we had no major agricultural exports, we should enjoy no major export restitutions.

11. Nevertheless, in spite of these difficulties, both the Labour Administration and its Conservative successor believed that the prize of entry into the Community was so great that we should have to come to terms with these financial arrangements, while naturally doing our utmost in the negotiations to mitigate and delay their impact. A specially strong consideration—and this was an argument we made much use of in the negotiations—was the desirability of ensuring if we could that the burdens we assumed did not start from too high a point or increase too rapidly. It was felt—and this was a point particularly strongly stressed by the Confederation of British Industry in the studies they made of the problems of entry—that too heavy burdens in the early stages, in terms of foreign exchange transfers to the Community budget or (to put it more realistically) in terms of the transfer of real resources from ourselves to our future partners, would force us to adopt restrictive policies of economic management which would cancel the beneficial 'dynamic' effects on our economy which we expected to flow from other consequences of our entry.

12. It also followed from the effect on us of the Community's finance regulation that our entry into the Community would confer very significant benefits, in terms of straight reductions of cost, on the existing Member States of the Community. Under the arrangements they had agreed at the beginning of 1970, their own contributions to the budget would be limited by certain keys and ceilings for a number of years, and they would not be obliged to hand over 90 per cent of all levies and customs duties until 1975. Further limitations on their contributions would operate until 1977. Accordingly, so long at least as these limitations continued to operate (indeed even thereafter, because of the effect of our contribution on the VAT element), and so long as the enlargement of the Community did not by itself lead to a significant increase of the budget (which was not anticipated), any major contribution to the budget from a new source that is to say from us—would have the simple effect of reducing the contributions required from each of the existing Member States by a proportionate amount. We made much of this argument in the negotiations. It was irrefutable and none of the Member States attempted to refute it, though they were equally reluctant to acknowledge or still more to quantify it. No doubt this benefit was highly welcome to them; but not surprisingly they refrained from saying so. An exception was M. Lardinois, Dutch Minister of Agriculture. At a Press conference in The Hague on 24 June, 1971, the day after we had reached agreement on our contribution to the budget at the Ministerial meeting in Luxembourg, M. Lardinois said that the Dutch contribution to the EEC would drop as a result of the admission of other countries. The Dutch budget in 1973 would benefit by 150 million florins.

13. A further factor complicating our position in the negotiations was that

the Community's financial provisions for agriculture were in the highest degree advantageous to two of our fellow candidates, Denmark and the Irish Republic, simply because they are large agricultural exporters. Together with the better access and increased prices they would enjoy for agricultural exports to other Community markets including especially ours, these financial provisions constituted perhaps the principal reason why these two countries wished to join the Community. Norway's position was closer to our own, but for various reasons this was for her a more marginal problem, and in any case she hoped—and may have succeeded—to be able to secure not insignificant compensations from Community agricultural funds in respect both of agriculture and fisheries.

14. To conclude this chapter on the background to Community Finance something should be said about the ratification of the Community's Treaty of April 1970 on the definitive finance regulation. It occurred to several of the Governments of the Five—especially the Germans, the Italians and the Dutch that the fact that the Community's decisions could only enter into force after the Treaty in which they were to be embodied had been formally ratified by the Parliaments of the Six might give them a useful means of exercising pressure on the French in connection with the opening and the progress of our negotiations. This idea was expressed in one or two quarters; and the French promptly reacted by turning the tables on their partners. Already on 18 February, 1970, when the main decisions on the finance regulation had been taken but still two months before they were embodied in a formal instrument, M. Schumann told the Foreign Affairs Commission of the French Assembly 'that the completion of the Common Market would not be fully achieved until the agreement had been ratified by the Parliaments of all Six Member States. These ratifications would enable the negotiations for the enlargement of the Community to enter their decisive phase.' Talking afterwards to the Press, the President of the Commission, M. de Broglie, commented that the negotiations between the Common Market and Great Britain would not be able to enter an active and definitive phase until the agricultural finance Treaty had been ratified by the Six.

15. In this tussle of wills, the French won easily. No more was heard of the Five using ratification as a weapon; and in so far as it was a weapon it was now firmly in French hands. From time to time, in the first six months of the negotiations, allusions were made to this French position; and from time to time we wondered to what extent we should attribute the slow progress of the negotiations in the last three months of 1970 to deliberate foot-dragging by the French until ratification should have been completed by their partners: their own ratification was exemplary in its promptitude. The Five wondered too; and there is no doubt that these French tactics materially accelerated the completion of ratification by the Italian and Dutch Parliaments, always the last to complete this process. They did so before the end of 1970. So the French got their way; but probably progress in the negotiations would have been only marginally faster, if at all, even if this problem had not existed.

18

Community Finance: The Struggle

Of all the problems of the negotiations, few gave rise to so little actual negotiation in the Conference itself as the most important problem of all, that of Community Finance. To be sure, there was very little actual negotiation in the Conference on New Zealand or sugar either, and virtually none on sterling. The general pattern of development for the really important questions turned out to be a fairly constant one. It consisted of preliminary investigation by the Commission on the basis of factual papers by us; a report by the Commission to the Council of Ministers of the Six; prolonged canvassing, in every conceivable quarter outside the Conference, of general possibilities and methods of advance; a precise proposal by us; an even longer period in which our proposal was criticised and defended in conversations everywhere and at every level, with nothing in the Conference but occasional formal statements; a continued absence until the very last moment of any precise proposals from the Community; and then a sudden final crunch at which the Community made proposals in the Conference and agreement was achieved. This was the pattern in the case of Community finance. The final negotiation occupied only a few minutes in the Conference in the early morning of 13 May and a few hours in the corridors of the Conference at Luxembourg on the last night of the meeting from 21–23 June, 1971; and its outcome was formally endorsed, as were the other fruits of that productive meeting, in a formal session of the Conference between 4.30 a.m. and 5 a.m. on 23 June.

2. This was after all an issue on which it was scarcely to be expected that formal and detailed discussion with the Commission or the Community could foster a gradual process of increasing mutual understanding and the gradual emergence of acceptable elements of a compromise. The options were too stark and clear from the start. Thus the whole issue gave rise to only one formal session of any significance with the Commission, when on 18 September, 1970, British representatives met with them with the purpose merely of elucidating the methodology of the paper we had circulated in July and the assumptions on which it was based. But the absence of formal discussions in the Conference or with the Commission by no means implies that there was any lack of contacts and conversation. On the contrary; throughout the 11 months from 22 July,

1970, when we tabled our first paper and 23 June, 1971, when we reached agreement, the subject of Community finance gave rise to a continual stream of discussion at every level and in every capital of the Community. This was especially the case after we had tabled our formal proposals in the Conference on 16 December, 1970. Then there was something to bite on; and everyone chewed away at our proposals with destructive enthusiasm for months. The documentation is enormous. Conversations with the staff of the Commission, with each of the Six Delegations in Brussels, with Ambassadors of the Six in London and their staffs, with Ministers of the Six on every occasion of contact and steadily with officials in the Six Community capitals—the records of them would fill volumes.

3. Studies of the most elaborate statistical nature were everywhere conducted, not least in London; principles were elaborated; arguments surged to and fro; and many blind alleys were explored. More and more as time passed, in private conversations, figures were bandied about. Our position remained steady for a number of months after we had tabled our proposals. The French position remained hard and unyielding for even longer. The Five tended to veer and vary. Of them all, the Italians were steadily the most helpful and moderate from our point of view; though even they made clear to us (in a special message from Signor Moro delivered on 15 February) that our proposal for a 3 per cent contribution in the first year of our membership was unnegotiable. The Dutch, early in 1971, took what seemed to us a hard and unhelpful line; though later on they became less demanding. The Germans, while occasionally saying that from their own point of view they scarcely minded how low our first contribution might be, insisted from the start that we had no hope of getting anything nearly as low as the opening contribution we had proposed. Typical of the German reaction at Ministerial level (it was usually harder at official level) were some remarks Herr Scheel made on 22 January, 1971, when Herr Brandt and he received Sir Roger Jackling. Herr Scheel said 'it was thought in the Community that the share we had suggested, 15 per cent, was not possible. It ought to be somewhere between 15 per cent and 21 per cent. We had suggested going up in equal steps from a start of about 3 per cent. This did not seem the right starting level either. We ought to start at 12 per cent or 10 per cent or even 8 per cent and then go up in equal steps to a higher final level.'

4. The Germans also showed special concern (as Herr Scheel did on the occasion just mentioned, and later it was taken up by others) lest our early contributions should be so low as to fail to cover the additional charges imposed on the Community by its enlargement, and thus involve them in greater expense. The Belgians were prodigal of principles and, we thought, rather over-ingenious without being positively helpful; the Luxembourgers usually moved somewhere between the Belgians and the French, though at one point, relatively early in the proceedings, they surprised themselves and everyone else when at a meeting of the Council of Ministers on 1 February, 1971, M. Thorn proposed that our contribution in the first year should be 5 per cent. Towards the end, something

like a consensus had developed among the Five, and was apparent in the final week before the crucial Ministerial meeting began on 21 June, 1971. By then the Five seemed separately to have concluded that our contribution in 1973 should lie somewhere between 7 per cent and 8 per cent and in 1977 should reach something like 18 per cent. The outcome we finally had to accept was 8.64 per cent in 1973 and 18.92 per cent in 1977.

5. The Commission played, from our point of view, a less helpful role in this crucial issue than in virtually any other. This was because of the extreme character of the proposals they decided to put forward in their 'vue d'ensemble' of 17 November, 1971, which will be described later on. Having nailed their flag to these excessive demands, they were inhibited from doing much to help us in later stages. Why did they make so extremely unhelpful a proposal, by far the most unsatisfactory proposal, from our point of view, of any put forward by the Commission on any subject throughout the entire negotiations? I fear it must be accepted that the reason was simply that the two Members of the Commission most concerned with this issue—M. Deniau because of his responsibility for the negotiations and M. Barre because of his responsibility for economic affairs were Frenchmen, who naturally paid a special regard to the views of the French Government. M. Barre seems to have hoped the negotiations would fail, and to have believed that one way to make them fail was to put forward proposals on Community finance which we could not possibly accept.

6. It is time to turn to the sequence of the negotiations. At the opening meeting of the Conference on 30 June, 1970, Mr. Barber's statement included a strong passage on Community finance. 'We have to work together to find a solution to this basic problem which will be fair and sound for the enlarged Community and for all its members. If I appear to labour this point, it is only because, unless such a solution is found, the burden on the United Kingdom could not be sustained and no British Government could contemplate joining.' On 22 July, the day after our first bilateral Ministerial meeting, we tabled in Brussels a paper on 'the Financial Arrangements in an Enlarged Community'. It was the product of many months consideration and analysis. In its estimates of the financial consequences of enlargement it contained no deliberate or conscious exaggeration whatever, though naturally enough it tended to make the worst of a good case. The Community found, or affected to find, its conclusions incredible; though reports reached us that in one or two quarters, including Paris, its analysis was in fact regarded as fair enough.

7. Our paper described its purpose as being 'to set out what the effects would be of applying the Community finance regulations without adjustment in a Community enlarged by the accession of the United Kingdom, Denmark, the Irish Republic and Norway. It contains the best and most realistic estimates which the British Government have been able to make. ... Detailed consideration was also given to the various changes in trade flows likely to follow from enlargement of the Community.' A number of other assumptions applied in our paper were explained; and in particular we explained why we had adopted

a figure of 4,500 million units of account as the likely total of the Community budget in 1978 (which was the year to which all the calculations in the paper were directed). This was perhaps a high figure. In the White Paper published in July 1971 we assumed a total Community budget in 1978 of £1,600 million or 3,840 million units of account. There were plausible reasons for this reduction of nearly 15 per cent in our 1978 forecast a year later. By July 1971 the prospect of a reduction of the rate of growth in Community agricultural expenditure seemed much better than it had 12 months earlier. Nevertheless, it must be admitted that the two estimates were designed to serve two rather different purposes.

8. In estimating the possible contributions in 1978 from Member States based on a proportion of Value-added Tax or of their Gross National Product, we used the growth assumptions from a recent OECD publication, and deduced that in 1978 our share of the GNP of the enlarged Community would be 17 per cent, whereas that of Italy, France and Germany would be 16 per cent, 25 per cent and 28½ per cent respectively. The results of all our assumptions and calculations were set out in a table giving our estimate of 'contributions to and receipts from the Community budget for a Community of Ten in 1978'. This table displayed our case. As the final paragraph of our paper said: 'The calculations summarised in Table 1 show that, if the Community's financial arrangements were applied without adjustment to a Community of Ten, the United Kingdom's total contribution to the Community's Budget would amount to some 1,375 million UAs, representing 31 per cent of all contributions. The receipts the United Kingdom could expect would amount to 250 million UAs, which would represent 6 per cent of total receipts. As a result the United Kingdom's net contribution to the Community's finances would exceed 1,100 million units of account.'

9. Within 10 days the main contents and conclusions of our paper had leaked, and thenceforward the nature of the problem was wide open to discussion not only in the Community but in the Press. In accordance with the procedural decisions of the Conference, the Commission was charged by the Six with studying our paper and making a report on it to the Council of Ministers. Their report was completed in October 1970. It was a paper about as long as ours but very different in character. It was more discursive and less statistical, and quite deliberately so. The Commission paper said that 'it would be pointless to engage in detailed discussions on hypothetical figures for 1978'. While producing few figures of their own the Commission sought, in what was a good but somewhat patronising paper, to demolish ours. They cast doubts on our assumptions about Gross National Product. They claimed we had under-estimated the likely growth of our 'intra-Community' trade, hence over-estimating the amount of our customs duties; and we had under-estimated the amount of customs duties which would be raised in the existing Member States in 1978. Our calculations about agricultural levies were 'particularly problematical'. Here again we had over-estimated our own prospective contributions and under-estimated those

of the Six. Moreover we had under-estimated our receipts from Community funds.

10. But the main burden of the Commission's paper was to argue that patterns of Community expenditure would change. The proportion of agricultural expenditure in the total was certain to diminish. The Commission put forward two alternative assumptions about total expenditure in 1978; in one of them non-agricultural expenditure would amount to 40 per cent and in the other to 60 per cent of the total budget. This would admittedly produce a higher total budget; but, as regards Community activities other than agriculture, 'it is precisely a country like Great Britain which can benefit to the greatest degree'. Thus, the paper concluded, on our own estimate of the structure of the budget in 1978, the United Kingdom's contribution would be nearer 25 per cent than 30 per cent; but if the structure of the budget altered as the Commission anticipated, then the United Kingdom's contribution would amount to something nearer 20 per cent than 25 per cent. And the United Kingdom's receipts from the budget would amount to something more like 12½ per cent to 15½ per cent than the mere 6 per cent we had calculated.

11. Above all, argued the Commission, we had under-estimated the dynamic effects of membership. 'Calculations more or less favourable towards one party or another lose their significance when seen in the perspective of the dynamic effects which the United Kingdom's accession must have.' All in all, this was a fair enough negotiating paper, which was no doubt what the Community regarded our own paper as having been; but it was hardly a dispassionate analysis. The prospect that in a mere six years the Community's agricultural expenditure would shrink from well over 90 per cent of the total budget to 60 per cent—still less to 40 per cent—struck us as barely plausible. Nevertheless some of the assumptions the paper expressed about changes in the pattern of Community expenditure and possible consequent benefits to us represent valuable hostages to fortune which could prove useful to us—if they prove false—in later years.

12. The Community decided to make this paper formally available to us in the Conference (it had of course reached us soon after its completion) and at a meeting of the Deputies on 4 November, 1970, they promised to transmit it to us. In doing so the Chairman of the Deputies, speaking on behalf of the Community, expressed their agreement with the general lines of the paper's conclusions and in particular their endorsement of paragraph 20 of the paper. This paragraph contained an important sentence declaring that 'should unacceptable situations arise within the present Community, or an enlarged Community, the very survival of the Community would demand that the institutions find equitable solutions'. In our proposals of 16 December we referred, as will be seen later, to this sentence. When, at a later stage, we decided that we could not hope to secure (as in our proposal of 16 December we requested) a formal reaffirmation in the Treaty of Accession of the 'concept underlying this statement' in order to protect us should arrangements on Community finance

work out badly, we decided to make do instead with the fact that the Community had already formally given us this assurance; and it was quoted in our White Paper of July 1971.[1]

13. Meanwhile the Commission had been preparing a further paper, described as a 'vue d'ensemble', concerning the transitional arrangements for Community enlargement. This paper, completed by the Commission on 17 November, 1970, contained proposals on the subject of Community finance which we found extremely harsh and unwelcome. The paper was never formally communicated to us, which was perhaps just as well from the Community's point of view since much of its contents was highly vulnerable to reasoned argument. But of course we had copies of the paper within a couple of days of its production; and the Community knew we had. The rules of the game, however, prevented us from ever formally referring to it save by phrases such as ideas which we believe to be current within the Community.

14. This paper contained one thing that was welcome—an acknowledgment, very much in passing, that contributions to the budget by the Six would decrease in consequence of our own contribution. This was the only occasion on which the Community ever acknowledged this simple arithmetical fact. The paper also contained—less welcome—a hint at the relationship between a full financial contribution and full voting rights. But its main contents, so far as Community finance was concerned, were two alternative 'possibilities'—they were not put forward as formal proposals—for our contributions to the budget over a five year transitional period. The paper was silent on the question whether we should enjoy additional years of 'correctives', on the pattern of the arrangements the Six had made for themselves, before reaching our final automatic level of contribution. The two 'possibilities' put forward were, first, that we should make a contribution of 21.5 per cent of the total budget in 1973 and stick to this scale for five years; or, second, that we should pay in 1973 '10 per cent to 15 per cent' of the budget, rising in 1977 to '20 per cent to 25 per cent'. The first and more outrageous of these 'possibilities' was arrived at by allotting to us an opening scale (on the analogy for those already agreed for the Six in respect of the year 1970) which would lie between the 28 for France and the 31.5 for Germany and would mean for Great Britain 'a scale of the order of 30, i.e. as a percentage,

[1] A comparison of the two papers with the benefit of hindsight redounds to the credit of the United Kingdom's estimates which turned out to be much closer to actual developments in the European Community's pattern of spending and raising revenue and their net impact on the United Kingdom than did those of the Commission. In particular the proportion of spending on agriculture did not drop nearly as fast, or as far, as the Commission speculated they would, despite the fact that the European Community initiated a programme of regional expenditure. And the rapid overall increase in the size of the budget meant that these percentages produced a much larger quantum of net burden to the United Kingdom. These Commission estimates, and the extent to which they were very wide of the mark, did indeed provide valuable underpinning to the case developed by the United Kingdom in 1979 and subsequently, that the situation was indeed unacceptable and that the survival of the Community demanded that its institutions should find an equitable solution.

for a Community of Ten, about 21.5 per cent'. The main argument adduced for the figure of 21.5 per cent was that it would situate 'from the beginning the budgetary participation of new Member countries at a sufficiently high level'. Moreover, it was 'the most simple way'. The alternative 'possibility' was arrived at by a more complicated argument which nevertheless contained at least one entirely arbitrary assumption, namely that the gap between the minima (levels for 1973) and the maxima (levels for 1977) should 'be selected in such a way as to avoid too sudden changes during the transitional period': that is to say, we must start at a high figure because we should have to end at a high figure.

15. We regarded both these possibilities, and above all the first of them, as extremely prejudicial and entirely unjustified. They were very far indeed from our own ideas. After the Treaty had been signed, I told a responsible member of the Commission staff that we had always regarded these proposals as extremely unfair. His defence of them was to take the lower bracket of the second alternative—that is to say 10 per cent to 20 per cent from 1973 to 1977—and to say: 'After all that was pretty close to where we ended up'. This is true; but I still believe that this was an extremely biased proposal by the Commission, which fell far below its normal standard of helpfulness throughout the negotiations. Naturally enough, the French immediately fastened on to the higher of the Commission's alternative 'possibilities' and for the next four months continued to argue that our opening contribution should be 21.5 per cent.

16. After this paper had been circulated within the Community we regarded it as very important that we should, with the least possible delay, make our own proposals on Community finance to the Conference. It might have been better if we had been able to make them before the Commission's paper was written; but we had concentrated on getting our proposals on New Zealand and sugar well launched first and planned to leave finance till towards the end of the year. We now feared that the Community might take the Commission's ideas (which naturally, like everything else, leaked pretty rapidly to the Press) as the basis for making an early formal proposal to us, from which it would then have been all the harder to shift them. In the light of later experience, these fears were probably exaggerated. As we have seen already, the Community in fact always proved incapable of making precise and concrete proposals except in reaction to proposals from us, and then only at an extremely late stage in the proceedings. Nevertheless, we urged our friends in the Community to see that it did not put forward any proposals until we had been able to table our own. In a statement in the House of Commons on 25 November, Mr. Rippon said that Members would have read Press reports concerning a 'recent major report by the Commission, not yet communicated to us'. Speaking of Community finance, he added: 'I very much hope that the Community will await the proposals which we intend to put forward on this point in the near future before themselves endorsing or adopting any position as their own.' At the Ministerial meeting on 8 December Mr. Rippon promised that our proposals would soon be forthcoming. Our proposals were approved by the Cabinet on 14 December.

We tabled a paper containing them in the Conference on 16 December. Mr. Rippon, partly in order to forestall possibly garbled leaks, made a statement in the House of Commons on 16 December describing our proposals. The text of our paper is reproduced in Appendix I.

17. A very brief description of our proposals will suffice here. We argued that the appropriate base key for the United Kingdom's contribution, to be reached in the fifth year of our membership, would be 13–15 per cent. We should build up to this key in equal annual steps starting from a notional zero per cent in the year before accession. (This led by simple arithmetic to a 2.6–3 per cent contribution in 1973, though in fact these figures were not mentioned in our paper.) We described our proposal as being not a bargaining position but 'a reasonable point on which to conclude'. We asked for three years of correctives after 1977, on precisely the same basis as the Six had agreed for themselves. We referred to the Commission's view, 'with which the Community Delegation specifically agreed', about unacceptable situations; and expressed our view that the concept underlying this statement should be recorded in a suitable manner in the Treaty of Accession. As early as 22 January, 1971, Herr Scheel, in the conversation with Sir Roger Jackling already referred to, said, with reference to this last proposal, that 'a guarantee clause with legally binding force could not be negotiated'.[2]

[2] One very important element of the proposal tabled by the United Kingdom was the absence of any reference to the option referred to in paragraph 7 of the Communiqué of The Hague Summit to a possible adaptation of the European Community's financial arrangements in the light of enlargement. By proposing a set of transitional arrangements, buttressed only by the 'unacceptable situations' statement, the UK effectively excluded any fundamental changes to the system. They did so on the basis of an analysis that it would in fact prove impossible to negotiate such changes, that proposing them might well enable the French to block a successful outcome to the accession negotiations as a whole and that to try and fail would leave the United Kingdom in a worse position than would otherwise be the case.

19

Community Finance: The Outcome

The tabling of our proposals changed the basis of later discussion of this subject. Our proposals were nowhere well received. We had not expected that they would be; but the generally critical and even hostile character of the reaction they provoked was, I think, somewhat worse than we had foreseen. In a Press conference on 21 January, 1971, M. Pompidou was asked by *The Times* correspondent in Paris whether he thought the negotiations had got off to a good start and in particular what he thought about British proposals on Community finance. He replied: 'We have often had occasion to say that France wanted, and believed in, Britain's entry into the Common Market. That is still my position, but of course it depends in the first place on the British. One must admit that the British have three qualities amongst others: humour, tenacity and realism. I have the feeling that we are still slightly in the humorous stage.' We for our part were convinced that our proposals were serious and reasonable, and that we must stick to them. In a minute of 21 December, 1970, to Mr. Rippon I wrote: 'I am sure we must not be daunted by the cries of indignation which arose in Community quarters when our finance proposals were unveiled ... I do not myself think it would much matter if we were still standing pat on these proposals by next April.'

2. We proceeded, in the few weeks after we had tabled our proposals and indeed over the next few months, to launch and maintain a major campaign through diplomatic and other channels to explain and justify our proposals. How far this succeeded it is hard to say; but the general view in the Community of our proposals remained extremely critical. In particular there was one concept on which they were based, which seemed to us reasonable and natural, which we never succeeded in getting anyone in the Community to accept as such. This was the concept that, as in other areas of transition such as tariffs, we should move by regular stages over the transitional period from the situation which existed before we joined the Community to that which would exist in the fifth year of our membership. Thus our proposals provided that we should pay 13 to 15 per cent of the budget in 1977. It seemed to us perfectly natural that one should work back from this position and move by regular annual stages from the position on the eve of our entry—when we should be paying nothing

to the position in 1977. It was this purely arithmetical concept which produced our proposed contribution of 2.6 per cent to 3 per cent in 1973. The Community resisted this concept with a variety of arguments, including the argument that this payment in the first year would be insufficient to meet our contribution to the Community's running expenses. But their main argument, which was put forward particularly by the French but to which most other members of the Community seemed regrettably receptive, was that we must make some kind of 'act of faith' and demonstration of our readiness to play our full part by paying considerably more in the first year of our membership than a linear progression, from zero in 1972 to whatever might be agreed on as the appropriate figure for 1977, would have produced for 1973. Our failure to persuade the Community to accept the logic of our approach conditioned, among other things, the rather high level of the first year's contribution to which we eventually had to agree.

3. In the Conference, after our proposals had been tabled, relatively little occurred. One or two brief formal statements of principle were made from the Community side; rather longer debating statements were made from ours. Mr. Rippon's statement on this subject to the Conference at the Ministerial meeting on 2 February is reproduced in Appendix I, as a good indication of the strength of our feelings and, so we believed, of our arguments at this stage. But the French continued to cleave to the higher of the Commission's two 'possibilities'—21.5 per cent from the start and throughout the transitional period—as their objective. In a statement in the Conference on 2 February setting out certain principles which they believed should apply to Community finance, the Community ended by declaring that 'the procedures for implementing this principle will be the subject of subsequent proposals by the Community'. For long we awaited these proposals in vain; and indeed, not long after this meeting, French representatives at meetings of the Six in Brussels began taking the line that the Community could say nothing more about Community finance until we had withdrawn our unacceptable proposals and replaced them with new ones. As late as 16 March M. Brunet, Director of Economic Affairs in the French Foreign Ministry, declared at a meeting of the Council of Ministers that the British should withdraw their proposals and submit new ones. This we declined to do, and in the end, as will be seen later on, the Community broke the deadlock with some proposals of their own.

4. I will summarise at this point some of the more significant arguments used by either side in the controversy, and some of our own plans which never came to fruition. The Community, and especially the French, made much of the argument that the level of our contribution in our final year of transition must be high enough to avoid the need for our making a large jump to our eventual automatic level of contribution. We for our part retorted that, while we accepted this, it was equally important for us to avoid making a large jump to a high contribution in the first transitional year. The Community's argument about 'no high jump at the end' seems in reality to have been based on two

things. First, a reluctance to believe that we were in fact ready to accept the Community's system of *ressources propres*. Though this acceptance followed from the position we had adopted at the outset about accepting Community decisions, and though we had made our acceptance of the *ressources propres* system explicit as early as the Ministerial meeting of 8 December, 1970, we had to repeat this acceptance several times before the Community really accepted our acceptance. This scepticism was based, second, on a conviction that in some way or other we intended if we could to undermine the Community system. This we knew we could not do; and indeed we had concluded that there was no prospect even of taking advantage of the possibility left open by The Hague Communiqué of 'unanimous adaptation', an opening we therefore never sought to exploit.

5. Another argument much used on the Community side involved pointing to the budgetary savings we should make through the phasing-out of deficiency payments for agriculture, and trying to portray this saving as a reasonable offset to our budgetary contribution to Community funds. We of course retorted that they were not comparing like with like, and that what concerned us about our budgetary contribution to the Community was not its effect on our domestic budget but its foreign exchange and resource transfer aspects. Another line used by the Community, even after it began to be generally accepted that our contributions throughout the transitional period would be limited by some arbitrary key or ceiling, was to calculate the levies and duties we should be likely to be collecting and to insist that our contributions, even in the transitional period, must be based on some relationship to them. This argument of course pointed to higher figures. An argument which weighed strongly with the French in private was the undesirability of having to pay twice in the negotiations; that is to say, of having to make concessions to their partners to reach an opening proposal and then having to abate it further in negotiation with us. In the end, as will be shown later, they avoided this dilemma.

6. On our side, we strongly pressed the argument about the savings each member of the Community would make as a result of our own contribution; while the Six could not rebut this argument, they contrived to avoid showing much interest in it. We also argued strongly the need for a period of correctives after 1977; and by the end of January 1971 the Italians, Dutch and Germans at least appeared to have accepted that there should be three years of correctives. Privately, we investigated various possibilities of alleviating the foreign exchange burden of whatever contributions we might in the end have to make, for example by seeking agreement that a proportion of the contribution should remain blocked in sterling, or should be used to establish a fund from which payments would be made to us for necessary operations based on Community purposes in this country. Here too, in the end, we had to conclude that there was no prospect of getting Community agreement to such ideas, and we never put them forward. Finally, in considering later developments, it is necessary to bear in mind that from about mid-March there was a reasonably clear understanding between ourselves and the French (though the Five knew nothing of it) that Mr.

Heath would in fact be meeting President Pompidou before long. This understanding became a major factor in the timing of developments from both sides.

7. Meanwhile, however, the tough stand taken both by ourselves and the French began to be slightly modified. Speaking at an off-the-record briefing for French journalists in Brussels on 2 February, M. Schumann indicated (though we did not learn this until a day or two later) that France might be prepared to consider an opening contribution from Britain in the region of 10 to 12 per cent. At a luncheon with Press correspondents in Brussels on 3 February, Mr. Rippon left the impression that he too would be prepared to think of a figure considerably higher than 3 per cent as a possible opening British bid. He was reported to have hinted at final agreement at 'perhaps around 8 per cent'. This was I am convinced—and I was there—a complete misunderstanding by the Press. What Mr. Rippon said was that 'if the Community came down to 10 per cent as an opening bid we would have another go at them'. The French were as embarrassed by the reports of what M. Schumann had said as we were by the reports of what Mr. Rippon was supposed to have said; and at the next meeting of Deputies some amusement was caused when both I and M. Bochet (presiding in M. Boegner's absence) assured each other that no attention must be paid to Press reports but only to what was formally stated in the Conference.

8. Be that as it may, the damage done by the misleading reports of Mr. Rippon's remarks to the Press spread far and wide, and thereafter there was even less disposition in the Community than before to take seriously our 3 per cent starting figure. In any case, Mr. Rippon felt that the time had come to indicate some flexibility on our part. Not long after, on 23 February, in a conversation with the Dutch Ambassador in London, Mr. Rippon said: 'It would not be worth talking about the idea of an initial British contribution of 10 per cent; nor perhaps 8 per cent; nor even 7 per cent; but somewhere around 5 per cent would not be unreasonable as a basis for discussion.'

9. The Ministerial meeting of 16 March passed with no progress on Community finance—indeed no discussion at all, except that we succeeded (in spite of M. Brunet's statement made earlier in the day at the meeting of the Council of Ministers and recorded above) in getting it accepted and recorded that the ball was in the Community's court and that it was up to them to make the next move. Frequent discussions continued throughout April among the Permanent Representatives in Brussels as to the line the Community should adopt. The French by the end of March were backing down a little from their insistence that 21.5 per cent must be our opening figure. Arguments continued as to how much we should need to pay to meet at least our share of 'the running costs' of the Community—Mr. Rippon had declared in a broadcast early in March, by way of comment on some allegations by M. Schumann, that if it could be demonstrated that our opening contribution would not meet this cost we would increase it—and it soon transpired that the Community could only prove that our 3 per cent offer would not meet our share by the rather strange expedient of classifying the whole of the Agricultural Guidance Fund as part of the

Community's running costs. We for our part had by now accepted that we should have to move well above our original opening bid. We had known this from the start; though we had perhaps not been ready in December to acknowledge even to ourselves that our move above 3 per cent would have to be as large as now, in April, appeared inevitable.

10. In a paper dated 29 April circulated to his Ministerial colleagues Mr. Rippon made new proposals. They were accepted in the AE Committee, and on 6 May the Cabinet agreed 'that if at the Ministerial meeting on 11–12 May the Community put forward proposals pointing to a gradual increase in our contributions to the budget from less than 10 per cent in the first year of membership to a level of up to 20 per cent in the fifth year, the Chancellor of the Duchy of Lancaster should indicate that we would regard these as a basis for negotiation'.

11. Meanwhile, on the previous day in Brussels, the French had made a new proposal in the Committee of Permanent Representatives: it is reproduced in Appendix I. This ingenious proposal was conceptual only. It used the concept of the Gross National Product of the candidate States—a concept we had often been told was entirely unacceptable in this context—to establish a point of departure; that point would rise (in theory it could also fall, but in our case was most unlikely to do so) very slightly year by year, as in the Community's own system, to establish for each of the five years of transition the candidates' theoretical full contribution. That contribution would then be abated, year by year, by a different percentage, which the French paper defined as N per cent in 1973, P per cent in 1974, and so on till 1977. The paper was silent on the question of further 'corrective years'. It was clear that, on this basis, the crucial question would be defining the annual percentage abatements.

12. This proposal had by 7 May been broadly accepted by the other five Members of the Community as having a constructive intent. At a meeting of the Council of Ministers on 10 May M. Giscard d'Estaing recommended the French proposal to his colleagues, and they accepted it. It was put to us by the Community in the early hours of 13 May, late in the course of the Ministerial meeting which achieved success on sugar and agricultural transition. By now it contained one important addition, on correctives after 1977. It admitted their possibility, but said the Community could make no proposals at this stage. Its language implied reluctance to accept as much as three 'corrective years'. Replying to the Community proposal, Mr. Rippon said he welcomed this initiative. 'I would therefore like to suggest that the Community should, as soon as possible make proposals for the percentage values they would wish to give to these letters. Provided these percentage values are fair and reasonable we shall have, I think, an acceptable basis for negotiation'. Thus the stage was set for a final negotiation on figures, once the conceptual framework of the French proposal had been developed to include them.

13. Just over a week later Mr. Heath and M. Pompidou met in Paris. They discussed the problem of Community finance at length; but did not attempt to

agree on a final settlement. It was accepted that this must be left for the Conference to resolve in June. Nevertheless, the understanding was reached that the French would accept a first year contribution from us of less than 10 per cent. How much less was not agreed: and as will be seen there was still a considerable margin to argue about. At this meeting too it was made clear to M. Pompidou that the question of New Zealand dairy products was of critical political importance for us. We accepted the consequence of this, namely that a link was from now on firmly established—we had long foreseen that it would be—between the solution to be found for New Zealand and the solution for Community finance. In the final stages of the Conference this link was made absolutely explicit, in that each proposal the Community put forward on New Zealand dairy products was stated to be dependent on the solution reached on the question of Community finance.

14. After the long struggle things moved, so far as Community finance was concerned, fairly peacefully to a close. The longer and harder battle was over New Zealand. At a meeting of the AE Committee on 3 June the Chancellor of the Exchequer said that 'the most important objective was to keep our contribution in the first two or three years of membership as low as possible and every effort should be made to prevent our contribution in 1973 exceeding $7\frac{1}{2}$–8 per cent of the Budget. The Committee accepted however that in order to reach agreement it might be necessary in the last resort to accept an initial contribution as high as $9\frac{1}{2}$ per cent.' On 17 June Mr. Soames was instructed to take the line with the French 'not only that double figures are out of the question but that we could not start near them'. He was not to suggest that it would be easy for us to improve on the $6\frac{1}{2}$ per cent figure mentioned by the Prime Minister in Paris. We could however probably come to meet the Community by accepting two rather than three corrective years. On the same day, at a meeting with the French Ambassador in London 'Mr. Rippon emphasised the political importance of a satisfactory settlement on New Zealand while M. de Courcel spoke of the need for a high opening British contribution to the Community budget as a test of our European intentions'. (By now all the Six were speaking of the link between New Zealand and Community finance.) Mr. Soames spoke to M. Schumann on 18 June. The conversation mainly concerned New Zealand. As for our financial contribution, M. Schumann said that, having gone as far as he had on New Zealand, he would have to ask us to agree to a first year's contribution of 9 per cent. Mr. Soames replied that he was afraid this would not be possible. Why should M. Schumann attach importance to our paying 9 per cent in the first year rather than in the second? Later that day, M. Schumann telephoned to the Ambassador to say he had seen the President and 'M. Pompidou agreed to his formula for New Zealand, provided we accepted an initial contribution of 9 per cent'.

15. Around midnight on 22–23 June in Luxembourg the Community put to us precise proposals. The question of New Zealand dairy products had already been virtually solved, but was still linked to the question of Community finance.

The French insisted that the proposals made on Community finance were not open to negotiation, unless we wanted to reopen the question of New Zealand. Their proposals provided for a contribution of 8.64 per cent in 1973, and 18.92 per cent in 1977. For some time negotiations continued outside the Conference, with M. Deniau and M. Wellenstein of the Commission expounding to us the Community's position and conveying to them our counter-proposals. We settled the basis of correctives in 1978 and 1979 but we could not move the Community on their main percentage proposals. Shortly before midnight on 22–23 June Mr. Rippon had received a telegram from the Prime Minister authorising him (provided there was a satisfactory settlement on New Zealand) to accept not more than nine per cent as our 1973 contribution. Accordingly, we accepted the Community's proposals. I will not set them out in detail here; they are fully described in the White Paper of July 1971 and in the Act of Accession.

20

The Common Commercial Policy

Joining the Community involved, in the main, acceptance of or adaptation to its existing policies. The most striking and complete of the Community's existing policies was of course its Common Agricultural Policy; and it was this policy from which almost all our main problems and difficulties derived. Thus the problems of sugar, New Zealand and Community finance, and indeed the problem of Fisheries also, were all created by the nature and consequences of the Community's Common Agricultural Policy. So were the problems of increased domestic food prices and of our own agricultural transition arrangements. So were most problems of traditional suppliers of our market, such as Australia. So were a large number of lesser but still important problems, such as that of animal health. In most other areas—economic and monetary, transport, social, regional, technical barriers to trade, energy, harmonisation of taxation, company law—the Community's common policies were fortunately still, at the time of our negotiations, relatively rudimentary, though beginning to develop fast. Free movement of labour was an advanced area, but it caused us few difficulties. Indeed apart from agriculture the only other major and fully developed common policy of the Community was its Common Commercial Policy. To this also we had to adapt ourselves, and a very large proportion indeed of our negotiations, from the very beginning to the very end, was concerned with this process.

2. The Community's Common Commercial Policy found expression in very much more than merely the Customs Union and the Common External Tariff. The Tariff itself had different origins in respect of products related to the European Coal and Steel Community and to Euratom. But apart from tariffs the Community had more or less fully developed rules in respect of, for instance, safeguards, drawback, dumping, State monopolies, fiscal duties and export credits. It had its own tariff nomenclature; it had special arrangements for tariff quotas. All these rules and others were developing all the time, not least during the period of our negotiations when, to give one example, the Community initiated its scheme of generalised preferences for the benefit of developing countries. In addition, the Community had a variety of agreements with third countries, both preferential and non-preferential, to which it was necessary that we should, with suitable adaptations and transitional arrangements, become a

party by the time of our accession. By virtue of Articles 4 and 108 of the Treaty of Accession, this exceedingly complex process was deferred to the period between the signature of the Treaty and its entry into force. And in respect of our own trade with the Commonwealth developing countries offered the '1963 options' (see Chapter 13), we secured a longer delay: a standstill till 31 January, 1975. We for our part had our own special trading arrangements which complicated the process of adaptation. They included Commonwealth Preference, EFTA and the Anglo-Irish Free Trade Agreement.

3. Sorting out the immense puzzle to which all this added up was a prolonged and exceedingly complex process. It was less spectacular as a rule, in the sense of attracting less public attention, than the major problems deriving from the Common Agricultural Policy. It was also less politically difficult; but it would be wrong to suppose that it was much less important. The interests involved were often of considerable magnitude to industry in this country. This led to a requirement for continual consultation and contact by Government Departments in London (principally of course the Department of Trade and Industry) with the industrial organisations and associations concerned, and often with individual major firms. But negotiating with the Community the many scores of issues deriving from the Common Commercial Policy was for two reasons rather easier than in the case of the Common Agricultural Policy.

4. First of all, there was never the same constant major interest on the part of a single Member State of the Community to overcome. The Common Agricultural Policy of course benefited other Member States besides France; indeed the benefits derived from it by the Netherlands are proportionately greater even than those derived from it by France. Nevertheless, defence of the Common Agricultural Policy in all its aspects, including especially sugar, dairy products and finance, was a peculiar interest of France; and consequently, in a very real sense, the agricultural and financial arrangements we sought were in continual opposition to the interests of France. No comparable situation prevailed in the case of the Common Commercial Policy and its various ramifications. Here and there an individual Member State had a major interest; but France as a rule no more than the rest. Such a major interest would be fought for; but it seldom engaged the obligatory loyalty of the whole Community to the same extent that the agricultural issues did. Sometimes, in the negotiations deriving from the Common Commercial Policy, the Community would endorse and defend a minor national interest of one of its members only in a rather perfunctory way. They would give it a run for a single round of negotiation; but if it met with firm resistance from us it was much more likely to be dropped than in an agricultural case.

5. The second major reason why negotiations on the Common Commercial Policy were rather easier than those on the Common Agricultural Policy was that, on the whole, the Community—just because there was no major single national interest involved—was much more open to persuasion by rational argument. If we had a good case to make it usually received fair consideration.

In this field, of course, as in every other, the usual strong force of inertia was on the side of existing Community arrangements. The Community's habitual complacent affection for everything on which it had agreed (deriving of course as usual from the difficulty of overturning bargains struck in the past on the basis of competing national interests, or modifying administrative arrangements to which the Six had grown accustomed) had to be overcome. But these obstacles could be overcome by persuasion and persistence, without the need, as a rule, to invoke major political pressure. Thus fairly few of these problems required to be raised at Ministerial meetings. The Commission moreover were able to play a more significant role than in some other fields, just because so many of the matters at issue involved the kind of expert and detailed study and argument which they are peculiarly competent to conduct. Thus many of the eventual solutions were worked out in direct contacts between our Delegation and the Commission.

6. To deal with all these matters even in summary form would require infinite space and much greater knowledge than I possess. I shall therefore in this chapter deal with only a few of them, and rather superficially at that. For this I must apologise to Mr. Denman of the United Kingdom Delegation in particular, and to his colleagues from the Department of Trade and Industry, who conducted our negotiations on these matters with the greatest ingenuity and tenacity. The results of their work are scattered all over the Treaty of Accession. Behind every one of Articles 31 to 49 of the Act of Accession, dealing with transitional measures in respect of the free movement of goods, lies an infinity of argument. And much of the outcome of all this argument was eventually precipitated elsewhere, for instance in Article 4 of the Act; in Articles 108 to 115; in Articles 117 to 119; in Articles 135 and 136; in Protocols Nos. 8 to 15 (the tariff quota arrangements) and in Protocols Nos. 22 and 23. There are further parts of the Treaty which derive exclusively from this work on the Common Commercial Policy, such as Annexes III and IV; and much of the content of Annexes I, II, V (last section only), VII, X and XI (all of which Annexes reflected in the main the work of the group on Secondary Legislation) derive from it also, as do a couple of the Declarations recorded in the Final Act of the Conference.

7. Some of the Commercial policy issues are dealt with elsewhere in this Report. A few are covered in Section 2 of Annex I on Secondary Legislation.* Chapters 8 and 9 contain a summary account of the way the negotiations as a whole developed. From these Chapters it will be seen that the list of issues deriving from the Common Commercial Policy given in paragraph 2 above was not exhaustive. To it should be added liberalisation lists and trade relations with State trading countries; trade agreements for the Asian Commonwealth countries not qualifying for association; charges having an equivalent effect to duties; travellers' franchise; Protocol XVII concluded under List G of Annex I to the Treaty of Rome ('Flying Machines'); and various problems deriving from the Anglo-Irish Free Trade Agreement. Chapter 11 of this Report has already

* Not printed

described in some detail how the most important question of all in the field of the Common Commercial Policy—the transitional arrangements agreed for industrial tariffs—was approached and settled. To complete the story on tariffs, I should record that a similar tariff timetable (in spite of our opening position, as stated by Mr. Brown in July 1967, that 'in the case of the European Coal and Steel Community we seek only a limited period of transition') was agreed for products covered by the Treaty establishing the Coal and Steel Community. By paragraph 2 (*b*) of Article 32 of the Act and Annex III thereto, a period of one year from entry into force was agreed for abolishing Customs duties on EURATOM products. By paragraph 3 of Article 32 of the Treaty and Annex IV thereto the first tariff reductions on products subject to contractual margins of Commonwealth Preference were deferred until 1 July, 1973. This broadly completed the programme for the reduction and abolition of tariffs.

8. I shall make no attempt, in this Chapter or elsewhere, to tell the story of most of the issues listed in paragraph 2 above, as supplemented in paragraph 7. The same must apply to the very important and complex question of cotton textiles, which could have become, but happily did not, a major problem of the negotiations. Here the trouble was caused by the widely differing import régimes of the Community on the one hand and the United Kingdom on the other, and was compounded by changes in our own policy which were taking place towards the end of 1971, due in part to the effect on the Lancashire industry of our then rising level of unemployment. A number of discussions on these matters took place between our Delegation and the Commission, but the problem was kept outside the Conference and eventually settled by an understanding relating to the way in which we would implement, on 1 January, 1974, the Community's Scheme of Generalised Preferences. But I must omit the details of this, as of much else; and accordingly this Chapter will be confined to three topics, of an uneven but fairly general importance: the general consideration of the principles of the Common Commercial Policy with which the negotiations began; the important question of tariff quotas; and the way in which our release from our obligations under the EFTA agreement was settled.

9. The first of these three subjects was one of little difficulty but a certain general interest. We decided at the outset of the negotiations that, as part of our policy of opening on a broad front, it would be desirable to raise the general issue of the Common Commercial Policy and our adaptation to it. What the Community wanted from us at this stage, and what we were prepared to give them, was a general assurance that we accepted the Common Commercial Policy, subject to any necessary adaptations and transitions, and a particular assurance that we accepted the principle, due shortly to enter into force, that in future all trade agreements between the Member States of the Community and third countries should be entered into not by any one of them individually but by the Community as a whole. The problem here was in the main that of trade agreements with the East European State trading countries. It may be

that the Community was particularly anxious to elicit from us a general acceptance of the Common Commercial Policy because such an acceptance had not been explicitly given in Mr. Brown's statement of July 1967, though he had in that statement declared our readiness to accept the Common External Tariff.

10. Our purpose in raising these general issues at the outset of the Conference was to begin with something relatively easy on which, in order to demonstrate progress, agreement could be reached on 27 October, 1970, the first Ministerial meeting of the Conference after the summer holidays. Accordingly, we opened a general debate on the Common Commercial Policy in the early meetings of the Deputies. After a few discussions the way was open for formal statements to be exchanged on 27 October between Herr Scheel and Mr. Rippon and recorded in the minutes of the Conference. These statements recorded our acceptance of the 'progressive standardisation' of agreements between Member States and third countries; and our acceptance of the Common Commercial Policy subject to its development. All this was indeed little more than shadow boxing, in the sense both that it had little substance and that it was staged for public display. It was a useful step forward; but no more than a necessary prelude to the many difficult and detailed problems the Common Commercial Policy was yet to throw up.

11. I have selected the question of tariff quotas for description in this Chapter for two reasons. First, because it was a matter of major importance in the negotiations. Second, because it provided—and in this it was almost unique in the negotiations—an example of orderly, rational and successful negotiation of a highly technical character. Most of our negotiating problems with the Community should ideally have been, but could not be, settled in the way in which the problem of tariff quotas was settled. It was tackled relatively dispassionately, because although there were quite serious conflicting material interests involved they were not such as to paralyse the Community and make it impossible for them to achieve common positions except under intense political pressure. It was also dealt with throughout by experts from all parties concerned and on the basis of a very thorough exercise to agree on the relevant facts. Not only the facts but solutions too were established by experts. This was almost the only important area of the negotiations in which experts on the Community side were given sufficient latitude by their Governments to exchange concessions and reach sensible conclusions. It was also—apart from the drafting of the Treaty—the only area in which the work was done by a multilateral group, with experts from the Commission, all the Member States and all the applicants working together.

12. This was also an area in which we profited from experience in the negotiations of 1961 to 1963. The Commentary on the Narrative Report on those negotiations, prepared by the senior members of the Delegation, contained the following passage:

'In the tariff field we think that there was too much rigidity in our position.

> In the Lord Privy Seal's opening statement we proposed that the common tariff on five important industrial materials [several more materials were added later] should be reduced to nil. We maintained this request unchanged for a very long time, although it became clear quite soon that it was not negotiable as it stood. Unfortunately, this appeared to give the impression that there was some special significance about a reduction of the tariff to nil, and that a substantial reduction to a figure greater than nil would not meet our needs. It became politically difficult to modify our request.'

In 1970 we avoided the mistake of asking for nil tariffs. We succeeded in most cases in getting something near enough in practice to such an outcome to meet our requirements. But by asking for tariff quotas instead of for nil tariffs as such we avoided a head-on collision with the sanctity of the Common External Tariff, and thus created a more friendly and rational atmosphere in which the problems at issue could be debated dispassionately, and principles were not at stake.[1]

13. We opened up the question in July 1970 by tabling a paper. I will quote its first three paragraphs, since they set out the problem briefly:

> 'As Her Majesty's Government have already made clear the United Kingdom is content to accept the Common External Tariff as it will stand after the Kennedy Round reductions have been made. But in a few cases this would mean a new charge on raw material supplies which would have damaging consequences for British industry. It was for this reason that our request for a series of nil tariffs played a prominent part in the 1961–63 negotiations. The Community will recall that some limited offers were made including some nil tariffs.
>
> 'In the interests of limiting the questions to be settled in the negotiations to a minimum, we do not this time intend to ask for any reductions in tariffs. Rather we hope that the problems of British industry in so far as they are not dealt with as a result of arrangements made for developing Commonwealth countries can be dealt with in the same way as the problems of the Member States were dealt with—by tariff quotas granted either under Protocols to List G or under Article 25 of the Treaty of Rome.
>
> 'Attached is a list of a dozen commodities where problems for the United Kingdom of the sort described would arise. We have set out in each case the facts as we see them of the tariff and the supply position and the nature of the problem. We would like to discuss this assessment with the Community in order first to arrive at a joint appreciation of the facts.'

14. The 12 commodities we listed were phosphorous, alumina, silicon carbide, wattle extract, plywood, woodpulp, newsprint, ferro-chrome, ferro-silicon,

[1] The distinction between asking for nil tariffs and for a tariff quota was more than just presentational. A nil tariff would apply to the whole European Community and would require the lowering of the protection of existing Member States. A tariff quota could be limited quantitatively or could be applied only to one applicant country (as phosphorous was to the UK); and it could have a tariff rate somewhere between nil and the rate under the Common External Tariff.

aluminium, lead and zinc. In addition, we asked separately that the temporary suspension of the Common External Tariff on tea to zero, which had been one of the few practical outcomes of the earlier negotiations and dated from an arrangement we made with the Community in 1963, should be made permanent. The Danes also asked for tariff quotas on five other products: but these caused little difficulty, and after examination the Danes were satisfied that no arrangements comparable to our tariff quota Protocols were needed for them. The problem with our 12 commodities arose of course from the fact that, while in some cases all and in others most (i.e. those from the Commonwealth or EFTA) of our supplies of them entered the United Kingdom duty free, they would be subject to duty under the Common External Tariff. This reflects not so much a more protectionist attitude on the part of the Community as a different supply situation. Their internal sources of raw and semi-fabricated materials are larger than ours. In the case of our own most important raw material—coal—we had for long had an absolute prohibition of imports.

15. Our requests for tariff quotas had an interest for others besides ourselves. In particular, they were of great importance to Canada, which is an important supplier of many of the commodities in question. These included phosphorus, since in 1967 the British firm which used to produce all the phosphorus used in the United Kingdom had decided to transfer all its phosphorus production to Newfoundland, thereby making the United Kingdom wholly dependent on supplies (which of course were free of duty) from Canada. We were not able to do much in the negotiations to safeguard Canada's agricultural exports to our market; it was all the more important therefore that, in the field of tariff quotas, we were able to secure arrangements which will go a long way to protect some of their exports to us of raw materials and semi-fabricated products. Moreover, though Canada had the major interest, there are other Commonwealth countries too who will benefit from these arrangements, including Australia and several developing countries. Another factor, a complicating or simplifying one depending on the outcome, was the position of Norway. They too supplied important quantities of some of these materials duty-free (under EFTA arrangements) to our market. If they entered the Community, there would be no problem; but if they did not there would be a problem. It was in the main the Norwegian situation which helped us to reach understandings in the cases of silicon carbide, ferro-silicon, ferro-chrome and aluminium, which avoided the need for special arrangements in the Treaty. However, Paragraph 1 of Article 49 of the Act of Accession—which reads: 'Protocols Nos. 8 to 15 annexed to this Act shall not preclude any alteration to or suspension of duties decided under Article 28 of the EEC Treaty'—remains as a fallback provision in case of need.

16. It took a long time to get negotiations on tariff quotas started. From September to November we regularly pressed at meetings of the Deputies for some progress, urging the special importance of demonstrating to British industry that their requirements were on the way to being met. No doubt in this period the Member States of the Community were engaged on the process, which we

had already completed, of consulting their own industries. Eventually, in November, a procedure was agreed by which a multilateral fact-finding group was established; and simultaneously the Community declared its position on 8 of the 13 commodities—that is to say the 12 plus tea. Work in the fact-finding group, chaired by the Commission, proceeded at several meetings; and from time to time one side or the other made statements at meetings of the Deputies about its views or requirements. In January 1971 we agreed on further procedures. When the Community had declared its position on the remaining five products, the fact-finding work should be completed; and thereafter a multilateral working group to negotiate solutions would be set up. Matters moved forward on this basis. On 23 February, at a meeting of the Deputies, the Community stated its position on the five outstanding products; Mr. Denman made a general statement at a Deputies' meeting on 9 March, by way of reaction to the Community's proposals; and the multilateral working group to negotiate solutions was then established and met for the first time on 19 March.

17. At this point the Chairmanship of the group was taken over from the Commission by M. Renaud of the French Delegation, who proved an excellent Chairman. The work of the group moved forward smoothly, based by now on elaborate agreed papers setting out the facts of current supply and prospective production. After several meetings, the whole issue returned, with a report from the group, to the Deputies on 4 May. By then agreement had been reached on how to deal with 9 of the 13 products. When the Deputies met again the following day, three more (phosphorus, wattle extract and plywood) were settled as a result of reasonable compromises; and only alumina remained. The results reached and the one outstanding issue were reported to the Ministerial meeting on 11 May. It proved impossible to settle the question of alumina at that meeting. But as a result of a concession by the Community further progress was made in a meeting of the multilateral group on 26 May. The matter was further discussed at a meeting of the Deputies on 1 June; there remained one difficulty with the Italians which we managed to overcome; and the question of alumina was formally settled at the Ministerial meeting on 7 June. I will not attempt to describe the very complicated outcome of all these negotiations on tariff quotas, since it is succinctly recorded in Protocols Nos. 8 to 15. We did not get everything we wanted; but we got enough to meet our principal requirements satisfactorily.

18. The third and final topic I have selected to describe in this Chapter is the way in which our release from our obligations under the EFTA agreement was settled. This problem was mainly, though not exclusively, a consequence of the Community's Common Commercial Policy. It had a long history. In the negotiations from 1961 to 1963, we had the 'London Declaration' of July 1961 hanging round our necks; and even if we had otherwise succeeded in our negotiations, this would have presented us with major problems. By it we had undertaken to our EFTA partners that none of us would enter the Community until satisfactory arrangements had been agreed for all. Early in 1967, as we approached our second application to join the Communities, we succeeded,

against much opposition from the EFTA neutrals led by Switzerland, in ridding ourselves of this burden; and the Communiqué issued after the meeting of the EFTA Ministerial Council in London in April of that year finally disposed of it. This was a necessary process, for the Community had developed and cherished a doctrine about the impossibility of 'double appartenance'.

19. Nevertheless, while we had gained, and our EFTA partners had reluctantly accepted, our freedom to enter the Community irrespective of the arrangements they might get, we did not in 1971 feel that it would be essential for us to have formally terminated our EFTA membership by the prospective date (1 January, 1973) of our entry into the Community. There were several reasons for this. First, we hoped that our proposal for a year's 'initiation period', and when it had been dropped the agreement we reached with the Community that we need not make our first moves towards the Common External Tariff until 1 January, 1974, would mean that no practical difficulty would arise if our formal membership of EFTA were to continue for a year after we had joined the Community. And it seemed to us difficult to arrange things otherwise, because, on the one hand, the EFTA Convention provided that a member could leave it on giving one year's notice; and, on the other hand, we did not feel we could give such notice until we were absolutely certain that we were about to enter the Community, and we could not be certain until the process of ratification had been completed. The provisions for denunciation in the EFTA Convention left no room for conditional notice.

20. Accordingly, before this problem arose in the negotiations, our line was that we would not wish to give notice of our intention to withdraw from EFTA until we were in a position to deposit our instrument of ratification of our Treaty of Accession to the Community, that it to say we intended to give a year's notice from the last day of 1972. But at the end of September 1971 the Community rather unexpectedly began to adopt the line that any period of simultaneous membership of both organisations was impermissible. At first we resisted this, and argued the case described above. We received some sympathy from the Germans, the Dutch and the Belgians; but the others, in particular the French and the Commission, took a different line. They argued—and we could not deny the validity of these arguments—that there would be real discrepancies and conflicting obligations, quite apart from the tariff field. Such matters as rules of origin, safeguard clauses, rules of competition and certain agricultural arrangements would involve us in conflicting obligations; and the Commission insisted that we could not properly remain subject to decisions of the EFTA Council when we had become members of the Community. On 12 October, at a meeting of the Deputies, Signor Bombassei made a communication to me (outside the Conference) which stated simply that the Community wished to inform the candidate States that, in its opinion, incompatibility would exist, from the entry into force of the Treaty of Accession, between membership of the Community and membership of EFTA. We had arranged that this communication should be made outside the Conference in order to limit the risk of public attention being attracted to it; and in this we succeeded.

21. The date was somewhat delicate. The debate in Parliament on the decision of principle to join the Community was due to begin little more than a week later; the EFTA Ministerial Council was due to meet in Geneva on 4 November. It was important that the problem should not become one of public controversy. We reviewed our policy, and came to the conclusion that we should have to accept the Community's argument. We decided that we would have to give notice of our withdrawal from EFTA before the end of 1971, so that we would cease to be members on 31 December, 1972. We assumed, rightly as it proved, that our EFTA partners would be prepared to agree that, if for any reason our membership of the Community were frustrated, our notice of withdrawal would be disregarded and we could continue as members of EFTA.

22. A difficulty arose because of the rather different position of Denmark and Norway. We told them that we intended to inform the EFTA Ministerial meeting on 4 November that we would give notice of withdrawal by the end of the year. They for their part, while understanding our problem, decided that they could not themselves give notice so early. We had already, by now, the 'decision of principle' of Parliament behind us; they had a much longer way to travel in their domestic procedures before they could take formal steps to terminate their membership of EFTA. The Danes in particular made clear that they could not give notice of withdrawal from EFTA without the approval of Parliament; and had no prospect of getting such approval at so early a stage.

23. We never gave a formal reply to the communication made to us by the Community on 12 October, though on 3 November I told Signor Bombassei privately of the action we were likely to take next day in Geneva. At the Geneva meeting, Mr. Rippon duly gave notice of our intention. Some of our EFTA partners were a bit disturbed, but rather less than we had anticipated. The Permanent Council of EFTA was asked to make practical proposals to find a way round the difficulties. In the end, EFTA accepted that we should give our notice before the end of the year, and that we should be welcomed back to the fold should it for any reason fail to take effect. They agreed also on a procedure to allow the Danes and Norwegians to give, at a much later stage, shorter notice which would nevertheless be accepted as compatible with the provisions of the Convention. On 17 December, 1971 our Ambassador in Stockholm gave formal notice, in accordance with the EFTA Convention, to the Swedish Government that we should withdraw from EFTA on 31 December, 1972.[1]

[1] The main reason why the problems that arose over EFTA in the 1970–72 accession negotiations were so much less than those that arose in 1961–63 was because of a fundamental shift in the European Community's attitude to the non-candidate EFTA countries. In the first negotiations, which took place shortly after the breakdown of the attempt to establish a Europe-wide free trade area including the members of both the European Community and EFTA, the Community's attitude was defensive and restrictive. By the time the second set of accession negotiations got under way the European Community was ready to contemplate the negotiation of free trade area agreements with each of the non-candidate EFTA countries. And a full set of such agreements were concluded during 1972–73.

21

The Other Communities

(by Mr. P. Shovelton)

Our aims and tactics for the European Coal and Steel Community (ECSC) and EURATOM had been worked out in detail by the Ministry of Technology before the start of the negotiations and, as with other subjects, had been cleared by the Working Group for Europe. Our major objective, whilst accepting fully the Treaty of Paris which established the ECSC and the Treaty of Rome which established EURATOM, was to make the minimum changes in the structure, powers and practices of the United Kingdom coal, steel and atomic energy industries and of the powers of Her Majesty's Government in relation to them. But there was a doubt in the case of steel. The Conservative Government, on their return to power in June 1970, were pledged 'progressively to reduce the involvement of the State in the nationalised industries, for example in the steel industry, so as to improve their competitiveness'. There was therefore some debate before the negotiations opened whether our objective should go so far as to maintain the existing organisation of the British Steel Corporation. It was decided, however, that no indication should be given of a possible change of attitude until United Kingdom policy had been worked out and it could be determined how valuable any concession might be to us. In the event Ministers concluded by the spring of 1971 that they had to maintain the structure of the British steel industry, and its division between the public and the private sectors, largely as they had found it. The status quo therefore remained the objective.

2. Otherwise the negotiating briefs raised certain specialised problems—adaptation to the ECSC coal and steel pricing rules, protection against third country coal imports to the United Kingdom under the guise of Community coal, EURATOM safeguards and controls, the compulsory declaration of nuclear patents and so on. But it was not anticipated that this part of the negotiations would give rise to much trouble or take very long. Over by Christmas was the common assumption. And upon entry it was assumed that we would be able to accept the Treaties with a very short transitional period. Merely a year was anticipated.

3. In the event things did not prove quite so simple. The main settlements were not reached until May 1971 for EURATOM and until June the same year for ECSC. Even then a number of issues were left over for later settlement and

the final agreements, including agreement on the terms of Treaty drafting, were not arrived at until the concluding days of the negotiations in January 1972. To a large extent this reflected the time spent by the 'experts' of the Six in discussions in their own Groupe CECA and the Groupe Atomique. The officials from the Ministries concerned in the different countries always seemed to take an inordinate time to prepare a particular line for the Permanent Representative seven though on our side we were usually able to respond from one meeting to the next.

A.—THE EUROPEAN COAL AND STEEL COMMUNITY

4. ECSC was one of the few subjects where at our first Ministerial meeting on 21 July it was agreed, in effect, that a specialist Working Group should be set up between the Commission and the United Kingdom. The actual terms of reference were—'Having taken the wishes of the United Kingdom Delegation into account the Community Delegation gives the Commission a mandate to draw up, in liaison with the United Kingdom Delegation, an inventory of the provisions and practices existing within the United Kingdom which would be contrary to the ECSC Treaty and to its implementing regulations.' This wording was hardly satisfactory as it failed to cover all the issues at stake—for example our participation in the separate ECSC financing system or in the ECSC Consultative Committee. The words also contained a rather unfortunate flavour of putting the United Kingdom in the dock. Nevertheless in the interests of a quick settlement at the end of the day of 21 July Mr. Barber, then leading the United Kingdom team, decided to accept them.

5. In the execution of their mandate the Commission prepared two lengthy questionnaires based upon a good deal of research which they had undertaken prior to the start of the negotiations. They sent them to us in mid-September 1970. There were 23 questions on coal and 29 on steel. The questions concentrated on the powers of the United Kingdom Government in relation to the nationalised coal and steel undertakings, the organisation of the undertakings, the degree to which they might be subsidised by the State, their methods of price-fixing, the degree of 'transparency' of prices, including freight rates, and the extent of commercial agreements or long-term contracts giving favourable terms to special customers. (Transparency is the Treaty of Paris term to denote 'openness' or 'availability for all to see'.) In addition there were certain special questions about the extent of any supplementary social security schemes in the steel sector, about the private steel companies (designed to elucidate whether there might be any unfair discrimination, in Treaty of Paris terms, between the public and the private sectors), about our methods of supply of iron ore, and our control over scrap supplies and imports of coal. We answered these questions carefully and extensively and gave the Commission a full set of the legislation and major State papers concerning the two industries as well as voluminous statistics.

6. It was in preparing the answers that the United Kingdom machinery we

had set in motion for associating our coal and steel undertakings with the negotiations first came into play. Under the chairmanship of the Ministry of Technology (later the Department of Trade and Industry) a Coal and Steel Advisory Group (CSAG) was established with representatives of the Foreign Office, the Ministry of Transport (later Department of the Environment), the National Coal Board (NCB), the British Steel Corporation (BSC) and the British Independent Steel Producers' Association. This Group functioned throughout the negotiations (and indeed right up to June 1972) in order to reach agreement on the settlement of problems concerned with entry. The Group proved a most valuable means of consulting the industries and, although serious differences of approach had to be resolved from time to time, it never proved necessary at any stage of the negotiations for the nationalised concerns or the private steel sector to make separate representations to Ministers.

7. The Commission's questionnaire was answered in October and two meetings in Brussels followed at which a DTI team answered supplementary questions from a team of Commission experts drawn from the Commission's Negotiating Task Force, and its Directorates-General III, IV, VII and XVII. By mid-November the Commission team were satisfied they had all the information and explanations they wanted and proceeded to draft their report for the Commission to send to the Council. This was their report and we were not involved in its drafting though we did manage to obtain a sight of it. The major question, over which the Commission took at least two meetings, was the size and structure of the BSC. The Commission had for some time, in operating Article 66 of the Treaty of Paris relating to the approval of mergers, worked by a rule 'that there would be a serious risk to the maintenance of effective competition if the share of production of the largest undertakings in the Community exceeded 12–13 per cent of Community production of crude steel and that it would carefully examine requests for authorisation for mergers exceeding this ceiling'. The question therefore arose what effect the existence of an undertaking of the size of the BSC, producing 24 million tons of steel a year, or 18 per cent of the total production of the enlarged Community, would have on this policy. All the members of the Commission were understood to be in favour of drawing the attention of the Council to this dilemma; some were in favour of recommending that the BSC should be split up so as to conform with the Community's policies on competition. In the end the Commission reported to the Council, just before Christmas 1970, in the following terms—'In the enlarged Community, the development of a merger process by reference to the existence of an undertaking of the size of the BSC must be avoided; in the long run such a process would lead to a limited number of large enterprises set up mainly within the frontiers of each of the States. Such a market structure would not be in accordance with the objectives of the Treaty of Paris'. In other words the outlook did not look too good for the United Kingdom negotiating position.

8. With the submission of the Commission's report to the Council, which

promptly referred it to the Permanent Representatives, who promptly referred it to the Groupe CECA (experts from the capitals of the Six at, roughly, Counsellor level), almost total silence fell on the ECSC part of the negotiations for over four months. We used the intervening period to lobby the members of the Groupe CECA, both in Brussels and in their own capitals, and in particular to let it be known at the level of the Permanent Representatives in Brussels that to provoke the issue of the size of the BSC in the Negotiating Conference itself would be to add an extremely difficult and delicate item to the major issues of the negotiation—and one with serious political undertones in the United Kingdom in view of the marginal number of Labour pro-Marketeer MPs from the steel (and for that matter coal) constituencies. The four month waiting period was also used to discuss with the Commission experts the extent and make-up of the ECSC financial reserves and the basis of the calculations on which we might expect to receive a request from the Community to contribute to these reserves. From these, as members, we would ultimately be gaining by way of grants for research and for 'readaptation' (i.e. the Community term for redundancy, resettlement and retraining benefits) and by way of loans for the development of coal and steel undertakings and for 'reconversion' (i.e. the setting up of other industries in declining coal mining and steelmaking areas). I return to this question of our contribution to the ECSC reserves later.

9. The next important date in the ECSC negotiation is 4 May, 1971. On that day the Community delegation tabled, at a Deputies' meeting, a most significant statement. This was the result of the Commission's December report, and of its study by the Groupe CECA and the Permanent Representatives. Most important of all the Community Delegation said that it was 'anxious to assure the United Kingdom Delegation that it does not intend to call into question either the size or the legal position as regards the ownership of the National Coal Board and of the British Steel Corporation'. For the rest the Community delegation sought an assurance that 'the British Government considers that it will be obliged to eliminate provisions and practices contrary to the Treaty of Paris very soon after its accession to the ECSC, without prejudice to the transitional measures necessary for implementing the Community rules'. And a detailed 'List of Incompatibilities' (i.e. 'the provisions and practices existing in the United Kingdom which are contrary to the ECSC Treaty and its implementing regulations') was attached to the Community statement. This referred to the incompatibility of the Secretary of State's powers of general direction over the nationalised industries, of giving a specific direction in the matter of prices arising out of a recommendation of the Iron and Steel Consumers' Council, of settling disputes between the public and private steel sectors, and of approving investment in the private steel sector after consulting the BSC; it drew attention, *inter alia*, to the extensive degree of incompatibility in the United Kingdom pricing practices, particularly those of steel, and to the fact that if the BSC continued not to pay dividends, while still having access to long-term financial resources, this could be incompatible with the Treaty.

10. On receipt of this document an earnest debate took place in the United Kingdom within the Coal and Steel Advisory Group. It was widely felt that the 'list of incompatibilities' should be dealt with seriatim and the United Kingdom position explained, or the Community position disputed, point by point. In particular it was considered desirable to explore the Community's views on pricing procedures—which, after the BSC size issue, was the key element in the negotiations. On the other hand the tactics of the negotiation as a whole dictated that ECSC issues should be swept up as quickly and quietly as possible; and the tactics of the ECSC part of the negotiation indicated that it might be far preferable in the long run to iron out some of the rough edges that stood between the Delegations either during the interim period or after entry when the United Kingdom would be represented both in the Commission and the Council and our negotiating position would thereby be immensely stronger. The informal but very strong advice of the Commission's Negotiating Task Force was not to raise the 'list of incompatibilities' point by point, and in particular not the pricing issue. If we did they feared that the ECSC negotiation would get bogged down in technicalities, that it would take months more to solve, and the final result might well be highly unpalatable to the British.

11. So, with this advice very much in mind the United Kingdom negotiating team, at a late hour in Brussels on 17 May, decided to make at the Deputies' Meeting the next day simply a short statement noting with satisfaction the intention of the Community not to call into question the size and legal ownership of the nationalised bodies, and undertaking to remove 'incompatibilities' either before or very soon after Accession; we also stated that we could accept the Treaty of Paris and its implementing regulations from the date of entry, subject to any transitional measures which might be agreed.

12. This last statement reflected a significant alteration in objective. It will be recalled that at the beginning of the negotiation we had said that we could accept the Treaty of Paris after a very short transitional period. Indeed the same statement had been made by the Labour Government in the Foreign Secretary's statement at the Western European Union meeting in The Hague in July 1967. The tactic had been to offer a very short transitional period perhaps a year—for ECSC (and certainly only a year for EURATOM) in return for the much longer transitional periods we wanted for agriculture, Commonwealth sugar, New Zealand dairy products and the full rigours of the Community financing system. But by May 1971 the irrelevance of this approach was evident. Many transitional periods had been settled already—the main industrial and agricultural tariff timetables, Commonwealth sugar and in the case of EURATOM (see below) we had said we could do without any transitional period at all. We were therefore free to revise our tactics on ECSC transition and go for exactly what we wanted—that is to say no transitional period at all for coal, where we required unrestricted access as soon as possible to the coal markets of the Six, and the longest possible period for hanging on to our own measures of steel protection—notably tariffs and scrap export control.

13. Thus on 1 June, at the next Deputies' meeting, we stated that we wanted the same period of transition for steel tariffs as had been agreed for industrial tariffs generally (i.e. up to July 1977—see Chapter 11) and we would like a five year transitional period during which we might, if we wished (though we were by no means certain that we did) maintain our scrap export controls (a similar request on this score having been made by the Danes, Norwegians and Irish). The Six had not replied to us by the time of the Luxembourg Ministerial meeting on 21–23 June and we therefore pressed for an answer on these points and for the whole ECSC negotiation to be cleared up, so far as the Ministerial level was concerned, at that meeting.

14. It was at this period too that the amount of our contribution to the ECSC reserve funds was settled. There was no dispute between the two sides that the amount of the reserves which should be taken as the basis of the calculation was, roughly, £90 million or 220 million units of account. Argument did develop, largely within the councils of the Six themselves, as to the proportion which we should be asked to contribute. The value of our coal and steel production amounted to some 27 per cent of the total Community production and the French in particular considered that on a proper actuarial basis we should pay 27 per cent of £114 million (i.e. £90 million plus 27 per cent of £90 million). Others were however prepared that we should simply pay the straight 27 per cent. And so it turned out. We were asked on 1 June to pay £24 million or 57 million units of account in three equal annual payments beginning on 1 January, 1973. This we accepted without question seeing that the demand could have been considerably higher and that we foresaw substantial benefits from the funds in view of the extent of the forthcoming rundown of our coal industry and the reorganisation of our steel industry. Indeed the more difficult question—which had to be settled this side of the Channel—was who should pay, Her Majesty's Government or the industries. The Treasury felt strongly that the latter should pay. But the industries, strongly backed by DTI, felt the opposite. The matter was decided by Ministers, against the Treasury, on the grounds that the coal and steel industries had not themselves applied for entry, that the benefits from the funds would accrue to other industries and to local authorities as well as coal and steel, and that it was important to keep the goodwill of the industries throughout the negotiations.

15. This then was the position reached by the time of the June Luxembourg Ministerial meeting. After a good deal of prodding on the first day of the meeting, the Six were induced to make a statement. They summarised the agreements reached so far at official level—no intention of calling in question the size of the NCB or BSC, expectation that we would remove the incompatibilities, amount of our contribution to the reserves, etc.—and then replied on the questions of tariffs and scrap. For tariffs they were willing to give us what we had asked—transition over the four and a half year period agreed for industrial tariffs generally. For the removal of our scrap export controls they were willing to give us a two year period of transition rather than the five year

period we had asked for. At the same time they emphasised that there were still certain ECSC items outstanding which they would return to in due course. Mr. Rippon in reply accepted the Six's offers on tariffs and scrap, and said that this now settled ECSC so far as Ministers were concerned and the remaining items could be agreed at the level of the Deputies.

16. It seemed therefore that at the end of the Luxembourg meeting ECSC as a subject in the negotiations had been satisfactorily settled. But the midsummer calm was soon to be shattered by two developments. *The Guardian* had at the time recently printed an article very critical of the ECSC by Professor Lindsay of the London School of Economics. It followed this up on 30 June with a front page article under the headline 'Britain to lose control of Coal to Six' which made it quite clear that the list of incompatibilities was in the hands of the author of the article, Mr. Mark Arnold Foster. And indeed shortly afterwards he transmitted it to an MP who deposited it in the Library of the House of Commons. The tenor and many of the facts in the article were immediately contradicted by a statement hurriedly issued by the Foreign Office, with the agreement of the DTI, the same evening. But this did not inhibit public debate. The points in Mr. Foster's and Professor Lindsay's articles were taken up immediately on the floor of the House and from now on every opportunity was taken by opponents of entry to point to the imagined horrific implications for the two industries if we were to go in.

17. Other newspapers and journals—the *Financial Times*, the *Sunday Times* and *The Economist*—endeavoured, with the aid of DTI, to put the record straight and in perspective. The *Financial Times* even went so far as to publish in full the list of incompatibilities and the Six's covering statement which had been tabled at the Conference meeting of 4 May, thereby trying to impress upon the public how little substance there was in Mr. Foster's and Professor Lindsay's allegations. *The Economist* wrote a strong article under the title 'The Coal and Steel Canard' and the *Sunday Times* one called 'Euro-Steel Horror—a damp squib'. These commentators emphasised that the Labour Government, as well as the Conservative Government, had announced their acceptance of the Treaty of Paris and the rules made under it, thus accepting that certain changes in the practices of, and the legislation affecting, our nationalised coal and steel industries would have to be made. It was in the light of this public debate and furore that more was put in the July White Paper (Cmnd. 4715) on ECSC than would otherwise have been the case. Paragraph 157 in particular was designed to answer the charge of loss of control.

18. The other development which shattered the short-lived calm of the Luxembourg settlement was the news, which came to the British negotiator through the Commission, that the Germans had not accepted our interpretation of the settlement so far as coal was concerned. In our view acceptance of the Treaty of Paris from the moment of accession meant freedom for coal exports as well as imports. The Germans on the other hand, within the terms of the proviso which the Six had allowed themselves at Luxembourg—namely that

they would have certain other issues to raise—considered themselves free to raise the question of the phasing out of the tariff and quota restrictions which they applied to coal. To some extent the matter was academic since the German practice is to allow coal imports free of duty and to raise the level of their quotas for coal imports whenever they have a need to import. But to us it was the principle that mattered—particularly in the highly charged atmosphere that existed in the United Kingdom following *The Guardian* articles. And before any bilateral discussion with the Germans could take place we had to go on record in the White Paper (para. 157) with the statement that 'Coal imports from Community countries will be free from restrictions, as will our coal exports to them'. It was therefore essential that a satisfactory understanding was reached with the Germans—and indeed with the other members of the Six—on this point.

19. A bilateral meeting was held with the Germans, with a representative of the NCB present, early in July. It then became clear that the German coal industry, worried by the size and competitive strength of the United Kingdom coal industry and, as they alleged, by the advantages in pricing terms of our State system of social security contributions, were using the point about tariffs and quotas as a negotiating device to secure in the Treaty of Accession a 'clause de sauvegarde' which they could use in later years if the NCB were to flood them (unlikely as this might seem) with cheap imports. A satisfactory understanding—based upon Article 2 (4) of the Transitional Provisions Convention of the Treaty of Paris—was reached with the Germans but then other difficulties appeared. The problem, having thus been stirred up in the Groupe CECA, prompted the Italians to say that they could not accept immediate abolition of tariffs for their hard-pressed coke industry. We overcame this hurdle by an undertaking that if the NCB proposed any coke exports to Italy up to July 1977 they would consult beforehand with the Italian authorities and an appropriate entry was read into the record of the Permanent Representatives. But the situation—and the wording of the safeguard clause—was still unresolved when the negotiations adjourned for the summer break.

20. When negotiations were resumed a strenuous effort was made in the context of Treaty drafting to clear up the outstanding items which the Six had had in mind at Luxembourg. Among these was the question of medium and long-term contracts entered into by the NCB and BSC which the Six feared might frustrate the operations of the Treaty and in particular its pricing rules. A great deal of further information, much of it of considerable commercial importance, was therefore passed over to the Commission to convince them (as it ultimately did) that fears on this point were unfounded. And the matter got swept up into the 'clause de sauvegarde' question, the latter having become for the Groupe CECA and the Six a hold-all which could embrace all the problems which might emerge in the immediate years after entry.

21. The wording of the safeguard clause, as first put to us at the beginning of October 1971, was highly objectionable and appeared, in theory, to put at

risk all the hard-won gains of the previous year of negotiations. The words could be held even to prejudice the basic position and structure of the nationalised industries. Great efforts were therefore required to convince the Six, bilaterally and collectively, of the impossibility of such a clause. These efforts were conducted outside the formal Conference, in order to minimise the risk of leaks. And in the end the words which eventually appeared in Article 134 of the Act of Accession were agreed on 24 November. Shortly afterwards the enlargement of the ECSC Consultative Committee, to a size which could accommodate all the members which the United Kingdom could reasonably ask for, was agreed. Finally minor matters affecting the adaptation of ECSC secondary legislation and the adjustment of ECSC international agreements to accommodate the United Kingdom were resolved. Thus by the end of 1971, over 18 months since the start of the negotiations, all the ECSC matters that had to be regulated in the Accession Treaty had been agreed, leaving over for settlement in the Interim Period other questions of almost equal importance—notably adaptation to the ECSC steel pricing system, the negotiation of Readaptation Conventions for both coal and steel under Article 56 of the Treaty of Paris and the exact United Kingdom representation on the new ECSC Consultative Committee. At the time of writing (June 1972) the first of these matters—steel pricing—has been settled while the other two are being sympathetically negotiated with the Commission.

22. The conclusion one must draw from the ECSC negotiations is that behind comparatively simple-looking subjects lie considerable dangers. The original brief for the negotiation proved in the event not to have taken sufficient account of the Six's standpoint or indeed of the seriousness and dedication which the experts of the Six countries and the Commission, many of whom had spent a lifetime on this work, would devote to this specialised subject. But the end result was satisfactory. In the July 1971 debate in the House of Lords on the White Paper Lord Robens, who had only recently left the post of Chairman of the NCB, said 'Entry will open up new opportunities for the British coal industry'. And in the October debate Lord Melchett, Chairman of the BSC, said 'I am personally convinced that we have negotiated good terms for entry. For my industry the key question of scrap supplies, tariffs, the structure of the industry and pricing have either been satisfactorily resolved or are being satisfactorily negotiated with the other Six countries involved.'

B.—EURATOM

23. As a subject for negotiation this was a good deal easier than ECSC. Indeed the difficulties were much more on the side of the Six since it was a subject over which they had been quarrelling amongst themselves for years. It was for this reason that at the first meeting of the United Kingdom Negotiating Conference on 21 July, 1970, they declined to set up a special Working Group, as we had proposed, to examine together the problems that might arise from

our acceptance of the EURATOM Treaty. And we had to wait until January 1971 for their first thoughts on the subject. It then became clear that there would be five main subjects to be dealt with in this part of the negotiations—a demand for compensation 'for our access to the acquired knowledge of EURATOM and the establishments of the Joint Research Centre (Ispra in Northern Italy, Karlsruhe in Germany, Petten in the Netherlands and Geel near Brussels); the question of nuclear safeguards, controls and inspection; the territorial application of the Treaty; the resolution of any problems stemming from the integration of each party into the other's nuclear agreements with third countries; and transition, including tariff transition. Certain other questions emerged at a later stage but these five remained the principal issues.

24. The demand for 'compensation' we promptly and firmly rejected—'We believe that the Community's stock of nuclear information, in so far as it has not become obsolete with the passage of time, is now public knowledge.' This firmness may have offended some devoted Commission servants of EURATOM but it came as no surprise to most Delegates. M. Boegner, the French Permanent Representative, said in an aside to the British negotiator 'I don't blame you!' So the Community changed tack, though it took them, in characteristic fashion, over two months to do so. They then suggested an exchange of information of 'equivalent value' This concept we accepted and several meetings were held with the Commission in the summer of 1971, on our side with representatives of the Atomic Energy Authority and the Central Electricity Generating Board present, to agree on the basis for such an exchange, which would take place on entry. There was, of course, an element of unreality, not to say farce, about these discussions, with the scientific experts on both sides realising that the actual value of knowledge we would gain from EURATOM would be very slight and that we would make quite certain that any information we handed over would be equally slight—in value, if not in volume. However, the face of EURATOM was at stake and the agreement was eventually dressed up in the splendid form in which it appears in Protocol No. 28 of the Treaty of Accession.

25. The safeguards question was potentially more tricky since we had to ensure, as a nuclear weapons State, with a special position in relation to the Non-Proliferation Treaty (NPT), that we did not accept, via the EURATOM Control system, any commitments from which we were exempted under the NPT. We based ourselves on the position of France which, though a signatory of the EURATOM Treaty, had always invoked to the full those Treaty provisions (Articles 24–28 and Article 84) which exclude defence activities from scrutiny by the Commission. But our position was further complicated in that, unlike France, we had both signed and ratified the NPT, and also volunteered to accept safeguards in the United Kingdom with exceptions related to our defence requirements. We therefore had to steer a careful course between accepting new and additional obligations which might be burdensome, and renouncing the offer which we had already made in the NPT context. An additional factor

which needed careful handling was that the five Member States who had signed the NPT were negotiating arrangements under which EURATOM safeguards would be applied in place of the International Atomic Energy Authority (IAEA) safeguards prescribed by the NPT. Their negotiations with IAEA were taking place simultaneously with ours with the Community, and the precise status of EURATOM in the Vienna negotiations represented an uncomfortable compromise between the Five's desire to get EURATOM safeguards accepted and their reluctance to entrust such delicate matters to the Commission.

26. In all this the French remained aloof and distant—while working very closely with us behind the scenes to ensure we did not weaken their position. So when questioned on our attitude we stated in the Conference that we entirely accepted that 'the system of control and inspection which applies under the EURATOM Treaty and which may apply under any Agreement eventually reached between the EURATOM countries and the International Atomic Energy Agency as a consequence of the talks now going on in Vienna, will apply to us'. Subsequently this statement was repeated, though with the words 'member countries of EURATOM' instead of 'EURATOM countries' (a subtlety which gave rise to great questionings and suspicions in the corridors of Brussels) by Mr. Rippon at the Ministerial meeting of 11 May. It was a statement of principle which, in the context of Treaty drafting, was subsumed in the wording of Article 4 of the 'Act Concerning the Conditions of Accession'.

27. The question of the application of the EURATOM Treaty to the 'non-European territories under their jurisdiction' (see Article 198 of the Treaty) boiled down to the case of Hong Kong, since no member of the Six, nor even the Commission, had any ambition to inspect, for example, the territory of St. Helena or the Falkland Islands to see whether nuclear material was being manufactured there. But Hong Kong was a different case as the Colony's ambition to install a nuclear reactor there was widely known. We pressed the Colony's case for exclusion, quoting in aid the Community's refusal to offer Hong Kong association under Part IV of the Treaty of Rome. Ultimately, after a good deal of lobbying in the corridors, the Community accepted the Colony's exclusion at the Ministerial meeting in Brussels on 11 May.

28. The problem of integrating each side into the third country agreements of the other was governed by Articles 105 and 106 of the EURATOM Treaty; and in order that the problem could be properly examined the relevant agreements, conventions and other documents had to be exchanged. For our part we sent the Commission in April 1971 seven copies (one for each Member State and one for the Commission) of 63 different agreements. We received from them 18 agreements. After making our examination we had no questions to raise and foresaw no difficulty in accepting their agreements. The Community, after eight months of diligent examination of the papers, made a statement on 22 December, 1971, containing three points—first that it would examine 'in a positive spirit' the extension of the Dragon Agreement due to expire by 30 September, 1972. (The Dragon project is an experimental reactor at Winfrith,

Dorset, which is funded partly by the United Kingdom, partly by EURATOM, and partly by Norway, Denmark, Sweden, Austria and Switzerland.) Second, that it would keep us informed of progress in the re-negotiation of the EURATOM/United States Agreement and take account of any wishes we might have. And third, that it would make a statement later 'on the question of the agreements concluded by the candidate countries in the nuclear field'. Eventually on 6 January—only a week before the guillotine was scheduled to come down on Treaty drafting—the Community informed us that 'they had no particular comments to make on the agreements we had given them'.

29. Finally transition. It will be recalled that from the WEU meeting in The Hague in July 1967 onwards Her Majesty's Government had said that they could accept the EURATOM Treaty with only a 12-month period of transition and at Luxembourg on 30 June, 1970, Mr. Barber reaffirmed this. As we got deeper into negotiation we decided that we could enter EURATOM without any period of transition at all-except for adoption of the special tariff régime applied to the nuclear materials set out in Annex IV of the Treaty (this proved to be Lists A1 and A2 of the Annex only and not List B which the Community told us had never been operated as a separate list). We decided that we needed one year to adapt to the Common External Tariff and to abolish tariffs for intra-Community nuclear trade. This proposal the Community accepted—a small concession in our favour since the trade in nuclear materials between this country and Europe, though not considerable, is in our favour.

30. These, then, were the principal subjects of the EURATOM negotiations. There were certain other matters. We accepted, for example, that the EURATOM Research programmes were part of the 'acquis communautaire' and therefore, by implication, that we would take part in them after accession. But it was also accepted that the programmes could be modified to take account of our membership; nor was any change proposed in the system whereby some programmes are 'common'—and are paid for out of the Community's budget and some are 'supplementary'—and only those countries pay who care to participate in them. Some problems also arose out of the examination of the Community's secondary legislation such as the rules for radiological protection, where it was accepted that the Community's system was less strict than ours and needed to be brought up to date to conform with the latest International Committee on Radiological Protection recommendations, and the question of a contribution to the capital of the EURATOM Supply Agency.

31. This body, which had been set up under the Treaty to operate a common supply and purchasing policy for ores, source materials and special fissile materials had been widely disregarded in the Community, particularly by the French who maintained that the Council had never confirmed its powers after the initial seven-year period referred to in Article 76. The Commission had taken France to the European Court on the question and in November 1971 the Court ruled against France. This fortified the Commission in raising the question of a contribution to the capital of the Agency from the acceding States.

Fortunately the Community themselves, influenced perhaps by the knowledge that any such demand would be an awkward irritant in the concluding stages of the negotiation, and having already at an early stage of the negotiations told us that Chapter VI of the Treaty was being revised, put the matter aside, 'reserving its position ... for the interim period'. No more has yet been heard of it.

32. It will be seen from this account that the EURATOM part of the negotiations, though a potential source of embarrassment to both sides, did not raise any really difficult or important problems. The subject was dominated at first by the demand for 'compensation' and, when that was swept aside, by a variety of international legal questions such as delighted the meticulous minds of the Commission experts and jurists and the Groupe Atomique. On the United Kingdom side the problems did not involve industry in the same acute way as did those of the ECSC. Thus there was no necessity to set up a Working Group on the analogy of the Coal and Steel Advisory Group. At the same time close contact was maintained by the DTI with the interests concerned—the Atomic Energy Authority, the Central Electricity Generating Board, the nuclear power construction companies, British Nuclear Fuels Ltd., and the British Nuclear Forum. But the really big problem of the development of nuclear power in Europe—that is to say the forging of trans-frontier industrial links which can develop and produce the nuclear power stations of the Europe of the future and sell them all over the world—fell outside the scope of the negotiations. This must now be the aim for nuclear collaboration with our partners in the enlarged Community.

22

Miscellaneous Questions I

This chapter, like Chapter 20 on the Common Commercial Policy, will be rather a superficial one. I shall deal in it, and in the next two chapters with a wide range of subjects which arose in the negotiations and are not covered by the preceding chapters. Once again I feel I should apologise to some of the members of the Delegation whose long and detailed work on many of these questions deserves a fuller record, especially to Mr. Bell of the Treasury for a very rudimentary account of the long negotiations on capital movements and the European Investment Bank. The space given to them here is in no way proportionate either to their difficulty or their importance.

A.—OTHER AGRICULTURAL QUESTIONS

2. The major agricultural questions dealt with in the preceding chapters—transitional arrangements, sugar, New Zealand and Community finance—were by no means the only agricultural questions which had to be settled in the negotiations. The arrangements reached for sugar and New Zealand were reached not in the interests of our own agriculture, or even of our consumers, but in the interests of producers in Commonwealth countries. Most of the numerous other agricultural questions we had to settle did however relate primarily to the interests of our own farmers and consumers, and to the difficult process of our adaptation to the Common Agricultural Policy. They are set out in the main in Articles 50 to 107 of the Treaty of Accession; but other important provisions are scattered through the Annexes, the Protocols and the Final Act.

3. The problems involved in many of these sectors and their outcome are described in Section 3 of Annex I to this Report.* This is because the problems there described were as a rule solved in the context of arranging for adaptations, or delays, in the work on the Community's agricultural secondary legislation. Many of the matters dealt with in Section 3 of Annex I (such as animal health and grain-based spirits) were not settled exclusively in the secondary legislation

* Not printed

exercise, but had to be pursued from time to time in the Conference at Deputies meetings, and in the case of animal health at a Ministerial meeting. In what follows I shall deal with some of the more significant agricultural questions which had, in the main, to be settled in the Conference rather than in the secondary legislation exercise.

(i) *Liquid milk, pigmeat and eggs*

4. Our problem here was in a sense a hangover from Mr. Brown's statement of July 1967, in which he had referred to milk, pigmeat and eggs as problems we would need to discuss with the Community. On the whole, by 1970, we rather wished he had not. We did not feel that problems in these areas would be especially difficult. There would indeed be problems of definition and transition; but there was no longer an overriding need to single out these commodities rather than numerous others with which we should have to deal in the course of working through the Community's regulations. But the objectives stated by Mr. Brown had of course been noted by the British farming community and had to be taken up in our negotiations as special subjects. Indeed they were special subjects, in the sense that milk, pigmeat and eggs together represent a high proportion of total British farm output.

5. We accordingly decided to raise them at the start. Mr. Barber did so in his statement to the first Ministerial meeting (21 July, 1970) and we pursued the matter in the early meetings of Deputies. The whole exercise was somewhat formal; and our objective was reduced to little more than. demonstrating, right from the start our concern with certain important aspects of domestic agriculture, and isolating one or two fairly simple but important matters on which we hoped to show progress by reaching conclusions at an early Ministerial meeting. We knew the more detailed problems involved in the Community's regulations on these commodities would have to be left for later. One important matter was however involved in these early exchanges, namely the future of the Milk Marketing Board and the compatibility of its activities with Community principles and practices. On this we reached a tolerably satisfactory result.

6. By the time of the Ministerial meeting of 27 October, 1970, exchanges with the Commission and in Deputies meetings had led to the preparation of statements which were then exchanged between Mr. Rippon and Herr Scheel. Mr. Rippon recalled that Mr. Barber had raised the problem of milk, pigmeat and eggs at the first Ministerial meeting on 21 July; referred to the discussions which had taken place and expressed the hope that agreement could now be reached on these matters, thus removing them from our future agenda. He proceeded to set out a number of understandings reached on milk, pigmeat and eggs and concluded that if Herr Scheel could confirm these then 'we need raise no further points on these items during the negotiations, except in the general context of transitional arrangements'. Herr Scheel replied with a previously agreed statement. Our objective of reaching an early agreement on

some important subjects had thus been achieved; and the statements exchanged on 27 October were annexed, 15 months later, to the Final Act of the Conference.

(ii) *The annual review*

7. This too was a hangover from the past, but in this case not only from Mr. Brown's statement of July 1967. In the earlier negotiations of 1961 to 1963 there had also been much discussion of the need for an annual review of agriculture in the enlarged Community. Our requirement to press this point on the Community derived from the importance which farmers in the United Kingdom have always attached to the annual review which, in accordance with the provisions of agricultural legislation, they hold with the Ministry of Agriculture in the process of fixing guaranteed prices for the ensuing year. Conditions in the Community were bound to be different, and the direct influence of agricultural producers on the determination of Community prices was likely to be rather less than hitherto in the United Kingdom—or at least to be expressed and achieved in different ways. But provisional agreement had been reached in the earlier negotiations on a declaration about an annual review, and it was necessary to repeat the process.

8. Once again, this was a matter which we decided to bring up at the start. Mr. Barber raised it on 21 July, 1970, and we had early contacts with the Commission and early exchanges of statements in the meetings of Deputies. The Community was concerned not to commit themselves to any mechanism which would give agricultural producers an even greater say in the process of fixing farm prices in the Community than, by various existing methods of informal consultation and political pressure, they already enjoy. We were concerned to go as far as we could to assure our producers that they would have some kind of formal part to play in the process. The result was a further exchange of statements between Herr Scheel and Mr. Rippon at the Ministerial meeting on 27 October, 1970, which was of course a compromise between the objectives of the two sides. It was, once again, useful as a sign of early progress of the Conference; and its terms, though not going as far as they would have wished, satisfied the National Farmers' Union. The agreement reached is recorded as a 'Declaration on the System for Fixing Community Farm Prices' included in the Final Act of the Conference.

(iii) *Hill farming*

9. Here too we had an obligation deriving from Mr. Brown's statement of July 1967, in which he had referred to the case of British hill farmers. This was a more substantial problem, since we feared that it would prove difficult to reconcile our various hill farming grants, which were indispensable to the viability of hill farmers, with the provisions of the Common Agricultural Policy. Nevertheless, there were times when we were half inclined to regret our commitment to raise the issue, and felt that it might have been wiser to avoid doing so ourselves in the negotiations—though of course had we not done so

the Community might have raised it—and to take our chance instead of preserving as much as we could of our system of grants for hill farmers from the much stronger position we should enjoy once we were in the Community. We felt reasonably sure that at the worst it would be a long time, and we could make it longer, before the Community could mount a successful attack on our system. We feared on the other hand that, if we did raise the matter in the negotiations, we might force the Community into an earlier challenge to a system so vital to an important section of our agriculture.

10. As things turned out, it was probably as well that we were committed to raise the question, since in the end we dealt with it rather satisfactorily. That we were able to do so was to a large extent a matter of good timing. For almost a year, we said nothing on the subject. But as the climax of the negotiations approached in the early summer of 1971, Ministers concluded that we must be able to show some satisfactory solution of our hill farming problem as part of the process of 'breaking the back of the negotiations' before the summer holidays. They wished also to be able to include a reassuring outcome on hill farming in the White Paper planned for July. The objective had been defined by Ministers as long ago as July 1970, and was that we should 'seek a firm assurance that we would be allowed to give continued assistance to our hill farmers, comparable in value to what they now received'.

11. By May 1971, when we judged the time was approaching to raise the issue, we had come to the conclusion that it was neither necessary nor desirable to seek explicit assurances from the Six about the hill farming grants. To do so, we felt, would almost certainly provoke the wrong answer. It would be wiser to go for an assurance in general terms instead. Accordingly, early in June, Mr. Kearns initiated discussions with the Commission in order to work out with them such a general assurance. The moment was propitious. We had settled agricultural transition and sugar three weeks earlier; Mr. Heath and M. Pompidou had just had their successful meeting; the stage was set for the final breakthrough at the Ministerial meeting planned for 21 and 22 June. Nevertheless, the fact that Mr. Kearns succeeded in working out with the Commission a draft declaration which met our purposes seems to me to be one of the more remarkable accomplishments of the negotiations; for there were a score of objections which the Commission, in normal times, would have been likely to raise. By 14 June we had a text provisionally agreed with the Commission, and we instructed our posts in the Six capitals of the Community to put it, and recommend it, to the Governments of the Member States. We explained that Mr. Rippon hoped to make this statement at the Ministerial meeting in Luxembourg, and that the Community would record their general agreement with our understanding as set out in it.

12. The reactions of the Six Governments were reasonably favourable, though not unmixed with hesitation. The Dutch, having no hills, were among the most suspicious. Nevertheless, we felt we had enough encouragement to proceed, and accordingly did so at the Ministerial meeting which opened on

21 June. There was still a lot of work to be done in the corridors, and the drafts of our statement and the Community's reply underwent certain changes. We had to embody in both of them words acknowledging that our hill farming problems must be dealt with in conformity with the Treaty and the Common Agricultural Policy. By the final session of the meeting, at 4.30 a.m. on 23 June, all had been fixed up, and Mr. Rippon made his statement to which M. Schumann gave the agreed reply. Both are recorded in the 'Declarations on Hill Farming' which form a part of the Final Act of the Conference. The outcome has certainly not left our hill farming arrangements immune from scrutiny or change in the enlarged Community; but the Community has given a general admission of their necessary character, and the exchange of statements undoubtedly gives us a much firmer basis on which to stand in the future than we could possibly have had without it.

(iv) *Animal health*

13. This was a field in which we had always foreseen difficulties. It was referred to (indirectly but consciously) in Mr. Brown's statement of July 1967 when he spoke of 'certain matters affecting the harmonisation of laws in the agricultural and food field', and suggested that matters such as this could be settled after we joined the Community. That hope, as explained earlier in this Report, was disappointed; so animal health like everything else had to be tackled in the negotiations. It was a problem of real economic and potentially considerable political difficulty. It was also a problem that affected the four candidate countries in different degrees. The Irish Republic in particular (and Norway too) had been able, thanks to their isolated geographical position, to preserve exceptionally high standards of animal health, and the Irish depended on their maintenance to be able to continue their important exports of meat and meat products to the United States. This trade would have been cut off immediately if the Irish had had to abandon their guaranteed immunity against foot and mouth disease. Northern Ireland was in the same position.

14. While the rest of the United Kingdom had no such complete immunity, we were in respect of foot and mouth disease in a very different position from the Community countries. We had always maintained a policy of eradicating the disease, when it occurred, by slaughter. The Community countries dealt with it by vaccination. Our cattle are unvaccinated. To have agreed to permit the entry of live vaccinated cattle from the Community into the United Kingdom would have put our whole system of protection against the disease at risk, and probably forced us to change our policy, at the cost of immense upheaval and expense and a real decline in health standards. It would probably also have cost us our valuable exports of breeding stock to many parts of the world. There were also problems affecting brucellosis, and deriving from different methods of conferring protection against tuberculosis. Swine fever and Newcastle Disease (fowl pest) were further problems. As the end of the negotiations approached, opponents of entry in this country were more and more inclined

to seize on problems with which they would not otherwise have been concerned, and to magnify them into major issues threatening our ability to secure Parliamentary approval of the terms of entry. This process developed furthest in the case of fisheries; but animal health was another problem which could have caused similar grave difficulties. It was a real problem to the farming community, and could easily have been magnified into a problem of threatening political dimensions.

15. The way in which it was solved is set out in Section 3 of Annex I to this Report,* but this solution was not reached without major delays and difficulties which were only overcome by political intervention at high levels. As with other matters where we knew that major modifications to Community principles or legislation would be required—such as the Channel Islands and the Isle of Man or fisheries—we decided from the outset to leave the question of animal health alone until a fairly late stage in the negotiations, by which time we hoped the habitual doctrinal rigidity of the Community might have grown less. The Irish were bolder, and circulated a long paper to the Community as early as December 1970. We were forced to bring the issue up much earlier than we had intended, as a result of the programme adopted in the secondary legislation group; and a full statement of our problems was made in that group at the end of March 1971, with the purpose simply of delaying detailed consideration of regulations until the Conference itself had made some progress. On 1 June, 1971, we raised the matter in the Deputies, circulated a longish paper and proposed 'that an expert multilateral body should be set up—as was done in the case of tariff quotas' to study the problem and report to the Conference. But nothing happened. By July there had been no movement, and in our White Paper of that month (paragraph 151) we recorded that animal health still remained to be settled. So far, we were not much worried by the lack of progress.

16. But the autumn sessions of the Conference began slipping by, and still nothing happened. Though we had meant to leave animal health till a late stage, we began to wonder whether we had not left it almost too late. The Community took no steps to establish the multilateral group we had requested; and meanwhile a group from the Member States, composed of veterinary experts, considered the problem. Veterinary experts seem to be more stubborn than most; and what we learnt of their progress suggested that in this case pride in the Community's existing regulations and determination not to modify them was even more pronounced than usual. The Commission was by now adopting a much more sympathetic and reasonable view; at a relatively early stage M. Rabot, Director General of Agriculture, was convinced that the right solution—the one eventually adopted—was that we should accept imports from the Community of meat but not of live animals. But no one seemed to have any influence on the vets from the Member States. We appealed to Signor Bombassei, President of the Conference of Deputies, to help us; we got our Embassy in Paris

* Not printed

to intervene with M. Bernard of the Elysée. Everywhere we received sympathetic reactions but the vets just soldiered on. At last on 24 November the Community, at a meeting of Deputies, made a proposal to us. This was in one sense useful, in that at least in its form the proposal provided the basis for eventual agreement; but its content was extremely unsatisfactory. We had known of the proposal in advance, so Mr. Kearns was able at once to explain why we could not accept the import of vaccinated cattle, which the Community was suggesting we should do not only for slaughter but also for fattening. He also expressed a number of other objections; and the outcome was agreement that we should pursue the matter with the Commission.

17. This was something, but not enough. On 3 November M. Schumann, in a conversation with Mr. Soames, discussed the problem of animal health. As so often, France was the key. This was partly because some people in France thought there would be opportunities for an export trade in French store cattle to our market to develop; still more because, once France relented, other defenders of Community orthodoxy could be relied on to withdraw. M. Schumann and Mr. Soames agreed that the best course would be for Mr. Soames to have a talk with the French Minister of Agriculture, followed by a meeting of senior officials from each side. As so often in the negotiations, we had had to summon Mr. Soames to the rescue. He and M. Cointat, French Minister of Agriculture, discussed the problem on 7 December, and immediately afterwards a meeting of British and French officials was held in Paris. M. Cointat yielded the essential point—namely that we should have to import Community meat but not live animals, except unvaccinated, in relation to which we could continue our existing quarantine practices. We were now close to the date of what we hoped would be the final Ministerial meeting—11 December. We accordingly on 9 December asked Mr. Soames to approach the French once again; to say we hoped to settle animal health at this meeting as well as fisheries; and that we would be willing to accept the Community's proposals of 24 November subject to a number of modifications. Mr. Soames had two conversations with M. Brunet, with satisfactory results. At the Ministerial meeting the question was settled, subject to a final tidying-up of texts at a later Deputies meeting and subject to the outcome of further discussions between the Community and the Irish.

18. The Irish, who had like us a Ministerial meeting with the Community on 11 December, did not accept the outcome on animal health, and arranged a further Ministerial meeting early in the New Year to press their additional requirements. This was satisfactory for us, since Northern Ireland needed better terms, and it was accepted that they would have the same arrangements as the Irish Republic. The main Irish objective was to escape the obligation to import even meat, which would have been enough to destroy their international status as an area free from foot and mouth disease and their valuable export trade in meat to the United States based on this status. Great Britain has refrained for 50 years from exporting meat to Northern Ireland in order to preserve its foot

and mouth immunity; and we naturally wanted the Community to adopt the same practice. At their Ministerial meeting early in January the Irish were successful (except in respect of poultry imports); and accordingly the arrangements were completed which are now set out in Articles 104 to 106 of the Treaty of Accession.

19. One of the crucial points about these arrangements, as in so many other cases, was their duration. We did not succeed in securing unlimited exemption from the Community's basic directives. In every case (except for one shorter period in respect of a Danish problem) the time granted for exemptions was five years. This may well prove insufficient. But there are reasonable prospects that we shall in fact, when the time comes, be able to secure a prolongation of special arrangements in the field of animal health if we can demonstrate that they are still necessary. Article 106 provides that the Commission is to submit a report and proposals for future action by 1 July, 1976; and the 'review of the situation in the Community as a whole and in its various parts' for which this report will provide a basis is to be 'carried out in the light of developments in the veterinary field'. It was by the end of the day fairly well accepted by the Community, though this is nowhere formally on record, that the object of the whole exercise should be to promote higher veterinary standards, not to degrade those prevailing in one part of the Community for the sake of conformity with the rest of it. After the Commission has reported, there will remain 18 months before the derogations provided for by the Treaty lapse. That should be time enough to ensure that the ensuing, and presumably more permanent, arrangements are satisfactory to us.[1]

B.—MONETARY AND FISCAL QUESTIONS

(i) *Capital movements*

20. Adapting ourselves to the two existing Community directives on the control of capital movements had long been regarded as likely to constitute a major problem in the negotiations. Although the Community's régime, as expressed in these directives, had by no means abolished all restrictions on capital movements between Member States, it was considerably more liberal than our own. It was however a régime which some members of the Community themselves conspicuously failed, from time to time, to apply; and there were indeed periods in the course of the negotiations, related to successive foreign exchange crises, when the arrangements of individual Member States for the control of capital movements were sharply modified. Calculations made in 1969 and early 1970, when the Labour Government's White Paper of February 1970

[1] In the event the review was held in 1975 and led to agreement on the general Community provisions which would replace the derogations. The Republic of Ireland was granted a derogation for a further five years.

was being prepared, indicated that the application by us of the Community's rules on capital movements was likely to involve us in a considerable balance of payments cost. The calculations were necessarily highly speculative; and might have produced different results had they been made a year later. Nevertheless it was clearly necessary to ask for transitional arrangements to ease the consequences of our adoption of the Community's régime. Another aspect of this question which we feared might cause difficulties was the relationship between our differing systems of control on capital movements to the sterling area and to the rest of the world; but, as recorded in Chapter 14 above, these difficulties were avoided.

21. I will not record in detail the course of our negotiations over capital movements. They occupied many months and many meetings. A great deal of elaborate investigation and a series of modified proposals had to be made before agreement was reached. Our eventual agreement with the Community is set out in Articles 120 and 124 to 126 of the Act of Accession, coupled with Section V of the document, embodied in the Final Act of the Conference, setting out agreed procedures for the period between the signature of the Treaty and its entry into force. The procedures agreed on in Articles 124 and 125 provided for our compliance by stages—after two years in one case, after 30 months in another, and after five years in a third—with the provisions of the two Community directives. These arrangements were regarded as sufficient to protect our interests.

(ii) *The European Investment Bank*

22. The arrangements required for us to join the European Investment Bank proved rather difficult to arrive at and took much time to agree. They were eventually embodied in Protocol No. 1 'On the Statute of the European Investment Bank' and took the form of a number of agreed amendments to the Statute together with provisions governing the amount of our contribution to the capital of the Bank, and the times at which and methods by which it should be paid. There were also provisions for appropriate changes in the composition of the Board of Governors of the Bank.

23. These arrangements were satisfactory in the end, though at times we felt the Community was driving rather a hard bargain. In retrospect, I feel we may perhaps have suffered a little by the fact that we were negotiating not directly with the Bank, but at one remove from it. Any concessions on the Community side were thus in practice scarcely within the power of the Deputies, or even the Ministers of the Community Governments, but within the power of the Bank itself. And our own contacts with and knowledge of the Bank were not extensive, with the possible consequence (I cannot prove it) that the Bank continued to entertain the rather suspicious and defensive attitude towards us which to some extent characterised the general attitude of the member governments at the outset, but which, after a few months, the fairly regular and intimate contacts of the Conference had succeeded in dispersing. While I believe

this comment on our negotiations about the Bank to be justified, I certainly do not want to give the impression that I think the outcome would necessarily have been different if our direct contacts with the Bank had been closer. Probably it would not.

(iii) *Fiscal harmonisation*

24. In this context, this meant Value-added Tax. We knew that joining the Community would oblige us to introduce a Value-added Tax. But we felt we would need a long transitional period before we could introduce it. Accordingly, at a fairly early stage in the Conference, we asked for a transitional period of five years. Though the Community never formally reacted to this proposal, we became aware fairly rapidly that they thought we had asked for too much. This was probably one of the reasons why, as described elsewhere in this Report, the Community's reaction to Mr. Rippon's proposal of 8 December on transitional periods was at first somewhat lukewarm. He then suggested five years both for industrial tariffs and for agriculture; and also for Value Added Tax. But this proved to be one of the few areas of the negotiation where our own domestic developments removed a problem. In his 1971 Budget Mr. Barber announced plans for the introduction of Value-added Tax in the United Kingdom early in 1973. Accordingly, at the Deputies meeting on 6 April, 1971, we were able to withdraw our request for a five-year transitional period for fiscal harmonisation.

C.—TRANSPORT

25. The Common Transport Policy of the Community was luckily not very highly developed by the time our negotiations ended. But there were already a number of rules in existence which we had to accept or adapt. What transpired is set out in Section 2 of Annex I.* I mention the question of transport here only to record that one of the Community's regulations, that concerning drivers' hours, caused us considerable economic difficulty which might, once again, have turned into a matter of political difficulty had we failed to get a tolerable solution. The Community had laid down in this regulation maximum hours of work for lorry drivers which were shorter than those customary in this country. These shorter hours happened also, no doubt by accident, to be just too short to enable a number of regular transport runs in this country (such as that bringing fruit and vegetables from the South-West to London) to be completed without a change of crew.

26. Accepting this regulation was bound to mean considerable extra expenditure for transport undertakings. We therefore asked at first for a delay of five years before we had to comply with it. After a long pause, the Community offered us two years. We countered with a request for four years, with the conscious objective of compromising on three. Eventually the Community offered

* Not printed

us three. By this time pressure from the transport industry had grown greater; and the Department of the Environment sought to persuade Mr. Rippon that we should hold out for four years. Informal exploration with the Community led to the conclusion that they would not come further to meet us; and eventually we were authorised to settle for a delay of three years.

23

Miscellaneous Questions II

A.—COMMONWEALTH QUESTIONS

There was no single country or territory of the Commonwealth which did not feel its interests to be threatened to a greater or lesser degree by the prospect of our entry into the Community. The threat, and the anxiety, differed from case to case. Earlier chapters of this Report have described how the main Commonwealth issues were solved. These were the questions of New Zealand, of sugar, of association for independent developing Commonwealth countries and of Part IV association for Commonwealth dependent territories. Canadian and Australian problems were covered to the best of our ability by the tariff quota arrangements and the provisions of paragraph 5 of Protocol No. 16. But a number of separate Commonwealth questions remained, and I will deal with the main ones fairly briefly in this section.

(i) *Asian Commonwealth countries*

2. It had been a Community doctrine since the earlier negotiations—on the whole for good reasons—that the major Asian countries of the Commonwealth did not qualify for any form of preferential association with the Community. In the earlier negotiations it had been recognised that it would be necessary to offer to conclude trade agreements between the Community and such of these countries as wished to have them. Our objective in 1970 was to revive the Community offer. For two of these countries—India and especially Ceylon—the suspension of the Community's duty on tea to zero from 1963 had been a major benefit; but other problems of course remained. We encountered no real difficulty in reviving the Community's offer; and the matter had been settled before the end of 1970. The Community's undertaking took the form of the 'Joint Declaration of Intent on the Development of Trade Relations with Ceylon, India, Malaysia, Pakistan and Singapore' which forms a part of the Final Act of the Conference. This declared the Community's readiness to examine the problems of these countries in the field of trade from the date of accession with a view to seeking appropriate solutions. The words 'trade agreements' are not in fact used in the Declaration, but such agreements are

evidently included among the possible solutions to be sought. The problem will have been further eased to some extent by the time this examination takes place by the Generalised Preference Schemes introduced by the Community and the candidate countries; and this factor is referred to in the Declaration. At the time of the signature of the Treaty Pakistan was still a unitary State, so the problem of fitting Bangladesh into this process remained for future settlement.[1]

(ii) *Hong Kong*

3. In the earlier negotiations, it had proved impossible to get the Community to agree either to include Hong Kong among Commonwealth dependent territories qualifying for Part IV Association or to contemplate any other arrangements to mitigate the effect of our entry into the Community on Hong Kong's trade. When the negotiations began in 1970, we were pessimistic about the chances of doing anything to help Hong Kong. Hong Kong imports into the Community had for years been strictly controlled, though more by national than by Community arrangements. Thus Hong Kong did reasonably well in some Community markets, but extremely badly in others, especially in France. The French have always been reluctant to extend any privileges to Hong Kong, affecting to regard it as a 'factory' rather than a territory. So the outlook seemed bleak.

4. It would have remained so but for two factors. First of all, the Community did not have an altogether clear conscience in declining to do anything for Hong Kong. It had always been a principle of the Community that the dependent territories of Member States should receive special treatment; Hong Kong was unquestionably a British dependent territory; and some at least of the members of the Community, and the Commission, found it hard to justify even to themselves that nothing whatever should be done for Hong Kong. The second factor was a slightly fortuitous one which enabled the first to come into play. This was the imminence of the introduction by the Community of a Generalised Preference Scheme. We concentrated accordingly on the inclusion of Hong Kong in the Community's Generalised Preference Scheme, though we knew that, should we secure this objective, there would inevitably be qualifications and limitations on the benefits afforded to Hong Kong's manufactured goods. A further argument which undoubtedly carried much weight with the Community was that if they were to include Hong Kong in their Generalised Preference Scheme the chances would be much better of other donors, including the United States and Japan, doing likewise, and thereby helping to spread

[1] In the event the enlarged European Community negotiated non-preferential commercial co-operation agreements with India, Pakistan, Sri Lanka and Bangladesh. It also in due course negotiated a co-operation agreement with the newly established Association of South East Asia Nations (ASEAN) which included not only the Asian Commonwealth countries in that region (Malaysia and Singapore) but also Indonesia, Thailand and the Philippines. In parallel, the European Community expanded its Generalised Preference Scheme to cover a number of products of particular importance to the exports of the Asian Commonwealth countries, e.g. plywood.

the pressure of Hong Kong's imports over wider markets. Whatever the reasons, the Community accepted without too much reluctance that Hong Kong should be included in their Generalised Preference Scheme, though with numerous exceptions and limitations. This was of material advantage to Hong Kong, and was accepted by the Colony as a reasonably satisfactory outcome. It was also the first outcome of our negotiations to take practical effect. The arrangement reached was not, of course, embodied in the Treaty of Accession, but operated from 1 July, 1971, when the Community's scheme of Generalised Preferences was inaugurated.

(iii) *Gibraltar*

5. Article 227 of the Treaty of Rome defines the area of applicability of the Treaty and its fourth paragraph declares that 'the provisions of this Treaty shall apply to the European territories for whose external relations a Member State is responsible'. This rather odd provision had little relevance to the existing Member States; it was in fact included in the Treaty almost by error. During the drafting of the Treaty Italy had a problem arising from the then status of Trieste; by the time the Treaty was signed in March 1957 the problem had vanished. But paragraph 4 of Article 227 remained in the Treaty and had only too clear and definite an application in our case; for on the face of it this Article should have settled, without more ado, the future relations with the Community of Gibraltar, the Channel Islands and the Isle of Man and even our sovereign base areas in Cyprus. Our problem was to take advantage of Article 227.4, but only to an appropriate extent.

6. We raised the problem of Gibraltar at an early stage in the autumn of 1970; and the arrangements we eventually reached were arrived at piecemeal over a long period. It is a fact of fairly major political significance that the Community from the outset did not boggle at the application of the Treaty to Gibraltar; and its application in principle was accepted at a very early stage. There is no doubt that this was extremely unwelcome to Spain, and the position achieved for Gibraltar within the enlarged Community may remain of significance in relation to the future of the colony. The Spaniards never raised this question with us; but there is no doubt that they did so from time to time with the Six, or some of them, and that they watched our arrangements for Gibraltar as they gradually developed with a jealous and disapproving eye.[2]

7. What we wanted for Gibraltar was that the Treaty should apply, but that certain provisions of it, which would have been either irrelevant or unnecessary and excessively complicated, should not apply. Gibraltar wished to retain her status as a free port; and this was achieved by her being excluded from the

[2] The fact that Gibraltar was part of the enlarged Community became highly relevant when the time came to negotiate Spain's accession to the European Community. The continued closure by Spain of its frontier with Gibraltar was clearly not consistent with its obligations under the Community treaties and the opening of that frontier was negotiated by the United Kingdom and Spain before the latter's accession negotiations were completed.

revised definition of the customs territory of the Community. This had the effect of ousting all the Community's legislation on the Common Commercial Policy from application to Gibraltar. Further exemptions are set out in Article 28 of the Act of Accession. This in particular lays down that the Common Agricultural Policy and the obligation to introduce a Value-added Tax shall not apply to Gibraltar unless the Council unanimously decides otherwise. For the rest, the rules of the Community will apply to Gibraltar, though for the most part they will have little relevance or effect.[3] But Gibraltar will be able to profit by the Community's rules on free movement of labour; and to this end the Declaration by the Government of the United Kingdom on the definition of the term 'nationals' incorporated in the Final Act of the Conference includes a definition of Gibraltar nationality.

(iv) *The New Hebrides*

8. An almost comic procedure had to be adopted to ensure the advantages of Part IV association to the New Hebrides. We included the territory in our list of dependent territories qualifying for such association; whereupon the Community observed in reply that 'the New Hebrides is an Anglo-French Condominium'. This was indeed true; and this was no doubt the reason why the New Hebrides had not benefited from Part IV association from the entry into force of the Treaty of Rome. It proved necessary to arrange that the French Government should join us in a simultaneous request to the Community that the New Hebrides should receive the status we had asked for. When this had been done the Community agreed, and 'the Anglo-French Condominium of the New Hebrides' is now, by virtue of paragraph 2 of Article 24 of the Act of Accession, included, along with a long list of exclusively British dependent territories (and some pieces of Antarctica owned by Norway), in the list of dependent territories in Annex IV of the Treaty of Rome.[4]

(v) *Papua and New Guinea*

9. Chapter 3 of Title III of Part Four of the Act of Accession consists of a single Article on 'Relations with Papua-New Guinea'. Papua is a 'territory of the Commonwealth of Australia'; New Guinea is a trust territory administered by Australia. In fact, the two territories are administered as one. Had they been administered by the United Kingdom, they would of course have qualified for Part IV association; but since they are administered by Australia we had no *locus standi* to bring their problems into our negotiations at all. Nevertheless, the Australian Government pressed us strongly from an early stage to secure some

[3] As Community law in the fields of financial services and company law was developed as part of the Single Market, the relevance and effect on Gibraltar became greater and gave rise to some problems over applying the legislation in the territory and also to friction between Gibraltar and Spain.

[4] After the New Hebrides became independent as Vanuatu, it joined the Lomé Convention, the successor arrangements to the Yaoundé Convention.

protection in our negotiations for the exports of Papua-New Guinea, a high proportion of which are directed to the British market.

10. We felt all the more disposed to do what we could to meet Australian wishes since we were conscious that in other respects, more important to Australia, we had not been able to secure safeguards as firm as the Australian Government would have wished. We therefore agreed to raise the matter with the Community, and Mr. Rippon did so at a Ministerial meeting. In spite of the rather unusual character of the case, and our strict lack of *locus standi*, the Community reacted sympathetically, thus proving once again how relatively ready they are to take account of the interests of developing territories. Article 116 of the Act of Accession provides in effect that existing trade patterns between the United Kingdom and Papua-New Guinea may continue until 31 December, 1977; and it provides also for the arrangements to be reviewed, in particular if Papua-New Guinea should become independent before that date.[5]

B.—THE CHANNEL ISLANDS AND THE ISLE OF MAN

11. Anyone reading Protocol No. 3 to the Treaty of Accession—the Protocol
44 on the Channel Islands and the Isle of Man—might well be surprised to discover how troublesome the approach to it had been. Its terms seem so simple, clear and straightforward; almost as though they could have been written without preliminary discussion. In fact they had produced, at least on our side, almost as much discussion as any of the most important issues of the whole negotiation. We had always known that we should have trouble over the Islands. On 9 June, 1970, I sent a minute to Mr. Thomson (who was then planning meetings with the Islanders: but the General Election intervened) warning him that this might prove one of the most intricate and awkward problems confronting us. So it did; but far more in our domestic preparations and our contacts with the Islanders than in our eventual dealings with the Community. For in fact, when we eventually raised the matter with the Community (and we deliberately left it till a late stage), we had relatively little trouble in getting what we wanted. The Commission throughout, including their legal experts, were helpful and accommodating; and none of the Member States of the Community made difficulties. They could have made plenty had they wanted to. As Mr. Wellenstein once remarked to me, the problem was that we, for a variety of historical reasons, had been ready to grant the Islands unique privileges and the best of all possible worlds; we could hardly expect the Community to do likewise. But in the end that was more or less what they did.

12. The experience of the Channel Islanders and the Manxmen themselves in relation to our negotiations was much the same as that of every other community outside the United Kingdom who felt threatened by the prospect

[5] Following its independence, Papua New Guinea became a member of the Lomé Convention, the successor arrangements to the Yaoundé Convention.

of our entry. Ever since 1961 they had feared a damaging upheaval in their prosperity and their status if we were to join the Community. As our negotiations approached in 1969, their fears revived, and right up to the moment of agreement with the Community in November 1971 cries of anguish and despair from the Islands assailed us. The Home Office is responsible in Whitehall for relations with the Islands, and they bore the brunt of the Islands' apprehensions. They maintained continual touch with the Islands' representatives and conducted prolonged and difficult correspondence with them. Part of the Islanders' anxieties, as in so many other cases, derived from the feeling that they had so little control over negotiations crucial to their fate. They are not part of the United Kingdom and thus are not, of course, represented in Parliament at Westminster. Yet they did not lack champions there, nor in the British Press. A major source of our concern about the whole problem was that it could easily have become, failing a satisfactory solution, an emotional and political issue of considerable proportions in the United Kingdom.

13. The problem was anything but straightforward. It arose partly from the inevitable fact that, if no special arrangement were made, paragraph 4 of Article 227 of the Treaty of Rome—'the provisions of this Treaty shall apply to the European territories for whose external relations a Member State is responsible'—would operate to apply the Treaty as a whole and all the Community's rules and regulations to the Islands. Yet even without Article 227 things would have been almost as bad. For if the Islands did not want to be altogether in, equally they could not afford, if we were in, to be altogether out. The Islands had separate problems and interests. The interests, for example, of Jersey and Guernsey conflicted sharply. What they all wanted was to be able to continue their free trade with the United Kingdom without interruption; to be able to maintain their special taxation régimes; not to have to introduce Value Added Tax; and more generally to avoid being saddled with excessively complex obligations, transcending their administrative resources and skill, as a result of our entry. There was only one civil servant on Sark; and he would have found it hard to apply all the Community's secondary legislation.

14. A further very important factor was the long-standing convention that the Government of the United Kingdom does not make its international agreements applicable to the Islands without their consent. The 'man in the street' in the Islands, of course, feared that in this case we might attempt to do so. Yet, if we went in and they stayed out, what would the consequence be? Could it be other than to force the Islands to declare a kind of independence? In the spring of 1970 Government Departments in Whitehall began a thorough examination of what such independence would in fact entail.

15. From the point of view of the Community the Islands were no doubt a small problem, but hardly one they could ignore. Their total population is about 170,000. Not much, but yet half the population of Luxembourg. Moreover the Islands are rather rich and prosperous, so that nothing could be hoped for from the Community's normal generosity to developing territories. The Islands had

moreover a certain notoriety as tax havens; and this was something the Community especially disliked. They had shown considerable suspicion, in the autumn of 1970, about this aspect of some of the smaller Commonwealth dependent territories in the Caribbean. Could we reasonably hope they would let the Channel Islands and the Isle of Man get away with it?

16. It must be confessed that, while the views of the Islands about their own objectives continually shifted and wavered, our views about the best means of settling the problem wavered a bit too. There was one constant element: a conviction that it would be prudent to defer raising the problem of the Islands until a late stage in the negotiations. We were convinced that we should have a better chance of getting them what they wanted after 'the back of the negotiations had been broken'; after our success seemed certain; and when, we hoped, the Community would have become less dogmatic and less apt to quibble about details. There can be no doubt that this delay was proved wise. But the penalty we had to pay for it was a prolongation and intensification of the Islanders' concern, and its transmission to an increasing extent to Parliament and the Press in the United Kingdom.

17. Already in 1967 we had examined every conceivable territory whose relations with the Community might give us something to build on in the case of the Channel Islands and the Isle of Man: San Marino, Andorra, Monaco, Corsica, St. Pierre and Miquelon, Lichtenstein, Heligoland and the Faroe Islands. But without avail. Article 227.4 applied inexorably to the Islands, but to none of these other territories. Yet, as time passed, it became clear that the Community was by no means so dogmatic about this provision in the Treaty as we had feared. They agreed to a qualified application of it to Gibraltar; they agreed to oust it altogether in respect of our sovereign base areas in Cyprus, where we reached the very sensible arrangement (recorded in a Declaration annexed to the Final Act) that their relations with the Community should be settled in the context not of our negotiations but of any agreement which the enlarged Community might reach with Cyprus. In retrospect, I think we were rather slow to take these hints as to the flexibility with which the Community was prepared to apply Article 227.4.

18. The objectives expressed by the different Islands frequently changed, and varied from Island to Island. In 1967 Jersey had declared that from their point of view membership would be disastrous; they wanted to stay out, but to be within the Common External Tariff. Guernsey, on the other hand, had asked to be brought in, though with many exemptions. The Isle of Man had taken the Jersey position: out, but within the Tariff. Sark, though within the Bailiwick of Guernsey, had adopted Jersey's position. As 1970 passed, the collective view of the Islands, in so far as there could be said to be one, tended more towards exclusion. All this was natural enough, and reflected the real dilemma. Should the Islands be in, but out? Or should they be out, but in?

19. As I have said, our own views wavered too. In the spring of 1970 there was some disposition to hope that we might succeed in getting through our

negotiations without the problem of the Islands coming up at all, and that we could sort things out later from within the Community. If we were to have a chance of this, the Islands must agree to keep quiet. But though some might have been prepared to attempt to do so, we knew that Jersey would do nothing of the kind: they were determined to air their anxieties as widely and loudly as they could, if necessary by sending a Delegation to Brussels. It soon in any case became apparent that we could not evade the issue in the negotiations; and we were already aware, with a certain apprehension, that the Commission was diligently accumulating information about the Islands. In July 1970 Ministers in the AE Committee decided that in principle we should have to seek concessions for the Islands during our negotiations; but that our actual requirements should be formulated later. As late as November 1970 the Home Office tended to favour 'exclusion in principle'; and by January of 1971 the views of all the Islands had hardened in this direction. Meanwhile an alternative idea which was to form our opening bid was beginning to find some favour in London: namely, that we should seek association for the Islands under Article 238 of the Treaty of Rome. Eventually at the end of January 1971 Ministers approved this course as our objective, or at least our opening bid.

20. But before this point was reached an important meeting had taken place, on 1 October, 1970, when Lord Windlesham of the Home Office (in Mr. Maudling's absence) and Mr. Rippon had met representatives from the Islands in London. Apart from helping to convince them of the importance we attached to their problems, this meeting was mainly significant for an assurance given in confidence to the Island representatives—and this confidence was admirably respected until they were released from it exactly one year later—to the effect that if any agreement we might reach with the Community proved unacceptable to any of the Islands, we would not try to force such an agreement upon it. This assurance was doubly valuable. It relieved a genuine anxiety. And it demonstrated that the fate of the Islanders was largely in their own hands. Thus too much opposition for its own sake could be dangerous: they might be taken at their word.

21. Throughout this period, and indeed for many months to come, nothing whatever happened in the Conference in Brussels. There was a good deal of curiosity, especially on the part of the Commission, about the problem and the way in which we intended to tackle it. In November 1970 we told them privately that we hoped the matter could remain in abeyance for some time yet, as we were still discussing it with the Islands. In the early months of 1971 we were subject to some pressure to define our position in the context of the redefinition of the customs territory of the enlarged Community; but once again the Commission forbore to oblige us to show our hand. At the end of May 1971, however, the Channel Islands and the Isle of Man got caught up in the anxiety Ministers then felt to make as much progress as possible on every outstanding issue in what was foreseen as the crucial Ministerial meeting in the second half of June. With the July White Paper and the impending Parliamentary debates in mind,

Ministers decided that we must raise the problem with the Community in June, 'without necessarily reaching final agreement by the end of June'.

22. Accordingly, we raised it at a meeting of the Deputies on 16 June. I made a statement promising that we would shortly circulate (we did so a week later) as a Conference document a factual paper setting out the problem in detail. The statement went on to give the reasons why the United Kingdom Government 'is of the opinion that the Channel Islands and the Isle of Man could not become a part of the Communities under Article 227.4 of the Treaty of Rome without severe and damaging consequences for them'. It concluded that in our view the problem could best be dealt with by a form of association between the Islands and the Community of the sort provided for under Article 238 of the Treaty of Rome. The Community undertook to study this statement and reply when they had formulated their view.

23. We were aware, before we made this proposal, that it was based on shaky legal foundations. Article 238 empowered the Community to conclude association agreements only 'with a third country, with a union of states or with an international organisation'. The Channel Islands and the Isle of Man were none of these. We were therefore not surprised (we had had ample warning) when, at a Deputies meeting on 28 July, the Community declared that it thought a solution based on Article 238 would be inappropriate. They went on to say that they thought that Article 227.4 was the appropriate provision of the Treaty (together with the corresponding provisions of the other two Treaties), so that 'the accession of the United Kingdom to the Communities would thus lead to the automatic application of the three Treaties to these territories. Nevertheless the Community Delegation would be prepared to examine such requests for derogations from the full application of the three Treaties to these territories as the United Kingdom Delegation might propose'. Accordingly the Community asked us to set out our position more clearly and specify to what extent we wished the Treaties to be applied to these Islands.

24. We knew in advance what the Community were going to say, so we were able to reply after a brief adjournment. In doing so we said that what we wanted in substance for these Islands was arrangements which would allow them to export industrial and agricultural goods free of customs duties and other charges of equivalent value to the United Kingdom and to the other members of the enlarged Community. We wished that the other provisions of the Treaty and subsequent decisions taken under it should not apply to the Islands. This reaction by the Community to our proposal for association, and our reply to it, proved in fact to be the opening of the door to the eventual solution; although not altogether surprisingly the Islanders, hearing that the first proposal we had made had been rejected, were inclined at first to feel that disaster was approaching.

25. For the next six weeks the summer holidays inhibited developments; and by the time work was resumed in mid-September we were once again in no hurry. The crucial debate in Parliament on 'the decision of principle' was due

in the second half of October; we did not want trouble over the Islands to disturb things, and we knew we could not settle the whole question before the debate. We told the Community informally that we would prefer to leave the question in abeyance in the Conference until November; but informal contacts with the Commission on the details of a possible solution continued with some intensity. In London, Mr. Maudling and Mr. Rippon held a further meeting with representatives of the Islands on 1 October, 1971. By now they were able to give the Islanders some reassurance about the likely outcome; and the meeting proved a successful one. A Press statement issued after it recorded that 'At the meeting, the Home Secretary repeated the assurance, made to the Island representatives in confidence at a meeting a year ago that if, when the terms negotiated on behalf of the Islands were known, any of the Islands did not wish to accept them, Her Majesty's Government would not impose upon it accession to the Community. The Chancellor of the Duchy said that he hoped that the final stage of negotiations would be reached in Brussels at the beginning of November when the terms would be ready to present to the Island Legislatures, and that he would be glad at that time to visit Jersey, Guernsey and the Isle of Man to help to elucidate them.'

26. What the Press statement did not say was that the Island representatives, while generally content with the solution which seemed to be emerging, pressed hard for further information as to what the position would be if they were to reject the terms which finally emerged. They were promised that a paper on this issue would be communicated to them. The paper was prepared, and its rather stark description of the consequences of rejection were somewhat modified by Ministers. Nevertheless, what remained was strong enough to constitute a powerful argument against rejection; and when late in October an official from the Home Office visited the Islands, the message he carried cannot have been without effect.

27. From now on all went smoothly, subject to a number of points of detail into which I need not enter. We were determined to ensure if we could that the Community should make a statement to us at the Ministerial meeting on 9 November which Mr. Rippon could accept. (We could not leave it till later if the Island Legislatures were to have time to discuss the outcome, and we were to be in time, as we then still hoped, to sign the Treaty before the end of the year.) This was arranged. We saw the final draft of their statement on 6 November; it proved satisfactory. Subject to asking for reciprocity (which of course we had always been prepared to give) the Community agreed to free movement of goods from the Islands to the enlarged Community; and suggested some other acceptable provisions. Mr. Rippon in reply expressed his gratitude for the response the Community had made to our proposals, adding that he 'interpreted the Community's statement to mean that only the measures necessary for the establishment and proper functioning of the trade régime would be rendered applicable to the Islands within the framework of Article 227, and that all other provisions of the Treaty would be excluded. As regards

agricultural products, the detailed application of the Common Agricultural Policy in the Islands would need to be agreed between us in due course'. He concluded that he would 'be happy to commend the arrangements which the Community had proposed to the authorities of the Islands. He would be visiting them for this purpose in the course of the next week'.

28. Mr. Rippon spent the morning of 18 November in the Isle of Man; that afternoon and next morning he was in Guernsey; and later on 19 November he visited Jersey. In each Island he addressed the Legislature. His explanations of the agreement reached were accepted with much satisfaction. Each of the five Legislatures involved proceeded to deliberate and decide on the arrangements, and their decisions had all been reached by 17 December. The votes in Alderney and Guernsey were unanimously in favour; in Jersey, the arrangements were carried by 51 votes to one; and in Sark by 27 to two. In the Isle of Man the necessary resolutions were carried without a division. On 17 December the Community were informed, at a Deputies meeting in Brussels, of the Islands' acceptance of the arrangements. It remained only to complete the drafting of Protocol No. 3. Its effect is not to negate the application of Article 227 of the Treaty of Rome, but to define the extent of such application, and to limit it very significantly. The last sub-paragraph of paragraph 2 of Article 1 of the Protocol is particularly important. Its effect is to leave till after our accession, and to a decision by a qualified majority vote of the Council of the enlarged Community, the determination of the conditions under which (which will mean in practice the extent to which) the rules of the Common Agricultural Policy will apply to the Islands.

C.—FREE MOVEMENT OF LABOUR AND NATIONALITY

29. The Community's provisions for free movement of labour did not in themselves cause us much difficulty in the negotiations and we were able to accept them. Some apprehension had been expressed in recent years about their consequences for us; but by the time the negotiations began it had on the whole died down. In particular, the trade union movement accepted the policy and did nothing to stimulate the fears expressed in some quarters that hordes of foreign workers would pour into this country from the Community. Occasionally the policy, and the fears associated with it, were used, by the Press or in Parliament, as a stick to beat the Government with; but no real campaign developed. The only substantial issue we raised in this area concerned Northern Ireland. Its Government was anxious to be able to preserve its 'maintenance of employment' legislation at least for a transitional period. We secured a transitional period of five years for this purpose.

30. But much more difficulty arose over the need to define British nationality, which derived mainly but not exclusively from the Community's rules concerning the free movement of labour. A definition of nationality was also required in respect of some other Community provisions, including those

concerned with establishment. We thought at first that it might be possible to define British nationality, for the purposes of the Treaty of Accession, as a part of the work on secondary legislation; and as this proceeded we gave the Commission a proposed definition of British nationality as early as April 1971. A good deal of technical discussion with the Commission ensued; and it became clear at a very early stage that the Community found it difficult to understand that there was no nationality of the United Kingdom as such, and was worried by the fact that our nationality is a nationality 'of the United Kingdom and Colonies'. Our handling of the whole matter, it should be recorded, was for some time inhibited by the fact that the Immigration Act 1971 was passing through Parliament. Not until it received the Royal Assent on 28 October, 1971, could we be quite confident of the legal basis on which we would have to proceed.

31. By the end of July 1971 our discussions with the Commission had led them to give us some advice which we welcomed. This was that the matter could not be satisfactorily settled in the context of secondary legislation; but that we should plan instead to make a unilateral declaration defining our nationals. There was a precedent for this, in that the Government of the German Federal Republic had made a similar declaration on the occasion of the signing of the Treaty of Rome. This approach had obvious advantages for us, since we could more easily maintain a principle to which we attached great importance, and which the Community in theory at least accepted, namely that definition of its nationals is a matter within the exclusive competence of the government concerned. We also felt that this method of proceeding would give us more control over a matter which could have become extremely sensitive and potentially damaging from a political point of view. Throughout our negotiations on this subject, which only concluded eight days before the Treaty of Accession was signed, one of our major objectives was to keep our proceedings as confidential as possible, and to avoid public attention being attracted to the difficulties which in fact arose. On the whole we succeeded in this objective; and in the end we achieved a satisfactory result.

32. The difficulties we encountered, which became acute from November 1971 onwards, arose almost exclusively from the Dutch. As early as 21 September Mr. Westerterp, Mr. de Koster's successor as Dutch State Secretary for Foreign Affairs, told Mr. Rippon in Brussels about 'anxiety in the Netherlands that British entry into the Community would lead to large numbers of Pakistanis (and presumably other coloured Commonwealth citizens) invading the Netherlands in search of jobs'. This anxiety increased over the next few months. The Dutch tried hard to infect the other member governments with the same anxiety. They had some success at first with the Germans (who later however withdrew from support of the Dutch) and to some extent also with the Belgians. But the other Community governments remained unconcerned; and in particular the French never made any trouble at all and on the whole supported us. So did the Commission, who continued to argue strongly against the legal validity and

political acceptability of proposals which the Dutch from time to time put forward within the Community.

33. We communicated our proposed Declaration defining United Kingdom nationals informally to the Community early in November, making clear our intention that we would make the Declaration at the time of the signing of the Treaty of Accession and that it should be annexed to the Final Act of the Conference. Much discussion ensued within the Community and as time passed the reasons for Dutch concern became clearer. They expressed them to us as based on a belief that our entry would give rise to an influx of coloured Commonwealth immigrants from the United Kingdom into the Community countries, and that Holland would be in the front line because of the high level of security benefits available there and also because, of all the Community countries, Holland was the one where English was most widely spoken. The Dutch also entertained exaggerated ideas of the scope of the problem. Some of their officials were convinced there were two million Pakistanis alone in the United Kingdom. (Holland being one of the avenues of illegal immigration into the United Kingdom, the Dutch had some experience of Pakistanis.) We did our best to disabuse them of false ideas, and to convince them that movement out of the United Kingdom into the Community by Commonwealth immigrants was extremely unlikely to occur on an appreciable scale; but the Dutch refused to be comforted. In fact, the Dutch concern was closely linked to the fact that during this particular period a large influx of immigrants from the Netherlands' own overseas territories (Surinam and the Antilles) to Holland was taking place. It was causing great concern on social grounds and strong pressure on the Netherlands Government to take some action to stem the tide.

34. Mainly because of the Dutch attitude, discussions within the Community on how to handle this problem made little progress in November, and we began to be concerned at the blockage, since we still hoped to be able to conclude our negotiations and sign the Treaty before the end of the year. We felt it essential that we should bring the matter formally to the Conference and give notice of the Declaration we intended to make. Mr. Rippon accordingly made a statement at the end of the Ministerial meeting of 29–30 November. He told the Conference that we proposed to make our Declaration on the occasion of the signing of the Treaty, and he read it to them. By this time we had modified the draft informally communicated at the beginning of the month by excluding from it a category to which almost the whole Community had taken exception, namely (in effect) citizens of other Commonwealth countries who might acquire citizenship of the United Kingdom and Colonies by virtue of qualifying as 'patrials' under the terms of the Immigration Act. But we had also added to it definitions of a Gibraltar national and of a Channel Islander and a Manxman, since these too had become necessary in the light of the progress we had made on arrangements for Gibraltar and for the Channel Islands and the Isle of Man. Mr. Rippon's statement, being made at the end of a somewhat acrimonious and unsuccessful all-night session devoted almost entirely to fisheries, attracted little

attention in the Press; though it did lead to some criticism when Mr. Rippon reported on the meeting to the House of Commons.

35. Meanwhile Dutch concern had intensified. They sent a senior official to London for discussions here on 26 November; and throughout December in the internal discussions of the Community they continued to seek Community agreement to some arrangement which would protect them from the dangers they feared. To express it briefly, what the Dutch sought all the time was a device by which they could distinguish between British nationals born in the United Kingdom and other British nationals; and we continued steadily to maintain that we could not possibly be a party to any arrangements which discriminated between one class of 'Citizens of the United Kingdom and Colonies' and another. The Dutch concern duly surfaced in rather alarmist articles in the Dutch Press on 8 December, and was taken up, though not extensively, in the British Press.

36. From about the middle of December on the Dutch had become isolated in the Community, but they continued to press their point. There were intensive exchanges, always outside the formal Conference and usually between myself and the Luxembourg President of the Deputies, during the series of Deputies meetings held in January. By 6 January a solution which we could accept had begun to emerge, and agreement was finally reached on 14 January. This provided that there would be no further alterations to our unilateral declaration; we would make it on the occasion of signature, the Conference would take note of it, and it would be annexed to the Final Act; but the Conference would adopt a common declaration which would also be annexed to the Final Act. This second declaration—the 'Joint Declaration on the Free Movement of Workers'—records that enlargement of the Community could give rise to certain difficulties for the social situation in one or more Member States in connection with the free movement of workers; and that Member States reserve the right, should difficulties of this nature arise, to bring the matter before the institutions of the Community in order to solve the problem in accordance with the provisions of the Treaties. In addition, a text was agreed for entry in the minutes of the Conference which recorded certain facts relating to our legislation on nationality and its administration in a form which we were able to accept. Citizens of Gibraltar were covered by our Declaration on Nationality; but our definition of a Channel Islander and a Manxman was removed from the Declaration and appears instead in Article 6 of Protocol No. 3 'on the Channel Islands and the Isle of Man'.

24

Miscellaneous Questions III

A.—INSTITUTIONS

Enlarging the Community necessarily affected the composition of its institutions; and since their composition had been laid down by Articles of the three Treaties establishing the three Communities, it was necessary to amend these Articles. It was in fact the question of institutions which involved most (but not all) of the 'adjustments to this Treaty' necessitated by the entry of new members which are referred to in Article 237 of the Treaty of Rome. The institutional adjustments agreed on are set out in Articles 10 to 23 of the Act of Accession. Although working out the new institutional arrangements was rather a slow process, it proved, as far as we were concerned, to be a matter of no difficulty whatever. Once the principle had been accepted—and no one challenged it—that we should have the same position in the institutions of the Community as France, Germany and Italy, the rest was little more than arithmetic and commonsense. Whether the other candidates had greater problems I do not know. They may have felt their votes (three each) should have been nearer to those of Belgium and the Netherlands (five each) than to that of Luxembourg (two). But this would have upset the carefully calculated formula for qualified majority voting set out in Article 14 of the Act of Accession.

2. The only potential difficulty we had foreseen in the institutional sphere never in fact arose in the Conference. This was the question of the ability of new members to exercise their rights, including their voting rights, in full in the institutions of the Community from the start in spite of any limitations on their obligations which the arrangements for transition might give them. This problem has been discussed already in paragraphs 12 to 15 of Chapter 10.

3. The Community clearly had considerably more trouble on their side in formulating their proposals on institutions than we did in accepting them. As it turned out, they made their proposals in a number of successive statements over the last seven or eight months of the negotiations. But probably their problem too was little more than a technical one, and consisted in the main of clearing their proposals with various Community institutions (the Court of Justice, the European Investment Bank or the Economic and Social Committee) which were both jealous of their rights and not geared to the rapid tempo of

decision which, in its later phases, our Conference had engendered. But when the Community eventually made proposals to us, we were almost invariably able to accept them without any qualification and fairly rapidly.

4. The new arrangements set out in Article 14 of the Act of Accession for qualified majority voting in the Council of Ministers deserve perhaps a word, though it is likely that, for some time to come at least, these arrangements will remain largely academic. The agreement reached by Mr. Heath and M. Pompidou in Paris in May 1971 about majority voting in the Community is likely to mean that, in practice and for the time being, unanimity will remain necessary on all important questions. In so far however as the new arrangements come to be applied, their most interesting features are, first, that two of the bigger countries will be able between them to produce enough votes to block a proposal; and, second, that the four bigger countries together could not carry a proposal by the Commission against the rest unless they were joined by at least one of the six smaller countries other than Luxembourg.

5. We did secure one arrangement in this process of institutional reform which suited us. It turned out that it suited the existing members too. It was agreed that a completely new Commission should take office on the enlargement of the Communities. Without this agreement the existing members of the Commission would have had the right to complete four-year terms from the date of their appointment in July 1970. We thought at one stage of making a proposal about the duration of the Presidency of the Council of Ministers. The problem we had in mind was that the alphabet condemns us to be the last of the 10 members of the enlarged Community to assume the Presidency of the Council. We shall in fact not do so until the second half of 1977. We thought of suggesting a four-month period, instead of a six-month period, for the Presidency; this would have brought us to the Chair in the first four months of 1976. But we discovered that the Member States all felt that six months was the minimum period needed to enable efficient operation by the Presidency, and that a shorter period would mean insufficient continuity and too frequent change. Indeed, there is a tendency among some of the Member States to feel that the Presidency should last for a year. Accordingly, we did not propose a change.

B.—SECONDARY LEGISLATION

6. I feel considerable compunction in dealing with secondary legislation only in a section of a chapter devoted to miscellaneous questions. For this was by no means a subordinate matter. On the contrary, it was a matter absolutely central to the successful outcome of the negotiations; and a matter of immense complexity and difficulty. Because of its crucial importance to the negotiations and to the whole process of our assumption of membership of the Community, I include at the end of this Report an annex (Annex I),* three sections of which

* Not printed

are devoted entirely to secondary legislation. These sections have been written by Mr. Christofas and by two other officials who worked for him on this task. It proved, as we had foreseen, to be a central task of the whole Conference, and to need all the time we had. We were therefore fortunate in being able to agree with the Community, at the very start of the negotiations, that this task should be put in hand at once. Mr. Christofas deserves the highest credit for the way in which he organised and conducted it. It should not be assumed that the matters dealt with in the secondary legislation group were all relatively trivial. On the contrary, many of them were of considerable economic importance. And in some cases failure to get the right terms would have involved us in serious political difficulties.

7. Given the full description of the work contained in Annex I, I need do no more here than refer to a very few of its features. One very useful by-product of the work on secondary legislation was that it enabled so many British officials from so many different Departments to come to Brussels and participate actively in the work of the Conference. As the introduction to Annex I records, nearly 140 different officials from 17 Departments visited Brussels at various times during the Conference for this purpose. The familiarity this task gave them, both with the working methods of the Community and with its rules and regulations, should prove valuable in the future.

8. Another great advantage we derived from the way in which the secondary legislation work was done was that the Conference itself was thereby relieved of the need to consider an immense variety of detailed problems, and enabled to concentrate by and large on a relatively small number of major issues. To be sure, many issues arising out of secondary legislation had to be brought up in the main Conference before they were settled; but these were only the tip of the iceberg, and the immense preponderance of questions was settled without reference higher up. As a further lesson of the secondary legislation work—and I think it is one which deserves to be taken seriously—I will record a view expressed to me by Mr. Christofas and quote from a letter in which he expressed it. The view he expressed was that we started the secondary legislation exercise by being 'much too honest'; by which he meant 'that we took our obligations under the Community's secondary legislation too literally and did not approach it with the concept of flexibility which in practice characterises the attitudes of the existing Member States towards the implementation of their obligations'. To illustrate his point Mr. Christofas wrote that 'we were, before the negotiations started, terribly worried about a Community Directive prohibiting the use of potatoes grown in soil infested with eel-worm. Fortunately this Directive did not come up in the secondary legislation exercise until we had grown in experience. The Directive provided that there should be a survey of all potato-growing soil to see what eel-worm existed. We were therefore able to view this Directive with equanimity because we could make the survey thorough, the area is (comparatively speaking) immense, eel-worms are small and hard to find,

and we would have very few staff available to carry out the survey. The survey could therefore go on very nearly indefinitely. As far as present practice is concerned, there is the apocryphal story of events in Corsica immediately after the adoption of the Community Wine Regulation, which was not particularly palatable to the Corsican wine-growers. The story runs that a French Junior Minister of Agriculture visited Corsica shortly thereafter and was nearly mobbed by the local wine-growers. He at once said: 'France will honour her undertaking to the Community to abide by the Regulation. But I guarantee that no Inspectors will come here for at least the next three years.'

9. To give a view from the other side about the work on secondary legislation, I will quote a passage from the book by Dr. Nass to which I have already referred in Chapter 4. Dr. Nass, a German official of the Commission, was himself mainly occupied with the secondary legislation exercise; and he describes it in the following paragraph:

> 'By virtue of the mandate given by the Council to the Commission to examine necessary technical adaptations of secondary legislation, the Delegation of the Commission proceeded, together with representatives of the candidate countries, to work its way—regulation by regulation, page by page, article by article, paragraph by paragraph—through the whole mass of Community law. This process, in the course of which enactments covering some 13,000 typewritten pages were studied, had a double purpose: the explanation of the content of all this law and the determination of the need for technical adaptations which might be rendered necessary by accession. For this work, proceeding week by week for a year and a half, it is perhaps inappropriate, given the eventual success of the negotiations, to seek a parallel in the task of Sisyphus: Sisyphus knew that the stone which he rolled up the hill would always roll down again, yet he toiled on despite certain failure. Perhaps this multilateral examination of the whole complex of secondary legislation should be compared rather to the resolute search for the true path through a labyrinth of rules of an extent hardly to be comprehended. Even though the British Delegation was as a rule exceedingly well-informed about the content of Community law, it was yet able through this process to profit by a great variety of suggestions and explanations. These in turn led in various special areas of the negotiations to proposals, to the withdrawal of proposals and above all to the not-putting-forward of proposals; and to some extent their fruit will have ripened only after accession has taken place.'[1]

[1] In subsequent enlargement negotiations not only did the volume of secondary legislation steadily and substantially increase, so that, by the 1990s, Dr. Nass's 13,000 typewritten pages had become some 55,000 or more, but the relative importance of that part of the accession negotiations became ever greater. This also had the effect of enhancing the Commission's role in these later negotiations.

C.—AUTHENTIC ENGLISH TEXTS

10. This was, with secondary legislation, the other area of the work of the Conference which involved detailed and meticulous work on an enormous scale. English was to become an official language of the enlarged Community—it did so, incidentally, without the question ever being raised in the Conference and by virtue simply of a technical adaptation to Community Regulation No. 1 of 1958. Thus not merely would all future acts of the Community require publication in English; but all its existing Regulations, Directives and other enactments which would still be in effect at the moment of enlargement would do so likewise, if only because English and Scottish courts would have to apply them and British subjects would have to be able to know their obligations. And the texts of these existing regulations, as well as of future ones, must not be merely accurate translations, but authentic texts, authenticated by the Community. For they would have legal force not only in the United Kingdom, but throughout the Community. In the same way, the three original Treaties establishing the three Communities, together with the later 'Fusion' and 'Budget' Treaties, would have to have authentic English texts (except in the case of the Treaty of Paris establishing the Coal and Steel Community, the original of which was drawn up in French only).

11. How this task was tackled is set out in Section 4 of Annex I,* written by Mr. A. Elkin who had the main responsibility for the work on our side. I will add only two comments to what he has written. First, the immense scale of the work involved is indicated by the fact that when, on 13 January, 1972, we published in London English texts of all Community legislation still in force, the publication consisted of 42 volumes with over 9,000 pages and cost £143. Nor, of course, were any of the texts then published authentic texts; they were merely the best English texts available at the time. Second, the work on authentic English texts, as Mr. Elkin's contribution makes clear, was by no means finished by the time of the signature of the Treaty. On the contrary, the great bulk of the work then still remained to be completed, and constitutes a major task which will occupy the remainder of 1972.

D.—DRAFTING THE TREATY OF ACCESSION

12. Annex II, by Mr. Ian Sinclair who was the Legal Adviser to our Delegation throughout the Conference, deals with the work of drafting the Treaty. This occupied exactly four months from September 1971 to January 1972, during which Mr. Sinclair based himself permanently in Brussels. It was a Herculean task performed under intense pressure. From a fairly early stage of the process the Treaty drafting group was meeting almost as much by night as throughout the day; and Mr. Sinclair's accomplishments were prodigious.

* Not printed

Mr. David Hannay, who was his principal lieutenant throughout the process, also deserves great credit for his work.

13. When the negotiations opened, no one had a clear idea what form the agreements reached in them would eventually take. It was not clear, for instance, whether there would be a single multilateral Treaty between the Community and all four candidate countries; or whether there would be four separate treaties between the Community and each of them. Nor was it clear whether provisions relating to each of the three Communities would or would not eventually appear in the same instrument. From a fairly early stage in the negotiations Mr. Sinclair had informal conversations with Community lawyers to try and establish a common view. As these conversations proceeded, a consensus began to emerge that the best solution would be to have a single multilateral Treaty for all purposes between the Member States of the Community and all four candidates. One of the strongest arguments in favour of this course was that it was much the simplest means of providing, which would clearly be necessary, that treaty bonds should be established not only between the Community and each of the candidates but between the candidates themselves. But it was of course an automatic consequence of the decision to have a multilateral Treaty (it would no doubt have been necessary in any case) that each of the candidates must be bound by each of the provisions it contained, even though they dealt, as was often the case, with the requirement or interest of one candidate only.

14. There was one awkward formal difficulty. The two Treaties of Rome, establishing the European Economic Community and the European Atomic Energy Community, had identical provisions for the admission of a new member; it was to be achieved by an agreement between the Member States and the applicant State. The Treaty of Paris on the other hand, which established the European Coal and Steel Community, provided that a new member should be admitted to that Community by virtue of a decision of its Council. This led to the somewhat awkward structure of the eventual Instruments of Accession. They consist, on the one hand, of a Treaty of Accession to the European Economic Community and the European Atomic Energy Community, composed of three Articles only; and, on the other hand, of a Decision of the Council of the European Communities admitting the applicants to the European Coal and Steel Community, composed likewise of three more or less identical Articles. To each of these two Instruments is annexed the identical text of the Act of Accession, which is made an integral part both of the Treaty and of the Decision. The Act contains all the substantive provisions resulting from the negotiations, together with a number of Protocols and Annexes.

15. Mr. Sinclair's Annex records that there were some 30 issues which could not be resolved in the drafting group and had, in the last stages of the Conference, to be referred up to the level of the Deputies. Resolving these outstanding points was the last major task of the Conference. It did not in the end prove quite so difficult as I had anticipated. At the 37th Deputies meeting (12–14 January) the less critical of these points were settled through a reasonable

process of give and take. About eight points remained for the final Deputies meeting on 17 and 18 January. Of these points, three or four were critical for us and three or four were critical for the Community. We had deliberately sought to construct the elements of a package. A point concerning the drafting of the Protocol on New Zealand was one of those outstanding. I have described the outcome on this in paragraphs 40 to 42 of Chapter 16. As I there recorded, we got in the end a package which secured our principal requirements; and I shall not enter further into the details here.

E.—THE INTERIM PERIOD

16. It had been accepted from the start of our negotiations that nearly a year would be required after we signed a Treaty of Accession before it would have been ratified by all concerned and could enter into force. It was accordingly obvious that a serious problem existed about developments in the Community in this interim period. We should be bound on entry by acts of the Community decided and adopted during this period. But we could not, by definition, negotiate about them with the Community during our accession negotiations; nor in the interim period should we be able to protect our interests from within the Community's institutions. It was therefore accepted by all concerned from an early stage that special arrangements would be required to protect the interests of the candidates during this interim period.

17. We broached the question some time before the summer holidays of 1971. At the Ministerial meeting of 7 June in Luxembourg Mr. Rippon raised it and proposed agreement that the Deputies should be instructed to work out a detailed statement of the arrangements which would be most appropriate. The Community accepted this proposal in principle. A few days later we circulated a paper designed to lead to the giving by Ministers, at their next meeting on 21 to 23 June, of a clear mandate to the Deputies. Informal contacts ensued in Brussels, but no agreed text had been worked out by the time of the next Ministerial meeting in Luxembourg; and indeed a text which the Community then put to us was not altogether satisfactory. Accordingly, on 22 June, we tabled a new proposal which, at the end of the meeting, the Community accepted. The elements of our proposal were that consultation should take place with the candidate States in the interim period before the Community took any decisions; the candidate States should accept a reciprocal obligation to consult the Community about any decisions of their own which might affect their obligations as prospective members; and the Deputies should propose appropriate machinery for this purpose.

18. Once again a good deal of informal consultation in Brussels ensued, and much internal deliberation by the Permanent Representatives. This, as so often, revealed the French as taking the hardest position; it also revealed the Commission as notably forthcoming and collaborative from our point of view. But, as had been easy to foresee, there was one point on which the Community was

agreed: namely, that what it called its 'autonomy of decision' must be preserved throughout the interim period. Thus the candidates would be consulted; but they would have no veto on the decisions of the Community. This was natural enough; and of course we never pressed for a veto. But the crucial question remains. What happens if, even after consultation has been raised to the Ministerial level, the Community and a candidate cannot agree, and the Community goes ahead in spite of the dispute? Fortunately, at the time of writing, this situation has not yet arisen. Perhaps it never will.[2]

19. By 28 July the Community had settled their problems and they stated their agreed position in a meeting of the Deputies. We had as usual seen it in advance; and in replying I was able to say that we regarded their statement as most helpful and positive. We asked however that it should be further considered at the next Deputies meeting after the summer holidays. On 14 September we accepted the Community's proposal. It was agreed that it should be put forward as a joint recommendation by the Deputies to Ministers at their meeting on 21 September; and it was then formally endorsed by the Conference.

20. Two other developments of some interest grew out of this process. I have already recorded that the Commission were extremely forthcoming—an attitude which led to the uttering of some very severe strictures on them at meetings of the Permanent Representatives by M. Boegner. But the Commission stuck to their guns and decided to inaugurate a separate procedure of their own, irrespective of the action of the Council, for information of and consultation with the candidates. Accordingly, after the exchanges in the Deputies meeting of 28 July, Mr. Wellenstein handed me a formal *aide-mémoire* from the Commission outlining their separate intentions, which were of a very practical and helpful kind.

21. The second significant development arising out of these exchanges was the acceptance of the concept of a 'cut-off date' for the consideration by the negotiating Conference of new Community decisions and enactments. We had realised for some time that we must, with the Community's agreement, establish a date after which Community enactments could not be considered by the Conference and must, accordingly, be considered under the procedure for the interim period. Otherwise, the negotiations could logically never end. The Community accepted this concept, and it was already expressed in the statement made by them on the interim period at the Deputies meeting of 28 July. The final paragraph of this statement read: 'For its part, the Community is prepared to provide for this machinery to be set up as soon as the negotiations are concluded, without waiting for the Accession Treaty to be signed.' This formula meant something more sensible than it said; and everybody knew that the

[2] It never did. At no time during the interim period did the Community take a decision overriding the views of the candidate countries. As the date of accession approached the dividing line between the existing Member States and the candidates became more blurred. At the Summit Meeting of Heads of State and Government in the autumn of 1972 held to define the way ahead for an enlarged Community no such distinction was made at all.

concept, in this context, of 'concluding the negotiations' must be arbitrarily interpreted. So it was; and though the negotiations continued until 18 January, we had fixed long before then the arbitrary date of 10 November by which they were, for the purposes of this formula, deemed to have concluded. This meant that those concerned with secondary legislation did not have to deal with any Community enactments published after 10 November, since to such enactments the interim procedure would apply.

22. The agreement we reached with the Community on the interim period is the last of the documents annexed to the Final Act of the Conference. It is documents entitled 'Procedure for the Adoption of Certain Decisions and Other Measures to be Taken During the Period Preceding Accession'. Section I of this document comprises the agreement on the interim period which I have been describing. The remaining seven sections record other agreements about action which is necessary before the entry into force of the Treaty of Accession. They provide for instance for the necessary work to be done during the interim period on the Community's third country agreements and its 'Article 220 Conventions'; for the status of the candidate countries in negotiations with the EFTA non-candidates and in negotiations to adjust the Community's existing preferential and non-preferential agreements; for action in the interim period necessitated by the Treaty on the Non-Proliferation of Nuclear Weapons; and for pre-accession consultations about capital movements. Finally, in the final sentence of the Final Act, agreement was recorded that the necessary measures would have been taken before the end of 1972 to ensure that Protocol No. 19 'On Spirituous Beverages Obtained from Cereals'—about which we had fought so long and so hard both in the Secondary Legislation Group and in the Conference—would enter into force on accession.

25

Fisheries: The Background

When our negotiations opened, the problem of fisheries did not exist; but we saw it coming. It came later the same day. From then on fisheries was a major problem. At first, we did not realise how difficult it would prove to solve it or how strong the political passions would be which it was to arouse. It became in the end one of the most important as well as one of the most difficult questions in the whole negotiation; and it was the last to be solved. It was a question which produced serious difficulties not only with the Community but between the candidate countries. As political pressures in the United Kingdom grew stronger, and as the complications caused by Norway's special position increased, we ourselves changed our objective and our tactics more than once. In the end we got what we needed; but failure to do so could have meant failure to enter the Community at all.

2. The question of fisheries was economic peanuts, but political dynamite. Its economic significance is shown in the following table:

VALUE OF OUTPUT OF FISHERIES SECTOR AS PERCENTAGE OF GROSS DOMESTIC PRODUCT AT FACTOR COST IN 1970

	Per cent
Norway	1.5
Denmark	0.6
Irish Republic	0.3 (in 1969)
United Kingdom	0.1

The reasons for its enormous political significance, which came more and more to the surface in 1970 and 1971 as time passed, were much more complicated. In a way, they go rather deep into the ancient tribal feelings of the European nations. Sea fisheries remain the only significant economic activity of developed countries which are a form not of harvesting or processing, but of hunting. So the feelings they arouse are both deep and ancient. As a fisherman myself I understand these feelings. If I ever find someone else engaged in fishing a pool which by law, convention or comity I have a better right to be fishing at that moment than he, I experience feelings of sheer rage. This rage gripped our fishing community, as they faced the prospect of foreigners being allowed to fish our coastal waters. Fishery limits have always been (to use a particularly horrible jargon word) an interface along which independent nations have encountered each other, through their fishermen, with the bitterest feelings. It is not a smooth interface but one full of teeth; it scrapes and clashes, grinds and gnashes. Fishermen of all countries are only too ready still to cut their rivals' gear, ram their boats or even shoot at them.[1]

3. These feelings were easily transmitted from the fishermen themselves to the rest of the country, who regard coastal fishermen at least with romantic affection They are tiny and powerless as economic units; and all the more popular for that. No small stretch of coastline is without a few fishing boats; and like the Home Guard in 1940 every fisherman pictured the combined fleets of the Six sailing up to his particular coast and sweeping all the fish away. The threat of foreigners 'fishing up to our beaches' inflamed not only the sea fishermen but the growing body of sea anglers who fish from boats or cast a line from beaches and rocks and piers; and the National Federation of Sea Anglers joined in with scores of fishermen's associations from every district and harbour to castigate the Community and the British Government. The Scots in particular felt a cherished expression of their national character to be at risk; and Devon and Cornwall were not far behind. Moreover, fishermen and their friends have votes; and a large proportion of constituencies have coastlines. The interests of our inshore fisheries and our distant water fisheries clashed over the access provisions of the Common Fisheries Policy, and in economic terms the latter (except in Scotland) are distinctly more important. But politically the inshore men won hands down. The trawlermen's votes might matter in Fleetwood, Hull or Grimsby; but that was nothing compared to the dozens of coastal constituencies which were up in arms. The views of the British Trawlers Federation or the White Fish Authority came to matter much less than those of the South Devon Shell Fishermen's Association, the Campbeltown Town Council, the Harwich Fishermen and Boatmen's Association, the Looe and Polperro Fishermen's Protection Society, the Lerwick Harbour Trust, the Burgh of Buckie, the Firth of Forth Fishermen's Association and the dozens of similar bodies which bombarded Members of Parliament and Ministers with their protests. As the issue became more and more inflamed throughout 1971, there was real doubt whether failure to reach acceptable arrangements on the fisheries issue would not lose enough favourable Conservative votes in the House of Commons (and some Labour votes too) to make approval of our entry impossible. The dynamite had become a time-bomb, which had to be defused.

[1] Another singular feature of the fishing industry was that catches in what local fishermen regarded as 'their' waters by fishing boats from other countries brought no economic nor fiscal benefit to the country in question since the catches were in most cases landed and processed in another country. This characteristic differentiated fisheries not only from agriculture but even from the off-shore oil and gas industry.

4. Typical of the political situation was the fact, for example, that two of the most ardent and early of European enthusiasts among British politicians—Lord Boothby and Mr. Grimond—came to feel so strongly on the subject that even their support for the policy of entry was in doubt. I refer to this with no particular approbation. I think that in this respect Lord Boothby and Mr. Grimond were rather typical of a number of European enthusiasts in public life who had always imagined that entering the Community would be an easy, pleasant and comfortable process. They had never bothered to discover how intensely technical and difficult the process was bound to be, and had relied too much on mere idealism and good fellowship to do the trick. Nevertheless, the way their position changed exemplified a most significant political fact.

5. Fisheries also became increasingly, in the last eight months of the negotiations, an issue which attracted the attention of all sorts of people and organisations who had no particular concern with or knowledge of the subject, but put their shoulders to the wheel in the general interest of embarrassing the Government and defeating its policy. The intense agitation developed by all concerned with fisheries was taken up and orchestrated by the general anti-Market lobby. It was noticeable that there was very little public concern or agitation about fisheries until the end of October 1970; then it suddenly developed from every quarter and grew steadily in volume and intensity until the final settlement was reached in December 1971.

6. There was one further political factor of some significance. As there was no Common Fisheries Policy before June 1970, the Labour Government had not had to face the issue. This was the only major problem where the Conservative Government could not claim that they had 'picked up the hand prepared by our predecessors'. So in this area not even the Labour pro-Marketeers felt any commitment to a particular policy or approach.

7. Fisheries was a matter in which each of the four candidates had a strong interest; but their interests and objectives differed from case to case. Fisheries were important for us, and especially for Scotland. They were of much greater economic importance for Denmark than for us, but the Danish catch came largely from outside their own coastal waters. Their main problem was to safeguard the interests of the Faroe Islands and Greenland, which depend almost exclusively on fisheries for their existence; and till almost the last moment the Danes remained ready to accept the access provisions of the policy for their own coastal waters, unless the Norwegians should get special limits for their adjacent southern coast. The Irish Republic (which has no distant water trawlers and therefore coastal fisheries only) regarded fisheries frankly as a political not an economic issue, but were convinced, and I dare say rightly, that if they could not get a satisfactory settlement they would lose their referendum. For Norway, the interest was greatest of all. Though relatively small, as the table in paragraph 1 shows, in Norway even the economic interest was significant. (1.5 per cent of Gross Domestic Product, which fisheries represented for them, should be contrasted with the 3 per cent of Gross Domestic Product which all agriculture

represents for us.) And for Norway the question had—quite apart from all the emotional overtones—a social and employment significance which was very real indeed. Immense stretches of the Norwegian coastline, especially the northern half, are virtually only peopled at all by small and isolated communities which genuinely depend almost entirely on fishing. The degree of dependence in the Norwegian case far transcended that in the case, for instance, of the Shetlands; though it too was real enough. Together with their other great problem in the negotiations, which was the unique position of their agriculture, a threat to fisheries constituted for Norway a threat to their whole way of life and indeed to the very presence of population in large parts of their country.

8. This provided the Norwegians with a powerful argument. Norway could not conceivably join the Community at all unless she got an acceptable settlement on fisheries. If she did not join the Community, then quite possibly Denmark would not do so either. But whether Denmark joined or not, Norway left out might over the course of time come to feel that her exclusion from the Community made nonsense of her inclusion in NATO. So an excluded Norway might turn to neutrality, thereby immensely weakening NATO's northern flank. This was a real concern, which we accepted and felt ourselves, and which had its effect on most members of the Community also, especially perhaps on the Germans. The Norwegians relied very much on the Germans, largely because the Federal Chancellor, Herr Brandt, knew their country so well and sympathised with their problems. He had spent years of exile in Norway and had indeed been for several years a Norwegian citizen. It is not easy to prove that this special relationship yielded, in the end, much of a dividend; but the Community as a whole was disposed from the start to acknowledge that Norway's fisheries were a special case. This created a problem for us, which played a major part from July 1971 in our approach to the negotiations. Could we—could the Danes or the Irish—accept that Norway should be given significantly better terms for fisheries than the rest ?

9. A few figures are needed to demonstrate what was at stake. To begin with, the total fish catch of the six Member States of the Community was very much less than half that of the four candidate countries. The Community is a major importer of fish; Norway and Denmark, and to some extent Ireland, are exporters of fish. The following is taken from a memorandum the Norwegians presented to the Six Member Governments of the Community and to the Commission on 3 June, 1970, four weeks before negotiations began: 'FAO fisheries statistics show that the total world fish catch was approximately 64 million tons in 1968. Aggregate landings in the EEC amounted to 2.2 million tons and in the four applicant countries to 5.4 million tons. The catch in Norway alone came that year to 2.8 million tons. The fish production in an enlarged Community will be more than tripled.' We had our interest too; and we put the discrepancy even higher. In a paper circulated to the Conference in October 1970 we wrote that 'total fish production in the Ten for all purposes would, on current figures, be four times that in the Six'. Although the United Kingdom's

catch was less than half Norway's by quantity, it was about the same in value, since most of the fish landed in the United Kingdom is used for human consumption, whereas a very high proportion of that landed in Norway and Denmark is reduced to fish meal and other products. In Norway 66 per cent and in Denmark 78 per cent of fish landings are processed into fish meal. Though our own fish catch had about the same value as that of Norway, and our catch of fish for human consumption was by a wide margin the largest of the Ten, it is only fair to remember that our population is about 15 times greater than Norway's. Of our total fish catch the inshore fishermen produced some 40 per cent. As for exports, Norway's exports of fish and fish products were worth about £95 million in 1969, and Denmark's were worth about £57 million in 1968. Thus whatever proportion of total Gross Domestic Product the output of fisheries might represent, exports of fish and fish products were really significant for these two countries. (The Danish figure excludes Greenland and the Faroes.) As for employment, there were in 1970 8,000 full-time fishermen in Scotland, of whom 6,400 worked in the inshore fleet. There were 17,600 full-time and 4,000 part-time fishermen in the United Kingdom as a whole. Denmark (once more excluding Greenland and the Faroes) had nearly 13,000 full-time fishermen. Norway had 23,000 full-time fishermen, and 25,000 half-time fishermen. If this problem was politically so acute in the United Kingdom, it is easy to see from some of the above figures how absolutely crucial it was for Norway. In Norway fisheries provided 2.4 per cent of total employment; and this should be contrasted, once again, with the 3 per cent of our working population engaged in agriculture.

10. There was a further important difference between the Norwegian situation and that of the other three candidates. The United Kingdom and the Irish Republic were parties to the 1964 European Fisheries Convention (as were the Member States of the Community, though the Convention contained a saving clause in respect of a possible future Common Fisheries Policy of the Community). Denmark was also a party (though not in respect of Greenland and the Faroes), but Norway was not. It was under the provisions of this Convention that we and the Irish had been able to establish exclusive 12-mile fishery rights in our coastal waters, defined by advantageous baseline provisions which had much enlarged them. But we had to agree to respect for an indefinite period the historic rights of a number of other European countries to continue fishing in the outer 6 miles of these waters. Thus this 6-mile strip is fished to a considerable extent, over different stretches and for different species, by fishermen from Belgium, France, Germany, the Netherlands, the Irish Republic and Norway. A number of these countries, and we too, had similar historic rights in Irish coastal waters. But Norway was not a party to the 1964 Convention. She had established her 12-mile fishery limits in 1961 and had since then succeeded in ousting other countries from them. Thus our own and German rights to fish in almost the whole of the Norwegians' outer belt expired in October 1970. The Norwegians regarded this as a triumph, and were determined the process should

not be reversed. This was a sore issue with our distant water fishery interests; and what they most wanted was to recover fishing rights in Norwegian and Faroese waters.

11. There was however one paradox in the attitude of all the candidates. They were not opposed to the Common Fisheries Policy as a whole. On the contrary, while detesting the provisions for common access to coastal waters, they all, in greater or less degree, liked and welcomed the marketing provisions, though all wanted to see them amended in some important respects. This is natural enough. For Norway and Denmark especially, as major fish exporters, free access to the Community market was of the highest importance; and if this were coupled with marketing rules which would help to maintain the price of fish it would be a major benefit. Our Embassy in Oslo reported at the end of January 1971 that the target prices for fish fixed that week by the Six were regarded by the Norwegians as very encouraging, since they were much higher than expected. 'The Norwegians were now awaiting, with bated breath, the fixing of the withdrawal prices.' The Danes were equally pleased by the marketing regulations. In a statement at their Ministerial meeting on 2 March, 1971, the Irish Foreign Minister told the Community that 'most aspects of the fisheries regulation are fully acceptable to us', but went on to except the provisions for common access. We too felt that the fisheries marketing regulations, if suitably modified, would suit our own interests well. And all the candidates, especially Norway and Denmark, felt that in one way or another the Common Fisheries Policy might enable them to profit marginally at least (or reduce their losses) by drawing on Community funds. Mr. Kleppe, Norwegian Minister of Trade, told Mr. Rippon on 16 July, 1971, that Norway 'hoped to recoup half of her contribution to Community Finance from fisheries'.

12. A further reason, and a good reason, for the bitterness felt by all the candidate countries about the Community's Common Fisheries Policy was the way in which and the time at which it came into existence. It did so late in the afternoon of 30 June, 1970, about eight hours only after the Community had opened its negotiations with the four candidates. The popular view was that these two events were not unconnected, and I have no doubt whatever that the popular view was right. Throughout the negotiations, at least when dealing with the Community or any of its members, Mr. Rippon referred to the timing of the inauguration of the Common Fisheries Policy as 'a coincidence'; but I do not suppose that anyone to whom he so described it supposed that he meant what he said, or failed to notice the inverted commas round the words. I will deal a little later with the reasons for supposing that it was not a coincidence.

13. Before doing so, it is necessary to go a little further into the background of the Community's Common Fisheries Policy. Article 38 of the Treaty of Rome, and the inclusion of fish in its Annex II, obliged the Community to develop a Common Fisheries Policy. That this obligation was taken seriously, even outside the Community, is proved by the exception granted, to which I have just referred, in the European Fisheries Convention of 1964. But in fact

the Community's progress towards a Common Fisheries Policy had been extraordinarily, and as events proved deceptively, slow. In the early 1960s much work was done on a Common Fisheries Policy but a line of approach acceptable to all the Six could not be found. In 1966 the Commission submitted some basic principles for a policy, which underwent much discussion among the Member States and even in the European Parliament; but not until May 1968 did the Commission put forward formal proposals. These included proposals for a common structures policy, including provisions for common access to national waters: and this became of course the nub of all our difficulties in 1970 and 1971. But nothing much happened. In theory, agreement should have been reached by the end of 1969, when the Community's transitional period ended. In fact, the matter only came before the Council in December 1969. Even then it was raised rather unexpectedly (by the French), and there still seemed little likelihood of early decisions. Incidentally, the Council before which these proposals came was the Council of Ministers of Agriculture. At no time before or after its adoption was the Common Fisheries Policy ever considered by the 'real' Council of Ministers, that is to say the Council of the Foreign Ministers. In spite of its crucial political consequences for the candidate countries, there is little or no evidence to show that the Common Fisheries Policy was handled by most of the Member States of the Community as other than a technical issue.

14. At the December Council meeting of the Ministers of Agriculture, the French secured agreement that the Council should adopt basic regulations before 30 April, 1970. In retrospect, it is fairly easy to see that what led to agreement on the Common Fisheries Policy was a change in the French attitude, and this was the first sign of the change. Hitherto the French had strongly resisted the Commission's proposal for common access to the national waters of Member States. But by about this time French fisheries policy was changing. Less emphasis was placed on their inshore fisheries and much more on their distant water fisheries; and a good deal of Government investment to equip a distant water fishing fleet had been taking place. But was this by itself enough to account for the change in French policy, which brought them into line with the Germans, the Dutch and the Belgians, all of whom, having short coastlines and few fish, had from the start been strong supporters of the common access provisions? If not, what else had changed? It is only too obvious. By December 1969, The Hague Conference had taken place; the enlargement of the Community had been accepted in principle; the Community was about to embark on its preparations of a common negotiating position. There can be no reasonable doubt that what led to the adoption of the Community's Common Fisheries Policy and its provisions (with very limited exceptions only) for common access to each other's waters 'right up to the beach' was the approach of the candidates.

15. The United Kingdom, Ireland, Denmark at least in respect of the Faroes and Greenland, and still more Norway—they all have rich coastal fisheries which had been kept in good condition by effective conservation measures. I

confess that, in April 1971, I felt some doubt of the assertion, by then almost universal in the claims of British critics, that 'the waters within our own fishing limits are teeming with fish, whereas there are none at all within the fishing limits of the present Community countries'. I asked for expert comments on this assertion, and the Ministry of Agriculture produced some fairly conclusive ones, the main evidence being the simple fact that Community waters do not attract foreign fishermen, whereas British waters do. They quoted, for instance, a Dutch official as having said to us early in 1971 that 'the Dutch inshore waters were so poor that they had neither expected, nor so far experienced, any influx of foreign vessels'. Throughout the negotiations no fishermen from the candidate countries showed the slightest interest in securing access, by means of the Common Fisheries Policy, to Community waters; whereas all Community fishermen (except for geographical reasons the Italians) showed the greatest eagerness to get into ours.

16. It is hard to find an official avowal from the Community side of this interest, though it is perhaps fair to record two occasions on which the Dutch at least betrayed their interest. On 9 July, 1971 (by which time we had just completed a switch in our negotiating position and had moved from our proposal for 6-mile limits to a proposal for a status quo), Mr. Hartogh, the senior official in the Netherlands Foreign Ministry concerned with Community affairs, told Sir Edward Tomkins that the idea of a status quo 'represented a retreat from our previous proposal and would be resisted by the Dutch Ministry of Agriculture, who considered that we had made an important concession in offering to open our waters between six and 12 miles to foreign fishermen and were anxious to take full advantage of it'. And again, when finally on 12 December, 1971, we reached a settlement on fisheries, there was some disappointment expressed in Holland. Our Embassy in The Hague reported on 15 December an article in a Dutch paper by the managing director of one of the largest Dutch herring fishing firms. He wrote that the agreement is a 'slap in the face of the Dutch herring fishers'. They had thought 'that we would end up with a 3-mile zone, and now we are stuck for 10 years with a settlement which includes every possible restriction'. The writer went on to say that the Dutch herring fishers' disappointment was not directed so much at Norwegian obstinacy as at the fact that Britain, starting from a very difficult negotiating position, had managed to make its views prevail on practically all fronts. 'The British have won and the Danes, French and Irish have profited from it. Not only is the result contrary to the Six's original concepts, but it has yielded no other advantages for the Dutch fishers than that they may continue to fish where they did before.' The writer complained particularly about the Dutch failure to obtain concessions off the Scottish coast near Aberdeen. It must I think be accepted that by June 1970 the main purpose of the Community's common access provisions for fisheries was, quite simply, to get into the candidates' coastal waters. For that matter no one, ourselves included, was immune from the itch to get into other people's waters. Even the Irish, when all was over, proclaimed

through 'fishery spokesmen' that 'access to the 6–12-mile limit off the British West Coast is regarded as a gain offsetting losses on the Irish East Coast'.

17. Yet was this selfish interest of small and special groups enough to cause the Six to adopt, at so provocative a moment, a policy so likely to cause major difficulties to the candidate countries? We have seen already that the Dutch, Germans and Belgians had long been anxious to secure access to French waters. A German official told a member of our Embassy in Bonn on 25 June, 1971, that 'the Germans had opened up Community waters after much effort'. Probably the Italians, Germans, Luxembourgers and Belgians, up to 30 June, 1970, treated the matter largely as a technical one, and left it to their Ministries of Agriculture. The Dutch did not. Our friends in Holland fought to block the policy but, as we shall see, they lost. The Commission was no doubt all in favour of adopting the policy, as another feather in the integrationist hat.

18. But what of the French? It was a change of policy by them which made possible the decision of 30 June, 1970. Were they unaware of its implications for us and the other candidates? It is hard to believe. They are too alert and well organised for that. Very likely, as we ourselves did at the time, they under-estimated the full political seriousness of the step they took. Maybe they felt there was no harm in erecting another hurdle for us to jump—with much benefit for them if we could be persuaded to do so, and a way out no doubt to be found if we could not, accompanied perhaps by payment by us in some other context. I remain reluctant to believe that the French Administration (though there may well have been important individual exceptions) saw this step as creating an obstacle which would keep us out. Nor do I believe the step would have been endorsed in the highest quarters had it been so regarded. Indeed it is most improbable that the matter was ever, at this stage, referred to the top in France. The Community was extraordinarily slow to wake up to the reality of the political problem the candidates had over fisheries. As late as 26 May, 1971, the Belgian Prime Minister, in conversation with Sir John Beith, admitted that he had never heard of the Community's fisheries regulations or the problem they caused.

19. To return to the Community. The deadline of 30 April, 1970, for agreement on a Common Fisheries Policy was not observed. A further Council of Ministers of Agriculture met on 27 and 28 April. At this meeting the French were still (perhaps for tactical reasons) maintaining their objection to granting access to national waters. The Agricultural Ministers met again one month later on 25 and 26 May, and again made little progress; but on this occasion M. Mondon, the French Minister of Transport (responsible for Fisheries), urged agreement by 30 June and said that it would not be a good thing if the enlargement negotiations started in the twilight of unfinished business. No decision was taken; but after a further agricultural Council of Ministers on 8 and 9 June the impression prevailed that movement had started at last, and that agreement on at least the principal elements of a Common Fisheries Policy was likely when the Ministers of Agriculture next met on 29 June.

20. On 3 June, the Norwegians had made representations to the Community Governments. They said they wished to present their views on a Common Fisheries Policy and suggested that no definite decisions should be taken until they had had such an opportunity. This approach was treated with some derision within the Community. The idea of an outside party, even a candidate for membership, being entitled to be consulted in the formulation of one of the Community's policies was still regarded as heresy. It was partly the reception received by the Norwegian approach which led us to decide, at that stage, not to make a similar one. Partly also we still doubted, after so many years had passed and so little had been done, whether in fact significant progress would be made by the Community. Partly also, it should be admitted in the light of hindsight, we did not foresee how grave the difficulties would be which agreement on a common access policy would cause us. In any case, the instructions we sent to our Posts in the Community on 19 June were no more than a request for an assessment of the situation; our Posts were not to give the impression that we were unduly disturbed. It is perhaps fair to record that these instructions were sent the day after the General Election, when there was much else to be done.[2]

21. On 22 June our Delegation in Brussels reported that 'it was still considered possible' that agreement in principle on the main points of the fisheries arrangements would be reached on 29 June. A few days later our fears were much allayed by a telegram from The Hague. A Dutch official assured our Embassy on 26 June that he did not expect that agreement would be reached on 29 June. The French had been taking the line that agreement was required before the enlargement negotiations began. This was not acceptable to the Dutch. The Dutch official went on to say that the Dutch Ministry of Agriculture were in fact anxious to reach agreement as soon as possible. Nevertheless, that Ministry accepted the view of the Ministry of Foreign Affairs that, politically speaking, it would be very bad timing to reach agreement one day before the opening of the enlargement negotiations. It would look like a kind of insult to the candidate countries. Mr. de Koster, with his close connections with Denmark and Norway, felt particularly strongly about this. Accordingly, the Dutch would not make the necessary effort to resolve the outstanding difficulties at the meeting on 29 June. The Dutch Minister for Agriculture, Mr. Lardinois, would not himself go to the meeting. This was in itself an indication that the Dutch Government were against reaching premature agreement. The Dutch official went on to say that, nevertheless, the Dutch Ministry of Agriculture were particularly insistent that there should be freedom for Community fishermen to fish in each country's coastal waters.

[2] Given the damaging consequences which followed from adoption of the Common Fisheries Policy both in the accession negotiations and subsequently, which included contributing to Norway's failure on two occasions to enter the European Community, it is difficult to avoid the conclusion that the lobbying undertaken by the candidate countries was woefully inadequate and mistaken, as was the judgment by the original Member States to proceed with the policy in that form and at that time.

22. We were still further reassured by another telegram from The Hague on 28 June. Sir Edward Tomkins reported he had received a message from Mr. de Koster the previous night confirming that Mr. Lardinois would not go to the meeting on 29 June and that the Dutch would not allow agreement to be reached at it. Lardinois had been 'rather difficult to move, since he felt himself bound by some sort of previous undertaking to Duhamel (the French Minister of Agriculture); but the Dutch Prime Minister fully supported Mr. de Koster's view.

23. Accordingly, though Mr. Barber's speech for the opening meeting on 30 June in Luxembourg was amended to include a reference to the fact that fisheries policy might prove a difficulty in the negotiations, we went to Luxembourg reasonably confident that no decisions on a Common Fisheries Policy were imminent. At 8 p.m. on 29 June in Luxembourg Mr. Barber and Mr. de Koster met. Mr. Barber asked about fisheries, to which because of recent events 'he intended to make a modest reference in his opening statement'. Mr. de Koster said that this was an important question. The Scandinavian countries felt very strongly about it. He hoped he had succeeded in blocking progress within the EEC on a question which vitally concerned the countries now seeking membership. The Dutch Minister of Agriculture would not be coming to Luxembourg and the official representing him would see to it that no real progress was made.

24. Next morning the opening meeting of the four candidates with the Community took place; and next afternoon the Six Ministers of Agriculture reached agreement in principle on a Common Fisheries Policy, including the principle of common access 'up to the beaches'. What had happened? Mr. Franke, the Director-General of the Dutch Ministry of Agriculture, had duly gone to Luxembourg on Mr. Lardinois' behalf and blocked agreement on fisheries on 29 June. But the Ministers of Agriculture agreed to meet again next day after the opening session of the negotiations with the candidate countries. Between the two meetings on 29 and 30 June, further Ministerial discussion took place in The Hague, as a result of which Mr. Lardinois believed he had succeeded in reversing the earlier Cabinet decision. Dr. Luns and Mr. de Koster were absent from these discussions; they were in Luxembourg. Accordingly, Mr. Lardinois proceeded to Luxembourg on 30 June for the resumed Council of Ministers meeting of the Ministers of Agriculture. Dr. Luns made efforts on 30 June through The Hague to have him restrained; but Mr. Lardinois was determined to press on regardless of his colleagues' views. The Germans apparently made a half-hearted attempt to block a decision but gave way when it became clear that the Dutch had changed their ground. France then made the necessary concessions on access and agreement was reached.

25. I have no doubt that Mr. de Koster was perfectly sincere in his efforts to block agreement and in his belief that he had succeeded. There can be little doubt that Mr. Lardinois had made a deal with M. Duhamel, who at the meeting on 30 June insisted that the French Delegation had to return to Paris with an agreement. As a footnote to these unfortunate proceedings, it is worth recording two things. First of all, Sir Patrick Hancock reported on 29 June from Rome

that the Embassy had not yet been able to sound out the Italians, since 'the officials concerned were on strike last week and are on holiday today'. This was really rather a pity; the Italians might well have helped. Second, we received a rather shamefaced, and indeed shameful, explanation from the Dutch. A member of their Permanent Representation in Brussels told a British official on 1 July that their original instructions had only required them to block agreement before the opening session of the enlargement negotiations.

26. Nevertheless, the Dutch later on had some rather unproductive qualms —presumably their Foreign Ministry regained a point from their Ministry of Agriculture. At a meeting of the Permanent Representatives on 21 September, 1970, the Dutch argued that some changes to the proposed fisheries regulation would be necessary as a result of enlargement, and they for their part would be ready to agree to consultations with candidate countries before 1 November, the date on which, at that time, it was hoped the Common Fisheries Policy would enter into force. But the Dutch received no support. A Council of Ministers meeting later that day agreed on formulae to be stated to the candidates, including the special formula for Norway (see paragraph 12 in Chapter 26). It was proposed that the special additional point for Norway should also be made to the other candidates; but the French insisted successfully that it should be made to the Norwegians alone.

26

Fisheries: The First Twelve Months

The decisions on a Common Fisheries Policy which M. Duhamel and Mr. Lardinois had between them forced through the Council of Ministers of Agriculture on 30 June, 1970, were outline decisions only. Unfortunately, the worst feature of them was the clearest: access 'up to the beaches'.[1] Most of the rest remained to be filled in. At a further meeting of the Agricultural Council of Ministers on 19 and 20 October the main marketing and structures regulations for fisheries, including those on access to national waters, were settled and it was agreed that they should come into force on 1 February, 1971. At this meeting, our Delegation reported from Brussels, 'no reference was made to the documents put in by applicant countries'. The Council set itself a time-limit of 31 December for agreeing the various implementing regulations; and the Commission was to press ahead with their preparation. These were in fact agreed without difficulty by the six Ministers of Agriculture at a further Council meeting in the last week of January 1971, and entered into force likewise on 1 February, 1971.

2. Our negotiations meanwhile proceeded with little reference to fish; and as it turned out the fisheries issue was not finally settled until the very last day of the negotiations on 18 January, 1972. It was never altogether absent either from the Conference, still less from our contacts with the Commission in Brussels and the Member States there and in their capitals. But only for two periods of some two months each was fisheries a major theme of the Conference. These periods were June and July 1971, and November 1971 to January 1972. In the first period it was the least important of four major issues under discussion. By the second period it had become the dominant outstanding issue.

3. Our original tactical concept had been that fisheries was one of the

[1] The judgment that it was the access provisions of the Common Fisheries Policy which were its single most damaging feature was fully borne out by later developments following enlargement. When the Community took the decision to extend fisheries limits to 200 miles in 1976 and when it subsequently (in 1986) included Spain and Portugal in the Common Fisheries Policy it was the access provisions of the basic policy which created the greatest difficulties. And these same provisions complicated and undermined the efforts to introduce effective conservation measures as fisheries stocks came under increasing pressure.

questions we preferred to leave until the end. We knew that in this area the Community's regulations would have to be very substantially changed. We thought therefore that fisheries could best be both tackled and settled after 'the back of the negotiations had been broken' and when everyone concerned, being confident of a successful outcome, would be more relaxed and less dogmatic. It proved impossible to stick to this timetable. Public concern and political pressure about fisheries had become so great by the spring of 1971 that Ministers decided, late in May, that an attempt must be made to settle the matter before the end of June, so that a satisfactory result on this as on the other major issues of the negotiations could be reported in the July White Paper and presented to Parliament for its debate that month.

4. Accordingly, we raised the issue in the Conference at the beginning of June, and pressed hard for a solution at the crucial Luxembourg Ministerial meeting of 21–23 June. We did not get one, though some progress was made. By the Ministerial meeting of 12 July we had changed our tactics and Mr. Rippon made a further long statement in the Conference. Thereafter, we tried to slow things down, and succeeded. We did not want, and we avoided, further discussion of fisheries in the Conference until the vote in Parliament on the 'decision of principle' had been taken at the end of October. Then the matter was taken up again as rapidly as possible, for there was not much time left. It needed three further Ministerial meetings to reach agreement. Finally, on 12 December, 1971, we reached an agreement with the Community which Denmark and Ireland also accepted. Norway did not.

5. What the eventual Norwegian settlement might be remained crucial to our own position; so even from our point of view the matter could not be finally concluded till after the Norwegians eventually also settled shortly after midnight on 15 January, 1972. Intense negotiations between ourselves, the Community, the Danes and the Irish were then still required, and final agreement acceptable to all parties was only reached on 18 January.

6. There was thus a long period of over 10 months in the early stages when fisheries was on the whole a dormant subject in the Conference. But it was during this period, from October 1970 onwards, that it came to life as an increasingly serious political problem in the United Kingdom. As the previous chapter has shown, this was not a matter on which the candidates found it easy to determine their objectives and their tactics. This applied to us as much as to the rest. Our first official assessment of the effects of the Common Fisheries Policy, completed early in October 1970, was that the United Kingdom fishing industry as a whole should benefit from it. Freedom of access to fishing grounds would reopen to our distant water fleet fishing grounds off Norway, from which they were on the point of being excluded, and the Faroes. Moreover, the entry of Norway and Denmark into the Community should divert some of the pressure on our market by their exports of fish which arrangements in EFTA entailed. On balance there should be some economic gain; but the reaction of our inshore fleet would be politically very serious. By February 1971 we were changing our

minds, largely because we feared that national measures that might be taken, for instance by Norway, consistently with the Common Fisheries Policy could effectively exclude us from Norwegian waters. Already at this stage the first glimmering of what later become our 6-mile proposal can be discerned in a paper prepared by the Ministry of Agriculture for the Working Group on Europe. The conclusion may seem slightly illogical; but at this stage we did not believe we should prove able to change the common policy as much as, in the end, we did.

7. Strangely enough, the Norwegians seem also, at first, to have been divided in their attitude to the Common Fisheries Policy. At the end of January 1971 our Embassy in Oslo reported that a sub-committee set up to examine the problem, consisting of officials and fishery representatives, had completed a report which revealed a division of opinion between the two groups. The fishery representatives insisted on maintaining the Norwegian 12-mile limit. The official representatives did not agree. They thought this could not possibly be negotiated; they underlined that Norway, as a formidable fish exporting country, had much to gain from access under the terms of the marketing regulation to the markets of the enlarged Community; and they believed that Norwegian interests in their coastal waters could be protected by national regulations compatible with the Common Fisheries Policy. It is interesting to notice how completely, in Britain as in Norway, the more or less rational considerations based on economic interest which influenced officials in the early stages came to be swept away by the powerful political pressures which developed.

8. In September the Norwegians circulated a document of over 100 pages to the Community setting out their problems. In mid-October we circulated a document of four pages outlining the problem as we saw it. This paper referred, however, to one of our main preoccupations at that time. It was a preoccupation which by no means concerned only fisheries. Though it was a general issue of some importance, I have so far made no reference to it in this Report; but it arose largely in the context of fisheries and so I will deal with it briefly here.

9. In making a statement at the first Ministerial meeting on 21 July, 1970, which embodied a general review of the main problems of the negotiations Mr. Barber concluded with a passage recorded in the records of the Conference as follows:

> 'On the question of the development of the Community, Mr. Barber wished to make a more general point. The United Kingdom certainly had no wish to impede the development of the Community. But successive British Governments had waited a long time for the opportunity to negotiate entry into the Community, and it would be somewhat difficult for public opinion in Britain to believe that joining the Communities really did mean a pooling of interests if they saw efforts made to hasten decisions in Community development from which the candidates for membership were excluded.'

10. This statement at once raised Community hackles. At the first Deputies meeting the following day, I was asked to explain in more detail what Mr. Barber

had meant by this passage. I did so at the next Deputies meeting on 16 September, explaining 'that we hoped that, in any new development on which the Six might decide to embark in the coming months, the candidates' interests could be fully taken into account by some process of consultation'. Herr Sachs, the German chairman, replied with a hard statement no doubt agreed by the Six in advance. He referred to M. Harmel's statement of 30 June, and on this basis declared that 'where formal decisions were taken by the Community during the period of negotiations, candidates would have to accept these just as they were being asked to accept other decisions taken under the treaties at earlier dates'.

11. This request for consultation with the candidates before the Community developed its policies proved, very rapidly, to be something which the Community was not at that stage ready to accept. They had to accept it later for the interim period between signature of the Treaty and its entry into force; but they were determined, during the period of the negotiations, to maintain their 'autonomy of decision' entirely untrammelled. We could not move them on this and soon ceased to press the point. But we had not quite dropped it by the time we circulated our paper on fisheries in October. Accordingly, its first paragraph read as follows:

> The United Kingdom Delegation recalls that at the meeting of Deputies on 1 October they noted the Community's willingness to take careful note of statements made or documents submitted by the applicant States on the common fisheries policy. The United Kingdom Delegation then pointed out that this fell short of the request by the United Kingdom that there should be some procedure for consultation about developments of major significance in Community policy, and in undertaking to submit this present paper reserved their right to return to this question as to other matters of Community development should decisions by the Council make that necessary. The United Kingdom Delegation repeat the suggestion made on that occasion that the Community might have discussions with the United Kingdom before further decisions were taken by the Council on the common fisheries policy.

The Community proved no readier to consult us over the development of their fisheries policy than over anything else; and before long we had ceased to hope or ask for consultation of this kind. Some description is given in the last paragraph of Chapter 25 of the Community's consideration of consultation on fisheries.

12. The only other significant event which occurred in the Conference in the autumn of 1971 [*sic*: 1970] concerned not us but Norway. At the first Norwegian Ministerial meeting with the Community on 22 September, the Community replied to a Norwegian statement in terms which went beyond those they had used in speaking to the other candidates about fisheries. They had told us, for instance, that they were willing to take careful note of statements made or

documents submitted by the applicant States on the Common Fisheries Policy. They said the same to Norway, but added that they were 'prepared to recognise, in due course, the attention which it will be appropriate to ascribe to the problems faced by Norway in the fisheries sector'. This recognition by the Community of Norway's special difficulties over fisheries, and of no one else's, was something to which the Norwegians clung. (The Danes were also confident of being able to negotiate special arrangements for Greenland and the Faroes.) From then on the Norwegians were convinced that, at least at the end of the day, the Community would be ready to offer them special terms and special concessions. This conviction, which in the end proved only marginally true, continued throughout the negotiations to complicate progress by the other candidates and led the Norwegians to adopt until the very last a somewhat reserved and highly individual attitude which made progress by anybody harder to achieve. There can be little doubt that, in the early stages, the Community believed they would be able to settle fisheries by fobbing us and the Irish off with very limited concessions, and then proceeding to offer more generous treatment to Norway, Greenland and the Faroes.

13. Very little more happened in the Conference, or even on its fringes, until May 1971. We had a series of meetings with the Commission, in January, February and April 1971, which usefully elucidated the Community's regulations and the possible avenues which might lead to a solution. In March the Norwegian Government, which had been pursuing its application for membership under a Prime Minister who opposed the policy, fell and was replaced by a Social Democratic Government under Mr. Bratteli, which was much more wholehearted in pursuing the same aim. But he included in his Cabinet a Minister of Fisheries, Mr. Hoem, who was to cause him much trouble later. Shortly after this change of Government, the Norwegians on 4 May, 1971, put forward a proposal. They said they were prepared to accept the Common Fisheries Policy, including its access provisions, provided the Community would accept that the right of fishing in waters under the jurisdiction of Member States should be confined to persons or firms established in such Member States. This was an ingenious proposal, under which of course the Norwegians hoped to be able to operate rules which would effectively have preserved their coastal waters for their own fishermen. They argued that in no other professional economic activity were nationals of one Member State permitted to operate within the jurisdiction of another except in compliance with the latter State's rules of establishment. The Norwegians could not see why coastal waters should be treated in this respect differently from land; the Community of course could. It was quite a shrewd approach. As the Norwegians well knew, the French themselves, in their earlier resistance to the attempts of the other Member States to get a fisheries policy with common access provisions, had taken the establishment point. Much discussion ensued on the Norwegian proposal; we borrowed part of their concept for our own proposals of June 1971; and indeed the concept survives in a modified form in the Articles of the Act of Accession dealing with

fisheries (paragraph 1 of Article 100). But the Norwegian proposal itself made no progress; the Community found all sorts of reasons of law and precedent for treating it as inadmissible; and eventually the Norwegians had to accept its failure.[2]

14. Meanwhile throughout the spring of 1971 political pressure on fisheries had been rising sharply in the United Kingdom. Ministers were beginning to feel we could not, as we had originally hoped, leave the matter over until the autumn of the year. Accordingly, when Mr. Heath and M. Pompidou met in Paris on 19 and 20 May, fisheries was one of the subjects which Mr. Heath raised. At this stage, he could do no more than describe the political difficulties it involved and explain that we could not accept the Community's Common Fisheries Policy without considerable modifications. But we already calculated that the French, who had only been somewhat marginally converted in the winter of 1969 and the spring of 1970 to change their line on fisheries, might prove an ally rather than an enemy in our efforts to change the Community's position. This in the end proved on the whole, though there were difficult periods, to be the case; and the discussion between Mr. Heath and M. Pompidou showed willingness on the latter's part to take account of our difficulties.

15. Before plunging into the record of the negotiations, which were now about to begin in earnest, it may be useful at this stage to draw attention to the way in which their eventual outcome is set out in the Treaty of Accession. The main provisions are contained in Articles 100 to 103 of the Act of Accession. But these by no means tell the whole story. It is necessary to look also at Protocol No. 2 (on the Faroe Islands); at Protocol No. 4 (on Greenland); and at Protocol No. 21 (on the Fisheries Régime for Norway). In addition, there is the 'Joint Declaration on the Fisheries Sector' which forms a part of the Final Act of the Conference. Nor does this complete the picture. There were several statements by the Community, by ourselves and by the other applicants, recorded in the minutes of various Ministerial and Deputies meetings, both in December 1971 and January 1972, which incorporated essential elements in the final balance of agreement eventually reached. It should be noted that, under Articles 25 to 27 of the Act of Accession, the Treaty of Accession does not apply to the Faroe Islands. The Danish Government can however, during the three years succeeding the Treaty's entry into force, give notice that the Treaty shall apply to the Faroe Islands.[3]

16. As already recorded in paragraph 3 above, Ministers came to the conclusion at the end of May that we must raise fisheries immediately in the

[2] The legal doubts on the European Community side were well justified. At a much later stage, in the 1990s, when the British government introduced similar legislation, it was ruled to be illegal by the European Court of Justice as being in contravention with the Treaty provisions on freedom of establishment.

[3] In the light of the negative views of the Faroese themselves, the Danish Government never did give such notice and neither the Treaty nor the Common Fisheries Policy ever applied to the Faroe Islands.

Conference in order if possible to get a settlement by the end of June. But what were we to propose? At this stage, we were still to some extent under the influence of our opening view that on balance the Community's fishery régime might prove advantageous to us. This concept had become crystallised in a notion referred to by representatives of the British Trawler Federation when they met the Minister of Agriculture on 8 July, 1971 (by which time, as we shall see, it was out of date). On that occasion the British Trawler Federation representatives referred to their previous willingness 'to advocate proposals which would represent a fair compromise between the interests of the deep-sea and inshore fleets'. This had meant, and still meant at the end of May 1971, that it remained one of our major objectives to ensure access for our distant water trawlers to the outer 6 miles of Norwegian coastal waters, from which they had been expelled seven months before. A joint memorandum by the Secretary of State for Scotland and the Minister of Agriculture, Fisheries and Food dated 25 May, 1971, recommended the policy we should adopt in the light of the need to settle if we could before the end of June, and recommended that we should make proposals at the Deputies meeting on 1 June. These recommendations were endorsed at a meeting of the AE Committee on 27 May. Already Ministers took the view that the ideal solution would be for the Community to agree to suspend the application of their Common Fisheries Policy to us pending agreement on a suitably adapted fisheries régime after our entry into the Communities'. But they did not believe this could be achieved. They accordingly endorsed the two Ministers' proposals that we should ask for exclusive fishery rights for our own fishermen within a limit of 6 miles round our coasts. This proposal was to be put forward at the Deputies meeting on 1 June; and this was done.

17. Our proposals naturally elicited no formal reaction from the Community. Later, it became clear that they had caused a certain amount of mouth-watering in some quarters, certainly including Holland; for after all we had offered a substantial concession to Community fishermen. But if our proposals were by no means unpopular in the Community, it was otherwise at home, in Ireland and in Norway. We informed the Danish, Irish and Norwegian Governments of our proposals very shortly before we made them on 1 June. On 3 June the Clyde Fishermen's Association addressed a letter to Mr. Rippon from Campbeltown which began: 'We are astounded at the news that you have thrown away 6 miles before entering the negotiating chamber.' This was typical of reactions in a number of quarters, including the Scottish Press. On 9 June Mr. Grimond wrote to Mr. Rippon: 'I repeat that I cannot understand how a Government which, when it was in Opposition, assured the fishermen that a 12-mile limit was essential, can now say that they are willing to abandon it.' Lord Boothby telephoned Mr. Rippon to express his concern; but strangely enough, in the light of his later attitude, was satisfied when told that certain areas of sea he felt should be protected (in particular the Minches) would be protected even under our 6-mile proposal by our agreed baselines. Most remarkable of all in the light of later attitudes was the outcome of a meeting held on 11 June in

Edinburgh by the Secretary of State for Scotland and his Parliamentary Secretary, Mr. Buchanan-Smith, with representatives of the Scottish Inshore Fisheries Association. After Mr. Buchanan-Smith had described and defended our 6-mile proposal, most of the Fisheries representatives said they were prepared, with much reluctance, to accept it.

18. The Irish did not say much; but at a Ministerial meeting they had with the Community on 7 June, they put forward an entirely different proposal, namely that Ireland should be allowed to preserve her status quo in respect of fishery limits until such time as an enlarged Community could negotiate new arrangements to apply to all its members. The Norwegians must have been most deeply aggrieved of all. Mr. Rippon had visited Oslo from 24 to 26 May. He had said nothing about our 6-mile proposal; he could not have done so for Ministers had not yet agreed it. He had told Norwegian Ministers that 'in June he hoped that it would be possible to get the Community to accept the need for a settlement and to agree that this could not be negotiated solely with Britain, since settlement needed to suit the Community of Ten'. But Norway of course immediately realised, when they heard of our 6-mile proposal, that we were after their waters. On 29 June Mr. Brenchley reported from Oslo 'an outburst' by the Norwegian Foreign Minister. He said 'he had the impression that Britain wished Norway to open its fisheries zone to British trawlers up to the 6-mile limit in order to win Parliamentary support for EEC membership from the constituencies interested in trawling'. He went on to say that the plain fact was that if Norway could not get an exclusive 12-mile limit they would stay out of the Common Market; and the British proposal meant that Britain 'would in effect be working directly against Norwegian membership of EEC'.

19. At our Ministerial meeting with the Community on 7 June, Mr. Rippon recommended our proposals to his colleagues and urged that the Conference should reach a conclusion at the next Ministerial meeting on 21 and 22 June. What we needed, he said, was recognition that the fisheries régime will need modification, together with a clear indication of the way in which the problems could be solved. M. Schumann replied that the Community had asked the Commission to study the matter and prepare proposals.

20. By 17 June the Commission had produced proposals. They offered the candidates 6 miles of exclusive fisheries for 5 years, then for a further 5 years on a more conditional basis, and then a review. But, somewhat strangely, they did not offer these concessions only to the candidates. The régime they proposed was to apply to all Member States of the enlarged Community, thus completely changing the policy on which the Community had agreed a year before. Fortunately for us Member States jibbed at these proposals. At a meeting of the Permanent Representatives on 17 June none was able to take a position on the Commission's proposals; but the Germans and Belgians objected to them in particular as representing a complete reversal of the existing Common Fisheries Policy, in that they would apply to the Six as well as to the candidates. The Germans were specially irritated with the French. A telegram from our Embassy

in Bonn of 13 July reported that the German Press was pointing out 'that the French extracted costly finance support measures in the fisheries sector as the price for agreeing to the common policy over Community waters. Now they want to cash in twice, by securing acceptance that the British request for a 6-mile limit be extended to the enlarged Community without reopening the fisheries support issue' A Dutch official, speaking to our Embassy in The Hague on 17 June, made it clear that the Dutch regarded the Commission's proposals as much too generous to us. We should be. offered 6-mile limits, but for only two years. The Dutch must later have regretted this attitude.

21. As the Ministerial meeting in Luxembourg on 21 and 22 June approached, we urged the Community that our primary requirement was to settle, at least in outline, at that meeting. We needed agreement in principle that there would be modification in respect of access and a clear indication of its nature. At a further meeting of the AE Committee on 17 June Ministers concluded that we should be ready to accept 6-mile limits at the Luxembourg meeting if we could get them for ten years with an effective review thereafter. Ministers noted (and this was an example of the type of economic argument which became increasingly irrelevant as time passed) that only 9 per cent by volume and 3 per cent by value of our fishing industry's catch was taken in our waters between 6 and 12 miles.[4]

22. At this point, it is worth noting two straws in the wind. Both became significant later. On 17 June there was a General Election in Iceland. The Leftwing parties won it, and formed a Government on 14 July. They were pledged to assert exclusive 50-mile fishery limits. The risk of this had already profoundly affected the attitude of the British Trawler Federation. Early in June the Ministry of Agriculture noted that 'their attitude to limits can be understood only if it is realised that they are conditioned not so much by thoughts of access to Norwegian or even Faroese and Greenland waters, as by fears of unilateral extension of limits by Iceland'. Also in June, and for the first time, a Member State asked for the derogation available under the Common Fisheries Policy—exclusive 3-mile limits for 5 years—to be applied to parts of its waters. It was France which asked this, in respect of most of her Mediterranean coast and part of her north-eastern coast.

23. As it turned out, and in spite of much pressure from us, we failed to reach any definitive agreement with the Community at the Ministerial meeting in Luxembourg from 21 to 23 June. So much else was achieved at this meeting that this failure was hardly noticed. We did however make one important advance. The Community declared that it recognised 'that in the perspective of enlargement it will be necessary to reconsider, for a period of time to be specified', the access provisions of the Common Fisheries régime. Mr. Rippon took note of this, and proposed that, since fisheries was a matter of major concern to all the

[4] This line of economic argument was not only invalidated by political pressure. It also rapidly became outdated as the distant water part of the industry was excluded from Icelandic water.

applicant countries, the next Ministerial meeting (which was fixed for 12 July) should be a multilateral one between the Community and all the candidates.

24. Our fellow candidates had already been taking up more intransigent positions than we. On 18 June we heard that Irish Embassies in the capitals of the Six had informed the Six Governments that the Irish Government would not accept the Commission's proposals for a revision of the Common Fisheries Policy. (These proposals had of course not yet been accepted by the Six, still less put forward by them in the Conference.) On the morning of 21 June, at a Ministerial meeting with the Six in Luxembourg, the Norwegians stated that the Commission's suggestions on fisheries, as they understood them, would not represent an acceptable solution for Norway. Thus there was clearly, at the meeting from 21–23 June, no basis for agreement with all the candidates. Nevertheless, there is no doubt that the Six believed, at least three days before the meeting, that there was a real chance of reaching agreement with us at this meeting, presumably on the basis of the Commission's proposals. They went so far as to arrange that Norwegian Ministers (whose meeting with the Community took place on the morning of 21 June) should remain in Luxembourg until the end of our meeting in case it should be possible for the Six, at a resumed session with the Norwegians, to announce their agreement with us. So we had, as things turned out, rather a lucky escape, due mainly to the fact that the Community could not agree on the Commission's proposals. Had they done so, their position would have been very close indeed to that adopted by British Ministers (see paragraph 21 above) and agreement might have been hard to avoid.

27

Fisheries: The Last Seven Months

Well before our Ministerial meeting on 21–23 June with the Community, we had realised that we were getting into a dangerous position on fisheries and would have to change course. The Irish had advanced a completely different proposal, namely the maintenance of the status quo. The Norwegians had rejected the Commission's move towards 6-mile limits. We had not made it sufficiently clear in our proposals of 1 June that we would not be ready to allow the other candidates to achieve significantly better settlements on fisheries than we; yet this was the case. We were in danger of allowing the impression to grow up in the Community that they could reach an early and final settlement with us on relatively easy terms and then, later on, give the others more. The Community had been given, by our insistence on settling if possible in June, the impression that we were up against an imperative political deadline imposed by our own Parliamentary requirements. Even though our unconcern at failure to agree in June disproved this, they were still strongly inclined to believe that we should be forced, by the need for Parliament to take a 'decision of principle' at the end of October, to settle fisheries before then. And it was perfectly clear that the Norwegians, the Danes and the Irish would be only too happy to let us do so and themselves postpone their fisheries arrangements until much later. Our awareness, already in June, of our dilemma is shown by the fact that though at the Ministerial meeting of 21–23 June we stuck to our 6-mile proposal, we already clearly indicated our feeling that perhaps a status quo solution might prove the better plan.

2. The Norwegians let it be known at once that they would not attend a multilateral Ministerial meeting such as Mr. Rippon had proposed for 12 July. On 25 June we suggested to them, the Irish and the Danes that we should hold separate bilateral discussions between officials on fisheries. The Norwegians refused again. By now we had concluded that we ought to move to adopt the status quo proposal put forward by the Irish. On 28 June we described our position in a telegram to Bonn. We said we needed agreement that the status quo would continue until renegotiation by the enlarged Community had taken place. If the Community regarded it as essential to define matters more precisely, then all the difficulties arising from the differing objectives of the various

candidate countries would be injected into the negotiations. At separate bilateral meetings with Irish and Danish officials in Brussels on 30 June we made it clear the status quo was now our objective. They were glad to hear it. But the Norwegians were not. Their Ambassador in London delivered an *aide-mémoire* to Mr. Ford on 30 June, which expressed the Norwegian Government's hope that Her Majesty's Government would not challenge the principle, which the Community had already accepted, of considering Norway as a special case in the field of fisheries. In handing his *aide-mémoire* over, the Ambassador made clear his Government would not be satisfied with a status quo solution. He also said that if Norway were unable to join the EEC but were left outside there would be a danger that she might be drawn into some new orbit.

3. The Norwegians had two main reasons for their refusal to accept a status quo solution, a refusal which they maintained until the end of the negotiations. The first reason was the one they frequently repeated to us. They said that while their own Ministers might accept that Norway would be in a strong enough position to protect her interests in an enlarged Community they could never possibly persuade their fishing Community that a small country such as Norway would not have her interests overwhelmed if she entered the Community without getting them protected in advance. The second reason was one they referred to less often, but it was probably just as strong. The Norwegian Minister of Commerce, Mr. Kleppe, admitted it in a conversation with Mr. Rippon in London on 16 July when he said 'that Norway was a major exporter of fish, and the status quo would mean no access for Norway to the markets of the present Community'. Mr. Kleppe had in mind a dogma of the Commission, which several of the Member States supported, to the effect that (as Mr. Wellenstein told Mr. Christofas as late as 30 October, 1971) 'the status quo was not acceptable. The reason was the indivisibility of access and marketing'.

4. But for the Norwegian attitude it is possible that some arrangement based on the status quo might have proved negotiable. It would have suited the other three candidates. The French at one stage made it perfectly clear that it would suit them. The other members of the Community might have been brought to accept it if the status quo had involved the maintenance of the position the Community had reached by 1 February, 1971, and if the situation had not been complicated by the fact that the Commission's proposals of June 1971 involved changes in access arrangements even for the Member States. Early in November the German Foreign Ministry told us they had concluded the status quo solution was the best, though the Federal Chancellor, out of deference to Norway, was still opposed to it. As it was, the idea of a status quo solution remained alive until a late stage in the negotiations, but was overtaken from 11 November, 1971, onwards by the emerging pattern of the eventual solution.

5. Ministers in London met again in the AE Committee on 8 July to consider a paper put forward by officials. Their decision was that at the Ministerial meeting on 12 July the Chancellor of the Duchy should propose a status quo solution. He should if necessary explain that we were not withdrawing our early

proposal based on the 6-mile limit, and would still be prepared to reach an agreement on this basis if it were also acceptable to all the other applicants. Already before this meeting we had told our Embassy in Oslo that we did not now expect to make significant progress on fisheries before the autumn.

6. Accordingly, Mr. Rippon's objective at the Ministerial meeting on 12 July was no longer to reach an agreement that day; it was to set out on a new course, and in fact to lay down something of a smokescreen to cover our manoeuvre. This he did in a long statement, which contained much argument to demonstrate the need to abide by the principles of the European Fisheries Convention of 1964. He put forward our proposal for a status quo solution and added: 'In making this proposal I have had very much in mind that ... it would be unreasonable to expect any of the applicant countries to agree unconditionally to a permanent settlement for themselves without knowing ... what the final outcome on the Common Fisheries Policy would involve in the enlarged Community as a whole'. We thus served notice on the Community that we were not prepared to accept any agreement with them without knowing exactly what would be agreed with the other candidates.

7. Meanwhile the Community, in its internal deliberations, had continued to debate the Commission's proposals of mid-June. As early as 1 July the French, at a meeting of the Permanent Representatives, insisted that any derogations to the Common Fisheries Policy must (as the Commission had proposed) apply to all Member States, while the other five Delegations took the line that they should apply only to the candidate countries, and thus not call into question the degree of liberalised access to Community waters already achieved This struggle continued for some months. But on 14 September a Dutch official told our Embassy in The Hague that in the interests of breaking the deadlock within the Six the Dutch had decided to give way to the French on this point; and at a meeting of the Council of Ministers on 21 September the other four gave way and the French won their battle. This was an important development both in form and in substance. For the first time the Community agreed to overturn one of its own existing policies; and in doing so they helped to lay the basis for the eventual agreement.

8. Things had been happening in Norway too. When Mr. Rippon had been in Oslo on 25 May Mr. Kleppe had informed him that the Norwegian Government was about to introduce a Bill which would forbid all trawling within their 12-mile limit. He added that this would mean that, even if free access were accepted by Norway, no trawlers would be allowed into their waters and therefore the main interest of foreign fishermen would disappear. These Norwegian measures took effect from 1 July. They banned trawlers above a certain size from Norwegian waters between 6 and 12 miles. This ban applied to some 10 per cent of the Norwegian fishing fleet; but would effectively exclude the entire British distant water fleet, even if access to these waters should be reopened to foreign fishermen. From now on Norwegian waters would in any case be unavailable to us; and the British Trawler Federation, accepting this fact as they

had to, more and more transferred their concern to the problem of a possible extension of Icelandic fishery limits. Norway continued to view our attitude with the utmost suspicion. On 14 July the Norwegian Minister of Foreign Affairs declared 'that Britain's change of approach made no difference to Norway's requirements or to the line of her negotiations with the Six'. Shortly afterwards an article in the Norwegian paper *Arbeiderbladet* declared that Britain was Norway's main opponent in the fisheries negotiations.

9. This was the situation when the Community, and the negotiations, closed down for the summer holidays of 1971. But in fact, hard though it was at the time to discern, some of the elements of the eventual solution had already begun to emerge. Thus in the discussion by Ministers at the AE Meeting on 8 July already referred to, reference was made to the possibility that, if Norway got special concessions, we might be able to obtain similar concessions for some of our own fishing grounds, for instance those around the Shetland Islands and parts of South-West England. And already before the end of July a few informal conversations with the Commission and others began to indicate that the way out might be notional 6-mile limits for all, with extensions to 12 miles for special areas.

10. After the holidays, the main concern of British officials was to persuade Ministers that it would be wiser to postpone any attempt to settle the fisheries problem until after the vote in Parliament at the end of October, and that we must give the Community no reason for supposing that our political situation required agreement on fisheries before that date. We avoided any discussion of fisheries at the next Ministerial meeting with the Community on 21 September. At a meeting that day with Signor Moro, the Italian President of the Conference, Mr. Rippon told him he hoped the Community would not put anything to us on this subject before the October debate; and he suggested that it would be best to leave fisheries until the next Ministerial meeting on 9 November. At a further meeting of the AE Committee on 30 September Ministers considered two papers, one by officials and one by the Secretary of State for Scotland and the Minister of Agriculture. The paper by the two Ministers recommended yet another change of course: namely that we should seek to negotiate permanent arrangements by which we could retain 12-mile fishery limits all round our coasts. In the light of our earlier proposals, Ministers concluded that this would be difficult to defend, and decided that the right course was to press ahead with our proposal for maintaining the status quo pending the negotiation of a new policy by the enlarged Community.

11. From October till January contacts and negotiation on fisheries became so intense, intricate and continuous that I shall attempt to describe no more than the broad outlines in the remainder of this chapter.

12. We had decided that it might pay us to concentrate some attention on the French, who by now were anything but dogmatic defenders of the Community's original Common Fisheries Policy. Early in October Mr. Rippon had a meeting in Paris with M. Chamant, the French Minister responsible for

fisheries. On 26 October a meeting between British and French officials to discuss the problem was also held in Paris. At this meeting there was some discussion of the question whether the principle of a settlement should be 12 miles with holes (exceptions inwards to 6 miles) or 6 miles with bumps (exceptions outwards to 12 miles). I believe these contacts probably paid off in December when, as so often, the real climax of negotiation came with the French in Paris rather than with the Six in Brussels. By October, discussions were proceeding fairly intensively between the Commission and the candidates on the marketing regulation for fish. We took part in these, and negotiations on many complex marketing issues continued until the very end of the Conference, partly in informal contacts with the Commission, partly in the secondary legislation exercise, and occasionally at Deputies meetings. The Norwegians, who had important special interests in this area, were likewise pursuing them with a good deal of success. I shall give no further account in this chapter of the work on the marketing regulation and its outcome; it is covered to some extent in paragraphs 43 to 49 of Section III of Annex I.*

13. The eventual solution was beginning more and more to take shape behind the scenes. In mid-October the Commission proposed a formula for defining the areas which should receive special treatment, that is to say 12-mile limits. The formula was most unsatisfactory to us—it was based on the concept of areas 'without a hinterland'—but it nevertheless contributed to moving things forward. Throughout the remainder of the negotiations, a large part of our effort was directed—against the Commission and most Member States supported by Norway and Denmark—to ensuring that the criteria to be employed by the Community in its eventual review of the initial arrangements should not be so expressed as to make it appear that the continuation of the exceptional régime might be available to Norway, Greenland and the Faroes but not to our own special areas. On 27 October Mr. Tickell, Mr. Rippon's Private Secretary, discussed fisheries in London with M. Leng, M. Deniau's Chef de Cabinet. If there was any possibility, said Mr. Tickell, of the Norwegians getting 12 miles round most of their coastline, we would probably want 12 miles round the Shetlands, Orkneys, Scotland and South-West England, and the Irish would certainly put in a bid for part of their coastline. M. Leng said that in that case the French would want 12 miles around Britanny. Mr. Tickell replied that would be up to them: we could scarcely object.

14. How agreement was eventually to be reached was still obscure. The Community was becoming more and more irritated with Norwegian passivity and stubbornness. The Danes too were growing unpopular in Brussels, for general reasons unconnected with fisheries. Their new Social Democratic Government, formed in October, seemed to Community purists to be rather too remote, Nordic and independent in some of its political pronouncements. Its Ministerial negotiator, Mr. Norgaard, had a less sure touch in dealing with

* Not printed

the Community than his predecessor Mr. Nyboe Andersen, and he was much grumbled about. Yet the thought persisted that it would be unavoidable to hold multilateral meetings between all the candidates and the Community to sort things out; and for some time it was assumed that the next Ministerial meeting on 9 November might have to have this character. Rather fortunately, neither it nor any of its successors did so.

15. Our own Parliamentary debate was held late in October, and the 'decision of principle' was taken by a very satisfactory majority without too much criticism of the absence of progress on fisheries. With this hurdle behind us, we even felt, as the Ministerial meeting of 9 November approached, that there was no need—because given the Norwegian position there was so little chance—to reach agreement on fisheries at it; and we accepted that at least one further Ministerial meeting would be required.

16. The Ministerial meeting on 9 November, while entirely harmonious so far as our own dealings with the Community were concerned, seemed at the time rather sterile; but in retrospect it can be seen to have achieved a good deal. At the morning session, the Community at length put forward a major proposal. Though in many respects still entirely unsatisfactory, it nevertheless proved the basis on which, after much amendment, agreement was eventually reached. The Community (observing that their proposal was based on the United Kingdom's proposal of June 1971 for 6-mile fishery limits) proposed that all the Member States should enjoy 6-mile limits for five years from the entry into force of the Accession Treaty; that for a second period of five years such 6-mile limits should also be available subject to considerable restrictions; that there should (subject of course to the preservation of 'historic rights') be a special régime providing for 12-mile limits in 'certain strictly limited geographical areas only' on the same basis of two successive five-year periods; and that the whole régime so established should be subject, at the end of 10 years, to a review and decisions about the future. What these decisions might be was narrowly circumscribed by criteria which indicated that 6-mile limits (let alone special areas with 12 miles) could only, after 10 years, be exceptional. As for the special areas to enjoy 12-mile limits, the Community proposed: 'As regards Norway, the areas North of Trondheim: as regards Denmark, the Faroe Islands and Greenland: as regards the United Kingdom, the Orkneys and the Shetland Islands.' For the Irish Republic, they proposed nothing.

17. Mr. Rippon, in a first reaction at the morning session, welcomed the Community's statement but criticised it in a number of respects. He amplified his criticisms in a further statement when the meeting was resumed the same evening. (It was in these two statements that we introduced shellfish and crustacea into the debate, later to be joined by salmon. They all had a long swim, but proved in the end red herrings. We hoped, in case we could not get 12-mile limits for Devon and Cornwall, to get something equivalent by reservation of these fish to coastal fishermen. In the end we did not need the device, but it survives in what the Irish got for their east coast.) After Mr. Rippon's second

statement, a further adjournment took place, and when the meeting was resumed Signor Moro said that the Community had examined Mr. Rippon's remarks. They much appreciated their spirit; but they were faced with the task of finding some common denominator between the wishes of the different applicant States. (Meetings the Community had been having the same day with the other candidates had shown both the Irish and the Norwegians to be extremely critical of their proposals.) Signor Moro accordingly proposed that there should be exploratory contacts between the candidate States and the Commission and a further Ministerial meeting on 29 November. This we accepted.

18. On the same day in Brussels Mr. Rippon had a meeting with four Norwegian Ministers. They continued to insist that Norway must have a permanent arrangement, and were not much impressed by Mr. Rippon's remark 'that it was better when dealing with the Community to go round a problem than to attack it head on'. Next day I held a meeting in Brussels to discuss the fisheries position with my Danish, Irish and Norwegian opposite numbers. As usual, the Norwegians were stubborn and still insisted on permanence. At the end of the meeting (in order to put pressure on the Norwegians to hurry up: they had been putting it about for some time that they would be quite content to continue negotiating on fisheries till March or April 1972) I said that if other candidate States were not able to resolve their problems in time to sign the Treaty by the end of the year the United Kingdom might be obliged to sign a Treaty with an escape clause allowing us to return to the question of fisheries in the light of developments with the other candidates. My Norwegian colleague, Mr. Sommerfeldt, said that this would be most unfortunate.

19. The crisis in the Community's relations with the Norwegians had indeed now opened. They had at last, but virtually for the first time, been brought to the point of negotiation; but on 9 November they had rejected not only the Community's proposals on fisheries but also proposals on their other main problem, agriculture, which the Community regarded as generous. There was much doubt, not least in France, whether the Norwegians really wanted to join the Community and whether the Community should make further concessions to enable them to do so. Here the argument about the effect of Norway's exclusion on NATO, of which we and no doubt the Germans frequently reminded the members of the Community, came into play; and it probably helped to produce the right outcome in the end. And we soon had, even in the fisheries context, a strong interest in Norwegian membership; for the Norwegians told us categorically on 7 December that if they did not join the Community they intended to extend their fisheries limits to 50 miles, and made very clear their distaste for our efforts to ensure Community assent to the proposition that no Member State should be free to extend its fisheries jurisdiction against other members.

20. It was already clear that much of the difficulty over Norway stemmed from dissension in the Norwegian Government. The Minister of Fisheries, Mr. Hoem, who before joining the Government in the spring of 1971 had worked

for the Raw Fish Sales Organisation in Tromso, was opposed to any concessions. The concessions the Norwegian Government was being pressed at this time to make were two-fold. First, recognition that any exceptions granted to them could not be manifestly permanent, but would be subject to some kind of review after 10 years. Second, that they could not enjoy 12-mile limits for their whole coastline, but would have to accept a theoretical 6-mile limit with major exceptions at 12 miles. These were presumably the concessions Mr. Hoem felt unable to make, and shortly after the Norwegian Government had finally accepted, on 15 January, 1972, an agreement with the Community, he resigned. It was feared that the Norwegian Minister of Agriculture might also resign, which could have put the Government in an impossible position; but luckily he accepted and defended the agreement on agriculture which the Norwegians reached in December, and stood by his colleagues.

21. As agreed at the Ministerial meeting on 9 November, the Commission proceeded to have discussions with the candidate countries. These proved from our point of view somewhat difficult. The Commission was always rather stubborn over fisheries; feeling it their obligation to defend as long as they could the crumbling common policy of the Community. Nevertheless our contacts with them helped. They agreed, which was a major point for us, that instead of two successive five-year periods with different conditions, they would recommend a single initial period of 10 years; they produced a much improved (though still inadequate) draft review clause; and they offered the Irish a first special 12-mile area—County Donegal. Nevertheless, as the Ministerial meeting fixed for 29 November approached, we did not feel that we had made sufficient progress.

22. By now, the main problem for Ministers in London was to determine the extent of the demand we should make for 12-mile limits; and to ensure that the Community accepted that in future no member would be free to extend its fisheries jurisdiction against other members beyond 12 miles. The Minister of Agriculture circulated a paper to the AE Committee which (while still to some extent hankering after universal and permanent 12-mile limits subject only to historic rights) recommended that we should settle for a 6-mile rule provided we received extensive 12-mile areas. On 24 November the AE Committee considered this paper. They provisionally decided we must seek exclusive 12-mile areas not only for the Shetlands and Orkneys but also for the whole of the Scottish north and east coast; for the north-cast coast of England from Berwick to Spurn Head; for an area including the whole of Devon and Cornwall and most of Wales; and for County Down. But this was felt to be asking a lot; and Mr. Prior and Mr. Campbell were invited to consider urgently with Mr. Rippon whether some stretches of coastline could be eliminated from this list. We did not in any case intend to seek 12-mile limits for Western Scotland, because, immensely important though the fishing grounds involved are, we regarded them as being adequately protected by the baselines deriving from the 1964 Convention which operated just as well with 6-mile limits as with 12-mile limits.

23. No final conclusion had been reached as to the extent of our bid before

Mr. Rippon left for the Ministerial meeting on 29 November. Late on the evening of 28 November Mr. Rippon met in Brussels with Danish, Irish and Norwegian Ministers and officials, including Mr. Hoem. The Norwegian Minister of Commerce, Mr. Kleppe, still took a very hard line, perhaps because of Mr. Hoem's presence. He still insisted on 12-mile limits for the whole Norwegian coast and on guaranteed permanency; Norway could accept no reversion to the present Common Fisheries Policy. Nor did he see why we should all be in such a hurry to settle. The Norwegians in any case had to carry out a major process of consultation with their Parliamentary committees and fishing organisations before they could accept any agreement.

24. This was a discouraging prelude to what proved to be a most discouraging meeting with the Community. Everything went wrong. On 29 November the Prime Minister sent a message from London to the Norwegian Prime Minister urging him to seek agreement with the Community. Soon after midnight that night the text of the Prime Minister's letter had leaked widely in Brussels among all the Community Delegations. The Norwegians admitted their responsibility, and were far more embarrassed than we. The sense of guilt they felt about this over the next few weeks may even have contributed to the eventual settlement. The Council of Ministers of the Six met among themselves all day on 29 November and only began their meeting with us late in the evening. By this time M. Schumann had already returned to Paris. He had an appointment with President Bongo of Gabon. This did not improve the atmosphere. When they met us the Community handed over a long proposal on fisheries based on their proposal of 9 November. It had been improved by provision for a single initial period of 10 years; but there was no advance on 12-mile areas (except for Ireland) and the review clause still left very much to be desired. Mr. Rippon at once rejected several features of the Community's proposal, and the meeting adjourned. Shortly before midnight the Foreign Office sent instructions to Paris explaining the position reached and asking the Embassy to ascertain if M. Boegner, who in M. Schumann's absence was representing France in Brussels, had authority to settle that night on a basis satisfactory to us.

25. It proved impossible for the Embassy to take effective steps that night; and it soon became clear in Brussels that M. Boegner was in a bad mood and determined not to budge. Contacts with M. Deniau and others in the corridors raised our hopes that we might achieve a satisfactory review clause; but he was unable to sell it to the Six. The meeting with us resumed at 2.45 a.m. on 30 November, when Signor Moro proposed on behalf of the Community that attempts to settle that night should be abandoned and a further Ministerial meeting held on 11 December. Mr. Rippon urged the Community not to give up; we believed the formula agreed with M. Deniau might yet be accepted by the Six. After further discussion among the Six, and further stonewalling by M. Boegner, the meeting was resumed at 6.15 a.m. Signor Moro urged 'a short breathing space' until 11 December. Mr. Rippon still refused to give in, and persuaded the Community to try once again. A further meeting was held at

12.45 p.m. on 30 November when Signor Moro put forward a slightly revised version of the Community's proposal. This at least added 'a part of the Scottish coastline' to the 12-mile areas proposed for us; but the review clause was little changed and made still more unacceptable by the insertion of the requirement that the Community's decision in 1982 at the expiry of the 10 year initial period must be a unanimous one (this insertion, we later heard, had been expressly asked for by M. Schumann). At this point Mr. Rippon abandoned hope and agreed that matters must stand over until 11 December. Naturally enough, the other three candidates had made equally little progress in their meetings, interspersed between ours, with the Community; and the Danes and Norwegians at least felt a sense of grievance (which was hardly justified) that we had monopolised the Community's attention throughout the night. The Norwegian Press published in the next few days strong criticisms of British attitudes and tactics.

26. The Brussels meeting had been a bad one. The German Ambassador in London gave Mr. Tickell on 1 December an account of the meeting he had received from Bonn: 'It had all been most disappointing. M. Schumann's departure before the first meeting with the candidates and subsequent French blocking tactics had been deplorable. Legalism of this kind helped no one, but M. Boegner had evidently found this the best way of obstructing progress. In addition the Italian Chairmanship had been defective in various ways, particularly on points of procedure. The British had naturally been exasperated, but this had caused our reaction at the end to be too brusque: sympathy had swung against us. It was not clear who was going to pick up the pieces or how.' But already Mr. Soames had begun to do so. He had been unable to contact M. Jobert of the Elysée on the night of 29/30 November, but he succeeded in seeing M. Schumann on the morning of 30 November before the meeting in Brussels had concluded. This was the beginning of the process of putting things together again, which took some time.

27. Since our latest difficulties came from the French, we proceeded to try and sort things out in Paris. Mr. Soames returned to London and after a meeting with the Prime Minister and other Ministers concerned went back to Paris with a message from the Foreign Secretary to M. Schumann. He was armed also with a revised review clause and full details of our 12-mile requirements, which, in the bad atmosphere of the Brussels meeting, Mr. Rippon had judged it prudent not to reveal. Mr. Soames saw M. Schumann on 3 December. They came close to agreement on the review clause. But when Mr. Soames 'produced the great map' M. Schumann professed to be deeply shocked by the extent of our 12-mile requirements. On 7 December we communicated our views on the review clause and details of our 12-mile requirements to the other Members of the Community; and on 8 December to the Commission. By now we were asking for 'the North and East coast of Scotland, the North-East coast of England down to Spurn Head, the South-West coast from Sidmouth to Aberdovey, and County Down.' Mr. Soames saw M. Schumann again on 8 December. We had

by now told the French that we were unlikely to be ready to attend a meeting in Brussels on 11 December unless we were convinced that a satisfactory conclusion would be reached. M. Schumann was still difficult over 12-mile limits. So were most of the other Members of the Community, except of course the Italians but including in particular the Dutch.

28. Gradually, through many contacts and communications in London and elsewhere, things began to improve. We gave up our request for 12-mile limits for the coast of South Wales. Mr. Soames and his staff continued to press the French. He had two conversations with M. Brunet, Director of Economic Affairs in the Quai d'Orsay, and he also spoke to M. Bernard of the Elysée. M. Bernard was encouraging, and advised us strongly to stick to the meeting arranged for Saturday, 11 December. By the time of Mr. Soames' second conversation with M. Brunet on 10 December, the latter was 'very accommodating'. He said that, as to limits, he 'thought that our new map with Wales out could form a basis for discussion'. We decided to stick to the meeting arranged for 11 December.

29. This meeting brought agreement. It took some time to reach, for it was not achieved until 6.30 a.m. on Sunday morning, 12 December. We had arranged to begin the proceedings by a short session at 9.30 a.m. at which Mr. Rippon put forward our full proposals on fisheries (as well as on animal health). A long adjournment with many informal contacts followed. In the end we got a satisfactory review clause; we got a statement from the Community, recorded in the minutes, making it clear that the Common Fisheries Policy would not permit any member of the enlarged Community to extend its fisheries jurisdiction against other members; and we got almost everything we wanted in respect of 12-mile limits. These caused the main struggle; but with two small exceptions British Ministers (Mr. Rippon, Mr. Prior and Mr. Buchanan-Smith) refused to budge. This was in my opinion the best example of the successful application of political pressure at the right time which the negotiations produced. The two concessions we had to make involved eliminating from the 12-mile area for North-Eastern England the 35 miles from Flamborough Head to Spurn Head and another 35 miles of the North Northumberland coast southwards from the Scottish border to Coquet Island. When we thus got 12-mile limits for over 100 miles of the North-Eastern coast of England, the Danes suddenly sprang to life and insisted on a corresponding 12-mile exemption for a stretch of their West coast. They got it. As often before, M. Schumann left the Conference early in the morning before it ended; and we feared his departure might produce deadlock as it had two weeks before. But it proved otherwise. The climax came at about 6 a.m. when M. Deniau, pursuing his mediating rounds, stuck his head round the corner of the door of Mr. Rippon's room and asked, on behalf of the Community, if we would mind, as part of the bargain, the French having 12-mile limits for four of the five Departments of Brittany and one Department of Normandy. Everybody in the room shouted 'No!': and agreement had been reached.

30. But not with Norway. The Danes and Irish settled with us, the Irish having achieved major exceptions in respect of 12-mile limits. The Norwegians, with a divided Cabinet, declined to settle and made it clear that they must ask for more. In a sense, the Norwegians had now at last achieved the position they had longed to be in for over a year: out on their own and able to fight for themselves to get something more than the rest. Their problem was that the rest had by now got so much that it was hard to see what more they could get for themselves.

31. The Norwegians arranged a further Ministerial meeting with the Community for 10 January, 1972. As a prelude to it, their Prime Minister, Mr. Bratteli, toured the capitals of the Six (except Bonn, since Herr Brandt had recently been in Oslo); and he also came to England and had talks with the Prime Minister at Chequers on 9 January. These went well, and Mr. Bratteli seemed satisfied that we would not oppose some moderate embellishments of an agreement with Norway going slightly beyond what we had got ourselves. We had long made it clear that we had to insist on comparable, not identical, treatment for Norway.

32. The Norwegian negotiations on fish—they had by now settled on agriculture—continued while we for our part completed at meetings of the Deputies the long and complicated process of wrapping up numerous final details in many fields and settling disputed points arising from the drafting of the Treaty. We and the Norwegians were still pressing a number of points on the fish marketing regulation, which one by one were settled. But when the Norwegians held their Ministerial meeting with the Community on 10 January, agreement was still not reached, though the session went on till 8 a.m. on the following day. By now the Norwegians had accepted that a small area of their southern coastline should have 6-mile limits only; though the dividing point had not yet been finally agreed. At the end of their Ministerial meeting the Norwegians did not reject the Community's position; but they did not accept it either, and insisted that they must return to Norway for further consultation.

33. The Norwegian Deputy, Mr. Sommerfelt, was sent back to Brussels for a final meeting at Deputy level on 14 January. He concluded an agreement with the Community in the early hours of the following morning. The Norwegians achieved agreement on Protocol No. 21 'on the Fisheries Régime for Norway' and on the Joint Declaration which was to form a part of the Final Act of the Conference. But their achievement did not carry them far beyond our own position; we and the Irish had made it abundantly clear that it would be unacceptable to us if it did. They did however receive formal reassurance that in 1982 the Community would take particular account of the problems facing Norway in the field of fisheries; and this assurance we were prepared to accept. A good deal of final manoeuvring was required between ourselves, the Danes and the Irish on the one hand and the Community on the other to ensure, as part of the process of 'multilateralisation', that nobody, in taking note of the agreement with Norway, made statements which would embarrass anybody

else. The Danes at one stage threatened to seek further 12-mile limits, as a reaction to the Norwegian success in extending their own so far to the south; but this the Community quashed. Everything was finally sorted out, but not until 18 January, the very last day of the negotiations.

34. Our own agreement with the Community had been reasonably well received in the United Kingdom, all the more so as the sudden shower of additional coastline with 12-mile limits came as an unexpected last-minute surprise. We described our achievement, after much calculation of local catches, as amounting to 'no change at all in the protection now afforded in areas from which about 95 per cent by value of the total inshore catch is taken'. But of course there was no lack of complaints. Every area with 6 miles only felt hardly treated; and protests arrived from Wales, Norfolk, Essex, Sussex, Hampshire, Dorset, North Northumberland and Galloway. But—and this was the crucial factor—the Scottish inshore fishermen accepted the deal. Our agreement did not affect the Isle of Man; that, under Protocol No. 3, remains to be settled later. But nevertheless the Isle of Man invited Mr. Rippon to become Admiral of the Manx Herring Fleet; and he agreed to do so.

PART III
OUR FRIENDS AND PARTNERS

28

Our Fellow Candidates

We had, on the whole, relatively little difficulty with our three fellow candidates, the Irish Republic, Norway and Denmark. Each of them had real difficulties with their home public opinion, which in Norway at least were about as grave as our own. In Denmark too public support for membership, which had been solid at the start, ebbed rather rapidly away as the negotiations progressed. Each of the other candidates, unlike ourselves, had to hold a referendum before it could join the Community. But each of them necessarily occupied a rather subordinate position in the eyes of the Community throughout the negotiations. This must have been galling for them, perhaps more so than we realised. Yet each of the three was completely dependent for the success of its application for membership on the success of ours. None of the three would have applied for membership had we not done so; almost certainly none of the three—there is perhaps an exceedingly marginal doubt in the case of Denmark—would have maintained its application had ours failed.

2. Thus the three other candidates, in spite of their own critical national interests which were at stake, found themselves condemned to tag along behind us. When a few months after the negotiations began a member of the Irish Delegation was asked how the Irish were getting on, he replied: 'Oh, we're riding along on the backs of the British.' The other candidates had fewer meetings with the Community, whether at Ministerial or Deputy level; perhaps each had half as many, or rather less, than we; their meetings were often even shorter than ours and were to a large extent concerned with agreements we had already reached with the Community, which the other candidates were asked to accept. Each of them (Denmark less than the other two) had a few important special interests, but progress on these had as a rule to await progress on the main questions of our own negotiations.

3. On the whole, there were few major clashes of interest between ourselves and the other candidates; but there were some in each case. Fisheries was perhaps the most significant of these cases, where Norway, and to a lesser extent Denmark in respect of the Faroes and Greenland, tried hard to get more than we. There was also an irreconcilable clash of interest between ourselves and Denmark over the duration of the transitional period for agriculture. The Danes wanted no

transitional period at all, or only a minimal one, but they had to accept the period we negotiated; and they did so without protest. One at least of our own major requirements in the negotiations—the protection in our market of New Zealand butter and cheese—conflicted with the interests of Denmark and the Irish Republic, as major producers and exporters of the same commodities. It is to the credit of both of them that they accepted without causing trouble our need to look after New Zealand; though of course both Denmark and the Irish Republic were much more strongly established in our market for dairy products than any of the Six, and thus could afford to be somewhat less concerned.

4. We kept closely in touch with the other candidates in Brussels throughout the negotiations, partly through reciprocal briefing arrangements after meetings which worked satisfactorily. There were also fairly regular contacts at Ministerial level in Brussels and elsewhere. With few exceptions (the main one being fisheries, already fully described in Chapters 25 to 27) the special aims and requirements of the other candidates caused us little trouble. On the whole, they succeeded in getting what they required to protect their interests. The text of the Act of Accession is full of special concessions and arrangements negotiated by each of the other three candidates, to match those negotiated by us. In particular, a number of Protocols deal with particular Irish, Norwegian or Danish interests; and so do some of the Declarations annexed to the Final Act of the Conference.

A. THE IRISH REPUBLIC

5. The Irish had no choice about entering the Community. In spite of political independence, their economic and commercial dependence on the United Kingdom is so great that they could not stay out of the Community if we went in nor go in if we stayed out. But though they had no choice, they had a strong preference. This preference was for the entry of both of us into the Community; and it was based mainly on one simple and strong reason. They wanted to go on selling to us as much, and if possible more, of their agricultural surpluses as they had always done; and they wanted to sell them at the much higher Community prices. The Irish Ambassador in London made this extremely clear to me in a conversation in March 1970. He said his country did not expect to increase its exports to other members of the Community very much; but they wanted to see the United Kingdom 'subjected to Community disciplines'.

6. Apart from their own strong economic interest, the Irish no doubt had a real political interest in establishing close and permanent links with a number of Western European countries and thus escaping to some extent from too exclusive an international relationship with us. They did not feel, and fortunately for them the Community did not feel either, any difficulties of scruples arising from their neutral status. In the same conversation, the Irish Ambassador told me that the defence implications of entry into the Community presented his Government with no difficulty. According to my record he said: 'Changes in the Irish Goverment—especially the departure of Mr. Aiken, who had been a

great man for neutrality—had altered the Irish attitude and the present Irish Government saw no difficulty about accepting defence commitments in Europe, even if it were to mean—and he hardly thought it would—membership of NATO.' The general attitude of the Community seems to have been that though the Irish Republic was neutral, it was less neutral than others; and the question of the compatibility of neutrality with membership of the Community, which caused the Swedes such nightmares, never troubled the Irish.

7. Before the negotiations began, the Irish were anxious to keep extremely close to us and explore our thinking. They probably felt at the time a little remote from Community developments. Three meetings with Irish officials for this purpose took place in London and Dublin, in December 1969 and in January and May 1970. A further similar meeting was held in the early stages of the negotiations, in October 1970. These meetings confirmed that there should be no insuperable difficulties arising from any clash between our interests, though it was clear that the problem of integrating the provisions of the Anglo-Irish Free Trade Agreement into our Community obligations might be complex.

8. We had been inclined to feel that the Irish might be reluctant to accept so long an agricultural transitional period as we should require; but it transpired before long that they would be perfectly content with something like five years for both agriculture and industry, which we eventually got. Their concern was of course the opposite of ours. They would have liked a relatively short agricultural transitional period (though even here they probably needed three years); but they wanted as long an industrial transitional period as possible, because they realised that membership of the Community was bound to put a severe strain on their industry, and indeed to eliminate altogether some of its less efficient elements.

9. The Irish Delegation in Brussels sometimes seemed imperfectly informed and occasionally rather at a loss in dealing with the Community. Nevertheless, they were smart enough when it came to dealing with their own special problems. Sometimes, we thought, a little too smart; for though on the whole we kept each other fully informed, there was a slight disposition on the part of the Irish, for which I hardly blame them, to keep some of their objectives and their ideas about timing to themselves. Where these special interests were concerned, the Irish were inclined to bide their time and then dart in suddenly to strike the Community iron when they judged it hot. It must have been tactics like these which secured the rather remarkable provisions of Article 88, authorising the Irish to subsidise butter consumption in the transitional period.

10. The problems which arose out of the Anglo-Irish Free Trade Agreement were in the end successfully solved both with the Irish and with the Community, though a good deal of complicated negotiation was necessary, especially with the former. One of the main issues concerned the Irish desire, eventually brought to fruition in Protocol No. 7, to protect their motor vehicle assembly industry. To secure this they had to make a concession to the Community which put them in breach of their obligations to us under the Free Trade Agreement.

This led to complicated negotiations in November 1971 between the Irish and us which produced a satisfactory outcome. Other problems in this context were concerned with rules of origin, safeguard clauses and dumping; they were also overcome in ways which met both our own and Irish requirements.

11. We had feared we might have difficulty with the Irish arising out of our requirement to preserve for at least five years the provisions of the Northern Ireland Safeguarding of Employment Act, since the reasons for which we wanted to do so were highly suspect in Dublin. Nevertheless, the fortunate fact that the Irish themselves decided that they must ask for a similar transitional period before they could accept the Community's free movement of labour rules meant that we each got our way without a clash.

12. The Irish had political difficulties over fisheries which were perhaps as great as our own; and this meant that, although once or twice we were out of step, our general approach to the problem over the last six months of the negotiations was pretty well identical. The Irish also had apprehensions (as did the Danes) about the Community's rules on establishment, relating mainly to the question of land purchase by foreigners. In the end they concluded they could live with things as they were, and would be able to protect their interest, in the interim period or after entry, in respect of worse things which they saw coming. On animal health their problems were even graver than ours; but in the end they got almost everything they wanted in this field, which was useful to us since we had to get, and did get, the same treatment for Northern Ireland. A problem arose over the determination of the Irish that their country should be designated in the Treaty simply as 'Ireland'. But since there were a number of cases of international agreements where we had already accepted such a designation, we made no trouble. The Irish language was also a problem. The Irish insisted that the Treaty of Accession itself must be drawn up and signed in Irish as well as in the other seven languages; but, after rather prolonged inability to make up their mind, they eventually decided to save themselves and everyone else immense trouble by not asking that Irish should become an official language of the Community. Another Irish accomplishment was the thwarting of our desire to have the Treaty of Accession signed in the United Kingdom (see paragraph 28 of Chapter 35).

13. An awkward and delicate problem arose for us when the Irish, in October 1971, got the Community to agree to the document which appears in the Treaty as Protocol No. 30 'on Ireland'. Could we accept that the Community should give to the Irish Republic these undertakings in respect of economic development, under-employment and regional differences, without asking for something similar for ourselves? If we did, would we not be subject to severe criticism from Scotland, Wales, Northern Ireland and other areas of the United Kingdom with regional problems?

14. This problem arose rather suddenly and unexpectedly, and was all the more awkward because it did so just at the moment in October 1971 when the long debate in Parliament leading up to the vote on the 'decision of principle

was about to begin. We did not feel that the Protocol the Irish had wrested from the Community was in fact of much real significance; we could no doubt ensure that the Community's principles to which it referred would be applied as much in our case as in that of any other member. But it looked bad to have Ireland seemingly singled out for special treatment. We decided, since there was no hope of our being offered anything comparable ourselves and since an intervention would probably not stop the Irish getting what they wanted, that we should not intervene. We felt we could justify this special treatment for the Irish Republic by pointing out that she would after all be much the poorest member of the enlarged Community; and taking the line that we did not believe that what the Irish had been granted added anything in substance to what would be the position of all members of the Community, old and new alike, in respect of regional policy. We warned the Commission and the Presidency before final agreement was reached with the Irish that we should take this line if questioned; and indeed we did so in the Debate in the House of Commons, where the Irish Protocol attracted some attention, though rather less than we had feared. Towards the end of the negotiations however, during the processes of 'multilateralisation' and Treaty drafting, we made a statement on 6 January, 1972, at a Deputies meeting. We said we did not object to the Irish Protocol; but we wished to make it clear that we would wish to call for an examination of any particular system of aid if the consequences should prove damaging to the domestic market of the United Kingdom and thus to the functioning of the Common Market. We asked, and it was agreed, that this statement should be recorded formally in the minutes of the Conference.

15. An awkward last-minute problem caused by the Irish arose over sugar. Here again they adopted their technique of suddenly stating a new requirement at a well-judged moment. At their final Ministerial meeting on 10 January, 1971, [*sic*: 1972] they pressed for an increase in their sugar production quota from 135,000 to 240,000 tons. We had warned the Commission, when a week or two earlier we heard of this Irish gambit, that if the Irish Republic were given a significantly higher quota we could no longer accept the quota fixed for us. When after a long dispute the Community agreed to raise the Irish quota by 15,000 tons, I received instructions to insist on a higher quota for ourselves too. This is the incident to which I referred in paragraph 19 of Chapter 3 as the only case 'in which the Delegation received instructions which it felt it had no chance of carrying out successfully.' After efforts prolonged over several days, but conducted exclusively through the Presidency so as to avoid the risk of publicity, it became apparent that the Community would not agree to any increase in our sugar production quota; and I was authorised to drop our request.

B. NORWAY

16. The negotiations for joining the Community involved profound difficulties for Norway. They led, half way through, to a change of Government;

towards the end it was by no means certain, even with their new Government, that Norway would reach an acceptable conclusion. She did so; but whether the outcome will be endorsed by the Norwegian referendum, and whether, if it is, the Norwegian Government will secure the necessary 75 per cent majority for ratification in Parliament, still remain in doubt.

17. The whole issue became extremely divisive in Norway, certainly not less than in the United Kingdom. The Norwegians were reasonably well satisfied with the position they had occupied, as members of EFTA, throughout the 'sixties. They would not by themselves have wished to turn things upside-down. But our own determination to join the Communities forced them to take a painful decision. Most responsible Norwegians felt that, if we joined, it would be decisively in their economic interest to do the same. To stay out if we went in, and still more if we and Denmark both went in, would, they calculated, gravely diminish the prospect of economic growth in Norway. Norwegian industry and shipping interests were strongly in favour of going in. In 1970, the Norwegian trade unions were also solidly in support. But the Norwegians had temperamental and historical problems which stood in the way. They were accustomed to remote and difficult conditions; their independence was fairly recent in date, and they were very proud of it; they felt separate from the rest of Europe, especially from Latin and Catholic Europe, and preferred to be so. The Danes, to some extent, really felt themselves a part of Western Europe in a way that the Norwegians did not. The Norwegian decision to join the Communities was a reluctant one, dictated very much more by the head than by the heart.

18. They had a further serious problem—a good deal more serious than in the case of Denmark who had it too—based on their Nordic association with Sweden and Finland and the extremely close interlocking of their industry with that of Sweden which had grown up through common membership of EFTA. Norway felt that her membership of the Community would be impossible unless Sweden secured satisfactory free trade arrangements with the Community which would enable Norway's trade with Sweden to continue without interruption. Yet if Sweden could obtain a satisfactory relationship with the Community without joining it, why should not Norway do the same? This dilemma placed Norway in a real difficulty. If Sweden got inadequate arrangements, Norway might not be able to join the Community; if Sweden got extremely good arrangements, the Norwegian public might not see why Norway should ask for anything different. The answer to this dilemma lay, though it was not easy for the Norwegian Government to make the point in public, in Norway's membership of NATO. Many Norwegians feared, and so did we and most members of the Community, that if Norway were excluded, or were to exclude herself, from the Community she might in course of time be attracted into a Nordic neutral zone, thus seriously weakening European defence.

19. With all these difficult and divisive issues to cope with, the Norwegians

felt it best to follow the dictates of their prudent temperament and to take things slowly. In 1967 they had put in their application for membership a couple of months later than we, the Irish or the Danes; and in 1970 and 1971 they were in no hurry. Throughout the negotiations their instinct was always to follow a slow and separate course. They felt their separate objectives, especially in agriculture and fisheries, could probably best be dealt with late in the negotiations when things had loosened up. Though they never said so, they probably devoutly wished that we would settle our own problems with the Community and then get out of Norway's way, leaving her to make separate arrangements with the Community at a later stage. Apart from tactics, it was natural that Norway, and indeed the other candidates, should wish to be seen to be successfully asserting their own interests in separate dealings with the Community, rather than to give the impression of being merely dragged in on British coat-tails.

20. Norway had relatively few special problems in the negotiations. Community finance was rather more of a problem for her than it was for Denmark or the Irish Republic; but nothing like so grave as for us. She was worried about establishment, she was closely concerned by and involved in our own negotiations for tariff quotas. But these issues were nothing compared with her concern over agriculture and fisheries. The most difficult problem for Norway had always been seen as the impact of membership on her agriculture. 13.4 per cent of Norway's active population was engaged in agriculture in 1970 (in fact, forestry and fishing are part-time occupations of many of those classified as farmers). Norway's agricultural problem was the reverse of ours. For geographical and climatic reasons, their agriculture is heavily subsidised and producer prices are on the whole considerably higher than those in the Community. But the problem of agriculture for Norway had always been, as the problem of fisheries became, a fundamental social question involving the very future of human settlement in large areas of their country. When the fisheries problem arose, Norway confronted immense new difficulties. Fisheries was a sensitive issue for them economically, but far more so politically. In 1967, when there was no Community Fisheries Policy, Norwegian fisheries interests had been in favour of membership: they foresaw that Norway as a member of the Community could take part in shaping a Fisheries Policy which would be much to her advantage. But when on 30 June, 1970, the Community adopted a policy providing for 'access up to the beaches' the fisheries problem for Norway was fundamentally changed.

21. Norway began the negotiations with a coalition Government of non-Socialist parties under a Prime Minister from the Centre Party, which represented the farming interest. In these early days, before all the difficulties arose, the policy of joining the Community was relatively popular in Norway. On 15 June, 1970, the Norwegian Parliament endorsed the Norwegian application for membership by 132 votes to 17, much more than the majority of 75 per cent which would be necessary for ratification. Yet of the 17 hostile votes,

10 came from the Government parties; and by the time the negotiations were ending, the hostile vote in Parliament had risen to 37, only one below the figure needed to block entry. A public opinion poll in the autumn of 1970 showed a majority of 51 per cent in favour of entry, with many 'don't knows'; but by July 1971 a similar poll showed 33 per cent for entry and 36 per cent against. Meanwhile the Government had changed, as a result of a crisis in February and March 1971 which arose directly out of the negotiations. The Prime Minister, Mr. Borten, caused the crisis himself by leaking a damaging report from the Norwegian Delegation in Brussels. He and his party had been insisting that Norway must secure some form of complete exemption from the Common Agricultural Policy; the Norwegian Delegation had reported that the Community would not accept this. The Government fell, and was succeeded by a Socialist Government under Mr. Bratteli which, though in a small minority in the Norwegian Parliament, pursued the negotiations with rather more energy and dedication than its predecessor.

22. But they still took their time. The Norwegian involvement with us in the problem of fisheries has been covered in some detail in Chapters 25 to 27 of this Report; here it is worth underlining once again that the way things developed gave rise, from time to time, to a good deal of bitterness directed against us from Norway. For agriculture, the Norwegians ground an agreement slowly and painfully out of the Community, and succeeded in forcing the Community to give them a good deal more than they had originally intended. Norwegian achievements in these two fields are recorded in Protocols 20 and 21 to the Act of Accession. One of their difficulties over fisheries, as recorded in Chapter 27, was that when at last they found themselves on their own, after we had settled, we had achieved so much that there was relatively little left for them to get.

23. Norway's final agreements with the Community, both on agriculture and fisheries, contained a paradoxical element. The Norwegians had always been the most stubborn of the candidates in seeking explicit and permanent exceptions to Community arrangements, the most sceptical of Mr. Rippon's doctrine that better results could be got by going round a problem than attacking it head-on, and the least ready to proclaim an act of faith in the Community's good intentions. They did succeed, uniquely, in getting agreement in their agricultural protocol 'that the transitional period could not solve these problems and that it is therefore necessary to envisage specific arrangements'. But their agricultural protocol, apart from this, provides a good example of the application of Mr. Rippon's doctrine. Contrary to what Mr. Borten had so long striven for, the protocol maintains that 'the system applied to Norwegian agriculture must be devised in such a way as not to compromise the functioning of the Common Agricultural Policy, and particularly of the common organisation of markets throughout the Community'. Thus the principle is laid down of conformity with the Community's policy; and the rest of the protocol states a large number of exceptions which were enough to meet Norway's needs. As for fisheries, the

eventual solution reached involved, in return for the text of Protocol No. 21, a unilateral statement by Norway recorded in the minutes of the Conference. In this the Norwegian representative declared, among other things: 'The Community is founded on confidence that its Council will not take measures contrary to the vital interests of Norway. The Community has just given Norway the solemn assurance that it will take particular account of Norwegian coastal fisheries after 1982. My Government regards this as a real guarantee.' Of all the candidates, Norway was the last from whom such a statement might have been anticipated.

24. Whether Norway will join the Community still remains uncertain. And it was primarily because of this uncertainty over Norway, though it attached to some extent to the other candidates too, that we insisted on having a provision in the Treaty which would protect membership for one or more of the candidates should it be rejected by one or more of the others. This is the 'entry into force' provision which appears in the last paragraph of Article 2 of the Treaty of Accession.[1]

C. DENMARK

25. Compared to Norway and ourselves, Denmark had a relatively easy passage into the Community. No country had suffered more direct damage than Denmark as a result of the Common Agricultural Policy of the Community; and her trading history made it inevitable that Denmark should detest a situation in which we and Germany, the two main traditional markets for her agricultural exports, were in different economic and trading organisations. So while Denmark would almost certainly never have applied for membership of the Community had we not done so ourselves, once we had done so her economic interest in our entry and her own was overwhelming. An official Danish paper published in 1970 compared Dutch and Danish prices for agricultural producers in the year 1968–69 and showed that Danish agricultural income would have been almost 50 per cent higher than it was had Dutch prices applied. Like the Irish, the Danes had an immense interest in increasing the prices they would receive for their agricultural exports in our market; but more than the Irish they had an interest in increasing their agricultural exports to the Six, especially Germany, and recovering the exports they had lost in the previous seven or eight years.

26. The Danes have a somewhat difficult constitutional position in relation

[1] The Norwegian referendum on 25 September, 1972, produced a negative result (46.5% in favour, 53.5% against) and Norway therefore did not join the European Community in 1973 (nor did it do so when another referendum was lost (47.7% in favour, 52.3% against) in 1994, when Austria, Sweden and Finland joined. The special entry into force provisions were thus triggered and implemented without further negotiation. Norway then negotiated its own free trade agreement with the enlarged European Community along lines similar to those negotiated with the EFTA non-candidate countries.

to the ratification of an agreement with the Community. Professor Nyboe Andersen explained it to Mr. Barber in a meeting on 30 June, 1970, in Luxembourg as follows: 'According to the Danish Constitution, an Agreement to join the Community would have to be accepted either by a majority of five-sixths of Parliament or, if only a simple majority could be obtained in Parliament, by a national referendum. In the case of a referendum the rule was that it could only be rejected if more than 30 per cent of those entitled to vote voted against.' When the negotiations began, the Danes felt reasonably confident of getting their five-sixths majority in Parliament, and certainly, should it be necessary, of winning a referendum. But like all the other candidates, the Danes experienced, throughout the negotiations, a steady falling-off in the popularity of joining the Community. This did not however go so far as to appear to put success in a referendum at risk.[2]

27. The Danes had few special problems. The Community's establishment rules caused them concern, since they feared they would permit too much agricultural land and too many houses in Denmark to be bought up by Germans. In the end, like the Irish, the Danes reached a position where they felt they would be able, after the negotiations were over, to protect this interest. They had the same problem as Norway over Nordic sentiment, though less acute. Nevertheless the arrangements Sweden might negotiate with the Community were critical for Denmark. It was the hope that by then the outcome for Sweden would be clear which led to the referenda in both Norway and Denmark being postponed till the autumn of 1972. They also had a problem, which dominated their concern over fisheries, with Greenland and the Faroes. Greenland and the Faroe Islands were, I suppose, much the same for the Danes as New Zealand and the sugar producers were for us; and in one sense they were worse, since Greenlanders and Faroese formed a part of the Danish Delegation for negotiations on fisheries. These negotiations have been sufficiently described already, and the Danes in the end got what they wanted.[3]

28. For the rest, subject to the disappointing necessity of having to accept, from their point of view, much too long a transitional period for agriculture, everything went reasonably smoothly and satisfactorily for the Danes, and our own relations with them throughout the negotiations remained cordial. Like the Norwegians, they too had a change of Government before the negotiations ended, but in their case as a result of a general election. In October 1971 a Social Democratic Government under Mr. Krag took office and carried on

[2] In the event a referendum was required and held on 2 October, 1972. The result was positive (63.4% in favour, 36.6% against). There was some controversy over the fact that the Danes had set the date of this referendum after the Norwegian one, thus depriving the Norwegians of any possible boost from a positive result in the Danish referendum.

[3] But not only did the Faroe Islands never enter the European Community, Greenland, which did enter under special provisions, was dissatisfied with its status. As a result a subsequent negotiation in 1982 led to Greenland leaving the European Community under provisions set out in a special protocol.

negotiations with the Community without much change. As already recorded, the new Government's attitude towards questions of European political unification, and possible future defence co-operation, caused some criticism and discontent in the Community; but this did not in the end affect the outcome (see paragraph 14 of Chapter 27).

29

Others Concerned

It was not only our fellow candidates who, among those outside the Community, influenced our negotiations. There was scarcely a country in the world, inside the Commonwealth or outside, which did not feel it had some significant trading interest at stake in their outcome. Relatively few such countries tried seriously to influence the negotiations; and fewer succeeded. This Report should however include some account of the way in which at least a few countries outside the Community impinged upon us. I have therefore selected three countries or groups of countries with which this chapter will be concerned. They are, first, the EFTA non-applicants; second, the United States; and third, Australia and Canada.

A. THE EFTA NON-APPLICANTS

2. The EFTA non-applicants—Sweden, Switzerland, Austria, Portugal Iceland and Finland—did not so much, as it turned out, influence the course of our negotiations as take part in shaping the background against which they proceeded. The Stockholm Convention of 1960 had defined, in its preamble, the aims of EFTA; and they included 'the promotion of closer economic co-operation between the members of the Organisation for European Economic Co-operation, including the members of the European Economic Community'. EFTA had thus always had, as one of its objectives, the reduction of the gap between its members and those of the European Economic Community. And much of the history of EFTA, ever since our first application for membership in 1961, had been concerned with the incompatible policies of those of its members who aspired to join the European Community and those who, mainly because of their neutrality, did not or could not do so.

3. It had for years been accepted by the Community that, should it be enlarged to include ourselves and other new members, it could not ignore the claims of members of EFTA who were not candidates for membership of the Community to establish at least a free trade relationship with it. This attitude was formally expressed by the Community in the Communiqué issued after The Hague Summit meeting of December 1969, paragraph 16 of which reads:

'As soon as negotiations with the applicant countries have been opened, discussions will be started with such other EFTA members as may request them on their position in relation to the EEC'.

4. The position the Community developed in relation to the EFTA non-applicants over the next six months was stated in M. Harmel's opening speech to the Conference on 30 June, 1970. He said: 'The Community is prepared to open discussions with the European States which are members of EFTA but which have not applied for membership of the Community, with a view to seeking possible solutions to the problems raised by enlargement, and thus to enable these States to contribute to the construction of Europe ... The Community could agree to discussions starting in the autumn with a meeting at Ministerial level with any of these countries which so desire. The agreements concluded with these countries would be binding on the enlarged Community. It will therefore be necessary to seek appropriate formulae which will enable the States which have applied for membership to be associated in due course with the preparation and conclusion of these agreements. The Community considers that it would be desirable, for practical reasons and in the interest of all the countries concerned, for these agreements to come into force at the same time as the accession treaties'.

5. The EFTA countries themselves had reached much the same position. I have already recorded in Chapter 20 that we had freed ourselves, in April 1967, of the obligations of the London Declaration of 1961. We were thus no longer obliged not to enter the Community until all our EFTA partners had negotiated satisfactory arrangements for themselves. But though we no longer had precise obligations to our EFTA partners in this regard, we had expressed common understandings which were of great importance to them. Thus successive meetings of the EFTA Ministerial Council, since the enlargement of the Community became once more a possibility in 1969, had recorded the common interest of all its members in maintaining the free trade which the Association had established; and the view that it would be desirable—but no more—that the agreements which non-applicant EFTA members might reach with the Community should enter into force at the same time as the Treaty of Accession admitting the applicant members of EFTA to membership of the Community.

6. It had thus become an important interest for us that the negotiations with the EFTA non-applicants should proceed as rapidly as possible. Fortunately, the constitutional and other preliminaries required before agreements with the EFTA non-applicants could enter into force would be less time-consuming than in the case of the candidates. It was already more or less accepted, when negotiations opened, that the Community would have exploratory discussions with the EFTA non-applicants in the course of our negotiations for membership; but would only start negotiations with them when our negotiations had concluded, or were about to conclude. This, it was hoped, would be at the end of 1971. It was foreseen that the first six or seven months of 1972 would be required to complete agreements between the Community and the non-

applicants; and that, if all went well, all the agreements of the candidates and the non-applicants alike could enter into force on 1 January, 1973.

7. The negotiations between the Community and the EFTA non-applicants were completed just before I completed this Report and the separate agreements (apart from that with Finland, delayed by the resignation of the Finnish Government) were signed on 22 July, 1972, exactly six months after the signature of our own Treaty of Accession. The negotiations proved in a number of respects just as complicated as our own, though they were in the main much more narrowly concerned with industrial trade. They were very different in character from our own in that they were conducted not by the Community as such, but by the Commission operating on the basis of a mandate from the Council of Ministers. We and the other candidates were closely associated with the conduct of these negotiations—not more closely than we needed to be, but sometimes too closely for comfort, since the way things went involved us from time to time in disputes with our non-applicant EFTA partners, the effects of which will, I hope, prove transient. Discussions between the EFTA non-candidates and the Community opened in November 1970; and led over the course of the next year to the definition of the mandate for the Commission for the opening of negotiations. The candidate countries were invited to approve this mandate in November 1971. They expressed certain reservations about the mandate, but agreed that negotiations should open as soon as possible on the basis it laid down. Such negotiations, separately with each of the six EFTA non-applicants, opened in December 1971 and went on intensively till July 1972.

8. We knew that there would be conflicts of interest between ourselves, the Community and our non-applicant EFTA partners in the course of these negotiations. But fortunately these conflicts were laid aside during our own negotiations. The main interest of all the EFTA non-applicants alike was that our own negotiations should finish as soon as possible to clear the way for theirs. Thus they did nothing to hold things up; and their critical interest in the course of the candidates' negotiations seems to have been satisfactorily catered for by the full briefing arrangements described in Chapter 6. The EFTA non-applicants themselves had sufficient opportunities, in the course of our negotiations, to develop their requirements and assess their chances in the course of their discussions with the Commission; and they were able to enter on their negotiations a month before ours ended. On the whole, they bore the ordeal of waiting without too much complaint or too many changes in their own positions.

9. The exception was Sweden, which agonised for many months throughout 1970 and 1971 as to whether it should not seek some much closer form of relationship with the Community, conceivably even membership itself, than the others wanted. In the end, as economic and monetary union, political unification, and even the remoter possibility of defence co-operation came more and more to the surface of the Community's future plans, Sweden decided that her neutrality compelled her to be content with the same objectives as her partners. In the process of coming to this decision the Swedes at one point came close

to asking us to use our influence with the Community to get them more than the others had asked for. We indicated we would find it hard to do so; and in the end they made no formal request. Nevertheless, it was the Swedish problem, in its reflection on the interests of two of the candidates, Denmark and Norway, which as recorded in the previous chapter remained, at least until agreement with Sweden was reached in July 1972, a significant issue still capable of affecting the enlargement of the Community.[1]

B. THE UNITED STATES

10. Before our negotiations began, and throughout their course, we felt the utmost concern as to the attitude, and possible actions, of the United States towards them. The United States could have taken action, or made demands on the Community or on ourselves, which might have complicated the negotiations in the highest degree or even frustrated their successful outcome. It seemed on the whole unlikely that they would do so. But the Community had become a cause of sufficient concern to enough powerful interests in the United States to make the risk a real one; and we watched for it with eternal vigilance. In the end, nothing the United States did or said during the negotiations had much effect upon them. But there was one moment when our anxiety became rather acute.

11. The history of the involvement of the United States with the European Community is a long one, longer in fact than our own. When it comes to be written in full, it may appear that the United States were almost more responsible for the birth of the European Community than the Europeans themselves, as a matter of deliberate policy and calculated intervention. Whether or not they deserve this imputation of paternity, the Americans were naturally anxious not to avow it. All the same, throughout the 'fifties and the early 'sixties, the Americans looked on the European Community with almost undiluted hope and pride. This halcyon atmosphere persisted throughout our own first negotiations from 1961–63, when the American Administration gave extremely strong, and perhaps too open, support to our aspirations for membership. After the failure, they recognised that, given the position in France, their support for us had been too openly avowed; and thereafter though still strong it was more carefully muted.

12. As the European Economic Community developed, some of its policies proved unwelcome in practice to the United States, especially of course the Common Agricultural Policy. The beginnings of American disillusion with the Community go back to 1963, and were first sharply expressed in the 'chicken

[1] The free-trade area agreements with the EFTA non-candidate countries, supplemented by a similar agreement with Norway, after the negative outcome of its referendum for membership, were superseded in 1992 by more far-reaching agreements with these countries, apart from Switzerland, establishing a European Economic Area and thus including them in the Single Market. In 1995, Austria, Finland and Sweden became full members of the Community.

war' of 1964. These troubles did not yet go deep. The eventual success of the Kennedy Round, coinciding almost exactly with our second application for membership in 1967, seemed to have restored harmony, and American support in 1967 for our second application, though less openly expressed, was as strong as it had been for our first. Though the relationship was somewhat clouded when the offer the Americans had made in the Kennedy Round to abolish the 'American Selling Price' for certain chemical imports proved unacceptable to Congress, this cloud weighed more on the Europeans than on the Americans.

13. In 1968 came the change of Administration, and it accelerated a change of personnel which had already gone far in the American Administration and had resulted in the gradual departure from positions of influence of many of the American champions of the Community, including above all Mr. George Ball. When President Nixon formed his Administration there were, in its upper echelons, including those of the State Department, relatively few people who had been closely concerned with American policy towards the Community 10 years earlier. Meanwhile, old causes of dispute had grown sharper and new ones had arisen. By the time, at the end of 1969, when our negotiations were about to be resumed, the Americans had a whole catalogue of complaints against the Community, and few people left in important official positions who were ready to forgive it its sins.

14. Fortunately for us, there was at least one figure in the American Administration who supported, because he had taken part in it and believed in it, the American policy of eight or ten years earlier: President Nixon himself. This was all the more fortunate in that Dr. Kissinger was not an enthusiast for European integration, though scarcely an opponent either. The State Department, apart from a few officials of middle rank, seemed to have become rather indifferent, while sharing many of the trade policy objections to Community practices which weighed so strongly with other Departments. The Department of Agriculture, the Department of Commerce, the Treasury and the Office of the Special Representative for Trade had all, in different degrees, become strongly opposed to certain aspects of Community policy, and sceptical whether the enlargement of the Community to include us would not, from the point of view of the United States, make things worse.

15. The main reasons for American disenchantment with the Community can be quickly summarised. They disliked the effect on their exports of the Common Agricultural Policy. They disliked the proliferation of preferential agreements between the Community and third States, and they detested the reverse preferences which the Community had obliged its developing partners in the Yaoundé Association to grant it. They saw these developments as a major threat to liberal world trade and the principles of the GATT. They were suspicious of increasingly effective measures of technical standardisation being developed by European countries as potential barriers to United States exports. This did not concern the Community alone, and the main American complaint in this field was against standardisation arrangements for electronic components

which were being worked out between the United Kingdom, France and Germany. They had convinced themselves that the Community's Value Added Tax system operated as a subsidy at the border for exports and a barrier for imports. They strongly disliked—and this had always been a doctrine even of the old Community enthusiasts—the prospect of preferential trading arrangements being offered to European neutrals who would not accept the aim of European political integration. They had become increasingly irritated by the difficulty of pinning the Community down as an effective negotiating partner. Since these American attitudes were potentially of such importance to us, I have reproduced in Appendix I a telegram of 20 June, 1970, from our Ambassador in Washington, Mr. Freeman, summarising the United States attitude towards the enlargement of the Community. This telegram was sent 10 days before our negotiations opened and two days after our General Election. It is a useful summary of the background of American policy which we had to watch with such care throughout our negotiations.

16. There was not much we could do to relieve these American apprehensions. It was possible to argue with them that they exaggerated the adverse effects the Community had had on their exports, even their agricultural exports. The latter had tended, between 1961 and 1970, to behave very much in the same way as their agricultural exports to the rest of the world; and though they had dropped between 1966 and 1969, they recovered sharply in 1970. In their trade as a whole with the Community, the United States had enjoyed a large surplus throughout the 'sixties; and this surplus, at over $2 billion in 1970, was nearly double what it had been in 1958. Nevertheless there were plenty of individual sectors in the United States which could point to difficulties and declines; and general arguments were of little comfort to them. One objective which our friends in the United States Administration urged us to bear in mind—and this idea is recommended in the last paragraph of the Washington telegram referred to above—was that we and the Community should declare our readiness to embark, after enlargement had been completed, on a new trade negotiation on a world scale with the United States. This idea remained a fruitful one, and eventually, late in 1971, helped to achieve a settlement of the crisis over the American dollar and the American import surcharge.[2]

17. At the highest level, the American attitude remained encouraging. On 8 May 1970, in a message to M. Rey, President of the Commission, President Nixon 'reaffirmed the full support of the United States for the renewed effort of broadening and strengthening the European Community'. Yet only six weeks before we had been perturbed to hear, from our Embassy in Washington, that papers were being prepared for a new review of United States policy towards Europe by the National Security Council; and we were warned that this would

[2] These world trade negotiations, known as the Tokyo Round, finally got under way in the autumn of 1973 and were brought to a successful conclusion in 1979. They resulted in a further substantial liberalisation of world trade and thus in a lowering of tariff and other barriers to trade between the United States and the European Communities.

be the opportunity for a counter-offensive by the Secretaries of Commerce and Agriculture in particular. The telegram from Washington referred to above warned us, in June, that 'increasingly, as the negotiations proceed, we are likely to become the recipients of United States representations'. Yet we felt confident that we had friends in the State Department at least who would try to prevent this or reduce it to a minimum. They felt, like Mr. Cleveland, Minister for Economic Affairs at the United States Embassy in London, who was a strong believer in the enlargement of the Community and on several occasions throughout our negotiations a helpful influence. In May 1970 he told me that his objective, during our negotiations, would be 'to keep us off your backs'; and I think he contributed to doing so.

18. Of all the causes of American concern listed above, their objections to the spread of the Community's preferential trade agreements was the one in respect of which we most feared American intervention, because it was a necessary part of our policy to secure the offer of association—that is to say preferential trade agreements—for a number of the developing countries of the Commonwealth. On 3 August, 1970, I had a conversation with Mr. Samuels, Under-Secretary of State for Economic Affairs in the State Department, in the course of which he complained that 'the Americans had counted 41 preferential agreements, including Yaoundé and those still under negotiation or likely to be the consequence of our admission'. At this time, and for the next few months, we were much concerned with the dangers of the 'Mills Bill' which was on its way through Congress; and from October 1970 onwards we had increasingly difficult and acrimonious discussions with the United States Administration over our own scheme for agricultural import levies. These soured the atmosphere of our relations, and appeared to have produced an awkward deadlock when an unexpected settlement was eventually achieved (thanks in no small measure to Mr. Cleveland) in March 1971. And it was in this period that the American intervention we had feared for so long eventually took place, on the one but last day of 1970. I will not describe it here since the American action and our first reaction to it are fully described in our telegram No. 4 to Washington of 1 January, 1971, reproduced in Appendix I.

19. We were alarmed by this American intervention, as our reaction showed, and not least because it had been addressed to the Member States of the Community as well. Only a few days before, on 17 December, 1970, the Prime Minister had discussed our European policy with President Nixon. The latter had indeed spoken about his trade policy and agricultural problems, but had been as firm as ever in support of our entry. We decided we should rub in our first reaction still more strongly. Instructions were sent to Washington, and Mr. Freeman, on 12 January, 1971, took the opportunity of his farewell call on Mr. Rogers, the Secretary of State, to bring the matter up and rehearse our arguments in detail. Mr. Rogers appeared to be somewhat contrite. He represented the American approach as being rather a routine one. 'He himself was surprised that we had been so surprised. They had thought that by taking action at a low

level they would avoid making too much of the problem.' Finally, Mr. Rogers asked Mr. Freeman to convey to the Foreign Secretary 'his dismay that you were dismayed'. Mr. Freeman reported that the American instructions had been 'authorised at an unbelievably low level' in the State Department, and were evidently sent without the knowledge of the White House.

20. Whether or not our sharp reaction contributed to checking further American interventions, none took place. Statements by the President himself, whenever he had occasion to make one, remained satisfactory and encouraging. When the President of the Commission, Signor Malfatti, visited Washington in April 1971, he was received by the President, who spoke in the most favourable terms of the prospect of enlarging the Community. After our breakthrough at the Ministerial meeting in Luxembourg from 21–23 June, President Nixon sent on 8 July an extremely warm message of congratulation to the Prime Minister. 'You know', he wrote, 'that the United States has long and consistently supported the enlargement and strengthening of the Community. The historic decision reached at Luxembourg reflects, I believe, a determination on the part of all concerned to lead Western Europe to that unity which will permit it to play its proper role in world affairs.' This harmony continued to prevail until our negotiations were over, when once again the President issued a statement in the most satisfactory terms. 'The United States has always supported the strengthening and enlargement of the European Community. Upon the occasion of this historic act, the President wishes to emphasise that this support is as strong as ever.' The 'closing of the gold window' on 15 August, 1971, the import surcharge, and all the accompanying difficulties revived our fears to some extent; but the extensive repercussions of these events impinged in no way upon our negotiations.[3]

C. AUSTRALIA AND CANADA

21. Fortunately for us, Australia and Canada were no longer, in 1970, in a position to exercise so great an influence on our negotiations for entry into the Community as they had in 1961. Like ours, their trade patterns had changed; and their dependence on the British market had grown much less. By 1970, the United States had become Australia's main supplier and Japan her main market. Moreover, in Australia as in Canada, popular and political attitudes towards the possibility of British entry into the Community had changed profoundly; it was by 1970 in general seen as something which Britain must be left to decide for herself. It might have some uncomfortable consequences, in terms of trade and in other ways, for Australia and Canada; but they would have to put up with them.

22. There was in any case little we could do for them; and it would have

[3] The United States thereafter pursued their grievances over the effects of enlargement through negotiations with the enlarged Community under Article XXIV:6 of the General Agreement on Tariff and Trade. This led to an agreed settlement in July 1974.

been futile to seek unattainable objectives. Our general brief on 'Negotiating Aims for the Commonwealth', circulated to Ministers on 30 June, 1970, recorded that 'the previous administration decided in 1967 that we should not aim at securing more for New Zealand (apart from the field of dairy products), Canada and Australia than the gradual application of tariffs and levies over whatever transitional periods are negotiated'. It added that the Canadian and Australian Governments appeared reconciled to this. Throughout the negotiations, we had on the whole the advantage of an extremely sympathetic attitude from the Canadian Government. The Australian Government was less co-operative. Their general attitude was sad and sour. They grumbled a good deal about the damage they would suffer; and from May to July 1971 their complaints and accusations rose to an embarrassing public crescendo, which however had died away before the end of the year.

23. Australia's trade problems concerned butter and cheese, sugar, canned and dried fruit and apples and pears. Unfortunately each of these commodities affected a politically significant group of producers in distinct areas of Australia. And the fact that the Country Party, representing the farming interest, was a partner in the Australian Coalition Government meant that political difficulties deriving from these commodities were bound to receive vociferous attention. It was in fact from successive leaders of the Country Party, Sir John McEwen and Mr. D. Anthony, that most of our troubles came. The former, the formidable 'Black Jack', was now 70 years old and had held his post for years. He loathed the European Community and made no secret of it. When he came to London in July 1970 he complained (he had a case) of the Community's policy of 'predatory subsidised dumping'. After a visit to Brussels later that month, when he saw a number of Members of the Commission, he was asked at a Press conference whether he had had a sympathetic hearing. He replied 'No'. The Community disliked Sir John McEwen as much as he disliked it. Nevertheless, when he saw Mr. Barber in London he was resigned rather than demanding. He urged merely that we should ask for as long a transitional period as possible and do our best to ensure, when we were a member, that the enlarged Community pursued liberal trading policies.

24. After this visit, and after Mr. Rippon's visit to Australia in September 1970, Australian interest in the negotiations seemed to flag. This was deceptive. But it is nevertheless true that the Australians seemed to take less trouble to present their case to us and to follow events in Brussels than many other Commonwealth Governments. In part, the reason may have been the attitude in London, of Sir Alexander Downer, who never concealed his detestation for the idea of British entry into the Community. He seemed to regard his task as consisting more in the making of hostile public speeches than in personally representing his country's case to Ministers or Government Departments. The Australian Mission in Brussels also gave the impression of relative disinterest, and seemed far less assiduous than, for instance, the Canadians in following what was going on.

25. When we presented our proposals on sugar to the Conference in November 1970, the Australians reacted with some rather sharp criticisms and an *aide-mémoire*; but in fact they must have known perfectly well ever since Mr. George Brown's statement of 4 July, 1967, that we would not seek to preserve privileged access for Queensland sugar to our market after 1974. Thereafter, all remained calm in our relations with Australia until the Ministerial meeting of 11–13 May, 1971, concluded. This was the meeting at which the two matters of most concern to Australia were settled: sugar, and the arrangements for agricultural transition including our agreement to accept Community Preference from the start. By now Sir John McEwen had resigned; but his successor, Mr. Anthony, reacted sharply. He visited Europe soon afterwards, and in a statement in Brussels on 4 June declared that 'despite repeated strong representations over a period of years of the problems for Australia, Britain had made little, if any, reference in their recent negotiations to these problems'. He saw Mr. Rippon in London on 18 June; and afterwards seriously misrepresented, in a public statement, what Mr. Rippon had said to him. The quarrel simmered on; and when Mr. Anthony saw Mr. Rippon again on 25 June he said Australia felt that British undertakings had not been honoured. The Australian Prime Minister, Mr. McMahon, had written a letter to Mr. Heath on 15 June. Mr. Heath replied on 2 July defending our conduct and concluded: 'I really must urge you that it is not to anyone's advantage to belittle what has been undertaken by the Community'.

26. What had been undertaken by the Community was, of course, the agreement relating to problems which might arise for certain third countries as a result of disruption of trade, now enshrined in paragraph 5 of Protocol No. 16 'on Markets and Trade in Agricultural Products'. We maintained that this would be of real advantage to Australia in respect of her exports to our market of dairy products, sugar and other commodities. We tried to put the situation in respect of Australia in perspective in paragraph 121 of the White Paper published on 7 July; but Mr. Anthony attacked the White Paper in a statement issued in Canberra next day. Not surprisingly, all this attracted much attention in the Press and led to many questions in Parliament.

27. There was a good deal of Australian politics in all this criticism, and fortunately the Australian Press was far from unanimous in endorsing the criticism of Australian Ministers. Before long the trouble began to die away. When in November the Australian Prime Minister Mr. McMahon visited London, there were no recriminations, and by now the Australian Government were content to embark on the bilateral discussions with us of commodity problems which Mr. Rippon had suggested in July. Luckily, we were able soon after to accomplish something of real value to Australia in respect of Papua-New Guinea. This was a matter on which the Australians had been pressing us since the summer of 1970. How things worked out has already been described in paragraphs 9 and 10 of Chapter 23. Satisfaction with what we got for them in this context helped to diminish the grievance the Australians had felt that we failed to get more in others.

28. No such difficulties were caused by our negotiations to our relations with Canada. As the White Paper of July 1971 recorded, in 1970 only 9 per cent of Canada's total exports came to the United Kingdom, compared with 17 per cent in 1960. (The corresponding figures in the case of Australia were 12 per cent and 25 per cent.) The Canadians were indeed concerned at the prospect of our joining the Community; but they had decided rather more firmly than had the Australians that they must make the best of it, while hoping that we would do what was possible to protect their interests. During the negotiations, there were frequent contacts and discussions with the Canadians at Ministerial and official level, in London, Brussels and Ottawa; and no real difficulties arose.

29. The main Canadian concern was one about which little could be done, though they often expressed it to us. It was that our entry into the Community would leave them still more conspicuously and irrevocably in the shadow of the United States, with its immense dominance over the Canadian economy. Unlike Australia, with its various possibilities of Pacific association, the Canadians saw no regional alternative to which they could turn; though they were already considering, and may yet pursue, ideas of closer links of one kind or another with the enlarged European Community.[4]

30. Probably the injury our entry will inflict on Canadian trade will be less than in the case of Australia. The likely consequences are set out in paragraph 122 of the White Paper of July 1971. This paragraph indeed makes clear that the mitigations we secured for Canadian exports by our tariff quota arrangements are important—certainly more important than those, by no means negligible though they were, which these arrangements offered to Australia. The Canadians, like the Australians, are extremely concerned about the operation of Protocol No. 16; but here too, as the White Paper makes clear, some of their most important traditional exports to our market such as hard wheat and malting barley have a better chance than some Australian exports of avoiding disruption.

31. The Canadian Government, while perhaps regretting our entry into the Community, took a clear decision not to oppose it and to make the best of it. This was exemplified by a warm message of congratulation which Mr. Trudeau sent to Mr. Heath (and to the Governments of the Member States) on the occasion of the signature of the Treaty of Accession.

[4] Canada negotiated a commercial and economic co-operation agreement with the enlarged Community which was concluded in 1976.

30

The Commission

The Report prepared on the earlier negotiations of 1961–63 recorded that, in the early stages, the Commission 'supplied the driving force necessary to get the negotiations going'. But it goes on to record that as the negotiations progressed the Commission played a progressively less dominant role, and from January 1962 onwards had ceased to supply the motive force of the negotiations. From 1970 to 1972, the position was different. At no time did the Commission play a dominant role or provide a driving force; but they played throughout an important and indeed an indispensable part, which tended to get more, not less, significant as the negotiations progressed.

2. It has already been recorded in this Report that, at the outset, the member countries were determined to emphasise that the Commission could only be the servant of the Six, not of the Conference as a whole. This was natural. The Commission are an institution of the Community; they had to operate as a part of the Community, which was negotiating as a whole with us and the other candidates. The Member States, with much help from the Commission, had drawn up their negotiating position in the first six months of 1970. They were determined that the Commission, like any of themselves, should not be allowed to stray outside it. For this reason, at least in the early stages, the Member States were suspicious of authorising contacts between ourselves and the Commission. We wanted to maximise such contacts. We had no doubt either of the Commission's professional competence or of its goodwill. We felt that the closer we could get to the Commission and the more we could win its confidence the more helpful it would become; and so on the whole it proved.

3. At first, we were only able to enter into discussion with the Commission on the basis of principles agreed by the Member States; and even then they emphasised that the only task the Commission could have was that of giving us information and clarification. We needed this; but we often needed advice from the Commission too on the best practical means of tackling particular problems. But by the early spring of 1971, as mutual confidence grew, the Member States relaxed; and behind the cloak of 'information and clarification' we came to be in increasingly close contact with the Commission on a great variety of issues throughout the remainder of the negotiations. For their part,

the Commission grew in confidence in their dealings with us as the attitude of the Member States became more tolerant. In the early stages, they had had to watch their step and carefully avoid any risk of arousing the Member States' suspicions.

4. M. Deniau had been designated as the Member of the Commission responsible for the negotiations (he also kept his responsibility for relations with the Associated States); and a special 'task force' of the staff of the Commission had been assembled to work under him. M. Deniau and his task force were responsible not only for negotiations with us and the other candidates, but also for the discussions and subsequent negotiations with the EFTA non-applicants. In these cases, very different from our own, the Commission, operating of course on the basis of a mandate from the Council of Ministers, acted as the sole negotiator for the Community.

5. Apart from M. Deniau, the other eight Members of the Commission played on the whole a relatively small part in the negotiations. This irked some of them, such as Signor Spinelli and Herr Dahrendorf, who were full of goodwill towards us and wanted to play a part. No doubt the Commission at its regular meetings discussed many of the problems of the negotiations and took collective decisions on them. But we had the impression that M. Deniau and his task force were able on the whole to operate without too much dependence on a collective view of the Commission as such. The Members of the Commission, given the procedure and character of the Conference, had much less opportunity to take part in its proceedings than they had had in the earlier negotiations. Since they are careful to operate only on a level of equality with the Ministers of the Member States, the Members of the Commission (including M. Deniau) could in any case only appear in the Conference on the occasion of Ministerial meetings. And they rapidly found that they were never, except in the case of M. Deniau himself and even in his case almost never during the formal meetings, called upon to take any part in or make any contribution to the proceedings of the Conference. As a result, most Members of the Commission soon ceased to attend the Ministerial meetings.

6. Apart from M. Deniau himself, the only Member of the Commission who played from time to time a significant part in the Commission's work on the negotiations was M. Barre, the French Vice-President responsible for economic and monetary affairs. He was closely involved in the question of sterling and the British economy; but as recorded in Chapter 14 his involvement ended rather unsuccessfully. He was probably also closely involved for the Commission in the background of the Community's work on Community finance. The President of the Commission, Signor Malfatti, rightly felt it his duty to concern himself with the negotiations as much as he could. M. Deniau and the Commission's task force seem to have tried occasionally to make use of him when the Commission wished to press a particular point in the Council of Ministers. But neither Signor Malfatti's knowledge of the subject matter nor his authority

among his colleagues was outstanding; and though he was full of goodwill I do not think it can be claimed that he made any outstanding contribution to the success of the negotiations. I was however told by Mr. Wellenstein, after they were over, that he had played a useful and effective part during the discussions of the Six in the course of the critical Ministerial meeting at Luxembourg from 21–23 June, 1971, in improving the Community's eventual offer on New Zealand dairy products.

7. Dr. Mansholt had played a major part in the earlier negotiations of 1961 to 1963, at all events in their final stages. Over the years, his public attitude to our membership had been one of strong and enthusiastic support; but his attitude to our individual problems had been ambivalent. When it came to a choice between protecting the principles of the Common Agricultural Policy which he had created or modifying them to make things easier for us, he was always inclined to prefer the former. As it turned out, he played virtually no part in the 1970–72 negotiations. Members of the Directorate-General for Agriculture of the Commission played a conspicuous part, as will be seen; but I do not think that Dr. Mansholt made much effort to guide or control them. He was in any case by 1971 rather a sick man who, though it was not generally realised, had to a large extent given up any close personal involvement in the details of Community affairs and preferred to deal with broad political objectives. He sometimes seemed remarkably ignorant of what was happening in our negotiations. As late as 15 November, 1971, he expressed surprise to Mr. Christofas 'that there was difficulty on the animal health front in the negotiations and asked what the trouble was'. Animal health had already by then been one of the major issues of the Conference for four or five months. But when Mr. Christofas had explained the problem it became clear that Dr. Mansholt was aware of the Irish aspects of it (he had discussed them in Dublin a few months before) but totally unaware of the rest.

8. The position of Members of the Commission in relation to the Governments of the countries whose nationals they are is always rather a difficult one—especially for French Commissioners. I certainly do not find it surprising that M. Barre and M. Deniau felt it necessary to take very close account in what they did of the policies of the French Government. Nothing else was to be expected. M. Barre, there can be little doubt, hoped that the negotiations would fail. He was perhaps taking more account of what French policy had been, and of what he would have liked it still to be, than of what it had become. M. Deniau was readier to move with the times. I have no doubt at all that right from the start he wished for the success of the negotiations, and did his best to bring it about. But he too had to be circumspect, and avoid committing himself too far too soon. For this and other reasons the main burden of the Commission's work on the negotiations was carried by the task force composed of its officials. M. Deniau could in any case only appear at Ministerial level; and I think he was content to keep his powder dry and to leave things to the task force, who gave

us the impression, subject of course to the loyal support they had to give and did give to the Community's general positions, of having a pretty free hand to develop ideas, procedures and possible solutions.

9. Mr. Edmond Wellenstein had been appointed leader of the task force. A former member of the Dutch Foreign Service, he had worked since it was first set up for the High Authority of the Coal and Steel Community, and had been its outstanding official. On the merger of the executives he had joined the Commission in Brussels as a Director-General; and it was generally felt that he was the best possible choice to lead the task force. I certainly share this view myself. I had got to know Mr. Wellenstein well in the early 'sixties in Luxembourg, which was an asset. He is a man of integrity and of immense energy, with excellent knowledge of the affairs and the ways of the Community. Above all, he was completely dedicated to the success of the negotiations and spared no effort to bring it about. Sometimes, he struck some of us as unnecessarily rigid and too devoted to Community principles. I make no such criticism myself. It was his duty to defend Community positions. Towards the end, and perhaps partly from the exhaustion of overwork, he may have stuck a little too long to positions we found awkward; but as a rule he was tirelessly ingenious in looking for and finding ways round awkward problems. I think we owe him a lot.

10. Mr. Wellenstein's two Deputies in the task force were M. de Kergorlay (a Frenchman) and Herr Caspari (a German), both of them very able and helpful. Herr Caspari presided with Mr. Christofas over the work on secondary legislation, and was also responsible in the Commission for the negotiations concerning the Coal and Steel Community. The task force numbered eight or ten officials in all, and could call on any Directorate-General of the Commission for reinforcement or special assistance as the negotiations might require. Another member of the task force who did exceptionally good work was M. Braun (a Luxembourger), who specialised on questions arising from the Common Commercial Policy. Formally outside the task force, but working in practice within it, were officials of the Agricultural Directorate-General of the Commission who were of course concerned in more, and more important, aspects of the negotiations than most of their colleagues. M. Rabot (a Frenchman), Director-General for Agriculture, led this group; and his principal and uncommonly able lieutenant was Herr von Verschuer (a German). M. Rabot and Mr. Kearns established excellent working relations which paid useful dividends. Signor Ruggiero, Chef de Cabinet to the President of the Commission, maintained close contact with the task force and provided a useful link. It can I think be said that none of these Commission officials, the Frenchmen among them no more than the rest, allowed their attitude to be influenced in any way by their nationality.

11. Helpful and ingenious though they were, the representatives of the Commission could not by definition be completely impartial. It was their duty to defend the interests of the Community. They thoroughly understood the interests of the Six Member States; and sometimes found ours hard to accept

as qualifying for accommodation. In spite of this, and more and more as time passed, they came to play a most helpful part, and to develop a strong commitment to success.

12. In evaluating the Commission's work on the negotiations, it would be wrong to consider only the work they did with us and the other candidates. They had of course played a major part in the preparation of the Community's negotiating position, which was based to a considerable extent on the two 'Opinions' prepared by the Commission in 1967 and 1969; and in this context at least they had been to some extent a 'driving force'. They continued throughout the Conference to play an active role in the deliberations of the Six Member States at every level, with M. Deniau normally representing them at meetings of the Council of Ministers and Mr. Wellenstein at meetings of the Permanent Representatives. As Dr. Nass records in his book already referred to, the special legal position of the Community as negotiator ousted the normal rule of its internal proceedings that its decisions must be based on a proposal of the Commission. Nevertheless, the Council of Ministers' Communiqué of 9 June, 1970, on procedure for the negotiations (see Appendix II) recorded that 'the Commission shall be invited to make proposals', and in practice the Commission made something like its usual contribution to the negotiating decisions which the Community took. The same Communiqué records that the Commission would only be authorised to negotiate on the decision of the Council

13. The Commission felt a special responsibility for progress, and spent much time calculating the timing of a possible major intervention. They felt the time might come when it would be up to them to make the main contribution to breaking the stalemate within the Six; but they also felt they could make a decisive move of this kind once only. Dr. Nass records that the Commission were pondering a major initiative at the beginning of May 1971, when the Conference seemed deadlocked; but the announcement on 8 May of the meeting between Mr. Heath and M. Pompidou intervened, and they held their hand.

14. In fact, initiatives by the Commission, and formal acts in the shape of papers put forward by them to the Six and sometimes passed on by the Six to the Conference, were relatively few; and only two of them were important. These were the Commission's comments on our paper on Community Finance and their 'Vue d'Ensemble' of November 1971. Neither of these papers—both have been described in the course of this Report—were particularly helpful to us, being written as they were in the early days of the Conference and probably inspired more than the Commission's later work by Members of the Commission dominated by the cautious and rather suspicious mood of the first few months. Parts of the second paper proved useful, such as its proposals for sugar and for the length of the transitional period; but its proposals on New Zealand and above all on Community finance were damaging.

15. It was not however in its formal acts, exemplified by papers of this kind, that the Commission proved most helpful, nor on the whole in relation to the

most important subjects of the negotiations, where the Member States kept control most jealously in their own hands. Even here, the Commission played a helpful part on sugar and (in the very last stages) on New Zealand; but not on Community finance, where they lacked any room for manoeuvre because of the extreme proposals they had put forward in their 'Vue d'Ensemble' of November 1970. It was rather in the extremely complicated work connected for instance with arrangements for agricultural transition, with aspects of the Common Commercial Policy and above all with secondary legislation, that the Commission came into their own and gave us indispensable help. They were also exceptionally helpful and forbearing over the Channel Islands and the Isle of Man. Over fisheries, where they felt obliged to do their utmost to preserve a common policy from disintegration, they proved rather rigid; but even here made certain contributions no one else could have made in the approach to the final solution.

31

The Five

Anyone who has read Part II of this Report should have acquired a fairly clear impression of the attitudes of the six Member Governments of the Community during the negotiations. And it is not difficult, nor is it wrong, to conclude that in the main our negotiations were a negotiation with France. Nevertheless, a rather more systematic and connected description is required than the necessarily disjointed chapters of Part II could give of the general position and attitude throughout the negotiations of each of the Governments of the members of the Community. This chapter will attempt this task in respect of the Five; and the next two chapters will deal with France.

2. The position of France was so overwhelmingly central to the negotiations, and the attitude adopted by the other five Governments was in so many individual cases a matter of relatively little consequence to the outcome, that it would be easy to conclude that what the Five thought and did hardly mattered. The account in the remainder of this chapter of their individual attitudes may tend in some respects to reinforce that impression. It should therefore be stated at the outset that such an impression would be completely false. If the attitude of the five Governments, or any particular one of them, cannot easily be seen to have been a determining factor in the outcome of any particular problem in the negotiations, yet their collective pressure helped in most cases to wear down more extreme French positions and bring the Community as a whole towards positions within reach of our requirements. Earlier in this Report I have described our regular tactic of trying to 'keep the crisis within the Six', and not let it become a crisis between the Six and us. This alone is enough to prove the value to us of the Five as the main agent for moderating French positions. Correspondingly of course the Five confronted the French with a recurring dilemma—that of the risk of having to 'pay twice', first in negotiation with them and then in negotiation with us.

3. Above all the strong and steady position of the Five over the years in favour of British membership of the Community was certainly one of the determining factors which eventually brought success. Our exclusion in 1963 led to prolonged stagnation in the Community. Had we been excluded again in 1971, the consequences might have been worse, provided such exclusion were seen as the

responsibility of France. While the French may not have been more than marginally and conditionally in favour of our entry (at all events up to the Heath-Pompidou meeting of May 1971), they were at least determined that, should our entry be frustrated, it must not if it could possibly be avoided be seen to have been frustrated by them. On 24 June, 1971, the day after the decisive Ministerial meeting in Luxembourg ended, President Pompidou gave a television interview. In the course of it he said: 'When I came to power, Europe was in fact in deadlock. Our European partners were no longer prepared to tolerate Britain's exclusion.' The collective attitude of the Five was something of which the French had to take account, and did take account.

A. GERMANY

4. In one respect, the negotiations for our entry involved a certain irony for the German Federal Republic. They wanted us in. They had believed, since The Hague Summit Conference, that the French were prepared to let us in. Yet they knew perfectly well that one reason, and perhaps the main reason, why the French were prepared to let us in was the French feeling that Germany was becoming too powerful and needed to be balanced, inside the Community, by us. This French feeling was exemplified in their detestation of the monetary policy of Professor Schiller, which reached a climax—at a very advantageous moment for us—when the Deutschemark was floated on 8 May, 1971. Yet French apprehensions about Germany were based not only on Germany's sheer economic weight; there was also the fact that Germany was at last, as demonstrated by the *Ostpolitik*, beginning to play an independent role in Europe and to prove the hollowness of the Gaullist belief that France alone, among the countries of Western Europe, could conduct a genuine dialogue and real negotiations with the Soviet Union. Thus for the Germans letting us in to the Community was, in a sense, helping the French to perform an anti-German act. But while the Germans saw this clearly enough—and indeed Herr Brandt made one or two delicate references to the point in public speeches—they did not in any way allow it to affect their favourable attitude to our membership.

5. Another factor which non-Germans should bear in mind in considering the German attitude in our negotiations was that they coincided closely with the development of the *Ostpolitik*, which was naturally enough a matter of absolutely absorbing interest to all Germans, whether politicians or private individuals. From our point of view, our entry into the Community was a primordial interest. From the German point of view, it could hardly be so in comparison with the *Ostpolitik*, which fundamentally affected the future of the German State and nation. For us, the *Ostpolitik* was an immensely important, and potentially risky, aspect of European development as a whole. For all Germans it was and is a family affair of transcendant personal interest, in comparison with which the enlargement of the Community, however important it might be and had to be described as being, must have taken a secondary place. Yet, fortunately for us,

it was necessary for the German Government to claim to see, and I think it truly did see, its East European policy as being rooted in a successful development of its West European policy. And the more controversial Herr Brandt's *Ostpolitik* became in Germany, the more strongly did the German opposition support the enlargement of the Community as a necessary corrective.

6. On the whole, there were few major German interests with which our entry conflicted; and the Germans proved ready, where such interests were at stake, not to press them too hard, much less hard than for instance the Dutch. We had a bit of trouble over our tariff quota for phosphorus, caused by the fact that the main producer within the Community is a German firm; but this was satisfactorily sorted out. The Germans were also strong protagonists of the common access provisions of the Fisheries Policy; but they did not press their interest too far. They developed, late in the negotiations, a rather unwelcome anxiety about competition from British imports of coal; but this too, as recorded in paragraphs 17 and 18 of Chapter 21, proved surmountable.

7. They had a general anxiety about the risk that our membership might involve them in extra costs. Not surprisingly, there is a fairly strong feeling in Germany that, because of their economic strength and large reserves, they have tended in various fields to become the milch-cow of the Community, always called upon to pay the major share of Community expenditure, especially but not only in the agricultural field. We may run up against this feeling later, in our efforts to establish regional and industrial policies in the enlarged Community. In our negotiations it was in part this feeling which led the Germans to be rather less generous to us in respect of Community finance than we had hoped; but this, as already described, was a case in which few if any members of the Community were ready to be forthcoming.

8. While on the subject of German interests, a strong interest of theirs should be mentioned which operated in our favour and is sometimes overlooked. This was their interest in terminating trade discrimination against them by the members of EFTA. It related partly to the desirability from their point of view of establishing free trade with the United Kingdom; but even more to that of doing so with the Nordic countries (especially Sweden) and above all with Switzerland and Austria. Germany is at the geographical centre of EFTA; and has been traditionally dominant in the markets of Scandinavia, Austria and Switzerland. A few figures will illustrate this point. German exports to the United Kingdom throughout the 1960s were less by value than their exports to either Sweden, Austria or Switzerland. In 1969, German exports to EFTA amounted to 22½ per cent of their total exports to all markets including the rest of the Community. The corresponding figure for the other five members of the Community was under 17 per cent. German exports to EFTA were considerably larger than those of the other five members of the Community put together. They were well over half Italian, Dutch and Belgian exports to all markets, and almost half French exports to all markets.

9. Moreover, in spite of their enormous exports to EFTA, the Germans have

done conspicuously less well in the markets of many EFTA countries between 1960 and 1970 than they would have wished. They did well in our market, raising their share of it over the period from 4 per cent to 6.1 per cent. They held their own, and slightly more, in the Swiss and Austrian markets, of which imports from Germany represented some 30 per cent and 40 per cent respectively. But in the markets of Sweden, Norway, Denmark, Finland and Portugal they had lost ground. The share of these markets taken by German imports dropped, between 1960 and 1970, from 20.6 per cent to 17.4 per cent. Yet over the same period the German share of world exports rose from 8.2 per cent to 10 per cent. These simple facts, which have been insufficiently regarded in this country, explain a good deal of German policy. They explain to a large extent Professor Erhard's strong desire through the early 1960s to widen the scope of European free trade. They explain likewise the German proposals of early 1968, after the second French veto, for a 'commercial arrangement', which we so much disliked and about which the Swiss, Austrians and Swedes were so enthusiastic.

10. In their general posture in the negotiations the Germans operated true to form. In a despatch from Brussels of 13 April, 1965, I wrote: 'After two years in Brussels, I am bound to record as one of my major impressions that it is surprising how relatively small a part German policy still appears to play in the major decisions of the Community. I do not mean to state that it plays a small part; this is certainly not the case. But it surprises me all the same that a country whose economic and industrial power weighs so heavily in the Community scale should not count more decisively in Community decisions.' I added: 'Whatever the reason, it is certain that Germany, more than any other Member State except perhaps Luxembourg and Belgium, feels uncomfortable in isolation and seldom maintains a solitary position for long.' Consistently with these attitudes, the Germans in our negotiations tended to play a resolutely unheroic part. They maintained their traditional low posture; they were careful never to get out in front, and if they happened to do so tended to draw back. German officials, with whom we remained in the closest contact throughout in Bonn and elsewhere, were intensely cautious, the most senior ones (Herr von Braun, State Secretary in the Foreign Ministry responsible for economic affairs, and Herr Sachs, the German Permanent Representative in Brussels) being perhaps the most cautious of all. Herr Scheel himself was a bit more adventurous and determined. At least we cannot complain that the Germans let us down, because they were careful to promise so little.

11. The real dilemma which confronted the Germans centred on their relationship with France, which had become over the last 10 years a matter of the utmost importance to them and was made even more so by their need to maintain French support for the *Ostpolitik*. In a letter to me of 11 November, 1970, Sir Roger Jackling wrote: 'It is clear that the Germans are not at all disposed to have an all-out row with the French for our sakes if they can see any way to avoid it.' In another letter to me of 24 March, 1971, he wrote that while the

Germans certainly wanted us in they were inclined to be reluctant champions, and asked why this was so. He gave the following answer:

> From the German point of view there are good reasons for this. The main one is that no one in the German Government wants to have to choose between preserving Franco-German relations and enlarging the Community. The Germans—and particularly the Auswartiges Amt—have had lots of practice at sitting on the fence. In de Gaulle's day they were always being told that before long they would have to choose between Paris and Washington. They always managed to avoid doing so. ... As the Germans see it, to come down on either side of the fence would represent a defeat for their policy. So they will go to great lengths to avoid doing so, in the hope that in the end they can have *both* a continuation of their good relations with France *and* the enlargement of the Community.

If this correctly described German policy, and I think it did, they were successful in securing both their objectives. There was some anxiety in Bonn, especially after the Heath-Pompidou meeting, that a revived Anglo-French entente might do harm to German interests. But this does not seem to have been felt in the higher levels of the Federal Government, where improved Anglo-French relations were accepted as desirable.

12. The somewhat negative appraisal the preceding paragraphs have given of German policy may have done it less than justice. I think it is almost certain that, had a real crisis arisen in the negotiations, Herr Brandt would have tried to intervene to ensure their success. As early as 24 November, 1970, when he was on a visit to Signor Colombo in Rome, Herr Brandt told a Reuter correspondent that 'if insuperable difficulties arose in the course of the negotiations then he and Colombo were agreed that the possibility of a summit of the Six to resolve these difficulties could not be excluded'. At the summit meeting of the Six at The Hague in December 1969 Herr Brandt had done much to secure French agreement to the enlargement of the Community; and he had no intention of abandoning what he had achieved. Mr. Heath's visit to Herr Brandt in Bonn at the beginning of April 1971, six weeks before his meeting with M. Pompidou, produced no surprises and no decisive turn in the negotiations. Nevertheless, it was of great importance, as a demonstration to France of the fact that our own and German policy were in accord and that the enlargement of the Community remained an important German objective.

13. Herr Brandt, in a sense, was always for us a powerful card of last resort. He was certainly much more disposed to intervene in our favour than his predecessor Dr. Kiesinger had been in 1967; and the French knew it. Herr Brandt told Mr. Heath in April 1971 that he was prepared to ask for a summit of the Six if the situation in June should turn critical; and he said he had so informed M. Pompidou. At this meeting, and again when he saw Mr. Heath in London on 6 May, Herr Brandt made it clear that he had no objection to a

bilateral meeting between Mr. Heath and M. Pompidou to bring the negotiations to a climax, and indeed hoped that such a meeting would take place. Throughout the negotiations, Herr Brandt continued to believe, in spite of all the difficulties encountered, that M. Pompidou wanted them to succeed. The outcome proved him right; but he was ready to act should he be proved wrong. In a sense, Herr Brandt played in the negotiations the role of 'a fleet in being'. It did not prove necessary to engage him; but he was prepared to engage if it should.

B. ITALY

14. Italy's attitude to our membership throughout the negotiations was uninterruptedly favourable and helpful. The Italians had a strong political interest in getting us in, and fortunately they had no strong economic interests to protect in the process. They wanted us to join the Community for a variety of reasons. First of all, they strongly disliked the tendency which had developed, or threatened to develop, in recent years for the Community to be dominated by the bilateral relationship between France and Germany. Second, they sincerely held flattering views about the contribution our democratic tradition and political stability could make to the future of the Community. Third, they had long disliked, largely for economic reasons connected with competition for their own agricultural products, the tendency of the Community to develop increasingly widespread special relations with countries of the Mediterranean basin; and they wanted to correct this bias by extending the Community to the North. The Italians had strongly supported our membership from 1961 to 1963. But I think their support was even stronger in 1970 to 1972 as a result of a reassessment of their interests which they had carried out after our renewed application for membership in 1967.

15. There were some minor economic interests in the fields of industrial and agricultural trade which the Italians could have pressed to our disadvantage. The main issues—sugar, dairy products and fisheries—fortunately involved relatively little clash of interest. But even where smaller interests caused difficulty, as they did occasionally in the field of tariff quotas or horticulture, the Italians were moderate and conciliatory in the way they pressed them. They were prepared consciously to subordinate minor economic interests to an overriding political objective. And in the most important field of all from our point of view, Community finance, the Italians would probably have been prepared to settle for a lower contribution from us than any other member of the Community envisaged. They warned us candidly that we had no hope of settling for our original bid, and told us we would have to go higher. But they would have been content with a smaller increase than the rest.

16. The question was occasionally raised whether this benevolent and helpful attitude by the Italian Government really yielded solid results. It is not easy to prove that it did. Nevertheless, I have little doubt that the steady influence the

Italians exerted on their fellow members throughout the whole negotiations had a definitely favourable effect on the outcome.

17. Italian political support for our membership had been most formally expressed in the Anglo-Italian Declaration of 28 April, 1969, which had been published over the signatures of Mr. Michael Stewart and Signor Nenni during President Saragat's State Visit to London. The Conservative Government endorsed this Declaration, much to Italian satisfaction. All Italian politicians in power from President Saragat downwards continued throughout 1970 and 1971 to express the strongest support for the enlargement of the Community; and even the Italian Communists gave occasional hints of marginal benevolence. The Italians, who hate being left out of things, might have been expected to be a little aggrieved when the Heath-Pompidou meeting was announced, for clearly it was expected to achieve so much without them. But they resisted the temptation, and warmly supported the meeting.

18. It was of real value to us that Signor Colombo became Prime Minister of Italy in August 1970 and remained in office until the negotiations were over. He understood the problems of the Community well, and he had a close relationship with Mr. Heath from the earlier negotiations. He did his best to move things forward in our favour. When he visited M. Pompidou in Paris at the end of January, 1971, he came away with a strong impression that M. Pompidou was not merely prepared to see the Community enlarged but positively wanted Britain to become a member. By the time Signor Colombo visited Bonn early in April, just before Mr. Heath's visit, he had become, in the light of the then deadlock in the negotiations, more worried and sceptical; and later in April he wrote to M. Pompidou, and Signor Moro wrote to M. Schumann, arguing strongly in favour of early progress. These pressures must have helped; though, as the Italians later told us, M. Pompidou's reply was disappointing, and simply re-stated the French position in uncompromising terms. A visit by Signor Colombo and Signor Moro to London had been arranged for the end of June; and we had thought that it might conceivably be a necessary part of the process of 'breaking the back of the negotiations' before the summer holidays. In fact, it took place a few days after the successful Ministerial meeting in Luxembourg; and was an occasion mainly for celebration and mutual congratulations.

19. The Italians held the Chairmanship of the Council of Ministers throughout the last six months of 1971. This was helpful to us. Signor Moro (who had undoubtedly played a helpful role in the crucial meetings of the Six during our Ministerial meeting in Luxembourg from 21 to 23 June) proved on the whole a good Chairman; and Italian impartiality in the fisheries question, which was the main issue of the last six months of 1971, was an asset. The Italian Permanent Representative in Brussels, Signor Bombassei, was an even better Chairman of the Conference at Deputy level. Hard-working, cheerful and optimistic, he was shrewd and effective in his conduct of business, invariably helpful to us, and thoroughly constructive in moving things forward.

C. THE NETHERLANDS

20. Our experience of Netherlands attitudes in the negotiations was to some extent an unfortunate one. This was not what we had expected; but perhaps our expectations had been too high. Over the previous ten years before 1970, the Dutch had acquired, and all the world knew it, the reputation of being the most courageous and determined supporters, in the whole Community, of our entry. They had good reasons for being so, not based on any special regard for our interests. The Dutch strongly disliked the domination of the Community by its larger Members, and thought our entry would produce a better balance. They looked on reviving German strength and influence with no satisfaction. They claimed to feel that the Community was too inward-looking (though in fact they had done much to make it so), and that they wanted to adopt a more open and outward attitude towards the rest of the world. For all these reasons they favoured our Membership, and also because, like the Italians, they felt we would bring a reliable element of democratic commitment and political stability into the Community. So the Dutch continued, as they had done for years, to proclaim their emphatic support for our membership.

21. What they did not proclaim, however, was that one of their strongest motives for having us in the Community was their desire to secure better access for Dutch agricultural exports to our market. Another, I fear, must have been to have a new major contributor to the budget of the Community, so much of which is spent on providing protection and support for Dutch agriculture. The negotiations were to show how strong these motives were, and how difficult the Dutch found it to subordinate them to their major political interest in enlargement. There was a clear dichotomy in Dutch policy. On the one hand Dr. Luns (who perhaps had not concerned himself closely enough with questions of economic interest) and Mr. de Koster gave our cause strong and apparently undiluted support. On the other hand Mr. Lardinois, Dutch Minister of Agriculture, was determined, in a dozen contexts, to get his pound of flesh. This conflict was never clearly resolved; but Mr. Lardinois won a lot of the tricks.

22. It had probably been easier for the Dutch to give us wholehearted support in 1961–63 than it had become by 1970–72. For in the earlier negotiations the Common Agricultural Policy scarcely existed, and the potential conflict of interest between them and us remained below the surface. In the intervening years Dr. Mansholt, himself Dutch Minister of Agriculture from 1945 to 1958, had been steadily creating the Common Agricultural Policy, which is no more than Dutch agricultural policy writ large; and by 1970 the Dutch had divided interests and divided feelings. Dr. Luns and Mr. de Koster, the two Ministers in the Dutch Foreign Office, remained (until they both unfortunately left the scene at the end of June 1971) strong and loyal supporters; and they did their best for us (unsuccessfully) over fisheries in June 1970 and (successfully) over sugar and New Zealand right up to June 1971. Our contacts with them were probably more intimate than those with any other Community Ministers. But Mr.

Lardinois, the Dutch Minister of Agriculture, proved by contrast the most troublesome of all the Community Ministers we had to deal with. Unfortunately, when a new Dutch Government was formed at the beginning of July 1971, he retained his portfolio. Dr. Luns left office altogether; Mr. de Koster became Minister of Defence. And for the remaining six months of the negotiations Mr. Lardinois' influence appeared to be unchecked by his new colleagues at the Dutch Foreign Office and remained in the ascendant.

23. Holland is an agricultural phenomenon. We tend to think of it as the country with the largest port in the world, with important oil, chemical and electronics industries, and with extensive tulip fields. We tend to overlook the extraordinary degree to which it depends on extremely efficient agricultural production and immense agricultural exports. The Common Agricultural Policy of the Community has been proportionately of greater advantage to the Netherlands than even to France. Netherlands exports of 'food, beverages and tobacco' in 1969 amounted to $2,310 million. Those of France amounted to $2,558 million. Take away wine, and Dutch agricultural exports are probably larger than French. Agricultural exports formed just over 23 per cent of total Dutch exports. In the case of France, they formed just over 17 per cent of total exports. Dutch agricultural exports are more than half United States agricultural exports by value. This extraordinary Dutch export accomplishment is based on extraordinary figures of agricultural production. Of all the countries in the Community, the Netherlands has the highest degree of agricultural self-sufficiency in respect of oats (138 per cent), vegetables (180 per cent), potatoes (122 per cent), cheese (226 per cent), butter (350 per cent), pigmeat (178 per cent) and poultry (343 per cent). Compared with these figures (all for the year 1968–69) France leads the self-sufficiency tables in respect of wheat, barley, maize, and beef and veal only, and in most cases with much smaller percentage figures than the Dutch. (Belgium leads on sugar.) Apart from the French, the Dutch are the only country in the Community which is more than self-sufficient in beef and veal. These figures prove the extent of the Dutch interest; and in the light of them it is hardly surprising that the Minister of Agriculture should be a powerful figure in the Dutch Cabinet.

24. Moreover, Dutch Ministers of Agriculture, and their officials, have traditionally maintained the closest possible working relations with their French opposite numbers. This is hardly surprising, since their interest in the Common Agricultural Policy of the Community so closely coincides. It was a bit unexpected that, as recorded in Chapter 25, it was Mr. Lardinois and his French colleagues who arranged between them to inaugurate the Common Fisheries Policy of the Community on 30 June, 1970. It was less surprising that their objectives in other areas of the negotiations were closely in accord. Thus Mr. Lardinois was quite as strong as the French in standing out for full Community preference in our market from the start, in resisting the maintenance of any quota restrictions in the British market and in pressing for what would have been in effect a four rather than a five-year period of transition for our agriculture. He went even

further than the French in strongly urging on us for months that our deficiency payments must cease altogether at the moment of entry; in his determination that our horticultural tariffs must be dismantled at the same speed as our industrial ones; and in claiming (when he saw Mr. Rippon in The Hague in April 1971) that we ought to restrain our domestic sugar production to its present level at least until 1978, 'since British farmers would find an expanded market for grain'. Open though he was in his demands, he was sometimes less than candid. He told Mr. Rippon on the same occasion that he doubted whether Scottish waters would be invaded by Community fishermen; yet it was of their exclusion from waters off Aberdeen that Dutch fishermen complained most strongly when all was over.

25. But though the Dutch and French Ministries of Agriculture kept closely in touch, the French do not seem to have informed the Dutch when they had decided to make a move. Thus the Dutch found themselves suddenly deprived of French support, early in the morning of 12 May in Brussels, over horticultural tariffs, and had to give way, after long telephone calls from Dr. Luns in Brussels to Mr. Lardinois in The Hague. At the same meeting the Dutch were probably taken by surprise when the French accepted six movements for our agricultural prices instead of five. Much later in the negotiations, the Dutch were left for a short time isolated in opposition to our 12-mile zones for fisheries limits after the French had accepted them.

26. In some other respects Mr. Lardinois adopted an even cruder approach. For months, in the early stages of the negotiations, he sought to blackmail us by rather crudely suggesting that we could not expect a full voice in the institutions of the Community unless we accepted virtually the whole agricultural policy on the day of our entry. He made the point when Mr. Rippon visited The Hague in October 1970. He told Mr. Rippon in London on 16 November, 1970 that if Britain would accept the obligations of the Common Agricultural Policy from 1 January, 1973, 'this would be an excellent thing. It would ensure that Britain would have the same voting power as other Members and this was what the Netherlands wished to see. If such a declaration could not be made, the French and even the Commission might oppose full voting rights for Britain.' Mr. Rippon replied that Britain was certainly not prepared to join the Community without full voting rights from the outset. Nevertheless, on returning to Holland, Mr. Lardinois repeated his thesis in a press interview. He was no doubt largely responsible for the rather hard line the Dutch (or some of the Dutch: Dr. Luns spoke with quite a different voice) took on our contribution to the Community budget; and he was the only Community representative who blurted out, immediately after a settlement had been reached, how large the budgetary saving was that the Dutch would enjoy even in the first year of our membership as a result of it (see paragraph 12 of Chapter 17).

27. Long before this, we had had some interesting exchanges with the Dutch on Community finance. As a result of what the Dutch Chargé d'Affaires in London told me on 19 January, 1971, we formed the impression that their position

on Community finance was, after the French, the hardest of all the Member States from our point of view. Accordingly, on 25 January, shortly before the meeting of the Council of Ministers on 1 February in which we feared things might move in the wrong direction on Community finance, Mr. Rippon sent a personal message to Dr. Luns. In it he said: 'We all have our economic interests to defend, and I do not want to claim that ours are more significant than yours. But in the context of our negotiations there is a difference. As far as I can see, your economic interests are certain to benefit, in more ways than one, from our entry into the Community ... Ours are bound to suffer, at least in the short run. Therefore unless we can achieve terms we regard as tolerable, in the short run as well as in the longer run, we shall not be able to enter the Community.' The covering telegram with which this message went to our Embassy in The Hague said: 'We cannot help feeling there is some danger of Dr. Luns losing interest in these matters as he approaches the end of his term as Foreign Minister, thus leaving the way open to the influence of Mr. Lardinois and the predominance of economic over political interests.'

28. Given the power and determination of Mr. Lardinois, we were indeed fortunate that Dr. Luns and Mr. de Koster remained in office until after the back of the negotiations had been broken in June 1971. (We were therefore fortunate that it took over two months to form a new Dutch Government after the elections at the end of April.) And I must at once qualify the strictures of the preceding paragraphs by recording once more that in two of the main agricultural issues of the negotiations the Dutch attitude was excellent from our point of view, indeed better than that of any other Community Member. These were sugar and New Zealand. On sugar, the Dutch were the only Member of the Community who insisted throughout that the Community should be prepared, after 1974. to accept from developing countries the quantities of sugar provided for under the Commonwealth Sugar Agreement. On New Zealand, they were from the start the most forthcoming and helpful of the Six. This does them credit, since the export of dairy products is so strong a Dutch interest; but I have already recorded that the Dutch line on New Zealand was the result of a victory by Mr. de Koster over Mr. Lardinois (see paragraph 17 of Chapter 16). Dr. Luns and Mr. de Koster, responding to a widely held Dutch view, were always in the forefront in demanding Community action to help developing countries. Early in the negotiations Mr. de Koster told us several times of his strong doubts of the wisdom of offering association to countries in the Caribbean, because he was convinced this would cause grave difficulties with the United States. But when the French at last came out in favour of such an offer, the Dutch joined them.

29. After the new Dutch Government was formed, the only major issue left in the negotiations was fisheries. On this the Dutch continued to be difficult, as sufficiently recorded in earlier chapters. It was the same with many of the relatively minor but still significant agricultural issues outstanding. The new Ministers in the Dutch Foreign Office, Mr. Schmelzer and Mr. Westerterp, made

no impact on the negotiations in Brussels and do not seem to have succeeded in restraining their agricultural colleague in The Hague. Given that the new Dutch Prime Minister had himself been, only a few years before, the Minister of Agriculture, this may have been a harder task than ever. But it remains the case that the Dutch continued to make trouble over several outstanding matters of agricultural transitional arrangements and over the drafting of the agricultural sections of the Treaty. Thus to the very last moment the Dutch were against us on the drafting of the articles concerning deficiency payments and safeguard clauses for disruption during the transitional period either to third country trade or in our own market. And in respect of pigmeat they succeeded in securing arrangements they knew to be awkward and embarrassing to us. They also. to change the subject for once from agriculture, made an uncommon fuss over nationality, as recorded in Chapter 23.

30. This is an unhappy record, all the more so as it contrasts so strongly with two things. First of all, with the strong and effective political support which the Dutch Government gave us over the general objective of our membership and over some at least of the most important problems such as sugar, sterling and New Zealand. Second, with the still surviving public impression that the Dutch remained throughout our negotiations our strongest and most disinterested champions.

D. BELGIUM

31. The Belgians did not play a very significant part in the negotiations. Of their goodwill to us there was never any doubt. But in so far as they aspired to a significant role, two difficulties confronted them. First, they do not carry much weight in the Community; second, they always find it extremely difficult, whatever their feelings may be on the merits of a case, to take up a position very far removed from that of France. This is so for a variety of good historical and political reasons; but it limited Belgian capacity to influence events. M. Davignon, Political Director in the Belgian Foreign Office, found an interesting rationalisation of this Belgian habit in a conversation with Sir John Beith on 7 December, 1970. Sir John Beith asked him why, in a particular case, the Belgians had adopted an intermediate position between the French and the other four. M. Davignon replied that this was in keeping with regular Belgian policy of avoiding the isolation of France. If another country had adopted the Belgian position, the Belgians could have joined the rest; but somebody had to prevent the French getting too far out on their own. This was an explanation we hardly found convincing.

32. M. Harmel was Foreign Minister throughout the negotiations, and he did his best by his lights to move things forward in a way satisfactory to us. But we never felt much confidence in him. Belgium is traditionally inclined—and who but the super Powers is immune?—to aspire to play a role above its station. M. Harmel always desired to be seen to be active. We felt, partly as a result of

experience in the Ministerial Council of Western European Union over the last few years, that he was over-disposed to accept unsatisfactory compromises; too inclined to cast himself in the role of a mediator; and too interested in launching and pursuing somewhat nebulous Belgian initiatives. For these reasons, we were probably lucky that the Belgians were in the chair of the Council of Ministers for one day only of our negotiations—the first day of all.

33. Fortunately for us, the Belgians had few special interests to defend in the negotiations. Their Minister for Agriculture, M. Héger, was as stubborn as most of his agricultural colleagues in other Community countries; and it was due to him that the Belgian position on New Zealand butter and cheese remained for months less generous than that of any other member of the Six except France. In the early stages, the Belgians had a special interest in trying to ensure that the Commission should be the principal negotiator for the Community; but this was thwarted by the other Five. They were also keen supporters of the access provisions of the Common Fisheries Policy; but here again their resistance to our requirements was not pressed too hard, much less hard than, for instance, by the Dutch. On Community finance, the Belgians were not helpful to us. They put forward figures at a meeting of the Six on 18 February, 1971, which, as it happens, were very close to the figures on which we concluded. The Belgians might well feel that this was an example of accurate foresight; we felt they might have been more generous. They were rather more inclined than most other members of the Community to fluctuate between optimism and pessimism; and in the period between the March and May Ministerial meetings of 1971, when the Germans, Italians, Dutch and Belgians all felt pessimistic about the outcome, the Belgians were perhaps the most pessimistic of all. Thus M. Vaes, the extremely sensible Secretary-General of the Belgian Foreign Ministry, told Sir John Beith on 23 March, 1971, that he had no doubt that the French statement on sterling was intended to torpedo the negotiations. When later things moved successfully towards a conclusion, the Belgians were happy to move with them; but they were never in the lead.

E. LUXEMBOURG

34. Luxembourg's weight in the Community is too small for us to have reasonably expected any significant contribution from them to success. But they always did their best within the limits imposed upon them, and were staunch public supporters of enlargement. Their Foreign Minister, M. Thorn, was an eloquent and busy advocate of our entry; but, in keeping with Luxembourg practice over the years, he found it difficult, on individual issues, to take up a position too far away from that of France. Nevertheless, the Luxembourgers, like the Belgians, contributed their share to the general pressure in the right direction which the Five collectively exercised on the French; and we have no cause to complain about their conduct in the negotiations.

35. They held the Chair of the Community from 1 January, 1972, and in

consequence their Permanent Representative, M. Dondelinger, was Chairman of the Deputies meetings which occupied so many days and nights between 6 and 18 January. These meetings probably lasted well over twice as long, and settled 10 times as many questions, as all the Deputies meetings held in the first six months of the negotiations under German chairmanship. M. Dondelinger proved an admirable Chairman, and gave us much help.

32

France: A General Appraisal

In paragraph 20 of Chapter 1 of this Report, I recorded my own view that M. Pompidou and the French Government effectively took, at The Hague Summit meeting of December 1969, the decision which admitted us to the Community. Several months, and several hundred files, after recording that opinion, I find that I still hold it. But we suffered from many anxieties and uncertainties on the way to success, as parts of this chapter will record. I make no claim to have been convinced throughout the negotiations that they were destined to succeed.

2. It is only fair to record however that Mr. Soames and our Embassy in Paris maintained consistently throughout, in their advice to London, that the French Government had taken a decision that it wished us to enter the Communities and would stick to this decision. In the earliest days this view was slightly qualified. In a despatch of 2 March, 1970, Mr. Soames wrote that M. Pompidou, since becoming President, had made foreign policy his private domain. He went on:

> M. Pompidou is no fervent European, but he sees the Common Market as here to stay and he intends to give priority to making it work. He understands in this respect what the General tended or tried to forget, that a nation's power and influence rest largely on the strength of its economic base. He is also prepared to see Britain join this Europe, provided that there is no trespass on vital French interests. In 1963, even after General de Gaulle's veto, and again in the course of the Presidential campaign in 1969, he said that we belonged there for historical and geographical reasons. He now realises that the Common Market's development, upon which he depends for both political and economic reasons, will continue to be frustrated so long as the question of the British candidature remains unresolved one way or the other. He is even today still not fully convinced that we really want to join the Communities; or, alternatively, that our aim in seeking to do so is not fundamentally to change them. But he thinks that Britain could help balance Germany (a problem which is increasingly preoccupying both M. Pompidou and his Ministers). He suspects that our view of the future development of

a political Europe is likely to be closer to that of the French than to that of the Five. He probably hopes also that, in the long term, there could be some beneficial Anglo-French understanding on defence, as well as in technological and other fields.

3. After negotiations opened four months later, and all through their ups and downs, Mr. Soames remained even more convinced than the above passage suggests that all would be well in the end. When he had an interview with M. Pompidou on 20 November, 1970, the President said that he wished Mr. Soames to be 'quite clear that he wanted these negotiations to succeed'. They then had an argument about the wisdom of our insistence on breaking the back of the negotiations before the next summer holidays. The French, said the President, would be in the chair for the first half of 1971 and he was determined that the negotiations should not become a battle between Britain and France. But when Mr. Soames insisted that we must have concrete results by the summer, the President said 'that there was no doubt in his mind that this would in fact come about'. As so often, the sun shone clearest at the top. If we in the Foreign Office sometimes, in the first 10 months of the negotiations, cast doubts (never I think fundamental ones) on Mr. Soames' optimism, it was because we were so conscious of the frost and fog and drizzle lower down.

4. One of the things which made us sceptical was the fact that, in spite of the important Ministerial changes which took place after M. Pompidou's election as President of France, and which in particular saw the departure of M. Couve de Murville from office and of M. Debré from the French Foreign Ministry, French officials in key positions concerned with our negotiations remained unchanged. The same senior officials who had loyally served General de Gaulle for years, and acted as his instruments in ensuring our continued exclusion from the Community, remained in the same posts. In the Quai d'Orsay M. Alphand remained Secretary-General, M. de Beaumarchais remained Director of Political Affairs, and M. Brunet remained Director of Economic Affairs. In London, Baron de Courcel remained French Ambassador, and in Brussels M. Boegner remained French Permanent Representative. All these officials remained in these posts until after the end of our negotiations. They had been highly effective, often ruthless, exponents of Gaullist policy. Could they, we wondered, really change their spots?

5. They did, but slowly and probably rather reluctantly, under the impulse which came slowly, but in the end decisively, from the top, from the Elysée. Baron de Courcel remained aloof, frigid and critical in London almost until the eve of the meeting between Mr. Heath and M. Pompidou. M. Brunet seemed to us for months to be pursuing as hard and unyielding a course, as one of the main authors of the instructions received by the French Permanent Representation in Brussels, as he had over the previous few years. M. Boegner seemed to be playing his hand in his habitual and highly effective way. Yet there were newer figures who played in the end a more decisive part—M. Jobert and

M. Bernard. M. Jobert above all, as Secretary-General of the Elysée and M. Pompidou's chief trouble-shooter, helped Mr. Soames on many occasions to sort things out when they threatened to go wrong. M. Bernard, economic adviser in the Elysée and head of the interdepartmental secretariat which co-ordinates French policy in the Community, played from our point of view a steadily more helpful part.

6. I pause for a moment here to write something about M. Boegner. He had been French Permanent Representative in Brussels for eight or nine years already when our negotiations opened in 1970. He is a man of great clarity of mind and strength of will. Next to M. Couve de Murville himself, he had been, it is not too much to say, the dominant figure in the Community in Brussels over recent years. One of the German officials concerned with our negotiations told a member of our Embassy in Bonn in the course of them that he was pursued by M. Boegner even in his dreams. Yet I never felt, as the negotiations proceeded, that M. Boegner gave us much cause for complaint. If he was hard, he was fair. He never misled us, and he sometimes even gave us sound advice. When he held the Chair in the Deputies meetings in the critical period of the negotiations—the first six months of 1971—he showed a great deal of effective energy in moving things forward as well as he could, so much so that it was hard to believe that he was consciously working for failure. After things changed, in May 1971, he did not change his attitude much. He continued to carry out his instructions with his usual astringent effectiveness, but seemed to be relieved that the negotiations were clearly on the road to success. When we finally ended the last session of all, at three o'clock in the morning of 18 January, 1972, the Conference adjourned for a short celebration. As M. Boegner and I toasted each other in champagne, he remarked: 'J'ai toujours été partisan de l'élargissement.' At that moment I was ready to believe anything. And in retrospect I still believe it, merely re-interpreting toujours to mean 'for the last two years'.

7. M. Schumann's attitude in the negotiations—not so much in formal meetings with us but in what we heard of the way he played his hand in meetings of the Council of Ministers—often alarmed us. He lacked M. Couve de Murville's icy indifference in the face of steady pressures from the Five, which often seemed to rattle him. At such moments he would make emphatic statements of French inability to move an inch further, and utter alarming threats about the consequences for the whole future of the negotiations if his colleagues continued to resist French views. But this seems to have been no more than a negotiating technique, and not a very effective one. Nevertheless, partly as a result of these attitudes of M. Schumann, and partly on the basis of reports by our Embassy in Paris, we had an uncomfortable impression, right up until May 1971, that everyone concerned in the French Administration up to and including M. Schumann himself were not really yet sure of the destination they were supposed to arrive at. They seemed to be waiting for a decision and clear guidance from the top; and it was long in coming.

8. Whatever M. Schumann might do in Brussels, he remained cordial and

reassuring in Paris—though his conversations with Mr. Soames sometimes betrayed that he was a good deal less well-informed than he should have been on the details of the issues involved. When, for instance, Mr. Soames had a long talk with him on 26 March, M. Schumann assured him there was no question of new issues raised by the French being designed to prepare for a French veto. He wanted, he said, to thank Her Majesty's Government for 'the way in which Mr. Rippon reacted over the French paper on sterling, both in what he had said publicly, and in the attitude which he had taken with the Five'. The long conversation which ensued seemed in some respects less reassuring; but in retrospect it seems to me to confirm the view that, at this stage in the negotiations, the French were deliberately biding their time and keeping things on ice. M. Schumann himself, though no doubt he had a directive to this effect, can hardly have known exactly why; for as the next chapter will show he was not informed of the impending meeting between Mr. Heath and M. Pompidou in May until the evening before its announcement.

9. The really critical period of the negotiations was the eight-week period between the exceptionally unproductive Ministerial meeting of 16 March, 1971, and the unexpectedly fruitful Ministerial meeting of 11–13 May, 1971. At this point all concerned with the negotiations felt a sense of doubt and crisis, the Five other Members of the Community just as much as ourselves. It was enhanced and sharpened by one or two extra ingredients which, at this point, the French threw into the pot. The most alarming, of course, was the sudden emergence, with M. Boegner's statement at a meeting of the Permanent Representatives on 18 March, of the question of sterling in what appeared to many to be a rather critical and dangerous form. Early in April 1971 the French began talking darkly to some of their Community partners about the extreme difficulty of the problems posed by the EFTA neutrals, and hinting that this might prove another insurmountable obstacle.

10. M. Brunet talked at length about the problem of the neutrals to Mr. Palliser in Paris on 10 April, saying that what was done for Switzerland was infinitely more important to France in the negotiations than what was done for New Zealand; and they could hardly settle the latter before they knew what would happen about the former. Mr. Palliser replied that there was a mood of grave mistrust in London, and, he thought, in other European capitals at the way in which the French seemed to be continually raising new problems, or at least raising problems in such a way as to imply that they were raising fresh obstacles. He hoped the French would do all they could to avoid injecting the problem of the neutrals into the negotiations in such a way as further to strengthen this climate of mistrust. In the event, nothing awkward developed from this French thesis, and they soon dropped it. But it was at the same time, and in the same conversation with Mr. Palliser, that M. Brunet suggested that it might be impossible to reach an agreement on sugar for Commonwealth developing countries without at the same time agreeing to do something in respect of groundnuts from France's African associates. In the light of the way

things developed, all these bogies, including sterling, seem to have been little more than parts of a French holding operation designed to keep things deadlocked until the meeting between Mr. Heath and M. Pompidou had been set up.

11. But they had a depressing effect, and not only on us. As for us, I wrote a letter on 18 March to Mr. Soames (before we had heard of that day's offensive by the French on sterling) commenting on the Ministerial meeting of 16 March, and still more on the position of deadlock within the Six which made it so sterile, and asking for his views. I wrote: 'Perhaps the French feel they are constructing the best negotiating position for themselves in preparation for the crunch. If they make concessions to their partners before the crunch, they fear that they will have to pay a second time when the crunch with us comes. They may also want to demonstrate to us the ineffectiveness of the Five in the hope that we will be the readier to do a deal direct with Paris.' Mr. Soames replied next day. His analysis was that the French were still building up a negotiating position with as many throw-away points as possible. But he felt that, of the four essential points, our contribution to the budget and the application of Community preference were far more important to the French than New Zealand or sugar. 'My guess is that Boegner has been told to stonewall on everything else (without actually provoking a major crisis among the Six) until these two vitally important issues seem to the French ripe for settlement.'

12. Some of the Five felt even more depressed than we as this uncomfortable period passed. I have already recorded in the last chapter a Belgian reaction to the French gambit on sterling. On 1 April a member of the German Foreign Ministry told a member of our Embassy in Bonn 'that the Foreign Ministry was still unsure whether the French were intent on raising one obstacle after another in order to spin out the negotiations and see them break down or not. Recently, they had referred rather ominously to the great problems posed by the EFTA non-candidates which must be solved before agreement on entry was reached.' But he went on to say that the Federal Chancellor, however, remained determinedly optimistic about French intentions. It was a day or two after this that Signor Colombo visited Bonn, much more worried about French intentions than he had been two months before.

13. One index however reassured us. Though they raised some awkward new topics, the French avoided raising any which could have been fundamentally dangerous. They never at any time suggested that questions of defence, or in particular questions concerning nuclear affairs, had to be discussed even on the margin of our negotiations. The French Ambassador called on the Foreign Secretary on 7 April: 'He said that in his view it would be undesirable for us to raise the question of defence in the context of our negotiations for entry into the EEC. I took him to be referring particularly to Anglo-French nuclear co-operation.'

14. We of course, as these awkward weeks passed, had less reason to be depressed than did the Five. We were already (even before the Ministerial meeting of 16 March) in contact with the French to prepare, as the next chapter will

record, the meeting between Mr. Heath and M. Pompidou. It was announced on 8 May; and real progress was made for the first time at the Ministerial meeting of 11–13 May. With the Heath-Pompidou meeting a week later and the two successful Ministerial meetings at Luxembourg in June, we were over the hump. My conclusion from all this is, as before, that the French had believed from the start in a successful outcome, but had been determined to ensure that, before it came, we should pass some pretty stiff tests to their satisfaction. They had presumably accepted our proposition that the back of the negotiations must be broken before the summer holidays of 1971. But in adopting this timescale they kept the privilege of determining the rhythm by which we should move along it firmly in their own hands. Almost immediately after his meeting with Mr. Heath, M. Pompidou made a State Visit to Belgium. On 25 May Sir John Beith reported information M. Davignon gave him about M. Pompidou's conversation with the Belgian Prime Minister. 'The President explained to the Belgians that he had in fact put his money on enlargement, and British entry, at The Hague meeting and that since then he had only been waiting for confirmation that the British Government were determined to play a fully European role and to give priority to this over their other interests in the world. The talks with Mr. Heath had given him the assurance he needed.'

15. I think M. Pompidou must have felt for some months that the climax of the negotiations must be a meeting between himself and Mr. Heath, and that the second half of May, or thereabouts, would be the best time for it. This meant that we and all the other parties to the negotiations had to be kept on rather uncomfortable tenterhooks throughout the previous six months. The French were in a position to dictate the pace of the negotiations, and that is what they did. After the Heath-Pompidou meeting things moved on a predictable course, subject to much awkwardness over fisheries, to a successful conclusion. In one sense, solving the remaining problems after June 1971 was even harder than it had been before. In the book I have several times referred to Dr. Nass who wrote: 'To some extent the certainty of the final outcome led to an even harder struggle over individual questions.' But from the Heath-Pompidou meeting onwards the final outcome was certain. In his public statements at his meeting with Mr. Heath and over the next few weeks M. Pompidou promised success. And he was as good as his word.

16. It is all the same at first sight a little strange that the French should have handled things in this way, subjecting ourselves and all Europe to months of unnecessary and agonising suspense. The French could well retort that they had accepted the timescale we ourselves had laid down, and saw to it that it was adhered to. This is true. One might indeed conclude that had we laid down a shorter timescale they would have conformed to that too, and that in a sense the work of the negotiations expanded to fill the time available for it. Two factors help perhaps to explain the French tactic of stonewalling and delay. First, from their point of view it paid off. By keeping firm control over the timing of developments and the sequence in which solutions of individual problems were

reached, the French were able to set up the final package which best suited them, and by doing so to oblige us to pay more on Community finance in return for getting what we needed on New Zealand. Second, it is I think true that the French take an unusual satisfaction in the conduct of negotiations for its own sake. They like the tensions it can engender, and the careful orchestration of innumerable themes. For the French, negotiation is an art form, or even a sport. When I finally left the Conference Hall in Luxembourg at about 6 a.m. on 23 June, 1971, after so much had been settled, I happened to run into M. Brunet. 'Congratulations,' he said. 'Vous avez très bien négocié.' It was as though we had just finished a particularly exciting, hard fought and enjoyable game of tennis.

17. This is perhaps the place to record the major part played in the success of our negotiations by Mr. Soames and the Embassy in Paris. All our Embassies in Community countries, and a number of our posts in other countries too, played their part; but because the position of France was so central to the outcome, it fell to Mr. Soames to play a very much bigger part than any other Ambassador. He was of course helped in doing so by his special status as a former Cabinet Minister and by his easy and frequent access to the Prime Minister and other Ministers in London. Nevertheless, just because we got into so many difficulties with the French, he was able to play and invariably did play an essential part in sorting them out. I will not repeat the details here; they have emerged in many chapters of Part II of this Report. But just to recapitulate it is worth recalling that Mr. Soames played an indispensable part not only in setting up the meeting between Mr. Heath and M. Pompidou, but in the settlements we reached on each one of the major issues—Community finance, sugar, sterling, New Zealand and fisheries—and on some of the smaller but stickier issues too, such as animal health.

33

The Road to the Heath–Pompidou Summit

In paragraphs 5 and 6 of Chapter 7 I have described the extent to which, as the negotiations opened, we already foresaw that some kind of summit meeting would prove necessary before they ended. We were thinking at that point more of a summit of the Seven (or possibly the Ten) than of the bilateral Anglo-French summit meeting which in the end took place. Already, we did not like the idea of a summit of the Six; though we foresaw that it might be hard to reach a summit of the Seven until the Six had had a summit meeting of their own.

2. The idea that a summit meeting would be necessary was anything but a British monopoly. Right from the start, the concept hung in the air, as something pretty obvious. Various participants in the negotiations took it up. The first was M. Harmel, always too apt, in our judgment, to seek opportunities for a Belgian initiative. Late in October 1970, as we very soon after learned, he made a bilateral approach to the French Government suggesting that the French, in their capacity as Chairman of the Council of Ministers of the Six from 1 January, 1971, should call a summit meeting of the Six in Paris early in the New Year. In M. Harmel's conception this summit meeting was to deal with a number of subjects; but among them was that of the enlargement negotiations. We did not like this idea; but having no formal cognisance of it we could naturally take no action. The first French responses of which we heard tended to be positive; but it seems that, by the end of November, M. Pompidou had in effect decided not to adopt M. Harmel's proposal. This may well have been, though we certainly could not even guess at this at the time, because he already felt that a bilateral summit meeting with Mr. Heath would be the better course.

3. Mr. Heath did indeed have a meeting with M. Pompidou in November, but it was a very short one. It took place after General de Gaulle's funeral, when M. Pompidou had so many Heads of State and Government to receive that he could devote a very short time only to each. His meeting with Mr. Heath lasted only 10 minutes. M. Pompidou said he hoped there would be an opportunity for a fuller discussion with Mr. Heath before long. Mr. Heath replied that he hoped too that they could meet again when M. Pompidou thought the time appropriate. Six months passed before the appropriate time arrived.

4. Even before Mr. Heath and M. Pompidou met on 12 November, we had received from a member of our Delegation in Brussels a report that in retrospect looks more significant than it did at the time. A French official told him on 10 November of a conversation that he had had with M. Bernard of the Elysée the previous week-end. M. Bernard had said it was essential that, at a certain stage, M. Pompidou and Mr. Heath should become involved and should be prepared to take the major political decisions. He therefore envisaged a Heath-Pompidou meeting in March or April.

5. The next act of the summit saga was played in Rome where on 24 and 25 November Herr Brandt paid a visit to Signor Colombo. I have already recorded in paragraph 12 of Chapter 31 Herr Brandt's public reference on this occasion to the fact that if insuperable difficulties arose in the negotiations a summit of the Six 'could not be excluded'. Signor Colombo appears to have felt the same way.

6. But, at least in respect of the idea of a summit of the Six, we did not. On 31 December, 1970, in the light of further reports and rumours since the Rome meeting, we sent guidance to our European posts on the subject of a summit meeting. The telegram containing this guidance is reproduced in Appendix I. In it we said we wished to discourage the idea of a further summit meeting of the Six, which would present two major dangers. First, once it had been decided to call such a meeting, negotiations in Brussels would be bound to stagnate pending decisions taken at it. Second, a summit meeting of the Six might define a position for the Community which would be too rigid to change and too disadvantageous for us to accept. We might, we said, in certain circumstances find a summit of the Seven (or the Ten) useful, though we could hardly hope to get it without a previous summit of the Six. If at a later stage negotiations in Brussels were to run into serious trouble, then a summit meeting might be desirable, but this could only be judged much later on.

7. By January 1971, we began to get reports from our Embassy in Paris that French officials of fairly senior rank closely concerned with our negotiations were beginning to speak rather freely of the necessity they saw of a meeting between Mr. Heath and M. Pompidou. February brought further such reports but no clear move from either side. In the second half of the month Mr. Soames had a long talk with M. Jobert. This made him think a meeting with M. Pompidou would be useful; and he saw M. Pompidou on 25 February. M. Pompidou said nothing about a possible meeting with the Prime Minister. He stressed that it was necessary that we should, at the end of the transitional period, be paying a much higher percentage of the Community Budget than we had proposed; and it was 'capital' that we should adopt Community Preference in full from the start. (When Mr. Soames called on M. Schumann on 12 March, he said he had the impression from talking to M. Pompidou that these were the two French priorities. M. Schumann said that this was interesting. He had not heard of it. He would talk to the President about it.) Mr. Soames's interview with M. Pompidou on 25 February ended with M. Pompidou saying

that he believed Mr. Heath's political thinking on Europe to be exactly in line with his own.

8. On 1 March Mr. Soames had a meeting in London with the Prime Minister. The Prime Minister asked Mr. Soames how in his view the outstanding issues of the negotiations would be resolved. Would it be a case of a summit of the Ten, with M. Pompidou in the chair, the outcome of which had been carefully prepared in advance; or would the right course be for him to have bilateral talks with M. Pompidou, and leave the negotiations to be concluded thereafter at Ministerial level at Brussels? Mr. Soames said his clear preference was for the latter. He thought that M. Pompidou would want to settle these matters himself with the Prime Minister. Mr. Soames suggested he should now see M. Jobert again and say that he had reported to the Prime Minister what M. Jobert had said, and that the Prime Minister agreed that an understanding between himself and M. Pompidou would be an important element in the negotiations, and that the timing of any meeting between them was important in view of the need to avoid the Brussels negotiations turning sour. The Prime Minister agreed that Mr. Soames should speak to M. Jobert on these lines.

9. Mr. Soames did so on 6 March, and reported the conversation in a letter of 10 March to Sir Denis Greenhill. He asked M. Jobert whether further thought had been given in the Elysée to the timing of any meeting between the Prime Minister and the President. M. Jobert thought such a meeting would have to be either before the Ministerial meeting of the Negotiating Conference fixed for May, or before that fixed for June. He felt they should wait and see how the March Ministerial meeting went and talk to each other again thereafter. M. Jobert asked Mr. Soames to say nothing to M. Schumann about these discussions.

10. Thus already ten days before the March Ministerial meeting a general understanding existed between us and the French that there should be a meeting between Mr. Heath and M. Pompidou. It took nearly two months more to fix it up definitely, and I shall give only a very abbreviated account of the further steps, which were rather complicated. There was a certain amount of polite fencing between us and the French as to who was the originator of the idea of the meeting, each side wishing to regard the proposal for a meeting as having come first from the other. For what it is worth, and it scarcely matters, I think the initiative lay with the French. It was certainly clearly on their side in a conversation which took place over lunch during the Ministerial meeting in Brussels on 16 March between Mr. Tickell, Mr. Rippon's Private Secretary, and M. Bernard of the Elysée. Mr. Tickell's record of this conversation is reproduced in Appendix I, partly for the light it throws on the French attitude towards the projected meeting, partly as an interesting snapshot of the general situation as it appeared at that point in time. Whether by then M. Bernard knew of the conversation of 6 March between M. Jobert and Mr. Soames I cannot tell.

11. On 31 March the Foreign Secretary and Mr. Rippon had a conversation with the Prime Minister, which led to Mr. Soames being asked to tell M. Jobert

that the Prime Minister agreed that it would be valuable if he and M. Pompidou could meet at a mutually convenient time. The latter part of May seemed a possibility, but Mr. Heath would prefer to reflect further before suggesting dates. In fact, the Prime Minister wished to conclude his meeting with Herr Brandt, early in April, before deciding the best date for his visit to Paris. The Prime Minister held several further meetings with the Foreign Secretary, Mr. Rippon and Mr. Soames during April. Mr. Soames remained in contact with M. Jobert and gradually plans grew firmer. When they met on 27 April it transpired, from the French side, that the most convenient dates for M. Pompidou would be those on which a visit to London by M. Schumann had been arranged—20 and 21 May.

12. Extremely delicate factors in the timing of the meeting were, inevitably, the effect it would have on the negotiations in Brussels; and the effect which the state of the negotiations in Brussels would have on it. We felt it would be undesirable for Mr. Heath and M. Pompidou to meet at a time when the Brussels negotiations were still completely deadlocked. We did not want the meeting to appear an occasion almost of last resort, designed to break such a deadlock. We thought, on the contrary, that the meeting could be more fruitful if significant movement in the Brussels negotiations had occurred before it took place. Therefore, it was obviously undesirable that it should take place before the next Ministerial meeting in Brussels, fixed for 11 and 12 May. Therefore again, it was highly desirable that significant movement should take place at that meeting as a prelude to the Heath-Pompidou meeting. Yet there was an obvious risk that fixing a meeting with M. Pompidou for a date after the Brussels meeting would mean that nothing would happen at the Brussels meeting. Furthermore, there was the problem of timing the announcement. If it was agreed to hold the meeting after the Brussels meeting on 11 and 12 May, should it be announced before that meeting, or only after it? If it was announced before, was there not a risk that at the Brussels meeting the Five might, as it were, stand aside and await developments in Paris ten days later?

13. These problems were discussed with the French. Agreement was reached that the Heath-Pompidou meeting should be after the Brussels meeting on 11 and 12 May; that it should be announced before the Brussels meeting; and that the Brussels meeting should if possible be the occasion of significant progress. The French adhered to this arrangement, and they and we both made moves which helped the Brussels meeting of 11–13 May to be the occasion of the first real breakthrough. The French move (on association for developing Commonwealth countries and hence indirectly on sugar) was not so significant as our move on Community Preference. Yet that it was a deliberate and conscious move to meet us is, in my opinion, demonstrated by the exchanges between Mr. Soames and M. Jobert recorded in paragraph 27 of Chapter 13.

15[*sic*]. M. Jobert continued to insist that M. Schumann and the Quai d'Orsay must be completely excluded both from the process of arranging the meeting and from the later process of preparing it. On 3 May the dates of

20 and 21 May were definitely fixed for the meeting and it was agreed to announce it on Saturday, 8 May. Mr. Soames pleaded that M. Schumann should be informed. It would be most embarrassing if he were only to learn at the last minute that his own dates for visiting London had been pre-empted for a different meeting in Paris. But M. Jobert was adamant: on the French side, no one outside the Elysée was to know anything. When Mr. Soames had called on M. Schumann on 21 April M. Schumann had said that he hoped that his visit to London would perhaps pave the way for a visit by the Prime Minister to M. Pompidou. Mr. Soames asked whether he could take it that this was the President's view. M. Schumann replied that he had not discussed it with the President: what he had said represented his own personal thought. 'He then said rather pointedly that perhaps I had discussed it with the President and I was able truthfully to say that I had not.' M. Schumann left Paris on 4 May for a visit to Moscow. He was due back late on the evening of 7 May. On 7 May Baron de Courcel was summoned from London to Paris by M. Jobert, informed of the announcement to be made next day and 'sworn to secrecy'. When M. Schumann got back that evening he too was told; and next afternoon the meeting was announced.

16. Mr. Heath's meeting with M. Pompidou was extremely thoroughly prepared. On their side, the Elysée kept the preparations strictly in their own hands, and asked that the same procedure should be followed on our side. So far as contacts with the French were concerned, it was; and preparatory discussions with French officials in Paris before the meeting were carried out for us by Mr. Armstrong, the Prime Minister's Private Secretary, and Mr. Thornton of the Cabinet Office. Papers were exchanged between the two sides, and an agenda drawn up. The Prime Minister, in London and at Chequers, devoted an immense amount of time to thorough briefing on and preparation for the visit. During the visit, Sir William Nield and all the senior official members of the British negotiating team were present in Paris, in case their advice should be needed; but it hardly was.

17. In this Report I have written, and I shall write here, very little about the content and the immediate outcome of the meeting between Mr. Heath and M. Pompidou. It was by far the most significant meeting that took place in the whole course of the negotiations. But this is not the place for a full account of it. I will record only that it was successful beyond our best expectations. M. Pompidou and Mr. Heath spent almost 11 hours talking to each other, almost the whole of which was *tête-à-tête* with only interpreters present. I reproduce in Appendix II, to document the results of the meeting, its Communiqué and the statements made by M. Pompidou and Mr. Heath at their final Press Conference; and, in Appendix I, an extract from Mr. Soames' despatch of 9 June, 1971,* giving his view about the background to the meeting.

18. Though these documents must suffice as an account of the meeting,

* See Appendix I

nevertheless I will add here a brief summary of its achievements. The meeting established, at the highest level on either side, broad understandings about the main outstanding issues of the negotiations in Brussels. It also established an agreed timetable. M. Pompidou said at the Press Conference that he believed the main issues could be settled in the Negotiating Conference in June. The meeting set to some extent the pattern of life in the future enlarged Community. Mr. Heath's acceptance of M. Pompidou's view about majority voting, and the safeguarding of the vital interests of any Member State, was something M. Pompidou was determined to have; it was also something Mr. Heath was not reluctant to give. The meeting avoided causing any offence to the other five members of the Community, all of whom, partly as a result of careful preparation and subsequent briefing from the British and French, but still more as a result of their own independent judgment, saw it as an indispensable step on the path to final success and felt no bitterness at all that matters of such great significance were being settled without them. The meeting inaugurated an Anglo-French reconciliation which the events of the previous 10 years had made most necessary and desirable.

19. It did one thing more. It deflated and dissipated a cloud in which much poison had gathered. To my mind, it is extremely fortunate that, at M. Pompidou's insistence, the question of the future of the French language in the enlarged Community was brought up and discussed by himself and Mr. Heath. The fact that English was bound to acquire equal status with French in an enlarged Community, and French fears that it might soon achieve a higher status, had lain for years behind earlier French determination to exclude us from the Community. Ever since I myself arrived in Brussels as Ambassador to the Communities, a few months after the breakdown of the first negotiations, I have felt that this had been, and was becoming increasingly, a major reason for our exclusion. It was seldom referred to in public; but it loomed and swelled in the background. It was extremely wholesome that M. Pompidou exposed to the air this boil which had festered so long and so deep. In fact, there was not much to be done about it. Mr. Heath gave such reassurances as he could; and M. Pompidou accepted that it is a fact of life that the English language is bound to play a large part in the workings of an enlarged Community.

20. Still better, he continued to talk openly and sensibly about the issue after his meeting with Mr. Heath. A few days later he made a State Visit to Belgium. He gave a Press Conference in Brussels on 26 May, in which perhaps he did the British too much honour. 'If it were only the British', said M. Pompidou, 'they would be able to manage in French, but there were also the Nordic countries.' There was no question of the French having any imperialist designs. He simply wanted French to resist the offensive of the English language and keep its place, at the same level as English, as a working language. The use of French would help the Community to remain as it is.

PART IV
REFLECTIONS ON THE NEGOTIATIONS

34

This Time the Luck Ran Our Way

Our negotiations with the Community from 1970 to 1972 seem in retrospect to have proceeded under a lucky star. And not only in retrospect; for my part, I was conscious throughout that the general movement of major events, and the general attitude of the major personalities involved, this time favoured success. Between 1961 and 1963 the opposite seems, looking back, to have been the case. Events and personalities conspired to diminish our prospects as time passed.

2. The mere fact that we had in 1970 a third chance to join the Community was in itself a piece of historic luck hardly to be hoped for. Often before it had seemed that the door could no longer be opened, or would only be opened when it was too late. In 1969, the Community was beginning to get on the move again. In another year or two, if it had continued effectively on its way without us, it might have been too late.

3. Part II of this Report shows, I think, that on the whole, during the negotiations themselves, we had several lucky chances and lucky escapes, and few misfortunes. But I shall be concerned in this chapter not with the internal context of the negotiations, but with the way in which a series of fortunate events external to them helped to create a climate of success.

4. The first and most important of these fortunate events—and in its timing a fortuitous one—was the resignation of General de Gaulle on 28 April, 1969. This removed from our path what would almost certainly have proved, had he remained in power, an irremovable obstacle. I know of no reason for supposing that, had he remained in power, General de Gaulle would ever have been prepared to tolerate our entry into the Community on a basis which would have been acceptable to his partners and to us. Even his death, on 9 November, 1970, was a favourable event. It is true of course that he had taken no part whatever in public affairs since his resignation. But his presence, while he survived, as a potential centre of opposition to the enlargement of the Community, or as a potential source of some devastating and not easily to be ignored pronouncement, must have acted to some extent as a factor inhibiting the freedom of action of his successor. But of course his resignation was more important. From that very day, in every quarter, it seemed to be accepted that the enlargement

of the Community had become possible once again and indeed was beginning to look likely.

5. Other personal changes which in general favoured our chances took place in consequence of de Gaulle's departure. M. Couve de Murville, the Prime Minister for the last 10 months of the General's reign, vanished from office; and with him vanished perhaps our next most skilful and indomitable opponent. He seems to have maintained his opposition to our entry into the Community throughout the period of the negotiations. M. Debré, another strong but less implacable opponent, was moved from the position of Foreign Minister to that of Minister of Defence, where he was less able to assert his original opposition to admitting us and appears gradually, as the negotiations proceeded, to have grown resigned to their success. His successor as Foreign Minister, M. Schumann, probably had a favourable bias towards our entry from the start. He was not the man to run ahead of a policy decision by President Pompidou; and from time to time his attitudes and interventions proved exasperating and seemed an obstacle to progress. Nevertheless, I think he felt a genuine satisfaction as things moved forward; and while we might certainly have had as French Foreign Minister someone more efficient and more forthcoming in the conduct of the negotiations, we could just as easily have had someone more obstructive.

6. On the German side, too, it was an advantage to us that Herr Brandt replaced Dr. Kiesinger as Federal Chancellor in October 1969 and remained in office throughout the negotiations. In 1967 and 1968, Dr. Kiesinger had proved himself unexpectedly unsympathetic to our desire to join the Community, and reluctant in any way to put at risk the harmonious development of Franco-German relations which he evidently regarded as taking a clear priority over the enlargement of the Community. Herr Brandt was ready to strike a different balance, as he made clear at the summit meeting of the Community in December 1969. He too placed a very high priority on Franco-German relations; but he seems to have been more determined that the Community must be enlarged, and more effective as an advocate of our case, than Dr. Kiesinger ever aspired to be.

7. Another piece of good fortune was Signor Colombo's appointment as Prime Minister of Italy in August 1970. He had played a specially helpful part in the earlier negotiations, and had relations of close confidence with Mr. Heath. He believed profoundly in the desirability of our membership. That the Italian Government played so sympathetic, and so effective, a part in the negotiations from 1970 to 1972 must have been due, in part at least, to his leadership.

8. Finally, while dealing with personalities, it is necessary to mention Mr. Heath. His return to the scene as Prime Minister in June 1970 was greeted in Europe as a signal that Britain really meant business, and a portent that he would finish the work he had had to leave unfinished in 1963. And while on the subject of luck and Mr. Heath, I will mention one pure coincidence. Some years

earlier, while on holiday in Spain, Mr. Heath happened to stay in the same hotel as M. Jobert. They got to know each other, and remained in touch. By 1970 M. Jobert was M. Pompidou's right-hand man, as Secretary-General of the Elysée. I have no doubt this accident helped.

9. But our good fortune showed itself in fields even more fundamental than that of the personalities involved. Perhaps the most fortunate event of all from our point of view was that we were able to open the negotiations 12 days after a General Election and the formation of a new Government. This meant that there could never (short of some quite unforeseeable contingency) be any doubt that the Government had time to carry its policy through. Two and a half years' time were needed from the opening of negotiations before we could actually enter the Communities. Short of a situation in which both major parties resolutely supported our entry into the Community and were broadly agreed on the terms which must be attained, this probably meant that to carry the policy of entry through to success any British Government would have had to start negotiations during the first year of its existence. Our good luck in starting immediately after a General Election was something which could hardly have been expected, and something which, though little regarded, was of enormous value.

10. Moreover, it would have been extremely difficult for any new British Administration to open negotiations during the first year of its period of office unless the ground had been prepared by its predecessor. The decision to apply for membership; its endorsement by Parliament; the necessarily deliberate response by the Community, involving, among much else, an opinion by the Commission; the preparation of negotiating positions by the Community and by ourselves—could all these have been completed within a year? As it was, all these stages had been completed by the time of the 1970 General Election, and the new Government was able to start negotiations immediately. Little time, it may be claimed, was wasted between two crucial dates: General de Gaulle's resignation on 28 April, 1969, and the enlargement of the Community foreseen for 1 January, 1973. When the General resigned, the British application was waiting—the processes of 1967 in the United Kingdom needed no repetition. And even though all was ready on our side, yet, had the General's resignation been delayed even by three months, we could hardly have begun negotiations as soon as we did, or entered the Community as soon as we shall.

11. Next in the catalogue of luck, and quite decisive in comparison with the negotiations of 1961–63 or the attempt at negotiations of 1967, was our balance of payments experience throughout the negotiations from 1970–72. The United Kingdom reserves increased in every month from October 1970 to May 1972—an unprecedented sequence. And the following table, showing the United Kingdom current balance of payments outturn from 1960–71, makes clear enough how fortunate we were in the last three years of the period compared to any earlier sequence of years.

UNITED KINGDOM BALANCE OF PAYMENTS: CURRENT BALANCE
£ million

1960	1961	1962	1963	1964	1965	1966	1967	1968	1969	1970	1971
−255	+6	+122	+124	−376	−52	+83	−298	−288	+440	+579	+952

12. The underlying and increasing strength of our total balance of payments throughout the years 1969–71, founded of course on the strength of the current balance, transformed our situation and our prospects in the eyes of the Community and indeed of ourselves. The rapid and massive reduction in our short-term and medium-term international indebtedness, which also characterised these years, had a corresponding effect. In the light of this performance, the serious doubts which the Community had entertained for so long as to our ability both to meet the costs of entry and to avoid becoming a burden on the Community's progress were significantly reduced. There were some in France who argued, even half-way through the negotiations, that while it might in principle be desirable for us to enter the Community, we simply could not afford the balance of payments costs involved. There were some in Britain too, and even within Whitehall. As our balance of payments grew stronger throughout 1970 and 1971, these arguments and doubts were stilled. They were discredited, as time passed, by the fact that our performance so much exceeded even our own forecasts; and as the forecasts were proved too pessimistic the case based on them crumbled. Thus in his Budget speech in 1971 the Chancellor of the Exchequer said: 'We can expect another sizeable current account surplus in 1971, but it is not likely to be as high as in 1970'. It turned out to be over 50 per cent higher.

13. There were other events which, as the negotiations proceeded, gave them welcome and unanticipated support. Just how much the success of our negotiations on New Zealand butter owed to the sudden melting away of the Community's butter surplus and the discovery, early in 1971, that the world faced a shortage of butter, it is not easy to say; but it certainly made a difference. More directly political were various landmarks in the development of relations between Germany and France, which also undoubtedly had a major effect in predisposing the French Government towards, or confirming it in, a more favourable attitude. Herr Brandt's independent *Ostpolitik* played a major part in affecting French attitudes. So did Franco-German disputes over economic and monetary policy, typified by the bad relations between M. Giscard d'Estaing and Professor Schiller (who at times played in our negotiations the part of a good angel unawares) and marked especially by the floating of the Deutschemark on 8 May, 1971, three days before the first breakthrough at a Ministerial meeting in Brussels, two weeks before Mr. Heath's meeting with President Pompidou, and just at the moment when the French Government had seemed to be particularly obsessed by the iniquities, not of the Deutschemark, but of sterling. In a different way, but also a favourable one, the crisis which opened on 15

August, 1971, when President Nixon 'closed the gold window' and imposed an import surcharge, undoubtedly contributed to making the atmosphere in our negotiations with the Community more favourable.

14. Finally, we were fortunate in that over the 19 months of our negotiations with the Community there was (at least after the new Italian Government was formed early in August 1970) only one change of Government among the member countries. This very unusual continuity helped us; and the one exception—the change of Government in the Netherlands in July 1971—had an unfortunate effect from our point of view (see Chapter 31).

35

Did We Make Mistakes?

The authors of the Report on the Brussels Negotiations of 1961–63 spent much time examining what mistakes we had made in those negotiations; and they concluded that there had been several. This was obviously prudent; and it had the conscious purpose of helping any future British negotiators who might have the good fortune to embark once again on the attempt to enter the Community. This time (while of course we are not quite in yet) so directly pragmatic a purpose can perhaps be disregarded. Nevertheless, it is I think right, in reflecting on the negotiations, to see if there were cases in which we made mistakes and, if so, how much it mattered. I am satisfied that we did not make many. I do not think that we tripped up seriously, if at all, over transitional periods and mechanisms (the acceptance of Community preference in full from the start was absolutely unavoidable); over sterling, tariff quotas, the European Coal and Steel Community and Euratom, or over sugar—though I will have something to say about the sugar settlement in the next chapter. We made a change of course in approaching a solution on the Channel Islands and the Isle of Man, but I will not classify our first approach as a mistake. On the contrary, making it and then changing it helped things forward to an excellent result. This, of the major issues, leaves only New Zealand, Fisheries and Community Finance on which I have some doubts.

2. As for New Zealand, though I have made clear in what I have already written that I think we got more for New Zealand than was necessary and had ourselves to pay a heavy price in order to do so, I do not even in retrospect see how we could have acted otherwise than we did. If we had cast the slightest doubt on the merits of the New Zealand case, or failed to attempt to secure the best possible result for them, we would have risked securing not too much, but far too little. It was in the last resort British political and public opinion about New Zealand which obliged us to fight their battles so hard and to pay the Community to give them so much. Only if British political and public opinion had been less concerned could we have afforded to settle for less for New Zealand; and we could take no steps to reduce the concern of British political and public opinion without fatally weakening our whole negotiating position on New Zealand's behalf.

3. Nevertheless, I still feel it is something of a blemish on the outcome that we ourselves had to pay so much on New Zealand's behalf. There is no doubt that we bought a satisfactory arrangement for New Zealand dairy products by agreeing to a less than satisfactory one on Community finance. But for the link with New Zealand, we might have got a considerably lower contribution for 1973 and a slightly lower one for 1977. Let us assume—it is a not implausible assumption—that we might have settled for a contribution of 7 per cent in 1973 and 18 per cent in 1977. On this basis, and assuming an average Community budget over the five years of £1,500 million, the New Zealand settlement will cost us, over the five years, about £100 million in foreign exchange.

4. On fisheries, I have no doubt at all that we made one mistake. I think we made one possible mistake at the very start and one major mistake as we went along. I am not so certain that, in the end, either of them mattered much, since I believe that on the whole the outcome on fisheries was and will prove satisfactory. The most I can say in criticism of the course we adopted is that we gave ourselves a lot of avoidable trouble.

5. The first mistake which, in the light of hindsight, I believe we may have made was in not trying harder than we did to stop the adoption of a Common Fisheries Policy. I have written at length about the genesis of the Community's Common Fisheries Policy in paragraphs 12 to 26 of Chapter 25. In paragraph 20 of that chapter I recorded that, though we sent certain instructions to our Community posts on 19 June, 1970, these instructions were not an attempt to get the Community to defer the adoption of a Common Fisheries Policy. They were rather a request for an assessment of the situation, on the basis of which we might have attempted to intervene later. I ought however to record that in a letter to me of 24 June, 1970, Mr. Kearns of the Ministry of Agriculture suggested rather stronger action. He did not ask that we should 'make a major fuss', or seek to prevent the Community from taking any decisions; but he suggested that 'a simple marker' would be sufficient to preserve our position. He suggested we should tell the Community Governments that it would be gravely misunderstood here if decisions were taken by the Council of Ministers on the eve of the opening of negotiations with us and before we had had the opportunity of discussing these matters with them. I replied next day arguing against such action; saying I felt our position was adequately protected even if the Community were to reach certain preliminary decisions; and expressing the view, largely in the light of the Community's reaction to a recent similar intervention by Norway, that an intervention by us might meet with a similar reaction and even give the Community the impression that there would be advantage in pressing ahead in this field.

6. Before this argument could be carried further we were reassured by hearing from our Embassy in The Hague (on 26 June) that the Dutch intended to ensure there would be no agreement on fisheries at the meeting of the six Ministers of Agriculture on 29 June. In the light of this reassurance we gave no further consideration to intervention.

7. Given the circumstances—and I repeat the point I made in Chapter 25 that we were within a week of the installation of the new Conservative Administration, and so many other problems pressed that fisheries were far from uppermost in our minds—I would not feel inclined to accept blame for our inaction. Nevertheless, I feel obliged to consider whether, had we taken action, we could have prevented the Community agreement of 30 June, 1970, on a Common Fisheries Policy.

8. I believe we could have at least postponed such an agreement; and if we could have postponed it from 30 June it is possible, though questionable, that we could have postponed it indefinitely. There was one line of argument we could have adopted which would I think have obliged the Community not to decide on the Common Fisheries Policy at least on 30 June. We could have said to them—and a message from Mr. Barber to the Foreign Ministers of the Six or even from Mr. Heath to their Heads of Government would have been the appropriate vehicle—that the kind of provisions on common access to coastal waters which we knew they were considering were bound to cause us great political difficulty. We could have appealed to them to take this political difficulty into account, and at least to ensure that the matter was not settled solely by the six Ministers of Agriculture, but thoroughly considered by the Foreign Ministers of the Community at the next regular meeting of the Council of Ministers. Such an appeal could hardly have been ignored; and I think that at least the Dutch and the Italians, and probably the Germans also, would have felt obliged to support our request.

9. But could we thereby have achieved more than a brief postponement? And if we achieved only a brief postponement, might we not have done our cause more harm than good by publicly demonstrating that the Community was not prepared to interrupt its progress on our account? It is easy in the light of the situation today to exaggerate what such an appeal might have achieved. It is necessary to remember the strong determination which animated every member of the Community at the time that 'approfondissement' must go on, regardless of the wishes and views of the candidates. The attitude of the Community on this point a month or two later is described in paragraph 11 of Chapter 26. It seems to me possible that, even though we might well have secured a postponement from 30 June, it would not have been a long one; and the Community would nevertheless before long have adopted a Common Fisheries Policy with its offensive access provisions. We would thus have suffered a rebuff; though conceivably our future negotiating position would have been strengthened.

10. I therefore do not set much store by this mistake, if it was one. But I have no doubt that, almost a year later, we made a major mistake, in putting to the Community the proposals we put to them on 1 June, 1971. What we then suggested was agreement on the basis of six-mile limits. Why did we propose six-mile limits? For exactly the same reason for which we objected so strongly to the access provisions of the Common Fisheries Policy. Those access provisions, and our proposals for six-mile limits, were both based on the desire to

acquire fishing rights in somebody else's coastal waters. When we put forward these proposals, we thought it worth our while to abandon exclusive fishing rights in our outer six-mile belt (where many foreign fishermen had rights in any case) if we could thereby secure access for our distant-water fleet to the outer six-mile belt of Norwegian waters, and possibly of Faroese and Greenland waters too. The pot was calling the kettle black.

11. Very soon, as Chapter 25 has shown, we realised we had made a mistake and hastily changed course. We were lucky to be able to do so. There was a real risk that the Community, had it moved more quickly as the Commission tried to make it, could have taken us at our word and accepted our six-mile proposals. Fortunately for us, the Member States were, in this case, slower off the mark than the Commission; they did not accept the Commission's proposal; and while they were still arguing about it we changed course and opted instead for the status quo, making it clear at the same time that we should not be able to accept any settlement relating to our own waters until we knew what settlements would be available for the other candidates.

12. All the same, I think we immensely increased our future difficulties by our proposal for six-mile limits. If we had simply sat tight, rejecting the temptation to seek access for our distant-water fishing fleet to other people's coastal waters, our future negotiating position would have been much simpler, easier and stronger. We should have been in line with the Irish and the Norwegians and could have avoided all the awkward and painful disputes with Norway which later ensued. Our line with the Community could have been: 'If you want our waters, come and get them: we are sticking to 12 miles.' On the basis of such a line, unanimously adopted by the Irish, the Norwegians and ourselves (and by the Danes at least in respect of the Faroe Islands and Greenland) we might well have succeeded in securing, in the end, a status quo solution. As it was, instead of standing firm on a simple 12-mile position and being, if necessary, argued out of a part of it, we gave away (as the Clyde Fishermen's Association complained) six miles at the start; and had painfully thereafter to negotiate our way upwards again to 12.

13. It can be argued, against the case I am putting, that our six-mile proposal proved in the end far from vain or useless, since in effect it formed the basis of the agreement eventually reached between the Community and all the candidates. This is true. Six-mile limits have become, under the agreement reached, the basic normal limits at least until 1982 both for the candidates and for the present members of the Community themselves; and it was probably our proposal which led to this result. But it could of course have been reached in other ways.

14. Why was our handling of the issue of fisheries more uncertain, and more faulty, than our handling of other issues? Part of the reason, no doubt, is to be found in the simple fact that we failed to foresee the way in which and the intensity with which political pressures on the question of fishing limits would develop in this country. We did not at the outset realise how acute the question

would become; and in part our retreat from our opening position and the gradual stepping up of our demands as time passed was due simply to the mounting political pressure exercised upon us. But I do not think this is the whole reason. If our handling of the fisheries question was from the start rather unsatisfactory and unsteady, it is partly because the question only came alive when the Community adopted its Common Fisheries Policy on 30 June, 1970. In almost all other fields of the negotiation we had had months and even years to prepare our positions, and in this time intensive study by and co-ordination between all Departments concerned had led to the adoption of positions on which, on the whole, we were able thereafter to stand reasonably firm.

15. Had there been a Common Fisheries Policy in existence a year before negotiations began, we should no doubt have had time for much more thorough consideration between Whitehall Departments; for more far-reaching consultation with the fishing industry; and for more thorough contacts and exploration with our fellow-candidates. These might not have resolved all difficulties. There were inherent difficulties in the situation greater than in most others—the clash of interests between our inshore and distant-water fishermen, and the potential clash of interests between the candidate countries. We might still have come up with positions we should have had to modify; but I think we would have found the basis for a more consistent approach than we adopted.

16. It may perhaps be objected that we did, after all, have almost a whole year between the adoption of the Common Fisheries Policy on 30 June, 1970, and our first proposals to the Conference on Fisheries on 1 June, 1971. Why could we not have gone through these processes of consultation perfectly adequately in that period? The answer, I am afraid, reveals a weakness in our organisation. The only people who could effectively initiate and carry out these policy-forming processes were the people who were themselves heavily engaged throughout that year in all the other multifarious tasks of the negotiations. All were agreed, till late in May 1971, that fisheries should be left to be dealt with in the last stages of the negotiations. This consensus had, I fear, led to a natural, but probably harmful, postponement of the effort needed to hammer out an appropriate policy; and when, in May 1971, we suddenly had to produce a policy, there was not time for all the detailed consideration it deserved, and the first policy we produced proved mistaken.

17. Did this matter? I have already recorded my view that the eventual outcome was satisfactory. But I concluded also that the somewhat devious and unpredictable course we steered involved us in much avoidable trouble. We should have realised sooner than we did, and drawn the conclusions from such realisation, that the Norwegian position was such that we had in fact no prospect at all of recovering our fishing rights in the outer six miles of their coastal waters. It should have been clear to us sooner than it was that the Norwegians would not enter the Community at all unless they could keep virtually the whole of their exclusive 12-mile limits; and that they were in a position to ensure, as in fact they did in June 1971, that even if they were to accept six-mile limits in

theory they could keep our fishermen outside their 12-mile limits in practice. Strangely enough, we already appear to have realised this latter point in May 1971; yet we still proceeded, quite illogically, to put forward our six-mile limits proposal. And when we later turned round, the Fisheries Departments sometimes sought to move too far in the other direction. Even after we had proposed a status quo, they sought from time to time to adopt a new objective—namely, guaranteed 12-mile limits all round our coasts in perpetuity. And at one stage they argued that if we had to accept 12-mile limits in certain areas only, at least we should seek to oust from them those foreign fishermen who enjoy historic rights in them.

18. I now come to the most important subject of all, Community finance. Here, if we did make mistakes, it certainly cannot be claimed that we did so for lack of knowledge or time to prepare. Yet in this field I think, in the light of hindsight, that we may have made two mistakes.

19. The first possible mistake—and I emphasise that I certainly do not, and I think no one can, feel sure about it—was in our opening proposal of 16 December, 1970. We suggested (to ignore, as it was ignored, the lower figure in our two brackets) that we should pay 3 per cent of the budget in 1973 and 15 per cent in 1977. There were perfectly good, logical and defensible reasons for our proposal. But, as I have described in earlier chapters, it received an exceedingly hostile reaction from virtually all quarters in the Community. This is certainly no argument for concluding that we were wrong to propose these figures. Nevertheless, proposing so low a figure, especially for 1973, led the Community as a whole to harden its heart against us and to determine that we must be compelled to accept a very much higher opening figure. Is it possible that the opening figure we eventually had to accept (8.64 per cent) could have been lower if we ourselves had proposed a higher opening figure than 3 per cent? No one can tell. It seems to me likely that we could have avoided—not that it mattered unduly—some of the bitterness our proposal engendered if we had made our opening figure somewhat higher. We could, for instance, have taken a figure such as 3 per cent for our fair share of the running costs of the Community and added our proposal on to that, thus opening, for instance, with something between 5 and 6 per cent as our proposed contribution for 1973 and something perhaps a little above 15 per cent as our proposed contribution for 1977. Let us suppose we had proposed a range of 6 per cent to 16 per cent. What might have been the outcome?

20. First of all, we should have deprived ourselves of a good deal of room for manoeuvre; and that would have been dangerous. We should have been nearer than our actual proposal left us to our limits in the shape of acceptable ceilings. From 6 per cent the Community might have pushed us up to a point not lower than 8.64 per cent, but higher. On the other hand, we should I believe have avoided the really bitter and hostile Community reactions which our actual proposal gave rise to; and a better atmosphere might have led to a better settlement. It might even have led to a quicker one; but I conclude we should

in fact hardly have reached agreement sooner, on the principle already referred to in Chapter 32 that the work of the negotiations was bound to expand to fill the time available for it. Nor do I think that by avoiding the extreme hostility our actual proposal engendered we could have prevented the French from linking New Zealand and Community finance to their advantage: the gambit was too obvious. It could even be argued that without the crisis atmosphere of January to May 1971 in the Conference, due largely to our proposal on Community finance, it would have been harder to set up the Heath–Pompidou meeting.

21. The argument is in fact a sterile one, and no conclusion is possible. I raise it only because, though during the negotiations I never doubted the wisdom of our proposal, I have, in studying since the negotiations ended the course of events, been impressed by its possible disadvantages. In the end, I do not believe the point is an important one, or that we can be convicted of a mistake. I conclude that we would probably have come out more or less where we did whatever our opening proposal had been.

22. But I suggested in paragraph 18 above that we may have made a second mistake on Community finance. This mistake, if it was one, was one which we made at the very last moment, in the early hours of 23 June in Luxembourg. By then the package, New Zealand against Community finance, had been well and truly set up by the French and by the Community. I have described in some detail in earlier chapters what happened; and I will recall the salient points here. On 10 June, 1971, M. Schumann told Mr. Soames that if the Community were to give the New Zealanders as much as 50 per cent of the milk equivalent of butter and cheese in 1977, then the French could not come below 9 per cent as the figure for our financial contribution in 1973. On 18 June he told Mr. Soames that the same minimum of 9 per cent must apply if the Community moved to 63 per cent milk equivalent in 1977. We got 8.64 per cent as our budgetary proportion for 1973 and 71 per cent milk equivalent for New Zealand in 1977; and on the face of it this suggests that we did considerably better than M. Schumann was contemplating a few days earlier.

23. As recorded in earlier chapters, the Community steadily, on the night of 22–23 June, 1971, repeated that the proposals they were making on New Zealand were subject to a satisfactory agreement on the British contribution to the Community budget. And when the Community eventually put forward, late that night, their proposals for the budget—8.64 per cent in 1973 and 18.92 per cent in 1977, which we eventually accepted—the French insisted that the proposals made on Community finance were not open to negotiation, unless we wanted to reopen the question of New Zealand.

24. The question I am now raising is whether we should, in spite of this threat, have negotiated rather harder and longer than we did on the Community's proposals which I have just described. We did seek to get them reduced; two or three hours were spent, after the New Zealand question had been conditionally agreed, in discussing (outside the Conference, with the Community's

mediators M. Deniau and Mr. Wellenstein of the Commission) the figures the Community had put forward; and in settling, not altogether satisfactorily from our point of view, the limits of our contribution in the two corrective years of 1978 and 1979. Throughout this period the Community remained hard on their figures of 8.64 per cent for 1973 and 18.92 per cent for 1977, with no sign of give. These were figures Mr. Rippon had authority to accept (see paragraph 10 of Chapter 19). He received fresh authority (see paragraph 15 of Chapter 19) just before midnight on 22–23 June to accept not more than 9 per cent as our 1973 contribution.

25. Should we have fought on longer than we did? Should we have kept the Conference going until 7 or 8 a.m., instead of concluding at 4.30 a.m.? In raising this question I come back to the point I made in paragraph 2 of Chapter 17, namely that each 0.1 per cent of the 1973 budget meant £1,400,000. If we could have driven the Community down to say 8.5 per cent for 1973 and 18.75 per cent for 1977, we should have saved a little over £10 million in foreign exchange spread over the five years 1973 to 1977. Could we have done it, without risking a reopening of the New Zealand question, which we had just settled conditionally on terms which were indeed immensely satisfactory, but about the reaction to which of the New Zealand Government we were still extremely apprehensive?

26. Looking back, over a year later, at that June morning, I fear my conclusion is that we ought to have gone on trying a little bit longer than we did. I gave no such advice at the time. On the contrary, influenced perhaps too much by the circumstances and strains of the previous 48 hours, I felt it was reasonable that, being within our authority, we should settle. I feel no confidence that if we had gone on for two or three hours longer we could have moved the Community even a millimetre. But I should feel happier now if we had held out a little longer than we did.

27. Failure is always a mistake, so this catalogue of errors should record our failure to achieve an objective which we adopted at one stage. It was decided in August 1971 that it would be a good idea for the Treaty of Accession to be signed in the United Kingdom, and that this might prove acceptable to all concerned. In the middle of that month we made the suggestion to the Community Governments and the Governments of the other candidates. It was nowhere received with much enthusiasm, with the one exception of Denmark. The Belgians had long hoped and planned for signature in Brussels; the Italians, since the Treaty of Rome had been signed in their capital, had hoped that the Treaty of Accession might be signed there too. Nevertheless, the Italian reaction to our proposal was the warmest we got from a member Government. The French and Dutch, and naturally the Belgians, were very reserved. The Luxembourgers said they would support us if the Belgians released them from their pledge of support for Brussels. The Germans blew hot and cold. The Norwegians did not react at all for a long time but eventually gave a guarded acceptance.

28. Before long it became clear that the main obstacle to signature in the United Kingdom were the Irish; and the hesitations which they discreetly expressed in one or two Community capitals were sympathetically received. Had the Irish been ready to agree, we might have got all the others to do so; but the Belgians were able to take advantage of the situation to persuade the Six, soon after mid-October, that the Community should favour Brussels. By the end of the month we had decided to withdraw our proposal and to accept Brussels ourselves.

36

Did We Get a Good Bargain?

It is necessary, in the first place, to accept that in a certain sense the whole of our long negotiations were peripheral, accidental and secondary. The general movement of events in 1969 and 1970 revived the opportunity, and was much more important than the negotiations themselves. What mattered was to get into the Community, and thereby restore our position at the centre of European affairs which, since 1958, we had lost. The negotiations were concerned only with the means of achieving this objective at an acceptable price. They therefore had to be concerned with the Community as we found it, as it happened to be. None of its policies was essential to us; many of them were objectionable. But in order to get in we had either to accept them, or to secure agreed adaptations of them, or to negotiate acceptable transitional arrangements. We would never, had we been in the Community, have allowed a situation to develop which made it so difficult, for instance, to ensure fair arrangements for New Zealand dairy products or developing Commonwealth sugar, or to create a situation of equity in respect of our contribution to the Budget. But given the way things had developed in the Community without us, these were problems we had to confront and settle. As Lord Boothby put it in a letter to *The Times* published on 17 April, 1972: 'If we have now to accept one thousand regulations which we played no part in framing, we have only ourselves to blame.'

2. In a debate in the House of Commons on 20 January, 1971, Sir Anthony Meyer said: 'It has been said by many honourable Members in the debate that everything depends on the terms. Frankly, I do not think that it depends on the terms at all. I believe that it would be in the interests of this country to join the EEC whatever the terms.' In a debate in the House of Lords on 27 July, 1971, the late Lord Crowther said: 'It has always been clear, ever since we committed our biggest political mistake for 200 years by refusing to be one of the founder-members of the Common Market, that we should have to pay a price to get in, and the price is very much lower than I expected it to be. But, in any case, you do not haggle over the subscription when you are invited to climb into a lifeboat. You scramble aboard while there is still a seat for you.'

3. For my part, I have much sympathy with these views. As I have said, we had to get in. But given the economic and political reality of so many of the

problems which confronted us, and the state of Parliamentary and public opinion in this country, it was of course quite impossible for the Government to be so cavalier about the terms of entry as Sir Anthony Meyer or Lord Crowther were prepared to be. We had to get terms which could be publicly shown to be reasonable, advantageous and not too onerous. Did we do so?

4. For my part, I feel able to answer this question with an absolutely unhesitating affirmative. In doing so, I admit that I am relying to a considerable extent on our ability to defend ourselves and our interests when we have become a member of the Community. It seems to me reasonable to do so. The experience of many years, including those of the negotiations, taught us, if it needed teaching, that the power of any country outside the Community to influence its decisions and actions is extremely limited. The experience of the members of the Community themselves since 1958 should have taught us that their own power to protect their interests from within the Community is sufficient. One of the main problems with public opinion in this country during the negotiations—and the other candidate countries had the same experience—was to convince sceptics that matters not finally settled in black and white during the negotiations, but left over for future settlement by the institutions of the enlarged Community, would in fact, when it came to the point, be capable of being settled satisfactorily. This was partly of course because opponents of entry seized on every deferred issue to prophesy eventual disaster. But it was due also to a natural reluctance of the British public to take for granted that it was safe or wise to rely on our own ability to protect ourselves, as a future member, against the ravening sharks who would then be our colleagues and partners. I think this feeling did less than justice either to our capacity for looking after ourselves, or to the attitude of our future partners, or to the way in which, over the years, the Community has in practice worked.

5. There are quite a lot of questions which the negotiations, and the Treaty of Accession, have left open for future settlement, or which will come up for future review after the provisions of a transitional period have expired. In respect of every one of them, opponents of our entry claimed to foresee defeat. This I do not accept. Thus, I have no doubt at all that we shall have a good chance of ensuring better access to the enlarged Community (in practice, to our own market) for developing Commonwealth sugar producers after 1974 under the arrangements we negotiated than we could ever have achieved if we had insisted on reaching in 1971 a quantitative settlement to guarantee access from 1974 onwards. Arrangements for sugar, and for other commodities in which the Commonwealth territories concerned and in particular those of the Caribbean are vitally interested, may prove easier to achieve if these countries are prepared to opt for association of the Yaoundé type. It may prove difficult to persuade them to do so; but even if we are compelled to protect the interests of these countries against the consequences of a perverse choice, we shall probably in practice be able to get them more reasonable terms than we could possibly have

got for them by attempting to thrash out the details of their requirements in the negotiations in 1971.[1]

6. New Zealand is another case the critics have seized on. Ample provision—I have already in this Report recorded almost too often that I regard it as too ample—has been made for their interests until the end of 1977. What happens thereafter? It will no doubt depend in the main on the development of milk production and consumption in the world as a whole over the next five years and on the question whether or no it proves possible to achieve the 'International Agreement on Milk Products' referred to in Article 4 of Protocol 18. But even if no such agreement is reached, and even if milk surpluses in an enlarged Community continue to be embarrassingly large, the New Zealanders have pretty good protection. 'Appropriate measures to ensure the maintenance, after 31 December, 1977, of exceptional arrangements in respect of imports of butter from New Zealand ... shall be determined by the Council acting unanimously on a proposal from the Commission.' Opponents of our entry have argued that this crucial provision of Protocol No. 18 could be satisfied by authorising New Zealand to export to our market, after 1977, a few tons only of butter. In the light of the way the Community works, and of the influence we shall be able to exert in it, I simply do not accept that this is a realistic forecast. We shall I am convinced be able, by 1977, to ensure decent treatment for New Zealand butter exports after that year, if New Zealand still requires and deserves it.[2]

7. Then there is the question of fisheries. Shall we in 1983 suddenly find, in spite of all the transitional provisions we negotiated for the first 10 years, that the Community insists on reverting to its policy as it was in 1971 and begins fishing up to our beaches'? Nothing seems to me more unlikely. And the probability that we shall, before 1983, be able to negotiate a continuing arrangement which satisfactorily safeguards our interests was immensely reinforced by the fact that in this case the original Community policy was fundamentally changed by the negotiations, and in particular by the fact that the French joined with us and the other candidates in securing still more far-reaching derogations from the access provisions of the Common Fisheries Policy. In all these questions, and most of all in that of fisheries where the derogation lasts 10 years, we shall have ample time to prepare and promote the protection of our future interests.[3]

[1] This judgement was certainly borne out by the course of events. The sugar protocol to the Lomé Convention (the successor to the Yaoundé Convention) provided for guaranteed access to the enlarged Community at prices above the current world market levels of 1.2 million tons of sugar. Provisions similar to these have been included in each of the subsequent re-negotiations of the Lomé Convention.

[2] This judgement too was vindicated. Successive extensions of the arrangements in Protocol 18, albeit at somewhat declining volumes, were agreed periodically thereafter.

[3] This judgement is less easy to justify. Understandably, it was made in ignorance of the successive negotiations required to adapt the Common Fisheries Policy to take account of fisheries zones to 200 miles and of the accession to the European Community of two new members, Spain

8. The same goes for three other questions where in theory the result of our negotiations leaves our present arrangements at risk in the future: animal health, colorants used in food and antibiotics used in animal feeding-stuffs. In theory, once again, the Community's original provisions could revive to our disadvantage. In practice, it seems to me exceedingly improbable that they will. It is even less likely, to my mind, that the Community will suddenly, in 1982 (see paragraph 14 of Section II of Annex I), compel us to abandon the use in the United Kingdom, should we wish to maintain them, of measurements such as the fathom or the furlong, the bushel or the dram, let alone the mile or the pint (see page 130 of Part II of Cmnd. 4862, the Treaty of Accession).

9. Nor am I perturbed by the fact that in some of these cases the decision whether or not to continue arrangements advantageous to us has to be taken unanimously by the Council of Ministers, whether the requirement for such unanimity be overtly expressed as in the New Zealand Protocol or slurred over as in some other instances. This was a special bogy in the public relations aspect of our negotiations. Whenever we had to admit that a future decision crucial to our interests might have to be taken unanimously by the members of the enlarged Community, many people immediately assumed that we should be voted down and forced to accept an unsatisfactory outcome. Quite apart from the fact that Mr. Heath and M. Pompidou agreed that questions affecting the vital interest of any Member State could not be decided by a majority vote against it, this is simply not the way in which the Community has worked in the past or will work in the future. It is true no doubt that there are cases in which, on a strict construction of the texts, a unanimous decision will be required to do something necessary to protect our interest, and that failing such a decision the transitional arrangements will lapse and be replaced by the full rigour of the provisions they mitigate. But I remain unrepentantly convinced that this simply will not happen, if we do not want it to.

10. In considering therefore whether we got a good bargain, I am on the whole rather complacent. We had to accept some unwelcome arrangements in relation to agricultural transition; and some Canadian and Australian exports will suffer for it, as well as some interests of our own. In many other fields too we got less than we wanted. But none of these defects appears to me to be vital. So in respect of New Zealand, sugar, sterling, transitional arrangements for industrial and agricultural trade, fisheries, the ECSC and EURATOM, the Channel Isles and the Isle of Man and a dozen other questions, I refuse to admit to any qualms. This leaves the usual joker: Community finance.

11. Did we in this case have to accept an excessively burdensome settlement? That it is burdensome I will certainly not deny, nor conceal my view that in insisting on so high a contribution from us the Member States of the Community were a good deal less than generous. Nevertheless, I do not feel any real

and Portugal, with large fishing fleets and sparse fishing resources, both of which developments, together with the loss to the United Kingdom's fisheries fleet of access to Icelandic waters, occurred well after this account of the accession negotiations was written.

apprehension about the future. First of all, there is a reasonable chance that the Community's expenditure on agriculture, in respect of which we shall have to pay so much and receive so little, will tend to diminish rather than increase as a proportion of the total wealth of the Member States including ourselves. Second, there is no reason whatever for us to regard what seem to be the natural consequences of the arrangements reached and set out in the Treaty of Accession as necessarily immutable. It may be hard, though not necessarily impossible, to change the actual text of the Treaty or the Community's Finance Regulation. We shall have therefore, if the need arises, to seek relief by changing some other element of the equation; probably the pattern of Community expenditure.

12. We shall no doubt have, for a year or two, to see how things go and how heavy the burden upon us turns out to be. Even though the starting point for our contribution to the Community Budget is higher than for a long time I hoped and expected it would have to be, nevertheless in the first year or two at least the burden will not be overwhelming. Should it look like becoming too great or too inequitable, we should not assume that the enlarged Community will not be prepared to look at it again, even had we no handle to prompt them to do so. In the past the existing members of the Community frequently adapted the burden of contributions between them to restore a rough equity; we should not assume that this cannot somehow be achieved in the future, even though the rigidities of the system of *ressources propres* will make it harder than it used to be.

13. We have in fact, however, two handles to crank the Community into action if need be; and we must be ready to use them if things look like going wrong. The first is the Community's assurance, admittedly not enshrined in the Treaty of Accession but plainly on the record none the less, that, as recorded in paragraph 96 of our White Paper of July 1971, 'if unacceptable situations should arise the very survival of the Community would demand that the institutions find equitable solutions'. The second consists of the rather rash and sweeping predictions made by the Commission (see paragraphs 9 to 11 of Chapter 18) that the burden on us of our contribution to the budget would be very much less serious than we had claimed. These views of the Commission, once again, have no contractual status; but they are on the record, and we can invoke them if things look like going seriously wrong.[4]

14. One problem we shall encounter is that because of the long delays

[4] In the event, this issue did have to be addressed again. The first attempt was in the renegotiation undertaken by the Labour Government which came to power in 1974, when the Corrective Mechanism which subsequently proved to be of no significant use, was agreed; then again in the long series of negotiations which began in 1979 and culminated in the Fontainebleau European Council in 1984 when an abatement mechanism which reduced the United Kingdom's net contribution to the budget by two-thirds was agreed. Both the Community's assurance given in 1970 and the fact that the Commission's original calculations proved far off the mark underpinned these decisions which were in fact fundamental derogations from the Community's Finance Regulation.

involved in payments for agricultural purposes from the Community's budget, and the slow accounting procedures of the Community, it takes a long time to establish the precise budgetary outturn of any particular year. We should nevertheless be able to estimate pretty closely how things are going, and to be in a position, if they are going intolerably from our point of view, to demonstrate it soon enough. We must be prepared to do so promptly should the need arise.

15. So even on the question of Community finance, undoubtedly the most important and the least satisfactory of all, I feel no real apprehension that we shall find ourselves compelled indefinitely to accept a fundamentally inequitable situation.

16. I must however conclude this brief assessment of the terms we got by pointing out that, in a different sense from that already suggested in paragraph 1 above, they are largely irrelevant. Our success in the Community will depend less on the nature of the Community and the character of the terms on which we enter it than on our own domestic success, and in particular our own economic performance. The Community certainly offers us opportunities. But nothing could be more misleading or more dangerous than to suppose that it offers us a certain remedy for our deficiencies or a panacea to cure the ills from which we have suffered. If life in the Community proves successful and satisfactory for us, it will not be because we have entered it on these terms or on those, but because we succeed in adapting ourselves to the new environment it will provide, taking advantage of the opportunities it will offer and conducting our own life and business successfully. If we fail to make a success of our new position as a member of the enlarged Community, then we would probably fail even more disastrously were we condemned to remain outside it.

ANNEX I

Secondary Legislation and Authentic English Text*

* Not printed

ANNEX II

The Work of the Treaty Drafting Group

(By Mr. I. Sinclair)

The Drafting Group was effectively established during the month of September 1971 as a consequence of the statement made to us in Deputies on 28 July and our reply of the same date. It was then agreed that sufficient common ground had been established to enable the work of drafting the Treaty complex to begin.

2. Accordingly, on 10 September, the Italian Presidency took the initiative in sending an invitation to representatives of the six original Member States, and of the four acceding States, to participate in a first meeting of the Drafting Group to be held on 20 September. From the outset, it was envisaged that this should be a multilateral group consisting of delegations from the Ten, assisted by a delegation representing the Commission and served by the Council Secretariat. Given the pattern suggested by the Community delegation for the structure of the Treaty complex—namely, a single multilateral Treaty covering accession to the EEC and Euratom to be signed by the Six Member States and the four acceding States combined with a separate ECSC decision covering accession to the ECSC, to both of which would be annexed a single 'Act' containing the conditions of accession and the adjustments to all three Community Treaties—it was inevitable that the Drafting Group should be constituted as a multilateral group composed of representatives of all 10 delegations.

3. Before the first meeting of the Drafting Group, we had informal discussions with the Italian Presidency in order to clarify a number of procedural points. Throughout the summer break, the Council Secretariat and the Commission had been preparing initial drafts of provisions to be included within the framework of the Treaty complex. We had had an informal exchange of views with the Commission at the beginning of August on the form and content of the various provisions which would have to be drafted on transitional tariff matters. This informal exchange of views was extremely helpful as it enabled us to feed into the Commission some initial thoughts about the drafting of these transitional tariff provisions.

4. It was made abundantly clear at the beginning of the work of the Drafting Group that the various drafts prepared initially by the Council Secretariat or the Commission according to the subject matter and then presented to the

candidate countries were to be considered as *Presidency* drafts, tabled on the authority of the Presidency alone. This made it possible for the delegations of the Six to take a full and active part in the discussions within the group, since there was no question of considering the drafts prepared as a basis for discussion as constituting a formal Community position. In general, this operated greatly to our advantage, since it was possible to effect amendments to the drafts presented as a basis for discussion without appearing to depart from a fixed Community position.

5. There was, however, one major disadvantage in the method of work followed by the Drafting Group. The representatives of the six original Member States insisted upon scrutinising the drafts prepared by the Commission and the Council Secretariat before authorising the Italian Presidency to transmit them formally to the candidate countries. This had the unfortunate but inevitable consequence of interposing a considerable delay between the preparation of a series of draft articles and their formal transmission to the candidate countries. This delay was particularly marked in the case of the draft articles on agricultural transition. Although the Commission had begun work on the preparation of a series of draft articles on agricultural transition early in September, it was not until the beginning of November that we formally received the Presidency proposals; and the Presidency proposals we then received were incomplete, in that they omitted drafts of important provisions on safeguards and on beef and veal.

6. Fortunately, in the later stages of the work of the Drafting Group, this process of internal consideration by the Six of drafts prepared by the Commission or the Council Secretariat was effectively abandoned. But it was regrettable that the Drafting Group was effectively inhibited from even beginning consideration of the series of draft articles on agricultural transition until the beginning of November.

7. The Drafting Group took two important procedural decisions which sensibly affected the manner in which it carried out its task. The first procedural decision, taken at the outset, was to establish a group of jurists/linguists which would work in parallel with the Drafting Group itself. The underlying concept was that the Drafting Group would seek to establish an agreed (or nearly agreed) text in French which would then be referred to the group of jurists/linguists for the preparation of the other language texts. In principle, this was obviously a sound decision since it would have been impossible for the Drafting Group itself to establish agreed texts in all eight language versions. Had the Drafting Group tried to do so, it would inevitably have spent most of its time discussing linguistic niceties. There was, however, one minor unfortunate consequence. It rapidly became impossible for the group of jurists/linguists to follow the work of the Drafting Group, and the result was that, on occasion, the jurists/linguists made modifications to texts which had been agreed within the Drafting Group only with the greatest difficulty; it was then necessary to reopen discussion in the Drafting Group to reverse the amendments made by the jurists/linguists.

8. The second significant procedural decision of the Drafting Group was taken at a much later stage. By mid-December, all delegations were expressing anxieties about how to incorporate within the framework of the Treaty complex the various decisions of the Conference concerning technical and other adaptations to Community secondary legislation. Although work on the examination of Community secondary legislation had begun at a very early stage in the negotiations, there had been serious delays in the consideration by the Six of reports submitted by the Commission on their contacts with the delegations of the candidate countries. Even as late as December, we were still awaiting statements from the Community at the level of Deputies on a wide range of points arising out of the examination of secondary legislation. Fortunately, the Drafting Group were able to reach fairly quickly a broad measure of agreement as to the precise manner in which the necessary provisions concerning delays in the application of secondary legislation, transitional measures and technical adaptations to Community acts should be incorporated within the structure of the Treaty complex. Having done so, the Drafting Group thereupon immediately set up a Sub-Group whose mandate was to draw up the necessary texts and ensure that the various points agreed in the Conference were faithfully reflected in those texts. This Sub-Group on secondary legislation, under the Chairmanship of Trojan (Netherlands), worked very effectively and relieved the main Drafting Group of the burden of scrutinising the detail of most of what is now contained in the Annexes to the Act concerning the Conditions of Accession and Adjustments to the Treaties.

9. The Drafting Group began its work in late September by taking up a set of draft articles prepared by the Council Secretariat on institutional questions. This set of draft articles gave rise to no problems of substance, and the Drafting Group was quickly able to record agreement on the texts, subject to completing them in the light of later Conference decisions. The Drafting Group then moved on to more difficult sectors, namely, a series of draft articles on 'principles' (now Articles 1–9 of the Act) and a series of draft articles on transitional tariff measures (now Articles 31–49 of the Act). In dealing with these rather more difficult areas, the pattern of work which was adopted was to have a first reading at which points of difficulty were ventilated. There was then a pause for reflection, followed by a second and third reading at which possible solutions to these points of difficulty were discussed. Alternative formulae were advanced by different delegations (sometimes orally and sometimes in writing) in an endeavour to reach agreement. Sometimes, the Commission or the Council Secretariat were instructed to prepare redrafts in the light of the discussions.

10. The early discussion in the Drafting Group was reasonably fruitful. We were able to secure considerable improvements in the first Presidency drafts on 'principles' and on transitional tariff measures; we also managed to secure lesser improvements in the series of draft articles on capital movements and external relations. However, the French became more and more unwilling to discuss substantive points, particularly when the Drafting Group began its

consideration of the series of draft articles on agricultural transition. It is possible that the French began to realise, about the beginning of November, that the Drafting Group was increasingly involving itself in questions of substance rather than of mere drafting. Thereafter, the French representative in the Drafting Group became increasingly rigid in his approach, insisting that even very minor matters on which no specific agreement had been recorded in the Conference must be referred up to the Conference for decision.

11. By mid-November, it had already become clear, principally as a result of the rigid attitude taken by the French, that a number of issues could not be resolved at the level of the Drafting Group. Particular problems had arisen in the consideration of the series of draft articles on agricultural transition. These were not drafting problems, but rather problems of substance which had either not been covered in the Conference 'agreement' on agricultural transition or had been covered by a vague general formula which was open to differing interpretations. It had been our hope to confine to the minimum the number of issues arising from the work of the Drafting Group which had to be referred up to the level of Deputies (or to higher authority within the Conference) for further guidance. However, by the third week in November, it was already apparent that at least six or seven issues of this nature could not be resolved within the framework of the Drafting Group; and it was therefore decided that we ourselves should make a series of statements on these issues in the Conference at the level of Deputies. Once this decision had been taken, it was inevitable that an increasing number of issues arising out of the work of the Drafting Group would have to be referred up to the level of Deputies for decision. The rigidity of the French position in the Drafting Group became even more pronounced. No doubt they took the view at this stage that there was no mileage for them in acceding to individual United Kingdom proposals in the Drafting Group and that some kind of overall package would have to be assembled at the level of Deputies. Accordingly, during the month of December it became increasingly difficult to resolve even minor problems in the Drafting Group, and the number of points which had to be referred up to the level of Deputies began to accumulate, amounting in the end to some 30 points in all. At this point of time, the Drafting Group was severely handicapped by the fact that, on the Community side, issues which the group had been unable to resolve had to be considered by the 'Deputies of Deputies' of the Six. The Deputies of Deputies were, however, fully occupied in December with matters still outstanding in the negotiations at the level of Deputies. Accordingly, the Drafting Group was unable to get new instructions on the points which it had been unable to settle. Although this did not materially delay the work of the Drafting Group (since it was continually having to consider new proposals based on more recent Conference decisions), it did contribute (though it was not the main factor) to the decision that the aim of signature before Christmas must be abandoned.

12. It was indeed only in the second week of January that the Drafting Group began to receive the conclusions reached by the Conference at the level of

Deputies on some of the outstanding treaty drafting points. The final series of Conference decisions on outstanding treaty drafting points did not reach the Drafting Group until 18 January, and this meant that a great deal of work had to be done in the last two weeks of the Conference so that the various language texts would be ready for signature on 22 January.

13. Another difficulty which the Drafting Group had to face was the fact that, on certain key issues, the Presidency did not table proposals until the very last moment. This was particularly true of the provisions concerning opposability of existing international agreements (now embodied in Article 5 of the Act) and the entry into force of the Treaty of Accession itself (now Article 2 of the Treaty). The Drafting Group was unable to consider the content of these key provisions until the beginning of the week commencing 17 January. Fortunately, at any rate so far as the entry into force provision was concerned, we had taken an initiative as far back as November to circulate informally the text of what we thought would be an appropriate provision for entry into force. In the event, the Community proposal differed in some material respects from what we had originally in mind, but it did sufficiently cover the one vital issue (the possibility of non-ratification by one of the candidate countries) to make it acceptable to us. Again, it was fortunate that the Community proposal on opposability of existing international agreements also proved to be acceptable to us.

14. In the later stages of the work of the Drafting Group, we were, as has already been indicated, able to advance matters by circulating informally, or by tabling formally, drafts of certain provisions. Thus, in addition to the entry into force provision, the content of the Protocol on the Channel Islands and the Isle of Man owed much to a draft which we circulated informally to Community delegations in December. We also took the initiative in January in tabling a draft of what has now become Protocol No. 19 on Spirituous Beverages obtained from Cereals.

15. I should perhaps say something about the internal arrangements made by the United Kingdom delegation for the consideration of the various proposals tabled in the Drafting Group. From the beginning, we instituted a system in Brussels whereby 70 copies of every document to be considered by the Drafting Group were distributed to selected recipients in Whitehall. Full reports were sent by telegram on every meeting of the Drafting Group and specific instructions were sought in separate telegrams on the basis of these reports and of documents which had been circulated. As the work of the Drafting Group intensified, there was increasing difficulty in obtaining instructions in time and, occasionally, we had to seek instructions by telephone. But the delegation in Brussels were admirably served in this respect, and I would like to pay tribute to the promptness with which Departments in London reacted to requests for instructions.

16. Finally, a few words about the performance of individual delegations in the Drafting Group. The *French* began well but were handicapped by a change in their representation at the end of October. The new French representative

(M. Hades-Lebel) had not participated in the negotiations and was not sufficiently familiar with the background to the 'agreements' reached in the Conference. It was also obvious that he was bound by rigid instructions and had little or no room for manoeuvre in the group. The *German* representative (von Stulpnagel) was in general helpful although on occasions he appeared to be acting under some rather peculiar instructions from Bonn. But we were usually able to find a sufficient measure of common ground with him after private discussion, and he was particularly helpful over the rather delicate issue of how to incorporate within the Treaty complex provisions relating to the treatment of sugar after 1975. The *Netherlands* representative (M. Vijverberg) put in a variable performance. When he was in the Netherlands seat in the period before Christmas, he was inclined to be over-voluble and to argue for hours over drafting points of no real significance; he was also singularly lacking in an understanding of our presentational difficulties. He disclosed to us at one stage that, on practically all issues, he was acting on his own initiative and not on instructions from The Hague. However, he suffered a sea-change when, after the New Year began, he became Chairman of the Drafting Group. In this capacity, he did a very good job in concentrating discussion on the main issues and in achieving agreement in the group on a number of difficult points. He is an effective lawyer whose abilities are seen to their best advantage when he is constrained by the obligations of chairmanship. The *Italian* representative (Conti) was in the Chair till the end of 1971. On the whole he was a reasonably effective Chairman, although at times inclined to let the discussion continue unnecessarily. The *Belgian* representative (Van Ommeslaghe) was a complete cypher. He spoke only when pressed to do so by the Chair, and then simply to support the French position. He asserted Belgian interests on only one occasion—on a minor point connected with the drafting of the Protocol on Motor Vehicles in Ireland. *Luxembourg* was not represented in the Drafting Group and, in consequence, agreed to the assumption of the Chair by the Netherlands representative after 1 January.

17. The performance put up by the *Commission* delegation was, in general, unconvincing. Fresi, who led for the Commission, was, at times, stubborn and lacking in sensitivity. He also insisted, sometimes at the cost of considerable delay, in fielding the appropriate experts from the Commission; and it was quite clear that some of the experts were not familiar with the general framework adopted for drafting the Treaty provisions. We were occasionally treated to the spectacle of representatives from the Commission contradicting each other at successive meetings. The *Council Secretariat*, on the other hand, operated very effectively. The Secretary of the Drafting Group (Bandilla) was an able and efficient official who organised very capably the flow of documents. Furthermore the representative from the legal services of the Council Secretariat (Puissochet) was consistently helpful, and displayed considerable flexibility on a number of points of difficulty.

18. Of the other candidate countries, the *Norwegians* were well represented

in the group. They generally gave us support on points which we had raised, but they were of course sensitive on fisheries. The *Irish* put in a patchy performance. They were inclined to waste time unnecessarily on linguistic points, and they raised a difficulty at the last moment by pressing for signature of the Protocol on Irish regional policy. But they were reasonably co-operative on points where their interests did not clash with ours. The *Danish* delegation in the Drafting Group maintained a fairly studious silence except on agriculture where, more often than not, their interests were opposed to ours.

19. To sum up, the Drafting Group operated reasonably efficiently, given the problems with which it was confronted as a result of the way in which the negotiations had been conducted. Its difficulties stemmed principally from the fact that some of the earlier 'agreements' recorded in the Conference, particularly on agricultural transition and sugar, were vague and open to varying interpretations. It was noticeable that far fewer difficulties arose in the Drafting Group in relation to those matters on which fairly precise texts had been agreed within the framework of the Conference (e.g. New Zealand and Community finance).

APPENDIX I

Confidential Documents
(Arranged in Chronological Order)

A

WASHINGTON TELEGRAM No. 1896 TO FOREIGN AND COMMONWEALTH OFFICE OF 20 JUNE, 1970.

(See Chapter 29, paragraph 14.)

UNITED STATES ATTITUDE TOWARDS EUROPEAN ECONOMIC COMMUNITIES ENLARGEMENT

In recent months there has been an increase in the amount of public criticism in this country of EEC commercial policies and practices. Similar criticism has been expressed in private by some senior members of the administration, particularly those whose responsibility is in the fields of trade and agriculture. These developments may have given the impression that the United States is weakening in its traditional support for closer unity in Europe and that there is even a possibility of a major reappraisal of American policy. With the negotiations for enlargement about to start, you may like to have my assessment of the significance of these developments and the effect they may have on the attitude of the administration.

2. President Nixon's policy was set out in his statement on United States foreign policy for the 1970s which was sent to Congress on 18 February. In this statement he declared his firm support for 'a strengthening and broadening of the European, Community', explicitly recognised that United States interests would be adversely affected by Europe's evolution, but accepted that 'the possible economic price of a truly unified Europe is outweighed by the gain in the political vitality of the West as a whole'. This was not a new policy. Since his inauguration, President Nixon has consistently declared his support for the concept of European unity, notably at his Press conference on 4 March, 1969, on returning from his European tour. At that time, and subsequently, although the view was taken that it would be unhelpful to us to emphasise publicly United States support of United Kingdom entry, the State Department, with the President's authority, took every opportunity to make this point privately to diplomats in Washington and through United States missions overseas to other

governments. The 18 February statement was therefore no more than confirmation of existing policy. But it had the added weight of being included in a formal declaration drawn up as a result of a major and comprehensive review of United States foreign policy. Moreover, for the first time, mention was made of the need for the United States to make 'sacrifices in the common interest' as a necessary corollary to European unity.

3. This policy has been publicly reaffirmed by the President and other senior officials on several occasions since February. From all that has been said privately to myself and members of my staff by officials of the administration, from the President downwards, in recent months, I am reasonably confident that it will be maintained, even when, as has always been anticipated, some sectors of the economy are adversely affected. Perhaps the most significant reaffirmation of the policy was contained in the President's letter of 11 May to Mr. Wilbur Mills, Chairman of the House Ways and Means Committee, at the start of the Committee's hearings on the Trade Bill (my telegram number 27 Saving). In this letter, addressed to an audience who might be expected to be critical of his European policy, the President formally restated his support for enlargement, while emphasising the hope that, in the process of enlargement, due regard would be given to the commercial interests of the United States.

4. It is these interests which, as the prospect of enlargement gets nearer, have become more vocal in their criticisms. Agricultural producers are concerned about the effect of the common agricultural policy and, even though this policy may not be the only (or even in every case the main) cause, are able to point to a fall in EEC imports of United States agricultural products during the last few years. American wheat growers, in particular, complain, with some justification, that the EEC's subsidised wheat exports are cutting them out of third markets. United States industry foresees that the development of greater efficiency on the part of the advanced technologically based industries in the EEC will result in increased competition both in European markets and in third countries. Although, with few exceptions, United States trade does not so far appear to have suffered much damage (in fact the overall figures show that the reverse is the case), it is very widely assumed, in industrial and agricultural circles, that it is already being adversely affected and will be so still further as a result of enlargement.

5. There are, in addition, complaints about the bilateral preferential agreements which the EEC has negotiated with Mediterranean countries and which are attacked as being contrary to GATT. Similar objections are heard against the association agreements with former dependent overseas territories, which are likely to be increased in number on our entry by extension to the territories of the Caribbean. All these agreements involve not only preferential treatment for imports into the Common Market, but also reverse preferences, in favour of EEC exports, in the territories themselves. A further potential source of criticism lies in the negotiations on the future relations between the non-candidate EFTA countries and the enlarged Community. The United States

position on these is not yet defined, any more than are those of the Community or of the countries themselves. Different United States interests are likely to pull in opposite directions, but at least it is clear that there will be strong pressure on the administration to resist arrangements which provide these countries with the commercial benefits of membership without their having to accept the political obligations.

6. Within the Administration, the Secretaries of Commerce and Agriculture are inevitably in the forefront of the critics of the EEC. They may also have some support from the Treasury, on balance of payments grounds and because they may see the EEC's proposals for monetary unity as conflicting with United States policy on more flexible exchange rates. There have been suggestions that these agencies consider their interests were not taken sufficiently into account when the 18 February policy statement was drafted. The fact is that, as is made clear in the statement, the President's policy was decided on broad political and strategic rather than on economic grounds. We must expect however that, within the framework of this decision, the Administration will take vigorous action to protect United States interests. Most of the American complaints have already been ventilated in the GATT or in bilateral contacts with the Commission or individual members of the Six. Increasingly, as the negotiations proceed, we are likely to become similarly the recipients of United States representations. Some of these will be on aspects of existing EEC policy for which, as members or potential members of the Community, we are bound to assume a share of responsibility. Others will be on matters which arise in the course of the negotiations as the economic consequences for the United States of enlargement become apparent. I have no doubt that, in cases where United States interests consider they are particularly hard hit, there will be pressures, which the Administration may find irresistible, for retaliation. (Wilbur Mills has recently reverted to the iniquities of the EEC 'border taxes'. He told me in confidence earlier this week of his intention of attaching an amendment to the Trade Bill providing for countervailing duties on Community imports into the United States which receive such rebates: if such a measure made headway it could result in a major row between the United States and the Community.) These representations will be much publicised and, because of the President's deliberate low profile policy of non-intervention in European affairs, may sometimes give the impression that a shift in United States attitude is imminent.

7. Moreover, although at present opposition to EEC policies and concern about the possible consequences of enlargement emanate mainly from groups defending specific commercial interests, there is some evidence that their views are beginning to crystallise into a more co-ordinated pattern of opposition. In particular there is some support for the view that in the long term the EEC may develop into a gigantic trading area which will effectively discriminate against United States interests through a network of special preferential trading arrangements, public procurement practices favouring Member States, industrial policies designed to foster advanced technology industries at the expense of

their American competitors, and new standardisation and certification procedures which will tend to exclude American products. A number of those who think on these lines also profess to be disappointed at the lack of progress towards political unity in Europe and draw the deduction that what is in fact being created is no more than a preferential trading zone which will not only harm American agricultural and industrial interests, but will ultimately destroy existing international understandings on how multilateral trading should be conducted. This pattern of thinking is to be found at the lower levels of some of the agencies dealing with international economic relations and may in due course have some influence at higher levels. Nevertheless, it is still my expectation that any action which the United States Administration may consider is necessary to take in defence of American interests will be directed against modalities and individual policies of the EEC and will not imply any reversal of the basic United States support for the Community as the instrument through which the desired goal of European unity can best be realised.

8. It follows that a primary objective of our diplomacy in the United States (if not the overriding one) must be to reinforce the President's commitment to this basic support. There are, I believe, three things we can do in the context both of our bilateral relations with the United States and of helping the President to defend his policy against critics within the Administration and in Congress. The first is that we should take every opportunity to emphasise the importance we attach to making progress with the political integration of Europe, including closer defence co-operation alongside the economic development, and that we should, moreover, try to ensure that such progress is seen to be made. The second is that, during the course of the enlargement negotiations, we should make it plain that we recognise the legitimate concern of the United States to ensure that damage to their interests is minimised and that we are prepared to do what we reasonably can to achieve this. I realise that, in carrying out this second recommendation, we should have to be careful to distinguish between those criticisms of Community policies and actions for which there may be some justification and those which are simply ill-informed or self-serving. This distinction may not always be easy to make, still less to put over to the Congress, but at least we may hope it will be apparent to the President and principal members of his Administration. I realise how careful we must be in public utterances while the negotiations are in progress. The fact, however, remains that the more we can make these two points in public, the more we shall give the President ammunition which he can use against our critics here. Thirdly, we might consider the possibility of proposing to the Six and the other candidate countries that we should, at an appropriate stage, together take the initiative to declare our support for a further round of multilateral trade negotiations following on enlargement. This idea has been suggested, in confidence, by a member of the White House staff who considers that such a declaration would evoke a broad and positive response in the United States and would help to reassure American opinion about long-term trends in the commercial policy

of an enlarged Community. Despite the difficulties, I believe it to be worth pursuing.

Foreign and Commonwealth Office pass Bonn, Paris, Brussels, Rome, UKDEL EEC, The Hague and saving to Luxembourg, Stockholm, Vienna, Berne, Oslo, Copenhagen, Helsinki and Dublin.

FREEMAN.

B

TIMETABLE OF EVENTS AND PAPER ON TIMING SUBMITTED BY Mr. J.A. ROBINSON ON 17 JULY, 1970.

(See Chapter 7, paragraphs 5 to 7.)

1 January, 1971	France assumes Presidency of the European Communities
July 1971	Italy assumes Presidency of the European Communities
Late summer/ early autumn 1971	Conclusion of negotiations on major questions of substance
December 1971/ February 1972	Accession agreements signed
Calendar 1972	Ratification of the accession instruments by the existing members of the Community and the candidate countries. Passage of the necessary legislation by Parliament
1 January, 1973	Entry becomes effective.

TIMING OF OUR MEMBERSHIP OF THE EUROPEAN COMMUNITIES

Community views

Harmel told Mr. Barber on 30 June that the prospects for a successful conclusion of our negotiations for entry should be evident by the end of 1970. De Koster on the previous day had told Mr. Barber that if the negotiations had not succeeded in 18 months they would have failed; and Scheel has said that every effort must be made to conclude negotiations by Christmas 1971. On 6 July, Luns is reported to have told the Press that it would be 'towards next April' that it would be possible to say whether negotiations would succeed. On a number of occasions the retiring President of the Commission (Rey) has said that he envisaged negotiations lasting until the end of 1971; ratification taking place during 1972 and British entry on 1 January, 1973. Barre, the hostile French Commissioner responsible for monetary affairs, said before Christmas that he anticipated negotiations lasting two years and ending in failure.

Our own working assumption

2. Against the background of views expressed in the Community and what has seemed from our point of view to be a reasonable expectation, we have

taken as the framework for planning purposes that we shall, if negotiations succeed, enter the Communities on 1 January, 1973.

3. There are three phases which we must go through, if we are to enter:

(a) the completion of negotiations on the substantive issues;
(b) the drawing up of an accession instrument in legal form;
(c) the ratification of this instrument and passage of the necessary legislation by Parliament.

There may be, and we would hope will be, some overlap between (a) and (b)—i.e. before the conclusion of substantive negotiations, it would be possible to begin work on casting results into a legal instrument of accession. But, although we shall have to prepare legislation in advance (and indeed an official Committee will begin work on this in the autumn), (c) will have to wait for the conclusion of (a) and (b). (Although preparation of legislation will begin this autumn, it will not be possible to present it to Parliament until an agreement with the Community is signed.) The time required to complete (a) is the most difficult to foresee, but it is the part of the accession process which we can most easily influence. (b) will require a number of months. We have thought it politic to allow 12 months for ratification; but the Six concluded ratification of the Rome Treaty in 9 months, and there is no reason why the same sort of time-scale should not suffice for ratification of our accession. Allowing for some overlap between (a) and (b) it therefore seems wise to plan on the assumption that we shall need some 15 months between the conclusion of the substantive negotiations and our formal entry.

Time required for the substantive negotiations

4. So the essential question is: how long will substantive negotiations take?

5. Harmel is almost certainly expecting too much when he says that the prospects for a successful conclusion should be evident by the end of this year. On the other hand, while negotiations could take 18 months, or longer, it is probably true that conclusions will be drawn about their likely success or failure well before the end of next year. The 1961–63 negotiations were probably within three months or so of concluding substantive work when de Gaulle broke them off, and they had at that time been going on for 15 months. De Gaulle then described them as 'interminable' and there were many who felt that they had gone on a long time. In 1961–63 we set out to negotiate about far more issues than we want to see covered this time.

6. We must therefore accept that, if for other reasons we want to play the negotiations long, we risk allowing boredom and disillusion to build up in the Community and thus contribute to the impression that the negotiations are bound to fail. If it is not clear by July 1971 that negotiations are within reach of success, it will be very difficult to revive belief in the possibility of success when the conference resumes in September 1971 after the summer break.

Other factors in the negotiations

7. Two other points involved in the negotiations are important. First, the Chairmanship on the Community side, which will be:

July–December, 1970—Germany
January–June, 1971—France
July–December, 1971—Italy
January–June, 1972—Luxembourg

The Italians in Brussels are not generally good in the chair; and at Ministerial level there is the continual risk of changes. It would probably be better to bring matters to a head under French Chairmanship not only because it will be more proficient, but also because having the chair may inhibit rather than enhance French tactics.

8. The longer negotiations go on, the more new decisions will be taken on Community policies without our participation, and the greater the risk that these new decisions will present us with new problems. This is especially so in monetary and industrial policy.

Factors not directly related to the negotiations

9. Before considering what we can do, and what it would be advisable to do to influence the timing of the point at which negotiations on substance are brought to a head, we should have in mind a number of facts not directly involved in the negotiations.

Elections:

10. (i) *our own elections* must take place at latest by mid-1975. If we suppose entry into the European Communities at the beginning of 1973, and even if we do not get an initial 'standstill' or 'initiation' period at the start of our transitional period, the disadvantageous consequences of membership will not have begun seriously to bite before the first half of 1975. Assuming a five year transitional period (we need not assume less and may get more), we should by 1975 be applying two-fifths of the increase in food prices involved in membership and paying over to Community funds some two-fifths of whatever is agreed as our base key for contributions (in money terms, this might mean payment of between $250 million and $300 million in 1975). Tariffs *vis-à-vis* the Community would also have been reduced by two-fifths. But the experience of the Community has shown that the effects of tariff reductions are discounted in advance. A considerable increase in trade between Britain and the other members of the enlarged Community could therefore be expected to have taken place before 1975. We would not be obliged to make any tax changes in 1975 (though we may choose to make them for other reasons);

(ii) *elections in France* next take place for the national Assembly in the late spring of 1973. (The next presidential election should be in June 1976.) It could be argued that, with the increasing economic strength and political independence of Germany, public opinion in France might be more inclined as time goes on to favour our accession, and to criticise French policies which prevented it, and that therefore the months immediately preceding the elections to the French National Assembly would be good ones in which to bring matters to a head. But the French Government, if it wants to be difficult, should not find it impossible to show that it is delaying matters for reasons of 'European' and French national interests and in any case it is difficult to believe that we could continue negotiations into the second half of 1972 with any hope of maintaining a belief in a successful outcome;

(iii) the next *elections in Germany* are in September-October 1973 and are not therefore likely to influence the outcome. But the prospects for the present coalition Government in Germany and in particular the fate of its Eastern policy could be an important factor. If it becomes clear that Germany's Eastern policy has failed or is not going to produce early results, it is likely that the German Government will be increasingly inclined to fall back on Germany's relationship with France, and be less inclined to stand up to French demands in the negotiations with us in Brussels;

(iv) the next Presidential *election in the United States* is not until November 1972. It would clearly be desirable to conclude our negotiations and enter the Communities well before then;

(v) the other Parliamentary elections in Europe are not likely to be an important factor. They are: in the Netherlands, between the spring of 1971 and the spring of 1972; in Italy, May 1973, at least; in Belgium, spring 1973 at least.

Our own economic position

11. Developments over the next few months could, of course, improve our economic prospects. But it would be most unwise to assume that our balance of payments will continue at its present strength beyond 1971. This means that there is a risk that we shall look to the Six less attractive as a partner as 1972 approaches, and that our task of convincing home public opinion that we can stand the cost of membership will be harder.

12. More general economic factors also point to a short rather than a long period for substantive negotiations. As long as the outcome of negotiations is uncertain, Governments and industry and agriculture will be unable to take planning decisions except on the basis of a guess as to the outcome. This will affect developments in world trade, where it will be difficult to reach conclusions, and in some cases even begin serious work, on further reductions in barriers to trade; and domestic and European industry, where the basis for investment and other decisions will be uncertain; and domestic agriculture where the direction which expansion should take will be impossible to plan.

Our ability to bring matters to a head

13. The central issue in the negotiations is our contribution to the Community's budget. Once that is settled in outline, it will be clear that the negotiations will succeed: there are not likely to be any other breaking points on either side. We cannot expect to get a satisfactory settlement of this issue within the context of the negotiating procedures which the Community are offering us—meetings at Ministerial level with the Council of Ministers, at senior official level with the Permanent Representatives of the Six and in working parties. The normal negotiating machinery will no doubt resolve the other issues in due course, and our work on Community finance can clear the ground by establishing the facts and by setting out the theoretical possibilities. But the breakthrough will come, if it comes at all, as a result of an appeal to the Six on Community finance at the highest level. This points to a suggestion from our side at the appropriate moment for a summit meeting to attempt to settle this issue in principle. It would be important that Pompidou himself should attend such a summit. Timing apart, there could be advantage in having him in the chair on the Community's side. To achieve this, in addition to inviting him, we must make sure that Brandt comes. That would be the occasion for deploying the political arguments and implications in an all out bid to get an acceptable settlement.

14. It will clearly be open to us, since we must ourselves take the initiative for such a conference, to choose our own moment, once we have allowed sufficient time for the groundwork to be covered. It should be possible to cover the groundwork in six months, mid-September to mid-March. So, in the light of the factors set out early in this note, the basic choice is between bringing matters to a head at a summit meeting before Easter or bringing matters to a head in May or June. (The latter date would still allow time following the summit to complete agreement on the outlines of a detailed settlement before the Community went on holiday a the end of July.)

15. Because success on the Community finance issue, if we achieve it, will mark the turning point and mean that the negotiations are bound to succeed, it should be our aim to bring any other essential issues (even though they may not be breaking points) to the boil at the same time. There are only two such issues: provision for New Zealand and provision for developing Commonwealth sugar producers. It so happens that both these issues will inevitably, because of the balance of payments and levy aspects involved in their solution, become associated with the Community finance issue.

Conclusion

16. The conclusions of this paper are:

(i) there is no reason, from the point of view of domestic political considerations, to delay the conclusion of the substance of negotiations beyond next July;

(ii) there are no other arguments for delaying beyond July 1971, and some important reasons for trying to conclude matters in substance one way or the other by then;

(iii) it will pay us—indeed it is the only way in which we shall get a satisfactory conclusion on the key issue of Community finance—to seek a summit meeting with the Community at a moment which to a large extent can be of our choosing between March and July of next year. From the point of view of our balance of payments prospects, and for considerations of economic planning generally, the early date is preferable. As far as it is possible to make a judgment now, nothing would be gained by deferring a decisive meeting from March until June. And a summit before the end of June would make it easier to commit Pompidou personally;

(iv) if this timetable is acceptable for planning purposes, it will not be too soon to start a major exercise with public opinion in September, though it will be important to keep some extra effort in reserve until the early part of next year.

C

RECORD OF A CONVERSATION BETWEEN Mr. RIPPON AND M. SCHUMANN IN PARIS ON 9 NOVEMBER, 1970.

(See Chapter 7, paragraph 14.)

Present:

Right Hon. Geoffrey Rippon, QC, MP	M. Maurice Schumann
HE Right Hon. Christopher Soames	HE M. Geoffroy de Courcel
Sir C. O'Neill	HE M. Boegner
Mr. Tickell	M. Alphand
	M. Cuvillier

M. Schumann asked how Mr. Rippon saw the next steps ahead.

2. *Mr. Rippon* said that the negotiations should be lifted on to the political level as soon as possible. He hoped that during the forthcoming French Chairmanship of the Council of Ministers the essentials of the negotiations could be settled as a result of Anglo/French co-operation and initiative. At the very least he hoped no one would think or have reason to think that the negotiations constituted another duel between Britain and France. There must be an agreement between the candidates and the members as a whole. As for the conduct of the negotiations he wished to repeat that we were not putting forward demands but rather discussing problems and the possible solutions to them. If the British and French did sometimes find themselves in conflict, it was perhaps because the French were better negotiators than their colleagues. It was therefore all the more important that there should be a broad Anglo/French consensus. Herr Brandt had said recently that Germany was the driving force for the enlargement of the Communities. This was not a healthy idea: we hoped

the French were equally forceful in that respect. *M. Schumann* interjected that Herr Brandt had been addressing the Bundestag. *Mr. Rippon* continued that, so far as he could judge, all were now agreed on the objective of enlargement. It had been argued that during the last negotiations we were not sufficiently single-minded and ready to draw the necessary conclusions. But whether this was true or not then, it was not true now, and we were ready to make the necessary sacrifices provided the right terms could be found. He had several times referred to the need for haste. Apart from his desire to see the essentials of a settlement during the French Chairmanship, there was also the political problem of how to present the negotiations to public opinion in Britain as in Europe. He did not want anyone ever again to have the occasion for saying that the negotiations were interminable. Public opinion simply would not understand how a matter of this historic importance for Europe could not be settled fairly quickly if the political will to succeed was present on both sides. No British political leader would like to face a Party conference next autumn with the same story which he had given to the Party Conferences this autumn; in other words that we were looking for fair terms and that when these were found they could be recommended to Parliament and the country.

3. *M. Schumann* said he hoped very much that it would be possible to decide the essentials of the negotiations during his Chairmanship. He nevertheless had to be cautious and could make no promises. It would be difficult to fix too clear a timetable in advance. *Mr. Rippon* said we should still do our best and make early success our objective. There were only four major problems: New Zealand dairy products, sugar, transitional arrangements and Community finance.

4. *M. Schumann* said that he did not know whether the answers on these four points would make a satisfactory package. The key problem was that of Community finance. The French approach was strictly practical: the French wanted all members to enjoy fair and competitive conditions on the same terms. There were provisions in the Treaty of Rome for all members to help each other in the event of unusual or special conditions of strain arising for any one of them. The French had used these provisions in the past and the British would be entitled to do so once they were full members. Was the British Government fully aware of this? *Mr. Rippon* said that no one wanted a bad apple in the barrel. It was reasonable for all concerned to make sure that there would not be one, or that conditions of entry did not make Britain one. *M. Schumann* repeated that there were sufficient safeguards in the Treaty of Rome and Britain could count on them if need should arise. *Mr. Rippon* said that it would be useful if the French could emphasise this. We did not want to play the numbers game any more than the French. But we had to have solid assurances. In the case of New Zealand for example, we wanted a continuing arrangement to help the New Zealanders, subject of course to review.

5. Mr. Rippon went on that in M. Harmel's original statement of 30 June, he had said that the Community would give us some guidelines on how to cope with Commonwealth problems. Those who criticised our proposals for New

Zealand or Commonwealth sugar should know that we had not yet received any such guidelines. We would in fact value them. He nevertheless wished to get away from the whole idea of the negotiations being a series of demands and counter-demands. We had to settle things between friends and allies. The British public was apprehensive about what would happen when we joined the Community, and these fears could only be allayed by discussing the major problems as we had discussed such minor ones as pig meat, eggs and liquid milk in a friendly and co-operative spirit. It was interesting that he faced questions in the House of Commons not on these questions where fears had generally been allayed but on others where fears remained lively.

6. Mr. Rippon continued that it would be mistaken to regard the problems over New Zealand dairy products and Commonwealth sugar as British problems. They were rather an aspect of the Community's relations with the outside world. *M. Schumann* said that this was an interesting thought. Perhaps relations with New Zealand and the Commonwealth sugar producers should be regarded in the same category as those with the non-candidate countries of EFTA. *Mr. Rippon* said that the vital requirement was to see all these problems from a Community point of view. We would be very ready to do so as soon as we were members.

7. Mr. Rippon said that he had so far spoken on the assumption that the negotiations would succeed. He did not like to think what would happen if they failed. There would certainly be a period of very sour relations between Britain and the members of the Community but he thought at the end of it we would have to take things up again. All this was avoidable and with M. Schumann's help could be avoided. *M. Schumann* said that the negotiations represented a great chance for Britain. So far as Europe was concerned it represented a risk but it was a risk that the French were ready to take for political more than economic reasons. *Mr. Rippon* replied that it was a great chance for Europe. The British were ready to take the same risk for the same reasons.

D

UNITED KINGDOM PAPER ON COMMUNITY FINANCE CIRCULATED TO THE CONFERENCE ON 16 DECEMBER, 1970.

(See Chapter 18, paragraph 16.)

Following the decisions of the first Ministerial meeting in Brussels on 21 July, the United Kingdom Delegation set out in a paper (GB/9/70 of 23 July) the best and most realistic estimates which the British Government have been able to make of the effect of applying the Community financial regulations without adjustment in a Community of Ten. At the meeting of Deputies on 4 November (summary of conclusions in GB/31/70) the Community Delegation communicated to the British Delegation a paper by the Commission (GB/33/70) with the comment that the Council of the Community agreed with the general lines of this paper's conclusions particularly those expressed in paragraph 20.

2. In his statement, at the third Ministerial meeting on 8 December, Mr. Rippon remarked on the consequences of the sort of ideas which have been reported as under consideration in the Community in this context. In particular, if enlargement took place on this sort of basis, there would be a straight reduction in the financial contribution of each Member State of the present Community of the order of 30 per cent, and this reduction would be in addition to substantially increased agricultural exports from the existing members of the Community to the United Kingdom at higher prices, as a result of changes in the pattern of trade following the accession of the world's largest food importer. The assumption by the United Kingdom of a large share of the budgetary burdens at present borne by the Member States of the Community would moreover take place in the early years of transition, when a new member like the United Kingdom would have to adapt to Community practice in many fields (some of which would by themselves involve a considerable burden to the United Kingdom's balance of payments) without the prospect of Community payments from which the United Kingdom could benefit significantly, and before the dynamic consequences of entry (to which the Commission have referred in their document GB/33/70) had taken effect.

3. Against the background of the sort of ideas which the United Kingdom Delegation believe to have been expressed by the Commission, the United Kingdom Delegation has considered making proposals which would be equally extreme. Since, on the basis of the calculations submitted to the Conference in document GB/9/70, or any broadly similar calculations, any base key for the United Kingdom over about 5½ per cent would involve a net gain to the existing members of the Community additional to the gain to them which our increased agricultural imports from them will represent, it would be understandable if we were to propose that the United Kingdom key should be of the order of 6 or 7 per cent.

4. But, as Mr. Rippon said at the third Ministerial meeting on 8 December, the United Kingdom wants to integrate into the Community system with the minimum disturbance to all concerned, and wishes for its part to conduct the negotiations without recourse to extreme bargaining positions. The United Kingdom Delegation consequently wishes to put forward proposals which represent a reasonable point on which to conclude.

5. The Commission's paper (GB/33/70) compared the United Kingdom with the Federal Republic of Germany as the member country of the Community whose economic structure was nearest that of the United Kingdom. While there are clearly a number of structural differences between our economy and that of the Federal Republic, we have nevertheless used two independent methods of comparing our prospective position in relation to the Community budget with that of the Federal Republic. Firstly, we have used the estimates in GB/9/70, which show that if the net transfer burden imposed on us by the end of the transitional period were to be no bigger, relative to our GNP, than that

which Germany would then be paying, our basic key would have to be fixed at about 13 per cent. Secondly, we have noted that Germany's base key has been set at a level which will mean that in 1977, the third year of full operation of the 'ressources propres' system, Germany's contribution will be limited to a rather smaller share of Community expenditure than her expected share of the Community's GNP, even though she will be receiving much larger benefits from Community expenditure than the United Kingdom could hope to receive. On this basis an equivalent key for the United Kingdom would be 15 per cent.

6. In the light of these comparisons and the considerations in paragraph 2 above, the United Kingdom Delegation proposes that the United Kingdom's base key should be in the range of 13–15 per cent.

7. We propose that this key should apply in the fifth year of our membership of the Communities; and that our contributions to the Community's budget should build up to this key over the first five years of our membership in equal annual steps starting from a notional zero per cent in the year before accession. After the period of five years of build-up to the basic key, the correctives provided for in decision number 243 of 21 April should limit variations in the United Kingdom's contribution from year to year for a further period of three years. This would follow precisely the arrangements on which the existing members of the Community agreed for themselves in April 1970; and the build-up to the key by steps follows the arrangements made by the Community in January 1962.

8. The United Kingdom Delegation is confident that the estimates in GB/9/70 give as fair a picture as is now possible of the likely consequences of applying to a Community of Ten the existing financial arrangements without modification. The United Kingdom Delegation has noted the view of the Community that they do not find these calculations give a valid picture of the results of applying the financial regulations in a Community of Ten in eight years' time. The United Kingdom Delegation further notes the Community's view that both the total amount of the Community budget for 1978 and the composition of its expenditure and the proportion of the different expenditures within it are uncertain; that the Community will undergo considerable transformation which should take shape precisely within the 10-year period dealt with in the United Kingdom paper GB/9/70; and that policy developments within the Community could result in an entirely different structure for the Community budget and for intra-Community transfers. We also note the Community's view that the Community's efforts to eliminate agricultural surpluses by a suitable prices policy and by structural reforms should lead to a better balance of markets and a reduction in certain agricultural expenditures; and that it would be abnormal, 10 years after the end of the transitional period, for agricultural expenditure to continue to constitute almost the whole of the Community budget.

9. While noting the Community's statement that, on the basis of a hypothetical budget of 6,700 million UA, the United Kingdom could be expected to receive between 12½ and 15½ per cent and pay nearer 20 per cent than

25 per cent, the United Kingdom Delegation is bound to be sceptical about these forecasts which are not substantiated by detailed argument. The United Kingdom Delegation consequently notes with satisfaction the view of the Commission, with which the Community delegation specifically agreed, that, 'should unacceptable situations arise within the present Community or an enlarged Community, the very survival of the Community would demand that the institutions find equitable solutions'. It is the United Kingdom's view that the concept underlying this statement should be recorded in a suitable manner in the agreement on the enlargement of the Communities.

E

FOREIGN AND COMMONWEALTH OFFICE TELEGRAM TO PARIS No. 718 of 31 DECEMBER, 1970, ON THE SUBJECT OF A SUMMIT MEETING.

(See Chapter 33, paragraph 6.)

EUROPEAN ECONOMIC COMMUNITIES NEGOTIATIONS: POSSIBLE FURTHER SUMMIT MEETING

There have been a number of reports in recent weeks that the possibility of holding a further summit of the Six during 1971 might be considered if the course of negotiations for our entry seemed to make this a desirable move. Of these reports the only one which became general knowledge was that arising out of the Brandt/Colombo talks at the end of November (Rome telegram No. 889).

2. This is not an idea to which we wish to give further currency at this stage. A summit of the Six would present two major dangers from the point of view of our negotiations:

(a) once it had been decided to call a summit of the Six, negotiations in Brussels would be bound to stagnate pending decisions to be taken at the summit;

(b) there would be a danger that the summit of the Six would conclude by defining a position for the Community to adopt in negotiations with us which would be too rigid to change and too disadvantageous for us to accept.

The second of these disadvantages would not attend a summit of Seven. And there might be circumstances in which we would find a summit of the Seven (or the Ten) useful. But we must recognise that we would be most unlikely to be able to achieve a summit meeting of the Seven without there having first been a summit meeting of the Six.

3. Whatever views we held on this question, they would be unlikely decisively to influence what the Six decide to do. And it is not something on which we want to volunteer views. If however you are asked for views, you should say that for the present we are satisfied with the pace of the negotiations in Brussels,

and feel that the best course for all concerned is to concentrate on maintaining the pace in Brussels and concluding negotiations there in substance by the middle of the year. The number of outstanding issues of importance is small and this timetable is perfectly feasible given goodwill. If at a later stage, and contrary to our hopes and expectations, negotiations in Brussels were to run into serious trouble then a summit meeting might be desirable. But this could only be judged at a much later stage and we would hope that it would not prove necessary at all. Were it to be held it would be most important that the arrangements should be such as to enable us to play a full part in the discussions: it would not help to resolve difficulties arising in the Brussels negotiations if a separate summit meeting of the Six simply led to a hardening of the Community's position.

DOUGLAS-HOME.

F

FOREIGN AND COMMONWEALTH OFFICE TELEGRAM TO WASHINGTON, No. 4 OF 1 JANUARY, 1971.

(See Chapter 29, paragraph 18.)

THE UNITED STATES AND COMMONWEALTH ASSOCIATION WITH THE EUROPEAN ECONOMIC COMMUNITIES

On 30 December in the course of a call on Gallagher to discuss other matters, Rogers (Economic Counsellor at the United States Embassy) raised the question of association with the EEC for Commonwealth African and Caribbean countries, ostensibly in the context of generalised preferences and international trade policy.

2. Speaking on instructions, he said that the United States Administration had strong objections to the offer of associate status to these countries, on the grounds that association would enlarge an already discriminatory trading *bloc* and would be a backward step in the liberalisation of world trade. The Americans would regard any such arrangement as contrary to Articles I and XXIV of GATT. It would be particularly unfortunate at a time when the Administration were doing their best to keep protectionist pressures in check. Moreover, Congress were beginning to adopt a more sympathetic attitude towards GATT, and this tendency might well be reversed if the EEC association arrangements were extended. Rogers said that his instructions were to put American views on record: Tresize would probably be in London on 14 and 15 January for discussions on our agricultural levy proposals and would wish to discuss the question then.

3. Gallagher rehearsed the history of our request for association for these countries. There was nothing new in what we were seeking. Moreover, while we were in favour of the widest possible measure of trade liberalisation, given

the Yaoundé Convention to which we would have to subscribe on joining the Community, it was inevitable that we would seek arrangements for Commonwealth countries enabling them to obtain free entry for their exports to the enlarged Community as compensation for the competition which they would face in the British market from the existing associates. We were simply safeguarding the interests of developing countries who would otherwise be placed at a disadvantage.

4. Sir Con O'Neill summoned Cleveland (Minister Economic at the United States Embassy) this morning. He said that the Chancellor of the Duchy had been advised of Rogers' approach, and was deeply concerned about its significance for the EEC negotiations as a whole.

5. Sir Con O'Neill repeated that there was nothing new in our seeking offers of association for Commonwealth countries. It had been agreed in principle in the 1961 negotiations: and the Community had made clear in their 1963 declaration of intent that options including association were available to territories economically comparable to the existing associates, quite irrespective of our negotiations. This offer had been open ever since and it was by virtue of it that Nigeria and East African Commonwealth countries had concluded association arrangements with the Community. Although therefore it was an essential part of our present negotiating position to obtain offers of association, all we were doing in effect was confirming the existing position. We had received confirmation that the options open under the declaration of intent held good and were available for nine African Commonwealth countries: there was no reason to suppose that they would not be confirmed in respect of other countries.

6. It was an essential part of our negotiating position since 1961 that we must be able to do something for countries in this position. This had been made clear in the first negotiations, again by Mr. George Brown in 1967 and by Mr. Barber in Luxembourg on 30 June, 1970. M. Harmel had said at the same meeting in Luxembourg that any country which wished to join the Community would have to accept the Community's existing arrangements. Among these arrangements was association under the Yaoundé Convention, and we could not accept this without seeking to protect the interests of comparable Commonwealth countries. Otherwise these countries would be at a severe disadvantage. The UNCTAD generalised preferences scheme would not cover their interests because of its relatively limited coverage.

7. The offer of association was a central part of the whole package which Her Majesty's Government would have to present to Parliament and public opinion in this country at the end of the negotiations. We felt there was some inconsistency between the strong objections now expressed by the American Government and the strong general support of our membership of the Community most recently expressed by President Nixon to the Prime Minister. We did not wish to be unduly alarmist but we felt that, given the nature of the package which we should have to achieve, there was some risk to the whole negotiation in the position now expressed by the United States Government.

8. Moreover, we were surprised that action should have been taken at this time. If we succeeded in our negotiating objective and if the Commonwealth countries concerned chose to accept association, then it would not be until the beginning of 1975 before it took effect. The countries concerned would participate, as we would, in the renegotiation of the Yaoundé Convention. In the meantime, in the event of Commonwealth countries accepting association, it was foreseen that there should be a freeze in existing trading relations with those countries. Sir Con O'Neill concluded by underlining the concern we all felt.

9. Cleveland said that whilst we were concerned with the negotiations the American concern was with the future of the world trading system. He rehearsed the objections that the Americans had always expressed on the Yaoundé Convention and association arrangements with, e.g. Tunisia and Morocco. He thought the timing of the present American approach was the result of concern in Washington about the gradual acquisition by the Community of 'a world-wide trading empire', which both worried those most interested in liberal trading arrangements and put arguments into the hands of protectionists.

10. The American attitude to generalised preferences had always been largely influenced by the thought that other preferential arrangements such as the Yaoundé Convention would wither away when it came into force. In this they had always been encouraged by the Germans and the Dutch but whenever Yaoundé had had to be renegotiated the French had insisted on a continuance of existing arrangements with no provision of degressivity. The thought that there might be a further but extended Yaoundé Convention, particularly one which maintained existing arrangements, caused them a great deal of difficulty. And he wondered whether, if other preferential arrangements did not disappear, the generalised preferences scheme could be acceptable to Congress at all.

11. Speaking strictly personally and as he emphasised without any instructions to do so, he said that the contradiction between bringing this issue up now and continued support of British entry into the Community was, he was sure, recognised by those in Washington who were concerned with the question of our negotiations. If therefore the decision had gone as it had it was perhaps because the Americans were having little success in getting other European countries to recognise that there was a genuine problem about the future of worldwide trading arrangements. The problem was a very real one and this was a symptom of it. We probably had to recognise that we were in disagreement on this occasion but he feared that there were going to be more such occasions unless more sensitivity was shown in Europe and in the United Kingdom about the American problems, especially their difficulties over the Common Agricultural Policy and British agricultural levies.

12. In response to a question from Sir Con O'Neill, Cleveland said that essentially the same approach had been made to the Commission and to the member Governments of the Community but not to other applicants and not 'so far' to the developing countries involved. The Commission had been told

that Tresize would wish to raise the question in the next round of talks between the United States and the Commission in the week after next.

13. Cleveland undertook to report to Washington what Sir Con O'Neill had said and added that he personally hoped that, now that the Americans had put their views on record there would be no American 'campaign', on the issue, though he would not bet on it. Some show of concern for Washington's problems in the United Kingdom particularly on our agricultural policy, would help those who were required to reconcile the conflicts between supporting British entry, as the President did, and nevertheless taking account of American interests, which was also part of the Presidential position.

14. Sir Con O'Neill commented that Cleveland had observed that in 1957 when the Community's association arrangements were first formulated in the Treaty of Rome, the Americans had not intervened, so as not to prejudice the conclusion of the Treaty. He thought they should now reflect whether they were not putting at risk the conclusion of another Treaty.

DOUGLAS-HOME.

G

FOREIGN AND COMMONWEALTH OFFICE TELEGRAM TO BONN No. 51 of 22 JANUARY, 1971.

(See Chapter 10, paragraph 14.)

Paragraph 7 *(c)* of my telegram under reference referred to the suggestion in some quarters of the Community that, if we make a low contribution to Community finance in the first year of our membership, we ought not to have a voice in Community institutions and decisions.

2. It is clear that this suggestion is still current in the Community, perhaps more widely than a month ago. It may be no more than an additional means of pressure on us to force our contribution upwards. But we must take it seriously and do our best to refute it. You should draw on the following additional arguments if you encounter this suggestion.

3. When the Community considered this question during their preparations for the negotiations in the first half of last year, we understand that they agreed that the applicant countries should participate in making decisions in the Community with full rights from the time of their entry, since they would have accepted the treaties and decisions of the Community and since the transitional measures which might be agreed would end within a fixed period of time. It was also agreed that the question of the applicant countries participating in decisions which might not be applicable to them could only be settled at the end of the negotiations.

4. While you should not quote this Community position verbatim (since it is an internal Community decision) you should say that we understand this broadly to be the position the Community have agreed, and point out that the

decision was not related to what a candidate country might have to do in any particular year of its transitional period, and specifically recognised the need for transitional measures which would not affect a candidate country's voting rights. On the contrary the Community's decision seems to have recognised, rightly, that virtually all decisions would affect candidates from the moment of entry. There might be some restricted fields in which decisions of the Community would not have an effect on us (for example decisions relating to the current Yaoundé Convention, since the Community propose, and we agree, that the *status quo* should be preserved until the end of 1974 in relation to the Yaoundé Convention and Commonwealth countries opting for association with the Community). But with this narrow exception we imagine the Community will stick to the decision they have taken and give us full rights from the start. You should leave no doubt that we could not accept membership without full rights from the moment of entry.

5. You could go on to ask whether those who suggest that our vote might be affected by the contribution we made to Community finance are seeking to relate the voting pattern in Community institutions to the various countries' contributions to Community finance. This would be a new departure in Community thinking, and would produce a voting pattern very different from that existing in the present Community. You might point out that Luxembourg at present enjoys a specific vote in all Community institutions and decisions on the basis of a key contribution to Community finance of 0.2 per cent. Our proposal would mean our paying between 13 and 15 times as much in the first (repeat first) year of our membership. We do not see why our voting rights should be linked to our contribution any more than are those of Luxembourg.

DOUGLAS-HOME.

H

Mr. RIPPON'S STATEMENT ON COMMUNITY FINANCE AT THE MINISTERIAL MEETING OF 2 FEBRUARY, 1971.

(See Chapter 19, paragraph 3.)

The mechanics of agricultural transition is of course only one of a number of questions on which we await the position of the Community on proposals which we have made at various stages over the last few months. There are 14 such questions. I will not weary you with a list of them. But I hope that the pace can now be quickened and that in March we can record agreement on a number of these questions. We should certainly now be considering urgently the two major questions of New Zealand dairy products and sugar from the developing Commonwealth countries.

I would like now to say something about Community finance and 'ressources propres'. Here I understand why you did not have more to tell me about the Community's position. We will study the statement you have made, recognising that it does not cover the whole field or constitute a formal proposal of the Community. Some of the first and informal reactions to our proposals within the Community make me feel that it is a very good thing that you are going to pursue further the consideration among yourselves of the issues involved.

I would like, with your permission, Mr. Chairman, to try to contribute something further to that consideration. Believe me that nothing we do here is more important for the success of this great enterprise than finding acceptable transitional arrangements in this field of Community finance.

I repeat: acceptable transitional arrangements. For that is all we are talking about. We have told you in the clearest terms and I have stated publicly in the House of Commons, that we are willing to accept the Community's system of 'ressources propres'. That is not in question. In my speech in the House on 20 January, 1971, I said 'We have already expressed our willingness to accept the Community's direct income system. There is no argument about it. I hope that is fully understood. What we now have to do is to determine how to deal with the transitional period'. (*Hansard* Vol. 809 No. 66 Col. 1081.) I repeat that statement for the benefit of the Conference. Nor are we seeking a mathematical limit to our budget contribution in the period after the three years of correctives for which the Community's arrangements provide. What we are seeking are five years of transition, after which we apply the system of 'ressources propres' as you will apply it after your current five years of transition, followed by three years of correctives for us as for each of you.

I sometimes have the impression that our decision to accept the Community's system, subject only to acceptable transitional arrangements, surprised some people in the Community. In the early months of our negotiation, we heard anxiety expressed lest the British Government ask for adaptations to the system itself, such as The Hague communiqué of December 1969 envisaged. Then as you will no doubt recall it was suggested that if only we could accept the system without such adaptations, the transitional arrangements would not raise important problems for the Community. For what mattered to the Community was that, at the end of a fixed period, we should apply the Community's system in full. There has been some discussion about this, but I think it is worth recalling that on 8 December the Community 'Noted with satisfaction the British position ... on the acceptance by the United Kingdom Government of the system of "ressources propres"'. So we have in effect been thanked by the Community for that undertaking. Now we hear less of that satisfaction from our friends in the Community. Instead we hear of new difficulties and new principles relating to the transitional arrangements. We have accepted the goal. What I have to ask is, is the Community now losing sight of it?

There is a clear choice for you to make. Either we agree between us transitional arrangements which will enable Britain to carry the large resource transfer burden involved for us in the Community's 'financial' system. This is what we have proposed. The alternative is that you seek to impose such burdens on us from the start that we should not be capable of adjusting ourselves to the system. We have given you a lot of information about the thinking which led us to make our proposals for transitional arrangements. They are fair and generous to the Community. No country represented here was required to pay as much as we have offered to pay in our first year of membership, until they had been members of the Community for eight years. And these are gross figures. We shall get little or nothing back in the first year or two of our membership and little enough thereafter on the present pattern of Community expenditure. As I think it is now accepted that the other candidate countries are not likely to involve net outgoings from Community funds, each of the existing member countries stands to gain financially from the moment of our entry. Of course the gain to which you can all look forward will be divided—not altogether evenly—between the member countries. But all will have the advantage of a substantial gain in resources at our expense and I repeat that this is the position even in the transitional period: even when we pay as we have proposed for our first year of membership, between 2.6 per cent and 3 per cent of the budget.

If any existing member of the Community can show that his country will suffer a financial burden at any stage after our accession as a result of our proposals we will revise them immediately. I say this, although, as I understand it, it is not a Community principle that new members must suffer some manifest disadvantage.

I have noticed that the feature of our proposals which has attracted most criticism is that we should move by equal and regular steps from a low starting point up to our basic key in the fifth year of our transitional period. Reference is made to Britain's 'opening bid of 3 per cent' and the impression is being created, not perhaps round this table but outside, that this is something completely inadequate. I cannot understand why. To take this line seems to me to involve the negation of the concept of transition which is the key to the success of these negotiations. In other fields, nobody is objecting to the concept of gradual movement from the position existing on the date of our entry. It is a natural concept, designed to preserve a principle on which the Community has laid so much stress—that of a general balance of mutual advantage. But when it comes to this field of contributions to the Community budget many people seem to think that a different principle must be applied and that for some reason new members must be required at the outset to make a major step towards the assumption of financial burdens, quite out of scale with the concept of steady and gradual movement, and in conflict with the principle of a general balance of mutual advantage. For it is perfectly clear that there will be no financial or other benefits in the first year of our membership which would be at all commensurate with the kind of massive initial payment which, it seems to be assumed in some quarters, we ought to make at the outset. And the principle of gradual progression is completely abandoned. Indeed, a United Kingdom contribution of 2.6–3 per cent would already mean a substantial transfer of resources from the United Kingdom to the rest of the Community.

I am sure that a dispassionate examination of our proposal will show that its basis lies not in humour, but in realism. Let me add, moreover, that the logic of the proposal that we should pay a high proportion of the budget in our first year entirely escapes me. On what principle is this proposal based? It appears to be based on no more than a general view that new members, to prove their solidarity with the Community, must be required to pay from the start a burdensome contribution to its funds. There is no relationship, in such a proposal, to the concept of a general balance of mutual advantage. Such a proposal, as I say, in my judgment, amounts to the very negation of the concept of transition. It is more like the painful initiation of a new entrant to a secret society.

Some people even suggest that because under our proposals our initial payment would be small in the first year compared to what it would be in later years, we should not from the outset enjoy our full status as a member of the Community. This argument about status and voting rights is another whose logic I do not perceive. And of course my colleagues will recognise that Britain's position in the institutions of the Community raises a very clear and simple political question: either Britain enjoys a full voice from the start in the institutions of the Community, or we do not join.

Each country represented here is, as I have demonstrated, going to gain resources from the moment of our entry.

Each country represented here may have made its own calculation of the extra resources it would gain from us in the first year of our membership if our key was one or two percentage points more. And it is always tempting to try for a little bit more. I beg my colleagues round this table to ensure that any such calculations take account of the gain which each member country would have to forgo if acceptable transitional arrangements cannot be agreed and these negotiations fail.

In a speech in Paris last May Mr. Heath spoke of the possibility that these negotiations might fail. He said 'Whatever the Government in power in Britain I do not believe that Parliament will approve a settlement which in the opinion of its members is unequal and unfair'. He added that there was no need for failure provided that the realities were clearly grasped. This meant that we in Britain should understand the nature of the Community which the Six had built. This we have tried to do right from the outset of these negotiations. Equally the realities of the situation required from the Community a willingness to show in negotiations with Britain the same foresight and imagination which had served them well in the past. That is what the debate on Community finance is about. We said clearly that we accepted the Community system. That seems at first scarcely to have been believed. And we said at the start that we had not wanted to put forward an extreme bargaining position. I think some people still find that difficult to believe. It is misunderstandings of this kind which lead to serious situations which no one wants.

I ask you to believe that our position on both points is clear and sincere: We accept your system after a transitional period but we must insist in return that the transitional arrangements be fair. Throughout the seven months which we have negotiated together and indeed in the position which we adopted at the outset, first Mr. Barber and then I on behalf of the British Government, have made every effort to meet Community concerns and principles and practices. You are concerned that transitional arrangements should be the general rule. We have accepted that. You were concerned that we should adapt to your system at the end of these transitional periods. We have accepted that. You have been anxious to avoid any suggestion of a new review clause. We have avoided that. We ask only for a repetition of an assurance which the Commission itself put forward and the Community itself has endorsed. You were anxious that the corpus of decisions taken under the Treaties should be accepted by the candidate countries. We have accepted that too: so that out of 2,500 regulations and decisions in force, very few indeed will call for special transitional measures.

In the remaining issues which these negotiations must resolve, if they are to succeed, the terms must be fair and honourable. In the field of Community finance, you know that at the end of a short period of years we shall be applying your system to the full. And you must also know the very great advantages which will flow from that for all of you. But if you deny us acceptable transitional arrangements you and we and all Europe will lose the ultimate goal.

I

MINUTE FROM Mr. RIPPON TO THE PRIME MINISTER OF 17 MARCH, 1971.

(See Chapter 7, paragraph 16.)

EUROPEAN ECONOMIC COMMUNITY NEGOTIATIONS AND YOUR VISIT TO BONN

You may like to have my impressions of the meetings here [i.e. in Brussels] this week and their implications for your talks with Brandt.

2. In over six hours of discussions between themselves on Monday on Commonwealth sugar, New Zealand dairy products and Community finance, the Community made no significant progress towards a common position. In each case the French took an extreme position, and although there are differences of detail in the views of the Five and the Commission, the French were on this occasion isolated, and seen to be isolated on all the three main issues remaining to be settled in our negotiations. The atmosphere during this discussion seems to have been poor, with some blunt speaking, and renewed criticism of Schumann's partisan chairmanship. And we are told that Scheel, Moro and Luns took virtually no part in the restricted meeting after dinner, to demonstrate their dislike of Schumann's positions and attitude.

3. Given that genuine progress could not be made, the outcome was not unsatisfactory both for our own meeting yesterday and in setting the scene for your talks with Brandt. The Six had their row without us; the French position is regarded as unreasonable by all her partners; and there are no half-baked

compromise proposals (which could not have been acceptable to us) on the table to mask the differences within the Community.

4. The resulting impatience and irritation on the Community side helped to give an easy passage to our proposal to try to reach agreement on the main issues in May. We all agreed to set aside 10, 11 and the afternoon and evening of 12 May for a series of meetings for this purpose and to envisage a further meeting later in the month if necessary. The meeting on the 10th will be one of the Six, without us. (But for the Germans, there would have been agreement to specify 18 May for this further meeting, and I have no doubt that we shall get it if we need it.)

5. People are, of course, asking themselves why the French isolated themselves so unreasonably. Some of the French delegation were not happy with their position, particularly on sugar. But, even if Schumann handled his position insensitively, it is obviously part of a deliberate strategy. I believe that the French are now constructing the best negotiating position for themselves in preparation for the crunch here, and also no doubt for any bilateral meeting with us. (There is some speculation here about the possibility of an Anglo-French meeting and I am sure that the sooner arrangements can be made and announced for your meeting with Pompidou—for which April is more than ever the right time—the easier it will be to present it as not being confined to Community issues. It might also be tactically wise to link this visit with plans to meet Colombo later on as part of the series.) The French fear that if they make concessions to their partners here before the crunch, they will have to pay a second time when the crunch with us comes. And they are right. They may also want to demonstrate to us the ineffectiveness of the Five in order to strengthen their position in talking to us.

6. All this—and particularly the timetable which the Conference has now adopted—means that your talks with Brandt could not have been better timed. Scheel was apparently helpful in the Community's internal discussions on Monday, particularly on New Zealand and sugar. But German officials from von Braun downwards show no desire to stand up to the French, and we shall need Brandt's support.

7. The main points to get across to Brandt seem to me to be:

(a) the importance of the timetable we have now all set ourselves;
(b) where our priorities lie;
(c) our views on summitry; and
(d) the importance of success for Germany's policies, as well as for the Community as a whole and for our own continuing position in European integration and co-operation in all fields.

8. As regards the timetable, we have June and July in reserve. But things could turn sour if they were to drag on for another four months. All the issues are now clear, and can be decided if there is the will.

9. You will want to let Brandt know that our priorities are low payments to

the fund in the early years; something more for New Zealand than degressivity to half her present exports of butter and cheese; and reasonable assurances for quantities of sugar from the developing Commonwealth as well as prices. In return we could move to a somewhat higher financial contribution at the end of our transitional period, and would try to meet French anxieties on Community preference in agriculture.

10. On summitry, I hope you will feel able to tell Brandt in confidence of your plans for meeting Pompidou. As I have said, there is already speculation here. And in any case Brandt should know that we see serious drawbacks in planning a summit of the Seven: I understand that Monnet may have written or be writing to Brandt to urge on him a summit of the Seven, which we do not want.

11. I am sending a copy of this minute to the Foreign and Commonwealth Secretary and to Sir Burke Trend.

GEOFFREY RIPPON.

J

MINUTE BY Mr. TICKELL TO SIR CON O'NEILL OF 18 MARCH, 1971: PRESIDENT POMPIDOU AND THE EUROPEAN ECONOMIC COMMUNITIES NEGOTIATIONS.

(See Chapter 33, paragraph 10.)

I lunched on 16 March with M. Jean René Bernard (Secretary-General of the French Inter-Ministerial Committee on Europe, and Chargé de Mission at the Elysée). We had a general talk about the state of the enlargement negotiations.

2. We spoke first about the Chancellor of the Duchy's visit to Canada and the United States and the American attitude towards enlargement of the Community. I made the point that it was not always appreciated in Brussels that we were negotiating on several fronts and that it was no easy matter to institute our interim system of agricultural levies. The fact that we had decided to introduce such a system now, with all its consequences for our relations with such countries as Canada and the United States, was of great political significance. We deserved credit for it. M. Bernard agreed that our efforts in this respect were not always fully appreciated.

3. I said that for us the central enigma of the negotiations was the attitude of President Pompidou. M. Bernard said that M. Pompidou did not know Britain or really understand English. M. Bernard regretted that the efforts which he and I (in another capacity) had made in 1969 to arrange a visit from M. Pompidou to Britain had been overtaken by the departure of General de Gaulle. M. Bernard said that M. Pompidou's ignorance of Britain did not mean that he did not want Britain to join the Community. He was anxious for the negotiations to succeed and was planning on the assumption that they would. Success

was very much in the French national interest. Failure would be a disaster for France and Europe but a catastrophe for Britain. The French would certainly be blamed for failure. France was everyone's scapegoat. I asked why the French were standing out on sugar. They seemed to want to be blamed. He replied that the present French position on sugar (which he implied was not for ever) was not unreasonable. But he admitted it was causing the French considerable embarrassment in their relations with the third world.

4. After some beating about the bush we spoke about the possibility of a meeting between M. Pompidou and Mr. Heath. I said that it would be very dangerous if it were not successful. M. Bernard said that it would require very careful preparation and, so far as the public was concerned, would have to cover the whole range of world problems. As regards the negotiations it was a single-barrelled gun which could only be fired once. I said we were well aware of this. The advantages and disadvantages of such a meeting were very evenly balanced. We then left the subject.

5. Later in our conversation M. Bernard reverted to it by asking: When are our bilateral talks to start? He said it was already clear that the essential issues had to be decided by the British and French. He was sure that we had a shopping list. I said that this was not the way in which we envisaged a meeting, if any, between President Pompidou and Mr. Heath. The question was whether such a meeting would be the best way of advancing the negotiations. The alternatives were for M. Pompidou and Mr. Heath to deal with each other through their respective Ministers (here M. Bernard indicated unmistakably that M. Schumann was not entirely an *interlocuteur valable*) or to allow the negotiations to continue as at present between the Six on one side and Britain on the other. At this point M. Bernard said quite clearly that he thought a bilateral meeting between President Pompidou and Mr. Heath would be necessary if the negotiations were to be successfully concluded.

6. I explained to M. Bernard some of the internal political considerations in Britain and I hope reassured him somewhat about British public opinion. I said for the May Ministerial meeting there simply had to be some positive result. Even if we did not then succeed in deciding all the essential issues, we must agree on something and give the British Government the assurance it had so far lacked that the negotiations would succeed. Once we had that assurance the negotiations would be transformed. M. Bernard asked when were we going to pull out the stops in our campaign to convince British public opinion. I said that the British had been bitten twice and were disinclined to risk the experience again until success was in sight. Then things would change very quickly.

7. M. Bernard said that President Pompidou did not face a problem with either his Parliament or public opinion. But he was subject to pressure from vested interests who were very ready to reproach the Government if those interests were sacrificed. So far as M. Pompidou was concerned, the best way in which he could convince the French, and in particular French industrialists, of the advantages of British entry was to demonstrate some tangible gain. The

gain he had in mind was access to the British market for French agricultural produce. Hence the French insistence on Community preference. This was more important to the French than anything else.

8. M. Bernard promised to keep in touch. As he left he assured me once more of M. Pompidou's will and belief that the negotiations should succeed.

C. C. C. TICKELL.

K

FRENCH PROPOSAL TO SIX OF 5 MAY, 1971, ON COMMUNITY FINANCE.

(See Chapter 19, paragraph 11.)

PROJET DE RÈGLEMENT FINANCIER: DISPOSITIONS APPLICABLES AUX NOUVEAUX ÉTATS MEMBRES

Les nouveaux États Membres appliquent, à compter du 1st janvier, 1973, les dispositions de la décision du 21 avril, 1970, relative aux ressources propres.

2. Les contributions financières des nouveaux États Membres prévues à l'Article 3—2 *e* de la décision du 21 avril, 1970, sont calculées à l'aide de la clé suivante:

Royaume-Uni	19.22%	A%
Danemark	2.54%	B%
Irelande	0.60%	C%
Norvège	1.81%	D%

3. Pour l'année 1973 la variation maximum de la part relative des nouveaux membres, telle qu'elle est fixée à l'Article 3—3 *e* de la décision du 21 avril, 1970, est calculée par rapport à la clé définie au paragraphe 2 ci-dessus.

4. Les participations, financières totales des nouveaux membres découlant des règles des paragraphes précedents, ne, sont appelées qu'à concurrence de:

N% en 1973
P% en 1974
Q% en 1975
R% en 1976
S% en 1977

A partir du 1er janvier, 1978, elles sont intégralement appelées.

5. Jusqu'au 1er janvier, 1978, la fraction du budget des Communautes non couverte par les participations financières des nouveaux membres est repartie entre les anciens membres selon les dispositions de la décision du 21 avril, 1970.

L

FOREIGN AND COMMONWEALTH OFFICE TELEGRAMS TO BONN Nos. 359 AND 360 OF 7 MAY, 1971, ON AGRICULTURAL TRANSITION AND COMMUNITY PREFERENCE.

(See Chapter 11, paragraph 9.)

(Telegram No. 359)

In the light of clarificatory talks which we have had with the Commission, we believe that it should be possible to reach agreement on agricultural transition and Community preference at the meetings with the Community in Brussels next week. But we must be sure in advance that if we make an effort to reach agreement with the Community, we shall not suffer a rebuff.

2. MIFT gives the text of a draft statement which Mr. Rippon would be prepared to make to the Conference on 11 May provided it was clear in advance that an approach on these lines would be acceptable to the member countries and the Commission, and could lead to an agreement.

3. Please hand a copy of this draft informally to the Government to which you are accredited/commission and speak on the following lines.

4. Following the agreement of the Community at deputy level that we should have clarificatory talks with the Commission, we have been able to get a clearer picture of the remaining problems in the field of agricultural transition and the possibility of introducing full Community preference in agricultural products on entry. We now think that we see the form which an agreement between the Community and ourselves could take. But the issues involved are extremely sensitive from the domestic political point of view, and we cannot proceed on these lines in Brussels next week if there is any risk of the Community rejecting our approach. We should therefore like the Government to which you are accredited/commission to consider the line in our draft statement (MIFT) and to let us know urgently whether an agreement on these lines would be acceptable to them. We regard the issues covered by our proposal as a whole, and an agreement must cover them all.

5. As will be seen, draft statement virtually constitutes basis of a full agreement in this field, including the question of five full years for agricultural transition. This is a question of the greatest political and presentational importance for us. It is no less important than the other points in our statement and we do not believe it is technically difficult to arrange.

6. If we get a discouraging reaction from the Government to which you are accredited/commission, we should have to think in terms of making a much more general statement which would look forward to further work being done at deputy level after next week's Ministerial meeting.

7. In speaking on these lines you should:

(a) Stress that there must be no advance disclosure;

(b) make it clear that our contacts with the Commission have been strictly confined to clarification.

DOUGLAS-HOME.

(Telegram No. 360)

Agricultural transition
(My immediately preceding telegram.)

The complex problems of Community preference and agricultural transition have been the subject of considerable discussion between us, both in the meetings of our deputies and in contacts between the British Delegation and the Commission. In recent weeks there have been, in meetings of our deputies, two major statements (on 9 March and 6 April respectively) from the Community side on which we commented in a statement on 21 April. More recently there have been some extremely useful technical contacts with the Commission for purposes of enlightenment and explanation, which have enabled us to consider more closely how far our joint objectives could be met within the ambiance of the institutions and procedures of an Enlarged Community.

2. As a result of these exchanges I think we are now in a position to reach agreement at this meeting on the main elements of a settlement, which would not only be an important achievement in itself but would facilitate agreement on other outstanding issues. I should like to set out the basis on which I believe this can be achieved.

3. You will remember that in the British statement of 21 April we made it plain, not only that we accepted the principle of Community preference, but that our concern was essentially to ensure that certain legitimate and important transitional objectives could be met, rather than with the particular modalities and measures for meeting them. We indicated, therefore, that we might be able to consider your basic approach to agricultural transition, including in particular your proposals on Community preference, as a basis for agreement if we could be clear that a limited number of practical problems could be solved. These were:

(a) Provision to avoid any significant disruption of third country trade in major agricultural products during the course of transition;
(b) provision for speedy corrective action to deal with possible difficulties arising in the markets of the Enlarged Community from the operation of the transitional mechanisms;
(c) a full five-year period and six steps for agricultural price adjustment;
(d) acceptable arrangements to deal with tariff items, particularly in the sensitive horticultural sector.

4. First as regards trade with third countries, it is our understanding on the basis of paragraph 3 of the statement by the Community Delegation on 9 March and subsequent discussions with the Commission that the Community

recognises that for certain commodities, particularly those of which imports into the United Kingdom are at present regulated by quantitative arrangements, and which would become subject to a levy system on British accession, significant volumes of trade with third countries could be at risk of serious disruption. It is our understanding however that in such cases it would be the intention of the Enlarged Community to take effective measures, which would vary with the circumstances of the commodity, the degree of risk, the market situation, etc., within the framework of the mechanisms of the common agricultural policy and through the appropriate institutions and procedures of the Enlarged Community. The means and extent of such action would be decided upon taking into account *inter alia* the current and prospective conditions and outlets on world markets and in the markets of the Enlarged Community and the likely effects on the third countries concerned of any sudden and significant changes in their trade, and also after taking account of any relevant international commodity arrangements.

5. If the Community can endorse this understanding and can formally confirm that this is a correct statement of their intention we could accept that this would be sufficient to meet our requirements.

6. Secondly, there is the question of corrective action to deal with possible difficulties arising in the operation of the transitional mechanisms. Malfunction of this system could cause disturbance in the markets of the Enlarged Community, distort conditions of trade and delay achievement of the agreed programme of price adjustment by the new members. And we stressed on 21 April the importance of the ability of the Enlarged Community to take rapid corrective action in such circumstances.

7. In our discussions with the Commission they have drawn our attention to the fact that in each of the regulations for establishing the common organisation of markets—and thus involving transition from a régime existing beforehand in each of the Member States to a régime based on these regulations—an article had been inserted in these same regulations designed to bring about this transition in the best conditions. By virtue of this article, it has been possible to adopt the measures necessary to that purpose for a period of one year as from the implementation of the regulation by the 'Commission/Management Committee' procedure. In the case of milk products, where experience revealed that this period of one year was too short because of the difficulties encountered, the Community extended by another year the effective period of this article.

8. We understand that all other adaptations of the Community régime are made in one of two ways:

(i) Either by amending regulations to modify regulations made previously: such amending regulations are adopted in accordance with the same procedure as that under which the basic regulations were established; or

(ii) By instruments adopted under a simpler procedure expressly provided for that purpose by the basic regulations. The Commission have drawn our attention to the large number of legal instruments of the Council and of the Commission which have appeared in the official journal of the Communities which illustrate the effectiveness of corrective action by the institutions of the Community, using these procedures.

9. Furthermore, the Commission reminded us of the statement made by the Community at the 18th Session of the Conference of Deputies concerning additional measures during the transitional period, and in particular, paragraph 8 of that declaration which deals with safeguard clauses.

10. In the light of these explanations by the Commission it is our understanding that, either by means of provisions on the lines of those which were applied in the case of milk products, or by the use other appropriate mechanisms and procedures of the Enlarged Community, there would be adequate provision for taking rapid corrective action during the transitional period should it prove necessary.

11. If you can, therefore, from the Community side, again formally confirm our understanding is correct and that all these ways of taking rapid corrective action would be available in the Enlarged Community this would meet our second requirement.

12. I turn now to our third point: that is the timetable for the adaptation of our agricultural prices to Community levels. As the British Delegation has emphasised in previous discussion, we attach the greatest importance, for political, economic and administrative reasons, to having for this purpose five years of transition with six price steps. We have to make a much bigger price adjustment than you made in your transition and anything less than the five years for which we are asking would create real difficulties for us. It is necessary to take account of the effects of sudden price increases on our consumers, and on the economy in general: the considerable adjustments which will have to be made by our producers, including the special difficulties faced by our horticultural industry: and the possible effects on certain major aspects of world trade. The consequences of disruption in any of these areas would be no more in the Community's interest than Britain's and the damage which abrupt price rises could cause to the valuable markets which the United Kingdom will otherwise offer to the Community does not need underlining. I do not believe that these conclusions will be denied and I must ask you to accept our basic proposals here.

13. Finally, there is the question of the arrangements for tariff items, and in particular for the sensitive horticultural sector. I need not recite the differing proposals which have been made previously nor repeat the reasons why we consider it so important to secure adequate arrangements particularly for horticultural products. What I should like to do is to put forward a comprehensive proposal which would, I hope, provide a mutually acceptable basis for agreement between us. What we now propose is that tariffs on horticultural items should be adjusted by five steps of 20 per cent, as you have proposed, but that

the first step should be on 1 January, 1974, as we have proposed. For other Annex II products we would then be prepared to accept a timetable at least as rapid as that proposed by the Community. However, in the interests of avoiding disruption of markets there would have to be provision, analogous to that which the Community have already proposed for the harmonisation of agricultural prices, for a limited flexibility in tariff movement in any one year. This would entail, as with prices, the possibility of modifying the programme of tariff movements within specified limits, on a non-cumulative basis, and through the institutions and procedures of the Enlarged Community, if it were agreed that circumstances were such as to justify such action.

14. As regards the special problem of apples and pears what we would propose is that our present quota system should be replaced by a system of compensatory amounts, reflecting the differences in price levels between Britain and the Community, which would be subject to the general provisions suggested by the Community for price harmonisation and thus phased out by the end of the transition period. The arrangements should be sufficient to safeguard the stability of the British market during the transitional period following the removal of quotas.

15. I believe that in these ways we can find a mutually acceptable basis for agreement which will in no sense take us outside the framework of the institutions and procedures of the Enlarged Community or the principles of the CAP and which would ensure the achievement of the legitimate and important objectives necessary during transition. If this proposition which I have made can be agreed as a whole we, for our part, can accept the general system of agricultural transition and the approach to Community preference set out in your statements of 9 March and 6 April. There remain a number of points of detail to be sorted out but we do not need to settle these now. If we can agree, as I have suggested, on the main essentials I would propose that we should instruct our officials to carry forward the task of working these out later at an appropriate stage.

16. I believe we have before us today, therefore, a real opportunity to settle a matter of major importance in the negotiations and that we should grasp it firmly. An agreement on this matter is extremely desirable not only in view of the importance of the subject itself but because I believe it would give real impetus to the negotiations as a whole.

DOUGLAS-HOME.

M

Mr. SOAMES'S DESPATCH OF 9 JUNE, 1971, ON THE HEATH-POMPIDOU MEETING.

(See Chapter 33, paragraph 17.)

Paris,
9 June, 1971

Sir,

The Prime Minister paid an official visit to Paris, as the guest of the President of the French Republic, from 19–21 May. He was accompanied by members of his personal staff and by a team of senior advisers concerned with European questions. He carried out a full programme, the bulk of which was devoted to four sessions of talks with President Pompidou. During these four meetings, which lasted about 11 hours and were almost entirely *tête-à-tête*, apart from the presence of interpreters, the two Heads of Government discussed the future of Europe in all its aspects and established the closeness of their thinking on many points. I have the honour in this despatch to recall briefly the preparations for this meeting; to describe the Prime Minister's programme while he was here and to offer some comment, tentative as this must necessarily be while we are still negotiating in Brussels, on the results which the Prime Minister's visit has achieved.

2. 'The President of the French Republic and the Prime Minister', said the communiqué announcing the visit on 8 May, 'consider that a meeting to discuss, matters of common interest would now be useful'—a delightfully bland formula to describe so momentous a decision. Ever since the French decision at The Hague summit meeting in December 1969 to agree to the opening of negotiations with Britain, it had, I think, been clear—to informed opinion among the Five no less than in Britain and France—that success in Brussels was likely to depend finally on agreement between Britain and France; and for such agreement to become possible, this had to form part of a broader reconciliation of the two countries, based on the mutual acknowledgment that our future interests lay in working together both in the fields covered by an enlarged Community, and in those where broader co-operation on a European scale is still in the future. Given the link between our entry and a broader Anglo/French reconciliation, and adding to the equation the last decade's history of Anglo/French differences, it had come to seem very likely, by an early stage in the resumed negotiations, that the best hope of achieving the twin objectives lay in a meeting between the French President and the British Prime Minister. But first the success of such a meeting had to be assured, for failure would have been disastrous.

3. It was in February that, during a talk with President Pompidou's Secretary-General at the Elysée, it became clear that the President foresaw a meeting with the Prime Minister which, if successful, would pave the way for agreement in Brussels. It remained to be seen whether the ingredients of success were there,

and to this end detailed discussions were begun. It was necessary to deal with the problem both of timing and of substance. There was the question of strategic timing—for how long should our two negotiating teams be obliged to conduct their war of attrition in Brussels, so as to show public opinion that the utmost had been done to defend each country's special interests? This was particularly important for President Pompidou as General de Gaulle's successor. Then there was the question of tactical timing—once the choice of the date had been narrowed, which particular negotiating meeting should it precede or follow, and when exactly should it be announced? On the substance, it was clear that the two Heads of Government would not wish to concern themselves solely with particular aspects of the negotiations, for this would be both to pre-empt the proper function of the Ministers negotiating in Brussels and to miss the opportunity for a real meeting of minds across a wider spectrum. It became clear that President Pompidou wished to be sure in his mind about our attitude on such broader issues as the future of European institutions, majority voting, the place of the French language in the enlarged Community, the provisions for France's former colonies when the time came to renegotiate the Yaoundé Convention—and the handling of sterling. On our side, the Prime Minister wished to expound to the President, and engage his interest in, the whole concept of united Europe and the role it should rightfully play in the world which has been cardinal to the Prime Minister's own thinking for the past 20 years. But it would also be unthinkable for the Prime Minister to spend two days at the Elysée without a discussion in depth leading to a meeting of minds on the detailed problems which remained to be solved in the negotiations.

4. Patient discussion of these and other aspects of the meeting was needed before agreement could be reached, both on the timing and on the agenda for a meeting between the two Heads of Government. With a secretiveness which is characteristic, but also because he believed, rightly, that he could not rely on some elements in the Quai d'Orsay not to disrupt the careful preparations if they knew about them, the President decided that the preliminary and preparatory contacts should be handled exclusively by his own personal staff at the Elysée. It has now become common knowledge that the Quai d'Orsay were kept in ignorance and that M. Schumann only learned of the impending meeting when he returned from a visit to Moscow a few hours before the announcement was to be made. Even the French Prime Minister was only informed the day before. There were, and must still remain, risks for us in this method of work, if only because of the bitterness it has undoubtedly engendered among certain of the senior French officials engaged in the negotiations, whose goodwill towards us has in any case always been questionable. But be that as it may, these discussions led both Her Majesty's Government and President Pompidou to decide that a meeting between the Prime Minister and the President was timely and that it would have every chance of success.

5. M. Pompidou had taken his time over this critical decision. By the end of 1969 he had calculated that it was necessary to allow negotiations to open with

the United Kingdom in order to secure the final stage of the Community's agricultural policy: and it was so agreed at The Hague summit. I am less certain how convinced he was at that time that it was in France's interest that the negotiations should succeed. But I believe his mind was already moving along the lines that, provided vital French negotiating objectives were adequately protected, then on balance success would be advantageous to France. What was quite certain from the start was that, if the negotiations should fail, M. Pompidou did not want to be blamed for this; and it became increasingly clear, as the negotiations went on, that if they did break down he would be hard put to it to avoid being cast as the man responsible for failure.

6. Developments outside the negotiating room reinforced the arguments in favour of allowing the negotiations to succeed. M. Pompidou was widely blamed for the fiasco of France's negotiations with Algeria, on the grounds that he should have intervened personally at a much earlier stage. Many commentators asked whether he might be going to make the same mistake over the Community's negotiations with Britain: this sort of criticism could only be answered by a 'positive' result in Brussels. Within the Community itself, the ructions over monetary and economic union reminded those few in France who have ever forgotten it, that their neighbour across the Rhine could not be content for ever to adopt the complaisant attitude towards France's pretentions within the Six which had satisfied Dr. Adenauer, under the spell of General de Gaulle. France's perennial mistrust of Germany was undoubtedly (however regrettable its consequences in other contexts) one of the more compelling factors which decided M. Pompidou to disregard the misgivings of the orthodox Gaullists and invite Mr. Heath to visit him in Paris.

7. In making the physical arrangements for the visit, the French authorities, under instructions from the Elysée, could not have been more co-operative. The President not only decided to entertain the Prime Minister to two meals at the Elysée, but intimated that, 'if invited', he would be glad to come to a meal at the Embassy. It is most unusual for a visiting Head of Government to be entertained directly by the President to more than one meal; and it is exceptional, except during a State Visit, for the President himself to go out for a meal to an Embassy. These arrangements were quickly noted by the Press of a country which, despite its claims of civil egalitarianism, in fact observes the nuances of protocol and social relations with an attention which recalls Byzantium. The cynic might have seen them as all part of a French contingency plan for ensuring that, if the talks should go awry, the French could not be blamed for not having bent over backwards to ensure their success. I myself never shared this cynical view; and with the talks turning out in the satisfactory way that they did, the social arrangements played their part in emphasising the unique nature of the visit and helped to highlight its success. In small ways it proved possible for us to reciprocate and to emphasise in return the 'European' spirit in which the visit was being undertaken; for example, in the Prime Minister's gesture in making his first speech on arrival in French, and in the menu for the luncheon

at the Embassy, which was not only French but specifically designed to appeal to the Auvergnat.

8. The Prime Minister, accompanied by four senior members of his party, arrived at Orly in an HS-125 at 6.15 p.m. on the afternoon of 19 May. He was welcomed by the French Prime Minister (M. Jacques Chaban-Delmas), the Secretary of State at the Quai d'Orsay (M. Jean de Lipokowski) and the appropriate military and civil French officials. I was present with members of my staff to greet the Prime Minister as he stepped on to French soil and to present M. Chaban-Delmas to him. M. Chaban-Delmas' speech of welcome was cordiality personified. He referred to the imperishable links formed, notably on the field of battle, between France and the United Kingdom; he told Mr. Heath that 'your coming to Paris to make Europe represents a very real and great hope'; and he expressed the desire that the Prime Minister's conversations with M. Pompidou would be fruitful. The Prime Minister in reply said he was convinced that Europe was now at a moment as historic as that of 20 years ago. The decisions to be taken in the weeks to come would be of determining significance for the political future of Europe: it was in this spirit that he came to his talks with the President of the French Republic. For him, these talks would be inspired by the desire to establish between them the closest understanding on the great problems which now faced the whole of Europe. The two Prime Ministers then drove together to the British Embassy, where M. Chaban-Delmas came in for a drink before taking his leave. Later in the evening we had a working dinner for the Prime Minister and several of his senior advisers.

9. On the following morning (20 May), the Prime Minister left the Embassy for the Elysée at 9.55 a.m., accompanied only by his interpreter (Mr. Michael Palliser, Minister at this Embassy), one of his private secretaries and myself. At the Elysée Mr. Heath was greeted by the Chief of Protocol (M. Senard), and was escorted by the Secretary-General to the Presidency (M. Jobert) to the President's office on the first floor, where M. Pompidou was waiting to receive him at the head of the staircase. Photographs were taken and the talks began with no one else present but interpreters. The four sessions were to take a total of some 11 hours.

10. The first session, which had been expected to finish at 12.30 p.m., in fact ran on until the working lunch, for which M. Pompidou was joined by M. Chaban-Delmas, M. Schumann and senior French officials, and the Prime Minister by his senior officials and by myself with two senior members of my staff. It had been the Prime Minister's intention to return to the Embassy between the first session of the talks and the luncheon: as it was, he did this instead before the afternoon session—though not before the two Heads of Government had been temporarily lost to view inside a crowd of Press photographers who interrupted their post-prandial coffee in an arbour in the Elysée garden, reminding M. Chaban-Delmas (a former rugby international) of the last encounter between France and Wales at Colombes.

11. After the second session of the talks in the afternoon the Prime Minister

returned to the Embassy. He left again 20 minutes later with the French Prime Minister for the Arc de Triomphe, where Mr. Heath laid a wreath on the tomb of the French Unknown Soldier. This gesture was much appreciated and like all the Prime Minister's public appearances received excellent Press and television coverage. From the Arc de Triomphe the Prime Minister drove directly to the Matignon for a talk, at which I accompanied him, with M. Chaban-Delmas.

12. The day concluded with the President and Mme. Pompidou's formal dinner at the Elysée. This furnished the familiar combination of outward glitter and of hard work behind the scenes, for the guests had no sooner risen from the dinner table than Mr. Heath found himself involved in a detailed discussion on certain monetary questions with M. Schumann. Before then, both the President and the Prime Minister had in their exchange of toasts lifted enough of the blanket of silence, which they had by mutual consent imposed on the results of their conversations until these were concluded, to reassure the assembled company that good progress was being made. While both were careful to stress it was not their aim to pre-empt the negotiations in Brussels, M. Pompidou felt able to say that on many of the essential points, and notably the general conception of Europe, including its organisation and objectives, his and Mr. Heath's views were 'sufficiently close for us to be able to continue; without pessimism'. The Prime Minister for his part said he believed that the negotiating problems could be settled to the satisfaction of all the partners concerned. This would leave clear the way to make a momentous step towards European unity. The best hope for that movement forward was for France and Britain to advance together in partnership with each other, as they had so often done in the past. The Prime Minister concluded by quoting the words he had spoken at Aachen (a reference which, as we have, subsequently seen reported, was not lost on German opinion) on another Ascension Day eight years before, when he received the Charlemagne.

13. The next day (21 May) began, as arranged, with the third session of *tête-à-tête* talks between the Prime Minister and the President. They were joined at noon by M. Chaban-Delmas. The President and Mme. Pompidou were then the guests of my wife and myself at the luncheon given at this Embassy in honour of the Prime Minister. M. and Mme. Pompidou were accompanied to this, for us at least, memorable occasion by the French Prime Minister with the Ministers of Defence, Foreign Affairs and Justice, and by Mme. Valéry Giscard d'Estaing (her husband, the Minister of Finance being absent in the United States). In my toast to the President of the French Republic, I had no hesitation in describing the visit we were witnessing as 'a historic event for Europe and the world'. The President in his response spoke of 'this mark of the renewal of confidence and warm feeling between our two countries'.

14. The remainder of the day had been left flexible. The Prime Minister had provisionally arranged to leave in the late afternoon, but further commitments intervened—and I am confident the Prime Minister would agree that

what may have proved *Morning Cloud*'s loss was at least, and emphatically, Europe's gain! The Prime Minister returned to the Elysée for a fourth and final session of talks with the President. We then had the unique experience of seeing the President of the French Republic and the British Prime Minister seated together at a table in the Salle des Fêtes at the Elysée (the same room in which eight years before General de Gaulle had pronounced his first veto on Britain's application), proclaiming the harmony of their views on the future of Europe, and their belief, to use President Pompidou's words, that 'it would be unreasonable to think that agreement between Britain and the EEC will not be reached in June'. The Prime Minister in turn referred to the 'very clear understanding of each other's points of view' which he and M. Pompidou had reached, and to his belief that the talks would prove 'of real and lasting benefit not only to Britain and France but to Europe as a whole'. And their joint achievement was epitomised in the final sentences of President Pompidou's statement (which the Prime Minister quoted on 24 May in the House of Commons): 'Many people believed that Great Britain was not and did not wish to become European and that Britain wanted to enter the Community only so as to destroy it or to divert it from its objectives. Many people also thought that France was ready to use every pretext to place in the end a fresh veto on Britain's entry. Well, ladies and gentlemen, you see before you tonight two men who are convinced of the contrary.' With these carefully chosen words the French President both offered to Britain the reassurance as to France's intentions about which we have so long been sceptical; and served notice on his own diehards that the received Gaullist doctrine regarding Britain's intentions (resurrected so recently on British and French television by M. Couve de Murville) was not a doctrine to which the President subscribes.

15. After taking leave of President Pompidou and M. Chaban-Delmas at the end of the Press conference, the Prime Minister returned once more to the Embassy. Here there was time for a quiet dinner before M. Schumann arrived to accompany Mr. Heath to Orly. As it was by now after sundown, there was no special military ceremony at the airport. The Prime Minister's aeroplane took off at 10.15 p.m. He was going straight from London Airport to Chequers, where he intended to spend the week-end preparing the statement about his visit which he was to make to the House of Commons the following Monday, 24 May.

16. That statement, which has been very well received in Paris, makes it superfluous and indeed inappropriate to attempt any further comment on the Prime Minister's talks with M. Pompidou in respect of the prospects for success in our negotiations with the Community. All I might perhaps add is that, when the Prime Minister referred in the House to the long, and careful preparation which had been needed before his visit, adding that he believed that this was the key to its success, he was, of course, only telling half the story. The other and the master key was the way in which the Prime Minister handled the talks themselves. This was something which no one else could have done for him,

and without which no amount of careful preparation could have served its purpose. Mr. Heath succeeded in dispelling the doubt and disbelief about Britain which M. Pompidou inherited from the General and which was kept alive by the naturally suspicious temperament of this crafty Auvergnat. And what the two men had to say to each other should, I hope and believe, prove enough to enable agreement to be reached in Brussels before the summer is out.

17. The spotlight labelled Enlargement has already shifted from Paris back to Luxembourg, Brussels—and Westminster. I therefore conclude this despatch with a reference to the subject which remains for this post our paramount preoccupation. It is a truism to say that, since the withdrawal from power of General de Gaulle and perhaps even before it, there has been an improvement in Anglo-French relations from the nadir of December 1967. This, grudging at first and almost fatally undermined by the 'Soames affair', has since acquired an encouraging momentum as the months have passed. It has been illustrated by, but by no means confined to, the increasing direct contacts which have been made between officials and Ministers of our two Governments, beginning as was natural with officials of the two foreign Ministries but soon extending to other departments of Whitehall and of the French Administration. Now that this process of rapprochement has received the seal of approval at the highest level, we can again talk about the *entente cordiale* without embarrassment.

18. The 'renewal of friendship and co-operation between Britain and France', of which the Prime Minister spoke in the House on 24 May, is a young although vigorous plant. President Pompidou's expressed desire to proceed with the building of a united Europe on the basis of an enlarged community has already begun to be translated into practice at the first of this month's two meetings between Britain and the Six. I firmly believe that M. Pompidou intends these meetings to be a success. For the future progress of Europe which will thereby become possible, an indispensable condition will be the closest degree of co-operation between Britain and France. As a result of the improvement in our relations over the past three years, the infrastructure to support such co-operation is already in place. The Prime Minister's visit has ensured that it can be fruitfully developed.

19. I am sending copies of this despatch to Her Majesty's Representatives at Bonn, Brussels, CODEL Brussels, Copenhagen, Dublin, The Hague, Luxembourg, Moscow, UKDEL NATO, Oslo, Rome and Washington.

I have, etc.,

C. SOAMES.

N

FOREIGN AND COMMONWEALTH OFFICE TELEGRAM TO BONN No. 469 OF 11 JUNE, 1971.

(See Chapter 7, paragraph 19.)

CODEL Brussels Telegram No. 461 and subsequent reports show that there is some misapprehension among the Five and in the Commission about the extent to which we have discussed bilaterally with the French solutions to the outstanding problems in the negotiations: and that in consequence there is a risk that the Five and the Commission will slacken their efforts on our behalf in the final stages of the negotiations and assume that we will be able to reach agreement bilaterally with the French behind the scenes if indeed we have not already done so.

2. You should therefore take an early opportunity to speak at an appropriate level to the Government to which you are accredited and the Commission on the following lines.

3. As we approach the vital meeting on 21–22 June, at which the outstanding major issues in the negotiations are to be settled, we look to all Governments in the Community and the Commission to play their part in achieving a satisfactory outcome.

4. We are aware that the speed with which the French Delegation in Luxembourg on 7 June agreed to our statement on sterling has led some to suppose that the main outstanding issues—particularly Community finance and New Zealand—might be resolved with similar ease.

5. This is unlikely to be so. Sterling, and the related issues, which the French had raised were matters in an altogether special category. They were not part of the negotiations proper. They had been raised essentially by the French alone. And they were not related to obligations which were laid down in the Treaty of Rome or in regulations or directives adopted under it.

6. The Communiqué issued after the Prime Minister's talks with President Pompidou on 20–21 May said of the discussion on economic, financial and monetary problems that they had produced a useful clarification of views which will provide a firm basis for the future. We believe that these discussions greatly helped in securing subsequent French acceptance of the statement made by Mr. Rippon in Luxembourg on 7 June as settling these matters.

7. But as regards the outstanding questions in the negotiations, including Community finance and New Zealand, no such special factors applied, and although these questions were discussed between the Prime Minister and President Pompidou, as the Government to which you are accredited knows, there was no attempt to reach agreement or understanding in detail, it being recognised that the right place to. resolve these matters was in the negotiating conference in Brussels and Luxembourg.

8. You should go on to say that we are conscious that there is a feeling in some quarters that Governments of the Five and the Commission risk being

exposed as more royalist than the king if they take up a firm stand on matters of vital concern to us in the next two weeks in Brussels and Luxembourg. You should say that you have instructions to assure them that there is no risk of this. We are working on the possibility of certain changes in the presentation of New Zealand's needs in the field of dairy products and may have something to say on this at the meeting of Deputies in Brussels on 16 June. But whatever changes in presentations and detail we can make, it is going to be essential that we get more than the quantities envisaged in the Netherlands/Italian/German/ Luxembourg position in terms of milk equivalent. And as regards Community finance, while we can certainly move well above 3 per cent as our opening bid, it is going to be essential to get a first year figure well below the 11½ per cent figure of which the French are talking.

9. My immediately following telegram contains the instructions to Her Majesty's Ambassador in Paris for a further talk with M. Schumann. He will no doubt draw on the points in this telegram as appropriate in talking to the French, and may indeed wish to let both the Elysée and Schumann know that we are speaking to the Five and to the Commission on these lines. We are sure that the French continue to agree with us that we must not give the other Community Governments and the Commission the impression—which would be quite false—that we are settling everything bilaterally behind their backs.

DOUGLAS-HOME.

APPENDIX II

Published Documents
(Arranged in Chronological Order)

A

LETTER FROM Mr. HAROLD WILSON OF 10 MAY, 1967, TO THE PRESIDENT OF THE COUNCIL OF MINISTERS OF THE EUROPEAN ECONOMIC COMMUNITY.

(See Chapter 1.)

Mr. President, *10 May, 1967.*

I have the honour, on behalf of Her Majesty's Government in the United Kingdom of Great Britain and Northern Ireland, to inform Your Excellency that the United Kingdom hereby applies to become a member of the European Economic Community under the terms of Article 237 of the Treaty establishing the European Economic Community.

Please accept, Mr. President, the assurance of my highest consideration.

HAROLD WILSON.

His Excellency Monsieur R. van Elslande.

[Similar letters of the same date were sent in respect of the European Coal and Steel Community and the European Atomic Energy Community.]

B

Mr. GEORGE BROWN'S STATEMENT AT THE MINISTERIAL COUNCIL MEETING OF WESTERN EUROPEAN UNION ON 4 JULY, 1967.

(See Chapters 1 and 2.)

1. The United Kingdom has applied to become a member of the three European Communities—the European Economic Community, the European Coal and Steel Community, and Euratom. I have been charged by Her Majesty's Government in the United Kingdom to make clear to the Member application and its Governments of the Communities the reasons for our application and its consequences as we see them.

2. We in Britain are conscious that this is a decisive moment in our history. The issue will shape our future for generations to come.

3. We believe the same is true for Europe as a whole. And we believe that the present opportunity may not easily come again. Unless Europe is united and strengthened she will not be able to meet the challenge of the world today. And we must all of us meet it, or Europe will drift further and further into the margin of events. None of us, I believe, envisages a role of that sort as being commensurate with the skills and wealth and wisdom of our Continent. The world as a whole too would surely be the loser. European civilisation has given so much to it in the past. It has so much still to give.

4. The European Communities are developing on an economic base. But we in Britain, no less than the present Members of the Communities, do not see the issues only in economic terms. The balance of economic advantage for us is a fine one. Some of the most decisive considerations for us have been political.

5. Together we now have the possibility of gradually building up between us a true unity of purpose and action. But political power, and the ability to assert a European influence on events, must grow out of economic strength. That is why we have laid particular emphasis in our approach to this question on the technological aspects.

6. An integrated market and continuing progress towards economic union, the removal of national barriers which at present obstruct European industry from reaching its full potential, and the consequent development of technological enterprises on a truly Continental scale—these are urgent requirements. I believe there is a close meeting of minds between us on these objectives. We are none of us big enough as individual countries to provide all the resources for development and research for which the sophisticated products of our times call with mounting insistence. Too often we have watched the enterprise and inventive genius of our scientists and technicians failing to attain their rightful fulfilment. The rewards go elsewhere, to those countries which can offer the vital element of a large enough market.

7. Britain's entry into the Communities would do much to redress the balance. In the preliminary discussions which the Prime Minister and I had with you earlier this year we found wide recognition that this was a common problem and one which we could contribute a lot to solve. In particular, our contribution in nuclear development for peaceful uses, in computers and in aircraft, should greatly strengthen the Community.

8. Of course there is some scope for progress through bilateral cooperation—for example with projects where respective Governments control the purchasing programmes. But the field here is limited. In the commercial field, and it is the greater part of the field, let us have no illusions: there is no alternative for Europe to the development of a larger commercial market in which Europe-wide industries and companies can freely operate without tariff or other barriers. This alone will allow effective technological development. Britain's

entry would bring the Communities within sight of attaining a market of three hundred million people—a population greater than either that of the United States or the Soviet Union. This, combined with our skills and research knowledge, would united be an extremely powerful unit. If we do not unite, then I believe that the 1970s will find Western Europe producing the conventional equipment of the 1960s and being forced to look outside Europe for the advanced equipment of the 1970s. But if we can achieve this unity, we can be confident that Europe will maintain a commanding position in the increasingly competitive markets of the world, with all that that implies, for the welfare and standard of living of our own peoples, and for our contribution to world development.

9. But, as I say, we are aiming at something far more than material prosperity. We see this leading to a greater political purpose for Western Europe. And if that purpose is to be realised, Britain must share it. We want, as soon as we can, to develop really effective political unity with our fellow West Europeans.

10. The advantages for all of us of this unity will reach far wider than Western Europe itself. We see this as a major step towards a reconciliation and a revival in that larger Europe which has remained too long divided between East and West. We see this unity as enabling us all to bring a powerful influence to bear in other fields—in the Western Alliance and in the world as a whole. We see it too as enabling us all to contribute more effectively to the needs of the developing world. We see it, in short, as power for peace.

11. The need becomes more urgent with every year that passes. As successive crises have arisen in one part of the world or another we have, I believe, all felt increasingly that Europe has not played the part it could and should. Europe has made a remarkable recovery since the war, but we must now look to greater unity for the additional strength which will enable Europe to play its full part in the future.

12. Similarly, the economic problems of the developing world grow heavier every day. We are each providing substantial aid already. But we cannot say that we are doing enough. The requirement here, no less than in the political field, is for the common approach which a united Europe could provide.

13. Britain now asks to join you. We share your objectives. We want to link our efforts with yours. So do other European countries. We are convinced that this is the right road forward.

14. Fears have been expressed that there would be some radical alterations in the nature of your Communities if we and other European countries were now to enter them. There will of course be changes. But they will be changes of dimension—a larger Community, a more powerful and more influential Europe. None of us should have anything to fear here—for this whole concept of size is, as I have explained, the essential element of that unity we aspire to. And above all that unity requires a common purpose and outlook, and a will to work together. We have already given assurances about this, and what I have to say today will confirm them. The fundamentals of the Communities will

remain unaffected, for we shall be accepting precisely the same treaty aims and obligations in letter and spirit as yourselves. We aim to create with you a unity, which will be all the greater because it will be built on the rich diversity of achievements and characteristics of European peoples who share a common purpose and a common resolve for peace.

15. I have set out, in brief, the reasons for Britain's application to join the Communities. The processes of argument and debate in Britain which led to our decision were long and arduous. The issues have been carefully weighed in full realisation of what is at stake. The massive vote which the Government received in the British House of Commons on 10th May in support of its application is the result.

16. We seek to reduce the area of negotiations to the minimum. Much useful preliminary work was in fact done in the series of discussions which the Prime Minister and I had with your Governments earlier this year. These discussions isolated the major issues and pointed to ways of resolving them.

17. We want to keep the negotiations as short as possible so that we can start work with you in the Communities at an early date.

18. I now turn from the reasons for our application to the issues to be dealt with in the course of negotiations.

19. I begin with the Treaties. They, and particularly the Treaty establishing the European Economic Community, are the pillars of the Community structure. We accept all three Treaties, subject only to the adjustments which are required to provide for the accession of a new member, for example our participation and voting in the Communities' institutions, and our contribution to its financial expenditure. I shall come in a moment to the particular issues on which we seek satisfaction but let me say at once that, subject to this. Her Majesty's Government accept without reserve all the aims and objectives of the three Treaties and will implement them.

20. I will go further. We recognise that the Community is a dynamic organisation which has already evolved and will continue to evolve. If it is to be true to the spirit of the Treaties which established it, the Community's institutions will develop and its activities will extend to wider fields beyond the activities covered by the existing provisions of the Treaties. We believe that Europe can emerge as a Community expressing its own point of view and exercising influence in world affairs, not only in the commercial and economic but also in the political and defence fields. We shall play our full part in this process. Indeed it is the realisation of this European potential which has, above all, aroused our desire to join the Communities. As a member we shall accept whatever responsibilities the evolving Community may decide to assume and we shall join as eagerly as other members in creating new opportunities for the expression of European unity.

21. The questions to be settled before our entry are few.

22. It has been generally recognised that all of us, you no less than we, will need a transitional period or periods to permit mutual adaptation to the

circumstances of an enlarged Community. I would like to propose, following your example at the outset of the Community's life, that the first year of the transitional period should be a standstill period. We see mutual advantage in following the example which you set in 1958.

23. There would be the further advantage that it could give other members of the European Free Trade Association seeking membership of, or association with, the Community time to conclude their negotiations. If in the event, any of these EFTA countries, or the Irish Republic, were, by the end of that twelve-month period, in sight of, or at least well advanced towards, agreement, I am confident that we could agree together on the obvious consequences for the tariff treatment we extend to them.

24. In the case of EURATOM we seek nothing more than this twelve-month initial period. In the case of the European Coal and Steel Community we seek only a limited period of transition. Thereafter we are prepared fully to implement these two Treaties and all the arrangements made under them.

25. There is nothing in our law and practice which is irreconcilable with Community requirements. Many of the necessary adaptations could be made immediately following on a twelve months standstill. In other cases, we shall be able to adapt our arrangements with very little delay; but some of the changes which we shall be called on to make, particularly in the field of agriculture, will be very considerable and an adequate period of adaptation will be needed. You needed it yourselves. What the period should be will be a matter for discussion with you.

26. So much for transitional periods, which are clearly something which you will want just as much as we in order to allow adaptations to take place over a reasonable period of time.

27. I now turn to certain other questions which we are convinced it is in our common interest to discuss together and resolve, beginning with those which I wish to raise in the field of agriculture.

28. First, there is the question of an annual review. When the Community and Britain negotiated in 1962, the Community readily agreed that it would be in the common interest that existing procedures should be developed to ensure that the Commission and the Council of Ministers were each year fully and accurately informed of the agricultural situation and prospects in the Community before taking decisions on the levels of common prices; and that these procedures should provide for taking effectively into account the views of the agricultural industry throughout the Community. A procedure for an annual agricultural review held in conjunction with the producer organisations could, we believe, contribute materially to the smooth running and effectiveness of the common agricultural policy.

29. Secondly there is milk. Here our aim is quite simple: that the Community arrangements should ensure that we have adequate supplies of liquid milk to meet demand for consumption throughout the year. I am sure you will recognise that, in conformity with the aims of the Treaty, we must be able to offer our

consumers a continued assurance of supplies. We believe that this can be done without upsetting present Community arrangements.

30. For pig meat and eggs, we should wish to see support arrangements to ensure adequate market stability in the enlarged Community.

31. As regards the financing of the common agricultural policy, on which we had most useful discussions with all the Six Governments and with the Commission earlier this year, I think it is recognised that the existing financial arrangements would put an inequitable burden on the United Kingdom. But those for the period after 1969 will necessarily be affected by our entry into the Community. We shall look forward to taking part as a full member of the Community in the negotiation of the agricultural finance arrangements for the period after the end of 1969, including the question of the aid which, in common with the members of the Community, we give to farmers in areas where there are special difficulties, for example in our case the hill farmers.

32. There are two main questions which arise in relation both to Commonwealth interests and to agriculture: sugar and New Zealand.

33. For sugar, as you know, we have an agreement with Commonwealth sugar producers which runs until the end of 1974. Your own transitional arrangements are due to expire six months later. The commitment we have under the Commonwealth Sugar Agreement is a contract which we must fulfil. We believe that the sugar exported to Britain under the Commonwealth Sugar Agreement can be accommodated within a reasonable production quota under existing Community arrangements, and without departure from the precedents which you have set for yourselves. We have also to look to the longer-term interests of the developing countries and territories many of whose economies are overwhelmingly dependent on their exports of sugar and we believe that it is in the Community's longer-term interest that we should do so. In due course, we shall wish to discuss with you how these interests can be safeguarded in the longer term.

34. Turning to New Zealand: in 1962, and again when the Prime Minister and I visited the capitals of the Community countries in the first months of this year, we found general recognition that her case was of an altogether special kind, and should be treated by the Community as such. I do not believe that this should present the Community with problems which we cannot resolve together. New Zealand's economy largely depends on her trade in butter, cheese and lamb. Because of the size of the British market for dairy produce, we believe that provisions for exports of butter and cheese from New Zealand would in no way be inconsistent with substantial benefits accruing to other members of a wider Community; and we shall need to discuss such provisions with you. In the case of cheese it may be found that in practice there will be little or no problem. But we could turn out to be wrong about this. So we shall ask you to agree to a review procedure to enable action to be taken if it is necessary. For butter, more precise provision will have to be made. I am confident that in discussions together we can find a constructive and realistic solution. Community

farmers have a strong interest with New Zealand in wishing to see the level of butter consumption maintained in Europe.

35. I now turn to the remaining questions relating to the Commonwealth.

36. During the 1961–63 negotiations between the Community and Britain it was provisionally agreed that, with one or two exceptions, association under Part IV of the Treaty of Rome would be appropriate for our dependent territories. We trust that you would still agree that for these territories this is the best arrangement. We should discuss together the position of any dependent territories for which association is not appropriate.

37. It was also provisionally agreed during the 1961–63 negotiations that association under what was later negotiated as the Yaoundé Convention should be open to independent Commonwealth countries in Africa and the Caribbean. The Community subsequently repeated this offer in the Declaration of Intent issued by the Council of Ministers of the Community in July 1963—a Declaration of Intent which was in no way dependent on Britain's becoming a member of the Community. I trust that we can quickly confirm that the alternatives contemplated in this declaration will be open to independent Commonwealth countries in Africa and in the Caribbean.

38. I realise that the Yaoundé Convention is due to expire in May, 1969. It would scarcely be practicable for the Commonwealth countries in question to negotiate accession to the present Yaoundé Convention. I therefore suggest that these countries should be allowed to continue their present trading arrangements with Britain until new arrangements come into force after the expiry of the Yaoundé Convention in the negotiation of which it should be open to them to take part.

39. Agreement was also reached in principle in the 1961–63 negotiations that there should be certain trading arrangements for developing independent Commonwealth countries for whom association was not thought appropriate. We hope it will be possible to revive that agreement.

40. Another aspect of Community development to which we referred in our preliminary talks with your Governments was capital movements. I believe the discussions we then had about this were particularly useful. We fully accept the obligations of membership of the Community in this field subject only to a transitional period during which we would by stages bring our policies into line with yours.

41. During our preliminary talks we referred to the problem of the possible leak of portfolio investment from the United Kingdom into third countries, particularly into North America. We have given further consideration to this problem and we would propose, if it proves necessary, to take action to deal with it ourselves, after consulting you as provided for in Article 70 (2) of the Treaty.

42. So far as tariffs are concerned we shall be prepared to accept the Common External Tariff as it will stand after the Kennedy Round reductions have been made. We shall of course also need to discuss how our tariff structure

will be adjusted to that of the Community within the period of adjustment to which I have referred earlier.

43. There will be a limited number of other points which will need to be considered. The points of this kind which we have in mind at present include our accession to the Agreements associating Greece and Turkey with the Community, and certain matters affecting the harmonisation of laws in the agricultural and food field: we think that most of these could be settled after we join the Community.

44. In all other fields we accept, as I have already made clear, the obligations of the Treaty establishing the European Economic Community and the regulations, directives and other decisions taken under it, subject only to a transitional period and, of course, to developments in the Community in the meantime.

45. I recognise that the Member States of the Community on their side may wish to propose other questions for consideration during our negotiations. We shall of course be perfectly ready to discuss these questions. I would only add this. I have set out fully and frankly the issues which we believe will require attention in negotiations to provide for our entry into the European Communities. Our list is not a formidable one. More than ever we hold to our view that it presents no questions to which an answer cannot reasonably be found in our common interest. I hope that, when the Community comes to respond, it will be as full and frank as I have been and will mention in full any additional points which you think should occupy the negotiations ahead. We shall then, between us, have a complete view at the outset of the task which faces us.

46. I will not make any suggestions at this stage about the procedures we might adopt for the conduct of those negotiations. I am sure that we shall be able to fall in with whatever is proposed.

47. It only remains for me to say that the British Government and those who will be responsible for the conduct of our negotiations with the Community will spare no effort to bring them to a successful and speedy conclusion. We are confident that you will do no less. It will be a negotiation, certainly, but with a difference. The wider interests of Europe must prevail. Europe as a whole can gain, or lose, from our endeavours. And Europe. already, is all of us.

48. This application is therefore not just a matter of economics and politics. The history and culture of our continent is the birthright of us all. We have all contributed to it and we all share in it. Our application flows from the historical development of our continent, from the sentiments, which, as Europeans, we all share and from the idea we all have of the part our continent should play in the world. Today the European spirit flows strongly in the movement towards a greater unity. Surely it is in the interests of all our countries that Britain should make her full contribution to this unity. With Britain as a member of the Community, Europe will be enabled to play a greater role in terms of power and influence, and to contribute in far greater measure not only to the development of her own potential but to that of the world as a whole.

49. The opportunity is now before us to take a decisive step towards this greater unity. I have pledged the full determination of my country to succeed in this task. History, I am sure, will judge us all harshly if we fail in this endeavour.

50. I hope that the statement which I have made to you this afternoon will help the Community in its consideration of our application and enable negotiations to open as soon as the opinion of the Commission has been given in September. I am therefore conveying formally the text of my statement to you, Herr Brandt, as Chairman of the single Council of Ministers of the European Communities. I shall also convey copies to the President of the Commission. I am also arranging for the text to be made public in the United Kingdom.

C

LETTER FROM PRESIDENT OF THE COUNCIL OF MINISTERS OF THE EUROPEAN COMMUNITIES TO Mr. HAROLD WILSON OF 19 DECEMBER, 1967.

(See Chapter 1.)

Brussels,
19 December, 1967.

Mr. Prime Minister,

In reply to your letter of 10 May, 1967, I have the honour, on behalf of the Council of the European Communities, to inform you of the following.

The Council has since July of this year at numerous meetings dealt extensively with the subject of your letter, namely membership of the United Kingdom of Great Britain and Northern Ireland in the European Communities. At the same time, the Commission, in accordance with Articles 237 of the Treaty of the European Economic Community, 205 of the Treaty of the European Atomic community and 98 of the Treaty of the European Coal and Steel Community, has addressed two opinions on this subject to the Council (on 29 September and 12 December, 1967).

In the view of the Commission, negotiations with the States which have applied for membership should be opened in the appropriate form. At the Council meeting on 18 and 19 December it was established that no Member State has raised objections in principle to the enlargement of the Communities. One Member State was however of the view that the enlargement of the Communities would fundamentally alter the nature and the method of work of the Communities.

At the same meeting, Five Member States have associated themselves with the above-mentioned view of the Commission. Furthermore, they have expressed themselves in favour of opening negotiations now with the United Kingdom of Great Britain and Northern Ireland with the objective of membership. One Member State is however of the opinion that the process of recovery of the

British economy must be completed, before the application of Great Britain can again be taken into consideration.

At the present stage, therefore, no unanimity could be achieved in the Council regarding the continuation of the procedure. I would however in addition like to point out to you that the Council has unanimously decided: the United Kingdom's request for membership remains on the Council's agenda.

Furthermore, may I allow myself to convey to you the unanimously agreed summary* which reproduces in full the results of the Council meeting on 18 and 19 December, 1967.

Permit me, Mr. Prime Minister, to express my most exceptional respect.

K. SCHILLER.

D

THE COMMUNIQUE OF THE HAGUE SUMMIT MEETING OF DECEMBER 1969.

(See Chapters 1 and 2.)

The following is the official English text:

1. On the initiative of the Government of the French Republic and at the invitation of the Netherlands Government, the Heads of State or Government and the Ministers for Foreign Affairs of the Member States of the European Communities met at The Hague on 1 and 2 December, 1969. The Commission of the European Communities was invited to participate in the work of the conference on the second day.

2. Now that the Common Market is about to enter upon its final stage, they considered that it was the duty of those who bear the highest political responsibility in each of the Member States to draw up a balance-sheet of the work already accomplished, to show their determination to continue it and to define the broad lines for the future.

3. Looking back on the road that has been traversed, and finding that never before have independent states pushed their co-operation further, they were unanimous in their opinion that by reason of the progress made, the Community has now arrived at a turning point in its history. Over and above the technical and legal sides of the problems involved, the expiry of the transitional period at the end of the year has, therefore, acquired major political significance. Entry upon the final stage of the Common Market not only means confirming the irreversible nature of the work accomplished by the Communities, but also means paving the way for a united Europe capable of assuming its responsibilities in the world of tomorrow and of making a contribution commensurate with its traditions and its mission.

4. The Heads of State or Government therefore wish to reaffirm their belief in the political objectives which give the Community its meaning and purport, their determination to carry their undertaking through to the end, and their

* Not printed.

confidence in the final success of their efforts. Indeed, they have a common conviction that a Europe composed of States which in spite of their different national characteristics, are united in their essential interests, assured of internal cohesion, true to its friendly relations with outside countries, conscious of the role it has to play in promoting the relaxation of international tension and the rapprochement among all peoples, and first and foremost among those of the entire European continent, is indispensable if a mainspring of development, progress and culture, world equilibrium and peace is to be preserved. The European Communities remain the original nucleus from which European unity has been developed and intensified. The entry of other countries of this continent to the Communities—in accordance with the provisions of the Treaties of Rome—would undoubtedly help the Communities to grow to dimensions more in conformity with the present state of world economy and technology. The creation of a special relationship with other European States which have expressed a desire to that effect would also contribute to this end. A development such as this would enable Europe to remain faithful to its traditions of being open to the world and increase its efforts on behalf of developing countries.

5. As regards the completion of the Communities, the Heads of State or Government reaffirmed the will of their Governments to pass from the transitional period to the final stage of the European Community and, accordingly, to lay down a definitive financial arrangement for the common agricultural policy by the end of 1969. They agreed progressively to replace, within the framework of this financial arrangement, the contributions of Member countries by their own resources, taking into account all the interests concerned, with the object of achieving in due course the integral financing of the Communities' budgets in accordance with the procedure provided for in Article 201 of the Treaty establishing the EEC and of strengthening the budgetary powers of the European Parliament. The problem of the method of direct elections is still being studied by the Council of Ministers.

6. They asked the Governments to continue without delay, within the Council, the efforts already made to ensure a better control of the market by a policy of agricultural production making it possible to limit budgetary charges.

7. The acceptance of a financial arrangement for the final stage does not exclude its adaptation by unanimous vote, in particular in the light of an enlarged Community and on condition that the principles of this arrangement are not infringed.

8. They reaffirmed their readiness to further the more rapid progress of the later development needed to strengthen the Community and promote its development into an economic union. They are of the opinion that the integration process should result in a Community of stability and growth. To this end they agreed that within the Council, on the basis of the memorandum presented by the Commission on 12 February, 1969, and in close collaboration with the latter, a plan in stages should be worked out during 1970 with a view

to the creation of an economic and monetary union. The development of monetary co-operation should depend on the harmonisation of economic policies. They agree to arrange for the investigation of the possibility of setting up a European Reserve Fund in which a joint economic and monetary policy would have to result.

9. As regards the technological activity of the Community, they reaffirmed their readiness to continue more intensively the activities of the Community with a view to co-ordinating and promoting industrial research and development in the principal sectors concerned, in particular by means of common programmes, and to supply the financial means for the purpose.

10. They further agreed on the necessity of making fresh efforts to work out in the near future a research programme for the European Atomic Energy Community designed in accordance with the exigencies of modern industrial management, and making it possible to ensure the most effective use of the common research centre.

11. They reaffirmed their interest in the establishment of a European university.

12. The Heads of State or Government acknowledge the desirability of reforming the Social Fund, within the framework of a closely concerted social policy.

13. They reaffirmed their agreement on the principle of the enlargement of the Community, as provided by Article 237 of the Treaty of Rome. In so far as the applicant States accept the treaties and their political finality, the decisions taken since the entry into force of the treaties and the options made in the sphere of development the Heads of State or Government have indicated their agreement to the opening of negotiations between the Community on the one hand and the applicant States on the other. They agreed that the essential preparatory work could be undertaken as soon as practically and conveniently possible. By common consent, the preparations would take place in a most positive spirit.

14. As soon as negotiations with the applicant countries have been opened, discussion will be started with such other EFTA members as may request them on their position in relation to the EEC.

15. They agreed to instruct the Ministers for Foreign Affairs to study the best way of achieving progress in the matter of political unification, within the context of enlargement. The Ministers would be expected to report before the end of July 1970.

16. All the creative activities and the actions conducive to European growth decided upon here will be assured of a better future if the younger generation is closely associated with them. The Governments are resolved to endorse this and the Communities will make provisions for it.

E
ANNOUNCEMENT OF COMPOSITION OF UNITED KINGDOM NEGOTIATING DELEGATION AT OFFICIAL LEVEL, 10 APRIL, 1970.

(See Chapter 1.)

The names of the senior members of the British Delegation appointed to negotiate for British entry into the European Communities are published today. As already announced, the Ministerial leader will be the Right Hon. George Thomson, MP, the Chancellor of the Duchy of Lancaster.

The Leader of the Delegation at the official level will be Sir Con O'Neill, KCMG, a Deputy Under-Secretary of State in the Foreign and Commonwealth Office. The other members will be:

Mr. G.R. Bell, CB, Third Secretary, Her Majesty's Treasury;
Mr. G.R. Denman, CMG, on promotion to Deputy Secretary, Board of Trade;
Mr. F.M. Kearns, CB, MC, Deputy Secretary, MAFF;
Mr. W.P. Shovelton, Under-Secretary, Ministry of Technology.

Mr. J.A. Robinson, CMG, a Counsellor in the Diplomatic Service, will also be a member of the Delegation. Its Legal Adviser will be Mr. I.M. Sinclair of the Foreign and Commonwealth Office. In addition, Sir James Marjoribanks, KCMG, Her Majesty's Ambassador to the European Communities in Brussels, and his Deputy, Mr. K.C. Christofas, CMG, MBE, Minister Plenipotentiary, will be nominated as members of the negotiating Delegation, but will also continue to discharge their duties with the Permanent United Kingdom Delegation to the Communities in Brussels.

Officials from other Departments (including the Home Office, Scottish Office and the Welsh Office) will be available to join the Delegation as required.

The necessary junior supporting staff to complete the negotiating Delegation is also being selected and appointed.

F
COMMUNIQUE OF 9 JUNE, 1970, OF THE COUNCIL OF MINISTERS.

(See Chapter 3.)

ENLARGEMENT: PROCEDURE FOR NEGOTIATIONS

'1. In implementation of the Communiqué of The Hague, the negotiations for membership shall be conducted, at all levels, for all questions and in accordance with a standard procedure, by the European Communities.

2. Accordingly, the Council of Ministers shall decide upon the common standpoint of the European Communities in respect of all problems raised by the negotiations for membership.

3. With a view to the adoption of a common standpoint for the European Communities, the Commission shall be invited to make proposals in respect of all problems raised by the negotiations for membership.

4. The relevant discussions of the Council shall, in implementation of Article 4 of the Treaty establishing a single Council and a single Commission of the European Communities, be prepared by the Permanent Representatives Committee.

5. The meetings for negotiations between the European Communities and the applicant States shall be presided over for the European Communities, at all levels, by the President in Office of the Council of the European Communities.

6. The common standpoint of the European Communities shall be set out and defended in negotiations with the applicant States either by the President in Office of the Council or, on the decision of the Council, and particularly where agreed Community policies are concerned, by the Commission.

7. The rules mentioned in paragraphs 5 and 6 above shall also apply where negotiations are conducted at the level of the Permanent Representatives or of Working Parties to be set up.

8. Further, the Council states its readiness to entrust the Commission with the task of seeking, in liaison with the applicant States, possible solutions to specific problems raised during the negotiations and to report thereon to the Council, which will give the Commission any directives required for this task to be pursued, with a view to working out the basis of an agreement to be submitted to the Council.

This provision shall in particular apply where agreed Community policies are concerned.'

G

LETTER FROM M. HARMEL TO Mr. MICHAEL STEWART OF 9 JUNE, 1970.
(See Chapter 1.)

Monsieur le Ministre et Cher Collègue,

J'ai l'honneur de porter à votre connaissance que, lors de sa session tenue à Luxembourg le 8 juin 1970, le Conseil des Communautés européennes a décidé, conformément à l'article 237 du Traité instituant la Communauté Economique Européenne, à l'article 205 du Traité instituant la Communauté Européenne de l'Energie Atomique et à l'article 98 du Traité instituant la Communauté Européenne du Charbon et de l'Acier, d'ouvrir entre les Communautés Européennes et le Royaume-Uni les négociations qui font l'objet de la demande d'adhésion que le Gouvernement de Sa Majesté a adressée au Conseil des Communautés européennes par ses lettres du 10 mai 1967.

En conséquence, j'ai l'honneur d'inviter le Gouvernement de Sa Majesté à une première réunion, le 30 juin 1970 à Luxembourg, pour l'ouverture des négociations. Sont également invités à cette réunion, les Gouvernements du Royaume du Danemark, d'Irlande et du Royaume de Norvège.

Je vous prie d'agréer, Monsieur le Ministre et Cher Collègue, l'expression de mes sentiments les meilleurs et de très haute considération.

P. HARMEL.

H

M. HARMEL'S STATEMENT AT THE OPENING OF NEGOTIATIONS ON 30 JUNE, 1970.

(See Chapter 2.)

DECLARATION

made by the Spokesman of the Communities,
His Excellency Pierre HARMEL,
President in Office of the Council,
at the first Ministerial Meeting between the European Communities and the States which have applied for membership of these Communities held at Luxembourg on 30 June, 1970.

Your Excellencies, Ladies and Gentlemen and dear colleagues,

On this important date for Europe, 30 June, 1970, the Council of Ministers of the European Communities is happy to welcome the representatives of the United Kingdom, Ireland, Denmark and Norway. I mention these countries in the order in which their applications were made.

Your States wish to become members of the Communities. That is why we are meeting with you today in order to open negotiations. As it is expressed in Article 237 of the Treaty of Rome, the object of these negotiations is to establish, by joint agreement between the Member States of the Communities and the applicant States, the conditions of admission and the consequential adjustments to the Treaties.

The Council of Ministers is well aware that it is performing at a happily chosen moment, one of the fundamental acts which mark Europe's march towards its unification.

A march, the first step of which was taken 24 years ago.

This was on 19 September, 1946, at Zürich. The ruins of our old continent had hardly ceased smoking when Winston Churchill, the first to do so, spoke there of reconciliation. We must, he said, re-create the European Family, and provide it with a structure which could well be christened the 'United States of Europe'.

The idea of Europe, so strongly supported by our peoples, then found its first expression in the establishment of the Parliament at Strasbourg. I mention the Council of Europe because, in its Parliament and its Committee of Ministers, it has for a long time brought together the 10 States represented here, and because it has always been the forum of human rights and of Parliamentary democracy in which the new Europe recognises its cornerstone.

But it was on 9 May, 1950, that the work of European integration which your States are now approaching was started. On that day, by the voice of Robert Schuman, the French Government proposed a limited but decisive step, that of placing French and German production of coal and steel under a common High Authority, in an organisation open to the participation of the other States of Europe. The economic union which was then commencing was an audacious attempt, now largely accomplished, in which a group of States is working towards the achievement, product by product, of the conditions proper to an internal market to which common rules will apply and ultimately common policies.

We have not met here to write the history of European integration, but to make it. It is not the moment therefore to recount successes and failures, the moments of creation and the delays which occurred, all the patience and impatience which adorns every political achievement.

We knew, from the beginning, that it would be a gradual achievement, for Robert Schuman had warned us: 'Europe will not be created all at once, nor as part of an overall design; it will be built through practical achievements that will first establish a sense of common purpose.'

The important thing is that Europe is progressing quite rapidly, and we can at least record, on the whole, with the six Heads of State or of Government of the Member States, at the summit meeting at The Hague on 2 December last, that, at the end of this quarter of a century 'the European States have never perhaps advanced their co-operation further'.

The Institutions of which you wish to become part are therefore engaged in a process of continuous creation; they are living communities which open with you the negotiations for your accession.

But people who live together must have the same objectives.

We believe, Ladies and Gentlemen, that our European aims coincide with yours; they are concerned with, although at once going beyond, the economic progress which our Governments expect from the enlargement of the Communities.

In addition to the material aims and their favourable social results for our peoples, the entry of four countries which are rich in long parliamentary and democratic traditions, will reinforce the central nucleus of Europe.

This central nucleus is more than ever necessary to the idea of total Europe. In Europe we must maintain and reinforce a type of civilisation and a political system which we do not aspire to impose on any State, but which in our eyes is the best guarantee of liberty and of the progress of our peoples.

Other States may perhaps gather round this nucleus in due course, thus taking part in an enterprise whose institutions are founded on the freely expressed will of the people.

But our common thoughts go further still. If we place the effort which is starting today in a world context, we are obliged to think of the role to be played and the duties to be performed by a Community of peoples, favoured by high intellectual, technical and material development, counting more than 250 million inhabitants, united by geography, tradition, history, culture and a common civilisation! To what new missions of peace, to what generous acts, may not such a Europe devote all the power born of its unity?

For the Six Member States of the Communities, these objectives, these political aims, are those which animate our Heads of States or of Government. They solemnly restated them at The Hague in terms which we should read once more: 'We have a common conviction that a Europe composed of States which, in spite of their different national characteristics, are united in their essential interests, assured of its internal cohesion, true to its friendly relations with outside countries, conscious of the role it has to play in promoting the relaxation of international tension and a rapprochement among all peoples, and first and foremost among those of the entire European continent, is indispensable if a mainspring of development, progress and culture, world equilibrium and peace is to be preserved.'

These, Ladies and Gentlemen, are the thoughts which inspire and fortify our wills as we set out for you the actual context in which these negotiations are situated, and how we would propose to conduct them.

II. THE CONTEXT OF THE NEGOTIATIONS

The context of the negotiations is that of a three-fold movement, decided upon at the summit meeting at The Hague: the transition to the final period of the Common Market, the internal development of the Communities, and their enlargement.

These three themes are not linked in such a way that one is a precondition for the others. Instead we must see in them three complementary aspects of the second decisive stage in the construction of Europe.

1. *Completion*

The proclamation at The Hague of the political will to move on to the final stage of the Common Market on 1 January, 1970, involved, in accordance with the Treaty, stamping the work accomplished in 12 years with an irreversible nature, by noting that the essential part of the objectives of the Treaty have been accomplished, comprising in particular the establishment of the customs union and of common policies in the fields of trade and agriculture, as also the abolition of obstacles to the free movement of persons, services and capital.

But the Council wanted to complete what had been achieved by far-reaching decisions:

(1) It wished to adopt the definitive financial regulation for the years to come, without excluding the possibility of adapting it unanimously, to meet the demands of an enlarged Community, but on condition that the principles of the regulation should not be changed.
(2) It also wished to decide that by 1975 the Communities will have their own resources to take the place of the annual financial contributions now paid by the Member States.

The latter decision has a considerable political import, since at the same time the powers of the European Parliament are extended both as regards the preparation of budgets, and their supervision and implementation. It will also be recalled that the Council is continuing work on the problem of the procedure for direct elections to the European Parliament.

These are the significant decisions which have marked the transition to the final stage.

2. *Internal development*

The second compartment of the triptych relates to the internal development of the Communities. It was necessary, not only to keep the old promises recorded in the Treaties, but to formulate new ones, in order to mark the progress of European integration. It was also at The Hague that renewed expression was given to the will to progress more rapidly with the subsequent development required to strengthen the Communities, and that these new developments were announced and construction started, mainly along the following lines:

(a) The Heads of State or of Government agreed that a multi-stage plan should be worked out during 1970 with a view to the creation of an economic and monetary union.
(b) As regards the technological activity of the Community, they reaffirmed their readiness to continue the Community's activities more intensively with a view to co-ordinating and promoting industrial research and development in the principal advanced sectors, in particular by means of common programmes, and to supply the financial means for the purpose.
(c) They further agreed on the necessity of making fresh efforts to work out in the near future a research programme for the European Atomic Energy Community designed in accordance with the exigencies of modern industrial management, and making it possible to ensure the most effective use of the Common Research Centre.
(d) They also acknowledged the desirability of reforming the social fund, within the framework of a close concertation of social policies.

Work on these various subjects, as on others, is being actively continued within the Community, and we may congratulate ourselves that discussions have since then been initiated with the applicant States, as with a certain number of other European countries, in the fields of technology, industrial research, and patents.

I refer to this work, because it is the Community's intention that, as the examination of these problems leads, within the Community, either to guidelines or to resolutions for action, these will be put to the applicant States in the negotiations as Community positions.

As for the decisions in question, the applicant States will be asked to accept them on the same basis as the other decisions which have been taken since the Treaties came into force.

Finally, attention must be drawn to the work which has been undertaken in accordance with paragraph 15 of the Communiqué issued at The Hague. Pursuant to this paragraph the Ministers of Foreign Affairs of the Member States of the Community are now studying the best methods of making progress in the field of political unification, while bearing the enlargement of the Communities in mind. And the applicant States have been kept informed of each stage in the progress of this work.

III. THE COMMUNITY'S POSITION

We must now describe to you the positions and procedures which the Community has decided upon for the purpose of the negotiations:

(a) We assume in principle that your States accept the Treaties and their political objectives, all the decisions of every type which have been taken since the Treaties came into force, and the choices made in the field of development.

These decisions also include the agreements concluded by the Community with third countries.

(b) Under these conditions, the Community wishes, at the opening of the negotiations, to state a certain number of principles which it intends to apply:

1. The rule which must necessarily govern the negotiations is that the solution of any problems of adjustment which may arise must be sought in the establishment of transitional measures and not in changes in the existing rules.
2. The object of the transitional measures will be to allow for the adjustments which prove to be necessary as a consequence of the enlargement. Their duration must be restricted to that required to achieve this aim. As a general rule, they must incorporate detailed timetables and must commence with an initial significant mutual tariff reduction on the entry into force of the accession treaties.
3. The transitional measures must be conceived in such a way as to ensure an overall balance of reciprocal advantages.

With this in mind, it will be necessary to ensure an adequate synchronisation of the progress of freedom of movement of industrial goods with the achievement of the agricultural common market. This consideration must be taken into account in respect of the duration of the transitional measures in the industrial and agricultural sectors.

4. In the field of trade, the duration of the transitional period should be the same for all the applicants.

5. In the other fields in which transitional measures prove to be necessary, the duration of such measures could, if possible and desirable, be varied according to their subject matter and the applicants involved. These questions will be examined during the negotiations.

6. The various accession treaties should come into force on the same date.

(c) It is the Community's opinion that the accession of new members will lead to the enlarged Community having new responsibilities towards developing countries, which it will have to meet in appropriate ways.

With this in view, the enlarged Community must be ready to continue its policy of association, both as regards the existing Associated African and Malagasy States and for the benefit of the independent African countries of comparable structure and level of development which request association with a view to promoting their economic and social development.

The enlargement of the Community and, with it, the possible extension of the policy of association should not lead to weakening of relations with the present Associated States.

The terms and conditions of association with all these African countries could be defined during negotiations which might take place at the same time as the renegotiations with the States at present associated with the Community, which are to be held as from 1 August, 1973.

In connection with the new responsibilities of the enlarged Community to which I have just referred, it would also be desirable for the Six and the Applicant States to consult each other, preferably in the initial stage of the negotiations, with a view to adopting a joint position on the problem of generalised preferences.

When, during the course of the negotiations we reach the most important problems concerning relations with the Commonwealth, we will suggest guidelines as regards Commonwealth countries other than the African countries which I have mentioned.

(d) The Community is prepared to open discussions with the European States which are members of EFTA but which have not applied for membership of the Community, with a view to seeking possible solutions to the problems raised by enlargement, and thus to enable these States to contribute to the construction of Europe.

With reference to these discussions, I would remind you that it follows from the decisions taken at The Hague that it is not possible to conceive of an enlarged Community except in equality of rights and obligations of all the Member States.

The Community could agree to discussions starting in the autumn with a meeting at Ministerial level with any of these countries which so desire.

The agreements concluded with these countries would be binding on the enlarged Community. It will therefore be necessary to seek appropriate formulae which will enable the States which have applied for membership to be associated in due course with the preparation and conclusion of these agreements.

The Community considers that it would be desirable, for practical reasons and in the interest of all the countries concerned, for these agreements to come into force at the same time as the accession treaties.

(e) The Community is aware that the applications for membership raise both problems peculiar to each of the Applicant States and problems which will have to be examined jointly.

The organisation of the negotiations must therefore take this situation into account, it being understood that, during the first stage in any case, most of the work will have to be done on a bilateral basis.

This situation raises the problem of providing each of the Applicant States with adequate information on the progress being made in the other negotiations.

The Community proposes to put forward appropriate suggestions to this end at a later date, so that the exchange of information and the necessary consultations take place to the satisfaction of all concerned.

(f) The statement which I have just made on the Community's position is not exhaustive and does not therefore touch on all the problems which will arise during the negotiations. I am thinking here, in particular, of the questions raised by the Treaty establishing the European Atomic Energy Community and the Treaty establishing the European Coal and Steel Community, and also of the discussions which we shall be having with the United Kingdom on certain special questions relating to the economic, monetary and financial problems connected with accession.

The Community will have the opportunity to set out its views on these questions in more detail during the negotiations.

(g) Finally, the Community will employ a uniform negotiating procedure at all levels and for all questions. This time, therefore, the negotiations will take place in the framework of a Conference between the Communities and the States which have applied for membership of the Communities.

IV. CONCLUSIONS

Your Excellencies, Ladies and Gentlemen and dear colleagues,

The work which we are undertaking today is of considerable importance for the destiny of Europe.

It is arousing among our peoples an interest and a hope which we must not, which we cannot, disappoint. if we have the political aims of the Treaties, the development of the Communities, so much at heart it is because we have the profound conviction that the European Communities have been the original nucleus around which European unity has taken shape, has burgeoned and will continue to grow unchecked in the future.

The enlargement of the Communities which we all wish to achieve together will give new dimensions and new possibilities to the undertaking which we have successfully brought thus far.

At present, we can only glimpse these prospects of future developments. But we must ensure that they trace a picture of the Europe of the future which will be attractive to our peoples, presenting not only a vision of increased prosperity, but also of human, social and cultural values.

Your Excellencies, Ladies and Gentlemen and dear colleagues, I have presented to you some of our reflections at this initial stage of our work.

I am certain that our views, together with the declarations which you may wish to make, can constitute a good start for the negotiations which are commencing under such excellent auspices.

The task which awaits our negotiators is vast; the problems which they will have to solve are numerous and complex. But their efforts, and ours, will be sustained by a common political will to spare no effort to reach agreement in the shortest possible time.

Community will do everything in its power to achieve this end.

I

Mr. BARBER'S STATEMENT AT THE OPENING OF NEGOTIATIONS ON 30 JUNE, 1970.

(See Chapter 2.)

MR. CHAIRMAN,

I should like to begin by saying what a pleasure it is to be able to start our proceedings here in Luxembourg, and to thank the Luxembourg Government for the facilities and the hospitality which they are so generously providing today.

2. May I also tell you, Mr. Chairman, since this is I believe the last day of your term of office as President of the Council of Ministers of the European Communities, how much we appreciate all that you and your colleagues have done in the last six months to enable us all to meet together now? Since your historic meeting at The Hague last December, held at the initiative of the President of the French Republic, we have all moved along converging paths to Luxembourg.

3. I would also like to pay tribute to Monsieur Rey for all that he and his colleagues in the European Commission have done for the cause of a united Europe, and for the enlargement of the European Communities. I know all the member Governments of the Communities will miss him; and so shall we.

4. Mr. Chairman, before I turn to the substance of today's meeting, I hope that I may be allowed a purely personal word. After 20 years of political life, I can think of no greater challenge than to conduct these negotiations on behalf

of Her Majesty's Government. I come new to the details of European affairs, but I have followed these matters for long enough to recognise, on the one hand, the great advantages for all of us if these negotiations succeed, but, on the other hand, our need to face up to the very real problems which, together, we shall have to solve.

5. None of us in this room knows whether we shall succeed—whether we shall ultimately be able to agree upon terms which are mutually acceptable. But at least we can say this. We meet today with goodwill on all sides and, I believe, with a determination on the part of all of us to do everything possible to reach a fair solution.

6. Nine years ago we began negotiations for membership of the European Communities. We entered those negotiations with high hopes, but they were not to be fulfilled. Then, in May 1967 the previous British Government applied to join. And now, today, I want my colleagues in the Communities to know that the new Government in Britain are confident that with goodwill these negotiations now beginning can succeed. Our task is, together, to work out terms which are fair. And if none of us loses sight of the compelling reasons for uniting and strengthening Europe—reasons which have grown stronger with the years—then fair terms will be found.

7. The fact is that none of us acting alone can gain the ends which we desire for our own people in terms of physical security or economic or social advance. Looking beyond our own frontiers, there are still dangers, and it is right that Europe should assume a greater share of responsibility for its own defence. That too is our joint concern.

8. And it is wholly unrealistic to separate the political and economic interests of Europe, because our place in the world, and our influence, will be largely determined by the growth of our resources and the pace of our technological development. Economic growth and technological development today require that we integrate our economies and our markets.

9. Europe must, of course, take full account of the views of its friends and allies in other parts of the world. But let none of us who is taking part in these negotiations lose sight of our common objective of European unity. And let no one who is not taking part think it could be in his interest that we should fail to achieve that objective. For given this base, we can not only hope for, but more effectively work for a closer and more fruitful relationship between East and West. We can do more to promote the growth of international trade. And we can make a fuller European contribution to solving the problems of less prosperous countries.

10. These are the reasons why we want a united Europe. We want Europe to prosper. But we do not seek prosperity for Europe alone, any more than you do. We believe with you that Europe still has its contribution to make beyond its own frontiers and we believe that Europe cannot make its full contribution unless the Communities are enlarged to include Britain.

11. The Governments of Denmark, the Irish Republic and Norway have

also decided to apply to join the Communities, and we warmly welcome their decisions. We also believe that a number of European countries which do not join the Communities as full members will nevertheless have a valuable contribution to make to many of our common objectives, and that it will therefore be in the interest of all of us that these countries should find a mutually satisfactory relationship with the enlarged Communities.

12. Both Mr. Heath, in a speech last month, and the previous British Government have made it clear that we accept the Treaties establishing the three European Communities and the decisions which have flowed from them. I confirm that this is the position of Her Majesty's Government, subject to the points to which I now turn.

13. The list of questions which we wish to see covered in negotiations remains the same as those put forward by the previous British Government in July 1967. For Euratom and the European Coal and Steel Community we seek only a very short transitional period. Adaptation to the obligations of the European Economic Community will clearly require more time than that. And it would be unrealistic not to face up to the fact, at the outset, that there are some very difficult problems to be solved. Our main problems, as you know, concern certain matters of agricultural policy; our contribution to Community budgetary expenditure; Commonwealth sugar exports; New Zealand's special problems; and certain other Commonwealth questions.

14. The position which the previous British Government took in July 1967 was, of course, subject to developments in the Community in the meantime. Fisheries policy may prove to be one such development. In the field of Community budgetary arrangements, recent developments have made the problems facing our membership more difficult. As you know, our predecessors had looked forward to Britain's taking part as a full member in the negotiation of the financial arrangements for the period after the end of 1969. Had we done so, the resulting agreement would no doubt have made fair provision for us as it has for each of the existing members of the Communities. But we were not party to your agreement. And the arrangements which must in any case be agreed to enable a new member to take part in the budgetary provisions of the European Communities will constitute one of the crucial elements in the negotiation on which we are embarking. When the European Commission gave its Opinion on our candidature in September 1967, it was recognised that the existing financial arrangements would, if applied to Britain, 'give rise to a problem of balance in sharing of financial burdens'. I think it will be generally agreed that the new decisions have for us made that problem of balance more severe. And so we have to work together to find a solution to this basic problem which will be fair and sound for the enlarged Community and for all its members. If I appear to labour this point, it is only because, unless such a solution is found, the burden on the United Kingdom could not be sustained and no British Government could contemplate joining. Moreover, without such a solution, the

whole basis of stability and confidence, essential to the further development of the Communities, would be lacking.

15. A few weeks ago Mr. Heath spoke about the future development of the Communities. He said that we shared your determination to go on from what has already been achieved into new spheres of co-operation beginning with economic and monetary matters, but at the same time laying the foundations for a new method of working together in foreign policy and defence. In all these problems, he added, we should seek to achieve solutions which are Community solutions. We welcome the moves which you have already made towards closer economic and monetary integration and are ready to play our full part. And there are other aspects of policy where we shall likewise welcome further progress; in industrial policy, in regional policy, and of course in the field of technology where we are already working together, but where so much more could be done once the Communities had been enlarged.

16. I have said enough today to show you that the new British Government is determined to work with you in building a Europe which has a coherent character of its own. If the Communities are to develop; and if we are to find Community solutions to our common problems, we shall need the machinery to take the decisions. That means sharing in the continued development of effective institutions—effective to do those things which our joint experience shows to be necessary and advantageous to all. That has always been our practical approach to institutional change. What matters—to you and to us—is that our objectives are the same, and we no less than you, will want the institutions to match those objectives.

17. I have said that we accept the Treaties and their objectives. But it is not simply a question for us of accepting what you have done. Like you we look to the future. As the Commission recognised in its Opinion of last October, the accession of additional countries will be of great value for the Communities both in their internal development and in the exercise of increased responsibilities in the world.

18. I have referred to the main points which we wish to see covered in negotiations. We hope the negotiations can be kept short and confined to essentials. I am told that the problems which you have been discussing for the last six months in preparation for these negotiations are very much the same as ours. So these are common problems for us and for you—how to enable an enlarged Community to function most effectively for the advantage of all. Our wish is to look together in the spirit of the Community for solutions which in the words of the Commission's Opinion of 1969 will ensure the cohesion and the dynamism which will be indispensable in an enlarged Community.

19. Mr. Chairman, after many years we now have the opportunity to realise together a Europe which has a coherent character of its own. We have the same defence interest; our political interests are growing every day progressively closer. As we develop new policies together we shall, as I have said, find it natural

to develop the institutional machinery which we shall need to execute those policies. If we can together succeed in the negotiations now begun then, as Sir Winston Churchill said, there will be no limit to the happiness, to the prosperity and glory which Europe's people will enjoy. So let none of us spare any effort in these negotiations. Inspired by goodwill and united by so many aims and hopes and interests, this time we can succeed.

20. Mr. Chairman, in view of the importance of this meeting I am arranging for the text of my statement to be made public in the United Kingdom.

J

COMMUNIQUE ISSUED ON 21 MAY AFTER THE MEETING BETWEEN Mr. HEATH AND M. POMPIDOU IN PARIS ON 19–21 MAY, 1971.

(See Chapter 33.)

The President of the French Republic and the Prime Minister of the United Kingdom held discussions *en tête-à-tête* in Paris on 20 and 21 May, 1971. Mr. Heath also called upon M. Chaban-Delmas on 20 May.

On the role of Europe following the enlargement of the European Economic Community the President of the Republic and the British Prime Minister had a thorough exchange which showed that their views were very close. They expressed in particular their determination to contribute through the enlarged and deepened Community to increasing European co-operation and to the development of distinctively European policies, in the first instance principally in economic matters and progressively in other fields.

The discussion led to a complete identity of view on the working and the development of the Community.

The President of the Republic and the British Prime Minister considered the range of economic, financial and monetary problems which could arise as a result of enlargement. They also discussed the progress of the European Community towards economic and monetary union, and its implications for existing financial relationships. The Prime Minister reaffirmed the readiness of Britain to participate fully and in a European spirit in this development. These discussions produced a useful clarification of views which will provide a firm basis for the future.

The President of the Republic and the British Prime Minister took note with satisfaction of the agreements recently reached at the Ministerial meeting between the Community and the United Kingdom on 11 and 12 May on agricultural and industrial matters, and particularly on the application of Community preference in the agricultural field.

The President of the Republic and the British Prime Minister considered that it was desirable and possible to reach early agreement on the main outstanding issues in the negotiations for British entry, particularly the problems relating to New Zealand and the British contribution to the Community budget.

The President of the Republic and the British Prime Minister expressed their joint desire to resolve the problems which will arise from the renewal of the Yaoundé Convention in a positive spirit and having regard to existing rights. It would equally be necessary to take account of the need to safeguard the interests of the countries who are, or will have the opportunity to become, signatories of that Convention and who are largely dependent upon the markets of the enlarged Community for their exports of sugar or other primary products.

K

STATEMENTS BY THE PRESIDENT OF THE FRENCH REPUBLIC AND THE PRIME MINISTER OF THE UNITED KINGDOM AT THEIR JOINT PRESS CONFERENCE AT THE ELYSEE, 21 MAY 1971.

(See Chapter 33.)

A. THE PRESIDENT

Je veux tout d'abord saluer la présence à Paris du premier ministre britannique. Cette rencontre avait été souhaitée par tous nos partenaires de la Communauté économique européenne qui n'avaient pas manqué de nous le faire savoir. Elle répondait d'ailleurs, je crois aussi le savoir, au désir du gouvernement britannique, et c'est de grand coeur et avec grand plaisir que j'ai donc invité le Premier britannique à venir. Durant deux jours, vous avez beaucoup patienté et nous avons beaucoup travaillé. Nous avons eu près de douze heures d'entretiens, c'est vous dire que tous les sujets ont été abordés et qu'ils ont tous été traités en profondeur.

Le but de ces entretiens n'était pas et ne pouvait pas être de résoudre toutes les questions qui sont en discussion à Bruxelles. Depuis le début des négociations sur l'adhésion des autres candidats, la France a toujours eu pour position que c'etait la Communauté qui négociait, que par conséquent la Communauté devait se mettre d'accord d'abord sur les propositions qu'elle faisait aux négociateurs britanniques.

C'est pourquoi nous n'avons pas réglé ces problèmes que nous n'étions pas qualifiés pour régler.

Vous ne me croirez pas si je vous disais que nous n'en avons pas parlé. Nous en avons donc parlé, nous avons confronté nos points de vues, nous avons surtout essayé de comprendre mutuellement les raisons profondes, économiques ou politiques, qu'avait chacun des deux gouvernements pour déterminer sa position. Comme vous le verrez par le communiqué qui va être distribué, ces questions ont été mentionnées et sont mentionnées pour l'essentiel dans le communiqué.

Tout ce que je puis dire, c'est qu'il serait à l'heure actuelle déraisonnable de penser qu'on ne parviendra pas à un accord entre la Grande Bretagne et la Communauté au cours des négociations du mois de juin prochain et que, en tout cas, l'esprit de nos conversations d'aujourd'hui et d'hier me permet de penser que ces négociations devraient aboutir.

Ne concluez pas cependant que M. Schumann et ses collègues de la Communauté, ainsi que Mr. Rippon, n'auront pas encore de longs moments à discuter. Ils en ont l'habitude et, vu de Paris, j'ai même l'impression qu'ils aiment cela.

Mais l'essentiel de nos conversations a été sur la conception générale de l'Europe, sur son organisation, sur son fonctionnement, sur ses perspectives et cela dans le cadre de tous les grands problèmes qui se posent dans le monde, entre les pays européens et les autres, et à l'intérieur de ces pays européens.

Sur un certain nombre de grands problèrnes, nous avons constaté que nos points de vue étaient analogues, et même identiques.

Sur d'autres, nous avons pu également constater que si certaines différences, divergences, pouvaient subsister, elles ne faisaient aucunement obstacle à une coopération, l'identité de nos vues sur le but à atteindre étant compète.

Je crois pouvoir dire que nous avons eu conscience, le premier britannique et moi-même, qu'il s'agissait là d'un moment important dans, l'histoire de nos deux nations et dans l'histoire des pays d'Europe occidentale. Nos entretiens, par leur longueur même, témoignent que nous avons voulu aller jusqu'au fond du problème. Commencés et poursuivis d'un bout à l'autre, dans la plus grande franchise et dans la plus grande liberté, ils se terminent dans la confiance. Cette confiance c'est celle, et ce doit être celle, que se font deux peuples et qu'ils font à leurs partenaires, actuels et futurs, au sein de la Communauté, pour construire une Europe composée de nations soucieuses de maintenir leur identité, mais décidées à travailler ensemble pour atteindre à une unité véritable, d'abord dans le domaine économique et progressivement dans tous les autres, y compris, bien entendu, dans le domaine politique.

Beaucoup de gens croyaient que la Grande Bretagne n'était pas et ne voulait pas devenir européenne, et qu'elle ne souhaitait entrer dans la Communauté que pour la détruire ou pour la détourner de ses fins. Beaucoup aussi croyaient que la France était prête à utiliser tous les prétextes pour opposer finalement un nouveau veto à l'entrée de la Grande Bretagne.

Eh bien, Mesdames et Messieurs, vous voyez devant vous ce soir deux hommes qui sont convaincus du contraire.

B. THE PRIME MINISTER

We have been carrying on our talks during these last two days in an atmosphere that has been outstandingly warm and friendly. And I want to begin by thanking you for the welcome you have given me here in Paris.

Our talks have been very full and wide-ranging, but we have not carried them on in the way of M. Schumann and Mr. Rippon in Brussels by debating all night. But this has not in any way derogated from their effectiveness.

Mr. President, I share your satisfaction with the outcome of these talks. You have said we have been able to consider the future of Europe, its nature, institutions, its place and its influence in the world, and we find ourselves in very close agreement in our views about these aspects of our own continent.

As a result of our talks I believe that we now have a very clear understanding of each other's points of view and a sympathetic knowledge of each other's problems. For my part I have no doubt at all that the discussions which we have had will prove of real and lasting benefit, not only to Britain and France but to Europe as a whole.

You have described the way in which we have examined the outstanding problems in the negotiations in Brussels. I share your satisfaction; as a result of this examination we both agree that it is not only desirable but also possible for our negotiators there to find acceptable solutions to these remaining problems and be able to do so during the month of June. The way is now open to them to do so.

Mr. President, I have long believed that Europe must grow steadily together in unity, and that Britain should be a part of that wider entity. I believe that only in this way can we secure the future peace of our continent and end for ever the quarrels which have brought such suffering upon our countries in the past.

Secondly, I believe that we can in this way advance the prosperity of all our peoples and take full advantage of the greater economic opportunities which lie before us.

And finally, I believe that only by working together can we play a full and worthy part in the outside world.

You and I, Mr. President, in these talks, have been very conscious of the responsibilities which France and Britain have both inherited in that outside world and both of us mean to go on fulfilling them. These are the beliefs which I personally have held throughout my political life. These are the beliefs, Mr. President, which have brought us together this week. These are the beliefs which, I am now convinced, after these talks, will carry us through to the conclusion of this great enterprise.

L

CONSULTATIONS WITH THE DEVELOPING MEMBER COUNTRIES OF THE COMMONWEALTH SUGAR AGREEMENT, 2–3 JUNE, 1971: COMMUNIQUE.

(See Chapter 13, paragraph 38.)

Representatives of the Governments of the United Kingdom, Antigua, Barbados, Fiji, Guyana, India, Jamaica, Kenya, Mauritius, Swaziland, Trinidad and Tobago, Uganda, St. Kitts-Nevis-Anguilla, British Honduras, and. of the East African Community and the Caribbean Free Trade Association met at Lancaster House from 2–3 June, 1971. In the light of consultations that took place, Commonwealth Ministers agreed on the following statement:

The Governments represented expressed their satisfaction at the Community's readiness to offer the Governments concerned a choice of forms of association or a trading agreement; and also at the readiness to recognise the United Kingdom's contractual commitments to all the CSA member countries up to the end of 1974.

They noted that, in negotiations with the enlarged Community on association or trading agreements, it would be open to the Governments concerned to act individually or collectively. They further noted that the negotiations were due to be concluded by 1975, and that pending conclusion their existing patterns of trade with the United Kingdom would be maintained.

There was a full discussion of the Community's offer made on sugar after 1974. The British delegation assured other delegations that the Community's proposals constitute a specific and moral commitment by the enlarged Community, of which the United Kingdom would be a part. The British Government and other Commonwealth Governments participating regard this offer as a firm assurance of a secure and continuing market in the enlarged Community on fair terms for the quantities of sugar covered by the Commonwealth Sugar Agreement in respect of all its existing developing member countries. The developing Commonwealth countries will continue to plan their future production on this basis.

On this basis, Commonwealth Ministers agreed to accept the Community's proposal and stated that they would proceed accordingly, it being further agreed that Mr. Rippon would so inform the Council of Ministers of the European Community at their forthcoming Ministerial meeting with the United Kingdom, and would communicate to the Community the text of the agreed statement.

In the course of the meeting, Mr. Rippon gave the assurance that it would be the firm policy of the British Government to ensure that the proposal of the Community would be implemented in accordance with the statement recorded above in the event of the United Kingdom joining the European Community.

While recognising that the present meeting was concerned with the arrangements to apply to the developing Commonwealth sugar producers after Britain's entry into an enlarged Community, the Government representatives stressed the importance of a continuing and viable International Sugar Agreement to all sugar-producing countries. They expressed the hope that the enlarged Community would participate actively to this end.

M

THE 'ACQUIS COMMUNAUTAIRE': TRANSLATION OF AN EXTRACT FROM 'ENGLANDS AUFBRUCH NACH EUROPA' BY Dr. K.O. NASS.

(See Chapter 4.)

In the negotiations in the years 1961–63 the treaties represented not indeed the only, but certainly the decisive, sector of European law which Great Britain had to accept. It was in consequence of this that these negotiations were concerned above all with these treaties. By 1970, the situation was fundamentally changed. An almost inconceivable flood of European law has since then been enacted and had to be accepted by the candidates. This included not only acts enacted by the European Commission, as well as those enacted by the Council of Ministers, whether they were regulations, decisions or directives, in so far as they were addressed to all Member States. It included in addition agreements, which the representatives of the Member States meeting in the Council had concluded, and also international treaties, whether they were concluded by the Community itself (as for example the Association Agreements with Morocco and Tunisia) or whether they were concluded simultaneously by the Community and the Member States (so-called Mixed Treaties), as for example the Yaoundé Association Agreement or the Association Agreements with Greece and Turkey.

Finally, the whole corpus of existing Community law, the so-called 'Acquis Communautaire', had to acquire, from the day of accession, the same effectiveness for the United Kingdom as for the present Member States of the European Community. This included the 'conclusions' of the Council in a narrower sense: decisions such as that of 9 February, 1971, on the phased establishment of an Economic and Monetary Union; unilateral declarations in the minutes of the Council made by Member States on the occasion of the enactment of particular acts; the decisions which the European Commission had addressed to individual Member States or to private undertakings, for example those concerning systems of State support or those dealing with competition; in addition, such directives and remaining formal decisions as were not addressed to all the Member States and which accordingly would not automatically enter into force in respect of the United Kingdom as European law, but which have nevertheless become a part of the European legal order and have thus acquired a certain formal character in relation even to those to whom they were not originally addressed. Moreover and above all the judgments of the European Court form part of this 'Acquis Communautaire', especially the authentic interpretations of the treaties which they contain, for example on the direct application of provisions of the treaties and on many other subjects.

In the same way as in the case of the judgments of the European Court, the principles which it had laid down in determining the nature of Community law would become binding on the Acceding States. Accordingly, European law would have to become an independent system of law for the Acceding States, not to be reckoned as a part either of national or of international law. In Great

Britain too Community law would have to have direct application, in so far as its nature calls for such application, and would have to enjoy, in the event of conflict, priority over national legal provisions of whatever standing. Nor would national rules of interpretation be available for the interpretation of this European law, unless they were such as to be common to all Member States; on the contrary, the objectives of the Community would in the first instance become the standard for the interpretation of Community law, and the unity of the system of European law would have to be protected by the application of the provisions of Article 177 of the Treaty of Rome, which oblige national courts to refer for interpretative judgments to the European Court.

The existing corpus of Community law contains, as may be seen from this list, both published and unpublished components. The latter were expressly communicated to the candidate States in the course of the negotiations; for the published acts they could refer to the Official Journal of the Communities. Also to be regarded as a part of the 'Acquis Communautaire' are certain existing elements of European customary law. Prudently, no attempt to establish the nature of these elements was made on the occasion of British accession. Nevertheless it was clear that the so-called 'Luxembourg Protocol' of January 1966—the 'agreement to disagree' of Luxembourg—was not included in this sphere.

The whole mass of law described and characterised above—for this was the basis of the negotiations—had to acquire in the United Kingdom, from the day of the enlargement of the Communities, the same effect and the same validity as in and for the Member States. And this had to hold good not only for such law as had already been enacted at the moment when the negotiations began; it applied even beyond that to any supplementary European law which might be enacted till the day of the signature of the Accession Treaty, and indeed for the period between that signature and the entry of the Accession Treaty into force.

It followed from this attitude of the Community that additional rules, to supplement or to alter those already in force, could not as a matter of principle be adopted as a part of the negotiations for accession ...

This attitude of the Community was clear, and certainly was not easy for the British to accept. Yet the British accepted it. They too must have said to themselves that it was impossible that, as part of the process of accession, the whole laborious unification process of 12 years of European work should be reopened. Yet they naturally knew that all the decisions taken in the Community of Six had in no respect whatever taken account of British interests, but were at best compromises between the existing Member States of the Community.

In the course of time legislative practices had grown up in the Community which must have appeared specially peculiar to the British, as for example the failure to use the occasion of amending European regulations for the enactment of completely revised regulations. The British were astonished to find that there is not even a consolidated version of the Treaty of Rome in force in the Community, from which the complete text of the Treaty valid at a given time, including all the amendments which have been made since it entered into force, can be easily ascertained. On the contrary, elaborate processes are frequently necessary to establish which provisions of the treaties or of secondary legislation are actually at the moment in force. The land of 'case law' has a special respect for written law; but the flood of regulations of the European institutions reduced it not a little.

Although the whole corpus of Community law took no account of British interests, and in spite of the different character of British and European legal structures, the British resigned themselves to the fact that it was not possible to undo the 12 years of Community development in the course of the accession negotiations.

N

MR. RIPPON'S STATEMENT ON STERLING AT THE MINISTERIAL MEETING OF 7 JUNE 1971, SUBSEQUENTLY ANNEXED TO THE ACT OF ACCESSION.

(see Chapter 14, paragraph 37.)

(a) We are prepared to envisage an orderly and gradual run-down of official sterling balances after our accession.

(b) We shall be ready to discuss after our entry into the Communities what measures might be appropriate to achieve a progressive alignment of the external characteristics and practices in relation to sterling with those of other currencies in the Community in the context of progress towards economic and monetary union in the enlarged Community, and we are confident that official sterling* can be handled in a way which will enable us to take our full part in that progress.

(c) In the meantime we shall manage our policies with a view to stabilising the official sterling balances in a way which would be consistent with these longer term objectives.

(d) I hope that the Community will regard this statement as disposing satisfactorily of the question of sterling and associated matters, leaving only arrangements for UK compliance with the Directives relating to capital movements under the Treaty of Rome to be settled in the course of the negotiations.

* 'Official sterling' means 'official sterling balances'

APPENDIX III

Chronological Summary

1967

January

16–17	Prime Minister (Mr. Wilson) and Foreign Secretary (Mr. Brown) visit Rome.
23	Prime Minister's speech to the Council of Europe.
24–25	Prime Minister and Foreign Secretary visit Paris.
31 Jan.–1 Feb.	Prime Minister and Foreign Secretary visit Brussels.

February

15–16	Prime Minister and Foreign Secretary visit Bonn.
26–27	Prime Minister and Foreign Secretary visit The Hague.

March

7–8	Prime Minister and Foreign Secretary visit Luxembourg.

May

2	Statement by Prime Minister in Parliament on Membership of the European Communities (Cmnd. 3269).
4	White Paper 'The Common Agricultural Policy of the European Economic Community' (Cmnd. 3274) published.
10	House of Commons Vote in favour of Application for membership of European Communities (Ayes 488, Noes 62).
11	Presentation of Application to President of Council of Ministers of European Communities (also Irish and Danish Applications). Appointment of Lord Chalfont to lead Negotiating Team.
16	General de Gaulle's Press conference.
29–30	Summit meeting of the Six in Rome.
31	White Paper 'The Legal and Constitutional Implications of United Kingdom Membership of the European Communities' (Cmnd. 3301) published.

June

7	British Application acknowledged by a letter from the President of the Council of Ministers to the Prime Minister.
18–20	Prime Minister visits Paris for talks with General de Gaulle.

July

1	Entry into force of the Fusion Treaty.
4	Mr. Brown's Statement to Western European Union (Cmnd. 3345) at The Hague.
10	Council of Ministers asks Commission to prepare 'Opinion'.
21	Presentation of Norwegian Application.
26	Request for negotiations put in by Sweden.

September

29	Commission 'Opinion' forwarded to Council of Ministers (published 7 October).

October

16–17	Herr Brandt visits Paris.
23–25	Dr. Kiesinger visits London.

November

14–15	Belgian Prime Minister and Foreign Minister visit London.
18	Devaluation of £ sterling.
27	General de Gaulle's Press conference.

December

4	M. Rey visits London for talks with Prime Minister and Foreign Secretary.
18–19	Meeting of Council of Ministers in Brussels at which French refuse to agree to opening of negotiations.
19	Letter from President of Council of Ministers (Herr Schiller) to Prime Minister informing him of outcome of meeting.
29	Foreign Secretary visits Rome.

1968

January

15	Benelux proposals for co-operation with applicant States.
19	Foreign Secretary visits Bonn.

February

16–18	Kiesinger/de Gaulle Meeting: Franco-German declaration on commercial arrangement.

19–20	Dutch Prime Minister and Foreign Minister visit London.
22	Italian proposals for co-operation with applicant States.
March	
11–12	Luxembourg Prime Minister visits London.
April	
2	Commission 'Opinion' on commercial arrangement (discussed by Council of Ministers on 5 April).
26	WEU Ministerial meeting discussed United Kingdom/EEC interim arrangements (in Paris).
May	
—	Unrest in France.
June	
23 and 30	Elections for French Assembly.
July	
9	WEU Ministerial Council meeting in Bonn discusses United Kingdom/EEC interim arrangements.
10	Pompidou resigns as Prime Minister; replaced by Couve de Murville on 11 July.
August	
30	Dr. Luns visits London.
September	
18	M. Harmel visits London.
October	
21–22	WEU Ministerial meeting in Rome discusses Harmel Plan.
November	
6	M. Debré presents French Government's view on commercial arrangement to Council of Ministers of Community.
14	WEU Foreign Ministers (minus France) meet in Brussels. Italian Government requested to draft paper on implementation of Harmel Plan.

1969

January	
27	United Kingdom/EURATOM Agreement extended for two years.

February

4	Conversation between Her Majesty's Ambassador, Paris, and General de Gaulle: Soames Affair begins.
12–13	Prime Minister/Kiesinger talks in Bonn: joint statement.

April

28	Resignation of General de Gaulle.

June

15	President Pompidou elected.
29	Second Yaoundé Convention signed.

July

22	Council requests Commission to prepare an up-to-date version of its 'Opinion'.

August

8	French devaluation.

September

24	Second Arusha Agreement signed.
28	Federal German elections.
30	Deutschemark floats.

October

1	Commission completes revised 'Opinion'.
5	Mr. George Thomson appointed Chancellor of the Duchy of Lancaster.
6	Mr. Marshall visits London (and returns again on 17th).
21	Herr Brandt becomes Federal Chancellor.
26/27	At midnight: Deutschemark revalued.

November

4	Council of Ministers of Community invites United Kingdom (and eight others) to participate in Aigrain Group on Technological Projects.

December

1–2	The Hague Summit.
23	Council agrees in principle on definitive arrangements for agricultural finance (*ressources propres*).
31	End of Transitional Period of Treaty of Rome.

1970

January

1	Belgian Presidency of Council of Ministers begins.
9–10	WEU Ministerial meeting, Brussels.
15–16	Chancellor of the Duchy of Lancaster visits Rome.
23	M. Schumann visits London.

February

7	Council reaches final agreement on *ressources propres*.
10	Publication of White Paper 'Britain and the European Communities: an Economic Assessment' (Cmnd. 4289).
24–25	Debate in House of Commons on Motion that 'this House take note of White Paper on Britain and the European Communities'. Agreed to by oral assent with one 'No' (Mrs. Ewing) noted in Hansard.

March

2–4	Herr Brandt visits London.
9–10	Meeting of Heads of Mission from Six capitals (in London).
11–12	Chancellor of the Duchy of Lancaster visits Brussels.
12–13	Chancellor of the Duchy of Lancaster visits Luxembourg.
19	Chancellor of the Duchy of Lancaster visits The Hague.

April

6–7	M. Barre visits London.
10	Announcement of appointment of British negotiating team.
13–14	Chancellor of the Duchy of Lancaster visits Bonn.
17–18	Chancellor of the Duchy of Lancaster visits Paris.
27–28	M. Thorn visits London.

May

14–15	Chancellor of the Duchy of Lancaster attends EFTA Ministerial meeting.
18–19	Signor Colombo visits London.
26–27	Mr. de Koster visits London.
29	Dissolution of Parliament.

June

5–6	WEU Ministerial meeting, Bonn. French returned to WEU (after a year's boycott).
9	President of Council of Ministers replies to United Kingdom application of 11 May, 1967, and invites United Kingdom to participate in formal Opening of Negotiations on 30 June.

8–9, 16–17	Talks in London with New Zealand officials.
18	General election in United Kingdom.
20	Mr. Anthony Barber made Chancellor of the Duchy of Lancaster.
30	Opening of negotiations between four applicants and European Communities at Luxembourg. Council of Ministers (of Agriculture) adopts resolution on establishment of a Common Fisheries Policy.

July

1	German Presidency begins.
2	Nine-Member Commission replaces fourteen-Member Commission.
Week beginning	
6	Mr. Marshall in London.
7–14	Mr. McEwen (Australian Deputy Prime Minister) in London.
16–17	Herr Scheel visits London.
20	Death of Mr. lain MacLeod.
21	First bilateral Ministerial meeting (United Kingdom/Six).
22	1st Deputies meeting.
28	Mr. Rippon replaces Mr. Barber as Chancellor of the Duchy of Lancaster.

August

6	Signor Colombo forms new Italian Government.
7	Northern Ireland Ministers visit London for talks on Common Market.
12	Signature of German-Soviet Treaty.

September

3	Meeting between Mr. Rippon and Caribbean Ministers in London.
4	M. Alphand visits London.
6–7	Mr. Rippon visits Bonn.
11–14	Mr. Rippon visits Hong Kong.
15–17	Mr. Rippon visits Australia.
16	2nd Deputies meeting.
17–22	Mr. Rippon visits New Zealand.
21	First Ministerial meeting (Ireland/Six).
22	First Ministerial meetings (Norway/Six and Denmark/Six).

October

1	3rd Deputies meeting.
2	Meeting in London between Mr. Rippon and Lord Windlesham, and representatives of Jersey, Guernsey and Isle of Man.

5 Herr von Braun visits London.
8 Werner Report on economic and monetary union completed.
13–14 Mr. Rippon visits Brussels.
14 4th Deputies meeting.
15 Final report of Werner Group transmitted to Council and Commission.
16 Mr. Rippon visits The Hague.
21 5th Deputies meeting.
27 Second Ministerial meeting (United Kingdom/Six).

November

4 6th Deputies meeting.
5–6 EFTA Ministerial meeting, Geneva.
6–9 Mr. Rippon visits Paris.
9 Death of General de Gaulle.
10 Sweden, Switzerland and Austria open discussions with Community.
12 Heath/Pompidou meeting at de Gaulle's funeral.
17 7th Deputies meeting.
23–25 Hong Kong representatives visit London for talks.
24 M. Giscard d'Estaing in London.
Portugal, Finland and Iceland open discussions with Community.
26–27 Mr. Mitchell Sharp visits London.

December

1 8th Deputies meeting.
2 Meeting of Ten Foreign Ministers in Brussels.
8 Third Ministerial meeting (United Kingdom/Six).
10–12 Mr. Rippon in Paris for Council of Europe Ministerial meeting.
14 EEC Council fails to reach agreement on proposals for implementation of Werner Plan, thereby failing to respect The Hague Summit deadline.
15 Second Ministerial meetings (Six/Ireland, Denmark and Norway).
16 Signor Moro visits London.
18 9th Deputies meeting.

1971

January

1 French Presidency begins. Entry into force of the Treaty

modifying budgetary provisions of the Treaty of Rome.

3–5 M. Deniau visits London.
7–9 Mr. Rippon visits Copenhagen.
10–12 Mr. Rippon visits Luxembourg—for WEU Ministerial meeting.
12 10th Deputies meeting.
21 President Pompidou's Press conference.
26–27 11th Deputies meeting.
27 Meeting in London between Mr. Rippon and Mr. Lightbourne, Jamaican Minister for Trade and Industry.
29 United Kingdom/EURATOM agreement prolonged for one year.

February

2 Fourth Ministerial meeting (Six/United Kingdom).
4–5 Herr Scheel visits London.
7–9 Mr. Rippon visits Jamaica.
9 Council of Ministers agrees on the establishment by stages of economic and monetary union.
9–12 Mr. Rippon visits Guyana.
10 12th Deputies meeting.
12–17 Mr. Rippon visits Trinidad and Tobago.
15–16 Visit to Court of Justice by a party of British legal experts led by Lord Wilberforce.
17–18 Mr. Rippon visits St. Lucia.
18–21 Mr. Rippon visits Barbados.
23 13th Deputies meeting.

March

2 Third Ministerial meetings (Six/Ireland and Denmark).
2–5 Signor Malfatti visits London.
4–5 Mr. Rippon visits Canada.
7–10 Mr. Rippon visits United States.
9 14th Deputies meeting.
10–11 M. Harmel visits London.
13 New Norwegian Government formed under Mr. Bratteli.
16 Fifth Ministerial meeting (Six/United Kingdom).
22 Sir James Marjoribanks leaves United Kingdom Delegation to the European Communities, Mr. Christofas assumes charge.
24 15th Deputies meeting.
27–30 Mr. Rippon visits Rome.
30 Third Ministerial meeting (Six/Norway).

April

4–6 Prime Minister visits Bonn (and goes on to Berlin).

6	16th Deputies meeting.
18–20	Mr. Rippon visits The Hague (WEU Ministerial meeting).
21	17th Deputies meeting.
28	18th Deputies meeting.
28	Dutch general election.

May

4–5	19th Deputies meeting.
5–6	Herr Brandt visits London
8	Announcement of Heath–Pompidou meeting.
11–13	Sixth Ministerial meeting (Six/United Kingdom). Agreement recorded on Commonwealth sugar, and on transitional arrangements in agricultural sector.
13–14	EFTA Ministerial meeting, Reykjavik (Mr. Rippon in Reykjavik from 13–16 May).
18	Foreign Secretary visits Paris for Meeting of Ten Foreign Ministers.
	20th Deputies meeting.
18–19	Mr. Marshall visits London.
19–21	Mr. Heath meets President Pompidou in Paris.
24–26	Mr. Rippon visits Oslo.

June

1	21st Deputies meeting.
2–3	Consultations with Commonwealth Sugar Producing Countries in London.
7	Fourth Ministerial meetings (Six/Ireland and Denmark), in Luxembourg.
7–8	Seventh Ministerial meeting (Six/United Kingdom), in Luxembourg.
	Agreement recorded on Sterling.
11–13	Mr. Rippon visits M. Deniau (for Blois).
15–16	Mr. Rippon visits Paris (for WEU Assembly).
16	22nd Deputies meeting.
17	Statement by Prime Minister in House of Commons on postponing 'decision of principle' until October.
21	Fourth Ministerial meeting (Six/Norway), in Luxembourg.
21–23	Eighth Ministerial meeting (Six/United Kingdom), in Luxembourg: Agreement is recorded on New Zealand dairy products and Community Finance.
28–29	Signor Colombo visits London.
29	23rd Deputies meeting.
30 June–2 July	Mr. Hartling (Danish Foreign Minister) visits London.

July

1	Italian Presidency begins.
6	New Dutch Government sworn in.
7	Publication of White Paper 'The United Kingdom and the European Communities' (Cmnd. 4715).
9	Signor Malfatti visits London.
12	Ninth Ministerial meeting (Six/United Kingdom): Fifth Ministerial meeting (Six/Ireland and Denmark).
20	24th Deputies meeting.
21–26	'Take Note' Debate in House of Commons, with motion agreed to without a vote.
27	Fifth Ministerial meeting (Six/Norway).
28	25th Deputies meeting.

August

15	President Nixon 'closes Gold Window'.

September

14	26th Deputies meeting.
21	Tenth Ministerial meeting (Six/United Kingdom).
23–28	Mr. Rippon visits Rome.
28	27th Deputies meeting.

October

1	Representatives of Channel Isles and Isle of Man received in London by Mr. Maudling and Mr. Rippon.
3–5	Mr. Rippon visits Strasbourg (EFTA and Council of Europe meetings).
5–6	Mr. Rippon visits Paris for talks with MM. Schumann, Chamant and Cointat.
11	New Danish Government takes office under Mr. Krag.
12	28th Deputies meeting.
18	Mr. Palliser arrives in Brussels to take up his post as Head of the United Kingdom Delegation to the European Communities.
19	Sixth Ministerial meetings (Six/Ireland and Norway), in Luxembourg.
21	Opening of Substantative debate in House of Commons on decision of principle to join the European Communities on the basis of the arrangements which have been negotiated.
27	29th Deputies meeting.
28	Closure of EEC Debate: House voted Ayes 356, Noes 244.

November

1–3	Mr. Rippon visits Bonn.
3	30th Deputies meeting.
3–5	Mr. Rippon visits Geneva for EFTA Ministerial meeting.
5–6	Foreign Secretary in Rome for Meeting of 10 Foreign Ministers.
7	General election in Belgium.
9	11th Ministerial meeting (Six/United Kingdom).
11–12	M. Schumann visits London.
12	Herr Dahrendorf visits London.
15–16	President, judges and senior officials of the European Court of Justice pay an official visit to London.
16	Multilateral Deputies meeting to discuss mandate for negotiations with EFTA non-applicant countries.
18	Mr. Rippon visits Isle of Man.
18–19	Mr. Rippon visits Guernsey and Jersey. Mr. Krag visits London.
20	Mr. Rippon visits Paris for WEU meeting.
24	31st Deputies meeting.
29–30	12th Ministerial meeting (Six/United Kingdom) (also Six/Norway, Six/Denmark and Six/Ireland): devoted to Fisheries, ends in deadlock.

December

3	First round of negotiations Six/Sweden, Switzerland and Austria takes place in Brussels.
7	32nd Deputies meeting.
11–12	13th Ministerial meeting (Six/United Kingdom) (also Six/Norway, Six/Denmark and Six/Ireland). Agreement on Fisheries policy reached, acceptable to Ireland and Denmark but not Norway.
13	First round of negotiations Six/Finland.
15	33rd Deputies meeting.
17	34th Deputies meeting. Notice given in Stockholm of United Kingdom withdrawal from EFTA at end of 1972.
17–19	First round of negotiations Six/Portugal, Iceland.
22	35th Deputies meeting.
29 Dec.–3 Jan.	Mr. Rippon visits New York to address Council on Foreign Relations.

1972

January

1	Luxembourg Presidency begins.

3–5	Mr. Rippon visits Los Angeles to address World Affairs Council.
5–7	Mr. Rippon speaks in New Orleans.
6–7	36th Deputies meeting.
7–11	Mr. Rippon visits Jamaica for talks with Mr. Lightbourne and other Ministers.
10–12	Ministerial meetings (Ireland/Six and Norway/Six).
12–14	37th Deputies meeting.
13	Publication in London (in 42 volumes) of the pre-accession series of secondary legislation of the Communities as at 10 November, 1971.
14–15	Final agreement on Fisheries reached at meeting with Norway at Deputies Level.
17–18	38th Deputies meeting.
21	New Belgian Government takes office.
22	Signature in Brussels of Treaty of Accession.
25	Presentation of European Communities Bill to House of Commons and First Reading.

Index